Learn JavaFX 17

Building User Experience and
Interfaces with Java

Second Edition

Kishori Sharan
Peter Späth

Apress®

Learn JavaFX 17: Building User Experience and Interfaces with Java

Kishori Sharan
Montgomery, AL, USA

Peter Späth
Leipzig, Sachsen, Germany

ISBN-13 (pbk): 978-1-4842-7847-5
https://doi.org/10.1007/978-1-4842-7848-2

ISBN-13 (electronic): 978-1-4842-7848-2

Managing Director, Apress Media LLC: Welmoed Spahr
Acquisitions Editor: Steve Anglin
Development Editor: Laura Berendson
Coordinating Editor: Mark Powers

Cover designed by eStudioCalamar

Cover image by Onder Ortel on Unsplash (www.unsplash.com)

Distributed to the book trade worldwide by Apress Media, LLC, 1 New York Plaza, New York, NY 10004, U.S.A. Phone 1-800-SPRINGER, fax (201) 348-4505, e-mail orders-ny@springer-sbm.com, or visit www.springeronline.com. Apress Media, LLC is a California LLC and the sole member (owner) is Springer Science + Business Media Finance Inc (SSBM Finance Inc). SSBM Finance Inc is a **Delaware** corporation.

For information on translations, please e-mail booktranslations@springernature.com; for reprint, paperback, or audio rights, please e-mail bookpermissions@springernature.com.

Apress titles may be purchased in bulk for academic, corporate, or promotional use. eBook versions and licenses are also available for most titles. For more information, reference our Print and eBook Bulk Sales web page at http://www.apress.com/bulk-sales.

Any source code or other supplementary material referenced by the author in this book is available to readers on GitHub via the book's product page, located at www.apress.com/9781484278475. For more detailed information, please visit http://www.apress.com/source-code.

Printed on acid-free paper

To my father-in-law Mr. Jim Baker
—Kishori Sharan

To my niece Alina
—Peter Späth

Table of Contents

ix

About the Authors

Kishori Sharan has earned a Master of Science in Computer Information Systems degree from Troy State University, Alabama. He is a Sun Certified Java 2 programmer. He has vast experience in providing training to professional developers in Java, JSP, EJB, and web technology. He has over ten years of experience in implementing enterprise-level Java applications.

Peter Späth graduated in 2002 as a physicist and soon afterward became an IT consultant, mainly for Java-related projects. In 2016, he decided to concentrate on writing books on various aspects, but with a main focus on software development. With two books about graphics and sound processing, three books on Android app development, and several books on Java development, the author continues his effort in writing software development–related literature.

About the Technical Reviewer

Preethi Vasudev earned an MS in Computer Information Systems and Cyber Security from Auburn University, Alabama. She is an Oracle-certified Java 8 programmer with more than 15 years of industry experience in investment banking, healthcare, and other areas. She is interested in Java and related technologies and enjoys participating in coding competitions.

Acknowledgments

My heartfelt thanks are due to my father-in-law, Jim Baker, for displaying extraordinary patience in reading the initial draft of the first few chapters of the book and his valuable suggestions for improving the material.

I thank my friend Richard Castillo for his hard work in reading the initial draft of the first 12 chapters of the book and weeding out several mistakes. Richard was instrumental in running all examples and pointing out errors. I also thank him for allowing me to use a few pictures in this book from his website www.digitizedchaos.com.

My wife, Ellen, was always patient when I spent long hours at my computer desk working on this book. I thank her for all her support to me in writing this book. She also deserves my sincere thanks for letting me sometimes seclude myself on weekends so I could focus on this book.

I also thank my family members and friends for their encouragement and support to me in writing this book: my elder brothers, Janki Sharan and Dr. Sita Sharan; my sister and brother-in-law, Ratna and Abhay; my nephews Babalu, Dabalu, Gaurav, Saurav, and Chitranjan; my friends Shivashankar Ravindranath, Kannan Somasekar, Mahbub Choudhury, Biju Nair, Srinivas Kakkera, Anil Kumar Singh, Chris Coley, Willie Baptiste, Rahul Jain, Larry Brewster, Greg Langham, LaTondra Okeke, Dinesh Sankala, Rahul Nagpal, Ravi Datla, and many more friends not mentioned here.

I thank the president of my company Up and Running Inc., Josh Bush, for his support and my wonderful, supportive coworkers—Preethi Vasudeva, Tanina Jones, Ann Wedgeworth, William Barnett, and Shannah Glenn—for their encouragement.

My sincere thanks are due to the wonderful team at Apress for their support during the publication of this book. Thanks to Mark Powers, the senior coordinating editor, and Matthew Moodie, the development editor, for providing excellent support. Thanks also to the technical reviewers Jeff Friesen, David Coffin, Wallace Jackson, Massimo Nardone, and Tri Phan for their insights and feedback during the editing process; they were instrumental in weeding out many technical errors and improving the material. I also thank the copy editors, Mary Bearden, Lori Cavanaugh, Lori Jacobs, and Karen Jameson, for their extraordinary efforts in editing the book and applying many corrections during a very short span of time. Last but not least, my sincere thanks to Steve Anglin, the lead editor at Apress, for taking the initiative for the publication of this book.

—Kishori Sharan

Many thanks to the Apress staff for offering me to write the JavaFX version 17 edition of this book. Thanks also to my friends for their patience concerning updates to my latest composition work, a classic style Tango for violin and cello. This work had to stand behind a little bit, so the JavaFX book's schedule could be held.

—Peter Späth

Introduction

Java had the support for developing GUI applications since its version 1.0 using the AWT (Abstract Window Toolkit). Later, AWT was replaced by Swing, which gave a little better user experience, but still lacked the modern-looking widgets and the support for a developer's productivity. Both AWT and Swing lacked the first-class support for data binding, efficient GUI rendering engines, easy-to-use 2D and 3D libraries for developers, and style sheet support. JavaFX was first released in 2008 as the tool to use for developing rich Internet applications (RIAs); it used a statically typed declarative language called *JavaFX Script*, which did not attract a lot of attention from Java developers. JavaFX 2.0, released in 2011, caught the Java community's attention when it dropped the support for JavaFX Script and supported writing JavaFX programs using the Java programming language. In its current version, JavaFX 17 is supported as an open source add-on that can be downloaded from the Gluon company's website. Now JavaFX 17 is considered a real successor for Swing for building the GUI application using the Java platform.

Learn JavaFX 17 shows you how to start developing rich client desktop applications in JavaFX 17 using your Java skills. It provides comprehensive coverage of the JavaFX 17 features. Each chapter starts with an introduction to the topic at hand. A step-by-step discussion of the topic with small snippets of code follows. At the end of the topic's discussion, a complete program is presented. Special care has been taken to present the topics in such a way that chapters can be read serially. The book contains numerous pictures to aid you in visualizing the GUI that is built at every step in the discussion.

The book starts with an introduction to JavaFX and its history. It lists the system requirements and the steps to start developing JavaFX applications. It shows you how to create a Hello World application in JavaFX, explaining every line of code in the process. Later in the book, advanced topics such as 2D and 3D graphics, charts, FXML, advanced controls, and printing are discussed.

I faced a few hurdles while writing the first edition of this book. As JavaFX 8 was being developed, JavaFX 2, the version before JavaFX 8, was the first release of JavaFX that used the Java programming language to write JavaFX code. There were a few bugs in JavaFX 2. Sometimes, it took me a couple of days of hard work to create an example to work with, only to realize that there was a bug in it. Later, if something did not work, I would look at the JIRA bug reports for JavaFX before spending too much time researching it myself. I had to fix bugs as I found them. It took me 18 months to finish this book, and, in the end, it was satisfying to see that what I had produced was a lot of useful material covering almost every topic in JavaFX so fully that readers could use it to learn and build a rich client application quickly using JavaFX. I hope you will enjoy the book and benefit greatly from it.

I believe that programming is simple if you learn it that way. Keeping this in mind, I kept the examples in the book as simple as possible, presenting them in as few lines as I could. The examples focus on the topic being discussed. I do not present complex GUI in my examples, keeping in mind that this could obscure the learning process of the topic at hand. I have seen books that contain examples that run four or five pages long, sometimes even longer; readers of such books (myself included) often get lost in trying to understand the logic of the program, thus forgetting what they were trying to learn in that section. Therefore, simple programs in this book are intended to help you learn JavaFX faster. The book includes many ready-to-run programs and even more pictures. Having more pictures than programs is evident from my approach in keeping the readers' interest the first priority. Almost every time I discuss a snippet of code producing a UI, I include the picture of the results of the UI, so readers are not left to their imaginations as to what the code snippet will produce. Having to run every snippet of code to see the output can hinder the learning rhythm.

Structure of the Book

The book contains 27 chapters covering all topics—from basic to advanced—in JavaFX. Chapters are arranged in an order that aids you to quickly learn JavaFX. I have used an incremental approach to teach JavaFX, assuming no prior GUI development knowledge. Each chapter starts with a section introducing the topic to be discussed in the chapter. Each section contains a bit of background of the features being discussed, followed with code snippets and a complete program.

What You Will Learn

This book will help you to learn

- What JavaFX 17 is and its history
- How to develop rich client desktop applications using JavaFX 17
- How to use properties, collections, colors, and styles
- How to use controls and handle events to build modern GUI applications
- How to use advanced controls such as TreeView, TableView, and TreeTableView
- How to access web pages in JavaFX applications
- How to draw 2D and 3D shapes and apply effects and transformations
- How to create animations and charts using the JavaFX 17 APIs
- How to add audios and videos to your applications
- How to create GUIs in JavaFX using FXML
- How to provide the printing capabilities using the JavaFX Print API

Who Is This Book For?

Learn JavaFX 17 was written for Java developers, with beginning to intermediate-level Java skills, who want to learn how to develop modern desktop GUI applications using JavaFX 17.

Source Code

Source code for this book can be accessed at github.com/apress/learn-javafx17.

CHAPTER 1

■ ■ ■

Getting Started

In this chapter, you will learn:

- What JavaFX is
- The history of JavaFX
- How to set up Eclipse IDE to work with a JavaFX application, and how to write your first JavaFX application
- How to pass parameters to a JavaFX application
- How to launch a JavaFX application
- The life cycle of a JavaFX application
- How to terminate a JavaFX application

What Is JavaFX?

JavaFX is an open source Java-based framework for developing rich client applications. It is comparable to other frameworks on the market such as Adobe AIR and Microsoft Blazor. JavaFX is also seen as the successor of Swing in the arena of graphical user interface (GUI) development technology in the Java platform. The JavaFX library is available as a public Java application programming interface (API). JavaFX contains several features that make it a preferred choice for developing rich client applications:

- JavaFX is written in Java, which enables you to take advantage of all Java features such as multithreading, generics, and lambda expressions. You can use any Java IDE of your choice, such as NetBeans or Eclipse, to author, compile, run, debug, and package your JavaFX application.

- JavaFX supports data binding through its libraries.

- JavaFX code can also be written using any Java virtual machine (JVM)–supported scripting language such as Kotlin, Groovy, and Scala.

- JavaFX offers two ways to build a user interface (UI): using Java code and using FXML. FXML is an XML-based scriptable markup language to define a UI declaratively. The Gluon company provides a tool called Scene Builder, which is a visual editor for FXML.

- JavaFX provides a rich set of multimedia support such as playing back audios and videos. It takes advantage of available codecs on the platform.

© Kishori Sharan and Peter Späth 2022
K. Sharan and P. Späth, *Learn JavaFX 17*, https://doi.org/10.1007/978-1-4842-7848-2_1

- JavaFX lets you embed web content in the application.

- JavaFX provides out-of-the-box support for applying effects and animations, which are important for developing gaming applications. You can achieve sophisticated animations by writing a few lines of code.

Behind the JavaFX API lie a number of components to take advantage of the Java native libraries and the available hardware and software. JavaFX components are shown in Figure 1-1.

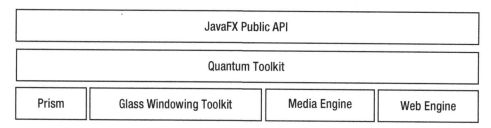

Figure 1-1. *Components of the JavaFX platform*

The GUI in JavaFX is constructed as a *scene graph*. A scene graph is a collection of visual elements, called nodes, arranged in a hierarchical fashion. A scene graph is built using the public JavaFX API. Nodes in a scene graph can handle user inputs and user gestures. They can have effects, transformations, and states. Types of nodes in a scene graph include simple UI controls such as buttons, text fields, two-dimensional (2D) and three-dimensional (3D) shapes, images, media (audio and video), web content, and charts.

Prism is a hardware-accelerated graphics pipeline used for rendering the scene graph. If hardware-accelerated rendering is not available on the platform, Java 2D is used as the fallback rendering mechanism. For example, before using Java 2D for rendering, it will try using DirectX on Windows and OpenGL on Mac, Linux, and Embedded Platforms.

The *Glass Windowing Toolkit* provides graphics and windowing services such as windows and the timer using the native operating system. The toolkit is also responsible for managing event queues. In JavaFX, event queues are managed by a single, operating system–level thread called *JavaFX Application Thread*. All user input events are dispatched on the JavaFX Application Thread. JavaFX requires that a live scene graph must be modified only on the JavaFX Application Thread.

Prism uses a separate thread, other than the JavaFX Application Thread, for the rendering process. It accelerates the process by rendering a frame while the next frame is being processed. When a scene graph is modified, for example, by entering some text in the text field, Prism needs to re-render the scene graph. Synchronizing the scene graph with Prism is accomplished using an event called a *pulse* event. A pulse event is queued on the JavaFX Application Thread when the scene graph is modified and it needs to be re-rendered. A pulse event is an indication that the scene graph is not in sync with the rendering layer in Prism, and the latest frame at the Prism level should be rendered. Pulse events are throttled at 60 frames per second maximum.

The media engine is responsible for providing media support in JavaFX, for example, playing back audios and videos. It takes advantage of the available codecs on the platform. The media engine uses a separate thread to process media frames and uses the JavaFX Application Thread to synchronize the frames with the scene graph. The media engine is based on *GStreamer*, which is an open source multimedia framework.

The web engine is responsible for processing web content (HTML) embedded in a scene graph. Prism is responsible for rendering the web contents. The web engine is based on *WebKit*, which is an open source web browser engine. HTML5, Cascading Style Sheets (CSS), JavaScript, and Document Object Model (DOM) are supported.

The Quantum toolkit is an abstraction over the low-level components of Prism, Glass, media engine, and web engine. It also facilitates coordination between low-level components.

> ■ **Note** Throughout this book, it is assumed that you have intermediate-level knowledge of the Java programming language, including lambda expressions and the new Time API (since Java 8).

History of JavaFX

JavaFX was originally developed by Chris Oliver at SeeBeyond, and it was called F3 (Form Follows Function). F3 was a Java scripting language for easily developing GUI applications. It offered declarative syntax, static typing, type inference, data binding, animation, 2D graphics, and Swing components. SeeBeyond was bought by Sun Microsystems, and F3 was renamed JavaFX in 2007. Oracle acquired Sun Microsystems in 2010. Oracle then open sourced JavaFX in 2013.

The first version of JavaFX was released in the fourth quarter of 2008. The version number jumped from 2.2 to 8.0. From Java 8, the version numbers of Java SE and JavaFX will be the same. The major versions for Java SE and JavaFX will be released at the same time as well. The current release for JavaFX is version 17.0. Starting with the release of Java SE 11, JavaFX no longer is part of the Java SE runtime library. From Java 11, you need to download and include the JavaFX libraries to compile and run your JavaFX programs. Table 1-1 contains a list of releases of JavaFX.

Table 1-1. *JavaFX Releases*

Release Date	Version	Comments
Q4, 2008	JavaFX 1.0	It was the initial release of JavaFX. It used a declaration language called JavaFX Script to write the JavaFX code.
Q1, 2009	JavaFX 1.1	Support for JavaFX Mobile was introduced.
Q2, 2009	JavaFX 1.2	–
Q2, 2010	JavaFX 1.3	–
Q3, 2010	JavaFX 1.3.1	–
Q4, 2011	JavaFX 2.0	Support for JavaFX Script was dropped. It used the Java language to write the JavaFX code. Support for JavaFX Mobile was dropped.
Q2, 2012	JavaFX 2.1	Support for Mac OS for desktop only was introduced.
Q3, 2012	JavaFX 2.2	–
Q1, 2014	JavaFX 8.0	The JavaFX version jumped from 2.2 to 8.0. JavaFX and Java SE versions will match from Java 8.
Q2, 2015	JavaFX 9.0	Some internal APIs made public, JEP253.
Q3, 2018	JavaFX 11.0.3	JavaFX no longer part of the Oracle Java JDK. JavaFX now a downloadable open source module provided by the Gluon company. Support for handheld and other embedded devices added as *ports*.
Q1, 2019	JavaFX 12.0.1	Bug fixes and some enhancements.
Q3, 2019	JavaFX 13.0	Bug fixes and some enhancements.

(continued)

Table 1-1. (*continued*)

Release Date	Version	Comments
Q1, 2020	JavaFX 14.0	Support HTTP/2 in WebView. More bug fixes and some enhancements.
Q3, 2020	JavaFX 15.0	Improved stability (memory management). More bug fixes and some enhancements.
Q1, 2021	JavaFX 16.0	JavaFX modules must be loaded from the module path, not the classpath (compiler warning). More bug fixes and some enhancements.
Q4, 2021	JavaFX 17.0.1	Minor enhancements and bug fixes.

The release notes show more details. You can see them at `https://github.com/openjdk/jfx/tree/master/doc-files`.

System Requirements

You need to have the following software installed on your computer:

- Java Development Kit 17, from Oracle, or OpenJDK.
- Eclipse IDE 2021-06 or later.
- The JavaFX 17 SDK for your platform, downloaded and extracted in a folder of your choice. Go to `https://openjfx.io/` for the documentation and download links.

▨ **Caution**   If you use Oracle's JDK, you need to enter a paid program in case you use the JDK for a commercial project. Consider using OpenJDK if you don't want that.

It is not necessary to have the Eclipse IDE to compile and run the programs in this book. You can use any other IDE, for example, NetBeans, JDeveloper, or IntelliJ IDEA. And, if this is your wish, you can work without any IDE at all, by just using the command line, maybe together with a build tool like Ant, Maven, or Grails.

The JavaFX distribution comes also in a bunch of prepackaged jmod files. However, as of the time of writing this edition, it was not possible to use them because of a CLASSPATH issue. You can give the JMODs a try, if you like. We will be using the SDK in this book, which consists of a bunch of Java modules packaged as jar files, alongside with platform-specific native libraries.

JavaFX Runtime Library

After you download and extract the JavaFX SDK distribution on your PC, you find the Java module JARs (javafx.base, javafx.graphics, etc.) together with platform-specific native libraries (.so files, .dll files, etc.) in the lib folder. For compiling and running JavaFX applications, you must refer to the JARs in this lib folder, and all the platform-specific native libraries must be present in the very same folder.

If you use an IDE and/or JavaFX tools, the JavaFX modules and libraries might be included and configured for you. If this is the case for you, watch out for the correct JavaFX version. The most reliable development setup, although maybe not the most convenient, is to use Eclipse for editing and compiling the Java files, providing the JavaFX libraries yourself, and *not* to use any special JavaFX features of the IDE.

JavaFX Source Code

Experienced developers sometimes prefer to look at the source code of the JavaFX library to learn how things are implemented behind the scenes.

The JavaFX SDK includes the sources—watch out for the src.zip file inside the lib folder. This is also the file you can use from inside Eclipse to attach JavaFX sources to the JavaFX API libraries—you can then use the F3 key in order to easily navigate to the JavaFX API class sources.

Your First JavaFX Application

Let's write your first JavaFX application. It should display the text "Hello JavaFX" in a window. I will take an incremental, step-by-step approach to explain how to develop this first application. I will add as few lines of code as possible and then explain what the code does and why it is needed.

Starting an Eclipse Project

Let us first see how to set up an Eclipse project in order to develop the JavaFX application.

■ **Note** If you use a different IDE, in order to see how to set up a JavaFX project you must consult the IDE's documentation.

Open Eclipse and use any workspace you like. Next, install the JRE from JDK 17 if you haven't done so already. To achieve that, go to the preferences and register the JRE, as shown in Figure 1-2.

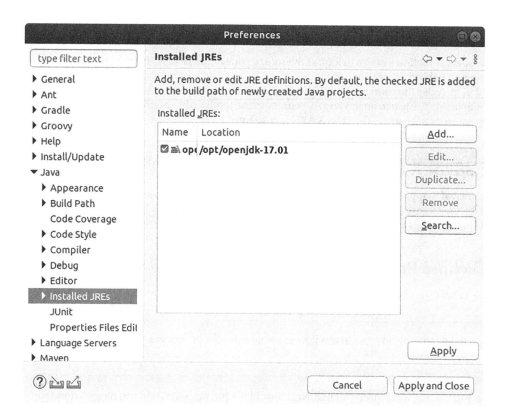

Figure 1-2. *Registering a JRE in Eclipse*

Start a new Java project named HelloFX. Make sure the New Project wizard creates a module-info. java file. There is a check box for that. In the project preferences, add all the module JARs from your JavaFX installation's lib folder; see Figure 1-3.

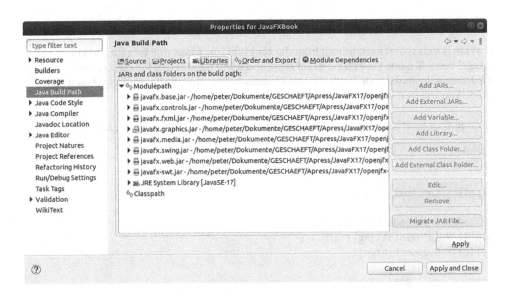

Figure 1-3. *Adding the JavaFX modules in Eclipse*

Make sure you add the JARs in the Modulepath section, not in the Classpath section.

As a last preparatory step, create a package com.jdojo.intro in the src folder—here, we add the application classes.

Setting Up a Module Info

In order for JavaFX to work correctly in a modularized environment, remember we added a module-info.java file inside the src folder, which is the same as saying "we use a modularized environment," we need to add a couple of entries in that file. Open it and change its contents to

```
module JavaFXBook {
        requires javafx.graphics;
        requires javafx.controls;
        requires java.desktop;
        requires javafx.swing;
        requires javafx.media;
        requires javafx.web;
        requires javafx.fxml;
        requires jdk.jsobject;

        opens com.jdojo.intro to javafx.graphics, javafx.base;
}
```

In the first line, as the module name, use whatever you entered while creating the project.

Creating the *HelloJavaFX* Class

A `JavaFX` application is a class that must inherit from the `Application` class that is in the `javafx.` `application` package. You will name your class `HelloFXApp`, and it will be stored in the `com.jdojo.intro` package. Listing 1-1 shows the initial code for the `HelloFXApp` class. Note that the `HelloFXApp` class will not compile at this point. You will fix it in the next section.

Listing 1-1. Inheriting Your JavaFX Application Class from the `javafx.application.Application` Class

```
// HelloFXApp.java
package com.jdojo.intro;

import javafx.application.Application;

public class HelloFXApp extends Application {
    public static void main(String[] args) {
        Application.launch(args);
    }
    // Application logic goes here
}
```

The program includes a package declaration, an import statement, and a class declaration. There is nothing like JavaFX in the code. It looks like any other Java application program. However, you have fulfilled one of the requirements of the JavaFX application by inheriting the `HelloFXApp` class from the Application class.

Overriding the *start()* Method

If you try compiling the `HelloFXApp` class, it will result in the following compile-time error: *HelloFXApp is not abstract and does not override abstract method start(Stage) in Application.* The error is stating that the Application class contains an abstract `start(Stage stage)` method, which has not been overridden in the `HelloFXApp` class. As a Java developer, you know what to do next: you either declare the `HelloFXApp` class as abstract or provide an implementation for the `start()` method. Here, let's provide an implementation for the `start()` method. The `start()` method in the `Application` class is declared as follows:

```
public abstract void start(Stage stage) throws java.lang.Exception
```

Listing 1-2 shows the revised code for the `HelloFXApp` class that overrides the `start()` method.

Listing 1-2. Overriding the `start()` Method in Your JavaFX Application Class

```
// HelloFXApp.java
package com.jdojo.intro;

import javafx.application.Application;
import javafx.stage.Stage;

public class HelloFXApp extends Application {
    public static void main(String[] args) {
        Application.launch(args);
    }
```

```
    @Override
    public void start(Stage stage) {
            // The logic for starting the application goes here
    }
}
```

In the revised code, you have incorporated two things:

- You have added one more import statement to import the Stage class from the javafx.stage package.

- You have implemented the start() method. The throws clause for the method is dropped, which is fine by the rules for overriding methods in Java.

The start() method is the entry point for a JavaFX application. It is called by the JavaFX application launcher. Notice that the start() method is passed an instance of the Stage class, which is known as the *primary stage* of the application. You can create more stages as necessary in your application. However, the primary stage is always created by the JavaFX runtime for you.

■ **Tip** Every JavaFX application class must inherit from the Application class and provide the implementation for the start(Stage stage) method.

Showing the Stage

Similar to a stage in the real world, a JavaFX stage is used to display a scene. A scene has visuals—such as text, shapes, images, controls, animations, and effects—with which the user may interact, as is the case with all GUI-based applications.

In JavaFX, the primary stage is a container for a scene. The stage look and feel is different depending on the environment your application is run in. You do not need to take any action based on the environment because the JavaFX runtime takes care of all the details for you. Since the application runs as a desktop application, the primary stage will be a window with a title bar and an area to display the scene.

The primary stage created by the application launcher does not have a scene. You will create a scene for your stage in the next section.

You must show the stage to see the visuals contained in its scene. Use the show() method to show the stage. Optionally, you can set a title for the stage using the setTitle() method. The revised code for the HelloFXApp class is shown in Listing 1-3.

Listing 1-3. Showing the Primary Stage in Your JavaFX Application Class

```
// HelloFXApp.java
package com.jdojo.intro;

import javafx.application.Application;
import javafx.stage.Stage;

public class HelloFXApp extends Application {
    public static void main(String[] args) {
            Application.launch(args);
    }
```

```
        @Override
        public void start(Stage stage) {
                // Set a title for the stage
                stage.setTitle("Hello JavaFX Application");

                // Show the stage
                stage.show();
        }
}
```

Launching the Application

You are now ready to run your first JavaFX application. Your IDE will probably have compiled your classes on the fly. Eclipse works this way.

Run the HelloFXApp class using the launcher from your Eclipse IDE. Click mouse-right on the class name, then invoke Run as ➤ Java Application. On a command line, for compiling and running you must add all the modulepath entries, which to show is beyond the introductory scope of this chapter.

If successfully launched, the application will display a window with a title bar as shown in Figure 1-4.

Figure 1-4. *The HelloFXApp JavaFX application without a scene*

The main area of the window is empty. This is the content area in which the stage will show its scene. Because you do not have a scene for your stage yet, you will see an empty area. The title bar shows the title that you have set in the start() method.

You can close the application using the Close menu option in the window title bar. Use Alt + F4 to close the window in Windows. You can use any other option to close the window as provided by your platform.

■ **Tip** The launch() method of the Application class does not return until all windows are closed or the application exits using the Platform.exit() method. The Platform class is in the javafx.application package.

You haven't seen anything exciting in JavaFX yet! You need to wait for that until you create a scene in the next section.

Adding a Scene to the Stage

An instance of the Scene class, which is in the javafx.scene package, represents a scene. A stage contains one scene, and a scene contains visual contents.

The contents of the scene are arranged in a tree-like hierarchy. At the top of the hierarchy is the *root* node. The root node may contain child nodes, which in turn may contain their child nodes, and so on. You must have a root node to create a scene. You will use a VBox as the root node. VBox stands for vertical box, which arranges its children vertically in a column. The following statement creates a VBox:

```
VBox root = new VBox();
```

▪ Tip   Any node that inherits from the `javafx.scene.Parent` class can be used as the root node for a scene. Several nodes, known as layout panes or containers such as VBox, HBox, Pane, FlowPane, GridPane, or TilePane, can be used as a root node. Group is a special container that groups its children together.

A node that can have children provides a getChildren() method that returns an ObservableList of its children. To add a child node to a node, simply add the child node to the ObservableList. The following snippet of code adds a Text node to a VBox:

```
// Create a VBox node
VBox root = new VBox();

// Create a Text node
Text msg = new Text("Hello JavaFX");

// Add the Text node to the VBox as a child node
root.getChildren().add(msg);
```

The Scene class contains several constructors. You will use the one that lets you specify the root node and the size of the scene. The following statement creates a scene with the VBox as the root node, with 300px width and 50px height:

```
// Create a scene
Scene scene = new Scene(root, 300, 50);
```

You need to set the scene to the stage by calling the setScene() method of the Stage class:

```
// Set the scene to the stage
stage.setScene(scene);
```

That's it. You have completed your first JavaFX program with a scene. Listing 1-4 contains the complete program. The program displays a window as shown in Figure 1-5.

Listing 1-4. A JavaFX Application with a Scene Having a Text Node

```
// HelloFXAppWithAScene.java
package com.jdojo.intro;

import javafx.application.Application;
import javafx.scene.Scene;
import javafx.scene.layout.VBox;
import javafx.scene.text.Text;
import javafx.stage.Stage;
```

```
public class HelloFXAppWithAScene extends Application {
    public static void main(String[] args) {
        Application.launch(args);
    }

    @Override
    public void start(Stage stage) {
        Text msg = new Text("Hello JavaFX");
        VBox root = new VBox();
        root.getChildren().add(msg);

        Scene scene = new Scene(root, 300, 50);
        stage.setScene(scene);
        stage.setTitle(
            "Hello JavaFX Application with a Scene");
        stage.show();
    }
}
```

Figure 1-5. *A JavaFX application with a scene having a Text node*

Improving the *HelloFX* Application

JavaFX is capable of doing much more than you have seen so far. Let's enhance the first program and add some more user interface elements such as buttons and text fields. This time, the user will be able to interact with the application. Use an instance of the Button class to create a button as shown:

```
// Create a button with "Exit" text
Button exitBtn = new Button("Exit");
```

When a button is clicked, an ActionEvent is fired. You can add an ActionEvent handler to handle the event. Use the setOnAction() method to set an ActionEvent handler for the button. The following statement sets an ActionEvent handler for the button. The handler terminates the application. You can use a lambda expression or an anonymous class to set the ActionEvent handler. The following snippet of code shows both approaches:

```
// Using a lambda expression
exitBtn.setOnAction(e -> Platform.exit());
```

```
// Using an anonymous class
import javafx.event.ActionEvent;
import javafx.event.EventHandler;
...
exitBtn.setOnAction(new EventHandler<ActionEvent>() {
        @Override
        public void handle(ActionEvent e) {
                Platform.exit();
        }
});
```

The program in Listing 1-5 shows how to add more nodes to the scene. The program uses the setStyle() method of the Label class to set the fill color of the Label to blue. I will discuss using CSS in JavaFX later.

Listing 1-5. Interacting with Users in a JavaFX Application

```
// ImprovedHelloFXApp.java
package com.jdojo.intro;

import javafx.application.Application;
import javafx.application.Platform;
import javafx.scene.Scene;
import javafx.scene.control.Button;
import javafx.scene.control.Label;
import javafx.scene.control.TextField;
import javafx.scene.layout.VBox;
import javafx.stage.Stage;

public class ImprovedHelloFXApp extends Application {
        public static void main(String[] args) {
                Application.launch(args);
        }

        @Override
        public void start(Stage stage) {
                Label nameLbl = new Label("Enter your name:");
                TextField nameFld = new TextField();

                Label msg = new Label();
                msg.setStyle("-fx-text-fill: blue;");

                // Create buttons
                Button sayHelloBtn = new Button("Say Hello");
                Button exitBtn = new Button("Exit");

                // Add the event handler for the Say Hello button
                sayHelloBtn.setOnAction(e -> {
                        String name = nameFld.getText();
                        if (name.trim().length() > 0) {
                                msg.setText("Hello " + name);
```

```
            } else {
                    msg.setText("Hello there");
            }
        });

        // Add the event handler for the Exit button
        exitBtn.setOnAction(e -> Platform.exit());

        // Create the root node
        VBox root = new VBox();

        // Set the vertical spacing between children to 5px
        root.setSpacing(5);

        // Add children to the root node
        root.getChildren().addAll(nameLbl, nameFld, msg,
                sayHelloBtn, exitBtn);

        Scene scene = new Scene(root, 350, 150);
        stage.setScene(scene);
        stage.setTitle("Improved Hello JavaFX Application");
        stage.show();
    }
}
```

The improved HelloFX program displays a window as shown in Figure 1-6. The window contains two labels, a text field, and two buttons. A VBox is used as the root node for the scene. Enter a name in the text field and click the Say Hello button to see a hello message. Clicking the Say Hello button without entering a name displays the message Hello there. The application displays a message in a Label control. Click the Exit button to exit the application.

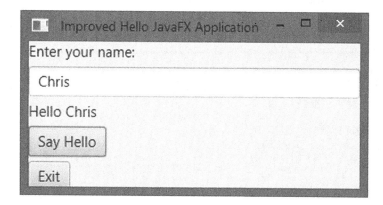

Figure 1-6. *A JavaFX application with a few controls in its scene*

Passing Parameters to a JavaFX Application

Like a Java application, you can pass parameters to a JavaFX application on the command line or via some launch configuration from an IDE.

The Parameters class, which is a static inner class of the Application class, encapsulates the parameters passed to a JavaFX application. It divides parameters into three categories:

- Named parameters
- Unnamed parameters
- Raw parameters (a combination of named and unnamed parameters)

You need to use the following three methods of the Parameters class to access the three types of parameters:

- Map<String, String> getNamed()
- List<String> getUnnamed()
- List<String> getRaw()

A parameter can be named or unnamed. A named parameter consists of a (name, value) pair. An unnamed parameter consists of a single value. The getNamed() method returns a Map<String, String> that contains the key-value pairs of the name parameters. The getUnnamed() method returns a List<String> where each element is an unnamed parameter value.

You pass only named and unnamed parameters to a JavaFX application. You do not pass raw type parameters. The JavaFX runtime makes all parameters, named and unnamed, passed to an application available as a List<String> through the getRaw() method of the Parameters class. The following discussion will make the distinction between the returned values from the three methods clear.

The getParameters() method of the Application class returns the reference of the Application. Parameters class. The reference to the Parameters class is available in the init() method of the Application class and the code that executes afterward. The parameters are not available in the constructor of the application as it is called before the init() method. Calling the getParameters() method in the constructor returns null.

The program in Listing 1-6 reads all types of parameters passed to the application and displays them in a TextArea. A TextArea is a UI node that displays multiple lines of text.

Listing 1-6. Accessing Parameters Passed to a JavaFX Application

```java
// FXParamApp.java
package com.jdojo.intro;

import java.util.List;
import java.util.Map;
import javafx.application.Application;
import javafx.scene.Group;
import javafx.scene.Scene;
import javafx.scene.control.TextArea;
import javafx.stage.Stage;

public class FXParamApp extends Application {
    public static void main(String[] args) {
        Application.launch(args);
    }
```

```
@Override
public void start(Stage stage) {
        // Get application parameters
        Parameters p = this.getParameters();
        Map<String, String> namedParams = p.getNamed();
        List<String> unnamedParams = p.getUnnamed();
        List<String> rawParams = p.getRaw();

        String paramStr = "Named Parameters: " + namedParams +
            "\n" +
            "Unnamed Parameters: " + unnamedParams + "\n" +
            "Raw Parameters: " + rawParams;

        TextArea ta = new TextArea(paramStr);
        Group root = new Group(ta);
        stage.setScene(new Scene(root));
        stage.setTitle("Application Parameters");
        stage.show();
    }
}
```

Let's look at a few cases of passing the parameters to the FXParamApp class. The output mentioned in the following cases is displayed in the TextArea control in the window when you run the FXParamApp class.

Case 1

The class is run as a stand-alone application using the following command:

```
java [options] com.jdojo.stage.FXParamApp Anna Lola
```

The preceding command passes no named parameters and two unnamed parameters: Anna and Lola. The list of the raw parameters will contain the two unnamed parameters. The output will be as shown:

```
Named Parameters: {}
Unnamed Parameters: [Anna, Lola]
Raw Parameters: [Anna, Lola]
```

Case 2

To pass a named parameter from the command line, you need to precede the parameter with exactly two hyphens (--). That is, a named parameter should be entered in the form

```
--key=value
```

The class is run as a stand-alone application using the command:

```
java [options] com.jdojo.stage.FXParamApp \
    Anna Lola --width=200 --height=100
```

The preceding command passes two named parameters: width=200 and height=100. It passes two unnamed parameters: Anna and Lola. The list of the raw parameters will contain four elements: two named parameters and two unnamed parameters. Named parameter values in the raw parameter list are preceded by two hyphens. The output will be as shown:

```
Named Parameters: {height=100, width=200}
Unnamed Parameters: [Anna, Lola]
Raw Parameters: [Anna, Lola, --width=200, --height=100]
```

Launching a JavaFX Application

Earlier, I touched on the topic of launching the JavaFX application while developing the first JavaFX application. This section gives more details on launching a JavaFX application.

Every JavaFX application class inherits from the Application class. The Application class is in the javafx.application package. It contains a static launch() method. Its sole purpose is to launch a JavaFX application. It is an overloaded method with the following two variants:

- static void launch(Class<? extends Application> appClass, String... args)

- static void launch(String... args)

Notice that you do not create an object of your JavaFX application class to launch it. The JavaFX runtime creates an object of your application class when the launch() method is called.

■ **Tip** Your JavaFX application class must have a no-args constructor; otherwise, a runtime exception will be thrown when an attempt is made to launch it.

The first variant of the launch() method is clear. You pass the class reference of your application class as the first argument, and the launch() method will create an object of that class. The second argument is comprised of the command-line arguments passed to the application. The following snippet of code shows how to use the first variant of the launch() method:

```
public class MyJavaFXApp extends Application {
    public static void main(String[] args) {
            Application.launch(MyJavaFXApp.class, args);
    }

    // More code goes here
}
```

The class reference passed to the launch() method does not have to be of the same class from which the method is called. For example, the following snippet of code launches the MyJavaFXApp application class from the MyAppLauncher class, which does not extend the Application class:

```
public class MyAppLauncher {
      public static void main(String[] args) {
              Application.launch(MyJavaFXApp.class, args);
      }

      // More code goes here
}
```

The second variant of the launch() method takes only one argument, which is the command-line argument passed to the application. Which JavaFX application class does it use to launch the application? It attempts to find the application class name based on the caller. It checks the class name of the code that calls it. If the method is called as part of the code for a class that inherits from the Application class, directly or indirectly, that class is used to launch the JavaFX application. Otherwise, a runtime exception is thrown. Let's look at some examples to make this rule clear.

In the following snippet of code, the launch() method detects that it is called from the main() method of the MyJavaFXApp class. The MyJavaFXApp class inherits from the Application class. Therefore, the MyJavaFXApp class is used as the application class:

```
public class MyJavaFXApp extends Application {
      public static void main(String[] args) {
              Application.launch(args);
      }

      // More code goes here
}
```

In the following snippet of code, the launch() method is called from the main() method of the Test class. The Test does not inherit from the Application class. Therefore, a runtime exception is thrown, as shown in the output below the code:

```
public class Test {
      public static void main(String[] args) {
              Application.launch(args);
      }

      // More code goes here
}
```

```
Exception in thread "main" java.lang.RuntimeException: Error: class Test is not a subclass
of javafx.application.Application
        at javafx.application.Application.launch(Application.java:308)
        at Test.main(Test.java)
```

In the following snippet of code, the launch() method detects that it is called from the run() method of the MyJavaFXApp$1 class. Note that the MyJavaFXApp$1 class is an anonymous inner class generated by the compiler, which is a subclass of the Object class, not the Application class, and it implements the Runnable interface. Because the call to the launch() method is contained within the MyJavaFXApp$1 class, which is not a subclass of the Application class, a runtime exception is thrown, as shown in the output that follows the code:

```
public class MyJavaFXApp extends Application {
        public static void main(String[] args) {
                Thread t = new Thread(new Runnable() {
                        public void run() {
                                Application.launch(args);
                        }
                });

                t.start();
        }

        // More code goes here
}
```

```
Exception in thread "Thread-0" java.lang.RuntimeException: Error: class MyJavaFXApp$1 is
not a subclass of javafx.application.Application
        at javafx.application.Application.launch(Application.java:211)
        at MyJavaFXApp$1.run(MyJavaFXApp.java)
        at java.lang.Thread.run(Thread.java:722)
```

Now that you know how to launch a JavaFX application, it's time to learn the best practice in launching a JavaFX application: limit the code in the main() method to only one statement that launches the application, as shown in the following code:

```
public class MyJavaFXApp extends Application {
        public static void main(String[] args) {
                Application.launch(args);

                // Do not add any more code in this method
        }

        // More code goes here
}
```

■ **Tip** The launch() method of the Application class must be called only once; otherwise, a runtime exception is thrown. The call to the launch() method blocks until the application is terminated.

The Life Cycle of a JavaFX Application

The JavaFX runtime creates several threads. At different stages in the application, threads are used to perform different tasks. In this section, I will only explain those threads that are used to call methods of the Application class during its life cycle. The JavaFX runtime creates, among other threads, two threads:

- JavaFX-Launcher
- JavaFX Application Thread

The launch() method of the Application class creates these threads. During the lifetime of a JavaFX application, the JavaFX runtime calls the following methods of the specified JavaFX Application class in order:

- The no-args constructor

- The init() method

- The start() method

- The stop() method

The JavaFX runtime creates an object of the specified Application class on the JavaFX Application Thread. The JavaFX Launcher Thread calls the init() method of the specified Application class. The init() method implementation in the Application class is empty. You can override this method in your application class. It is not allowed to create a Stage or a Scene on the JavaFX Launcher Thread. They must be created on the JavaFX Application Thread. Therefore, you cannot create a Stage or a Scene inside the init() method. Attempting to do so throws a runtime exception. It is fine to create UI controls, for example, buttons or shapes.

The JavaFX Application Thread calls the start(Stage stage) method of the specified Application class. Note that the start() method in the Application class is declared abstract, and you must override this method in your application class.

At this point, the launch() method waits for the JavaFX application to finish. When the application finishes, the JavaFX Application Thread calls the stop() method of the specified Application class. The default implementation of the stop() method is empty in the Application class. You will have to override this method in your application class to perform your logic when your application stops.

The code in Listing 1-7 illustrates the life cycle of a JavaFX application. It displays an empty stage. You will see the first three lines of the output when the stage is shown. You will need to close the stage to see the last line of the output.

Listing 1-7. The Life Cycle of a JavaFX Application

```
// FXLifeCycleApp.java
package com.jdojo.intro;

import javafx.application.Application;
import javafx.scene.Group;
import javafx.scene.Scene;
import javafx.stage.Stage;

public class FXLifeCycleApp extends Application {
    public FXLifeCycleApp() {
        String name = Thread.currentThread().getName();
        System.out.println("FXLifeCycleApp() constructor: " +
            name);
    }

    public static void main(String[] args) {
        Application.launch(args);
    }
```

```
@Override
public void init() {
        String name = Thread.currentThread().getName();
        System.out.println("init() method: " + name);
}

@Override
public void start(Stage stage) {
        String name = Thread.currentThread().getName();
        System.out.println("start() method: " + name);

        Scene scene = new Scene(new Group(), 200, 200);
        stage.setScene(scene);
        stage.setTitle("JavaFX Application Life Cycle");
        stage.show();
}

@Override
public void stop() {
        String name = Thread.currentThread().getName();
        System.out.println("stop() method: " + name);
}
}
```

```
FXLifeCycleApp() constructor: JavaFX Application Thread
init() method: JavaFX-Launcher
start() method: JavaFX Application Thread
stop() method: JavaFX Application Thread
```

Terminating a JavaFX Application

A JavaFX application may be terminated explicitly or implicitly. You can terminate a JavaFX application explicitly by calling the Platform.exit() method. When this method is called, after or from within the start() method, the stop() method of the Application class is called, and then the JavaFX Application Thread is terminated. At this point, if there are only daemon threads running, the JVM will exit. If this method is called from the constructor or the init() method of the Application class, the stop() method may not be called.

A JavaFX application may be terminated implicitly, when the last window is closed. This behavior can be turned on and turned off using the static setImplicitExit(boolean implicitExit) method of the Platform class. Passing true to this method turns this behavior on. Passing false to this method turns this behavior off. By default, this behavior is turned on. This is the reason that in most of the examples so far, applications were terminated when you closed the windows. When this behavior is turned on, the stop() method of the Application class is called before terminating the JavaFX Application Thread. Terminating the JavaFX Application Thread does not always terminate the JVM. The JVM terminates if all running nondaemon threads terminate. If the implicit terminating behavior of the JavaFX application is turned off, you must call the exit() method of the Platform class to terminate the application.

Summary

JavaFX is an open source Java-based GUI framework that is used to develop rich client applications. It is the successor of Swing in the arena of GUI development technology on the Java platform.

The GUI in JavaFX is shown in a stage. A stage is an instance of the Stage class. A stage is a window in a desktop application. A stage contains a scene. A scene contains a group of nodes (graphics) arranged in a tree-like structure.

A JavaFX application inherits from the Application class. The JavaFX runtime creates the first stage called the primary stage and calls the start() method of the application class passing the reference of the primary stage. The developer needs to add a scene to the stage and make the stage visible inside the start() method.

You can launch a JavaFX application using the launch() method of the Application class.

During the lifetime of a JavaFX application, the JavaFX runtime calls predefined methods of the JavaFX Application class in a specific order. First, the no-args constructor of the class is called, followed by calls to the init() and start() methods. When the application terminates, the stop() method is called. You can terminate a JavaFX application by calling the Platform.exit() method.

The next chapter will introduce you to properties and binding in JavaFX.

CHAPTER 2

■ ■ ■

Properties and Bindings

In this chapter, you will learn:

- What a property is in JavaFX

- How to create a property object and use it

- The class hierarchy of properties in JavaFX

- How to handle the invalidation and change events in a property object

- What a binding is in JavaFX and how to use unidirectional and bidirectional bindings

- About the high-level and low-level binding APIs in JavaFX

This chapter discusses the properties and binding support in Java and JavaFX. If you have experience using the JavaBeans API for properties and binding, you can skip the first few sections, which discuss the properties and binding support in Java, and start with the section "Understanding Properties in JavaFX."

The examples of this chapter lie in the `com.jdojo.binding` package. In order for them to work, you must add a corresponding line to the `module-info.java` file:

```
...
opens com.jdojo.binding to javafx.graphics, javafx.base;
...
```

What Is a Property?

A Java class can contain two types of members: *fields* and *methods*. Fields represent the state of objects, and they are declared private. Public methods, known as *accessors*, or *getters* and *setters*, are used to read and modify private fields. In simple terms, a Java class that has public accessors, for all or part of its private fields, is known as a Java *bean*, and the accessors define the properties of the bean. Properties of a Java bean allow users to customize its state, behavior, or both.

Java beans are observable. They support property change notification. When a public property of a Java bean changes, a notification is sent to all interested listeners.

In essence, Java beans define reusable components that can be assembled by a builder tool to create a Java application. This opens the door for third parties to develop Java beans and make them available to others for reuse.

A property can be read-only, write-only, or read/write. A ready-only property has a getter but no setter. A write-only property has a setter but no getter. A read/write property has a getter and a setter.

Java IDEs and other builder tools (e.g., a GUI layout builder) use introspection to get the list of properties of a bean and let you manipulate those properties at design time. A Java bean can be visual or nonvisual. Properties of a bean can be used in a builder tool or programmatically.

The JavaBeans API provides a class library, through the java.beans package, and naming conventions to create and use Java beans. The following is an example of a Person bean with a read/write name property. The getName() method (the getter) returns the value of the name field. The setName() method (the setter) sets the value of the name field:

```java
// Person.java
package com.jdojo.binding;

public class Person {
        private String name;

        public String getName() {
                return name;
        }

        public void setName(String name) {
                this.name = name;
        }
}
```

By convention, the names of the getter and setter methods are constructed by appending the name of the property, with the first letter in uppercase, to the words *get* and *set*, respectively. The getter method should not take any parameters, and its return type should be the same as the type of the field. The setter method should take a parameter whose type should be the same as the type of the field, and its return type should be void.

The following snippet of code manipulates the name property of a Person bean programmatically:

```java
Person p = new Person();
p.setName("John Jacobs");
String name = p.getName();
```

Some object-oriented programming languages, for example, C#, provide a third type of class member known as a *property*. A property is used to read, write, and compute the value of a private field from outside the class. C# lets you declare a Person class with a Name property as follows:

```csharp
// C# version of the Person class
public class Person {
        private string name;

        public string Name {
                get { return name; }
                set { name = value; }
        }
}
```

In C#, the following snippet of code manipulates the name private field using the Name property; it is equivalent to the previously shown Java version of the code:

```
Person p = new Person();
p.Name = "John Jacobs";
string name = p.Name;
```

If the accessors of a property perform the routine work of returning and setting the value of a field, C# offers a compact format to define such a property. You do not even need to declare a private field in this case. You can rewrite the Person class in C# as shown here:

```
// C# version of the Person class using the compact format
public class Person {
        public string Name { get; set; }
}
```

So, what is a property? A *property* is a publicly accessible attribute of a class that affects its state, behavior, or both. Even though a property is publicly accessible, its use (read/write) invokes methods that hide the actual implementation to access the data. Properties are observable, so interested parties are notified when its value changes.

■ **Tip**   In essence, properties define the public state of an object that can be read, written, and observed for changes. Unlike other programming languages, such as C#, properties in Java are not supported at the language level. Java support for properties comes through the JavaBeans API and design patterns. For more details on properties in Java, please refer to the JavaBeans specification, which can be downloaded from www.oracle.com/java/technologies/javase/javabeans-spec.html.

Apart from simple properties, such as the name property of the Person bean, Java also supports *indexed*, *bound*, and *constrained* properties. An indexed property is an array of values that are accessed using indexes. An indexed property is implemented using an array data type. A bound property sends a notification to all listeners when it is changed. A constrained property is a bound property in which a listener can veto a change.

What Is a Binding?

In programming, the term *binding* is used in many different contexts. Here, I want to define it in the context of *data binding*. Data binding defines a relation between data elements (usually variables) in a program to keep them synchronized. In a GUI application, data binding is frequently used to synchronize the elements in the data model with the corresponding UI elements.

Consider the following statement, assuming that x, y, and z are numeric variables:

```
x = y + z;
```

The preceding statement defines a binding between x, y, and z. When it is executed, the value of x is synchronized with the sum of y and z. A binding also has a time factor. In the preceding statement, the value of x is bound to the sum of y and z and is valid at the time the statement is executed. The value of x may not be the sum of y and z before and after the preceding statement is executed.

Sometimes, it is desired for a binding to hold over a period. Consider the following statement that defines a binding using listPrice, discounts, and taxes:

```
soldPrice = listPrice - discounts + taxes;
```

For this case, you would like to keep the binding valid forever, so the sold price is computed correctly, whenever listPrice, discounts, or taxes change.

In the preceding binding, listPrice, discounts, and taxes are known as *dependencies*, and it is said that soldPrice is bound to listPrice, discounts, and taxes.

For a binding to work correctly, it is necessary that the binding is notified whenever its dependencies change. Programming languages that support binding provide a mechanism to register listeners with the dependencies. When dependencies become invalid or they change, all listeners are notified. A binding may synchronize itself with its dependencies when it receives such notifications.

A binding can be an *eager binding* or a *lazy binding*. In an eager binding, the bound variable is recomputed immediately after its dependencies change. In a lazy binding, the bound variable is not recomputed when its dependencies change. Rather, it is recomputed when it is read the next time. A lazy binding performs better compared to an eager binding.

A binding may be *unidirectional* or *bidirectional*. A unidirectional binding works only in one direction; changes in the dependencies are propagated to the bound variable. A bidirectional binding works in both directions. In a bidirectional binding, the bound variable and the dependency keep their values synchronized with each other. Typically, a bidirectional binding is defined only between two variables. For example, a bidirectional binding, x = y and y = x, declares that the values of x and y are always the same.

Mathematically, it is not possible to define a bidirectional binding between multiple variables uniquely. In the preceding example, the sold price binding is a unidirectional binding. If you want to make it a bidirectional binding, it is not uniquely possible to compute the values of the list price, discounts, and taxes when the sold price is changed. There are an infinite number of possibilities in the other direction.

Applications with GUIs provide users with UI widgets, for example, text fields, check boxes, and buttons, to manipulate data. The data displayed in UI widgets have to be synchronized with the underlying data model and vice versa. In this case, a bidirectional binding is needed to keep the UI and the data model synchronized.

Understanding Binding Support in JavaBeans

Before I discuss JavaFX properties and binding, let's take a short tour of binding support in the JavaBeans API. You may skip this section if you have used the JavaBeans API before.

Java has supported binding of bean properties since its early releases. Listing 2-1 shows an Employee bean with two properties, name and salary.

Listing 2-1. An Employee Java Bean with Two Properties Named name and salary

```
// Employee.java
package com.jdojo.binding;

import java.beans.PropertyChangeListener;
import java.beans.PropertyChangeSupport;

public class Employee {
        private String name;
        private double salary;
        private PropertyChangeSupport pcs = new PropertyChangeSupport(this);
```

```java
    public Employee() {
            this.name = "John Doe";
            this.salary = 1000.0;
    }

    public Employee(String name, double salary) {
            this.name = name;
            this.salary = salary;
    }

    public String getName() {
            return name;
    }

    public void setName(String name) {
            this.name = name;
    }

    public double getSalary() {
            return salary;
    }

    public void setSalary(double newSalary) {
            double oldSalary = this.salary;
            this.salary = newSalary;

            // Notify the registered listeners about the change
            pcs.firePropertyChange("salary", oldSalary, newSalary);
    }

    public void addPropertyChangeListener(
                    PropertyChangeListener listener) {
            pcs.addPropertyChangeListener(listener);
    }

    public void removePropertyChangeListener(
                    PropertyChangeListener listener) {
            pcs.removePropertyChangeListener(listener);
    }

    @Override
    public String toString() {
            return "name = " + name + ", salary = " + salary;
    }
}
```

Both properties of the Employee bean are read/write. The salary property is also a bound property. Its setter generates property change notifications when the salary changes.

Interested listeners can register or deregister for the change notifications using the addPropertyChangeListener() and removePropertyChangeListener() methods. The PropertyChangeSupport class is part of the JavaBeans API that facilitates the registration and removal of property change listeners and firing of the property change notifications.

Any party interested in synchronizing values based on the salary change will need to register with the Employee bean and take necessary actions when it is notified of the change.

Listing 2-2 shows how to register for salary change notifications for an Employee bean. The output below it shows that salary change notification is fired only twice, whereas the setSalary() method is called three times. This is true because the second call to the setSalary() method uses the same salary amount as the first call, and the PropertyChangeSupport class is smart enough to detect that. The example also shows how you would bind variables using the JavaBeans API. The tax for an employee is computed based on a tax percentage. In the JavaBeans API, property change notifications are used to bind the variables.

Listing 2-2. An EmployeeTest Class That Tests the Employee Bean for Salary Changes

```java
// EmployeeTest.java
package com.jdojo.binding;

import java.beans.PropertyChangeEvent;

public class EmployeeTest {
    public static void main(String[] args) {
        final Employee e1 = new Employee("John Jacobs", 2000.0);

        // Compute the tax
        computeTax(e1.getSalary());

        // Add a property change listener to e1
        e1.addPropertyChangeListener(
                EmployeeTest::handlePropertyChange);

        // Change the salary
        e1.setSalary(3000.00);
        e1.setSalary(3000.00); // No change notification is sent.
        e1.setSalary(6000.00);
    }

    public static void handlePropertyChange(PropertyChangeEvent e) {
        String propertyName = e.getPropertyName();

        if ("salary".equals(propertyName)) {
            System.out.print("Salary has changed. ");
            System.out.print("Old:" + e.getOldValue());
            System.out.println(", New:" +
                        e.getNewValue());
            computeTax((Double)e.getNewValue());
        }
    }

    public static void computeTax(double salary) {
        final double TAX_PERCENT = 20.0;
        double tax = salary * TAX_PERCENT/100.0;
        System.out.println("Salary:" + salary + ", Tax:" + tax);
    }
}
```

```
Salary:2000.0, Tax:400.0
Salary has changed. Old:2000.0, New:3000.0
Salary:3000.0, Tax:600.0
Salary has changed. Old:3000.0, New:6000.0
Salary:6000.0, Tax:1200.0
```

Understanding Properties in JavaFX

JavaFX supports properties, events, and binding through *properties* and *binding* APIs. Properties support in JavaFX is a huge leap forward from the JavaBeans properties.

All properties in JavaFX are observable. They can be observed for invalidation and value changes. There can be read/write or read-only properties. All read/write properties support binding.

In JavaFX, a property can represent a value or a collection of values. This chapter covers properties that represent a single value. I will cover properties representing a collection of values in Chapter 3.

In JavaFX, properties are objects. There is a property class hierarchy for each type of property. For example, the IntegerProperty, DoubleProperty, and StringProperty classes represent properties of int, double, and String types, respectively. These classes are abstract. There are two types of implementation classes for them: one to represent a read/write property and one to represent a wrapper for a read-only property. For example, the SimpleDoubleProperty and ReadOnlyDoubleWrapper classes are concrete classes whose objects are used as read/write and read-only double properties, respectively.

The following is an example of how to create an IntegerProperty with an initial value of 100:

```
IntegerProperty counter = new SimpleIntegerProperty(100);
```

Property classes provide two pairs of getter and setter methods: get()/set() and getValue()/setValue(). The get() and set() methods get and set the value of the property, respectively. For primitive type properties, they work with primitive type values. For example, for IntegerProperty, the return type of the get() method and the parameter type of the set() method are int. The getValue() and setValue() methods work with an object type; for example, their return type and parameter type are Integer for IntegerProperty.

■ **Tip** For reference type properties, such as StringProperty and ObjectProperty<T>, both pairs of getter and setter work with an object type. That is, both get() and getValue() methods of StringProperty return a String, and set() and setValue() methods take a String parameter. With autoboxing for primitive types, it does not matter which version of getter and setter is used. The getValue() and setValue() methods exist to help you write generic code in terms of object types.

The following snippet of code uses an IntegerProperty and its get() and set() methods. The counter property is a read/write property as it is an object of the SimpleIntegerProperty class:

```
IntegerProperty counter = new SimpleIntegerProperty(1);
int counterValue = counter.get();
System.out.println("Counter:" + counterValue);
```

```
counter.set(2);
counterValue = counter.get();
System.out.println("Counter:" + counterValue);
```

```
Counter:1
Counter:2
```

Working with read-only properties is a bit tricky. A ReadOnlyXXXWrapper class wraps two properties of XXX type: one read-only and one read/write. Both properties are synchronized. Its getReadOnlyProperty() method returns a ReadOnlyXXXProperty object.

The following snippet of code shows how to create a read-only Integer property. The idWrapper property is read/write, whereas the id property is read-only. When the value in idWrapper is changed, the value in id is changed automatically:

```
ReadOnlyIntegerWrapper idWrapper = new ReadOnlyIntegerWrapper(100);
ReadOnlyIntegerProperty id = idWrapper.getReadOnlyProperty();

System.out.println("idWrapper:" + idWrapper.get());
System.out.println("id:" + id.get());

// Change the value
idWrapper.set(101);

System.out.println("idWrapper:" + idWrapper.get());
System.out.println("id:" + id.get());
```

```
idWrapper:100
id:100
idWrapper:101
id:101
```

■ **Tip** Typically, a wrapper property is used as a private instance variable of a class. The class can change the property internally. One of its methods returns the read-only property object of the wrapper class, so the same property is read-only for the outside world.

You can use seven types of properties that represent a single value. The base classes for those properties are named as XXXProperty, read-only base classes are named as ReadOnlyXXXProperty, and wrapper classes are named as ReadOnlyXXXWrapper. The values for XXX for each type are listed in Table 2-1.

Table 2-1. *List of Property Classes That Wrap a Single Value*

Type	XXX Value
int	Integer
long	Long
float	Float
double	Double
boolean	Boolean
String	String
Object	Object

A property object wraps three pieces of information:

- The reference of the bean that contains it

- A name

- A value

When you create a property object, you can supply all or none of the preceding three pieces of information. Concrete property classes, named like SimpleXXXProperty and ReadOnlyXXXWrapper, provide four constructors that let you supply combinations of the three pieces of information. The following are the constructors for the SimpleIntegerProperty class:

```
SimpleIntegerProperty()
SimpleIntegerProperty(int initialValue)
SimpleIntegerProperty(Object bean, String name)
SimpleIntegerProperty(Object bean, String name, int initialValue)
```

The default value for the initial value depends on the type of the property. It is zero for numeric types, false for boolean types, and null for reference types.

A property object can be part of a bean, or it can be a stand-alone object. The specified bean is the reference to the bean object that contains the property. For a stand-alone property object, it can be null. Its default value is null.

The name of the property is its name. If not supplied, it defaults to an empty string.

The following snippet of code creates a property object as part of a bean and sets all three values. The first argument to the constructor of the SimpleStringProperty class is this, which is the reference of the Person bean, the second argument—"name"—is the name of the property, and the third argument—"Li"—is the value of the property:

```
public class Person {
        private StringProperty name = new SimpleStringProperty(
                this, "name", "Li");
            // More code goes here...
}
```

Every property class has getBean() and getName() methods that return the bean reference and the property name, respectively.

Using Properties in JavaFX Beans

In the previous section, you saw the use of JavaFX properties as stand-alone objects. In this section, you will use them in classes to define properties. Let's create a Book class with three properties: ISBN, title, and price, which will be modeled using JavaFX property classes.

In JavaFX, you do not declare the property of a class as one of the primitive types. Rather, you use one of the JavaFX property classes. The title property of the Book class will be declared as follows. It is declared private as usual:

```
public class Book {
        private StringProperty title = new SimpleStringProperty(this,
                "title", "Unknown");
}
```

You declare a public getter for the property, which is named, by convention, as XXXProperty, where XXX is the name of the property. This getter returns the reference of the property. For our title property, the getter will be named titleProperty as shown in the following:

```
public class Book {
        private StringProperty title = new SimpleStringProperty(this,
                "title", "Unknown");

        public final StringProperty titleProperty() {
                return title;
        }
}
```

The preceding declaration of the Book class is fine to work with the title property, as shown in the following snippet of code that sets and gets the title of a book:

```
Book b = new Book();
b.titleProperty().set("Harnessing JavaFX 17.0");
String title = b.titleProperty().get();
```

According to the JavaFX design patterns, and not for any technical requirements, a JavaFX property has a getter and a setter that are similar to the getters and setters in JavaBeans. The return type of the getter and the parameter type of the setter are the same as the type of the property value. For example, for StringProperty and IntegerProperty, they will be String and int, respectively. The getTitle() and setTitle() methods for the title property are declared as follows:

```
public class Book {
        private StringProperty title = new SimpleStringProperty(this,
                "title", "Unknown");

        public final StringProperty titleProperty() {
                return title;
        }

        public final String getTitle() {
                return title.get();
        }
```

```
        public final void setTitle(String title) {
                this.title.set(title);
        }
}
```

Note that the getTitle() and setTitle() methods use the title property object internally to get and set the title value.

■ **Tip** By convention, getters and setters for a property of a class are declared final. Additional getters and setters, using JavaBeans naming convention, are added to make the class interoperable with the older tools and frameworks that use the old JavaBeans naming conventions to identify the properties of a class.

The following snippet of code shows the declaration of a read-only ISBN property for the Book class:

```
public class Book {
        private ReadOnlyStringWrapper ISBN =
                new ReadOnlyStringWrapper(this, "ISBN", "Unknown");

        public final String getISBN() {
                return ISBN.get();
        }

        public final ReadOnlyStringProperty ISBNProperty() {
                return ISBN.getReadOnlyProperty();
        }

        // More code goes here...
}
```

Notice the following points about the declaration of the read-only ISBN property:

- It uses the ReadOnlyStringWrapper class instead of the SimpleStringProperty class.

- There is no setter for the property value. You may declare one; however, it must be private.

- The getter for the property value works the same as for a read/write property.

- The ISBNProperty() method uses ReadOnlyStringProperty as the return type, not ReadOnlyStringWrapper. It obtains a read-only version of the property object from the wrapper object and returns the same.

For the users of the Book class, its ISBN property is read-only. However, it can be changed internally, and the change will be reflected in the read-only version of the property object automatically.

Listing 2-3 shows the complete code for the Book class.

Listing 2-3. A Book Class with Two Read/Write and a Read-Only Properties

```java
// Book.java
package com.jdojo.binding;

import javafx.beans.property.DoubleProperty;
import javafx.beans.property.ReadOnlyStringProperty;
import javafx.beans.property.ReadOnlyStringWrapper;
import javafx.beans.property.SimpleDoubleProperty;
import javafx.beans.property.SimpleStringProperty;
import javafx.beans.property.StringProperty;

public class Book {
        private StringProperty title = new SimpleStringProperty(this,
                "title", "Unknown");
        private DoubleProperty price = new SimpleDoubleProperty(this,
                "price", 0.0);
        private ReadOnlyStringWrapper ISBN = new ReadOnlyStringWrapper(this,
                "ISBN", "Unknown");

        public Book() {
        }

        public Book(String title, double price, String ISBN) {
                this.title.set(title);
                this.price.set(price);
                this.ISBN.set(ISBN);
        }

        public final String getTitle() {
                return title.get();
        }

        public final void setTitle(String title) {
                this.title.set(title);
        }

        public final StringProperty titleProperty() {
                return title;
        }

        public final double getprice() {
                return price.get();
        }

        public final void setPrice(double price) {
                this.price.set(price);
        }

        public final DoubleProperty priceProperty() {
                return price;
        }
```

```
        public final String getISBN() {
                return ISBN.get();
        }

        public final ReadOnlyStringProperty ISBNProperty() {
                return ISBN.getReadOnlyProperty();
        }
}
```

Listing 2-4 tests the properties of the Book class. It creates a Book object, prints the details, changes some properties, and prints the details again. Note the use of the ReadOnlyProperty parameter type for the printDetails() method. All property classes implement, directly or indirectly, the ReadOnlyProperty interface.

The toString() methods of the property implementation classes return a well-formatted string that contains all relevant pieces of information for a property. I did not use the toString() method of the property objects because I wanted to show you the use of the different methods of the JavaFX properties.

Listing 2-4. A Test Class to Test Properties of the Book Class

```
// BookPropertyTest.java
package com.jdojo.binding;

import javafx.beans.property.ReadOnlyProperty;

public class BookPropertyTest {
        public static void main(String[] args) {
                Book book = new Book("Harnessing JavaFX", 9.99,
                        "0123456789");

                System.out.println("After creating the Book object...");

                // Print Property details
                printDetails(book.titleProperty());
                printDetails(book.priceProperty());
                printDetails(book.ISBNProperty());

                // Change the book's properties
                book.setTitle("Harnessing JavaFX 17.0");
                book.setPrice(9.49);

                System.out.println(
                        "\nAfter changing the Book properties...");

                // Print Property details
                printDetails(book.titleProperty());
                printDetails(book.priceProperty());
                printDetails(book.ISBNProperty());
        }
```

```
        public static void printDetails(ReadOnlyProperty<?> p) {
                String name = p.getName();
                Object value = p.getValue();
                Object bean = p.getBean();
                String beanClassName = (bean == null)?
                        "null":bean.getClass().getSimpleName();
                String propClassName = p.getClass().getSimpleName();

                System.out.print(propClassName);
                System.out.print("[Name:" + name);
                System.out.print(", Bean Class:" + beanClassName);
                System.out.println(", Value:" + value + "]");
        }
}
```

```
After creating the Book object...
SimpleStringProperty[Name:title, Bean Class:Book, Value:Harnessing JavaFX]
SimpleDoubleProperty[Name:price, Bean Class:Book, Value:9.99]
ReadOnlyPropertyImpl[Name:ISBN, Bean Class:Book, Value:0123456789]

After changing the Book properties...
SimpleStringProperty[Name:title, Bean Class:Book, Value:Harnessing JavaFX 17.0]
SimpleDoubleProperty[Name:price, Bean Class:Book, Value:9.49]
ReadOnlyPropertyImpl[Name:ISBN, Bean Class:Book, Value:0123456789]
```

Understanding the Property Class Hierarchy

It is important to understand a few core classes and interfaces of the JavaFX properties and binding APIs before you start using them. Figure 2-1 shows the class diagram for core interfaces of the properties API. You will not need to use these interfaces directly in your programs. Specialized versions of these interfaces and the classes that implement them exist and are used directly.

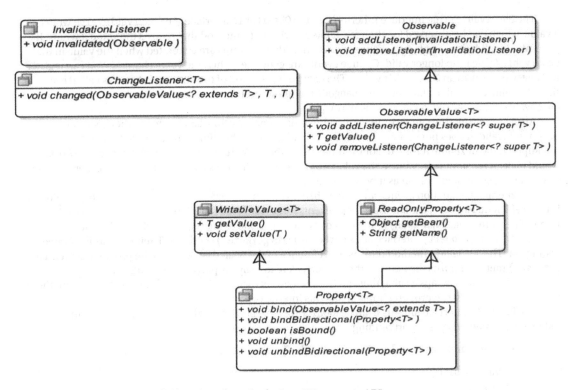

Figure 2-1. *A class diagram for core interfaces in the JavaFX property API*

Classes and interfaces in the JavaFX properties API are spread across different packages. Those packages are javafx.beans, javafx.beans.binding, javafx.beans.property, and javafx.beans.value.

The Observable interface is at the top of the properties API. An Observable wraps content, and it can be observed for invalidations of its content. The Observable interface has two methods to support this. Its addListener() method lets you add an InvalidationListener. The invalidated() method of the InvalidationListener is called when the content of the Observable becomes invalid. An InvalidationListener can be removed using its removeListener() method.

■ **Tip** All JavaFX properties are observable.

An Observable should generate an invalidation event only when the status of its content changes from valid to invalid. That is, multiple invalidations in a row should generate only one invalidation event. Property classes in the JavaFX follow this guideline.

■ **Tip** The generation of an invalidation event by an Observable does not necessarily mean that its content has changed. All it means is that its content is invalid for some reason. For example, sorting an ObservableList may generate an invalidation event. Sorting does not change the contents of the list; it only reorders the contents.

The ObservableValue interface inherits from the Observable interface. An ObservableValue wraps a value, which can be observed for changes. It has a getValue() method that returns the value it wraps. It generates invalidation events and change events. Invalidation events are generated when the value in the ObservableValue is no longer valid. Change events are generated when the value changes. You can register a ChangeListener to an ObservableValue. The changed() method of the ChangeListener is called every time the value of its value changes. The changed() method receives three arguments: the reference of the ObservableValue, the old value, and the new value.

An ObservableValue can recompute its value lazily or eagerly. In a lazy strategy, when its value becomes invalid, it does not know if the value has changed until the value is recomputed; the value is recomputed the next time it is read. For example, using the getValue() method of an ObservableValue would make it recompute its value if the value was invalid and if it uses a lazy strategy. In an eager strategy, the value is recomputed as soon as it becomes invalid.

To generate invalidation events, an ObservableValue can use lazy or eager evaluation. A lazy evaluation is more efficient. However, generating change events forces an ObservableValue to recompute its value immediately (an eager evaluation) as it has to pass the new value to the registered change listeners.

The ReadOnlyProperty interface adds getBean() and getName() methods. Their use was illustrated in Listing 2-4. The getBean() method returns the reference of the bean that contains the property object. The getName() method returns the name of the property. A read-only property implements this interface.

A WritableValue wraps a value that can be read and set using its getValue() and setValue() methods, respectively. A read/write property implements this interface.

The Property interface inherits from ReadOnlyProperty and WritableValue interfaces. It adds the following five methods to support binding:

- void bind(ObservableValue<? extends T> observable)

- void unbind()

- void bindBidirectional(Property<T> other)

- void unbindBidirectional(Property<T> other)

- boolean isBound()

The bind() method adds a unidirectional binding between this Property and the specified ObservableValue. The unbind() method removes the unidirectional binding for this Property, if one exists.

The bindBidirectional() method creates a bidirectional binding between this Property and the specified Property. The unbindBidirectional() method removes a bidirectional binding.

Note the difference in the parameter types for the bind() and bindBidirectional() methods. A unidirectional binding can be created between a Property and an ObservableValue of the same type as long as they are related through inheritance. However, a bidirectional binding can only be created between two properties of the same type.

The isBound() method returns true if the Property is bound. Otherwise, it returns false.

■ **Tip** All read/write JavaFX properties support binding.

Figure 2-2 shows a partial class diagram for the integer property in JavaFX. The diagram gives you an idea about the complexity of the JavaFX properties API. You do not need to learn all of the classes in the properties API. You will use only a few of them in your applications.

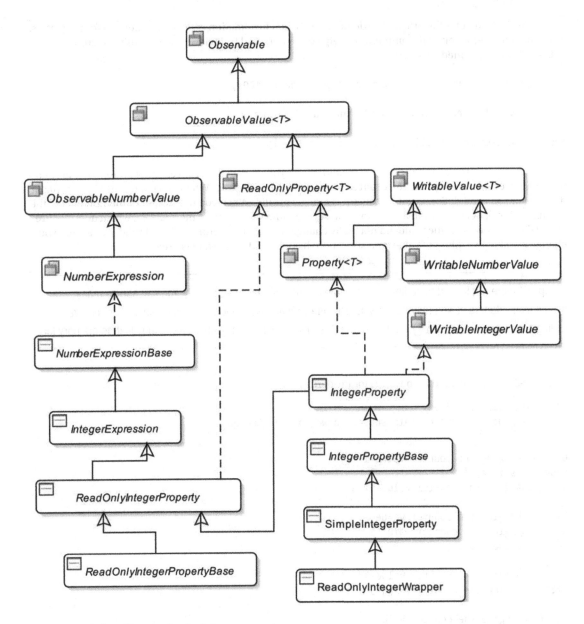

Figure 2-2. *A class diagram for the integer property*

Handling Property Invalidation Events

A property generates an invalidation event when the status of its value changes from valid to invalid for the first time. Properties in JavaFX use lazy evaluation. When an invalid property becomes invalid again, an invalidation event is not generated. An invalid property becomes valid when it is recomputed, for example, by calling its get() or getValue() method.

Listing 2-5 provides the program to demonstrate when invalidation events are generated for properties. The program includes enough comments to help you understand its logic. In the beginning, it creates an IntegerProperty named counter:

```
IntegerProperty counter = new SimpleIntegerProperty(100);
```

An InvalidationListener is added to the counter property:

```
counter.addListener(InvalidationTest::invalidated);
```

When you create a property object, it is valid. When you change the counter property to 101, it fires an invalidation event. At this point, the counter property becomes invalid. When you change its value to 102, it does not fire an invalidation event, because it is already invalid. When you use the get() method to read the counter value, it becomes valid again. Now you set the same value, 102, to the counter, which does not fire an invalidation event, as the value did not really change. The counter property is still valid. At the end, you change its value to a different value, and sure enough, an invalidation event is fired.

■ **Tip**   You are not limited to adding only one invalidation listener to a property. You can add as many invalidation listeners as you need. Once you are done with an invalidation listener, make sure to remove it by calling the removeListener() method of the Observable interface; otherwise, it may lead to memory leaks.

Listing 2-5. Testing Invalidation Events for Properties

```
// InvalidationTest.java
// Listing part of the example sources download for the book
```

```
Before changing the counter value-1
Counter is invalid.
After changing the counter value-1

Before changing the counter value-2
After changing the counter value-2
Counter value = 102

Before changing the counter value-3
After changing the counter value-3

Before changing the counter value-4
Counter is invalid.
After changing the counter value-4
```

Handling Property Change Events

You can register a ChangeListener to receive notifications about property change events. A property change event is fired every time the value of a property changes. The changed() method of a ChangeListener receives three values: the reference of the property object, the old value, and the new value.

Let's run a similar test case for testing property change events as was done for invalidation events in the previous section. Listing 2-6 has the program to demonstrate change events that are generated for properties.

Listing 2-6. Testing Change Events for Properties

```java
// ChangeTest.java
package com.jdojo.binding;

import javafx.beans.property.IntegerProperty;
import javafx.beans.property.SimpleIntegerProperty;
import javafx.beans.value.ObservableValue;

public class ChangeTest {
    public static void main(String[] args) {
        IntegerProperty counter = new SimpleIntegerProperty(100);

        // Add a change listener to the counter property
        counter.addListener(ChangeTest::changed);

        System.out.println("\nBefore changing the counter value-1");
        counter.set(101);
        System.out.println("After changing the counter value-1");

        System.out.println("\nBefore changing the counter value-2");
        counter.set(102);
        System.out.println("After changing the counter value-2");

        // Try to set the same value
        System.out.println("\nBefore changing the counter value-3");
        counter.set(102); // No change event is fired.
        System.out.println("After changing the counter value-3");

        // Try to set a different value
        System.out.println("\nBefore changing the counter value-4");
        counter.set(103);
        System.out.println("After changing the counter value-4");
    }

    public static void changed(ObservableValue<? extends Number> prop,
                               Number oldValue,
                               Number newValue) {
        System.out.print("Counter changed: ");
        System.out.println("Old = " + oldValue +
                ", new = " + newValue);
    }
}
```

```
Before changing the counter value-1
Counter changed: Old = 100, new = 101
After changing the counter value-1

Before changing the counter value-2
Counter changed: Old = 101, new = 102
After changing the counter value-2

Before changing the counter value-3
After changing the counter value-3

Before changing the counter value-4
Counter changed: Old = 102, new = 103
After changing the counter value-4
```

In the beginning, the program creates an IntegerProperty named counter:

```
IntegerProperty counter = new SimpleIntegerProperty(100);
```

There is a little trick in adding a ChangeListener. The addListener() method in the IntegerPropertyBase class is declared as follows:

```
void addListener(ChangeListener<? super Number> listener)
```

This means that if you are using generics, the ChangeListener for an IntegerProperty must be written in terms of the Number class or a superclass of the Number class. Three ways to add a ChangeListener to the counter property are shown as follows:

```
// Method-1: Using generics and the Number class
counter.addListener(new ChangeListener<Number>() {
        @Override
        public void changed(ObservableValue<? extends Number> prop,
                            Number oldValue,
                            Number newValue) {
            System.out.print("Counter changed: ");
            System.out.println("Old = " + oldValue +
                    ", new = " + newValue);
        }});

// Method-2: Using generics and the Object class
counter.addListener( new ChangeListener<Object>() {
        @Override
        public void changed(ObservableValue<? extends Object> prop,
                            Object oldValue,
                            Object newValue) {
            System.out.print("Counter changed: ");
            System.out.println("Old = " + oldValue +
                    ", new = " + newValue);
        }});
```

```
// Method-3: Not using generics. It may generate compile-time warnings.
counter.addListener(new ChangeListener() {
        @Override
        public void changed(ObservableValue prop,
                            Object oldValue,
                            Object newValue) {
                System.out.print("Counter changed: ");
                System.out.println("Old = " + oldValue +
                        ", new = " + newValue);
        }});
```

Listing 2-6 uses the first method, which makes use of generics; as you can see, the signature of the changed() method in the ChangeTest class matches with the changed() method signature in method-1. I have used a lambda expression with a method reference to add a ChangeListener as shown:

```
counter.addListener(ChangeTest::changed);
```

The preceding output shows that a property change event is fired when the property value is changed. Calling the set() method with the same value does not fire a property change event.

Unlike generating invalidation events, a property uses an eager evaluation for its value to generate change events, because it has to pass the new value to the property change listeners. The next section discusses how a property object evaluates its value, if it has both invalidation and change listeners.

Handling Invalidation and Change Events

You need to consider performance when you have to decide between using invalidation listeners and change listeners. Generally, invalidation listeners perform better than change listeners. The reason is twofold:

- Invalidation listeners make it possible to compute the value lazily.

- Multiple invalidations in a row fire only one invalidation event.

However, which listener you use depends on the situation at hand. A rule of thumb is that if you read the value of the property inside the invalidation event handler, you should use a change listener instead. When you read the value of a property inside an invalidation listener, it triggers the recomputation of the value, which is automatically done before firing a change event. If you do not need to read the value of a property, use invalidation listeners.

Listing 2-7 has a program that adds an invalidation listener and a change listener to an IntegerProperty. This program is a combination of Listings 2-5 and 2-6. The output below it shows that when the property value changes, both events, invalidation and change, are always fired. This is because a change event makes a property valid immediately after the change, and the next change in the value fires an invalidation event and, of course, a change event too.

Listing 2-7. Testing Invalidation and Change Events for Properties Together

```
// ChangeAndInvalidationTest.java
// Listing part of the example sources download for the book
```

```
Before changing the counter value-1
Counter is invalid.
Counter changed: old = 100, new = 101
After changing the counter value-1

Before changing the counter value-2
Counter is invalid.
Counter changed: old = 101, new = 102
After changing the counter value-2

Before changing the counter value-3
After changing the counter value-3

Before changing the counter value-4
Counter is invalid.
Counter changed: old = 102, new = 103
After changing the counter value-4
```

Using Bindings in JavaFX

In JavaFX, a binding is an expression that evaluates to a value. It consists of one or more observable values known as its *dependencies*. A binding observes its dependencies for changes and recomputes its value automatically. JavaFX uses lazy evaluation for all bindings. When a binding is initially defined or when its dependencies change, its value is marked as invalid. The value of an invalid binding is computed when it is requested next time, usually using its get() or getValue() method. All property classes in JavaFX have built-in support for binding.

Let's look at a quick example of binding in JavaFX. Consider the following expression that represents the sum of two integers x and y:

```
x + y
```

The expression, x + y, represents a binding, which has two dependencies: x and y. You can give it a name sum as

```
sum = x + y
```

To implement the preceding logic in JavaFX, you create two IntegerProperty variables: x and y:

```
IntegerProperty x = new SimpleIntegerProperty(100);
IntegerProperty y = new SimpleIntegerProperty(200);
```

The following statement creates a binding named sum that represents the sum of x and y:

```
NumberBinding sum = x.add(y);
```

A binding has an isValid() method that returns true if it is valid; otherwise, it returns false. You can get the value of a NumberBinding using the methods intValue(), longValue(), floatValue(), and doubleValue() as int, long, float, and double, respectively.

The program in Listing 2-8 shows how to create and use a binding based on the preceding discussion. When the sum binding is created, it is invalid and it does not know its value. This is evident from the output. Once you request its value, using the sum.initValue() method, it computes its value and marks itself as valid. When you change one of its dependencies, it becomes invalid until you request its value again.

Listing 2-8. Using a Simple Binding

```java
// BindingTest.java
package com.jdojo.binding;

import javafx.beans.binding.NumberBinding;
import javafx.beans.property.IntegerProperty;
import javafx.beans.property.SimpleIntegerProperty;

public class BindingTest {
        public static void main(String[] args) {
                IntegerProperty x = new SimpleIntegerProperty(100);
                IntegerProperty y = new SimpleIntegerProperty(200);

                // Create a binding: sum = x + y
                NumberBinding sum = x.add(y);

                System.out.println("After creating sum");
                System.out.println("sum.isValid(): " + sum.isValid());

                // Let us get the value of sum, so it computes its value and
                // becomes valid
                int value = sum.intValue();

                System.out.println("\nAfter requesting value");
                System.out.println("sum.isValid(): " + sum.isValid());
                System.out.println("sum = " + value);

                // Change the value of x
                x.set(250);

                System.out.println("\nAfter changing x");
                System.out.println("sum.isValid(): " + sum.isValid());

                // Get the value of sum again
                value = sum.intValue();

                System.out.println("\nAfter requesting value");
                System.out.println("sum.isValid(): " + sum.isValid());
                System.out.println("sum = " + value);
        }
}
```

```
After creating sum
sum.isValid(): false

After requesting value
sum.isValid(): true
sum = 300

After changing x
sum.isValid(): false

After requesting value
sum.isValid(): true
sum = 450
```

A binding, internally, adds invalidation listeners to all of its dependencies (Listing 2-9). When any of its dependencies become invalid, it marks itself as invalid. An invalid binding does not mean that its value has changed. All it means is that it needs to recompute its value when the value is requested next time.

In JavaFX, you can also bind a property to a binding. Recall that a binding is an expression that is synchronized with its dependencies automatically. Using this definition, a bound property is a property whose value is computed based on an expression, which is automatically synchronized when the dependencies change. Suppose you have three properties, x, y, and z, as follows:

```
IntegerProperty x = new SimpleIntegerProperty(10);
IntegerProperty y = new SimpleIntegerProperty(20);
IntegerProperty z = new SimpleIntegerProperty(60);
```

You can bind the property z to an expression, x + y, using the bind() method of the Property interface as follows:

```
z.bind(x.add(y));
```

Note that you cannot write z.bind(x + y) as the + operator does not know how to add the values of two IntegerProperty objects. You need to use the binding API, as you did in the preceding statement, to create a binding expression. I will cover the details of the binding API shortly.

Now, when x, y, or both change, the z property becomes invalid. The next time you request the value of z, it recomputes the expression x.add(y) to get its value.

You can use the unbind() method of the Property interface to unbind a bound property. Calling the unbind() method on an unbound or never bound property has no effect. You can unbind the z property as follows:

```
z.unbind();
```

After unbinding, a property behaves as a normal property, maintaining its value independently. Unbinding a property breaks the link between the property and its dependencies.

Listing 2-9. Binding a Property

```java
// BoundProperty.java
package com.jdojo.binding;

import javafx.beans.property.IntegerProperty;
import javafx.beans.property.SimpleIntegerProperty;

public class BoundProperty {
        public static void main(String[] args) {
            IntegerProperty x = new SimpleIntegerProperty(10);
            IntegerProperty y = new SimpleIntegerProperty(20);
            IntegerProperty z = new SimpleIntegerProperty(60);
            z.bind(x.add(y));
            System.out.println("After binding z: Bound = " + z.isBound() +
                ", z = " + z.get());

            // Change x and y
            x.set(15);
            y.set(19);
            System.out.println("After changing x and y: Bound = " +
                    z.isBound() + ", z = " + z.get());
            // Unbind z
            z.unbind();

            // Will not affect the value of z as it is not bound to
                // x and y anymore
            x.set(100);
            y.set(200);
            System.out.println("After unbinding z: Bound = " +
                    z.isBound() + ", z = " + z.get());
        }
}
```

```
After binding z: Bound = true, z = 30
After changing x and y: Bound = true, z = 34
After unbinding z: Bound = false, z = 34
```

Unidirectional and Bidirectional Bindings

A binding has a direction, which is the direction in which changes are propagated. JavaFX supports two types of binding for properties: *unidirectional binding* and *bidirectional binding*. A unidirectional binding works only in one direction; changes in dependencies are propagated to the bound property and not vice versa. A bidirectional binding works in both directions; changes in dependencies are reflected in the property and vice versa.

The bind() method of the Property interface creates a unidirectional binding between a property and an ObservableValue, which could be a complex expression. The bindBidirectional() method creates a bidirectional binding between a property and another property of the same type.

Suppose that x, y, and z are three instances of `IntegerProperty`. Consider the following bindings:

```
z = x + y
```

In JavaFX, the preceding binding can only be expressed as a unidirectional binding as follows:

```
z.bind(x.add(y));
```

Suppose you were able to use bidirectional binding in the preceding case. If you were able to change the value of z to 100, how would you compute the values of x and y in the reverse direction? For z being 100, there are an infinite number of possible combinations for x and y, for example, (99, 1), (98, 2), (101, –1), (200, –100), and so on. Propagating changes from a bound property to its dependencies is not possible with predictable results. This is the reason that binding a property to an expression is allowed only as a unidirectional binding.

Unidirectional binding has a restriction. Once a property has a unidirectional binding, you cannot change the value of the property directly; its value must be computed automatically based on the binding. You must unbind it before changing its value directly. The following snippet of code shows this case:

```
IntegerProperty x = new SimpleIntegerProperty(10);
IntegerProperty y = new SimpleIntegerProperty(20);
IntegerProperty z = new SimpleIntegerProperty(60);
z.bind(x.add(y));

z.set(7878); // Will throw a RuntimeException
```

To change the value of z directly, you can type the following:

```
z.unbind();   // Unbind z first
z.set(7878); // OK
```

Unidirectional binding has another restriction. A property can have only one unidirectional binding at a time. Consider the following two unidirectional bindings for a property z. Assume that x, y, z, a, and b are five instances of `IntegerProperty`:

```
z = x + y
z = a + b
```

If x, y, a, and b are four different properties, the bindings shown earlier for z are not possible. Think about x = 1, y = 2, a = 3, and b = 4. Can you define the value of z? Will it be 3 or 7? This is the reason that a property can have only one unidirectional binding at a time.

Rebinding a property that already has a unidirectional binding unbinds the previous binding. For example, the following snippet of code works fine:

```
IntegerProperty x = new SimpleIntegerProperty(1);
IntegerProperty y = new SimpleIntegerProperty(2);
IntegerProperty a = new SimpleIntegerProperty(3);
IntegerProperty b = new SimpleIntegerProperty(4);
IntegerProperty z = new SimpleIntegerProperty(0);

z.bind(x.add(y));
System.out.println("z = " + z.get());
```

```
z.bind(a.add(b)); // Will unbind the previous binding
System.out.println("z = " + z.get());
```

```
z = 3
z = 7
```

A bidirectional binding works in both directions. It has some restrictions. It can only be created between properties of the same type. That is, a bidirectional binding can only be of the type x = y and y = x, where x and y are of the same type.

Bidirectional binding removes some restrictions that are present for unidirectional binding. A property can have multiple bidirectional bindings at the same time. A bidirectional bound property can also be changed independently; the change is reflected in all properties that are bound to this property. That is, the following bindings are possible, using the bidirectional bindings:

```
x = y
x = z
```

In the preceding case, the values of x, y, and z will always be synchronized. That is, all three properties will have the same value, after the bindings are established. You can also establish bidirectional bindings between x, y, and z as follows:

```
x = z
z = y
```

Now a question arises. Will both of the preceding bidirectional bindings end up having the same values in x, y, and z? The answer is no. The value of the right-hand operand (see the preceding expressions, for example) in the last bidirectional binding is the value that is contained by all participating properties. Let me elaborate this point. Suppose x is 1, y is 2, and z is 3, and you have the following bidirectional bindings:

```
x = y
x = z
```

The first binding, x = y, will set the value of x equal to the value of y. At this point, x and y will be 2. The second binding, x = z, will set the value of x to be equal to the value of z. That is, x and z will be 3. However, x already has a bidirectional binding to y, which will propagate the new value 3 of x to y as well. Therefore, all three properties will have the same value as that of z. The program in Listing 2-10 shows how to use bidirectional bindings.

Listing 2-10. Using Bidirectional Bindings

```java
// BidirectionalBinding.java
package com.jdojo.binding;

import javafx.beans.property.IntegerProperty;
import javafx.beans.property.SimpleIntegerProperty;

public class BidirectionalBinding {
        public static void main(String[] args) {
            IntegerProperty x = new SimpleIntegerProperty(1);
            IntegerProperty y = new SimpleIntegerProperty(2);
            IntegerProperty z = new SimpleIntegerProperty(3);
```

```
        System.out.println("Before binding:");
        System.out.println("x=" + x.get() + ", y=" + y.get() +
                ", z=" + z.get());

        x.bindBidirectional(y);
        System.out.println("After binding-1:");
        System.out.println("x=" + x.get() + ", y=" + y.get() +
                ", z=" + z.get());

        x.bindBidirectional(z);
        System.out.println("After binding-2:");
        System.out.println("x=" + x.get() + ", y=" + y.get() +
                ", z=" + z.get());

        System.out.println("After changing z:");
        z.set(19);
        System.out.println("x=" + x.get() + ", y=" + y.get() +
                ", z=" + z.get());

        // Remove bindings
        x.unbindBidirectional(y);
        x.unbindBidirectional(z);
        System.out.println(
                "After unbinding and changing them separately:");
        x.set(100);
        y.set(200);
        z.set(300);
        System.out.println("x=" + x.get() + ", y=" + y.get() +
                ", z=" + z.get());
    }
}
```

```
Before binding:
x=1, y=2, z=3
After binding-1:
x=2, y=2, z=3
After binding-2:
x=3, y=3, z=3
After changing z:
x=19, y=19, z=19
After unbinding and changing them separately:
x=100, y=200, z=300
```

Unlike a unidirectional binding, when you create a bidirectional binding, the previous bindings are not removed because a property can have multiple bidirectional bindings. You must remove all bidirectional bindings using the unbindBidirectional() method, calling it once for each bidirectional binding for a property, as shown here:

```
// Create bidirectional bindings
x.bindBidirectional(y);
x.bindBidirectional(z);

// Remove bidirectional bindings
x.unbindBidirectional(y);
x.unbindBidirectional(z);
```

Understanding the Binding API

Previous sections gave you a quick and simple introduction to bindings in JavaFX. Now it's time to dig deeper and understand the binding API in detail. The binding API is divided into two categories:

- High-level binding API
- Low-level binding API

The high-level binding API lets you define binding using the JavaFX class library. For most use cases, you can use the high-level binding API.

Sometimes, the existing API is not sufficient to define a binding. In those cases, the low-level binding API is used. In the low-level binding API, you derive a binding class from an existing binding class and write your own logic to define a binding.

The High-Level Binding API

The high-level binding API consists of two parts: the Fluent API and the Bindings class. You can define bindings using only the Fluent API, only the Bindings class, or by combining the two. Let's look at both parts, first separately and then together.

Using the Fluent API

The Fluent API consists of several methods in different interfaces and classes. The API is called *Fluent* because the method names, their parameters, and return types have been designed in such a way that they allow writing the code fluently. The code written using the Fluent API is more readable as compared to code written using nonfluent APIs. Designing a fluent API takes more time. A fluent API is more developer friendly and less designer friendly. One of the features of a fluent API is *method chaining*; you can combine separate method calls into one statement. Consider the following snippet of code to add three properties x, y, and z. The code using a nonfluent API might look as follows:

```
x.add(y);
x.add(z);
```

Using a Fluent API, the preceding code may look as shown in the following, which gives readers a better understanding of the intention of the writer:

```
x.add(y).add(z);
```

Figure 2-3 shows a class diagram for the IntegerBinding and IntegerProperty classes. The diagram has omitted some of the interfaces and classes that fall into the IntegerProperty class hierarchy. Class diagrams for long, float, and double types are similar.

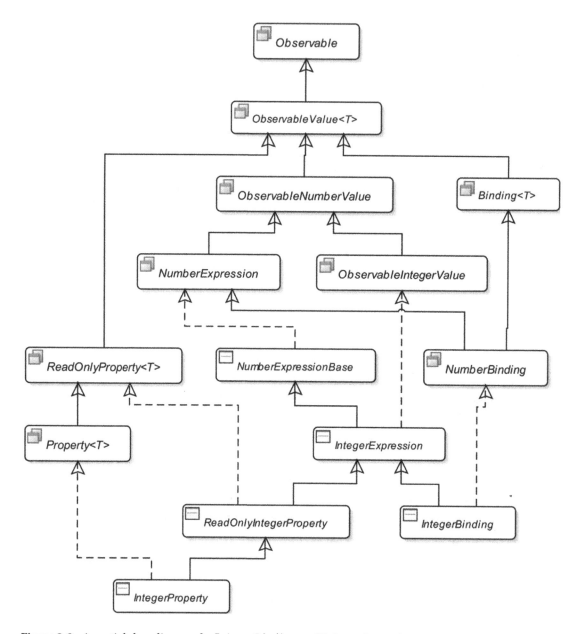

Figure 2-3. *A partial class diagram for* `IntegerBinding` *and* `IntegerProperty`

Classes and interfaces from the `ObservableNumberValue` and `Binding` interfaces down to the `IntegerBinding` class are part of the fluent binding API for the int data type. At first, it may seem as if there were many classes to learn. Most of the classes and interfaces exist in properties and binding APIs to avoid boxing and unboxing of primitive values. To learn the fluent binding API, you need to focus on `XXXExpression` and `XXXBinding` classes and interfaces. The `XXXExpression` classes have the methods that are used to create binding expressions.

The *Binding* Interface

An instance of the Binding interface represents a value that is derived from one or more sources known as dependencies. It has the following four methods:

- public void dispose()
- public ObservableList<?> getDependencies()
- public void invalidate()
- public boolean isValid()

The dispose() method, whose implementation is optional, indicates to a Binding that it will no longer be used, so it can remove references to other objects. The binding API uses weak invalidation listeners internally, making the call to this method unnecessary.

The getDependencies() method, whose implementation is optional, returns an unmodifiable ObservableList of dependencies. It exists only for debugging purposes. This method should not be used in production code.

A call to the invalidate() method invalidates a Binding. The isValid() method returns true if a Binding is valid. Otherwise, it returns false.

The *NumberBinding* Interface

The NumberBinding interface is a marker interface whose instance wraps a numeric value of int, long, float, or double type. It is implemented by DoubleBinding, FloatBinding, IntegerBinding, and LongBinding classes.

The *ObservableNumberValue* Interface

An instance of the ObservableNumberValue interface wraps a numeric value of int, long, float, or double type. It provides the following four methods to get the value:

- double doubleValue()
- float floatValue()
- int intValue()
- long longValue()

You used the intValue() method provided in Listing 2-8 to get the int value from a NumberBinding instance. The code you use would be

```
IntegerProperty x = new SimpleIntegerProperty(100);
IntegerProperty y = new SimpleIntegerProperty(200);

// Create a binding: sum = x + y
NumberBinding sum = x.add(y);
int value = sum.intValue(); // Get the int value
```

The *ObservableIntegerValue* Interface

The ObservableIntegerValue interface defines a get() method that returns the type-specific int value.

The *NumberExpression* Interface

The NumberExpression interface contains several convenience methods to create bindings using a fluent style. It has over 50 methods, and most of them are overloaded. These methods return a Binding type such as NumberBinding, BooleanBinding, and so on. Table 2-2 lists the methods in the NumberExpression interface. Most of the methods are overloaded. The table does not show the method arguments.

Table 2-2. *Summary of the Methods in the NumberExpression Interface*

Method Name	Return Type	Description
add() subtract() multiply() divide()	NumberBinding	These methods create a new NumberBinding that is the sum, difference, product, and division of the NumberExpression, and a numeric value or an ObservableNumberValue.
greaterThan() greaterThanOrEqualTo() isEqualTo() isNotEqualTo() lessThan() lessThanOrEqualTo()	BooleanBinding	These methods create a new BooleanBinding that stores the result of the comparison of the NumberExpression and a numeric value or an ObservableNumberValue. Method names are clear enough to tell what kind of comparisons they perform.
negate()	NumberBinding	It creates a new NumberBinding that is the negation of the NumberExpression.
asString()	StringBinding	It creates a StringBinding that holds the value of the NumberExpression as a String object. This method also supports locale-based string formatting.

The methods in the NumberExpression interface allow for mixing types (int, long, float, and double) while defining a binding, using an arithmetic expression. When the return type of a method in this interface is NumberBinding, the actual returned type would be of IntegerBinding, LongBinding, FloatBinding, or DoubleBinding. The binding type of an arithmetic expression is determined by the same rules as the Java programming language. The results of an expression depend on the types of the operands. The rules are as follows:

- If one of the operands is a double, the result is a double.

- If none of the operands is a double and one of them is a float, the result is a float.

- If none of the operands is a double or a float and one of them is a long, the result is a long.

- Otherwise, the result is an int.

Consider the following snippet of code:

```
IntegerProperty x = new SimpleIntegerProperty(1);
IntegerProperty y = new SimpleIntegerProperty(2);
NumberBinding sum = x.add(y);
int value = sum.intValue();
```

The number expression x.add(y) involves only int operands (x and y are of int type). Therefore, according to the preceding rules, its result is an int value, and it returns an IntegerBinding object. Because the add() method in the NumberExpression specifies the return type as NumberBinding, a NumberBinding type is used to store the result. You have to use the intValue() method from the ObservableNumberValue interface. You can rewrite the preceding snippet of code as follows:

```
IntegerProperty x = new SimpleIntegerProperty(1);
IntegerProperty y = new SimpleIntegerProperty(2);

// Casting to IntegerBinding is safe
IntegerBinding sum = (IntegerBinding)x.add(y);
int value = sum.get();
```

The NumberExpressionBase class is an implementation of the NumberExpression interface. The IntegerExpression class extends the NumberExpressionBase class. It overrides methods in its superclass to provide a type-specific return type.

The program in Listing 2-11 creates a DoubleBinding that computes the area of a circle. It also creates a DoubleProperty and binds it to the same expression to compute the area. It is your choice whether you want to work with Binding objects or bound property objects. The program shows you both approaches.

Listing 2-11. Computing the Area of a Circle from Its Radius Using a Fluent Binding API

```java
// CircleArea.java
package com.jdojo.binding;

import javafx.beans.binding.DoubleBinding;
import javafx.beans.property.DoubleProperty;
import javafx.beans.property.SimpleDoubleProperty;

public class CircleArea {
    public static void main(String[] args) {
        DoubleProperty radius = new SimpleDoubleProperty(7.0);

        // Create a binding for computing area of the circle
        DoubleBinding area =
                radius.multiply(radius).multiply(Math.PI);

        System.out.println("Radius = " + radius.get() +
                ", Area = " + area.get());

        // Change the radius
        radius.set(14.0);
        System.out.println("Radius = " + radius.get() +
                ", Area = " + area.get());

        // Create a DoubleProperty and bind it to an expression
        // that computes the area of the circle
        DoubleProperty area2 = new SimpleDoubleProperty();
        area2.bind(radius.multiply(radius).multiply(Math.PI));
        System.out.println("Radius = " + radius.get() +
                ", Area2 = " + area2.get());
    }
}
```

```
Radius = 7.0, Area = 153.93804002589985
Radius = 14.0, Area = 615.7521601035994
Radius = 14.0, Area2 = 615.7521601035994
```

The *StringBinding* Class

The class diagram containing classes in the binding API that supports binding of String type is depicted in Figure 2-4.

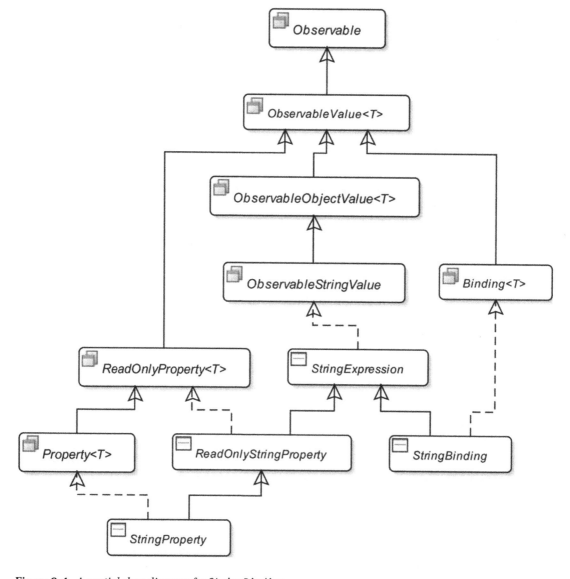

Figure 2-4. *A partial class diagram for StringBinding*

The ObservableStringValue interface declares a get() method whose return type is String. The methods in the StringExpression class let you create binding using a fluent style. Methods are provided to concatenate an object to the StringExpression, compare two strings, and check for null, among others. It has two methods to get its value: getValue() and getValueSafe(). Both return the current value. However, the latter returns an empty String when the current value is null.

The program in Listing 2-12 shows how to use StringBinding and StringExpression classes. The concat() method in the StringExpression class takes an Object type as an argument. If the argument is an ObservableValue, the StringExpression is updated automatically when the argument changes. Note the use of the asString() method on the radius and area properties. The asString() method on a NumberExpression returns a StringBinding.

Listing 2-12. Using StringBinding and StringExpression

```java
// StringExpressionTest.java
package com.jdojo.binding;

import java.util.Locale;
import javafx.beans.binding.StringExpression;
import javafx.beans.property.DoubleProperty;
import javafx.beans.property.SimpleDoubleProperty;
import javafx.beans.property.SimpleStringProperty;
import javafx.beans.property.StringProperty;

public class StringExpressionTest {
        public static void main(String[] args) {
            DoubleProperty radius = new SimpleDoubleProperty(7.0);
            DoubleProperty area = new SimpleDoubleProperty(0);
            StringProperty initStr = new SimpleStringProperty(
                    "Radius = ");

            // Bind area to an expression that computes the area of
            // the circle
            area.bind(radius.multiply(radius).multiply(Math.PI));

            // Create a string expression to describe the circle
            StringExpression desc = initStr.concat(radius.asString())
                .concat(", Area = ")
                .concat(area.asString(Locale.US, "%.2f"));

            System.out.println(desc.getValue());

            // Change the radius
            radius.set(14.0);
            System.out.println(desc.getValue());
        }
}
```

```
Radius = 7.0, Area = 153.94
Radius = 14.0, Area = 615.75
```

The *ObjectExpression* and *ObjectBinding* Classes

Now it's time for ObjectExpression and ObjectBinding classes to create bindings of any type of objects. Their class diagram is very similar to that of the StringExpression and StringBinding classes. The ObjectExpression class has methods to compare objects for equality and to check for null values. The program in Listing 2-13 shows how to use the ObjectBinding class.

Listing 2-13. Using the ObjectBinding Class

```java
// ObjectBindingTest.java
package com.jdojo.binding;

import javafx.beans.binding.BooleanBinding;
import javafx.beans.property.ObjectProperty;
import javafx.beans.property.SimpleObjectProperty;

public class ObjectBindingTest {
        public static void main(String[] args) {
            Book b1 = new Book("J1", 90, "1234567890");
            Book b2 = new Book("J2", 80, "0123456789");
            ObjectProperty<Book> book1 = new SimpleObjectProperty<>(b1);
            ObjectProperty<Book> book2 = new SimpleObjectProperty<>(b2);

            // Create a binding that computes if book1 and book2 are equal
            BooleanBinding isEqual = book1.isEqualTo(book2);
            System.out.println(isEqual.get());

            book2.set(b1);
            System.out.println(isEqual.get());
        }
}
```

```
false
true
```

The *BooleanExpression* and *BooleanBinding* Classes

The BooleanExpression class contains methods such as and(), or(), and not() that let you use boolean logical operators in an expression. Its isEqualTo() and isNotEqualTo() methods let you compare a BooleanExpression with another ObservableBooleanValue. The result of a BooleanExpression is true or false.

The program in Listing 2-14 shows how to use the BooleanExpression class. It creates a boolean expression, x > y && y <> z, using a fluent style. Note that the greaterThan() and isNotEqualTo() methods are defined in the NumberExpression interface. The program only uses the and() method from the BooleanExpression class.

Listing 2-14. Using BooleanExpression and BooleanBinding

```java
// BooelanExpressionTest.java
package com.jdojo.binding;

import javafx.beans.binding.BooleanExpression;
import javafx.beans.property.IntegerProperty;
import javafx.beans.property.SimpleIntegerProperty;

public class BooelanExpressionTest {
        public static void main(String[] args) {
            IntegerProperty x = new SimpleIntegerProperty(1);
            IntegerProperty y = new SimpleIntegerProperty(2);
            IntegerProperty z = new SimpleIntegerProperty(3);

            // Create a boolean expression for x > y && y <> z
            BooleanExpression condition =
                    x.greaterThan(y).and(y.isNotEqualTo(z));

            System.out.println(condition.get());

            // Make the condition true by setting x to 3
            x.set(3);
            System.out.println(condition.get());
        }
}
```

```
false
true
```

Using Ternary Operation in Expressions

The Java programming language offers a ternary operator, (condition?value1:value2), to perform a ternary operation of the form *when-then-otherwise*. The JavaFX binding API has a When class for this purpose. The general syntax of using the When class is shown here:

```
new When(condition).then(value1).otherwise(value2)
```

The condition must be an ObservableBooleanValue. When the condition evaluates to true, it returns value1. Otherwise, it returns value2. The types of value1 and value2 must be the same. Values may be constants or instances of ObservableValue.

Let's use a ternary operation that returns a String even or odd depending on whether the value of an IntegerProperty is even or odd, respectively. The Fluent API does not have a method to compute modulus. You will have to do this yourself. Perform an integer division by 2 on an integer and multiply the result by 2. If you get the same number back, the number is even. Otherwise, the number is odd. For example, using an integer division, (7/2)*2, results in 6, and not 7. Listing 2-15 provides the complete program.

Listing 2-15. Using the When Class to Perform a Ternary Operation

```java
// TernaryTest.java
package com.jdojo.binding;

import javafx.beans.binding.When;
import javafx.beans.property.IntegerProperty;
import javafx.beans.property.SimpleIntegerProperty;
import javafx.beans.binding.StringBinding;

public class TernaryTest {
        public static void main(String[] args) {
            IntegerProperty num = new SimpleIntegerProperty(10);
            StringBinding desc =
                    new When(num.divide(2).multiply(2).isEqualTo(num))
                                    .then("even")
                                    .otherwise("odd");

            System.out.println(num.get() + " is " + desc.get());

            num.set(19);
            System.out.println(num.get() + " is " + desc.get());
        }
}
```

```
10 is even
19 is odd
```

Using the *Bindings* Utility Class

The Bindings class is a helper class to create simple bindings. It consists of more than 150 static methods. Most of them are overloaded with several variants. I will not list or discuss all of them. Please refer to the online JavaFX API documentation to get the complete list of methods. Table 2-3 lists the methods of the Bindings class and their descriptions. It has excluded methods belonging to collections binding.

Table 2-3. Summary of Methods in the Bindings Class

Method Name	Description
add() subtract() multiply() divide()	They create a binding by applying an arithmetic operation, indicated by their names, on two of its arguments. At least one of the arguments must be an ObservableNumberValue. If one of the arguments is a double, its return type is DoubleBinding; otherwise, its return type is NumberBinding.
and()	It creates a BooleanBinding by applying the boolean and to two of its arguments.
bindBidirectional() unbindBidirectional()	They create and delete a bidirectional binding between two properties.
concat()	It returns a StringExpression that holds the value of the concatenation of its arguments. It takes a varargs argument.
convert()	It returns a StringExpression that wraps its argument.
createXXXBinding()	It lets you create a custom binding of XXX type, where XXX could be Boolean, Double, Float, Integer, String, and Object.
equal() notEqual() equalIgnoreCase() notEqualIgnoreCase()	They create a BooleanBinding that wraps the result of comparing two of its arguments being equal or not equal. Some variants of the methods allow passing a tolerance value. If two arguments are within the tolerance, they are considered equal. Generally, a tolerance value is used to compare floating-point numbers. The ignore case variants of the methods work only on String type.
format()	It creates a StringExpression that holds the value of multiple objects formatted according to a specified format String.
greaterThan() greaterThanOrEqual() lessThan() lessThanOrEqual()	They create a BooleanBinding that wraps the result of comparing arguments.
isNotNull isNull	They create a BooleanBinding that wraps the result of comparing the argument with null.
max() min()	They create a binding that holds the maximum and minimum of two arguments of the method. One of the arguments must be an ObservableNumberValue.
negate()	It creates a NumberBinding that holds the negation of an ObservableNumberValue.
not()	It creates a BooleanBinding that holds the inverse of an ObservableBooleanValue.
or()	It creates a BooleanBinding that holds the result of applying the conditional or operation on its two ObservableBooleanValue arguments.
selectXXX()	It creates a binding to select a nested property. The nested property may be of the type a.b.c. The value of the binding will be c. The classes and properties involved in the expression like a.b.c must be public. If any part of the expression is not accessible, because they are not public or they do not exist, the default value for the type, for example, null for Object type, an empty String for String type, 0 for numeric type, and false for boolean type, is the value of the binding. (Later, I will discuss an example of using the select() method.)
when()	It creates an instance of the When class taking a condition as an argument.

Most of our examples using the Fluent API can also be written using the Bindings class. The program in Listing 2-16 is similar to the one in Listing 2-12. It uses the Bindings class instead of the Fluent API. It uses the multiply() method to compute the area and the format() method to format the results. There may be several ways of doing the same thing. For formatting the result, you can also use the Bindings.concat() method, as shown here:

```
StringExpression desc = Bindings.concat("Radius = ",
    radius.asString(Locale.US, "%.2f"),
    ", Area = ", area.asString(Locale.US, "%.2f"));
```

Listing 2-16. Using the Bindings Class

```
// BindingsClassTest.java
package com.jdojo.binding;

import java.util.Locale;
import javafx.beans.binding.Bindings;
import javafx.beans.binding.StringExpression;
import javafx.beans.property.DoubleProperty;
import javafx.beans.property.SimpleDoubleProperty;

public class BindingsClassTest {
        public static void main(String[] args) {
            DoubleProperty radius = new SimpleDoubleProperty(7.0);
            DoubleProperty area = new SimpleDoubleProperty(0.0);

            // Bind area to an expression that computes the area of
            // the circle
            area.bind(Bindings.multiply(
                    Bindings.multiply(radius, radius), Math.PI));

            // Create a string expression to describe the circle
            StringExpression desc = Bindings.format(Locale.US,
                "Radius = %.2f, Area = %.2f", radius, area);

            System.out.println(desc.get());

            // Change the radius
            radius.set(14.0);
            System.out.println(desc.getValue());
        }
}
```

```
Radius = 7.00, Area = 153.94
Radius = 14.00, Area = 615.75
```

Let's look at an example of using the selectXXX() method of the Bindings class. It is used to create a binding for a nested property. In the nested hierarchy, all classes and properties must be public. Suppose you have an Address class that has a zip property and a Person class that has an addr property. The classes are shown in Listings 2-17 and 2-18, respectively.

Listing 2-17. An Address Class

```java
// Address.java
package com.jdojo.binding;

import javafx.beans.property.SimpleStringProperty;
import javafx.beans.property.StringProperty;

public class Address {
        private StringProperty zip = new SimpleStringProperty("36106");

        public StringProperty zipProperty() {
                return zip;
        }
}
```

Listing 2-18. A Person Class

```java
// Person.java
package com.jdojo.binding;

import javafx.beans.property.ObjectProperty;
import javafx.beans.property.SimpleObjectProperty;

public class Person {
        private ObjectProperty<Address> addr =
                new SimpleObjectProperty(new Address());

        public ObjectProperty<Address> addrProperty() {
                return addr;
        }
}
```

Suppose you create an ObjectProperty of the Person class as follows:

```java
ObjectProperty<Person> p = new SimpleObjectProperty(new Person());
```

Using the Bindings.selectString() method, you can create a StringBinding for the zip property of the addr property of the Person object as shown here:

```java
// Bind p.addr.zip
StringBinding zipBinding = Bindings.selectString(p, "addr", "zip");
```

The preceding statement gets a binding for the StringProperty zip, which is a nested property of the addr property of the object p. A property in the selectXXX() method may have multiple levels of nesting. You can have a selectXXX() call like

```java
StringBinding xyzBinding = Bindings.selectString(x, "a", "b", "c", "d");
```

▪ **Note** JavaFX API documentation states that `Bindings.selectString()` returns an empty `String` if any of its property arguments is inaccessible. However, the runtime returns `null`.

Listing 2-19 shows the use of the `selectString()` method. The program prints the values of the `zip` property twice: once for its default value and once for its changed value. At the end, it tries to bind a nonexistent property `p.addr.state`. Binding to a nonexistent property leads to an exception.

Listing 2-19. Using the `selectXXX()` Method of the `Bindings` Class

```
// BindNestedProperty.java
// Listing part of the example sources download for the book
```

```
36106
35217
null
Aug. 21, 2021 10:41:56 AM com.sun.javafx.binding.SelectBinding$SelectBindingHelper
getObservableValue
WARNING: Exception while evaluating select-binding [addr, state]
java.lang.NoSuchMethodException: com.jdojo.binding.BindNestedProperty$Address.getState()
    at java.base/java.lang.Class.getMethod(Class.java:2195)
    ...
    at  JavaFXBook/
    com.jdojo.binding.BindNestedProperty.main(BindNestedProperty.java:57)
```

Combining the Fluent API and the *Bindings* Class

While using the high-level binding API, you can use the fluent and `Bindings` class APIs in the same binding expression. The following snippet of code shows this approach:

```
DoubleProperty radius = new SimpleDoubleProperty(7.0);
DoubleProperty area = new SimpleDoubleProperty(0);

// Combine the Fluent API and Bindings class API
area.bind(Bindings.multiply(Math.PI, radius.multiply(radius)));
```

Using the Low-Level Binding API

The high-level binding API is not sufficient in all cases. For example, it does not provide a method to compute the square root of an `Observable` number. If the high-level binding API becomes too cumbersome to use or it does not provide what you need, you can use the low-level binding API. It gives you power and flexibility at the cost of a few extra lines of code. The low-level API allows you to use the full potential of the Java programming language to define bindings.

Using the low-level binding API involves the following three steps:

1. Create a class that extends one of the binding classes. For example, if you want to create a DoubleBinding, you need to extend the DoubleBinding class.

2. Call the bind() method of the superclass to bind all dependencies. Note that all binding classes have a bind() method implementation. You need to call this method passing all dependencies as arguments. Its argument type is a varargs of Observable type.

3. Override the computeValue() method of the superclass to write the logic for your binding. It calculates the current value of the binding. Its return type is the same as the type of the binding, for example, it is double for a DoubleBinding, String for a StringBinding, and so forth.

Additionally, you can override some methods of the binding classes to provide more functionality to your binding. You can override the dispose() method to perform additional actions when a binding is disposed. The getDependencies() method may be overridden to return the list of dependencies for the binding. Overriding the onInvalidating() method is needed if you want to perform additional actions when the binding becomes invalid.

Consider the problem of computing the area of a circle. The following snippet of code uses the low-level API to do this:

```
final DoubleProperty radius = new SimpleDoubleProperty(7.0);
DoubleProperty area = new SimpleDoubleProperty(0);

DoubleBinding areaBinding = new DoubleBinding() {
    {
        this.bind(radius);
    }

    @Override
    protected double computeValue() {
        double r = radius.get();
        double area = Math.PI * r * r;
        return area;
    }
};

area.bind(areaBinding); // Bind the area property to the areaBinding
```

The preceding snippet of code creates an anonymous class, which extends the DoubleBinding class. It calls the bind() method, passing the reference of the radius property. An anonymous class does not have a constructor, so you have to use an instance initializer to call the bind() method. The computeValue() method computes and returns the area of the circle. The radius property has been declared final, because it is being used inside the anonymous class.

The program in Listing 2-20 shows how to use the low-level binding API. It overrides the computeValue() method for the area binding. For the description binding, it overrides the dispose(), getDependencies(), and onInvalidating() methods as well.

Listing 2-20. Using the Low-Level Binding API to Compute the Area of a Circle

```
// LowLevelBinding.java
// Listing part of the example sources download for the book
```

```
Radius = 7.00, Area = 153.94
Description is invalid.
Radius = 14.00, Area = 615.75
```

Using Bindings to Center a Circle

Let's look at an example of a JavaFX GUI application that uses bindings. You will create a screen with a circle, which will be centered on the screen, even after the screen is resized. The circumference of the circle will touch the closer sides of the screen. If the width and height of the screen are the same, the circumference of the circle will touch all four sides of the screen.

Attempting to develop the screen, with a centered circle, without bindings is a tedious task. The Circle class in the javafx.scene.shape package represents a circle. It has three properties—centerX, centerY, and radius—of the DoubleProperty type. The centerX and centerY properties define the (x, y) coordinates of the center of the circle. The radius property defines the radius of the circle. By default, a circle is filled with black color.

You create a circle with centerX, centerY, and radius set to the default value of 0.0 as follows:

```
Circle c = new Circle();
```

Next, add the circle to a group and create a scene with the group as its root node as shown here:

```
Group root = new Group(c);
Scene scene = new Scene(root, 150, 150);
```

The following bindings will position and size the circle according to the size of the scene:

```
c.centerXProperty().bind(scene.widthProperty().divide(2));
c.centerYProperty().bind(scene.heightProperty().divide(2));
c.radiusProperty().bind(Bindings.min(scene.widthProperty(),
    scene.heightProperty()).divide(2));
```

The first two bindings bind the centerX and centerY of the circle to the middle of the width and height of the scene, respectively. The third binding binds the radius of the circle to the half (see divide(2)) of the minimum of the width and the height of the scene. That's it! The binding API does the magic of keeping the circle centered when the application is run.

Listing 2-21 has the complete program. Figure 2-5 shows the screen when the program is initially run. Figure 2-6 shows the screen when the screen is stretched horizontally. Try stretching the screen vertically and you will notice that the circumference of the circle touches only the left and right sides of the screen.

Listing 2-21. Using the Binding API to Keep a Circle Centered in a Scene

```
// CenteredCircle.java
// Listing part of the example sources download for the book
```

Figure 2-5. *The screen when the* CenteredCircle *program is initially run*

Figure 2-6. *The screen when the screen for the* CenteredCircle *program is stretched horizontally*

Summary

A Java class may contain two types of members: fields and methods. Fields represent the state of its objects, and they are declared private. Public methods, known as accessors, or getters and setters, are used to read and modify private fields. A Java class having public accessors for all or part of its private fields is known as a Java bean, and the accessors define the properties of the bean. Properties of a Java bean allow users to customize its state, behavior, or both.

JavaFX supports properties, events, and binding through properties and binding APIs. Properties support in JavaFX is a huge leap forward from the JavaBeans properties. All properties in JavaFX are observable. They can be observed for invalidation and value changes. You can have read/write or read-only properties. All read/write properties support binding. In JavaFX, a property can represent a value or a collection of values.

A property generates an invalidation event when the status of its value changes from valid to invalid for the first time. Properties in JavaFX use lazy evaluation. When an invalid property becomes invalid again, an invalidation event is not generated. An invalid property becomes valid when it is recomputed.

In JavaFX, a binding is an expression that evaluates to a value. It consists of one or more observable values known as its dependencies. A binding observes its dependencies for changes and recomputes its value automatically. JavaFX uses lazy evaluation for all bindings. When a binding is initially defined or when its dependencies change, its value is marked as invalid. The value of an invalid binding is computed when it is requested next time. All property classes in JavaFX have built-in support for binding.

A binding has a direction, which is the direction in which changes are propagated. JavaFX supports two types of binding for properties: unidirectional binding and bidirectional binding. A unidirectional binding works only in one direction; changes in dependencies are propagated to the bound property, not vice versa. A bidirectional binding works in both directions; changes in dependencies are reflected in the property and vice versa.

The binding API in JavaFX is divided into two categories: high-level binding API and low-level binding API. The high-level binding API lets you define binding using the JavaFX class library. For most use cases, you can use the high-level binding API. Sometimes, the existing API is not sufficient to define a binding. In those cases, the low-level binding API is used. In the low-level binding API, you derive a binding class from an existing binding class and write your own logic to define the binding.

The next chapter will introduce you to observable collections in JavaFX.

CHAPTER 3

■ ■ ■

Observable Collections

In this chapter, you will learn:

- What observable collections in JavaFX are
- How to observe observable collections for invalidations and changes
- How to use observable collections as properties

The examples of this chapter lie in the com.jdojo.collections package. In order for them to work, you must add a corresponding line to the module-info.java file:

```
...
opens com.jdojo.collections to javafx.graphics, javafx.base;
...
```

What Are Observable Collections?

Observable collections in JavaFX are extensions to collections in Java. The *collections* framework in Java has the List, Set, and Map interfaces. JavaFX adds the following three types of observable collections that may be observed for changes in their contents:

- An observable list
- An observable set
- An observable map

JavaFX supports these types of collections through three new interfaces:

- ObservableList
- ObservableSet
- ObservableMap

These interfaces inherit from List, Set, and Map from the java.util package. In addition to inheriting from the Java collection interfaces, JavaFX collection interfaces also inherit the Observable interface. All JavaFX observable collection interfaces and classes are in the javafx.collections package. Figure 3-1 shows a partial class diagram for the ObservableList, ObservableSet, and ObservableMap interfaces.

© Kishori Sharan and Peter Späth 2022
K. Sharan and P. Späth, *Learn JavaFX 17*, https://doi.org/10.1007/978-1-4842-7848-2_3

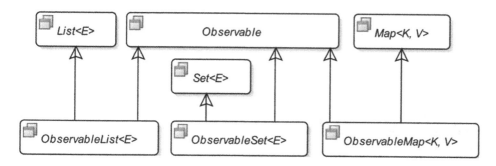

Figure 3-1. *A partial class diagram for observable collection interfaces in JavaFX*

The observable collections in JavaFX have two additional features:

- They support invalidation notifications as they are inherited from the Observable interface.

- They support change notifications. You can register change listeners to them, which are notified when their contents change.

The javafx.collections.FXCollections class is a utility class to work with JavaFX collections. It consists of all static methods.

JavaFX does not expose the implementation classes of observable lists, sets, and maps. You need to use one of the factory methods in the FXCollections class to create objects of the ObservableList, ObservableSet, and ObservableMap interfaces.

■ **Tip** In simple terms, an observable collection in JavaFX is a list, set, or map that may be observed for invalidation and content changes.

Understanding *ObservableList*

An ObservableList is a java.util.List and an Observable with change notification features. Figure 3-2 shows the class diagram for the ObservableList interface.

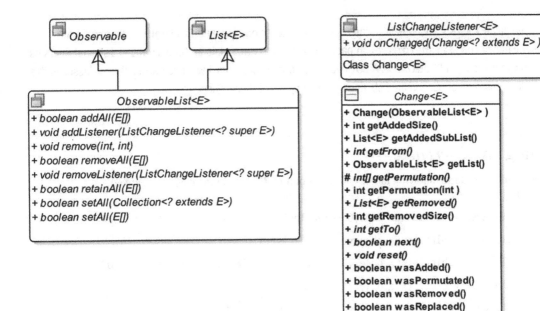

Figure 3-2. *A class diagram for the* ObservableList *interface*

■ **Tip** The methods filtered() and sorted() are missing in the diagram. You can use them for filtering and sorting the list elements. For details, see the API documentation.

The addListener() and removeListener() methods in the ObservableList interface allow you to add and remove ListChangeListeners, respectively. Other methods perform operations on the list, which affect multiple elements.

If you want to receive notifications when changes occur in an ObservableList, you need to add a ListChangeListener interface whose onChanged() method is called when a change occurs in the list. The Change class is a static inner class of the ListChangeListener interface. A Change object contains a report of the changes in an ObservableList. It is passed to the onChanged() method of the ListChangeListener. I will discuss list change listeners in detail later in this section.

You can add or remove invalidation listeners to or from an ObservableList using the following two methods that it inherits from the Observable interface:

- void addListener(InvalidationListener listener)

- void removeListener(InvalidationListener listener)

Note that an ObservableList contains all of the methods of the List interface as it inherits them from the List interface.

▒ **Tip**   The JavaFX library provides two classes named `FilteredList` and `SortedList` that are in the `javafx.collections.transformation` package. A `FilteredList` is an `ObservableList` that filters its contents using a specified `Predicate`. A `SortedList` sorts its contents. I will not discuss these classes in this chapter. All discussions of observable lists apply to the objects of these classes as well.

Creating an *ObservableList*

You need to use one of the following factory methods of the `FXCollections` class to create an `ObservableList`:

- `<E> ObservableList<E> emptyObservableList()`

- `<E> ObservableList<E> observableArrayList()`

- `<E> ObservableList<E> observableArrayList(Collection<? extends E> col)`

- `<E> ObservableList<E> observableArrayList(E... items)`

- `<E> ObservableList<E> observableList(List<E> list)`

- `<E> ObservableList<E> observableArrayList(Callback<E, Observable[]> extractor)`

- `<E> ObservableList<E> observableList(List<E> list, Callback<E, Observable[]> extractor)`

The `emptyObservableList()` method creates an empty, unmodifiable `ObservableList`. Often, this method is used when you need an `ObservableList` to pass to a method as an argument and you do not have any elements to pass to that list. You can create an empty `ObservableList` of `String` as follows:

```
ObservableList<String> emptyList = FXCollections.emptyObservableList();
```

The `observableArrayList()` method creates an `ObservableList` backed by an `ArrayList`. Other variants of this method create an `ObservableList` whose initial elements can be specified in a `Collection` as a list of items or as a `List`.

The last two methods in the preceding list create an `ObservableList` whose elements can be observed for updates. They take an extractor, which is an instance of the `Callback<E, Observable[]>` interface. An extractor is used to get the list of `Observable` values to observe for updates. I will cover the use of these two methods in the "Observing an ObservableList for Updates" section.

Listing 3-1 shows how to create observable lists and how to use some of the methods of the `ObservableList` interface to manipulate the lists. At the end, it shows how to use the `concat()` method of the `FXCollections` class to concatenate elements of two observable lists.

Listing 3-1. Creating and Manipulating Observable Lists

```
// ObservableListTest.java
package com.jdojo.collections;

import javafx.collections.FXCollections;
import javafx.collections.ObservableList;
```

```java
public class ObservableListTest {
    public static void main(String[] args) {
        // Create a list with some elements
        ObservableList<String> list =
                FXCollections.observableArrayList("one", "two");
        System.out.println("After creating list: " + list);

        // Add some more elements to the list
        list.addAll("three", "four");
        System.out.println("After adding elements: " + list);

        // You have four elements. Remove the middle two
        // from index 1 (inclusive) to index 3 (exclusive)
        list.remove(1, 3);
        System.out.println("After removing elements: " + list);

        // Retain only the element "one"
        list.retainAll("one");
        System.out.println("After retaining \"one\": " + list);

        // Create another ObservableList
        ObservableList<String> list2 =
            FXCollections.<String>observableArrayList(
                "1", "2", "3");

        // Set list2 to list
        list.setAll(list2);
        System.out.println("After setting list2 to list: " +
                list);

        // Create another list
        ObservableList<String> list3 =
            FXCollections.<String>observableArrayList(
                "ten", "twenty", "thirty");

        // Concatenate elements of list2 and list3
        ObservableList<String> list4 =
                FXCollections.concat(list2, list3);
        System.out.println("list2 is " + list2);
        System.out.println("list3 is " + list3);
        System.out.println(
                "After concatenating list2 and list3:" + list4);
    }
}
```

```
After creating list: [one, two]
After adding elements: [one, two, three, four]
After removing elements: [one, four]
After retaining "one": [one]
After setting list2 to list: [1, 2, 3]
list2 is [1, 2, 3]
list3 is [ten, twenty, thirty]
After concatenating list2 and list3:[1, 2, 3, ten, twenty, thirty]
```

Observing an *ObservableList* for Invalidations

You can add invalidation listeners to an ObservableList as you do to any Observable. Listing 3-2 shows how to use an invalidation listener with an ObservableList.

■ **Tip** In the case of the ObservableList, the invalidation listeners are notified for every change in the list, irrespective of the type of a change.

Listing 3-2. Testing Invalidation Notifications for an ObservableList

```java
// ListInvalidationTest.java
package com.jdojo.collections;

import javafx.beans.Observable;
import javafx.collections.FXCollections;
import javafx.collections.ObservableList;

public class ListInvalidationTest {
    public static void main(String[] args) {
        // Create a list with some elements
        ObservableList<String> list =
            FXCollections.observableArrayList("one", "two");

        // Add an InvalidationListener to the list
        list.addListener(ListInvalidationTest::invalidated);

        System.out.println("Before adding three.");
        list.add("three");
        System.out.println("After adding three.");

        System.out.println("Before adding four and five.");
        list.addAll("four", "five");
        System.out.println("Before adding four and five.");
```

```
                System.out.println("Before replacing one with one.");
                list.set(0, "one");
                System.out.println("After replacing one with one.");
        }

        public static void invalidated(Observable list) {
                System.out.println("List is invalid.");
        }
}
```

```
Before adding three.
List is invalid.
After adding three.
Before adding four and five.
List is invalid.
Before adding four and five.
Before replacing one with one.
List is invalid.
After replacing one with one.
```

Observing an *ObservableList* for Changes

Observing an ObservableList for changes is a bit tricky. There could be several kinds of changes to a list. Some of the changes could be exclusive, whereas some can occur along with other changes. Elements of a list can be permutated, updated, replaced, added, and removed. You need to be patient in learning this topic because I will cover it in bits and pieces.

You can add a change listener to an ObservableList using its addListener() method, which takes an instance of the ListChangeListener interface. The changed() method of the listeners is called every time a change occurs in the list. The following snippet of code shows how to add a change listener to an ObservableList of String. The onChanged() method is simple; it prints a message on the standard output when it is notified of a change:

```
// Create an observable list
ObservableList<String> list = FXCollections.observableArrayList();

// Add a change listener to the list
list.addListener(new ListChangeListener<String>() {
        @Override
        public void onChanged(ListChangeListener.Change<? extends String>
                        change) {
            System.out.println("List has changed.");
        }
});
```

Listing 3-3 contains the complete program showing how to detect changes in an ObservableList. It uses a lambda expression with a method reference, which are features of Java 8, to add a change listener. After adding a change listener, it manipulates the list four times, and the listener is notified each time, as is evident from the output that follows.

75

Listing 3-3. Detecting Changes in an ObservableList

```java
// SimpleListChangeTest.java
package com.jdojo.collections;

import javafx.collections.FXCollections;
import javafx.collections.ListChangeListener;
import javafx.collections.ObservableList;

public class SimpleListChangeTest {
        public static void main(String[] args) {
            // Create an observable list
            ObservableList<String> list =
                    FXCollections.observableArrayList();

            // Add a change listener to the list
            list.addListener(SimpleListChangeTest::onChanged);

            // Manipulate the elements of the list
            list.add("one");
            list.add("two");
            FXCollections.sort(list);
            list.clear();
        }

        public static void onChanged(
                ListChangeListener.Change<? extends String> change) {
            System.out.println("List has changed");
        }
}
```

```
List has changed.
List has changed.
List has changed.
List has changed.
```

Understanding the *ListChangeListener.Change* Class

Sometimes, you may want to analyze changes to a list in more detail rather than just knowing that the list has changed. The ListChangeListener.Change object that is passed to the onChanged() method contains a report to a change performed on the list. You need to use a combination of its methods to know the details of a change. Table 3-1 lists the methods in the ListChangeListener.Change class with their categories.

Table 3-1. *Methods in the* `ListChangeListener.Change` *Class*

Method	Category
`ObservableList<E> getList()`	General
`boolean next()` `void reset()`	Cursor movement

`boolean wasAdded()`
`boolean wasRemoved()`
`boolean wasReplaced()`
`boolean wasPermutated()`
`boolean wasUpdated()`
	Change type

`int getFrom()` `int getTo()`	Affected range
`int getAddedSize()` `List<E> getAddedSubList()`	Addition
`List<E> getRemoved()` `int getRemovedSize()`	Removal
`int getPermutation(int oldIndex)`	Permutation

The `getList()` method returns the source list after changes have been made. A `ListChangeListener.Change` object may report a change in multiple chunks. This may not be obvious at first. Consider the following snippet of code:

```
ObservableList<String> list = FXCollections.observableArrayList();

// Add a change listener here...

list.addAll("one", "two", "three");
list.removeAll("one", "three");
```

In this code, the change listener will be notified twice: once for the `addAll()` method call and once for the `removeAll()` method call. The `ListChangeListener.Change` object reports the affected range of indexes. In the second change, you remove two elements that fall into two different ranges of indexes. Note that there is an element "two" between the two removed elements. In the second case, the `Change` object will contain a report of two changes. The first change will contain the information that, at index 0, the element "one" has been removed. Now, the list contains only two elements with the index 0 for the element "two" and index 1 for the element "three". The second change will contain the information that, at index 1, the element "three" has been removed.

A `Change` object contains a cursor that points to a specific change in the report. The `next()` and `reset()` methods are used to control the cursor. When the `onChanged()` method is called, the cursor points before the first change in the report. Calling the `next()` method the first time moves the cursor to the first change in the report. Before attempting to read the details for a change, you must point the cursor to the change by calling the next() method. The next() method returns true if it moves the cursor to a valid change. Otherwise, it returns false. The reset() method moves the cursor before the first change. Typically, the next() method is called in a while loop, as shown in the following snippet of code:

```
ObservableList<String> list = FXCollections.observableArrayList();
...
// Add a change listener to the list
list.addListener(new ListChangeListener<String>() {
    @Override
    public void onChanged(ListChangeListener.Change<? extends String>
            change) {
        while(change.next()) {
            // Process the current change here...
        }
    }
});
```

In the change type category, methods report whether a specific type of change has occurred. The wasAdded() method returns true if elements were added. The wasRemoved() method returns true if elements were removed. The wasReplaced() method returns true if elements were replaced. You can think of a replacement as a removal followed by an addition at the same index. If wasReplaced() returns true, both wasRemoved() and wasAdded() return true as well. The wasPermutated() method returns true if elements of a list were permutated (i.e., reordered) but not removed, added, or updated. The wasUpdated() method returns true if elements of a list were updated.

Not all five types of changes to a list are exclusive. Some changes may occur simultaneously in the same change notification. The two types of changes, permutations and updates, are exclusive. If you are interested in working with all types of changes, your code in the onChanged() method should look as follows:

```
public void onChanged(ListChangeListener.Change change) {
        while (change.next()) {
                if (change.wasPermutated()) {
                        // Handle permutations
                }
                else if (change.wasUpdated()) {
                        // Handle updates
                }
                else if (change.wasReplaced()) {
                        // Handle replacements
                }
                else {
                        if (change.wasRemoved()) {
                                // Handle removals
                        }
                        else if (change.wasAdded()) {
                                // Handle additions
                        }
                }
        }
}
```

In the affected range type category, the getFrom() and getTo() methods report the range of indexes affected by a change. The getFrom() method returns the beginning index, and the getTo() method returns the ending index plus one. If the wasPermutated() method returns true, the range includes the elements that were permutated. If the wasUpdated() method returns true, the range includes the elements that were updated. If the wasAdded() method returns true, the range includes the elements that were added. If the wasRemoved() method returns true and the wasAdded() method returns false, the getFrom() and getTo() methods return the same number—the index where the removed elements were placed in the list.

The getAddedSize() method returns the number of elements added. The getAddedSubList() method returns a list that contains the elements added. The getRemovedSize() method returns the number of elements removed. The getRemoved() method returns an immutable list of removed or replaced elements. The getPermutation(int oldIndex) method returns the new index of an element after permutation. For example, if an element at index 2 moves to index 5 during a permutation, the getPermutation(2) will return 5.

This completes the discussion about the methods of the ListChangeListener.Change class. However, you are not done with this class yet! I still need to discuss how to use these methods in actual situations, for example, when elements of a list are updated. I will cover handling updates to elements of a list in the next section. I will finish this topic with an example that covers everything that was discussed.

Observing an *ObservableList* for Updates

In the "Creating an *ObservableList*" section, I had listed the following two methods of the FXCollections class that create an ObservableList:

- `<E> ObservableList<E> observableArrayList(Callback<E, Observable[]> extractor)`

- `<E> ObservableList<E> observableList(List<E> list, Callback<E, Observable[]> extractor)`

If you want to be notified when elements of a list are updated, you need to create the list using one of these methods. Both methods have one thing in common: they take a Callback<E,Observable[]> object as an argument. The Callback<P,R> interface is in the javafx.util package. It is defined as follows:

```
public interface Callback<P,R> {
        R call(P param)
}
```

The Callback<P,R> interface is used in situations where further action is required by APIs at a later suitable time. The first generic type parameter specifies the type of the parameter passed to the call() method, and the second one specifies the return type of the call() method.

If you notice the declaration of the type parameters in Callback<E,Observable[]>, the first type parameter is E, which is the type of the elements of the list. The second parameter is an array of Observable. When you add an element to the list, the call() method of the Callback object is called. The added element is passed to the call() method as an argument. You are supposed to return an array of Observable from the call() method. If any of the elements in the returned Observable array changes, listeners will be notified of an "update" change for the element of the list for which the call() method had returned the Observable array.

Let's examine why you need a Callback object and an Observable array to detect updates to elements of a list. A list stores references of its elements. Its elements can be updated using their references from anywhere in the program. A list does not know that its elements are being updated from somewhere else. It needs to know the list of Observable objects, where a change to any of them may be considered an update to its elements. The call() method of the Callback object fulfills this requirement. The list passes every element to the call() method. The call() method returns an array of Observable. The list watches for any changes to the elements of the Observable array. When it detects a change, it notifies its change listeners that its element associated with the Observable array has been updated. The reason this parameter is named *extractor* is that it extracts an array of Observable for an element of a list.

Listing 3-4 shows how to create an ObservableList that can notify its change listeners when its elements are updated.

Listing 3-4. Observing a List for Updates of Its Elements

```java
// ListUpdateTest.java
package com.jdojo.collections;

import java.util.List;
import javafx.beans.Observable;
import javafx.beans.property.IntegerProperty;
import javafx.beans.property.SimpleIntegerProperty;
import javafx.collections.FXCollections;
import javafx.collections.ListChangeListener;
import javafx.collections.ObservableList;
import javafx.util.Callback;

public class ListUpdateTest {
    public static void main(String[] args) {
        // Create an extractor for IntegerProperty.
        Callback<IntegerProperty, Observable[]> extractor =
                (IntegerProperty p) -> {
            // Print a message to know when it is called
            System.out.println("The extractor is called for " + p);
            // Wrap the parameter in an Observable[] and return it
            return new Observable[]{p};
        };
        // Create an empty observable list with a callback to
        // extract the observable values for each element of the list
        ObservableList<IntegerProperty> list =
            FXCollections.observableArrayList(extractor);

        // Add two elements to the list
        System.out.println("Before adding two elements...");
        IntegerProperty p1 = new SimpleIntegerProperty(10);
        IntegerProperty p2 = new SimpleIntegerProperty(20);
        list.addAll(p1, p2); // Will call the call() method of the
                        // extractor - once for p1 and once for p2.
        System.out.println("After adding two elements...");

        // Add a change listener to the list
        list.addListener(ListUpdateTest::onChanged);

        // Update p1 from 10 to 100, which will trigger
        // an update change for the list
        p1.set(100);
    }
```

```java
    public static void onChanged(
            ListChangeListener.Change<? extends IntegerProperty>
                change) {
        System.out.println("List is " + change.getList());

        // Work on only updates to the list
        while (change.next()) {
            if (change.wasUpdated()) {
                // Print the details of the update
                System.out.println("An update is detected.");

                int start = change.getFrom();
                int end = change.getTo();
                System.out.println("Updated range: [" + start +
                        ", " + end + "]");

                List<? extends IntegerProperty> updatedElementsList;
                updatedElementsList =
                        change.getList().subList(start, end);

                System.out.println("Updated elements: " +
                        updatedElementsList);
            }
        }
    }
}
```

```
Before adding two elements...
The extractor is called for IntegerProperty [value: 10]
The extractor is called for IntegerProperty [value: 20]
After adding two elements...
List is [IntegerProperty [value: 100], IntegerProperty [value: 20]]
An update is detected.
Updated range: [0, 1]
Updated elements: [IntegerProperty [value: 100]]
```

The main() method of the ListUpdateTest class creates an extractor that is an object of the Callback<IntegerProperty, Observable[]> interface. The call() method takes an IntegerProperty argument and returns the same by wrapping it in an Observable array. It also prints the object that is passed to it.

The extractor is used to create an ObservableList. Two IntegerProperty objects are added to the list. When the objects are being added, the call() method of the extractor is called with the object being added as its argument. This is evident from the output. The call() method returns the object being added. This means that the list will watch for any changes to the object (the IntegerProperty) and notify its change listeners of the same.

A change listener is added to the list. It handles only updates to the list. At the end, you change the value for the first element of the list from 10 to 100 to trigger an update change notification.

A Complete Example of Observing an *ObservableList* for Changes

This section provides a complete example that shows how to handle the different kinds of changes to an ObservableList.

Our starting point is a Person class as shown in Listing 3-5. Here, you will work with an ObservableList of Person objects. The Person class has two properties: firstName and lastName. Both properties are of the StringProperty type. Its compareTo() method is implemented to sort Person objects in ascending order by the first name then by the last name. Its toString() method prints the first name, a space, and the last name.

Listing 3-5. A Person Class with Two Properties Named firstName and lastName

```java
// Person.java
package com.jdojo.collections;

import javafx.beans.property.SimpleStringProperty;
import javafx.beans.property.StringProperty;

public class Person implements Comparable<Person> {
        private StringProperty firstName = new SimpleStringProperty();
        private StringProperty lastName = new SimpleStringProperty();

        public Person() {
                this.setFirstName("Unknown");
                this.setLastName("Unknown");
        }

        public Person(String firstName, String lastName) {
                this.setFirstName(firstName);
                this.setLastName(lastName);
        }

        // Complete listing part of the example sources download for
        // the book
        ...
}
```

The PersonListChangeListener class, as shown in Listing 3-6, is a change listener class. It implements the onChanged() method of the ListChangeListener interface to handle all types of change notifications for an ObservableList of Person objects.

Listing 3-6. A Change Listener for an ObservableList of Person Objects

```java
// PersonListChangeListener.java
// Listing part of the example sources download for the book
```

The ListChangeTest class, as shown in Listing 3-7, is a test class. It creates an ObservableList with an extractor. The extractor returns an array of firstName and lastName properties of a Person object. That means when one of these properties is changed, a Person object as an element of the list is considered updated, and an update notification will be sent to all change listeners. It adds a change listener to the list. Finally, it makes several kinds of changes to the list to trigger change notifications. The details of a change notification are printed on the standard output.

This completes one of the most complex discussions about writing a change listener for an ObservableList. Aren't you glad that JavaFX designers didn't make it more complex?

Listing 3-7. Testing an ObservableList of Person Objects for All Types of Changes

```
// ListChangeTest.java
// Listing part of the example sources download for the book
```

```
Before adding Li Na: []
Change Type: Added
Added Size: 1
Added Range: [0, 1]
Added List: [Li Na]
After adding Li Na: [Li Na]

Before adding Vivi Gin and Li He: [Li Na]
Change Type: Added
Added Size: 2
Added Range: [1, 3]
Added List: [Vivi Gin, Li He]
After adding Vivi Gin and Li He: [Li Na, Vivi Gin, Li He]

Before sorting the list:[Li Na, Vivi Gin, Li He]
Change Type: Permutated
Permutated Range: [0, 3]
index[0] moved to index[1]
index[1] moved to index[2]
index[2] moved to index[0]
After sorting the list:[Li He, Li Na, Vivi Gin]

Before updating Li Na: [Li He, Li Na, Vivi Gin]
Change Type: Updated
Updated Range : [1, 2]
Updated elements are: [Li Smith]
After updating Li Smith: [Li He, Li Smith, Vivi Gin]

Before replacing Li He with Simon Ng: [Li He, Li Smith, Vivi Gin]
Change Type: Replaced
Change Type: Removed
Removed Size: 1
Removed Range: [0, 1]
Removed List: [Li He]
Change Type: Added
Added Size: 1
Added Range: [0, 1]
Added List: [Simon Ng]
After replacing Li He with Simon Ng: [Simon Ng, Li Smith, Vivi Gin]

Before setAll(): [Simon Ng, Li Smith, Vivi Gin]
Change Type: Replaced
Change Type: Removed
```

```
Removed Size: 3
Removed Range: [0, 3]
Removed List: [Simon Ng, Li Smith, Vivi Gin]
Change Type: Added
Added Size: 3
Added Range: [0, 3]
Added List: [Lia Li, Liz Na, Li Ho]
After setAll(): [Lia Li, Liz Na, Li Ho]

Before removeAll(): [Lia Li, Liz Na, Li Ho]
Change Type: Removed
Removed Size: 1
Removed Range: [0, 0]
Removed List: [Lia Li]
Change Type: Removed
Removed Size: 1
Removed Range: [1, 1]
Removed List: [Li Ho]
After removeAll(): [Liz Na]
```

Understanding *ObservableSet*

If you survived learning the ObservableList and list change listeners, learning about the ObservableSet will be easy! Figure 3-3 shows the class diagram for the ObservableSet interface.

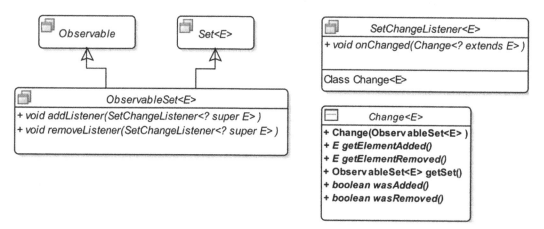

Figure 3-3. *A class diagram for the ObservableSet interface*

It inherits from the Set and Observable interfaces. It supports invalidation and change notifications, and it inherits the methods for the invalidation notification support from the Observable interface. It adds the following two methods to support change notifications:

- void addListener(SetChangeListener<? super E> listener)

- void removeListener(SetChangeListener<? super E> listener)

An instance of the SetChangeListener interface listens for changes in an ObservableSet. It declares a static inner class named Change, which represents a report of changes in an ObservableSet.

■ **Note** A set is an unordered collection. This section shows the elements of several sets in outputs. You may get a different output showing the elements of sets in a different order than shown in those examples.

Creating an *ObservableSet*

You need to use one of the following factory methods of the FXCollections class to create an ObservableSet:

- `<E> ObservableSet<E> observableSet(E... elements)`

- `<E> ObservableSet<E> observableSet(Set<E> set)`

- `<E> ObservableSet<E> emptyObservableSet()`

Since working with observable sets does not differ much from working with observable lists, we do not further investigate on this topic. You can consult the API documentation and the example classes in the com.jdojo.collections package to learn more about observable sets.

Understanding *ObservableMap*

Figure 3-4 shows the class diagram for the ObservableMap interface. It inherits from the Map and Observable interfaces. It supports invalidation and change notifications. It inherits the methods for the invalidation notification support from the Observable interface, and it adds the following two methods to support change notifications:

- `void addListener(MapChangeListener<? super K, ? super V> listener)`

- `void removeListener(MapChangeListener<? super K, ? super V> listener)`

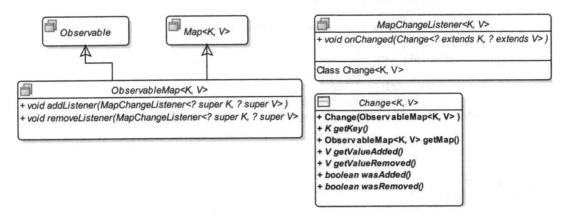

Figure 3-4. *A class diagram for the* ObservableMap *interface*

An instance of the MapChangeListener interface listens for changes in an ObservableMap. It declares a static inner class named Change, which represents a report of changes in an ObservableMap.

85

Creating an *ObservableMap*

You need to use one of the following factory methods of the FXCollections class to create an ObservableMap:

- `<K,V> ObservableMap<K, V> observableHashMap()`
- `<K,V> ObservableMap<K, V> observableMap(Map<K, V> map)`
- `<K,V> ObservableMap<K,V> emptyObservableMap()`

The first method creates an empty observable map that is backed by a HashMap. The second method creates an ObservableMap that is backed by the specified map. Mutations performed on the ObservableMap are reported to the listeners. Mutations performed directly on the backing map are not reported to the listeners. The third method creates an empty unmodifiable observable map. Listing 3-8 shows how to create ObservableMaps.

Listing 3-8. Creating ObservableMaps

```java
// ObservableMapTest.java
package com.jdojo.collections;

import java.util.HashMap;
import java.util.Map;
import javafx.collections.FXCollections;
import javafx.collections.ObservableMap;

public class ObservableMapTest {
        public static void main(String[] args) {
            ObservableMap<String, Integer> map1 =
                    FXCollections.observableHashMap();

            map1.put("one", 1);
            map1.put("two", 2);
            System.out.println("Map 1: " + map1);

            Map<String, Integer> backingMap = new HashMap<>();
            backingMap.put("ten", 10);
            backingMap.put("twenty", 20);

            ObservableMap<String, Integer> map2 =
                    FXCollections.observableMap(backingMap);
            System.out.println("Map 2: " + map2);
        }
}
```

```
Map 1: {two=2, one=1}
Map 2: {ten=10, twenty=20}
```

Since working with observable maps does not differ much from working with observable lists and sets, we do not further investigate on this topic. You can consult the API documentation and the example classes in the com.jdojo.collections package to learn more about observable maps.

Properties and Bindings for JavaFX Collections

The ObservableList, ObservableSet, and ObservableMap collections can be exposed as Property objects. They also support bindings using high-level and low-level binding APIs. Property objects representing single values were discussed in Chapter 2. Make sure you have read that chapter before proceeding in this section.

Understanding *ObservableList* Property and Binding

Figure 3-5 shows a partial class diagram for the ListProperty class. The ListProperty class implements the ObservableValue and ObservableList interfaces. It is an observable value in the sense that it wraps the reference of an ObservableList. Implementing the ObservableList interface makes all of its methods available to a ListProperty object. Calling methods of the ObservableList on a ListProperty has the same effect as if they were called on the wrapped ObservableList.

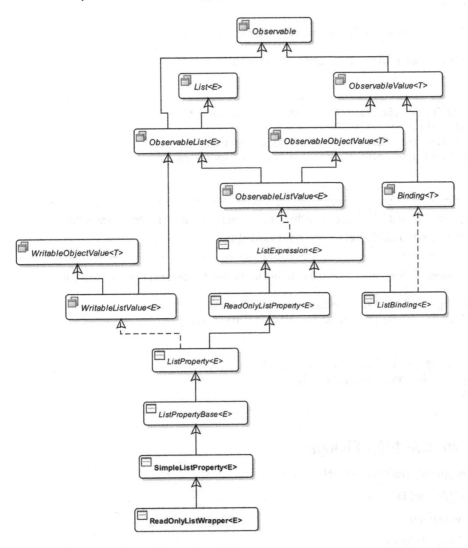

Figure 3-5. *A partial class diagram for the* ListProperty *class*

You can use one of the following constructors of the SimpleListProperty class to create an instance of the ListProperty:

- SimpleListProperty()

- SimpleListProperty(ObservableList<E> initialValue)

- SimpleListProperty(Object bean, String name)

- SimpleListProperty(Object bean, String name, ObservableList<E> initialValue)

One of the common mistakes in using the ListProperty class is not passing an ObservableList to its constructor before using it. A ListProperty must have a reference to an ObservableList before you can perform a meaningful operation on it. If you do not use an ObservableList to create a ListProperty object, you can use its set() method to set the reference of an ObservableList. The following snippet of code generates an exception:

```
ListProperty<String> lp = new SimpleListProperty<String>();

// No ObservableList to work with. Generates an exception.
lp.add("Hello");
```

```
Exception in thread "main" java.lang.UnsupportedOperationException
        at java.util.AbstractList.add(AbstractList.java:148)
        at java.util.AbstractList.add(AbstractList.java:108)
        at javafx.beans.binding.ListExpression.add(ListExpression.java:262)
```

■ **Tip**   Operations performed on a ListProperty that wraps a null reference are treated as if the operations were performed on an immutable empty ObservableList.

The following snippet of code shows how to create and initialize a ListProperty before using it:

```
ObservableList<String> list1 = FXCollections.observableArrayList();
ListProperty<String> lp1 = new SimpleListProperty<String>(list1);
lp1.add("Hello");

ListProperty<String> lp2 = new SimpleListProperty<String>();
lp2.set(FXCollections.observableArrayList());
lp2.add("Hello");
```

Observing a *ListProperty* for Changes

You can attach three types of listeners to a ListProperty:

- An InvalidationListener

- A ChangeListener

- A ListChangeListener

All three listeners are notified when the reference of the ObservableList, which is wrapped in the ListProperty, changes or the content of the ObservableList changes. When the content of the list changes, the changed() method of ChangeListeners receives the reference to the same list as the old and new value. If the wrapped reference of the ObservableList is replaced with a new one, this method receives references of the old list and the new list. To handle the list change events, please refer to the "Observing an *ObservableList* for Changes" section in this chapter.

The program in Listing 3-9 shows how to handle all three types of changes to a ListProperty. The list change listener handles the changes to the content of the list in a brief and generic way. Please refer to the "Observing an *ObservableList* for Changes" section in this chapter on how to handle the content change events for an ObservableList in detail.

Listing 3-9. Adding Invalidation, Change, and List Change Listeners to a ListProperty

```
// ListPropertyTest.java
// Listing part of the example sources download for the book
```

```
Before addAll()
List property is invalid.
List Property has changed. Old List: [one, two, three], New List: [one, two, three]
Action taken on the list: Added. Removed: [], Added: [one, two, three]
After addAll()

Before set()
List property is invalid.
List Property has changed. Old List: [one, two, three], New List: [two, three]
Action taken on the list: Replaced. Removed: [one, two, three], Added: [two, three]
After set()

Before remove()
List property is invalid.
List Property has changed. Old List: [three], New List: [three]
Action taken on the list: Removed. Removed: [two], Added: []
After remove()
```

Binding the *size* and *empty* Properties of a *ListProperty*

A ListProperty exposes two properties, size and empty, which are of type ReadOnlyIntegerProperty and ReadOnlyBooleanProperty, respectively. You can access them using the sizeProperty() and emptyProperty() methods. The size and empty properties are useful for binding in GUI applications. For example, the model in a GUI application may be backed by a ListProperty, and you can bind these properties to the text property of a label on the screen. When the data changes in the model, the label will be updated automatically through binding. The size and empty properties are declared in the ListExpression class.

The program in Listing 3-10 shows how to use the size and empty properties. It uses the asString() method of the ListExpression class to convert the content of the wrapped ObservableList to a String.

Listing 3-10. Using the size and empty Properties of a ListProperty Object

```java
// ListBindingTest.java
package com.jdojo.collections;

import javafx.beans.property.ListProperty;
import javafx.beans.property.SimpleListProperty;
import javafx.beans.property.SimpleStringProperty;
import javafx.beans.property.StringProperty;
import javafx.collections.FXCollections;

public class ListBindingTest {
        public static void main(String[] args) {
            ListProperty<String> lp =
                        new SimpleListProperty<>(FXCollections.observableArrayList());

            // Bind the size and empty properties of the ListProperty
            // to create a description of the list
            StringProperty initStr = new SimpleStringProperty("Size: " );
            StringProperty desc = new SimpleStringProperty();
            desc.bind(initStr.concat(lp.sizeProperty())
                            .concat(", Empty: ")
                            .concat(lp.emptyProperty())
                            .concat(", List: ")
                            .concat(lp.asString()));

            System.out.println("Before addAll(): " + desc.get());
            lp.addAll("John", "Jacobs");
            System.out.println("After addAll(): " + desc.get());
        }
}
```

```
Before addAll(): Size: 0, Empty: true, List: []
After addAll(): Size: 2, Empty: false, List: [John, Jacobs]
```

Binding to List Properties and Content

Methods to support high-level binding for a list property are in the ListExpression and Bindings classes. Low-level binding can be created by subclassing the ListBinding class. A ListProperty supports two types of bindings:

- Binding the reference of the ObservableList that it wraps

- Binding the content of the ObservableList that it wraps

The bind() and bindBidirectional() methods are used to create the first kind of binding. The program in Listing 3-11 shows how to use these methods. As shown in the following output, notice that both list properties have the reference of the same ObservableList after binding.

Listing 3-11. Binding the References of List Properties

```java
// BindingListReference.java
package com.jdojo.collections;

import javafx.beans.property.ListProperty;
import javafx.beans.property.SimpleListProperty;
import javafx.collections.FXCollections;

public class BindingListReference {

    public static void main(String[] args) {
        ListProperty<String> lp1 =
            new SimpleListProperty<>(
                    FXCollections.observableArrayList());
        ListProperty<String> lp2 =
            new SimpleListProperty<>(
                    FXCollections.observableArrayList());

        lp1.bind(lp2);

        print("Before addAll():", lp1, lp2);
        lp1.addAll("One", "Two");
        print("After addAll():", lp1, lp2);

        // Change the reference of the ObservableList in lp2
        lp2.set(FXCollections.observableArrayList("1", "2"));
        print("After lp2.set():", lp1, lp2);

        // Cannot do the following as lp1 is a bound property
        // lp1.set(FXCollections.observableArrayList("1", "2"));
        // Unbind lp1
        lp1.unbind();
        print("After unbind():", lp1, lp2);

        // Bind lp1 and lp2 bidirectionally
        lp1.bindBidirectional(lp2);
        print("After bindBidirectional():", lp1, lp2);

        lp1.set(FXCollections.observableArrayList("X", "Y"));
        print("After lp1.set():", lp1, lp2);
    }

    public static void print(String msg, ListProperty<String> lp1,
            ListProperty<String> lp2) {
        System.out.println(msg);
        System.out.println("lp1: " + lp1.get() + ", lp2: " +
                lp2.get() + ", lp1.get() == lp2.get(): " +
                (lp1.get() == lp2.get()));
        System.out.println("--------------------------");
    }
}
```

```
Before addAll():
lp1: [], lp2: [], lp1.get() == lp2.get(): true
--------------------------
After addAll():
lp1: [One, Two], lp2: [One, Two], lp1.get() == lp2.get(): true
--------------------------
After lp2.set():
lp1: [1, 2], lp2: [1, 2], lp1.get() == lp2.get(): true
--------------------------
After unbind():
lp1: [1, 2], lp2: [1, 2], lp1.get() == lp2.get(): true
--------------------------
After bindBidirectional():
lp1: [1, 2], lp2: [1, 2], lp1.get() == lp2.get(): true
--------------------------
After lp1.set():
lp1: [X, Y], lp2: [X, Y], lp1.get() == lp2.get(): true
--------------------------
```

The bindContent() and bindContentBidirectional() methods let you bind the content of the ObservableList that is wrapped in a ListProperty to the content of another ObservableList in one direction and both directions, respectively. Make sure to use the corresponding methods, unbindContent() and unbindContentBidirectional(), to unbind contents of two observable lists.

■ **Tip** You can also use methods of the Bindings class to create bindings for references and contents of observable lists.

It is allowed, but not advisable, to change the content of a ListProperty whose content has been bound to another ObservableList. In such cases, the bound ListProperty will not be synchronized with its target list. Listing 3-12 shows examples of both types of content binding.

Listing 3-12. Binding Contents of List Properties

```java
// BindingListContent.java
package com.jdojo.collections;

import javafx.beans.property.ListProperty;
import javafx.beans.property.SimpleListProperty;
import javafx.collections.FXCollections;

public class BindingListContent {

    public static void main(String[] args) {
        ListProperty<String> lp1 =
            new SimpleListProperty<>(
                    FXCollections.observableArrayList());
        ListProperty<String> lp2 =
            new SimpleListProperty<>(
                    FXCollections.observableArrayList());
```

```java
        // Bind the content of lp1 to the content of lp2
        lp1.bindContent(lp2);

        /* At this point, you can change the content of lp1. However,
         * that will defeat the purpose of content binding, because
         * the content of lp1 is no longer in sync with the content of
         * lp2.
         * Do not do this:
         * lp1.addAll("X", "Y");
         */
        print("Before lp2.addAll():", lp1, lp2);
        lp2.addAll("1", "2");
        print("After lp2.addAll():", lp1, lp2);

        lp1.unbindContent(lp2);
        print("After lp1.unbindContent(lp2):", lp1, lp2);

        // Bind lp1 and lp2 contents bidirectionally
        lp1.bindContentBidirectional(lp2);

        print("Before lp1.addAll():", lp1, lp2);
        lp1.addAll("3", "4");
        print("After lp1.addAll():", lp1, lp2);

        print("Before lp2.addAll():", lp1, lp2);
        lp2.addAll("5", "6");
        print("After lp2.addAll():", lp1, lp2);
    }

    public static void print(String msg, ListProperty<String> lp1,
            ListProperty<String> lp2) {
        System.out.println(msg + " lp1: " + lp1.get() +
            ", lp2: " + lp2.get());
    }
}
```

```
Before lp2.addAll(): lp1: [], lp2: []
After lp2.addAll(): lp1: [1, 2], lp2: [1, 2]
After lp1.unbindContent(lp2): lp1: [1, 2], lp2: [1, 2]
Before lp1.addAll(): lp1: [1, 2], lp2: [1, 2]
After lp1.addAll(): lp1: [1, 2, 3, 4], lp2: [1, 2, 3, 4]
Before lp2.addAll(): lp1: [1, 2, 3, 4], lp2: [1, 2, 3, 4]
After lp2.addAll(): lp1: [1, 2, 3, 4, 5, 6], lp2: [1, 2, 3, 4, 5, 6]
```

Binding to Elements of a List

ListProperty provides so many useful features that I can keep discussing this topic for at least 50 more pages! I will wrap this topic up with one more example.

It is possible to bind to a specific element of the ObservableList wrapped in a ListProperty using one of the following methods of the ListExpression class:

- ObjectBinding<E> valueAt(int index)

- ObjectBinding<E> valueAt(ObservableIntegerValue index)

The first version of the method creates an ObjectBinding to an element in the list at a specific index. The second version of the method takes an index as an argument, which is an ObservableIntegerValue that can change over time. When the bound index in the valueAt() method is outside the list range, the ObjectBinding contains null.

Let's use the second version of the method to create a binding that will bind to the last element of a list. Here, you can make use of the size property of the ListProperty in creating the binding expression. The program in Listing 3-13 shows how to use the valueAt() method.

Listing 3-13. Binding to the Elements of a List

```
// BindingToListElements.java
// Listing part of the example sources download for the book
```

```
List:[], Last Value: null
List:[John], Last Value: John
List:[John, Donna, Geshan], Last Value: Geshan
List:[John, Donna], Last Value: Donna
List:[], Last Value: null
```

Understanding *ObservableSet* Property and Binding

A SetProperty object wraps an ObservableSet. Working with a SetProperty is very similar to working with a ListProperty. I am not going to repeat what has been discussed in the previous sections about properties and bindings of an ObservableList. The same discussions apply to properties and bindings of ObservableSet. The following are the salient points to remember while working with a SetProperty:

- The class diagram for the SetProperty class is similar to the one shown in Figure 3-5 for the ListProperty class. You need to replace the word "List" with the word "Set" in all names.

- The SetExpression and Bindings classes contain methods to support high-level bindings for set properties. You need to subclass the SetBinding class to create low-level bindings.

- Like the ListProperty, the SetProperty exposes the size and empty properties.

- Like the ListProperty, the SetProperty supports bindings of the reference and the content of the ObservableSet that it wraps.

- Like the ListProperty, the SetProperty supports three types of notifications: invalidation notifications, change notifications, and set change notifications.

- Unlike a list, a set is an unordered collection of items. Its elements do not have indexes. It does not support binding to its specific elements. Therefore, the SetExpression class does not contain a method like valueAt() as the ListExpression class does.

You can use one of the following constructors of the SimpleSetProperty class to create an instance of the SetProperty:

- SimpleSetProperty()
- SimpleSetProperty(ObservableSet<E> initialValue)
- SimpleSetProperty(Object bean, String name)
- SimpleSetProperty(Object bean, String name, ObservableSet<E> initialValue)

The following snippet of code creates an instance of the SetProperty and adds two elements to the ObservableSet that the property wraps. In the end, it gets the reference of the ObservableSet from the property object using the get() method:

```
// Create a SetProperty object
SetProperty<String> sp = new SimpleSetProperty<String>(FXCollections.observableSet());

// Add two elements to the wrapped ObservableSet
sp.add("one");
sp.add("two");

// Get the wrapped set from the sp property
ObservableSet<String> set = sp.get();
```

The program in Listing 3-14 demonstrates how to use binding with SetProperty objects.

Listing 3-14. Using Properties and Bindings for Observable Sets

```
// SetBindingTest.java
// Listing part of the example sources download for the book
```

```
Before sp1.add(): Size: 0, Empty: true, Set: []
After sp1.add(): Size: 2, Empty: false, Set: [Jacobs, John]
Called sp1.bindContent(sp2)...
Before sp2.add(): sp1: [], sp2: []
After sp2.add(): sp1: [1], sp2: [1]
After sp1.unbindContent(sp2): sp1: [1], sp2: [1]
Before sp2.add(): sp1: [1], sp2: [1]
After sp2.add(): sp1: [1, 2], sp2: [2, 1]
```

Understanding *ObservableMap* Property and Binding

A MapProperty object wraps an ObservableMap. Working with a MapProperty is very similar to working with a ListProperty. I am not going to repeat what has been discussed in the previous sections about properties and bindings of an ObservableList. The same discussions apply to properties and bindings of ObservableMap. The following are the salient points to remember while working with a MapProperty:

- The class diagram for the MapProperty class is similar to the one shown in Figure 3-5 for the ListProperty class. You need to replace the word "List" with the word "Map" in all names and the generic type parameter <E> with <K, V>, where K and V stand for the key type and value type, respectively, of entries in the map.

- The MapExpression and Bindings classes contain methods to support high-level bindings for map properties. You need to subclass the MapBinding class to create low-level bindings.

- Like the ListProperty, the MapProperty exposes size and empty properties.

- Like the ListProperty, the MapProperty supports bindings of the reference and the content of the ObservableMap that it wraps.

- Like the ListProperty, the MapProperty supports three types of notifications: invalidation notifications, change notifications, and map change notifications.

- The MapProperty supports binding to the value of a specific key using its valueAt() method.

Use one of the following constructors of the SimpleMapProperty class to create an instance of the MapProperty:

- SimpleMapProperty()

- SimpleMapProperty(Object bean, String name)

- SimpleMapProperty(Object bean, String name, ObservableMap<K,V> initialValue)

- SimpleMapProperty(ObservableMap<K,V> initialValue)

The following snippet of code creates an instance of the MapProperty and adds two entries. In the end, it gets the reference of the wrapped ObservableMap using the get() method:

```
// Create a MapProperty object
MapProperty<String, Double> mp =
        new SimpleMapProperty<String, Double>(FXCollections.observableHashMap());

// Add two entries to the wrapped ObservableMap
mp.put("Ken", 8190.20);
mp.put("Jim", 8990.90);

// Get the wrapped map from the mp property
ObservableMap<String, Double> map = mp.get();
```

The program in Listing 3-15 shows how to use binding with MapProperty objects. It shows the content binding between two maps. You can also use unidirectional and bidirectional simple binding between two map properties to bind the references of the maps they wrap.

Listing 3-15. Using Properties and Bindings for Observable Maps

```
// MapBindingTest.java
// Listing part of the example sources download for the book
```

```
Ken Salary: null
Before mp1.put(): Size: 0, Empty: true, Map: {}, Ken Salary: null
After mp1.put(): Size: 3, Empty: false, Map: {Jim=9800.8, Lee=6000.2, Ken=7890.9}, Ken
Salary: 7890.9
```

```
Called mp1.bindContent(mp2)...
Before mp2.put(): Size: 0, Empty: true, Map: {}, Ken Salary: null
After mp2.put(): Size: 2, Empty: false, Map: {Cindy=7800.2, Ken=7500.9}, Ken
Salary: 7500.9
```

Summary

JavaFX extends the collections framework in Java by adding support for observable lists, sets, and maps that are called observable collections. An observable collection is a list, set, or map that may be observed for invalidation and content changes. Instances of the ObservableList, ObservableSet, and ObservableMap interfaces in the javafx.collections package represent observable interfaces in JavaFX. You can add invalidation and change listeners to instances of these observable collections.

The FXCollections class is a utility class to work with JavaFX collections. It consists of all static methods. JavaFX does not expose the implementation classes of observable lists, sets, and maps. You need to use one of the factory methods in the FXCollections class to create objects of the ObservableList, ObservableSet, and ObservableMap interfaces.

The JavaFX library provides two classes named FilteredList and SortedList that are in the javafx.collections.transformation package. A FilteredList is an ObservableList that filters its contents using a specified Predicate. A SortedList sorts its contents.

The next chapter will discuss how to create and customize stages in JavaFX applications.

CHAPTER 4

■ ■ ■

Managing Stages

In this chapter, you will learn:

- How to get details of screens such as their number, resolutions, and dimensions
- What a stage is in JavaFX and how to set bounds and styles of a stage
- How to move an undecorated stage
- How to set the modality and opacity of a stage
- How to resize a stage and how to show a stage in full-screen mode

The examples of this chapter lie in the com.jdojo.stage package. In order for them to work, you must add a corresponding line to the module-info.java file:

```
...
opens com.jdojo.stage to javafx.graphics, javafx.base;
...
```

Knowing the Details of Your Screens

The Screen class in the javafx.stage package is used to get the details, for example, dots-per-inch (DPI) setting and dimensions of user screens (or monitors). If multiple screens are hooked up to a computer, one of the screens is known as the primary screen and others as nonprimary screens. You can get the reference of the Screen object for the primary monitor using the static getPrimary() method of the Screen class with the following code:

```
// Get the reference to the primary screen
Screen primaryScreen = Screen.getPrimary();
```

The static getScreens() method returns an ObservableList of Screen objects:

```
ObservableList<Screen> screenList = Screen.getScreens();
```

You can get the resolution of a screen in DPI using the getDpi() method of the Screen class as follows:

```
Screen primaryScreen = Screen.getPrimary();
double dpi = primaryScreen.getDpi();
```

You can use the getBounds() and getVisualBounds() methods to get the bounds and visual bounds, respectively. Both methods return a Rectangle2D object, which encapsulates the (x, y) coordinates of the upper-left and the lower-right corners, the width, and the height of a rectangle. The getMinX() and getMinY() methods return the x and y coordinates of the upper-left corner of the rectangle, respectively. The getMaxX() and getMaxY() methods return the x and y coordinates of the lower-right corner of the rectangle, respectively. The getWidth() and getHeight() methods return the width and height of the rectangle, respectively.

The bounds of a screen cover the area that is available on the screen. The visual bounds represent the area on the screen that is available for use, after taking into account the area used by the native windowing system such as task bars and menus. Typically, but not necessarily, the visual bounds of a screen represent a smaller area than its bounds.

If a desktop spans multiple screens, the bounds of the nonprimary screens are relative to the primary screen. For example, if a desktop spans two screens with the (x, y) coordinates of the upper-left corner of the primary screen at (0, 0) and its width 1600, the coordinates of the upper-left corner of the second screen would be (1600, 0).

The program in Listing 4-1 prints the screen details when it was run on a Windows desktop with two screens. You may get a different output. Notice the difference in height for bounds and visual bounds for one screen and not for the other. The primary screen displays a task bar at the bottom that takes away some part of the height from the visual bounds. The nonprimary screen does not display a task bar, and therefore its bounds and visual bounds are the same.

■ **Tip**   Although it is not mentioned in the API documentation for the Screen class, you cannot use this class until the JavaFX launcher has started. That is, you cannot get screen descriptions in a non-JavaFX application. This is the reason that you would write the code in the start() method of a JavaFX application class. There is no requirement that the Screen class needs to be used on the JavaFX Application Thread. You could also write the same code in the init() method of your class.

Listing 4-1. Accessing Screen Details

```java
// ScreenDetailsApp.java
package com.jdojo.stage;

import javafx.application.Application;
import javafx.application.Platform;
import javafx.collections.ObservableList;
import javafx.geometry.Rectangle2D;
import javafx.stage.Screen;
import javafx.stage.Stage;

public class ScreenDetailsApp extends Application  {
        public static void main(String[] args) {
                Application.launch(args);
        }

        public void start(Stage stage) {
                ObservableList<Screen> screenList = Screen.getScreens();
                System.out.println("Screens Count: " + screenList.size());
```

```
                // Print the details of all screens
                for(Screen screen: screenList) {
                        print(screen);
                }

                Platform.exit();
        }

        public void print(Screen s) {
                System.out.println("DPI: " + s.getDpi());

                System.out.print("Screen Bounds: ");
                Rectangle2D bounds = s.getBounds();
                print(bounds);

                System.out.print("Screen Visual Bounds: ");
                Rectangle2D visualBounds = s.getVisualBounds();
                print(visualBounds);
                System.out.println("----------------------");
        }

        public void print(Rectangle2D r) {
                System.out.format("minX=%.2f, minY=%.2f, width=%.2f,
                        height=%.2f%n",
                        r.getMinX(), r.getMinY(),
                        r.getWidth(), r.getHeight());
        }
}
```

```
Screens Count: 2
DPI: 96.0
Screen Bounds: minX=0.00, minY=0.00, width=1680.00, height=1050.00
Screen Visual Bounds: minX=0.00, minY=0.00, width=1680.00, height=1022.00
----------------------
DPI: 96.0
Screen Bounds: minX = 1680.00, minY=0.00, width= 1680.00, height=1050.00
Screen Visual Bounds: minX = 1680.00, minY=0.00, width= 1680.00, height=1050.0
----------------------
```

What Is a Stage?

A stage in JavaFX is a top-level container that hosts a scene, which consists of visual elements. The Stage class in the javafx.stage package represents a stage in a JavaFX application. The primary stage is created by the platform and passed to the start(Stage s) method of the Application class. You can create additional stages as needed.

■ **Tip**   A stage in a JavaFX application is a top-level container. This does not necessarily mean that it is always displayed as a separate window. For this book's purpose however, a stage corresponds to a window, unless otherwise noted.

Figure 4-1 shows the class diagram for the Stage class, which inherits from the Window class. The Window class is the superclass for several window-line container classes. It contains the basic functionalities that are common to all types of windows (e.g., methods to show and hide the window; set x, y, width, and height properties; set the opacity of the window; etc.). The Window class defines x, y, width, height, and opacity properties. It has show() and hide() methods to show and hide a window, respectively. The setScene() method of the Window class sets the scene for a window. The Stage class defines a close() method, which has the same effect as calling the hide() method of the Window class.

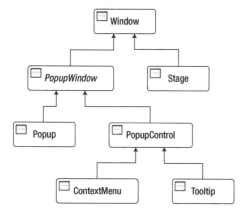

Figure 4-1. *The class diagram for the Stage class*

A Stage object must be created and modified on the JavaFX Application Thread. Recall that the start() method of the Application class is called on the JavaFX Application Thread, and a primary Stage is created and passed to this method. Note that the primary stage that is passed the start() method is not shown. You need to call the show() method to show it.

Several aspects of working with stages need to be discussed. I will handle them one by one from the basic to the advanced level in the sections that follow.

Showing the Primary Stage

Let's start with the simplest JavaFX application, as shown in Listing 4-2. The start() method has no code. When you run the application, you do not see a window, nor do you see output on the console. The application runs forever. You will need to use the system-specific keys to cancel the application. If you are using Windows, use your favorite key combination Ctrl + Alt + Del to activate the task manager! If you are using the command prompt, use Ctrl + C.

Listing 4-2. An Ever-Running JavaFX Application

```
// EverRunningApp.java
package com.jdojo.stage;
```

```
import javafx.application.Application;
import javafx.stage.Stage;

public class EverRunningApp extends Application {
        public static void main(String[] args) {
                Application.launch(args);
        }

        @Override
        public void start(Stage stage) {
                // Do not write any code here
        }
}
```

To determine what is wrong with the program in Listing 4-2, you need to understand what the JavaFX application launcher does. Recall that the JavaFX Application Thread is terminated when the Platform. exit() method is called or the last shown stage is closed. The JVM terminates when all nondaemon threads die. The JavaFX Application Thread is a nondaemon thread. The Application.launch() method returns when the JavaFX Application Thread terminates. In the preceding example, there is no way to terminate the JavaFX Application Thread. This is the reason the application runs forever.

Using the Platform.exit() method in the start() method will fix the problem. The modified code for the start() method is shown in Listing 4-3. When you run the program, it exits without doing anything meaningful.

Listing 4-3. A Short-Lived JavaFX Application

```
// ShortLivedApp.java
package com.jdojo.stage;

import javafx.application.Application;
import javafx.application.Platform;
import javafx.stage.Stage;

public class ShortLivedApp extends Application {
        public static void main(String[] args) {
                Application.launch(args);
        }

        @Override
        public void start(Stage stage) {
                Platform.exit(); // Exit the application
        }
}
```

Let's try to fix the ever-running program by closing the primary stage. You have only one stage when the start() method is called, and closing it should terminate the JavaFX Application Thread. Let's modify the start() method of the EverRunningApp with the following code:

```
@Override
public void start(Stage stage) {
        stage.close(); // Close the only stage you have
}
```

Even with this code for the start() method, the EverRunningApp runs forever. The close() method does not close the stage if the stage is not showing. The primary stage was never shown. Therefore, adding a stage.close() call to the start() method did not do any good. The following code for the start() method would work. However, this will cause the screen to flicker as the stage is shown and closed:

```
@Override
public void start(Stage stage) {
      stage.show();  // First show the stage
      stage.close(); // Now close it
}
```

■ **Tip**   The close() method of the Stage class has the same effect as calling the hide() method of the Window class. The JavaFX API documentation does not mention that attempting to close a not showing window has no effect.

Setting the Bounds of a Stage

The bounds of a stage consist of four properties: x, y, width, and height. The x and y properties determine the location (or position) of the upper-left corner of the stage. The width and height properties determine its size. In this section, you will learn how to position and size a stage on the screen. You can use the getters and setters for these properties to get and set their values.

Let's start with a simple example as shown in Listing 4-4. The program sets the title for the primary stage before showing it. When you run this code, you would see a window with the title bar, borders, and an empty area. If other applications are open, you can see their content through the transparent area of the stage. The position and size of the window are decided by the platform.

■ **Tip**   When a stage does not have a scene and its position and size are not set explicitly, its position and size are determined and set by the platform.

Listing 4-4. Displaying a Stage with No Scene and with the Platform Default Position and Size

```
// BlankStage.java
package com.jdojo.stage;

import javafx.application.Application;
import javafx.stage.Stage;

public class BlankStage extends Application {
      public static void main(String[] args) {
            Application.launch(args);
      }
```

```
    @Override
    public void start(Stage stage) {
            stage.setTitle("Blank Stage");
            stage.show();
    }
}
```

Let's modify the logic a bit. Here, you will set an empty scene to the stage without setting the size of the scene. The modified start() method would look as follows:

```
import javafx.scene.Group;
import javafx.scene.Scene;
...
@Override
public void start(Stage stage) {
    stage.setTitle("Stage with an Empty Scene");
    Scene scene = new Scene(new Group());
    stage.setScene(scene);
    stage.show();
}
```

Notice that you have set a Group with no children nodes as the root node for the scene, because you cannot create a scene without a root node. When you run the program in Listing 4-4 with the preceding code as its start() method, the position and size of the stage are determined by the platform. This time, the content area will have a white background, because the default background color for a scene is white.

Let's modify the logic again. Here, let's add a button to the scene. The modified start() method would be as follows:

```
import javafx.scene.control.Button;
...
@Override
public void start(Stage stage) {
    stage.setTitle("Stage with a Button in the Scene");
    Group root = new Group(new Button("Hello"));
    Scene scene = new Scene(root);
    stage.setScene(scene);
    stage.show();
}
```

When you run the program in Listing 4-4 with the preceding code as its start() method, the position and size of the stage are determined by the computed size of the scene. The content area of the stage is wide enough to show the title bar menus or the content of the scene, whichever is bigger. The content area of the stage is tall enough to show the content of the scene, which in this case has only one button. The stage is centered on the screen, as shown in Figure 4-2.

Figure 4-2. *A stage with a scene that contains a button where the size of the scene is not specified*

Let's add another twist to the logic by adding a button to the scene and set the scene width and height to 300 and 100, respectively, as follows:

```
@Override
public void start(Stage stage) {
        stage.setTitle("Stage with a Sized Scene");
        Group root = new Group(new Button("Hello"));
        Scene scene = new Scene(root, 300, 100);
        stage.setScene(scene);
        stage.show();
}
```

When you run the program in Listing 4-4 with the preceding code as its start() method, the position and size of the stage are determined by the specified size of the scene. The content area of the stage is the same as the specified size of the scene. The width of the stage includes the borders on the two sides, and the height of the stage includes the height of the title bar and the bottom border. The stage is centered on the screen, as shown in Figure 4-3.

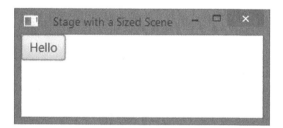

Figure 4-3. *A stage with a scene with a specified size*

Let's add one more twist to the logic. You will set the size of the scene and the stage using the following code:

```
@Override
public void start(Stage stage) {
        stage.setTitle("A Sized Stage with a Sized Scene");
        Group root = new Group(new Button("Hello"));
        Scene scene = new Scene(root, 300, 100);
        stage.setScene(scene);
        stage.setWidth(400);
        stage.setHeight(100);
        stage.show();
}
```

When you run the program in Listing 4-4 with the preceding code as its start() method, the position and size of the stage are determined by the specified size of the stage. The stage is centered on the screen, and it will then look like the one shown in Figure 4-4.

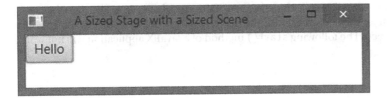

Figure 4-4. *A sized stage with a sized scene*

■ **Tip** The default centering of a stage centers it horizontally on the screen. The y coordinate of the upper-left corner of the stage is one-third of the height of the screen minus the height of the stage. This is the logic used in the `centerOnScreen()` method in the `Window` class.

Let me recap the rules for positioning and resizing a stage. If you do not specify the bounds of a stage and

- It has no scene, its bounds are determined by the platform.

- It has a scene with no visual nodes, its bounds are determined by the platform. In this case, the size of the scene is not specified.

- It has a scene with some visual nodes, its bounds are determined by the visual nodes in the scene. In this case, the size of the scene is not specified, and the stage is centered on the screen.

- It has a scene and the size of the scene is specified, its bounds are determined by the specified size of the scene. The stage is centered on the screen.

If you specify the size of the stage but not its position, the stage is sized according to the set size and centered on the screen, irrespective of the presence of a scene and the size of the scene. If you specify the position of the stage (x, y coordinates), it is positioned accordingly.

■ **Tip** If you want to set the width and height of a stage to fit the content of its scene, use the `sizeToScene()` method of the `Window` class. The method is useful if you want to synchronize the size of a stage with the size of its scene after modifying the scene at runtime. Use the `centerOnScreen()` method of the `Window` class to center the stage on the screen.

If you want to center a stage on the screen horizontally as well as vertically, use the following logic:

```
Rectangle2D bounds = Screen.getPrimary().getVisualBounds();
double x = bounds.getMinX() + (bounds.getWidth() - stage.getWidth())/2.0;
double y = bounds.getMinY() + (bounds.getHeight() - stage.getHeight())/2.0;
stage.setX(x);
stage.setY(y);
```

Be careful in using the preceding snippet of code. It makes use of the size of the stage. The size of a stage is not known until the stage is shown for the first time. Using the preceding logic before a stage is shown will not really center the stage on the screen. The following start() method of a JavaFX application will not work as intended:

```
@Override
public void start(Stage stage) {
        stage.setTitle("A Truly Centered Stage");
        Group root = new Group(new Button("Hello"));
        Scene scene = new Scene(root);
        stage.setScene(scene);

        // Wrong!!!! Use the logic shown below after the stage.show() call
        // At this point, stage width and height are not known. They are NaN.
        Rectangle2D bounds = Screen.getPrimary().getVisualBounds();
        double x = bounds.getMinX() + (bounds.getWidth() -
                stage.getWidth())/2.0;
        double y = bounds.getMinY() + (bounds.getHeight() -
                stage.getHeight())/2.0;
        stage.setX(x);
        stage.setY(y);

        stage.show();
}
```

Initializing the Style of a Stage

The area of a stage can be divided into two parts: content area and decorations. The content area displays the visual content of its scene. Typically, decorations consist of a title bar and borders. The presence of a title bar and its content varies depending on the type of decorations provided by the platform. Some decorations provide additional features rather than just an aesthetic look. For example, a title bar may be used to drag a stage to a different location; buttons in a title bar may be used to minimize, maximize, restore, and close a stage; or borders may be used to resize a stage.

In JavaFX, the style attribute of a stage determines its background color and decorations. Based on styles, you can have the following five types of stages in JavaFX:

- Decorated

- Undecorated

- Transparent

- Unified

- Utility

A *decorated* stage has a solid white background and platform decorations. An *undecorated* stage has a solid white background and no decorations. A *transparent* stage has a transparent background and no decorations. A *unified* stage has platform decorations and no border between the client area and decorations; the client area background is unified with the decorations. To see the effect of the unified stage style, the scene should be filled with Color.TRANSPARENT. Unified style is a conditional feature. A *utility* stage has a solid white background and minimal platform decorations.

■ **Tip** The style of a stage specifies only its decorations. The background color is controlled by its scene background, which is solid white by default. If you set the style of a stage to TRANSPARENT, you will get a stage with a solid white background, which is the background of the scene. To get a truly transparent stage, you will need to set the background color of the scene to null using its setFill() method.

You can set the style of a stage using the initStyle(StageStyle style) method of the Stage class. The style of a stage must be set before it is shown for the first time. Setting it the second time, after the stage has been shown, throws a runtime exception. By default, a stage is decorated.

The five types of styles for a stage are defined as five constants in the StageStyle enum:

- StageStyle.DECORATED
- StageStyle.UNDECORATED
- StageStyle.TRANSPARENT
- StageStyle.UNIFIED
- StageStyle.UTILITY

Listing 4-5 shows how to use these five styles for a stage. In the start() method, you need to uncomment only one statement at a time, which initializes the style of the stage. You will use a VBox to display two controls: a Label and a Button. The Label displays the style of the stage. The Button is provided to close the stage, because not all styles provide a title bar with a close button. Figure 4-5 shows the stage using four styles. The contents of windows in the background can be seen through a transparent stage. This is the reason that when you use the transparent style, you will see more content that has been added to the stage.

Listing 4-5. Using Different Styles for a Stage

```java
// StageStyleApp.java
package com.jdojo.stage;

import javafx.application.Application;
import javafx.scene.Scene;
import javafx.scene.control.Button;
import javafx.scene.control.Label;
import javafx.scene.layout.VBox;
import javafx.scene.paint.Color;
import javafx.stage.Stage;
import javafx.stage.StageStyle;
import static javafx.stage.StageStyle.DECORATED;
import static javafx.stage.StageStyle.UNDECORATED;
import static javafx.stage.StageStyle.TRANSPARENT;
import static javafx.stage.StageStyle.UNIFIED;
import static javafx.stage.StageStyle.UTILITY;

public class StageStyleApp extends Application {
    public static void main(String[] args) {
        Application.launch(args);
    }
```

```
    @Override
    public void start(Stage stage) {
            // A label to display the style type
            Label styleLabel = new Label("Stage Style");

            // A button to close the stage
            Button closeButton = new Button("Close");
            closeButton.setOnAction(e -> stage.close());

            VBox root = new VBox();
            root.getChildren().addAll(styleLabel, closeButton);
            Scene scene = new Scene(root, 100, 70);
            stage.setScene(scene);

            // The title of the stage is not visible for all styles.
            stage.setTitle("The Style of a Stage");

            /* Uncomment one of the following statements at a time */
            this.show(stage, styleLabel, DECORATED);
            //this.show(stage, styleLabel, UNDECORATED);
            //this.show(stage, styleLabel, TRANSPARENT);
            //this.show(stage, styleLabel, UNIFIED);
            //this.show(stage, styleLabel, UTILITY);
    }

    private void show(Stage stage, Label styleLabel, StageStyle style) {
            // Set the text for the label to match the style
            styleLabel.setText(style.toString());

            // Set the style
            stage.initStyle(style);

            // For a transparent style, set the scene fill to null.
            // Otherwise, the content area will have the default white
            // background of the scene.
            if (style == TRANSPARENT) {
                stage.getScene().setFill(null);
                stage.getScene().getRoot().setStyle(
                    "-fx-background-color: transparent");
            } else if(style == UNIFIED) {
                stage.getScene().setFill(Color.TRANSPARENT);
            }

            // Show the stage
            stage.show();
    }
}
```

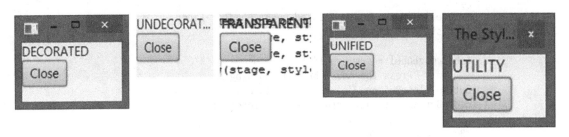

Figure 4-5. A stage using different styles

Moving an Undecorated Stage

You can move a stage to a different location by dragging its title bar. In an undecorated or transparent stage, a title bar is not available. You need to write a few lines of code to let the user move this kind of stage by dragging the mouse over the scene area. Listing 4-6 shows how to write the code to support dragging of a stage. If you change the stage to be transparent, you will need to drag the stage by dragging the mouse over only the message label, as the transparent area will not respond to the mouse events.

This example uses mouse event handling. I will cover event handling in detail in Chapter 9. It is briefly presented here to complete the discussion on using different styles of a stage.

Listing 4-6. Dragging a Stage

```
// DraggingStage.java
package com.jdojo.stage;

import javafx.application.Application;

import javafx.scene.Scene;
import javafx.scene.control.Button;
import javafx.scene.control.Label;
import javafx.scene.input.MouseEvent;
import javafx.scene.layout.VBox;

import javafx.stage.Stage;
import javafx.stage.StageStyle;

public class DraggingStage extends Application {
        private Stage stage;
        private double dragOffsetX;
        private double dragOffsetY;

        public static void main(String[] args) {
                Application.launch(args);
        }

        @Override
        public void start(Stage stage) {
                // Store the stage reference in the instance variable to
```

```
            // use it in the mouse pressed event handler later.
            this.stage = stage;

            Label msgLabel = new Label(
                    "Press the mouse button and drag.");
            Button closeButton = new Button("Close");
            closeButton.setOnAction(e -> stage.close());

            VBox root = new VBox();
            root.getChildren().addAll(msgLabel, closeButton);

            Scene scene = new Scene(root, 300, 200);

            // Set mouse pressed and dragged even handlers for the
            // scene
            scene.setOnMousePressed(e -> handleMousePressed(e));
            scene.setOnMouseDragged(e -> handleMouseDragged(e));

            stage.setScene(scene);
            stage.setTitle("Moving a Stage");
            stage.initStyle(StageStyle.UNDECORATED);
            stage.show();
    }

    protected void handleMousePressed(MouseEvent e) {
            // Store the mouse x and y coordinates with respect to the
            // stage in the reference variables to use them in the
            // drag event
            this.dragOffsetX = e.getScreenX() - stage.getX();
            this.dragOffsetY = e.getScreenY() - stage.getY();
    }

    protected void handleMouseDragged(MouseEvent e) {
            // Move the stage by the drag amount
            stage.setX(e.getScreenX() - this.dragOffsetX);
            stage.setY(e.getScreenY() - this.dragOffsetY);
    }
}
```

The following snippet of code adds the mouse pressed and mouse dragged event handlers to the scene:

```
scene.setOnMousePressed(e -> handleMousePressed(e));
scene.setOnMouseDragged(e -> handleMouseDragged(e));
```

When you press the mouse in the scene (except the button area), the handleMousePressed() method is called. The getScreenX() and getScreenY() methods of the MouseEvent object return the x and y coordinates of the mouse with respect to the upper-left corner of the screen. Figure 4-6 shows a diagrammatic view of the coordinate systems. It shows a thin border around the stage. However, when you run the example code, you will not see any border. This is shown here to distinguish the screen area from the stage area. You store the x and y coordinates of the mouse with respect to the stage's upper-left corner in instance variables.

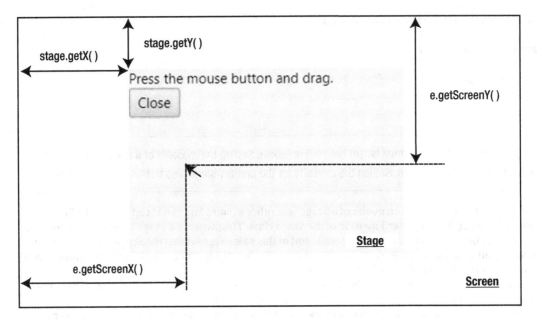

Figure 4-6. *Computing the mouse coordinates with respect to the stage*

When you drag the mouse, the handleMouseDragged() method is called. The method computes and sets the position of the stage using the position of the mouse when it was pressed and its position during the drag.

Initializing Modality of a Stage

In a GUI application, you can have two types of windows: modal and modeless. When a modal window is displayed, the user cannot work with other windows in the application until the modal window is dismissed. If an application has multiple modeless windows showing, the user can switch between them at any time.

JavaFX has three types of modality for a stage:

- None
- Window modal
- Application modal

The modality of a stage is defined by one of the following three constants in the Modality enum in the javafx.stage package:

- NONE
- WINDOW_MODAL
- APPLICATION_MODAL

You can set the modality of a stage using the initModality(Modality m) method of the Stage class as follows:

```
// Create a Stage object and set its modality
Stage stage = new Stage();
```

```
stage.initModality(Modality.WINDOW_MODAL);

/* More code goes here.*/

// Show the stage
stage.show();
```

░ **Tip** The modality of a stage must be set before it is shown. Setting the modality of a stage after it has been shown throws a runtime exception. Setting the modality for the primary stage also throws a runtime exception.

A Stage can have an owner. An owner of a Stage is another Window. You can set an owner of a Stage using the initOwner(Window owner) method of the Stage class. The owner of a Stage must be set before the stage is shown. The owner of a Stage may be null, and in this case, it is said that the Stage does not have an owner. Setting an owner of a Stage creates an owner-owned relationship. For example, a Stage is minimized or hidden if its owner is minimized or hidden, respectively.

The default modality of a Stage is NONE. When a Stage with the modality NONE is displayed, it does not block any other windows in the application. It behaves as a modeless window.

A Stage with the WINDOW_MODAL modality blocks all windows in its owner hierarchy. Suppose there are four stages: s1, s2, s3, and s4. Stages s1 and s4 have modalities set to NONE and do not have an owner; s1 is the owner of s2; s2 is the owner of s3. All four stages are displayed. If s3 has its modality set to WINDOW_MODAL, you can work with s3 or s4, but not with s2 and s1. The owner-owned relationship is defined as s1 to s2 to s3. When s3 is displayed, it blocks s2 and s1, which are in its owner hierarchy. Because s4 is not in the owner hierarchy of s3, you can still work with s4.

░ **Tip** The modality of WINDOW_MODAL for a stage that has no owner has the same effect as if the modality is set to NONE.

If a Stage with its modality set to APPLICATION_MODAL is displayed, you must work with the Stage and dismiss it before you can work with any other windows in the application. Continuing with the same example from the previous paragraph of displaying four stages, if you set the modality of s4 to APPLICATION_MODAL, the focus will be set to s4, and you must dismiss it before you can work with other stages. Notice that an APPLICATION_MODAL stage blocks all other windows in the same application, irrespective of the owner-owned relationships.

Listing 4-7 shows how to use different modalities for a stage. It displays the primary stage with six buttons. Each button opens a secondary stage with a specified modality and owner. The text of the buttons tells you what kind of secondary stage they will open. When the secondary stage is shown, try clicking the primary stage. When the modality of the secondary stage blocks the primary stage, you will not be able to work with the primary stage; clicking the primary stage will set the focus back to the secondary stage.

Listing 4-7. Using Different Modalities for a Stage

```
// StageModalityApp.java
package com.jdojo.stage;

import javafx.application.Application;
```

```java
import javafx.scene.Scene;
import javafx.scene.control.Button;
import javafx.scene.control.Label;
import javafx.scene.layout.VBox;
import javafx.stage.Stage;
import javafx.stage.Modality;
import static javafx.stage.Modality.NONE;
import static javafx.stage.Modality.WINDOW_MODAL;
import static javafx.stage.Modality.APPLICATION_MODAL;
import javafx.stage.Window;

public class StageModalityApp extends Application {
    public static void main(String[] args) {
        Application.launch(args);
    }

    @Override
    public void start(Stage stage) {
        /* Buttons to display each kind of modal stage */
        Button ownedNoneButton = new Button("Owned None");
        ownedNoneButton.setOnAction(e -> showDialog(stage, NONE));

        Button nonOwnedNoneButton = new Button("Non-owned None");
        nonOwnedNoneButton.setOnAction(e ->
                showDialog(null, NONE));

        Button ownedWinButton = new Button("Owned Window Modal");
        ownedWinButton.setOnAction(e ->
                showDialog(stage, WINDOW_MODAL));

        Button nonOwnedWinButton =
                new Button("Non-owned Window Modal");
        nonOwnedWinButton.setOnAction(e ->
                showDialog(null, WINDOW_MODAL));

        Button ownedAppButton =
                new Button("Owned Application Modal");
        ownedAppButton.setOnAction(e ->
                showDialog(stage, APPLICATION_MODAL));

        Button nonOwnedAppButton =
                new Button("Non-owned Application Modal");
        nonOwnedAppButton.setOnAction(e ->
                showDialog(null, APPLICATION_MODAL));

        VBox root = new VBox();
        root.getChildren().addAll(
                ownedNoneButton, nonOwnedNoneButton,
                ownedWinButton, nonOwnedWinButton,
                ownedAppButton, nonOwnedAppButton);
        Scene scene = new Scene(root, 300, 200);
```

```
                stage.setScene(scene);
                stage.setTitle("The Primary Stage");
                stage.show();
        }

        private void showDialog(Window owner, Modality modality) {
                // Create a Stage with specified owner and modality
                Stage stage = new Stage();
                stage.initOwner(owner);
                stage.initModality(modality);

                Label modalityLabel = new Label(modality.toString());
                Button closeButton = new Button("Close");
                closeButton.setOnAction(e -> stage.close());

                VBox root = new VBox();
                root.getChildren().addAll(modalityLabel, closeButton);
                Scene scene = new Scene(root, 200, 100);
                stage.setScene(scene);
                stage.setTitle("A Dialog Box");
                stage.show();
        }
}
```

Setting the Opacity of a Stage

The opacity of a stage determines how much you can see through the stage. You can set the opacity of a stage using the setOpacity(double opacity) method of the Window class. Use the getOpacity() method to get the current opacity of a stage.

The opacity value ranges from 0.0 to 1.0. Opacity of 0.0 means the stage is fully translucent; opacity of 1.0 means the stage is fully opaque. Opacity affects the entire area of a stage, including its decorations. Not all JavaFX runtime platforms are required to support opacity. Setting opacity on the JavaFX platforms that do not support opacity has no effect. The following snippet of code sets the opacity of a stage to half-translucent:

```
Stage stage = new Stage();
stage.setOpacity(0.5); // A half-translucent stage
```

Resizing a Stage

You can set whether a user can or cannot resize a stage by using its setResizable(boolean resizable) method. Note that a call to the setResizable() method is a *hint* to the implementation to make the stage resizable. By default, a stage is resizable. Sometimes, you may want to restrict the use to resize a stage within a range of width and height. The setMinWidth(), setMinHeight(), setMaxWidth(), and setMaxHeight() methods of the Stage class let you set the range within which the user can resize a stage.

■ **Tip** Calling the setResizable(false) method on a Stage object prevents the user from resizing the stage. You can still resize the stage programmatically.

It is often required to open a window that takes up the entire screen space. To achieve this, you need to set the position and size of the window to the available visual bounds of the screen. Listing 4-8 provides the program to illustrate this. It opens an empty stage, which takes up the entire visual area of the screen.

Listing 4-8. Opening a Stage to Take Up the Entire Available Visual Screen Space

```java
// MaximizedStage.java
package com.jdojo.stage;

import javafx.application.Application;
import javafx.geometry.Rectangle2D;
import javafx.scene.Group;
import javafx.scene.Scene;
import javafx.stage.Screen;
import javafx.stage.Stage;

public class MaximizedStage extends Application {
    public static void main(String[] args) {
        Application.launch(args);
    }

    @Override
    public void start(Stage stage) {
        stage.setScene(new Scene(new Group()));
        stage.setTitle("A Maximized Stage");

        // Set the position and size of the stage equal to the
        // position and size of the screen
        Rectangle2D visualBounds =
                Screen.getPrimary().getVisualBounds();
        stage.setX(visualBounds.getMinX());
        stage.setY(visualBounds.getMinY());
        stage.setWidth(visualBounds.getWidth());
        stage.setHeight(visualBounds.getHeight());

        // Show the stage
        stage.show();
    }
}
```

Showing a Stage in Full-Screen Mode

The Stage class has a fullScreen property that specified whether a stage should be displayed in full-screen mode. The implementation of full-screen mode depends on the platform and profile. If the platform does not support full-screen mode, the JavaFX runtime will simulate it by displaying the stage maximized and undecorated. A stage may enter full-screen mode by calling the `setFullScreen(true)` method. When a stage enters full-screen mode, a brief message is displayed about how to exit the full-screen mode: you will need to press the ESC key to exit full-screen mode. You can exit full-screen mode programmatically by calling the `setFullScreen(false)` method. Use the `isFullScreen()` method to check if a stage is in full-screen mode.

Showing a Stage and Waiting for It to Close

You often want to display a dialog box and suspend further processing until it is closed. For example, you may want to display a message box to the user with options to click yes and no buttons, and you want different actions performed based on which button is clicked by the user. In this case, when the message box is displayed to the user, the program must wait for it to close before it executes the next sequence of logic. Consider the following pseudo-code:

```
Option userSelection = messageBox("Close", "Do you want to exit?", YESNO);
if (userSelection == YES) {
        stage.close();
}
```

In this pseudo-code, when the `messageBox()` method is called, the program needs to wait to execute the subsequent `if` statement until the message box is dismissed.

The `show()` method of the `Window` class returns immediately, making it useless to open a dialog box in the preceding example. You need to use the `showAndWait()` method, which shows the stage and waits for it to close before returning to the caller. The `showAndWait()` method stops processing the current event temporarily and starts a nested event loop to process other events.

■ **Tip** The `showAndWait()` method must be called on the JavaFX Application Thread. It should not be called on the primary stage or a runtime exception will be thrown.

You can have multiple stages open using the `showAndWait()` method. Each call to the method starts a new nested event loop. A specific call to the method returns to the caller when all nested event loops created after this method call have terminated.

This rule may be confusing in the beginning. Let's look at an example to explain this in detail. Suppose you have three stages: s1, s2, and s3. Stage s1 is opened using the call `s1.showAndWait()`. From the code in s1, stage s2 is opened using the call `s2.showAndWait()`. At this point, there are two nested event loops: one created by `s1.showAndWait()` and another by `s2.showAndWait()`. The call to `s1.showAndWait()` will return only after both s1 and s2 have been closed, irrespective of the order they were closed. The `s2.showAndWait()` call will return after s2 has been closed.

Listing 4-9 contains a program that will allow you to play with the `showAndWait()` method call using multiple stages. The primary stage is opened with an Open button. Clicking the Open button opens a secondary stage using the `showAndWait()` method. The secondary stage has two buttons—Say Hello and Open—which will, respectively, print a message on the console and open another secondary stage. A message is printed on the console before and after the call to the `showAndWait()` method. You need to open multiple secondary stages, print messages by clicking the Say Hello button, close them in any order you want, and then look at the output on the console.

Listing 4-9. Playing with the showAndWait() Call

```java
// ShowAndWaitApp.java
package com.jdojo.stage;

import javafx.application.Application;
import javafx.scene.Scene;
import javafx.scene.control.Button;
import javafx.scene.layout.VBox;
import javafx.stage.Stage;

public class ShowAndWaitApp extends Application {
    protected static int counter = 0;
    protected Stage lastOpenStage;

    public static void main(String[] args) {
        Application.launch(args);
    }

    @Override
    public void start(Stage stage) {
        VBox root = new VBox();
        Button openButton = new Button("Open");
        openButton.setOnAction(e -> open(++counter));
        root.getChildren().add(openButton);
        Scene scene = new Scene(root, 400, 400);
        stage.setScene(scene);
        stage.setTitle("The Primary Stage");
        stage.show();

        this.lastOpenStage = stage;
    }

    private void open(int stageNumber) {
        Stage stage = new Stage();
        stage.setTitle("#" + stageNumber);

        Button sayHelloButton = new Button("Say Hello");
        sayHelloButton.setOnAction(
            e -> System.out.println(
                "Hello from #" + stageNumber));

        Button openButton = new Button("Open");
        openButton.setOnAction(e -> open(++counter));

        VBox root = new VBox();
        root.getChildren().addAll(sayHelloButton, openButton);
        Scene scene = new Scene(root, 200, 200);
        stage.setScene(scene);
        stage.setX(this.lastOpenStage.getX() + 50);
        stage.setY(this.lastOpenStage.getY() + 50);
        this.lastOpenStage = stage;
```

```java
        System.out.println("Before stage.showAndWait(): " +
                stageNumber);

        // Show the stage and wait for it to close
        stage.showAndWait();

        System.out.println("After stage.showAndWait(): " +
                stageNumber);
    }
}
```

■ **Tip** JavaFX does not provide a built-in window that can be used as a dialog box (a message box or a prompt window). You can develop one by setting the appropriate modality for a stage and showing it using the showAndWait() method.

Summary

The Screen class in the javafx.stage package is used to obtain the details, such as the DPI setting and dimensions, of the user's screens hooked to the machine running the program. If multiple screens are present, one of the screens is known as the primary screen, and the others are the nonprimary screens. You can get the reference of the Screen object for the primary monitor using the static getPrimary() method of the Screen class.

A stage in JavaFX is a top-level container that hosts a scene, which consists of visual elements. The Stage class in the javafx.stage package represents a stage in a JavaFX application. The primary stage is created by the platform and passed to the start(Stage s) method of the Application class. You can create additional stages as needed.

A stage has bounds that comprise its position and size. The bounds of a stage are defined by its four properties: x, y, width, and height. The x and y properties determine the location (or position) of the upper-left corner of the stage. The width and height properties determine its size.

The area of a stage can be divided into two parts: content area and decorations. The content area displays the visual content of its scene. Typically, decorations consist of a title bar and borders. The presence of a title bar and its content varies depending on the type of decorations provided by the platform. You can have five types of stages in JavaFX: decorated, undecorated, transparent, unified, and utility.

JavaFX allows you to have two types of windows: modal and modeless. When a modal window is displayed, the user cannot work with other windows in the application until the modal window is dismissed. If an application has multiple modeless windows showing, the user can switch between them at any time. JavaFX defines three types of modality for a stage: none, window modal, and application modal. A stage with none as its modality is a modeless window. A stage with window modal as its modality blocks all windows in its owner hierarchy. A stage with application modal as its modality blocks all other windows in the application.

The opacity of a stage determines how much you can see through the stage. You can set the opacity of a stage using its setOpacity(double opacity) method. The opacity value ranges from 0.0 to 1.0. Opacity of 0.0 means the stage is fully translucent; the opacity of 1.0 means the stage is fully opaque. Opacity affects the entire area of a stage, including its decorations.

You can set a hint whether a user can resize a stage by using its setResizable(boolean resizable) method. The setMinWidth(), setMinHeight(), setMaxWidth(), and setMaxHeight() methods of the Stage class let you set the range within which the user can resize a stage. A stage may enter full-screen mode by calling its setFullScreen(true) method.

You can use the show() and showAndWait() methods of the Stage class to show a stage. The show() method shows the stage and returns, whereas the showAndWait() method shows the stage and blocks until the stage is closed.

The next chapter will show you how to create scenes and work with scene graphs.

CHAPTER 5

Making Scenes

In this chapter, you will learn:

- What a scene and a scene graph are in a JavaFX application
- About different rendering modes of a scene graph
- How to set the cursor for a scene
- How to determine the focus owner in a scene
- How to use the `Platform` and `HostServices` classes

The examples of this chapter lie in the `com.jdojo.scene` package. In order for them to work, you must add a corresponding line to the `module-info.java` file:

```
...
opens com.jdojo.scene to javafx.graphics, javafx.base;
...
```

What Is a Scene?

A *scene* represents the visual contents of a stage. The Scene class in the `javafx.scene` package represents a scene in a JavaFX program. A Scene object is attached to, at the most, one stage at a time. If an already attached scene is attached to another stage, it is first detached from the previous stage. A stage can have, at the most, one scene attached to it at any time.

A scene contains a scene graph that consists of visual nodes. In this sense, a scene acts as a container for a scene graph. A scene graph is a tree data structure whose elements are known as *nodes*. Nodes in a scene graph form a parent-child hierarchical relationship. A node in a scene graph is an instance of the `javafx.scene.Node` class. A node can be a branch node or a leaf node. A branch node can have children nodes, whereas a leaf node cannot. The first node in a scene graph is called the *root* node. The root node can have children nodes; however, it never has a parent node. Figure 5-1 shows the arrangement of nodes in a scene graph. Branch nodes are shown in rounded rectangles and leaf nodes in rectangles.

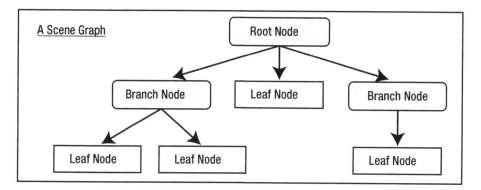

Figure 5-1. *The arrangement of nodes in a scene graph*

The JavaFX class library provides many classes to represent branch and leaf nodes in a scene graph. The Node class in the javafx.scene package is the superclass of all nodes in a scene graph. Figure 5-2 shows a partial class diagram for classes representing nodes.

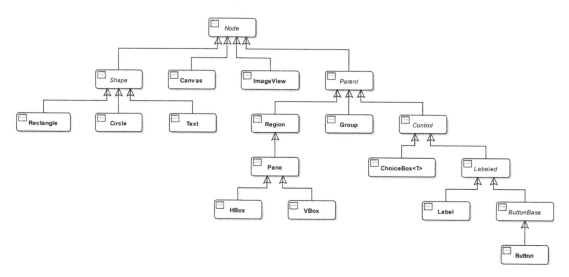

Figure 5-2. *A partial class diagram for the* javafx.scene.Node *class*

A scene always has a root node. If the root node is resizable, for example, a Region or a Control, it tracks the size of the scene. That is, if the scene is resized, the resizable root node resizes itself to fill the entire scene. Based on the policy of a root node, the scene graph may be laid out again when the size of the scene changes.

A Group is a nonresizable Parent node that can be set as the root node of a scene. If a Group is the root node of a scene, the content of the scene graph is clipped by the size of the scene. If the scene is resized, the scene graph is not laid out again.

Parent is an abstract class. It is the base class for all branch nodes in a scene graph. If you want to add a branch node to a scene graph, use objects of one of its concrete subclasses, for example, Group, Pane, HBox, or VBox. Classes that are subclasses of the Node class, but not the Parent class, represent leaf nodes, for example, Rectangle, Circle, Text, Canvas, or ImageView. The root node of a scene graph is a special branch node that is the topmost node. This is the reason you use a Group or a VBox as the root node while creating a Scene object. I will discuss classes representing branch and leaf nodes in detail in Chapters 10 and 12. Table 5-1 lists some of the commonly used properties of the Scene class.

Table 5-1. *Commonly Used Properties of the Scene Class*

Type	Name	Property and Description
ObjectProperty<Cursor>	cursor	It defines the mouse cursor for the Scene.
ObjectProperty<Paint>	fill	It defines the background fill of the Scene.
ReadOnlyObjectProperty<Node>	focusOwner	It defines the node in the Scene that owns the focus.
ReadOnlyDoubleProperty	height	It defines the height of the Scene.
ObjectProperty<Parent>	root	It defines the root Node of the scene graph.
ReadOnlyDoubleProperty	width	It defines the width of the Scene.
ReadOnlyObjectProperty<Window>	window	It defines the Window for the Scene.
ReadOnlyDoubleProperty	x	It defines the horizontal location of the Scene on the Window.
ReadOnlyDoubleProperty	y	It defines the vertical location of the Scene on the window.

Graphics Rendering Modes

The scene graph plays a vital role in rendering the content of a JavaFX application on the screen. Typically, two types of APIs are used to render graphics on a screen:

- Immediate mode API

- Retained mode API

In the immediate mode API, the application is responsible for issuing the drawing commands when a frame is needed on the screen. The graphics are drawn directly on the screen. When the screen needs to be repainted, the application needs to reissue the drawing commands to the screen. Java2D is an example of the immediate mode graphics-rendering API.

In the retained mode API, the application creates and attaches drawing objects to a graph. The graphics library, not the application code, retains the graph in memory. Graphics are rendered on the screen by the graphics library when needed. The application is responsible only for creating the graphic objects—the "what" part; the graphics library is responsible for storing and rendering the graphics—the "when" and "how" parts. The retained mode rendering API relieves developers of writing the logic for rendering the graphics. For example, adding or removing part of a graphic from a screen is simple by adding or removing a graphic object from the graph using high-level APIs; the graphics library takes care of the rest. In comparison to the immediate mode, the retained mode API uses more memory, as the graph is stored in memory. The JavaFX scene graph uses retained mode APIs.

You might think that using the immediate mode API would always be faster than using the retained mode API because the former renders graphics directly on the screen. However, using the retained mode API opens the door for optimizations by the class library that is not possible in the immediate mode where every developer is in charge of writing the logic as to what and when it should be rendered.

Figures 5-3 and 5-4 illustrate how immediate and retained mode APIs work, respectively. They show how a text, Hello, and a hexagon are drawn on the screen using the two APIs.

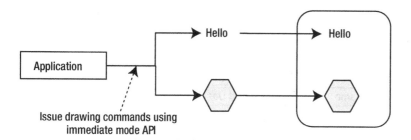

Figure 5-3. *An illustration of the immediate mode API*

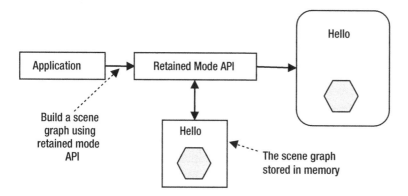

Figure 5-4. *An illustration of the retained mode API*

Setting the Cursor for a Scene

An instance of the `javafx.scene.Cursor` class represents a mouse cursor. The `Cursor` class contains many constants, for example, `HAND`, `CLOSED_HAND`, `DEFAULT`, `TEXT`, `NONE`, `WAIT`, for standard mouse cursors. The following snippet of code sets the `WAIT` cursor for a scene:

```
Scene scene;
...
scene.setCursor(Cursor.WAIT);
```

You can also create and set a custom cursor to a scene. The `cursor(String name)` static method of the `Cursor` class returns a standard cursor if the specified name is the name of a standard cursor. Otherwise, it treats the specified name as a URL for the cursor bitmap. The following snippet of code creates a cursor from a bitmap file named `mycur.png`, which is assumed to be in the `CLASSPATH`:

```
// Create a Cursor from a bitmap
URL url = getClass().getClassLoader().getResource("mycur.png");
Cursor myCur = Cursor.cursor(url.toExternalForm());
scene.setCursor(myCur);

// Get the WAIT standard cursor using its name
Cursor waitCur = Cursor.cursor("WAIT")
scene.setCursor(waitCur);
```

The Focus Owner in a Scene

Only one node in a scene can be the focus owner. The focusOwner property of the Scene class tracks the Node class that has the focus. Note that the focusOwner property is read-only. If you want a specific node in a scene to be the focus owner, you need to call the requestFocus() method of the Node class.

You can use the getFocusOwner() method of the Scene class to get the reference of the node having the focus in the scene. A scene may not have a focus owner, and in that case, the getFocusOwner() method returns null. For example, a scene does not have a focus owner when it is created but is not attached to a window.

It is important to understand the distinction between a focus owner and a node having focus. Each scene may have a focus owner. For example, if you open two windows, you will have two scenes, and you can have two focus owners. However, only one of the two focus owners can have the focus at a time. The focus owner of the active window will have the focus. To check if the focus owner node also has the focus, you need to use the focused property of the Node class. The following snippet of code shows the typical logic in using the focus owner:

```
Scene scene;
...
Node focusOwnerNode = scene.getFocusOwner();
if (focusOwnerNode == null) {
        // The scene does not have a focus owner
}
else if (focusOwnerNode.isFocused()) {
        // The focus owner is the one that has the focus
}
else {
        // The focus owner does not have the focus
}
```

Table 5-2. *Methods of the Platform Class*

Method	Description
void exit()	It terminates a JavaFX application.
boolean isFxApplicationThread()	It returns true if the calling thread is the JavaFX Application Thread. Otherwise, it returns false.
boolean isImplicitExit()	It returns the value of the implicit implicitExit attribute of the application. If it returns true, it means that the application will terminate after the last window is closed. Otherwise, you need to call the exit() method of this class to terminate the application.
boolean isSupported(ConditionalFeature feature)	It returns true if the specified conditional feature is supported by the platform. Otherwise, it returns false.
void runLater(Runnable runnable)	It executes the specified Runnable on the JavaFX Application Thread. The timing of the execution is not specified. The method posts the Runnable to an event queue and returns immediately. If multiple Runnables are posted using this method, they are executed in the order they are submitted to the queue.
void setImplicitExit(boolean value)	It sets the implicitExit attribute to the specified value.

Understanding the *Platform* Class

The Platform class in the javafx.application package is a utility class used to support platform-related functionalities. It consists of all static methods, which are listed in Table 5-2.

The runLater() method is used to submit a Runnable task to an event queue, so it is executed on the JavaFX Application Thread. JavaFX allows developers to execute some of the code only on the JavaFX Application Thread. Listing 5-1 creates a task in the init() method that is called on the JavaFX Launcher Thread. It uses the Platform.runLater() method to submit the task to be executed on the JavaFX Application Thread later.

■ **Tip** Use the Platform.runLater() method to execute a task that is created on a thread other than the JavaFX Application Thread but needs to run on the JavaFX Application Thread.

Listing 5-1. Using the Platform.runLater() Method

```java
// RunLaterApp.java
package com.jdojo.scene;

import javafx.application.Application;
import javafx.application.Platform;
import javafx.scene.Group;
import javafx.scene.Scene;
import javafx.stage.Stage;

public class RunLaterApp extends Application {
        public static void main(String[] args) {
                Application.launch(args);
        }

        @Override
        public void init() {
                System.out.println("init(): " +
                        Thread.currentThread().getName());

                // Create a Runnable task
                Runnable task = () ->
                        System.out.println("Running the task on the "
                    + Thread.currentThread().getName());

                // Submit the task to be run on the JavaFX Application
                // Thread
                Platform.runLater(task);
        }
}
```

```
        @Override
        public void start(Stage stage) throws Exception {
                stage.setScene(new Scene(new Group(), 400, 100));
                stage.setTitle("Using Platform.runLater() Method");
                stage.show();
        }
}
```

```
init(): JavaFX-Launcher

Running the task on the JavaFX Application Thread
```

Some features in a JavaFX implementation are optional (or conditional). They may not be available on all platforms. Using an optional feature on a platform that does not support the feature does not result in an error; the optional feature is simply ignored. Optional features are defined as enum constants in the ConditionalFeature enum in the javafx.application package, as listed in Table 5-3.

Table 5-3. Constants Defined in the ConditionalFeature Enum

Enum Constant	Description
EFFECT	Indicates the availability of filter effects, for example, reflection, shadow, etc.
INPUT_METHOD	Indicates the availability of the text input method.
SCENE3D	Indicates the availability of 3D features.
SHAPE_CLIP	Indicates the availability of clipping of a node against an arbitrary shape.
TRANSPARENT_WINDOW	Indicates the availability of the full window transparency.

Suppose your JavaFX application uses 3D GUI on user demand. You can write your logic for enabling 3D features as shown in the following code:

```
import javafx.application.Platform;
import static javafx.application.ConditionalFeature.SCENE3D;
...
if (Platform.isSupported(SCENE3D)) {
        // Enable 3D features
}
else {
        // Notify the user that 3D features are not available
}
```

Knowing the Host Environment

The HostServices class in the javafx.application package provides services related to the launching environment (desktop for this book) hosting the JavaFX application. You cannot create an instance of the HostServices class directly. The getHostServices() method of the Application class returns an instance of the HostServices class. The following is an example of how to get an instance of HostServices inside a class that inherits from the Application class:

```
HostServices host = getHostServices();
```

The HostServices class contains the following methods:

- String getCodeBase()

- String getDocumentBase()

- String resolveURI(String base, String relativeURI)

- void showDocument(String uri)

The getCodeBase() method returns the code base uniform resource identifier (URI) of the application. In a stand-alone mode, it returns the URI of the directory that contains the JAR file used to launch the application. If the application is launched using a class file, it returns an empty string.

The getDocumentBase() method returns the URI of the document base. It returns the URI of the current directory for the application launched in stand-alone mode.

The resolveURI() method resolves the specified relative URI with respect to the specified base URI and returns the resolved URI.

The showDocument() method opens the specified URI in a new browser window. Depending on the browser preference, it may open the URI in a new tab instead. The following snippet of code opens the Yahoo! home page:

```
getHostServices().showDocument("http://www.yahoo.com");
```

The program in Listing 5-2 uses all of the methods of the HostServices class. It shows a stage with two buttons and host details. One button opens the Yahoo! home page and another shows an alert box. The output shown on the stage will vary depending on how the application is launched.

Listing 5-2. Knowing the Details of the Host Environment for a JavaFX Application

```java
// KnowingHostDetailsApp.java
package com.jdojo.scene;

import java.util.HashMap;
import java.util.Map;
import javafx.application.Application;
import javafx.application.HostServices;
import javafx.scene.Group;
import javafx.scene.Scene;
import javafx.scene.control.Button;
import javafx.scene.control.Label;
import javafx.scene.layout.VBox;
import javafx.stage.Modality;
import javafx.stage.Stage;
import javafx.stage.StageStyle;
```

```java
public class KnowingHostDetailsApp extends Application {
        public static void main(String[] args) {
                Application.launch(args);
        }

        @Override
        public void start(Stage stage) {
                String yahooURL = "http://www.yahoo.com";
                Button openURLButton = new Button("Go to Yahoo!");
                openURLButton.setOnAction(e →
                        getHostServices().showDocument(yahooURL));

                Button showAlert = new Button("Show Alert");
                showAlert.setOnAction(e -> showAlert());

                VBox root = new VBox();

                // Add buttons and all host related details to the VBox
                root.getChildren().addAll(openURLButton, showAlert);

                Map<String, String> hostdetails = getHostDetails();
                for(Map.Entry<String, String> entry :
                                hostdetails.entrySet()) {
                    String desc = entry.getKey() + ": " +
                            entry.getValue();
                    root.getChildren().add(new Label(desc));
                }

                Scene scene = new Scene(root);
                stage.setScene(scene);
                stage.setTitle("Knowing the Host");
                stage.show();
        }

        protected Map<String, String> getHostDetails() {
                Map<String, String> map = new HashMap<>();
                HostServices host = this.getHostServices();

                String codeBase = host.getCodeBase();
                map.put("CodeBase", codeBase);

                String documentBase = host.getDocumentBase();
                map.put("DocumentBase", documentBase);

                String splashImageURI =
                        host.resolveURI(documentBase, "splash.jpg");
                map.put("Splash Image URI", splashImageURI);

                return map;
        }
```

```
        protected void showAlert() {
                Stage s = new Stage(StageStyle.UTILITY);
                s.initModality(Modality.WINDOW_MODAL);

                Label msgLabel = new Label("This is an FX alert!");
                Group root = new Group(msgLabel);
                Scene scene = new Scene(root);
                s.setScene(scene);

                s.setTitle("FX Alert");
                s.show();
        }
}
```

Summary

A scene represents the visual contents of a stage. The Scene class in the javafx.scene package represents a scene in a JavaFX program. A Scene object is attached to at the most one stage at a time. If an already attached scene is attached to another stage, it is first detached from the previous stage. A stage can have at the most one scene attached to it at any time.

A scene contains a scene graph that consists of visual nodes. In this sense, a scene acts as a container for a scene graph. A scene graph is a tree data structure whose elements are known as nodes. Nodes in a scene graph form a parent-child hierarchical relationship. A node in a scene graph is an instance of the javafx.scene.Node class. A node can be a branch node or a leaf node. A branch node can have children nodes, whereas a leaf node cannot. The first node in a scene graph is called the root node. The root node can have children nodes; however, it never has a parent node.

An instance of the javafx.scene.Cursor class represents a mouse cursor. The Cursor class contains many constants, for example, HAND, CLOSED_HAND, DEFAULT, TEXT, NONE, WAIT, for standard mouse cursors. You can set a cursor for the scene using the setCursor() method of the Scene class.

Only one node in a scene can be the focus owner. The read-only focusOwner property of the Scene class tracks the node that has the focus. If you want a specific node in a scene to be the focus owner, you need to call the requestFocus() method of the Node class. Each scene may have a focus owner. For example, if you open two windows, you will have two scenes, and you may have two focus owners. However, only one of the two focus owners can have the focus at a time. The focus owner of the active window will have the focus. To check if the focus owner node also has the focus, you need to use the focused property of the Node class.

The Platform class in the javafx.application package is a utility class used to support platform-related functionalities. It contains methods for terminating the application, checking if the code being executed is executed on the JavaFX Application Thread, and so on.

The HostServices class in the javafx.application package provides services related to the launching environment (desktop for this book) hosting the JavaFX application. You cannot create an instance of the HostServices class directly. The getHostServices() method of the Application class returns an instance of the HostServices class.

The next chapter will discuss nodes in detail.

CHAPTER 6

■ ■ ■

Understanding Nodes

In this chapter, you will learn:

- What a node is in JavaFX
- About the Cartesian coordinate system
- About the bounds and bounding box of nodes
- How to set the size of a node and how to position a node
- How to store user data in a node
- What a managed node is
- How to transform node's bounds between coordinate spaces

The examples of this chapter lie in the `com.jdojo.node` package. In order for them to work, you must add a corresponding line to the `module-info.java` file:

```
...
opens com.jdojo.node to javafx.graphics, javafx.base;
...
```

What Is a Node?

Chapter 5 introduced you to scenes and scene graphs. A scene graph is a tree data structure. Every item in a scene graph is called a *node*. An instance of the `javafx.scene.Node` class represents a node in the scene graph. Note that the Node class is an abstract class, and several concrete classes exist to represent a specific type of nodes.

A node can have subitems (also called children), and these nodes are called branch nodes. A branch node is an instance of the Parent, whose concrete subclasses are Group, Region, and WebView. A node that cannot have subitems is called a *leaf node*. Instances of classes such as Rectangle, Text, ImageView, and MediaView are examples of leaf nodes. Only a single node within each scene graph tree will have no parent, which is referred to as the *root node*. A node may occur at the most once anywhere in the scene graph.

A node may be created and modified on any thread if it is not yet attached to a scene. Attaching a node to a scene and subsequent modification must occur on the JavaFX Application Thread.

A node has several types of bounds. Bounds are determined with respect to different coordinate systems. The next section will discuss the Cartesian coordinate system in general; the following section explains how Cartesian coordinate systems are used to compute the bounds of a node in JavaFX.

The Cartesian Coordinate System

If you have studied (and still remember) the Cartesian coordinate system from your coordinate geometry class in high school, you may skip this section.

The Cartesian coordinate system is a way to define each point on a 2D plane uniquely. Sometimes, it is also known as a *rectangular coordinate system*. It consists of two perpendicular, directed lines known as the x-axis and the y-axis. The point where the two axes intersect is known as the *origin*.

A point in a 2D plane is defined using two values known as its x and y coordinates. The x and y coordinates of a point are its perpendicular distances from the y-axis and x-axis, respectively. Along an axis, the distance is measured as positive on one side from the origin and as negative on the other side. The origin has (x, y) coordinates, such as (0, 0). The axes divide the plane into four quadrants. Note that the 2D plane itself is infinite and so are the four quadrants. The set of all points in a Cartesian coordinate system defines the *coordinate space* of that system.

Figure 6-1 shows an illustration of the Cartesian coordinate system. It shows a point P having x and y coordinates of x1 and y1. It shows the type of values for the x and y coordinates in each quadrant. For example, the upper-right quadrant shows (+, +), meaning that both x and y coordinates for all points in this quadrant will have positive values.

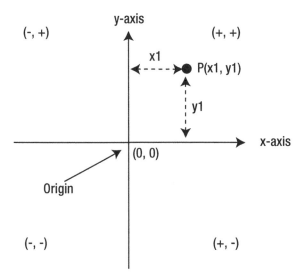

Figure 6-1. *A two-dimensional Cartesian coordinate system used in coordinate geometry*

A transformation is a mapping of points in a coordinate space to the same coordinate space, preserving a predefined set of geometric properties. Several types of transformations can be applied to points in a coordinate space. Some examples of transformation types are *translation, rotation, scaling,* and *shearing*.

In a translation transformation, a fixed pair of numbers is added to the coordinates of all points. Suppose you want to apply translation to a coordinate space by (a, b). If a point had coordinates (x, y) before translation, it will have the coordinate of (x + a, y + b) after translation.

In a rotation transformation, the axes are rotated around a pivot point in the coordinate space, and the coordinates of points are mapped to the new axes. Figure 6-2 shows examples of translation and rotation transformations.

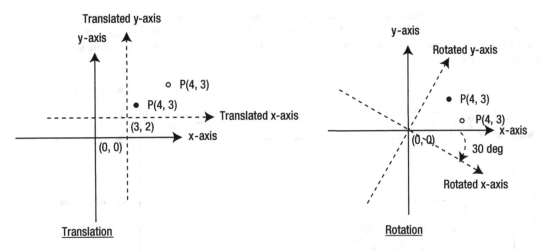

Figure 6-2. *Examples of translation and rotation transformations*

In Figure 6-2, axes before the transformations are shown in solid lines, and axes after the transformations are shown in dashed lines. Note that the coordinates of point P at (4, 3) remain the same in the translated and rotated coordinate spaces. However, the coordinates of the point relative to the original coordinate space change after the transformation. The point in the original coordinate space is shown in a solid black fill color, and in the transformed coordinate space, it is shown without a fill color. In the rotation transformation, you have used the origin as the pivot point. Therefore, the origins for the original and the transformed coordinate space are the same.

Cartesian Coordinate System of a Node

Each node in a scene graph has its own coordinate system. A node uses a Cartesian coordinate system that consists of an x-axis and a y-axis. In computer systems, the values on the x-axis increase to the right, and the values on y-axis increase downward, as shown in Figure 6-3. Typically, when showing the coordinate system of nodes, the negative sides of the x-axis and y-axis are not shown, even though they always exist. The simplified version of the coordinate system is shown on the right part of Figure 6-3. A node can have negative x and y coordinates.

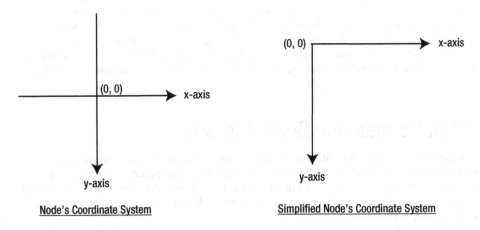

Figure 6-3. *The coordinate system of nodes*

In a typical GUI application, nodes are placed within their parents. A root node is the ultimate parent of all nodes, and it is placed inside a scene. The scene is placed inside a stage, and the stage is placed inside a screen. Each element comprising a window, from nodes to the screen, has its own coordinate system, as shown in Figure 6-4.

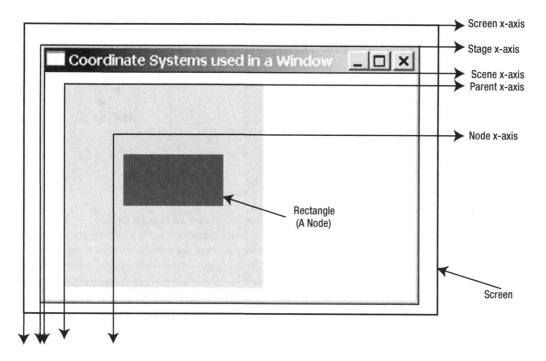

Figure 6-4. *Coordinate systems of all elements comprising a GUI window*

The outermost rectangular area with a thick black border is the screen. The rest is a JavaFX stage with a region and a rectangle. The region has a light gray background color, and a rectangle has a blue background color. The region is the parent of the rectangle. This simple window uses five coordinate spaces as indicated in Figure 6-4. I have labeled only the x-axes. All y-axes are vertical lines meeting the respective x-axes at their origins.

What are the coordinates of the upper-left corner of the rectangle? The question is incomplete. The coordinates of a point are defined relative to a coordinate system. As shown in Figure 6-4, you have five coordinate systems at play and, hence, five coordinate spaces. Therefore, you must specify the coordinate system in which you want to know the coordinates of the upper-left corner of the rectangle. In a node's coordinate system, they are (10, 15); in a parent's coordinate system, they are (40, 45); in a scene's coordinate system, they are (60, 55); in a stage's coordinate system, they are (64, 83); in a screen's coordinate system, they are (80, 99).

The Concept of Bounds and Bounding Box

Every node has a geometric shape, and it is positioned in a coordinate space. The size and the position of a node are collectively known as its *bounds*. The bounds of a node are defined in terms of a bounding rectangular box that encloses the entire geometry of the node. Figure 6-5 shows a triangle, a circle, a rounded rectangle, and a rectangle with a solid border. Rectangles around them, shown with a dashed border, are the bounding boxes for those shapes (nodes).

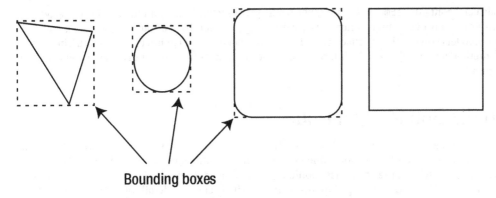

Bounding boxes

Figure 6-5. *The bounding rectangular box defining the geometric shape of nodes*

The area (area in a 2D space and volume in a 3D space) covered by the geometric shape of a node and its bounding box may be different. For example, for the first three nodes in Figure 6-5, counting from the left, the areas of the nodes and their bounding boxes are different. However, for the last rectangle, without rounded corners, its area and that of its bounding box are the same.

An instance of the javafx.geometry.Bounds class represents the bounds of a node. The Bounds class is an abstract class. The BoundingBox class is a concrete implementation of the Bounds class. The Bounds class is designed to handle bounds in a 3D space. It encapsulates the coordinates of the upper-left corner with the minimum depth in the bounding box and the width, height, and depth of the bounding box. The methods getMinX(), getMinY(), and getMinZ() are used to get the coordinates. The three dimensions of the bounding box are accessed using the getWidth(), getHeight(), and getDepth() methods. The Bounds class contains the getMaxX(), getMaxY(), and getMaxZ() methods that return the coordinates of the lower-right corner, with the maximum depth, in the bounding box.

In a 2D space, the minX and minY define the x and y coordinates of the upper-left corner of the bounding box, respectively, and the maxX and maxY define the x and y coordinates of the lower-right corner, respectively. In a 2D space, the values of the z coordinate and the depth for a bounding box are zero. Figure 6-6 shows the details of a bounding box in a 2D coordinate space.

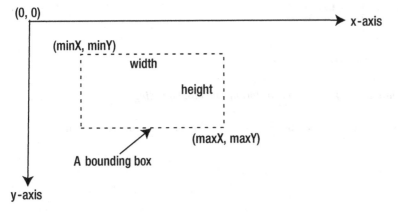

Figure 6-6. *The makings of a bounding box in a 2D space*

The Bounds class contains isEmpty(), contains(), and intersects() utility methods. The isEmpty() method returns true if any of the three dimensions (width, height, or depth) of a Bounds is negative. The contains() method lets you check if a Bounds contains another Bounds, a 2D point, or a 3D point. The intersects() method lets you check if the interior of a Bounds intersects the interior of another Bounds, a 2D point, or a 3D point.

Knowing the Bounds of a Node

So far, I have covered topics such as coordinate systems, bounds, and bounding boxes related to a node. That discussion was to prepare you for this section, which is about knowing the bounds of a node. You might have guessed (though incorrectly) that the Node class should have a getBounds() method to return the bounds of a node. It would be great if it were that simple! In this section, I will discuss the details of different types of bounds of a node. In the next section, I will walk you through some examples.

Figure 6-7 shows a button with the text "Close" in three forms.

Figure 6-7. *A button with and without an effect and a transformation*

The first one, starting from the left, has no effects or transformations. The second one has a drop shadow effect. The third one has a drop shadow effect and a rotation transformation. Figure 6-8 shows the bounding boxes representing the bounds of the button in those three forms. Ignoring the coordinates for now, you may notice that the bounds of the button change as effects and transformations are applied.

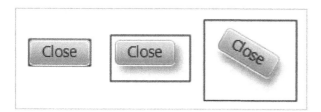

Figure 6-8. *A button with and without an effect and a transformation with bounding boxes*

A node in a scene graph has three types of bounds defined as three read-only properties in the Node class:

- layoutBounds
- boundsInLocal
- boundsInParent

When you are trying to understand the three types of the bounds of a node, you need to look for three points:

- How the (minX, minY) values are defined. They define the coordinates of the upper-left corner of the bounding box described by the Bounds object.

- Remember that coordinates of a point are always defined relative to a coordinate space. Therefore, pay attention to the coordinate space in which the coordinates, as described in the first step, are defined.

- What properties of the node—geometry, stroke, effects, clip, and transformations—are included in a particular type of bounds.

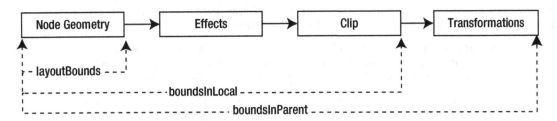

Figure 6-9. *Factors contributing to the size of a node*

Figure 6-9 shows the properties of a node contributing to the bounds of a node. They are applied from left to right in order. Some node types (e.g., Circle, Rectangle) may have a nonzero stroke. A nonzero stroke is considered part of the geometry of a node for computing its bounds.

Table 6-1 lists the properties that contribute to a particular type of the bounds of a node and the coordinate space in which the bounds are defined. The boundsInLocal and boundsInParent of a node are also known as its *physical bounds* as they correspond to the physical properties of the node. The layoutBounds of a node is known as the *logical bounds* as it is not necessarily tied to the physical bounds of the node. When the geometry of a node is changed, all bounds are recomputed.

Table 6-1. *Contributing Properties to the Bounds of a Node*

Bounds Type	Coordinate Space	Contributors
layoutBounds	Node (Untransformed)	Geometry of the node Nonzero stroke
boundsInLocal	Node (Untransformed)	Geometry of the node Nonzero stroke Effects Clip
boundsInParent	Parent	Geometry of the node Nonzero stroke Effects Clip Transformations

---

▪ **Tip** The boundsInLocal and BoundsInParent are known as physical or visual bounds as they correspond to how the node looks visually. The layoutBounds is also known as the *logical bounds* as it does not necessarily correspond to the physical bounds of the node.

The *layoutBounds* Property

The layoutBounds property is computed based on the geometric properties of the node in the *untransformed* local coordinate space of the node. Effects, clip, and transformations are not included. Different rules, depending on the resizable behavior of the node, are used to compute the coordinates of the upper-left corner of the bounding box described by the layoutBounds:

- For a resizable node (a Region, a Control, and a WebView), the coordinates for the upper-left corner of the bounding box are always set to (0, 0). For example, the (minX, minY) values in the layoutBounds property are always (0, 0) for a button.

- For a nonresizable node (a Shape, a Text, and a Group), the coordinates of the upper-left corner of the bounding box are computed based on the geometric properties. For a shape (a rectangle, a circle, etc.) or a Text, you can specify the (x, y) coordinates of a specific point in the node relative to the untransformed coordinate space of the node. For example, for a rectangle, you can specify the (x, y) coordinates of the upper-left corner, which become the (x, y) coordinates of the upper-left corner of the bounding box described by its layoutBounds property. For a circle, you can specify the centerX, centerY, and radius properties, where centerX and centerY are the x and y coordinates of the center of the circle, respectively. The (x, y) coordinates of the upper-left corner of the bounding box described by the layoutBounds for a circle are computed as (centerX - radius, centerY - radius).

The width and height in layoutBounds are the width and height of the node. Some nodes let you set their width and height; but some compute them automatically for you and let you override them.

Where do you use the layoutBounds property of a node? Containers allocate spaces to lay out child nodes based on their layoutBounds. Let's look at an example as shown in Listing 6-1. It displays four buttons in a VBox. The first button has a drop shadow effect. The third button has a drop shadow effect and a 30-degree rotation transformation. The second and the fourth buttons have no effect or transformation. The resulting screen is shown in Figure 6-10. The output shows that irrespective of the effect and transformation, all buttons have the same layoutBounds values. The size (width and height) in the layoutBounds objects for all buttons is determined by the text of the button and the font, which is the same for all buttons. The output may differ on your platform.

Listing 6-1. Accessing the layoutBounds of Buttons with and Without Effects

```java
// LayoutBoundsTest.java
package com.jdojo.node;

import javafx.application.Application;
import javafx.scene.Scene;
import javafx.scene.control.Button;
import javafx.scene.effect.DropShadow;
import javafx.scene.layout.VBox;
import javafx.stage.Stage;
```

```java
public class LayoutBoundsTest extends Application {
        public static void main(String[] args) {
                Application.launch(args);
        }

        @Override
        public void start(Stage stage) {
                Button b1 = new Button("Close");
                b1.setEffect(new DropShadow());

                Button b2 = new Button("Close");

                Button b3 = new Button("Close");
                b3.setEffect(new DropShadow());
                b3.setRotate(30);

                Button b4 = new Button("Close");

                VBox root = new VBox();
                root.getChildren().addAll(b1, b2, b3, b4);

                Scene scene = new Scene(root);
                stage.setScene(scene);
                stage.setTitle("Testing LayoutBounds");
                stage.show();

                System.out.println("b1=" + b1.getLayoutBounds());
                System.out.println("b2=" + b2.getLayoutBounds());
                System.out.println("b3=" + b3.getLayoutBounds());
                System.out.println("b4=" + b4.getLayoutBounds());
        }
}
```

```
b1=BoundingBox [minX:0.0, minY:0.0, minZ:0.0, width:57.0, height:23.0, depth:0.0,
maxX:57.0, maxY:23.0, maxZ:0.0]
b2=BoundingBox [minX:0.0, minY:0.0, minZ:0.0, width:57.0, height:23.0, depth:0.0, maxX:57.0,
maxY:23.0, maxZ:0.0]
b3=BoundingBox [minX:0.0, minY:0.0, minZ:0.0, width:57.0, height:23.0, depth:0.0, maxX:57.0,
maxY:23.0, maxZ:0.0]
b4=BoundingBox [minX:0.0, minY:0.0, minZ:0.0, width:57.0, height:23.0, depth:0.0,
maxX:57.0, maxY:23.0, maxZ:0.0]
```

Figure 6-10. *The layoutBounds property does not include the effects and transformations*

Sometimes, you may want to include the space needed to show the effects and transformations of a node in its layoutBounds. The solution for this is easy. You need to wrap the node in a Group and the Group in a container. Now the container will query the Group for its layoutBounds. The layoutBounds of a Group is the union of the boundsInParent for all its children. Recall that (see Table 6-1) the boundsInParent of a node includes the space needed for showing effects and transformation of the node. If you change the statement

```
root.getChildren().addAll(b1, b2, b3, b4);
```

in Listing 6-1 to

```
root.getChildren().addAll(new Group(b1), b2, new Group(b3), b4);
```

the resulting screen is shown in Figure 6-11. This time, VBox allocated enough space for the first and the third groups to account for the effect and transformation applied to the wrapped buttons.

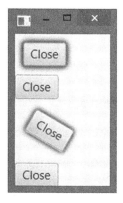

Figure 6-11. *Using a Group to allocate space for effects and transformations of a node*

■ **Tip** The layoutBounds of a node is computed based on the geometric properties of a node. Therefore, you should not bind such properties of a node to an expression that includes the layoutBounds of the node.

The *boundsInLocal* Property

The boundsInLocal property is computed in the untransformed coordinate space of the node. It includes the geometric properties of the node, effects, and clip. Transformations applied to a node are not included.

Listing 6-2 prints the layoutBounds and boundsInLocal of a button. The boundsInLocal property includes the drop shadow effect around the button. Notice that the coordinates of the upper-left corner of the bounding box defined by the layoutBounds are (0.0, 0.0), and they are (-9.0, -9.0) for the boundsInLocal. The output may be a bit different on different platforms as the size of nodes is computed automatically based on the platform running the program.

Listing 6-2. Accessing the boundsInLocal Property of a Node

```java
// BoundsInLocalTest.java
package com.jdojo.node;

import javafx.application.Application;
import javafx.scene.Scene;
import javafx.scene.control.Button;
import javafx.scene.effect.DropShadow;
import javafx.scene.layout.VBox;
import javafx.stage.Stage;

public class BoundsInLocalTest extends Application {
    public static void main(String[] args) {
        Application.launch(args);
    }

    @Override
    public void start(Stage stage) {
        Button b1 = new Button("Close");
        b1.setEffect(new DropShadow());

        VBox root = new VBox();
        root.getChildren().addAll(b1);

        Scene scene = new Scene(root);
        stage.setScene(scene);
        stage.setTitle("Testing LayoutBounds");
        stage.show();

        System.out.println("b1(layoutBounds)=" +
            b1.getLayoutBounds());
        System.out.println("b1(boundsInLocal)=" +
            b1.getBoundsInLocal());
    }
}
```

```
b1(layoutBounds)=BoundingBox [minX:0.0, minY:0.0, minZ:0.0, width:57.0, height:23.0,
depth:0.0, maxX:57.0, maxY:23.0, maxZ:0.0]
b1(boundsInLocal)=BoundingBox [minX:-9.0, minY:-9.0, minZ:0.0, width:75.0, height:42.0,
depth:0.0, maxX:66.0, maxY:33.0, maxZ:0.0]
```

When do you use the boundsInLocal of a node? You would use boundsInLocal when you need to include the effects and the clip of a node. Suppose you have a Text node with a reflection and you want to center it vertically. If you use the layoutBounds of the Text node, it will only center the text portion of the node and would not include the reflection. If you use the boundsInLocal, it will center the text with its reflection. Another example would be checking for collisions of balls that have effects. If a collision between two balls occurs when one ball moves inside the bounds of another ball that include their effects, use the boundsInLocal for the balls. If a collision occurs only when they intersect their geometric boundaries, use the layoutBounds.

The *boundsInParent* Property

The boundsInParent property of a node is in the coordinate space of its parent. It includes the geometric properties of the node, effects, clip, and transformations. It is rarely used directly in code.

Bounds of a Group

The computation of layoutBounds, boundsInLocal, and boundsInParent for a Group is different from that of a node. A Group takes on the collection bounds of its children. You can apply effects, clip, and transformations separately on each child of a Group. You can also apply effects, clip, and transformations directly on a Group, and they are applied to all of its children nodes.

The layoutBounds of a Group is the union of the boundsInParent of all its children. It includes effects, clip, and transformations applied directly to the children. It does not include effects, clip, and transformations applied directly to the Group. The boundsInLocal of a Group is computed by taking its layoutBounds and including the effects and clip applied directly to the Group. The boundsInParent of a Group is computed by taking its boundsInLocal and including the transformations applied directly to the Group.

When you want to allocate space for a node that should include effects, clip, and transformations, you need to try wrapping the node in a Group. Suppose you have a node with effects and transformations and you only want to allocate layout space for its effects, not its transformations. You can achieve this by applying the effects on the node and wrapping it in a Group and then applying the transformations on the Group.

A Detailed Example on Bounds

In this section, I will walk you through an example to show how the bounds of a node are computed. You will use a rectangle and its different properties, effects, and transformations in this example.

Consider the following snippet of code that creates a 50 by 20 rectangle and places it at (0, 0) in the local coordinate space of the rectangle. The resulting rectangle is shown in Figure 6-12, which shows the axes of the parent and the untransformed local axes of the node (the rectangle in this case), which are the same at this time:

```
Rectangle r = new Rectangle(0, 0, 50, 20);
r.setFill(Color.GRAY);
```

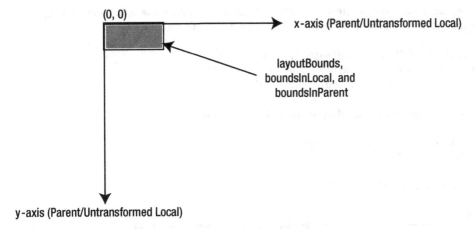

Figure 6-12. *A 50 by 20 rectangle placed at (0, 0) with no effects and transformations*

Three types of bounds of the rectangle are the same, as follows:

```
layoutBounds[minX=0.0, minY=0.0, width=50.0, height=20.0]
boundsInLocal[minX=0.0, minY=0.0, width=50.0, height=20.0]
boundsInParent[minX=0.0, minY=0.0, width=50.0, height=20.0]
```

Let's modify the rectangle to place it at (75, 50) as follows:

```
Rectangle r = new Rectangle(75, 50, 50, 20);
```

The resulting node is shown in Figure 6-13.

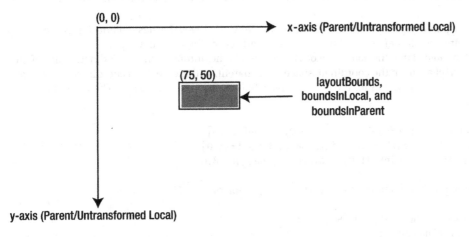

Figure 6-13. *A 50 by 20 rectangle placed at (75, 50) with no effects and transformations*

The axes for the parent and the node are still the same. All bounds are the same, as follows. The upper-left corner of all bounding boxes has moved to (75, 50) with the same width and height:

```
layoutBounds[minX=75.0, minY=50.0, width=50.0, height=20.0]
boundsInLocal[minX=75.0, minY=50.0, width=50.0, height=20.0]
boundsInParent[minX=75.0, minY=50.0, width=50.0, height=20.0]
```

Let's modify the rectangle and give it a drop shadow effect, as follows:

```
Rectangle r = new Rectangle(75, 50, 50, 20);
r.setEffect(new DropShadow());
```

The resulting node is shown in Figure 6-14.

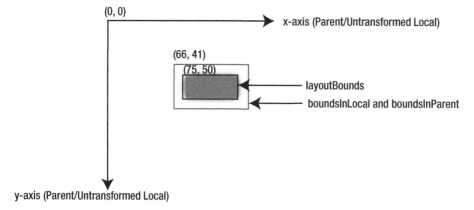

Figure 6-14. *A 50 by 20 rectangle placed at (75, 50) with a drop shadow and no transformations*

The axes for the parent and the node are still the same. Now, the layoutBounds did not change. To accommodate the drop shadow effect, the boundsInLocal and boundsInParent have changed, and they have the same values. Recall that the boundsInLocal is defined in the untransformed coordinate space of the node and the boundsInParent in the coordinate space of the parent. In this case, both coordinate spaces are the same. Therefore, the same values for the two bounds define the same bounding box. The values for the bounds are as follows:

```
layoutBounds[minX=75.0, minY=50.0, width=50.0, height=20.0]
boundsInLocal[minX=66.0, minY=41.0, width=68.0, height=38.0]
boundsInParent[minX=66.0, minY=41.0, width=68.0, height=38.0]
```

Let's modify the previous rectangle to have a (x, y) translation of (150, 75) as follows:

```
Rectangle r = new Rectangle(75, 50, 50, 20);
r.setEffect(new DropShadow());
r.getTransforms().add(new Translate(150, 75));
```

The resulting node is shown in Figure 6-15. A transformation (a translation, in this case) transforms the coordinate space of the node, and as a result, you see the node being transformed. In this case, you have three coordinate spaces to consider: the coordinate space of the parent and the untransformed and transformed coordinate spaces of the node. The layoutBounds and boundsInParent are relative to the untransformed local coordinate space of the node. The boundsInParent is relative to the coordinate space of the parent. Figure 6-15 shows all coordinate spaces at play. The values for the bounds are as follows:

```
layoutBounds[minX=75.0, minY=50.0, width=50.0, height=20.0]
boundsInLocal[minX=66.0, minY=41.0, width=68.0, height=38.0]
boundsInParent[minX=216.0, minY=116.0, width=68.0, height=38.0]
```

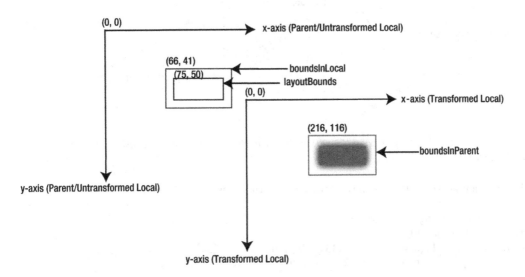

Figure 6-15. *A 50 by 20 rectangle placed at (75, 50) with a drop shadow and a (150, 75) translation*

Let's modify the rectangle to have a (x, y) translation of (150, 75) and a 30-degree clockwise rotation:

```
Rectangle r = new Rectangle(75, 50, 50, 20);
r.setEffect(new DropShadow());
r.getTransforms().addAll(new Translate(150, 75), new Rotate(30));
```

The resulting node is shown in Figure 6-16. Notice that the translation and rotation have been applied to the local coordinate space of the rectangle, and the rectangle appears in the same position relative to its transformed local coordinate axes. The layoutBounds and boundsInLocal remained the same because you did not change the geometry of the rectangle and the effects. The boundsInParent has changed because you added a rotation. The values for the bounds are as follows:

```
layoutBounds[minX=75.0, minY=50.0, width=50.0, height=20.0]
boundsInLocal[minX=66.0, minY=41.0, width=68.0, height=38.0]
boundsInParent[minX=167.66, minY=143.51, width=77.89, height=66.91]
```

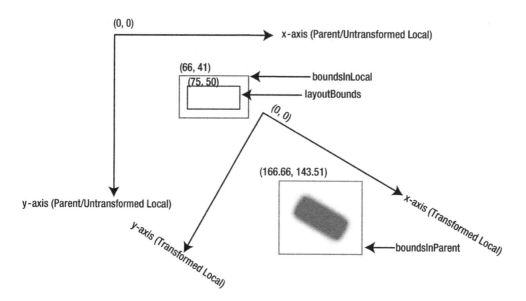

Figure 6-16. *A 50 by 20 rectangle placed at (75, 50) with a drop shadow, a (150, 75) translation, and a 30-degree clockwise rotation*

As the last example, you will add scale and shear transformations to the rectangle:

```
Rectangle r = new Rectangle(75, 50, 50, 20);
r.setEffect(new DropShadow());
r.getTransforms().addAll(new Translate(150, 75), new Rotate(30),
                    new Scale(1.2, 1.2), new Shear(0.30, 0.10));
```

The resulting node is shown in Figure 6-17.

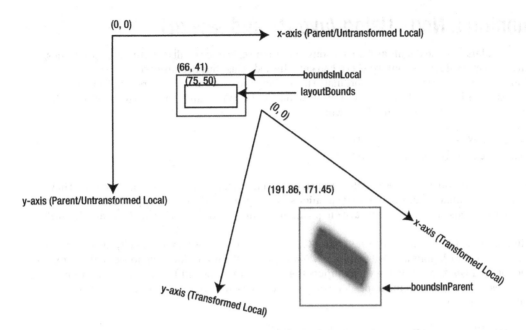

Figure 6-17. *A 50 by 20 rectangle placed at (75, 50) with a drop shadow, a (150, 75) translation, a 30-degree clockwise rotation, a 1.2 in x and y scales, and a 0.30 x shear and 0.10 y shear*

Notice that only boundsInParent has changed. The values for the bounds are as follows:

```
layoutBounds[minX=75.0, minY=50.0, width=50.0, height=20.0]
boundsInLocal[minX=66.0, minY=41.0, width=68.0, height=38.0]
boundsInParent[minX=191.86, minY=171.45, width=77.54, height=94.20]
```

For a beginner, it is not easy to grasp the concepts behind different types of bounds of a node. A beginner is one who is learning something for the first time. I started out as a beginner while learning about bounds. During the learning process, another beautiful concept and hence its implementation in a JavaFX program came about. The program, which is a very detailed demo application, helps you understand visually how bounds are affected by changing the state of a node. You can save the scene graph with all coordinate axes. You can run the NodeBoundsApp class as shown in Listing 6-3 to see all the examples in this section in action.

Listing 6-3. Computing the Bounds of a Node

```java
// NodeBoundsApp.java
package com.jdojo.node;
...
public class NodeBoundsApp extends Application {
        // The code for this class is not included here as it is very big.
        // Please refer to the source code. You can download the source code
        // for all programs in this book from
          // http://www.apress.com/source-code
}
```

Positioning a Node Using *layoutX* and *layoutY*

If you do not understand the details and the reasons behind the existence of all layout-related properties, laying out nodes in JavaFX is as confusing as it can get. The Node class has two properties, layoutX and layoutY, to define the translation of its coordinate space along the x-axis and y-axis, respectively. The Node class has translateX and translateY properties that do the same thing. The final translation of the coordinate space of a node is the sum of the two:

```
finalTranslationX = layoutX + translateX
finalTranslationY = layoutY + translateY
```

Why do you have two properties to define translations of the same kind? The reason is simple. They exist to achieve the similar results in different situations. Use layoutX and layoutY to position a node for a stable layout. Use translateX and translateY to position a node for a dynamic layout, for example, during animation.

It is important to keep in mind that the layoutX and layoutY properties do not specify the final position of a node. They are translations applied to the *coordinate space* of the node. You need to factor the minX and minY values of the layoutBounds when you compute the value of layoutX and layoutY to position a node at a particular position. To position the upper-left corner of the bounding box of a node at finalX and finalY, use the following formula:

```
layoutX = finalX - node.getLayoutBounds().getMinX()
layoutY = finalY - node.getLayoutBounds().getMinY()
```

■ **Tip** The Node class has a convenience method, relocate(double finalX, double finalY), to position the node at the (finalX, finalY) location. The method computes and sets the layoutX and layoutY values correctly, taking into account the minX and minY values of the layoutBounds. To avoid errors and misplacement of nodes, I prefer using the relocate() method over the setLayoutX() and setLayoutY() methods.

Sometimes, setting the layoutX and layoutY properties of a node may not position them at the desired location inside its parent. If you are caught in this situation, check the parent type. Most parents, which are the subclasses of the Region class, use their own positioning policy, ignoring the layoutX and layoutY settings of their children. For example, HBox and VBox use their own positioning policy, and they will ignore the layoutX and layoutY values for their children.

The following snippet of code will ignore the layoutX and layoutY values for two buttons, as they are placed inside a VBox that uses its own positioning policy. The resulting layout is shown in Figure 6-18.

```
Button b1 = new Button("OK");
b1.setLayoutX(20);
b1.setLayoutY(20);

Button b2 = new Button("Cancel");
b2.setLayoutX(50);
b2.setLayoutY(50);

VBox vb = new VBox();
vb.getChildren().addAll(b1, b2);
```

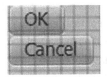

Figure 6-18. *Two buttons using layoutX and layoutY properties and placed inside a VBox*

If you want to have full control on positioning a node within its parent, use a Pane or a Group. A Pane is a Region, which does not position its children. You will need to position the children using the layoutX and layoutY properties. The following snippet of code will lay out two buttons as shown in Figure 6-19, which shows the coordinate grid in which lines are placed 10px apart:

```
Button b1 = new Button("OK");
b1.setLayoutX(20);
b1.setLayoutY(20);

Button b2 = new Button("Cancel");
b2.setLayoutX(50);
b2.setLayoutY(50);

Group parent = new Group(); //Or. Pane parent = new Pane();
parent.getChildren().addAll(b1, b2);
```

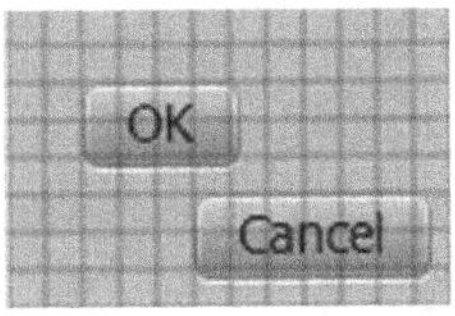

Figure 6-19. *Two buttons using layoutX and layoutY properties and placed inside a Group or a Pane*

Setting the Size of a Node

Every node has a size (width and height), which may be changed. That is, every node can be resized. There are two types of nodes: *resizable* nodes and *nonresizable* nodes. Aren't the previous two sentences contradictory? The answer is yes and no. It is true that every node has the potential to be resized. However, by a resizable node, it is meant that a node can be resized by its parent during layout. For example, a button is a resizable node, and a rectangle is a nonresizable node. When a button is placed in a container, for example, in an HBox, the HBox determines the best size for the button. The HBox resizes the button depending on how much space is needed for the button to display and how much space is available to the HBox. When a rectangle is placed in an HBox, the HBox does not determine its size; rather, it uses the size of the rectangle specified by the application.

■ **Tip** A resizable node can be resized by its parent during a layout. A nonresizable node is not resized by its parent during a layout. If you want to resize a nonresizable node, you need to modify its properties that affect its size. For example, to resize a rectangle, you need to change its width and height properties. Regions, Controls, and WebView are examples of resizable nodes. Group, Text, and Shapes are examples of nonresizable nodes.

How do you know if a node is resizable? The isResizable() method in the Node class returns true for a resizable node; it returns false for a nonresizable node.

The program in Listing 6-4 shows the behavior of resizable and nonresizable nodes during a layout. It adds a button and a rectangle to an HBox. After you run the program, make the stage shorter in width. The button becomes smaller up to a point when it displays an ellipsis (...). The rectangle remains the same size all the time. Figure 6-20 shows the stage at three different points during resizing.

Listing 6-4. A Button and a Rectangle in an HBox

```java
// ResizableNodeTest.java
package com.jdojo.node;

import javafx.application.Application;
import javafx.scene.Scene;
import javafx.scene.control.Button;
import javafx.scene.layout.HBox;
import javafx.scene.paint.Color;
import javafx.scene.shape.Rectangle;
import javafx.stage.Stage;

public class ResizableNodeTest extends Application {
        public static void main(String[] args) {
                Application.launch(args);
        }

        @Override
        public void start(Stage stage) {
                Button btn = new Button("A big button");
                Rectangle rect = new Rectangle(100, 50);
                rect.setFill(Color.WHITE);
                rect.setStrokeWidth(1);
                rect.setStroke(Color.BLACK);

                HBox root = new HBox();
                root.setSpacing(20);
                root.getChildren().addAll(btn, rect);

                Scene scene = new Scene(root);
                stage.setScene(scene);
                stage.setTitle("Resizable Nodes");
                stage.show();
```

```
            System.out.println("btn.isResizable(): " +
                    btn.isResizable());
            System.out.println("rect.isResizable(): " +
                    rect.isResizable());
    }
}
```

```
btn.isResizable(): true
rect.isResizable(): false
```

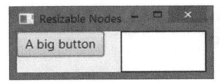 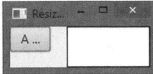 

Figure 6-20. *A button and a rectangle shown in full size and after resizing the stage*

Resizable Nodes

The actual size of a resizable node is determined by two things:

- The sizing policy of the container in which the node is placed

- The sizing range specified by the node itself

Each container has a resizing policy for its children. I will discuss the resizing policy of containers in Chapter 10. A resizable node may specify a range for its size (width and height), which should be taken into account by an *honoring* container for laying out the node. A resizable node specifies three types of sizes that constitute the range of its size:

- Preferred size

- Minimum size

- Maximum size

The *preferred size* of a node is its ideal width and height to display its contents. For example, a button in its preferred size would be big enough to display all its contents, based on the current properties such as the image, text, font, and text wrapping. The *minimum size* of a node is the smallest width and height that it would like to have. For example, a button in its minimum size would be big enough to display the image and an ellipsis for its text. The *maximum size* of a node is the largest width and height that it would like to have. In the case of a button, the maximum size of a button is the same as its preferred size. Sometimes, you may want to extend a node to an unlimited size. In those cases, the maximum width and height are set to Double.MAX_VALUE.

Most of the resizable nodes compute their preferred, minimum, and maximum sizes automatically, based on their contents and property settings. These sizes are known as their *intrinsic sizes*. The Region and Control classes define two constants that act as sentinel values for the intrinsic sizes of nodes. Those constants are

- USE_COMPUTED_SIZE

- USE_PREF_SIZE

Both constants are of double type. The values for USE_COMPUTED_SIZE and USE_PREF_SIZE are –1 and Double.NEGATIVE_INFINITY, respectively. It was not documented as to why the same constants were defined twice. Maybe the designers did not want to move them up in the class hierarchy, as they do not apply to all types of nodes.

If the size of a node is set to the sentinel value USE_COMPUTED_SIZE, the node will compute that size automatically based on its contents and properties settings. The USE_PREF_SIZE sentinel value is used to set the minimum and maximum sizes if they are the same as the preferred size.

The Region and Control classes have six properties of the DoubleProperty type to define preferred, minimum, and maximum values for their width and height:

- prefWidth

- prefHeight

- minWidth

- minHeight

- maxWidth

- maxHeight

By default, these properties are set to the sentinel value USE_COMPUTED_SIZE. That means nodes compute these sizes automatically. You can set one of these properties to override the intrinsic size of a node. For example, you can set the preferred, minimum, and maximum width of a button to be 50 pixels as follows:

```
Button btn = new Button("Close");
btn.setPrefWidth(50);
btn.setMinWidth(50);
btn.setMaxWidth(50);
```

The preceding snippet of code sets preferred, minimum, and maximum widths of the button to the same value that makes the button horizontally nonresizable.

The following snippet of code sets the minimum and maximum widths of a button to the preferred width, where the preferred width itself is computed internally:

```
Button btn = new Button("Close");
btn.setMinWidth(Control.USE_PREF_SIZE);
btn.setMaxWidth(Control.USE_PREF_SIZE);
```

■ **Tip** In most cases, the internally computed values for preferred, minimum, and maximum sizes of nodes are fine. Use these properties to override the internally computed sizes only if they do not meet the needs of your application. If you need to bind the size of a node to an expression, you would need to bind the prefWidth and prefHeight properties.

How do you get the actual preferred, minimum, and maximum sizes of a node? You might guess that you can get them using the getPrefWidth(), getPrefHeight(), getMinWidth(), getMinHeight(), getMaxWidth(), and getMaxHeight() methods. But you should not use these methods to get the actual sizes of a node. These sizes may be set to the sentinel values, and the node will compute the actual sizes internally. These methods return the sentinel values or the override values. Listing 6-5 creates two buttons and overrides the preferred intrinsic width for one of them to 100 pixels. The resulting screen is shown in Figure 6-21. The following output proves that these methods are not very useful to learn the actual sizes of a node for layout purposes.

Listing 6-5. Using getXXXWidth() and getXXXHeight() Methods of Regions and Controls

```java
// NodeSizeSentinelValues.java
package com.jdojo.node;

import javafx.application.Application;
import javafx.scene.Scene;
import javafx.scene.control.Button;
import javafx.scene.layout.VBox;
import javafx.stage.Stage;

public class NodeSizeSentinelValues extends Application {
    public static void main(String[] args) {
        Application.launch(args);
    }

    @Override
    public void start(Stage stage) {
        Button okBtn = new Button("OK");
        Button cancelBtn = new Button("Cancel");

        // Override the intrinsic width of the cancel button
        cancelBtn.setPrefWidth(100);

        VBox root = new VBox();
        root.getChildren().addAll(okBtn, cancelBtn);

        Scene scene = new Scene(root);
        stage.setScene(scene);
        stage.setTitle("Overriding Node Sizes");
        stage.show();

        System.out.println("okBtn.getPrefWidth(): " +
                okBtn.getPrefWidth());
        System.out.println("okBtn.getMinWidth(): " +
                okBtn.getMinWidth());
        System.out.println("okBtn.getMaxWidth(): " +
                okBtn.getMaxWidth());

        System.out.println("cancelBtn.getPrefWidth(): " +
                cancelBtn.getPrefWidth());
        System.out.println("cancelBtn.getMinWidth(): " +
                cancelBtn.getMinWidth());
        System.out.println("cancelBtn.getMaxWidth(): " +
                cancelBtn.getMaxWidth());
    }
}
```

155

```
okBtn.getPrefWidth(): -1.0
okBtn.getMinWidth(): -1.0
okBtn.getMaxWidth(): -1.0
cancelBtn.getPrefWidth(): 100.0
cancelBtn.getMinWidth(): -1.0
cancelBtn.getMaxWidth(): -1.0
```

Figure 6-21. *Buttons using sentinel and override values for their widths*

To get the actual sizes of a node, you need to use the following methods in the Node class. Note that the Node class does not define any properties related to sizes. The size-related properties are defined in the Region, Control, and other classes.

- double prefWidth(double height)

- double prefHeight(double width)

- double minWidth(double height)

- double minHeight(double width)

- double maxWidth(double height)

- double maxHeight(double width)

Here, you can see another twist in getting the actual sizes of a node. You need to pass the value of its height to get its width and vice versa. For most nodes in JavaFX, width and height are independent. However, for some nodes, the height depends on the width and vice versa. When the width of a node depends on its height or vice versa, the node is said to have a *content bias*. If the height of a node depends on its width, the node has a *horizontal content bias*. If the width of a node depends on its height, the node has a *vertical content bias*. Note that a node cannot have both horizontal and vertical content biases, which will lead to a circular dependency.

The getContentBias() method of the Node class returns the content bias of a node. Its return type is the javafx.geometry.Orientation enum type, which has two constants: HORIZONTAL and VERTICAL. If a node does not have a content bias, for example, Text or ChoiceBox, the method returns null.

All controls that are subclasses of the Labeled class, for example, Label, Button, or CheckBox, have a HORIZONTAL content bias when they have the text wrapping property enabled. For some nodes, their content bias depends on their orientation. For example, if the orientation of a FlowPane is HORIZONTAL, its content bias is HORIZONTAL; if its orientation is VERTICAL, its content bias is VERTICAL.

You are supposed to use the above-listed six methods to get the sizes of a node for layout purposes. If a node type does not have a content bias, you need to pass –1 to these methods as the value for the other dimension. For example, a ChoiceBox does not have a content bias, and you would get its preferred size as follows:

```
ChoiceBox choices = new ChoiceBox();
...
double prefWidth = choices.prefWidth(-1);
double prefHeight = choices.prefHeight(-1);
```

For those nodes that have a content bias, you need to pass the biased dimension to get the other dimension. For example, for a button, which has a HORIZONTAL content bias, you would pass –1 to get its width, and you would pass its width value to get its height as follows:

```
Button b = new Button("Hello JavaFX");

// Enable text wrapping for the button, which will change its
// content bias from null (default) to HORIZONTAL
b.setWrapText(true);
...
double prefWidth = b.prefWidth(-1);
double prefHeight = b.prefHeight(prefWidth);
```

If a button does not have the text wrap property enabled, you can pass –1 to both methods prefWidth() and prefHeight(), as it would not have a content bias.

The generic way to get the width and height of a node for layout purposes is outlined as follows. The code shows how to get the preferred width and height, and the code would be similar to get minimum and maximum width and height of a node:

```
Node node = get the reference of the node;
...
double prefWidth = -1;
double prefHeight = -1;

Orientation contentBias = b.getContentBias();

if (contentBias == HORIZONTAL) {
        prefWidth = node.prefWidth(-1);
        prefHeight = node.prefHeight(prefWidth);
} else if (contentBias == VERTICAL) {
        prefHeight = node.prefHeight(-1);
        prefWidth = node.prefWidth(prefHeight);
} else {
        // contentBias is null
        prefWidth = node.prefWidth(-1);
        prefHeight = node.prefHeight(-1);
}
```

Now you know how to get the specified values and the actual values for the preferred, minimum, and maximum sizes of a node. These values indicate the range for the size of a node. When a node is laid out inside a container, the container tries to give the node its preferred size. However, based on the container's policy and the specified size of the node, the node may not get its preferred size. Instead, an honoring container will give a node a size that is within its specified range. This is called the *current size*. How do you get the current size of a node? The Region and Control classes define two *read-only* properties, width and height, that hold the values for the current width and height of a node.

Now let's see all these methods in action. Listing 6-6 places a button in an HBox, prints different types of sizes for the button, changes some properties, and prints the sizes of the button again. The following output shows that as the preferred width of the button becomes smaller, its preferred height becomes bigger.

Listing 6-6. Using Different Size-Related Methods of a Node

```java
// NodeSizes.java
package com.jdojo.node;

import javafx.application.Application;
import javafx.scene.Scene;
import javafx.scene.control.Button;
import javafx.scene.layout.HBox;
import javafx.stage.Stage;

public class NodeSizes extends Application {
        public static void main(String[] args) {
                Application.launch(args);
        }

        @Override
        public void start(Stage stage) {
                Button btn = new Button("Hello JavaFX!");

                HBox root = new HBox();
                root.getChildren().addAll(btn);

                Scene scene = new Scene(root);
                stage.setScene(scene);
                stage.setTitle("Sizes of a Node");
                stage.show();

                // Print button's sizes
                System.out.println("Before changing button properties:");
                printSizes(btn);

                // Change button's properties
                btn.setWrapText(true);
                btn.setPrefWidth(80);
                stage.sizeToScene();

                // Print button's sizes
                System.out.println(
                        "\nAfter changing button properties:");
                printSizes(btn);

        }

        public void printSizes(Button btn) {
                System.out.println("btn.getContentBias() = " +
                        btn.getContentBias());

                System.out.println("btn.getPrefWidth() = " +
                        btn.getPrefWidth() +
                   ", btn.getPrefHeight() = " + btn.getPrefHeight());
```

```java
            System.out.println("btn.getMinWidth() = " +
                    btn.getMinWidth() +
                ", btn.getMinHeight() = " + btn.getMinHeight());

            System.out.println("btn.getMaxWidth() = " +
                    btn.getMaxWidth() +
                ", btn.getMaxHeight() = " + btn.getMaxHeight());

            double prefWidth = btn.prefWidth(-1);
            System.out.println("btn.prefWidth(-1) = " + prefWidth +
                ", btn.prefHeight(prefWidth) = " +
                    btn.prefHeight(prefWidth));

            double minWidth = btn.minWidth(-1);
            System.out.println("btn.minWidth(-1) = " + minWidth +
                ", btn.minHeight(minWidth) = " +
                    btn.minHeight(minWidth));

            double maxWidth = btn.maxWidth(-1);
            System.out.println("btn.maxWidth(-1) = " + maxWidth +
                ", btn.maxHeight(maxWidth) = " +
                        btn.maxHeight(maxWidth));

            System.out.println("btn.getWidth() = " + btn.getWidth() +
                ", btn.getHeight() = " + btn.getHeight());
        }
}
```

```
Before changing button properties:
btn.getContentBias() = null
btn.getPrefWidth() = -1.0, btn.getPrefHeight() = -1.0
btn.getMinWidth() = -1.0, btn.getMinHeight() = -1.0
btn.getMaxWidth() = -1.0, btn.getMaxHeight() = -1.0
btn.prefWidth(-1) = 107.0, btn.prefHeight(prefWidth) = 22.8984375
btn.minWidth(-1) = 37.0, btn.minHeight(minWidth) = 22.8984375
btn.maxWidth(-1) = 107.0, btn.maxHeight(maxWidth) = 22.8984375
btn.getWidth() = 107.0, btn.getHeight() = 23.0

After changing button properties:
btn.getContentBias() = HORIZONTAL
btn.getPrefWidth() = 80.0, btn.getPrefHeight() = -1.0
btn.getMinWidth() = -1.0, btn.getMinHeight() = -1.0
btn.getMaxWidth() = -1.0, btn.getMaxHeight() = -1.0
btn.prefWidth(-1) = 80.0, btn.prefHeight(prefWidth) = 39.796875
btn.minWidth(-1) = 37.0, btn.minHeight(minWidth) = 22.8984375
btn.maxWidth(-1) = 80.0, btn.maxHeight(maxWidth) = 39.796875
btn.getWidth() = 80.0, btn.getHeight() = 40.0
```

The list of methods to get or set sizes of resizable nodes is not over. There are some convenience methods that can be used to perform the same task as the methods discussed in this section. Table 6-2 lists the size-related methods with their defining classes and usage.

Table 6-2. *Size-Related Methods of Resizable Nodes*

Methods/Properties	Defining Class	Usage
Properties: prefWidth prefHeight minWidth minHeight maxWidth maxHeight	Region, Control	They define the preferred, minimum, and maximum sizes. They are set to sentinel values by default. Use them to override the default values.
Methods: double prefWidth(double h) double prefHeight(double w) double minWidth(double h) double minHeight(double w) double maxWidth(double h) double maxHeight(double w)	Node	Use them to get the actual sizes of nodes. Pass –1 as the argument if the node does not have a content bias. Pass the actual value of the other dimension as the argument if the node has a content bias. Note that there are no corresponding properties to these methods.
Properties: width height	Region, Control	These are *read-only* properties that hold the current width and height of resizable nodes.
Methods: void setPrefSize(double w, double h) void setMinSize(double w, double h) void setMaxSize(double w, double h)	Region, Control	These are convenience methods to override the default computed width and height of nodes.
Methods: void resize(double w, double h)	Node	It resizes a node to the specified width and height. It is called by the parent of the node during a layout. You should not call this method directly in your code. If you need to set the size of a node, use the setMinSize(), setPrefSize(), or setMaxSize() methods instead. This method has no effect on a nonresizable node.
Methods: void autosize()	Node	For a resizable node, it sets the layout bounds to its current preferred width and height. It takes care of the content bias. This method has no effect on a nonresizable node.

Nonresizable Nodes

Nonresizable nodes are not resized by their parents during layout. However, you can change their sizes by changing their properties. Nonresizable nodes (e.g., all shapes) have different properties that determine their sizes. For example, the width and height of a rectangle, the radius of a circle, and the (startX, startY) and (endX, endY) of a line determine their sizes.

There are several size-related methods defined in the Node class. Those methods have no effect when they are called on nonresizable nodes or they return their current size. For example, calling the resize(double w, double h) method of the Node class on a nonresizable node has no effect. For a nonresizable node, the prefWidth(double h), minWidth(double h), and maxWidth(double h) methods in the Node class return its layoutBounds width; whereas prefHeight(double w), minHeight(double w), and maxHeight(double w) methods return its layoutBounds height. Nonresizable nodes do not have content bias. Pass –1 to all these methods as the argument for the other dimension.

Storing User Data in a Node

Every node maintains an observable map of user-defined properties (key/value pairs). You can use it to store any useful information. Suppose you have a TextField that lets the user manipulate a person's name. You can store the originally retrieved person's name from the database as the property of the TextField. You can use the property later to reset the name or to generate an UPDATE statement to update the name in the database. Another use of the properties would be to store micro help text. When a node receives the focus, you can read its micro help property and display it, for example, in a status bar, to help the user understand the use of the node.

The getProperties() method of the Node class returns an ObservableMap<Object, Object> in which you can add or remove properties for the node. The following snippet of code adds a property "originalData" with a value "Advik" to a TextField node:

```
TextField nameField = new TextField();
...
ObservableMap<Object, Object> props = nameField.getProperties();
props.put("originalData", "Advik");
```

The following snippet of code reads the value of the "originalData" property from the nameField node:

```
ObservableMap<Object, Object> props = nameField.getProperties();
if (props.containsKey("originalData")) {
        String originalData = (String)props.get("originalData");
} else {
        // originalData property is not set yet
}
```

The Node class has two convenience methods, setUserData(Object value) and getUserData(), to store a user-defined value as a property for a node. The value specified in the setUserData() method uses the same ObservableMap to store the data that are returned by the getProperties() method. The Node class uses an internal Object as the key to store the value. You need to use the getUserData() method to get the value that you store using the setUserData() method, as follows:

```
nameField.setUserData("Saved"); // Set the user data
...
String userData = (String)nameField.getUserData(); // Get the user data
```

■ **Tip** You cannot access the user data of a node directly except by using the `getUserData()` method. Because it is stored in the same `ObservableMap` returned by the `getProperties()` method, you can get to it indirectly by iterating through the values in that map.

The Node class has a `hasProperties()` method. You can use it to see whether any properties are defined for the node.

What Is a Managed Node?

The Node class has a managed property, which is of type `BooleanProperty`. By default, all nodes are managed. The laying out of a managed node is managed by its parent. A `Parent` node takes into account the `layoutBounds` of all its managed children when it computes its own size. A `Parent` node is responsible for resizing its managed resizable children and positioning them according to its layout policy. When the `layoutBounds` of a managed child changes, the relevant part of the scene graph is relaid out.

If a node is unmanaged, the application is solely responsible for laying it out (computing its size and position). That is, a `Parent` node does not lay out its unmanaged children. Changes in the `layoutBounds` of an unmanaged node do not trigger the relayout above it. An unmanaged `Parent` node acts as a *layout root*. If a child node calls the `Parent.requestLayout()` method, only the branch rooted by the unmanaged `Parent` node is relaid out.

■ **Tip** Contrast the `visible` property of the Node class with its managed property. A `Parent` node takes into account the `layoutBounds` of all its invisible children for layout purposes and ignores the unmanaged children.

When would you use an unmanaged node? Typically, you do not need to use unmanaged nodes in applications because they need additional work on your part. However, just know that they exist and you can use them, if needed.

You can use an unmanaged node when you want to show a node in a container without the container considering its `layoutBounds`. You will need to size and position the node yourself. Listing 6-7 demonstrates how to use unmanaged nodes. It uses an unmanaged Text node to display a micro help when a node has the focus. The node needs to have a property named `"microHelpText"`. When the micro help is shown, the layout for the entire application is not disturbed as the Text node to show the micro help is an unmanaged node. You place the node at an appropriate position in the `focusChanged()` method. The program registers a change listener to the `focusOwner` property of the scene, so you show or hide the micro help Text node when the focus inside the scene changes. The resulting screens, when two different nodes have focus, are shown in Figure 6-22. Note that positioning the Text node, in this example, was easy as all nodes were inside the same parent node, a `GridPane`. The logic to position the Text node becomes complex if nodes are placed inside different parents.

Listing 6-7. Using an Unmanaged Text Node to Show Micro Help

```
// MicroHelpApp.java
package com.jdojo.node;

import javafx.application.Application;
import javafx.application.Platform;
```

```java
import javafx.beans.value.ObservableValue;
import javafx.geometry.VPos;
import javafx.scene.Node;
import javafx.scene.Scene;
import javafx.scene.control.Button;
import javafx.scene.control.Label;
import javafx.scene.control.TextField;
import javafx.scene.layout.GridPane;
import javafx.scene.paint.Color;
import javafx.scene.text.Font;
import javafx.scene.text.Text;
import javafx.stage.Stage;

public class MicroHelpApp extends Application {
        // An instance variable to store the Text node reference
        private Text helpText = new Text();

        public static void main(String[] args) {
                Application.launch(args);
        }

        @Override
        public void start(Stage stage) {
                TextField fName = new TextField();
                TextField lName = new TextField();
                TextField salary = new TextField();

                Button closeBtn = new Button("Close");
                closeBtn.setOnAction(e -> Platform.exit());

                fName.getProperties().put("microHelpText",
                        "Enter the first name");
                lName.getProperties().put("microHelpText",
                        "Enter the last name");
                salary.getProperties().put("microHelpText",
                    "Enter a salary greater than $2000.00.");

                // The help text node is unmanaged
                helpText.setManaged(false);
                helpText.setTextOrigin(VPos.TOP);
                helpText.setFill(Color.RED);
                helpText.setFont(Font.font(null, 9));
                helpText.setMouseTransparent(true);

                // Add all nodes to a GridPane
                GridPane root = new GridPane();

                root.add(new Label("First Name:"), 1, 1);
                root.add(fName, 2, 1);
                root.add(new Label("Last Name:"), 1, 2);
                root.add(lName, 2, 2);
```

```java
            root.add(new Label("Salary:"), 1, 3);
            root.add(salary, 2, 3);
            root.add(closeBtn, 3, 3);
            root.add(helpText, 4, 3);

            Scene scene = new Scene(root, 300, 100);

            // Add a change listener to the scene, so you know when
                // the focus owner changes and display the micro help
            scene.focusOwnerProperty().addListener(
                (ObservableValue<? extends Node> value,
                        Node oldNode, Node newNode)
                    -> focusChanged(value, oldNode, newNode));
            stage.setScene(scene);
            stage.setTitle("Showing Micro Help");
            stage.show();
        }

    public void focusChanged(ObservableValue<? extends Node> value,
                Node oldNode, Node newNode) {
            // Focus has changed to a new node
            String microHelpText =
                    (String)newNode.getProperties().get("microHelpText");

            if (microHelpText != null &&
                            microHelpText.trim().length() > 0)  {
                helpText.setText(microHelpText);
                helpText.setVisible(true);

                // Position the help text node
                double x = newNode.getLayoutX() +
                    newNode.getLayoutBounds().getMinX() -
                    helpText.getLayoutBounds().getMinX();
                double y = newNode.getLayoutY() +
                    newNode.getLayoutBounds().getMinY() +
                    newNode.getLayoutBounds().getHeight() -
                    helpText.getLayoutBounds().getMinX();

                helpText.setLayoutX(x);
                helpText.setLayoutY(y);
                helpText.setWrappingWidth(
                            newNode.getLayoutBounds().getWidth());
            }
            else {
                helpText.setVisible(false);
            }
        }
    }
```

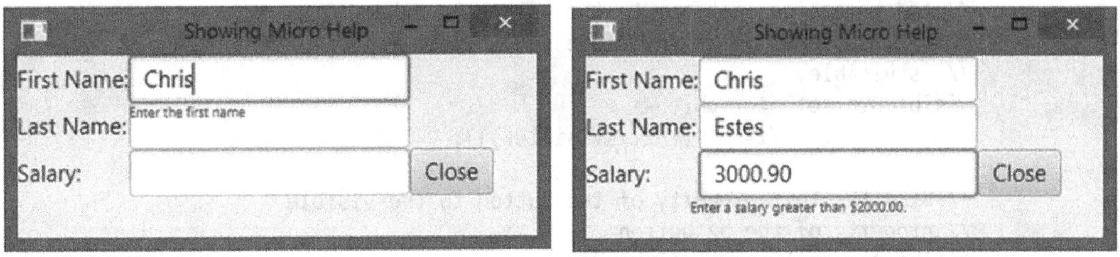

Figure 6-22. *Using an unmanaged Text node to show micro help*

Sometimes, you may want to use the space that is used by a node if the node becomes invisible. Suppose you have an HBox with several buttons. When one of the buttons becomes invisible, you want to slide all buttons from right to left. You can achieve a slide-up effect in VBox. Achieving sliding effects in HBox and VBox (or any other containers with relative positioning) is easy by binding the managed property of the node to the visible property. Listing 6-8 shows how to achieve the slide-left feature in an HBox. It displays four buttons. The first button is used to make the third button, b2, visible and invisible. The managed property of the b2 button is bound to its visible property:

```
b2.managedProperty().bind(b2.visibleProperty());
```

When the b2 button is made invisible, it becomes unmanaged, and the HBox does not use its layoutBounds in computing its own layoutBounds. This makes the b3 button slide to the left. Figure 6-23 shows two screenshots when the application is run.

Listing 6-8. Simulating the Slide-Left Feature Using Unmanaged Nodes

```java
// SlidingLeftNodeTest.java
package com.jdojo.node;

import javafx.application.Application;
import javafx.beans.binding.When;
import javafx.scene.Scene;
import javafx.scene.control.Button;
import javafx.scene.layout.HBox;
import javafx.stage.Stage;

public class SlidingLeftNodeTest extends Application {
    public static void main(String[] args) {
        Application.launch(args);
    }

    @Override
    public void start(Stage stage) {
        Button b1 = new Button("B1");
        Button b2 = new Button("B2");
        Button b3 = new Button("B3");
        Button visibleBtn = new Button("Make Invisible");
```

165

```
            // Add an action listener to the button to make
            // b2 visible if it is invisible and invisible if it
            // is visible
            visibleBtn.setOnAction(e ->
                    b2.setVisible(!b2.isVisible()));

            // Bind the text property of the button to the visible
            // property of the b2 button
            visibleBtn.textProperty().bind(
                    new When(b2.visibleProperty())
            .then("Make Invisible")
            .otherwise("Make Visible"));

            // Bind the managed property of b2 to its visible
            // property
            b2.managedProperty().bind(b2.visibleProperty());

            HBox root = new HBox();
            root.getChildren().addAll(visibleBtn, b1, b2, b3);

            Scene scene = new Scene(root);
            stage.setScene(scene);
            stage.setTitle("Sliding to the Left");
            stage.show();
    }
}
```

Figure 6-23. *Simulating the slide-left feature for the B2 button*

Transforming Bounds Between Coordinate Spaces

I have already covered coordinate spaces used by nodes. Sometimes, you may need to translate a Bounds or a point from one coordinate space to another. The Node class contains several methods to support this. The following transformations of a Bounds or a point are supported:

- Local to parent

- Local to scene

- Parent to local

- Scene to local

The localToParent() method transforms a Bounds or a point in the local coordinate space of a node to the coordinate space of its parent. The localToScene() method transforms a Bounds or a point in the local coordinate space of a node to the coordinate space of its scene. The parentToLocal() method transforms a Bounds or a point in the coordinate space of the parent of a node to the local coordinate space of the node. The sceneToLocal() method transforms a Bounds or a point in the coordinate space of the scene of a node to the local coordinate space of the node. All methods have three overloaded versions; one version takes a Bounds as an argument and returns the transformed Bounds; another version takes a Point2D as an argument and returns the transformed Point2D; another version takes the x and y coordinates of a point and returns the transformed Point2D.

These methods are sufficient to transform the coordinate of a point in one coordinate space to another within a scene graph. Sometimes, you may need to transform the coordinates of a point in the local coordinate space of a node to the coordinate space of the stage or screen. You can achieve this using the x and y properties of the Scene and Stage classes. The (x, y) properties of a scene define the coordinates of the top-left corner of the scene in the coordinate space of its stage. The (x, y) properties of a stage define the coordinates of the top-left corner of the stage in the coordinate space of the screen. For example, if (x1, y1) is a point in the coordinate space of the scene, (x1 + x2, y1 + y2) defines the same point in the coordinate space of the stage, where x2 and y2 are the x and y properties of the stage, respectively. Apply the same logic to get the coordinate of a point in the coordinate space of the screen.

Let's look at an example that uses transformations between the coordinate spaces of a node, its parent, and its scene. A scene has three Labels and three TextFields placed under different parents. A red, small circle is placed at the top-left corner of the bounding box of the node that has the focus. As the focus changes, the position of the circle needs to be computed, which would be the same as the position of the top-left corner of the current node, relative to the parent of the circle. The center of the circle needs to coincide with the top-left corner of the node that has the focus. Figure 6-24 shows the stage when the focus is in the first name and last name nodes. Listing 6-9 has the complete program to achieve this.

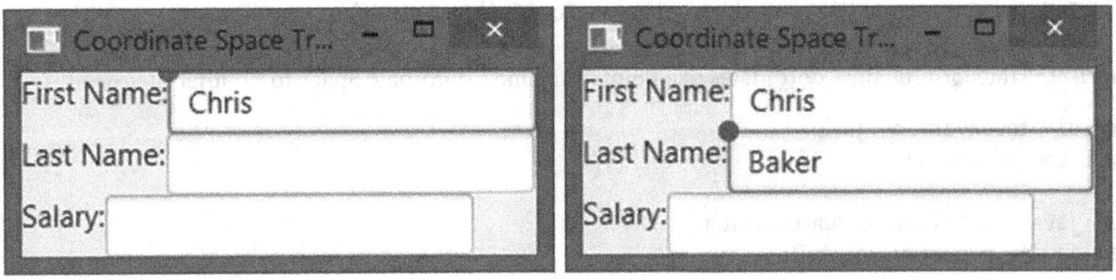

Figure 6-24. *Using coordinate space transformations to move a circle to a focused node*

The program has a scene consisting of three Labels and TextFields. A pair of a Label and a TextField is placed in an HBox. All HBoxes are placed in a VBox. An unmanaged Circle is placed in the VBox. The program adds a change listener to the focusOwner property of the scene to track the focus change. When the focus changes, the circle is placed at the top-left corner of the node that has the focus.

The placeMarker() contains the main logic. It gets the (x, y) coordinates of the top-left corner of the bounding box of the node in focus in the local coordinate space:

```
double nodeMinX = newNode.getLayoutBounds().getMinX();
double nodeMinY = newNode.getLayoutBounds().getMinY();
```

It transforms the coordinates of the top-left corner of the node from the local coordinate space to the coordinate space of the scene:

```
Point2D nodeInScene = newNode.localToScene(nodeMinX, nodeMinY);
```

Now the coordinates of the top-left corner of the node are transformed from the coordinate space of the scene to the coordinate space of the circle, which is named marker in the program:

```
Point2D nodeInMarkerLocal = marker.sceneToLocal(nodeInScene);
```

Finally, the coordinate of the top-left corner of the node is transformed to the coordinate space of the parent of the circle:

```
Point2D nodeInMarkerParent = marker.localToParent(nodeInMarkerLocal);
```

At this point, the nodeInMarkerParent is the point (the top-left corner of the node in focus) relative to the parent of the circle. If you relocate the circle to this point, you will place the top-left corner of the bounding box of the circle to the top-left corner of the node in focus:

```
marker.relocate(nodeInMarkerParent.getX(), nodeInMarkerParent.getY())
```

If you want to place the center of the circle to the top-left corner of the node in focus, you will need to adjust the coordinates accordingly:

```
marker.relocate(
    nodeInMarkerParent.getX() + marker.getLayoutBounds().getMinX(),
    nodeInMarkerParent.getY() + marker.getLayoutBounds().getMinY());
```

Listing 6-9. Transforming the Coordinates of a Point from One Coordinate Space to Another

```
// CoordinateConversion.java
package com.jdojo.node;

import javafx.application.Application;
import javafx.geometry.Point2D;
import javafx.scene.Node;
import javafx.scene.Scene;
import javafx.scene.control.Label;
import javafx.scene.control.TextField;
import javafx.scene.layout.HBox;
import javafx.scene.layout.VBox;
import javafx.scene.paint.Color;
import javafx.scene.shape.Circle;
import javafx.stage.Stage;

public class CoordinateConversion extends Application {
        // An instance variable to store the reference of the circle
        private Circle marker;

        public static void main(String[] args) {
                Application.launch(args);
        }
```

```
@Override
public void start(Stage stage) {
        TextField fName = new TextField();
        TextField lName = new TextField();
        TextField salary = new TextField();

        // The Circle node is unmanaged
        marker = new Circle(5);
        marker.setManaged(false);
        marker.setFill(Color.RED);
        marker.setMouseTransparent(true);

        HBox hb1 = new HBox();
        HBox hb2 = new HBox();
        HBox hb3 = new HBox();
        hb1.getChildren().addAll(
                new Label("First Name:"), fName);
        hb2.getChildren().addAll(new Label("Last Name:"), lName);
        hb3.getChildren().addAll(new Label("Salary:"), salary);

        VBox root = new VBox();
        root.getChildren().addAll(hb1, hb2, hb3, marker);

        Scene scene = new Scene(root);

        // Add a focus change listener to the scene
        scene.focusOwnerProperty().addListener(
            (prop, oldNode, newNode) -> placeMarker(newNode));

        stage.setScene(scene);
        stage.setTitle("Coordinate Space Transformation");
        stage.show();
}

public void placeMarker(Node newNode) {
        double nodeMinX = newNode.getLayoutBounds().getMinX();
        double nodeMinY = newNode.getLayoutBounds().getMinY();
        Point2D nodeInScene =
                newNode.localToScene(nodeMinX, nodeMinY);
        Point2D nodeInMarkerLocal =
                marker.sceneToLocal(nodeInScene);
        Point2D nodeInMarkerParent =
                marker.localToParent(nodeInMarkerLocal);

        // Position the circle approperiately
        marker.relocate(
                nodeInMarkerParent.getX()
                    + marker.getLayoutBounds().getMinX(),
            nodeInMarkerParent.getY()e
                    + marker.getLayoutBounds().getMinY());
}
}
```

169

Summary

A scene graph is a tree data structure. Every item in a scene graph is called a node. An instance of the javafx.scene.Node class represents a node in the scene graph. A node can have subitems (also called children), and such a node is called a branch node. A branch node is an instance of the Parent class whose concrete subclasses are Group, Region, and WebView. A node that cannot have subitems is called a leaf node. Instances of classes such as Rectangle, Text, ImageView, and MediaView are examples of leaf nodes. Only a single node within each scene graph tree will have no parent, which is referred to as the root node. A node may occur at the most once anywhere in the scene graph.

A node may be created and modified on any thread if it is not yet attached to a scene. Attaching a node to a scene and subsequent modification must occur on the JavaFX Application Thread. A node has several types of bounds. Bounds are determined with respect to different coordinate systems. A node in a scene graph has three types of bounds: layoutBounds, boundsInLocal, and boundsInParent.

The layoutBounds property is computed based on the geometric properties of the node in the *untransformed* local coordinate space of the node. Effects, clip, and transformations are not included. The boundsInLocal property is computed in the untransformed coordinate space of the node. It includes the geometric properties of the node, effects, and clip. Transformations applied to a node are not included. The boundsInParent property of a node is in the coordinate space of its parent. It includes the geometric properties of the node, effects, clip, and transformations. It is rarely used directly in code.

The computation of layoutBounds, boundsInLocal, and boundsInParent for a Group is different from that of a node. A Group takes on the collection bounds of its children. You can apply effects, clip, and transformations separately on each child of a Group. You can also apply effects, clip, and transformations directly on a Group, and they are applied to all its children nodes. The layoutBounds of a Group is the union of the boundsInParent of all its children. It includes effects, clip, and transformations applied directly to the children. It does not include effects, clip, and transformations applied directly to the Group. The boundsInLocal of a Group is computed by taking its layoutBounds and including the effects and clip applied directly to the Group. The boundsInParent of a Group is computed by taking its boundsInLocal and including the transformations applied directly to the Group.

Every node maintains an observable map of user-defined properties (key/value pairs). You can use it to store any useful information. A node can be managed or unmanaged. A managed node is laid out by its parent, whereas the application is responsible for laying out an unmanaged node.

The next chapter will discuss how to use colors in JavaFX.

CHAPTER 7

■ ■ ■

Playing with Colors

In this chapter, you will learn:

- How colors are represented in JavaFX
- What different color patterns are
- How to use an image pattern
- How to use a linear color gradient
- How to use a radial color gradient

The examples of this chapter lie in the com.jdojo.color package. In order for them to work, you must add a corresponding line to the module-info.java file:

```
...
opens com.jdojo.color to javafx.graphics, javafx.base;
...
```

This is the first time we use files from the resources folder. In order to simplify access to the resource files, we introduce a utility class in package com.jdojo.util:

```java
package com.jdojo.util;

import java.io.File;
import java.io.IOException;
import java.net.URL;

public class ResourceUtil {
    // Where the resources directory is, seen from current working
    // directory. This differs from build tool to build tool, and
    // from IDE to IDE, so you might have to adapt this.
    private final static String RSRC_PATH_FROM_CURRENT_DIR = "bin";

    public static URL getResourceURL(String inResourcesPath) {
        var fStr = (RSRC_PATH_FROM_CURRENT_DIR +
            "/resources/" +
            inResourcesPath).replace("/", File.separator);
        try {
            return new File(fStr).getCanonicalFile().toURI().toURL();
        } catch (IOException e) {
```

```
                System.err.println("Cannot fetch URL for '" +
                    inResourcesPath + "'");
                System.err.println("""
                    If the path is correct, try to adapt the
                    RSRC_PATH_FROM_CURRENT_DIR constant in class
                    ResourceUtil""".stripIndent());
                e.printStackTrace(System.err);
                return null;
            }
    }

    public static String getResourceURLStr(String inResourcesPath) {
        return getResourceURL(inResourcesPath).toString();
    }

    public static String getResourcePath(String inResourcesPath) {
        var fStr = (RSRC_PATH_FROM_CURRENT_DIR +
            "/resources/" +
            inResourcesPath).replace("/", File.separator);
        return new File(fStr).getAbsolutePath();
    }
}
}
```

Understanding Colors

In JavaFX, you can specify color for text and background color for regions. You can specify a color as a uniform color, an image pattern, or a color gradient. A uniform color uses the same color to fill the entire region. An image pattern lets you fill a region with an image pattern. A color gradient defines a color pattern in which the color varies along a straight line from one color to another. The variation in a color gradient can be linear or radial. I will present examples using all color types in this chapter. Figure 7-1 shows the class diagram for color-related classes in JavaFX. All classes are included in the javafx.scene.paint package.

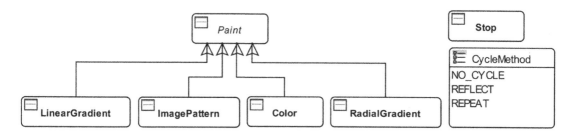

Figure 7-1. *The class diagram of color-related classes in JavaFX*

The Paint class is an abstract class, and it is the base class for other color classes. It contains only one static method that takes a String argument and returns a Paint instance. The returned Paint instance would be of the Color, LinearGradient, or RadialGradient class, as shown in the following code:

```
public static Paint valueOf(String value)
```

You will not use the valueOf() method of the Paint class directly. It is used to convert the color value read in a String from the CSS files. The following snippet of code creates instances of the Paint class from Strings:

```
// redColor is an instance of the Color class
Paint redColor = Paint.valueOf("red");

// aLinearGradientColor is an instance of the LinearGradient class
Paint aLinearGradientColor = Paint.valueOf("linear-gradient(to bottom right, red, black)" );

// aRadialGradientColor is an instance of the RadialGradient class
Paint aRadialGradientColor =    Paint.valueOf("radial-gradient(radius 100%, red, blue, black)");
```

A uniform color, an image pattern, a linear color gradient, and a radial color gradient are instances of the Color, ImagePattern, LinearGradient, and RadialGradient classes, respectively. The Stop class and the CycleMethod enum are used while working with color gradients.

■ **Tip** Typically, methods for setting the color attribute of a node take the Paint type as an argument, allowing you to use any of the four color patterns.

Using the Color Class

The Color class represents a solid uniform color from the RGB color space. Every color has an alpha value defined between 0.0 and 1.0 or 0 and 255. An alpha value of 0.0 or 0 means the color is completely transparent, and an alpha value of 1.0 or 255 denotes a completely opaque color. By default, the alpha value is set to 1.0. You can have an instance of the Color class in three ways:

- Using the constructor
- Using one of the factory methods
- Using one of the color constants declared in the Color class

The Color class has only one constructor that lets you specify the RGB and opacity in the range [0.0;1.0]:

```
public Color(double red, double green, double blue, double opacity)
```

The following snippet of code creates a completely opaque blue color:

```
Color blue = new  Color(0.0, 0.0, 1.0, 1.0);
```

You can use the following static methods in the Color class to create Color objects. The double values need to be between 0.0 and 1.0 and int values between 0 and 255:

- Color color(double red, double green, double blue)
- Color color(double red, double green, double blue, double opacity)
- Color hsb(double hue, double saturation, double brightness)
- Color hsb(double hue, double saturation, double brightness, double opacity)

- Color rgb(int red, int green, int blue)

- Color rgb(int red, int green, int blue, double opacity)

The valueOf() and web() factory methods let you create Color objects from strings in web color value formats. The following snippet of code creates blue Color objects using different string formats:

```
Color blue = Color.valueOf("blue");
Color blue = Color.web("blue");
Color blue = Color.web("#0000FF");
Color blue = Color.web("0X0000FF");
Color blue = Color.web("rgb(0, 0, 255)");
Color blue = Color.web("rgba(0, 0, 255, 0.5)"); // 50% transparent blue
```

The Color class defines about 140 color constants, for example, RED, WHITE, TAN, and BLUE, among others. Colors defined by these constants are completely opaque.

Using the *ImagePattern* Class

An image pattern lets you fill a shape with an image. The image may fill the entire shape or use a tiling pattern. Here are the steps you would use to get an image pattern:

1. Create an Image object using an image from a file.

2. Define a rectangle, known as the anchor rectangle, relative to the upper-left corner of the shape to be filled.

The image is shown in the anchor rectangle and is then resized to fit the anchor rectangle. If the bounding box for the shape to be filled is bigger than that of the anchor rectangle, the anchor rectangle with the image is repeated within the shape in a tiling pattern.

You can create an object of the ImagePattern using one of its constructors:

- ImagePattern(Image image)

- ImagePattern(Image image, double x, double y, double width, double height, boolean proportional)

The first constructor fills the entire bounding box with the image without any pattern. The second constructor lets you specify the x and y coordinates, width, and height of the anchor rectangle. If the proportional argument is true, the anchor rectangle is specified relative to the bounding box of the shape to be filled in terms of a unit square. If the proportional argument is false, the anchor rectangle is specified in the local coordinate system of the shape. The following two calls to the two constructors would produce the same result:

```
ImagePatterm ip1 = new ImagePattern(anImage);
ImagePatterm ip2 = new ImagePattern(anImage, 0.0, 0.0, 1.0, 1.0, true);
```

For the example here, you will use the image shown in Figure 7-2. It is a 37px by 25px blue rounded rectangle. It can be found in the resources/picture/blue_rounded_rectangle.png file under the source code folder.

Figure 7-2. *A blue rounded rectangle*

Using that file, let's create an image pattern, using the following code:

```
Image img = create the image object...
ImagePattern p1 = new ImagePattern(img, 0, 0, 0.25, 0.25, true);
```

The last argument in the `ImagePattern` constructor set to `true` makes the bounds of the anchor rectangle, 0, 0, 0.25, and 0.25, to be interpreted proportional to the size of the shape to be filled. The image pattern will create an anchor rectangle at (0, 0) of the shape to be filled. Its width and height will be 25% of the shape to be filled. This will make the anchor rectangle repeat four times horizontally and four times vertically. If you use the following code with the preceding image pattern, it will produce a rectangle as shown in Figure 7-3:

```
Rectangle r1 = new Rectangle(100, 50);
r1.setFill(p1);
```

Figure 7-3. *Filling a rectangle with an image pattern*

If you use the same image pattern to fill a triangle with the following snippet of code, the resulting triangle will look like the one shown in Figure 7-4:

```
Polygon triangle = new Polygon(50, 0, 0, 50, 100, 50);
triangle.setFill(p1);
```

Figure 7-4. *Filling a triangle with an image pattern*

How would you fill a shape completely with an image without having a tiling pattern? You would need to use an `ImagePattern` with the proportional argument set to true. The center of the anchor rectangle should be at (0, 0), and its width and height should be set to 1 as follows:

```
// An image pattern to completely fill a shape with the image
ImagePatterm ip = new ImagePattern(yourImage, 0.0, 0.0, 1.0, 1.0, true);
```

The program in Listing 7-1 shows how to use an image pattern. The resulting screen is shown in Figure 7-5. Its `init()` method loads an image in an `Image` object and stores it in an instance variable. If the image file is not found in the `CLASSPATH`, it prints an error message and quits.

Listing 7-1. Using an Image Pattern to Fill Different Shapes

```java
// ImagePatternApp.java
package com.jdojo.color;

import com.jdojo.util.ResourceUtil;
import javafx.application.Application;
import javafx.scene.Scene;
import javafx.scene.image.Image;
import javafx.scene.layout.HBox;
import javafx.scene.paint.ImagePattern;
import javafx.scene.shape.Circle;
import javafx.scene.shape.Rectangle;
import javafx.stage.Stage;

public class ImagePatternApp extends Application {
    private Image img;

    public static void main(String[] args) {
        Application.launch(args);
    }

    @Override
    public void init() {
        // Create an Image object
        final String imgPath = ResourceUtil.getResourceURLStr(
            "picture/blue_rounded_rectangle.png");
        img = new Image(imgPath);
    }

    @Override
    public void start(Stage stage) {
        // An anchor rectangle at (0, 0) that is 25% wide and 25% tall
        // relative to the rectangle to be filled
        ImagePattern p1 = new ImagePattern(img, 0, 0, 0.25, 0.25, true);
        Rectangle r1 = new Rectangle(100, 50);
        r1.setFill(p1);

        // An anchor rectangle at (0, 0) that is 50% wide and 50% tall
        // relative to the rectangle to be filled
        ImagePattern p2 = new ImagePattern(img, 0, 0, 0.5, 0.5, true);
        Rectangle r2 = new Rectangle(100, 50);
        r2.setFill(p2);

        // Using absolute bounds for the anchor rectangle
        ImagePattern p3 = new ImagePattern(img, 40, 15, 20, 20, false);
        Rectangle r3 = new Rectangle(100, 50);
        r3.setFill(p3);
```

```
// Fill a circle
ImagePattern p4 = new ImagePattern(img, 0, 0, 0.1, 0.1, true);
Circle c = new Circle(50, 50, 25);
c.setFill(p4);

HBox root = new HBox();
root.getChildren().addAll(r1, r2, r3, c);

Scene scene = new Scene(root);
stage.setScene(scene);

stage.setTitle("Using Image Patterns");
stage.show();
    }
}
```

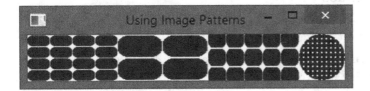

Figure 7-5. *Filling different shapes with image patterns*

Understanding Linear Color Gradient

A linear color gradient is defined using an axis known as a *gradient line*. Each point on the gradient line is of a different color. All points on a line that is perpendicular to the gradient line have the same color, which is the color of the point of intersection between the two lines. The gradient line is defined by a starting point and an ending point. Colors along the gradient line are defined at some points on the gradient line, which are known as *stop-color points* (or stop points). Colors between two stop points are computed using interpolation.

The gradient line has a direction, which is from the starting point to the ending point. All points on a line perpendicular to the gradient line that pass through a stop point will have the color of the stop point. For example, suppose you have defined a stop point P1 with a color C1. If you draw a line perpendicular to the gradient line passing through the point P1, all points on that line will have the color C1.

Figure 7-6 shows the details of the elements constituting a linear color gradient. It shows a rectangular region filled with a linear color gradient. The gradient line is defined from the left side to the right side. The starting point has a white color, and the ending point has a black color. On the left side of the rectangle, all points have the white color, and on the right side, all points have the black color. In between the left and the right sides, the color varies between white and black.

177

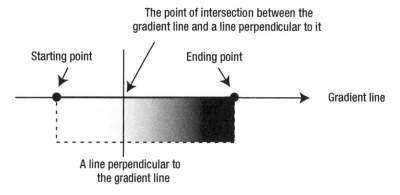

Figure 7-6. *The details of a linear color gradient*

Using the *LinearGradient* Class

In JavaFX, an instance of the LinearGradient class represents a linear color gradient. The class has the following two constructors. The types of their last arguments are different:

- LinearGradient(double startX, double startY, double endX, double endY, boolean proportional, CycleMethod cycleMethod, List<Stop> stops)

- LinearGradient(double startX, double startY, double endX, double endY, boolean proportional, CycleMethod cycleMethod, Stop... stops)

The startX and startY arguments define the x and y coordinates of the starting point of the gradient line. The endX and endY arguments define the x and y coordinates of the ending point of the gradient line.

The proportional argument affects the way the coordinates of the starting and ending points are treated. If it is true, the starting and ending points are treated relative to a unit square. Otherwise, they are treated as absolute values in the local coordinate system. The use of this argument needs a little more explanation.

Typically, a color gradient is used to fill a region, for example, a rectangle. Sometimes, you know the size of the region, and sometimes you will not. The value of this argument lets you specify the gradient line in relative or absolute form. In relative form, the region is treated as a unit square. That is, the coordinates of the upper-left and the lower-right corners are (0.0, 0.0) and (1.0, 1.0), respectively. Other points in the regions will have x and y coordinates between 0.0 and 1.0. Suppose you specify the starting point as (0.0, 0.0) and the ending point as (1.0, 0.0). It defines a horizontal gradient line from left to right. The starting and ending points of (0.0, 0.0) and (0.0, 1.0) define a vertical gradient line from top to bottom. The starting and ending points of (0.0, 0.0) and (0.5, 0.0) define a horizontal gradient line from the left to the middle of the region.

When the proportional argument is false, the coordinate values for the starting and ending points are treated as absolute values with respect to the local coordinate system. Suppose you have a rectangle of width 200 and height 100. The starting and ending points of (0.0, 0.0) and (200.0, 0.0) define a horizontal gradient line from left to right. The starting and ending points of (0.0, 0.0) and (200.0, 100.0) define a diagonal gradient line from the top-left corner to the bottom-right corner.

The cycleMethod argument defines how the regions outside the color gradient bounds, defined by the starting and ending points, should be filled. Suppose you define the starting and ending points with the proportional argument set to true as (0.0, 0.0) and (0.5, 0.0), respectively. This covers only the left half of the region. How should the right half of the region be filled? You specify this behavior using the `cycleMethod` argument. Its value is one of the enum constants defined in the `CycleMethod` enum:

- `CycleMethod.NO_CYCLE`

- `CycleMethod.REFLECT`

- `CycleMethod.REPEAT`

The cycle method of `NO_CYCLE` fills the remaining region with the terminal color. If you have defined color a stop point only from the left to the middle of a region, the right half will be filled with the color that is defined for the middle of the region. Suppose you define a color gradient for only the middle half of a region, leaving the 25% at the left side and 25% at the right side undefined. The `NO_CYCLE` method will fill the left 25% region with the color that is defined at the 25% distance from left and the right 25% region with the color defined at the 25% distance from right. The color for the middle 50% will be determined by the color-stop points.

The cycle method of `REFLECT` fills the remaining regions by reflecting the color gradient, as start-to-end and end-to-start, from the nearest filled region. The cycle method of `REPEAT` repeats the color gradient to fill the remaining region.

The `stops` argument defines the color-stop points along the gradient line. A color-stop point is represented by an instance of the `Stop` class, which has only one constructor:

```
Stop(double offset, Color color)
```

The offset value is between 0.0 and 1.0. It defines the relative distance of the stop point along the gradient line from the starting point. For example, an offset of 0.0 is the starting point, an offset of 1.0 is the ending point, an offset of 0.5 is in the middle of the starting and ending points, and so forth. You define at least two stop points with two different colors to have a color gradient. There are no limits on the number of stop points you can define for a color gradient.

That covers the explanation for the arguments of the `LinearGradient` constructors. So let's look at some examples on how to use them.

The following snippet of code fills a rectangle with a linear color gradient, as shown in Figure 7-7:

```
Stop[] stops = new Stop[]{new Stop(0, Color.WHITE), new Stop(1, Color.BLACK)};
LinearGradient lg = new LinearGradient(0, 0, 1, 0, true, NO_CYCLE, stops);
Rectangle r = new Rectangle(200, 100);
r.setFill(lg);
```

Figure 7-7. *A horizontal linear color gradient with two stop points: white at starting and black at ending point*

You have two color-stop points. The stop point in the beginning is colored white and that of the end is colored black. The starting point (0, 0) and ending point (1, 0) define a horizontal gradient from left to right. The `proportional` argument is set to `true`, which means the coordinate values are interpreted as relative to a unit square. The cycle method argument, which is set to `NO_CYCLE`, has no effect in this case as your gradient bounds cover the entire region. In the preceding code, if you want to set the proportional argument value to false, to have the same effect, you would create the LinearGradient object as follows. Note the use of 200 as the x coordinate for the ending point to denote the end of the rectangle width:

```
LinearGradient lg = new LinearGradient(0, 0, 200, 0, false, NO_CYCLE, stops);
```

Let's look at another example. The resulting rectangle after running the following snippet of code is shown in Figure 7-8:

```
Stop[] stops = new Stop[]{new Stop(0, Color.WHITE), new Stop(1, Color.BLACK)};
LinearGradient lg = new LinearGradient(0, 0, 0.5, 0, true, NO_CYCLE, stops);
Rectangle r = new Rectangle(200, 100);
r.setFill(lg);
```

Figure 7-8. *A horizontal linear color gradient with two stop points: white at starting and black at midpoint*

In this code, you have made a slight change. You defined a horizontal gradient line, which starts at the left side of the rectangle and ends in the middle. Note the use of (0.5, 0) as the coordinates for the ending point. This leaves the right half of the rectangle with no color gradient. The cycle method is effective in this case as its job is to fill the unfilled regions. The color at the middle of the rectangle is black, which is defined by the second stop point. The NO_CYCLE value uses the terminal black color to fill the right half of the rectangle.

Let's look at a slight variant of the previous example. You change the cycle method from NO_CYCLE to REFLECT, as shown in the following snippet of code, which results in a rectangle as shown in Figure 7-9. Note that the right half region (the region with undefined gradient) is the reflection of the left half:

```
Stop[] stops = new Stop[]{new Stop(0, Color.WHITE), new Stop(1, Color.BLACK)};
LinearGradient lg = new LinearGradient(0, 0, 0.5, 0, true, REFLECT, stops);
Rectangle r = new Rectangle(200, 100);
r.setFill(lg);
```

Figure 7-9. *A horizontal linear color gradient with two stop points: white at starting and black at midpoint and REFLECT as the cycle method*

Let's make a slight change in the previous example so the ending point coordinate covers only one-tenth of the width of the rectangle. The code is as follows, and the resulting rectangle is shown in Figure 7-10.

The right 90% of the rectangle is filled using the REFLECT cycle method by alternating end-to-start and start-to-end color patterns:

```
Stop[] stops = new Stop[]{new Stop(0, Color.WHITE), new Stop(1, Color.BLACK)};
LinearGradient lg = new LinearGradient(0, 0, 0.1, 0, true, REFLECT, stops);
Rectangle r = new Rectangle(200, 100);
r.setFill(lg);
```

Figure 7-10. *A horizontal linear color gradient with two stop points: white at starting and black at one-tenth point and REFLECT as the cycle method*

Now let's look at the effect of using the REPEAT cycle method. The following snippet of code uses an ending point at the middle of the width of the rectangle and a cycle method of REPEAT. This results in a rectangle as shown in Figure 7-11. If you set the ending point to one-tenth of the width in this example, it will result in a rectangle as shown in Figure 7-12.

```
Stop[] stops = new Stop[]{new Stop(0, Color.WHITE), new Stop(1, Color.BLACK)};
LinearGradient lg = new LinearGradient(0, 0, 0.5, 0, true, REPEAT, stops);
Rectangle r = new Rectangle(200, 100);
r.setFill(lg);
```

Figure 7-11. *A horizontal linear color gradient with two stop points: white at starting and black at midpoint and REPEAT as the cycle method*

Figure 7-12. *A horizontal linear color gradient with two stop points: white at starting and black at one-tenth point and REPEAT as the cycle method*

You could also define more than two stop points, as shown in the following snippet of code. It divides the distance between the starting and the ending points on the gradient line into four segments, each by 25% of the width. The first segment (from left) will have colors between red and green, the second between green and blue, the third between blue and orange, and the fourth between orange and yellow. The resulting rectangle is shown in Figure 7-13. If you are reading a printed copy of the book, you may not see the colors.

```
Stop[] stops = new Stop[]{new Stop(0, Color.RED),
                          new Stop(0.25, Color.GREEN),
                          new Stop(0.50, Color.BLUE),
                          new Stop(0.75, Color.ORANGE),
                          new Stop(1, Color.YELLOW)};
LinearGradient lg = new LinearGradient(0, 0, 1, 0, true, NO_CYCLE, stops);
Rectangle r = new Rectangle(200, 100);
r.setFill(lg);
```

Figure 7-13. *A horizontal linear color gradient with five stop points*

You are not limited to defining only horizontal color gradients. You can define a color gradient with a gradient line with any angle. The following snippet of code creates a gradient from the top-left corner to the bottom-right corner. Note that when the proportional argument is true, (0, 0) and (1, 1) define the (x, y) coordinates of the top-left and bottom-right corners of the region:

```
Stop[] stops = new Stop[]{new Stop(0, Color.WHITE), new Stop(1, Color.BLACK)};
LinearGradient lg = new LinearGradient(0, 0, 1, 1, true, NO_CYCLE, stops);
Rectangle r = new Rectangle(200, 100);
r.setFill(lg);
```

The following snippet of code defines a gradient line between (0, 0) and (0.1, 0.1) points. It uses the REPEAT cycle method to fill the rest of the region. The resulting rectangle is shown in Figure 7-14.

```
Stop[] stops = new Stop[]{new Stop(0, Color.WHITE), new Stop(1, Color.BLACK)};
LinearGradient lg = new LinearGradient(0, 0, 0.1, 0.1, true, REPEAT, stops);
Rectangle r = new Rectangle(200, 100);
r.setFill(lg);
```

Figure 7-14. *An angled linear color gradient with two stop points: white at the starting point (0, 0) and black at the ending point (0.1, 0.1) with REPEAT as the cycle method*

Defining Linear Color Gradients Using a String Format

You can also specify a linear color gradient in string format using the static method valueOf(String colorString) of the LinearGradient class. Typically, the string format is used to specify a linear color gradient in a CSS file. It has the following syntax:

linear-gradient([gradient-line], [cycle-method], color-stops-list)

The arguments within square brackets ([and]) are optional. If you do not specify an optional argument, the comma that follows also needs to be excluded. The default value for the gradient-line argument is "to bottom." The default value for the cycle-method argument is NO_CYCLE. You can specify the gradient line in two ways:

- Using two points—the starting point and the ending point

- Using a side or a corner

The syntax for using two points for the gradient line is

from point-1 to point-2

The coordinates of the points may be specified in percentage of the area or in actual measurement in pixels. For a 200px wide by 100px tall rectangle, a horizontal gradient line may be specified in the following two ways:

from 0% 0% to 100% 0%

or

from 0px 0px to 200px 0px

The syntax for using a side or a corner is

to side-or-corner

The side-or-corner value may be top, left, bottom, right, top left, bottom left, bottom right, or top right. When you define the gradient line using a side or a corner, you specify only the ending point. The starting point is inferred. For example, the value "to top" infers the starting point as "from bottom," the value "to bottom right" infers the starting point as "from top left," and so forth. If the gradient-line value is missing, it defaults to "to bottom."

The valid values for the cycle-method are repeat and reflect. If it is missing, it defaults to NO_CYCLE. It is a runtime error to specify the value of the cycle-method argument as NO_CYCLE. If you want it to be NO_CYCLE, simply omit the cycle-method argument from the syntax.

The color-stops-list argument is a list of color stops. A color stop consists of a web color name and, optionally, a position in pixels or percentage from the starting point. Examples of lists of color stops are

- white, black

- white 0%, black 100%

- white 0%, yellow 50%, blue 100%

- white 0px, yellow 100px, red 200px

When you do not specify positions for the first and the last color stops, the position for the first one defaults to 0% and the second one to 100%. So, the color stop lists "white, black" and "white 0%, black 100%" are fundamentally the same.

If you do not specify positions for any of the color stops in the list, they are assigned positions in such a way that they are evenly placed between the starting point and the ending point. The following two lists of color stops are the same:

- white, yellow, black, red, green

- white 0%, yellow 25%, black 50%, red 75%, green 100%

You can specify positions for some color stops in a list and not for others. In this case, the color stops without positions are evenly spaced between the preceding and following color stops with positions. The following two lists of color stops are the same:

- white, yellow, black 60%, red, green

- white 0%, yellow 30%, black 50%, red 80%, green 100%

If a color stop in a list has its position set less than the position specified for any previous color stops, its position is set equal to the maximum position set for the previous color stops. The following list of color stops sets 10% for the third color stop, which is less than the position of the second color stop (50%):

white, yellow 50%, black 10%, green

This will be changed at runtime to use 50% for the third color stop as follows:

white 0%, yellow 50%, black 50%, green 100%

Now let's look at some examples. The following string will create a linear gradient from top to bottom with NO_CYCLE as the cycle method. Colors are white and black at the top and bottom, respectively:

linear-gradient(white, black)

This value is the same as

linear-gradient(to bottom, white, black)

Figure 7-15. *Creating a linear color gradient using the string format*

The following snippet of code will create a rectangle as shown in Figure 7-15. It defines a horizontal color gradient with the ending point midway through the width of the rectangle. It uses repeat as the cycle method:

```
String value = "from 0px 0px to 100px 0px, repeat, white 0%, black 100%";
LinearGradient lg2 = LinearGradient.valueOf(value);
Rectangle r2 = new Rectangle(200, 100);
r2.setFill(lg2);
```

The following string value for a linear color gradient will create a diagonal gradient from the top-left corner to the bottom-right corner filling the area with white and black colors:

```
"to bottom right, white 0%, black 100%"
```

Understanding Radial Color Gradient

In a radial color gradient, colors start at a single point, transitioning smoothly outward in a circular or elliptical shape. The shape, let's say a circle, is defined by a center point and a radius. The starting point of colors is known as the *focus point of the gradient*. The colors change along a line, starting at the focus point of the gradient, in all directions until the periphery of the shape is reached. A radial color gradient is defined using three components:

- A gradient shape (the center and radius of the gradient circle)
- A focus point that has the first color of the gradient
- Color stops

The focus point of the gradient and the center point of the gradient shape may be different. Figure 7-16 shows the components of a radial color gradient. The figure shows two radial gradients: in the left side, the focus point and the center point are located at the same place; in the right side, the focus point is located horizontally right to the center point of the shape.

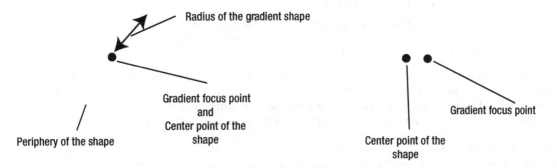

Figure 7-16. *Elements defining a radial color gradient*

The focus point is defined in terms of a focus angle and a focus distance, as shown in Figure 7-17. The focus angle is the angle between a horizontal line passing through the center point of the shape and a line joining the center point and the focus point. The focus distance is the distance between the center point of the shape and the focus point of the gradient.

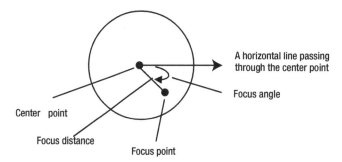

Figure 7-17. *Defining a focus point in a radial color gradient*

The list of color stops determines the value of the color at a point inside the gradient shape. The focus point defines the 0% position of the color stops. The points on the periphery of the circle define the 100% position for the color stops. How would you determine the color at a point inside the gradient circle? You would draw a line passing through the point and the focus point. The color at the point will be interpolated using the nearest color stops on each side of the point on the line.

Using the *RadialGradient* Class

An instance of the RadialGradient class represents a radial color gradient. The class contains the following two constructors that differ in the types of their last argument:

- RadialGradient(double focusAngle, double focusDistance, double centerX, double centerY, double radius, boolean proportional, CycleMethod cycleMethod, List<Stop> stops)

- RadialGradient(double focusAngle, double focusDistance, double centerX, double centerY, double radius, boolean proportional, CycleMethod cycleMethod, Stop... stops)

The focusAngle argument defines the focus angle for the focus point. A positive focus angle is measured clockwise from the horizontal line passing through the center point and the line connecting the center point and the focus point. A negative value is measured counterclockwise.

The focusDistance argument is specified in terms of the percentage of the radius of the circle. The value is clamped between –1 and 1. That is, the focus point is always inside the gradient circle. If the focus distance sets the focus point outside the periphery of the gradient circle, the focus point that is used is the point of intersection of the periphery of the circle and the line connecting the center point and the set focus point.

The focus angle and the focus distance can have positive and negative values. Figure 7-18 illustrates this: it shows four focus points located at 80% distance, positive and negative, from the center point and at a 60-degree angle, positive and negative.

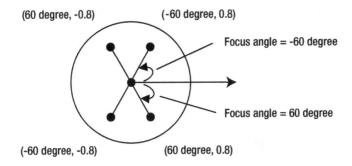

Figure 7-18. *Locating a focus point with its focus angle and focus distance*

The centerX and centerY arguments define the x and y coordinates of the center point, respectively, and the radius argument is the radius of the gradient circle. These arguments can be specified relative to a unit square (between 0.0 and 1.0) or in pixels.

The proportional argument affects the way the values for the coordinates of the center point and radius are treated. If it is true, they are treated relative to a unit square. Otherwise, they are treated as absolute values in the local coordinate system. For more details on the use of the proportional argument, please refer to the section "Using the *LinearGradient* Class" earlier in this chapter.

■ **Tip** JavaFX lets you create a radial gradient of a circular shape. However, when the region to be filled by a radial color gradient has a nonsquare bounding box (e.g., a rectangle) and you specify the radius of the gradient circle relative to the size of the shape to be filled, JavaFX will use an elliptical radial color gradient. This is not documented in the API documentation of the RadialGradient class. I will present an example of this kind shortly.

The cycleMethod and stops arguments have the same meaning as described earlier in the section on using the LinearGradient class. In a radial color gradient, stops are defined along lines connecting the focus point and points on the periphery of the gradient circle. The focus point defines the 0% stop point, and the points on the circle periphery define 100% stop points.

Let's look at some examples of using the RadialGradient class. The following snippet of code produces a radial color gradient for a circle as shown in Figure 7-19:

```
Stop[] stops = new Stop[]{new Stop(0, Color.WHITE), new Stop(1, Color.BLACK)};
RadialGradient rg = new RadialGradient(0, 0, 0.5, 0.5, 0.5, true, NO_CYCLE, stops);
Circle c = new Circle(50, 50, 50);
c.setFill(rg);
```

Figure 7-19. *A radial color gradient with the same center point and focus point*

The zero value for the focus angle and focus distance locates the focus point at the center of the gradient circle. A true `proportional` argument interprets the center point coordinates (0.5, 0.5) as (25px, 25px) for the 50 by 50 rectangular bounds of the circle. The radius value of 0.5 is interpreted as 25px, and that places the center of the gradient circle at the same location as the center of the circle to fill. The cycle method of `NO_CYCLE` has no effect in this case as the gradient circle fills the entire circular area. The color stop at the focus point is white, and at the periphery of the gradient circle, it is black.

The following snippet of code specifies the radius of the gradient circle as 0.2 of the circle to be filled. This means that it will use a gradient circle of 10px (0.2 multiplied by 50px, which is the radius of the circle to be filled). The resulting circle is shown in Figure 7-20. The region of the circle beyond the 0.2 of its radius has been filled with the color black, as the cycle method was specified as `NO_CYCLE`:

```
Stop[] stops = new Stop[]{new Stop(0, Color.WHITE), new Stop(1, Color.BLACK)};
RadialGradient rg = new RadialGradient(0, 0, 0.5, 0.5, 0.2, true, NO_CYCLE, stops);
Circle c = new Circle(50, 50, 50);
c.setFill(rg);
```

Figure 7-20. *A radial color gradient with the same center point and focus point having a gradient circle with a radius of 0.20*

Now let's use the cycle method of `REPEAT` in the preceding snippet of code. The resulting circle is shown in Figure 7-21.

```
Stop[] stops = new Stop[]{new Stop(0, Color.WHITE), new Stop(1, Color.BLACK)};
RadialGradient rg = new RadialGradient(0, 0, 0.5, 0.5, 0.2, true, REPEAT, stops);
Circle c = new Circle(50, 50, 50);
c.setFill(rg);
```

Figure 7-21. *A radial color gradient with the same center point and focus point, a gradient circle with a radius of 0.20, and the cycle method as REPEAT*

So now let's use a different center point and focus point. Use a 60-degree focus angle and 0.2 times the radius as the focus distance as in the following code. The resulting circle is shown in Figure 7-22. Notice the 3D effect you get by moving the focus point away from the center point.

```
Stop[] stops = new Stop[]{new Stop(0, Color.WHITE), new Stop(1, Color.BLACK)};
RadialGradient rg =
    new RadialGradient(60, 0.2, 0.5, 0.5, 0.2, true, REPEAT, stops);
Circle c = new Circle(50, 50, 50);
c.setFill(rg);
```

Figure 7-22. *A radial color gradient using different center and focus points*

Now let's fill a rectangular region (nonsquare) with a radial color gradient. The code for this effect follows, and the resulting rectangle is shown in Figure 7-23. Notice the elliptical gradient shape used by JavaFX. You have specified the radius of the gradient as 0.5 and the proportional argument as true. Since your rectangle is 200px wide and 100px tall, it results in two radii: one along the x-axis and one along the y-axis, giving rise to an ellipse. The radii along the x- and y-axes are 100px and 50px, respectively.

```
Stop[] stops = new Stop[]{new Stop(0, Color.WHITE), new Stop(1, Color.BLACK)};
RadialGradient rg =
    new RadialGradient(0, 0, 0.5, 0.5, 0.5, true, REPEAT, stops);
Rectangle r = new Rectangle(200, 100);
r.setFill(rg);
```

Figure 7-23. *A rectangle filled with a radial color gradient with a proportional argument value of true*

If you want a rectangle to be filled with a color gradient of a circular shape rather than elliptical shape, you should specify the proportional argument as false, and the radius value will be treated in pixels. The following snippet of code produces a rectangle, as shown in Figure 7-24:

```
Stop[] stops = new Stop[]{new Stop(0, Color.WHITE), new Stop(1, Color.BLACK)};
RadialGradient rg =
    new RadialGradient(0, 0, 100, 50, 50, false, REPEAT, stops);
Rectangle r = new Rectangle(200, 100);
r.setFill(rg);
```

Figure 7-24. *A rectangle filled with a radial color gradient with a proportional argument value of false*

How can you fill a triangle or any other shape with a radial color gradient? The shape of a radial gradient, circular or elliptical, depends on several conditions. Table 7-1 shows the combinations of the criteria that will determine the shape of a radial color gradient.

Table 7-1. *Criteria Used to Determine the Shape of a Radial Color Gradient*

Proportional Argument	Bounding Box for the Filled Region	Gradient Shape
true	Square	Circle
true	Nonsquare	Ellipse
false	Square	Circle
false	Nonsquare	Circle

I should emphasize here that, in the preceding discussion, I am talking about the bounds of the regions to be filled, not the region. For example, suppose you want to fill a triangle with a radial color gradient. The bounds of the triangle will be determined by its width and height. If the triangle has the same width and height, its bounds take a square region. Otherwise, its bounds take a rectangular region.

The following snippet of code fills a triangle with vertices (0.0, 0.0), (0.0, 100.0), and (100.0, 100.0). Notice that the bounding box for this triangle is a 100px by 100px square. The resulting triangle is the left one shown in Figure 7-25.

```
Stop[] stops = new Stop[]{new Stop(0, Color.WHITE), new Stop(1, Color.BLACK)};
RadialGradient rg =
    new RadialGradient(0, 0, 0.5, 0.5, 0.2, true, REPEAT, stops);
Polygon triangle = new Polygon(0.0, 0.0, 0.0, 100.0, 100.0, 100.0);
triangle.setFill(rg);
```

 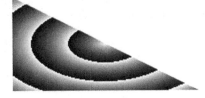

100px X 100px   200px X 100px

Figure 7-25. *Filling triangles with radial color gradients of circular and elliptical shapes*

The triangle in the right side of Figure 7-25 uses a rectangular bounding box of 200px by 100px, which is produced by the following snippet of code. Notice that the gradient uses an elliptical shape:

```
Polygon triangle = new Polygon(0.0, 0.0, 0.0, 100.0, 200.0, 100.0);
```

Finally, let's look at an example of using multiple color stops with the focus point on the periphery of the circle, as shown in Figure 7-26. The code to produce the effect is as follows:

```
Stop[] stops = new Stop[]{
    new Stop(0, Color.WHITE),
    new Stop(0.40, Color.GRAY),
    new Stop(0.60, Color.TAN),
    new Stop(1, Color.BLACK)};
RadialGradient rg =
    new RadialGradient(-30, 1.0, 0.5, 0.5, 0.5, true, REPEAT, stops);
Circle c = new Circle(50, 50, 50);
c.setFill(rg);
```

Figure 7-26. *Using multiple color stops in a radial color gradient*

Defining Radial Color Gradients in String Format

You can also specify a radial color gradient in string format by using the static method valueOf(String colorString) of the RadialGradient class. Typically, the string format is used to specify a radial color gradient in a CSS file. It has the following syntax:

```
radial-gradient([focus-angle], [focus-distance], [center], radius, [cycle-method], color-
stops-list)
```

The arguments within square brackets are optional. If you do not specify an optional argument, the comma that follows needs to be excluded as well.

The default value for focus-angle and focus-distance is 0. You can specify the focus angle in degrees, radians, gradians, and turns. The focus distance is specified as a percentage of the radius. Examples are as follows:

- focus-angle 45.0deg

- focus-angle 0.5rad

- focus-angle 30.0grad

- focus-angle 0.125turn

- focus-distance 50%

The center and radius arguments are specified in a percentage relative to the region being filled or in absolute pixels. You cannot specify one argument in a percentage and the other in pixels. Both must be specified in the same unit. The default value for center is (0, 0) in the unit. Examples are as follows:

- center 50px 50px, radius 50px

- center 50% 50%, radius 50%

The valid values for the cycle-method argument are repeat and reflect. If this is not specified, it defaults to NO_CYCLE.

A list of color stops is specified using colors and their positions. Positions are specified as a percentage of distance on a line from the focus point to the periphery of the shape of the gradient. Please refer to the earlier discussion on specifying the color stops in a linear color gradient for more details. Examples are as follows:

- white, black

- white 0%, black 100%

- red, green, blue

- red 0%, green 80%, blue 100%

The following snippet of code will produce a circle, as shown in Figure 7-27:

```
String colorValue =
   "radial-gradient(focus-angle 45deg, focus-distance 50%, " +
   "center 50% 50%, radius 50%, white 0%, black 100%)";
RadialGradient rg = RadialGradient.valueOf(colorValue);
Circle c = new Circle(50, 50, 50);
c.setFill(rg);
```

Figure 7-27. *Using string format for specifying a radial color gradient*

Summary

In JavaFX, you can specify text color and background color for regions. You can specify a color as a uniform color, an image pattern, or a color gradient. A uniform color uses the same color to fill the entire region. An image pattern lets you fill a region with an image pattern. A color gradient defines a color pattern in which the color varies along a straight line from one color to another. The variation in a color gradient can be linear or radial. All classes are included in the javafx.scene.paint package.

The Paint class is an abstract class, and it is the base class for other color classes. A uniform color, an image pattern, a linear color gradient, and a radial color gradient are instances of the Color, ImagePattern, LinearGradient, and RadialGradient classes, respectively. The Stop class and the CycleMethod enum are used when working with color gradients. You can specify colors using instances of one of these classes or in string forms. When you use a CSS to style nodes, you specify colors using string forms.

An image pattern lets you fill a shape with an image. The image may fill the entire shape or use a tiling pattern.

A linear color gradient is defined using an axis known as a gradient line. Each point on the gradient line is of a different color. All points on a line that is perpendicular to the gradient line have the same color, which is the color of the point of intersection between the two lines. The gradient line is defined by a starting point and an ending point. Colors along the gradient line are defined at some points on the gradient line, which are known as stop-color points (or stop points). Colors between two stop points are computed using interpolation. The gradient line has a direction, which is from the starting point to the ending point. All points on a line perpendicular to the gradient line that passes through a stop point will have the color of the stop point. For example, suppose you have defined a stop point P1 with a color C1. If you draw a line perpendicular to the gradient line passing through the point P1, all points on that line will have the color C1.

In a radial color gradient, colors start at a single point, transitioning smoothly outward in a circular or elliptical shape. The shape is defined by a center point and a radius. The starting point of colors is known as the focus point of the gradient. The colors change along a line, starting at the focus point of the gradient, in all directions until the periphery of the shape is reached.

The next chapter will show you how to style nodes in a scene graph using CSS.

CHAPTER 8

■ ■ ■

Styling Nodes

In this chapter, you will learn:

- What a cascading style sheet is
- The difference between styles, skins, and themes
- Naming conventions of Cascading Style Sheets styles in JavaFX
- How to add style sheets to a scene
- How to use and override the default style sheet in a JavaFX application
- How to add inline styles for a node
- About the different types of cascading style sheet properties
- About cascading style sheets style selectors
- How to look up nodes in a scene graph using cascading style sheets selectors
- How to use compiled style sheets

The examples of this chapter lie in the `com.jdojo.style` package. In order for them to work, you must add a corresponding line to the `module-info.java` file:

```
...
opens com.jdojo.style to javafx.graphics, javafx.base;
...
```

What Is a Cascading Style Sheet?

A cascading style sheet (CSS) is a language used to describe the presentation (the look or the style) of UI elements in a GUI application. CSS was primarily developed for use in web pages for styling HTML elements. It allows for the separation of the presentation from the content and behavior. In a typical web page, the content and presentation are defined using HTML and CSS, respectively.

JavaFX allows you to define the look (or the style) of JavaFX applications using CSS. You can define UI elements using JavaFX class libraries or FXML and use CSS to define their look.

CSS provides the syntax to write rules to set the visual properties. A rule consists of a *selector* and a set of *property-value* pairs. A selector is a string that identifies the UI elements to which the rules will be applied. A property-value pair consists of a property name and its corresponding value separated by a colon (:).

© Kishori Sharan and Peter Späth 2022
K. Sharan and P. Späth, *Learn JavaFX 17*, https://doi.org/10.1007/978-1-4842-7848-2_8

Two property-value pairs are separated by a semicolon (;). The set of property-value pairs is enclosed within curly braces ({ }) preceded by the selector. An example of a rule in CSS is as follows:

```
.button {
        -fx-background-color: red;
        -fx-text-fill: white;
}
```

Here, .button is a selector, which specifies that the rule will apply to all buttons; -fx-background-color and -fx-text-fill are property names with their values set to red and white, respectively. When the preceding rule is applied, all buttons will have the red background color and white text color.

■ **Tip**   Using CSS in JavaFX is similar to using CSS with HTML. If you have worked with CSS and HTML before, the information in this chapter will sound familiar. Prior experience with CSS is not necessary to understand how to use CSS in JavaFX. This chapter covers all of the necessary material to enable you to use CSS in JavaFX.

What Are Styles, Skins, and Themes?

A CSS rule is also known as a *style*. A collection of CSS rules is known as a *style sheet*. *Styles*, *skins*, and *themes* are three related, and highly confused, concepts.

Styles provide a mechanism to separate the presentation and content of UI elements. They also facilitate grouping of visual properties and their values, so they can be shared by multiple UI elements. JavaFX lets you create styles using JavaFX CSS.

Skins are collections of application-specific styles, which define the appearance of an application. *Skinning* is the process of changing the appearance of an application (or the skin) on the fly. JavaFX does not provide a specific mechanism for skinning. However, using the JavaFX CSS and JavaFX API, available for the Scene class and other UI-related classes, you can provide skinning for your JavaFX application easily.

Themes are visual characteristics of an operating system that are reflected in the appearance of UI elements of all applications. For example, changing the theme on the Windows operating system changes the appearance of UI elements in all applications that are running. To contrast skins and themes, skins are application specific, whereas themes are operating system specific. It is typical to base skins on themes. That is, when the current theme is changed, you would change the skin of an application to match the theme. JavaFX has no direct support for themes.

A Quick Example

Let's look at a simple, though complete, example of using style sheets in JavaFX. You will set the background color and text color of all buttons to red and white, respectively. The code for the styles is shown in Listing 8-1.

Listing 8-1. The Content of the File buttonstyles.css

```
.button {
    -fx-background-color: red;
    -fx-text-fill: white;
}
```

Save the content of Listing 8-1 in a `buttonstyles.css` file under the `resources\css` directory. In order to access the resources folder from inside the code, we again use the `ResourceUtil` utility class we introduced at the beginning of Chapter 7.

A scene contains an `ObservableList` of string URLs of style sheets. You can get the reference of the `ObservableList` using the `getStylesheets()` method of the `Scene` class. The following snippet of code adds the URL for the `buttonstyles.css` style sheet to the scene:

```
Scene scene;
...
scene.getStylesheets().add(
    "file://path/to/folder/resources/css/buttonstyles.css");
```

The `ResourceUtil` class helps us to build the correct URL path.

Listing 8-2 contains the complete program, which shows three buttons with a red background and white text. If you get the following warning message and do not see the buttons in red background with white text, it indicates that you have not placed the `resources\css` directory in the correct folder; see the `ResourceUtil` class.

```
WARNING: com.sun.javafx.css.StyleManager loadStylesheetUnPrivileged Resource "resources/
css/buttonstyles.css" not found.
```

Listing 8-2. Using a Style Sheet to Change the Background and Text Colors for Buttons

```java
// ButtonStyleTest.java
package com.jdojo.style;

import com.jdojo.util.ResourceUtil;

import javafx.application.Application;
import javafx.scene.Scene;
import javafx.scene.control.Button;
import javafx.scene.layout.HBox;
import javafx.stage.Stage;

public class ButtonStyleTest extends Application {
    public static void main(String[] args) {
        Application.launch(args);
    }

    @Override
    public void start(Stage stage) {
        Button yesBtn = new Button("Yes");
        Button noBtn = new Button("No");
        Button cancelBtn = new Button("Cancel");

        HBox root = new HBox();
        root.getChildren().addAll(yesBtn, noBtn, cancelBtn);

        Scene scene = new Scene(root);
```

```
        // Add a style sheet to the scene
        var url = ResourceUtil.getResourceURLStr("css/buttonstyles.css");
        scene.getStylesheets().add(url);

        stage.setScene(scene);
        stage.setTitle("Styling Buttons");
        stage.show();
    }
}
```

Naming Conventions in JavaFX CSS

JavaFX uses slightly different naming conventions for the CSS style classes and properties. CSS style class names are based on the simple names of the JavaFX classes representing the node in a scene graph. All style class names are lowercased. For example, the style class name is button for the Button class. If the class name for the JavaFX node consists of multiple words, for example, TextField, a hyphen is inserted between two words to get the style class name. For example, the style classes for the TextField and CheckBox classes are text-field and check-box, respectively.

■ **Tip** It is important to understand the difference between a JavaFX class and a CSS style class. A JavaFX class is a Java class, for example, javafx.scene.control.Button. A CSS style class is used as a selector in a style sheet, for example, button in Listing 8-1.

Property names in JavaFX styles start with -fx-. For example, the property name font-size in normal CSS styles becomes -fx-font-size in JavaFX CSS style. JavaFX uses a convention to map the style property names to the instance variables. It takes an instance variable; it inserts a hyphen between two words; if the instance variable consists of multiple words, it converts the name to the lowercase and prefixes it with -fx-. For example, for an instance variable named textAlignment, the style property name would be -fx-text-alignment.

Adding Style Sheets

You can add multiple style sheets to a JavaFX application. Style sheets are added to a scene or parents. Scene and Parent classes maintain an observable list of string URLs linking to style sheets. Use the getStylesheets() method in the Scene and Parent classes to get the reference of the observable list and add additional URLs to the list. The following code would accomplish this:

```
// Add two style sheets, ss1.css and ss2.css to a scene
Scene scene = ...
scene.getStylesheets().addAll(
    "file://.../resources/css/ss1.css",
    "file://.../resources/css/ss2.css");

// Add a style sheet, vbox.css, to a VBox (a Parent)
VBox root = new VBox();
root.getStylesheets().add("file://.../vbox.css");
```

You have to substitute the "..." by the correct path, or again use the ResourceUtil class. Of course, you can also use http:// URLs, in case the style sheets are available through the Internet.

Default Style Sheet

In previous chapters, you developed JavaFX applications with UI elements without the use of any style sheets. However, the JavaFX runtime was always using a style sheet behind the scenes. The style sheet is named modena.css, which is known as the *default style sheet* or the *user-agent style sheet*. The default look that you get for a JavaFX application is defined in the default style sheet.

The modena.css file is packaged in the JavaFX runtime javafx.controls.jar file. If you want to know the details of how styles are set for specific nodes, you need to look at the modena.css file. You can extract this file using the following command:

```
jar -xf javafx.controls.jar ^
    com/sun/javafx/scene/control/skin/modena/modena.css
```

This command places the modena.css file in the com\sun\javafx\scene\control\skin\modena directory under the current directory. Note that the jar command is in the JAVA_HOME\bin directory.

Prior to JavaFX 8, Caspian was the default style sheet. Caspian is defined in the jfxrt.jar file in the file named com/sun/javafx/scene/control/skin/caspian/caspian.css. Since JavaFX 8, Modena is the default style sheet. The Application class defines two String constants named STYLESHEET_CASPIAN and STYLESHEET_MODENA to represent the two themes. Use the following static methods of the Application class to set and get the application-wide default style sheet:

- public static void setUserAgentStylesheet(String url)

- public static String getUserAgentStylesheet()

Use the setUserAgentStylesheet(String url) method to set an application-wide default. A value of null will restore the platform default style sheet. The following statement sets Caspian as the default style sheet:

```
Application.setUserAgentStylesheet(Application.STYLESHEET_CASPIAN);
```

Use the getUserAgentStylesheet() method to return the current default style sheet for the application. If one of the built-in style sheets is the default, it returns null.

Adding Inline Styles

CSS styles for a node in a scene graph may come from style sheets or an inline style. In the previous section, you learned how to add style sheets to the Scene and Parent objects. In this section, you will learn how to specify an inline style for a node.

The Node class has a style property that is of the StringProperty type. The style property holds the inline style for a node. You can use the setStyle(String inlineStyle) and getStyle() methods to set and get the inline style of a node.

There is a difference between a style in a style sheet and an inline style. A style in a style sheet consists of a selector and a set of property-value pairs, and it may affect zero or more nodes in a scene graph. The number of nodes affected by a style in a style sheet depends on the number of nodes that match the selector of the style. An inline style does not contain a selector. It consists of only set property-value pairs. An inline style affects the node on which it is set. The following snippet of code uses an inline style for a button to display its text in red and bold:

```
Button yesBtn = new Button("Yes");
yesBtn.setStyle("-fx-text-fill: red; -fx-font-weight: bold;");
```

Listing 8-3 displays six buttons. It uses two VBox instances to hold three buttons. It places both VBox instances into an HBox. Inline styles are used to set a 4.0px blue border for both VBox instances. The inline style for the HBox sets a 10.0px navy border. The resulting screen is shown in Figure 8-1.

Listing 8-3. Using Inline Styles

```java
// InlineStyles.java
package com.jdojo.style;

import javafx.application.Application;
import javafx.geometry.Insets;
import javafx.scene.Scene;
import javafx.scene.control.Button;
import javafx.scene.layout.HBox;
import javafx.scene.layout.VBox;
import javafx.stage.Stage;

public class InlineStyles extends Application {
        public static void main(String[] args) {
                Application.launch(args);
        }

        @Override
        public void start(Stage stage) {
                Button yesBtn = new Button("Yes");
                Button noBtn = new Button("No");
                Button cancelBtn = new Button("Cancel");

                // Add an inline style to the Yes button
                yesBtn.setStyle(
                        "-fx-text-fill: red; -fx-font-weight: bold;");

                Button openBtn = new Button("Open");
                Button saveBtn = new Button("Save");
                Button closeBtn = new Button("Close");

                VBox vb1 = new VBox();
                vb1.setPadding(new Insets(10, 10, 10, 10));
                vb1.getChildren().addAll(yesBtn, noBtn, cancelBtn);

                VBox vb2 = new VBox();
                vb2.setPadding(new Insets(10, 10, 10, 10));
                vb2.getChildren().addAll(openBtn, saveBtn, closeBtn);

                // Add a border to VBoxes using an inline style
                vb1.setStyle(
                        "-fx-border-width: 4.0; -fx-border-color: blue;");
                vb2.setStyle(
                        "-fx-border-width: 4.0; -fx-border-color: blue;");
```

```
        HBox root = new HBox();
        root.setSpacing(20);
        root.setPadding(new Insets(10, 10, 10, 10));
        root.getChildren().addAll(vb1, vb2);

        // Add a border to the HBox using an inline style
        root.setStyle(
                "-fx-border-width: 10.0; -fx-border-color: navy;");

        Scene scene = new Scene(root);
        stage.setScene(scene);
        stage.setTitle("Using Inline Styles");
        stage.show();
    }
}
```

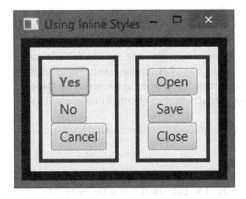

Figure 8-1. *A button, two VBox instances, and an HBox using inline styles*

Priorities of Styles for a Node

In a JavaFX application, it is possible, and very common, for the visual properties of nodes to come from multiple sources. For example, the font size of a button can be set by the JavaFX runtime, style sheets can be added to the parent and the scene of the button, an inline style can be set for the button, and programmatically can be added using the setFont(Font f) method. If the value for the font size of a button is available from multiple sources, JavaFX uses a rule to decide the source whose value is to be used.

Consider the following snippet of code along with the stylespriorities.css style sheet whose content is shown in Listing 8-4:

```
Button yesBtn = new Button("Yes");
yesBtn.setStyle("-fx-font-size: 16px");
yesBtn.setFont(new Font(10));

Scene scene = new Scene(yesBtn);
scene.getStylesheets().addAll(
    "file://pat/to/resources/css/stylespriorities.css");
...
```

Listing 8-4. The Content of the `stylespriorities.css` File

```
.button {
        -fx-font-size: 24px;
        -fx-font-weight: bold;
}
```

What will be the font size of the button? Will it be the default font size set by the JavaFX runtime, 24px, declared in the `stylespriorities.css`, 16px set by the inline style, or 10px set by the program using the `setFont()` method? The correct answer is 16px, which is set by the inline style.

The JavaFX runtime uses the following priority rules to set the visual properties of a node. The source with a higher priority that has a value for a property is used:

- Inline style (the highest priority)

- Parent style sheets

- Scene style sheets

- Values set in the code using the JavaFX API

- User agent style sheets (the lowest priority)

The style sheet added to the parent of a node is given higher priority than the style sheets added to the scene. This enables developers to have custom styles for different branches of the scene graph. For example, you can use two style sheets that set properties of buttons differently: one for buttons in the scene and one for buttons in any `HBox`. Buttons in an `HBox` will use styles from its parent, whereas all other buttons will use styles from the scene.

The values set using the JavaFX API, for example, the `setFont()` method, have the second lowest priority.

▪ **Note** It is a common mistake to set the same properties of a node in a style sheet and code using the Java API. In that case, the styles in the style sheet win, and developers spend countless hours trying to find the reasons why the properties set in the code are not taking effect.

The lowest priority is given to style sheets used by the user agent. What is a user agent? A user agent, in general, is a program that interprets a document and applies style sheets to the document to format, print, or read. For example, a web browser is a user agent that applies default formatting to HTML documents. In our case, the user agent is the JavaFX runtime, which uses the `modena.css` style sheet for providing the default look for all UI nodes.

▪ **Tip** The default font size that is inherited by nodes is determined by the system font size. Not all nodes use fonts. Fonts are used by only those nodes that display text, for example, a `Button` or a `CheckBox`. To experiment with the default font, you can change the system font and check it in code using the `getFont()` method of those nodes.

Listing 8-5 demonstrates the priority rules for choosing a style from multiple sources. It adds the style sheet, as shown in Listing 8-4, to the scene. The resulting screen is shown in Figure 8-2.

Listing 8-5. Testing Priorities of Styles for a Node

```java
// StylesPriorities.java
package com.jdojo.style;

import com.jdojo.util.ResourceUtil;

import javafx.application.Application;
import javafx.scene.Scene;
import javafx.scene.control.Button;
import javafx.scene.layout.HBox;
import javafx.scene.text.Font;
import javafx.stage.Stage;

public class StylesPriorities extends Application {
    public static void main(String[] args) {
        Application.launch(args);
    }

    @Override
    public void start(Stage stage) {
        Button yesBtn = new Button("Yes");
        Button noBtn = new Button("No");
        Button cancelBtn = new Button("Cancel");

        // Change the font size for the Yes button
        // using two methods: inline style and JavaFX API
        yesBtn.setStyle("-fx-font-size: 16px");
        yesBtn.setFont(new Font(10));

        // Change the font size for the No button using the JavaFX API
        noBtn.setFont(new Font(8));

        HBox root = new HBox();
        root.setSpacing(10);
        root.getChildren().addAll(yesBtn, noBtn, cancelBtn);

        Scene scene = new Scene(root);

        // Add a style sheet to the scene
        var url = ResourceUtil.getResourceURLStr(
            "css/stylespriorities.css");
        scene.getStylesheets().addAll(url);

        stage.setScene(scene);
        stage.setTitle("Styles Priorities");
        stage.show();
    }
}
```

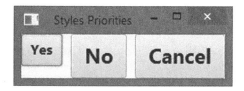

Figure 8-2. *Nodes using styles from different sources*

The font size value for the Yes button comes from four sources:

- Inline style (16px)

- Style sheet added to the scene (24px)

- JavaFX API (10px)

- Default font size set by the user agent (the JavaFX runtime)

The Yes button gets a 16px font size from its inline style, because that has the highest priority. The font size value for the No button comes from three sources:

- Style sheet added to the scene (24px)

- JavaFX API (10px)

- Default font size set by the user agent (the JavaFX runtime)

The No button gets a 24px font size from the style sheet added to the scene because that has the highest priority among the three available sources.

The font size value for the Cancel button comes from two sources:

- Style sheet added to the scene (24px)

- Default font size set by the user agent (the JavaFX runtime)

The Cancel button gets a 24px font size from the style sheet added to the scene, because that has the highest priority between the two available sources. The text for all buttons are shown in bold, because you have used the "-fx-font-weight: bold;" style in the style sheet, and this property value is not overridden by any other sources.

At this point, several questions may arise in your mind:

- How do you let the Cancel button use the default font size that is set by the JavaFX runtime?

- How do you use one font size (or any other properties) for buttons if they are inside an HBox and use another font size if they are inside a VBox?

You can achieve all these and several other effects using appropriate selectors for a style declared in a style sheet. I will discuss different types of selectors supported by JavaFX CSS shortly.

Inheriting CSS Properties

JavaFX offers two types of inheritance for CSS properties:

- Inheritance of CSS property types

- Inheritance of CSS property values

In the first type of inheritance, all CSS properties declared in a JavaFX class are inherited by all its subclasses. For example, the Node class declares a cursor property, and its corresponding CSS property is -fx-cursor. Because the Node class is the superclass of all JavaFX nodes, the -fx-cursor CSS property is available for all node types.

In the second type of inheritance, a CSS property for a node may inherit its value from its parent. The parent of a node is the container of the node in the scene graph, not its JavaFX superclass. The values of some properties of a node are inherited from its parent by default, and for some, the node needs to specify explicitly that it wants to inherit the values of the properties from its parent.

You can specify inherit as the value for a CSS property of a node if you want the value to be inherited from its parent. If a node inherits a CSS property from its parent by default, you do not need to do anything, that is, you do not even need to specify the property value as inherit. If you want to override the inherited value, you need to specify the value explicitly (overriding the parent's value).

Listing 8-6 demonstrates how a node inherits the CSS properties of its parent. It adds two buttons, OK and Cancel, to HBox. The following CSS properties are set on the parent and the OK button. No CSS properties are set on the Cancel button:

```
/* Parent Node (HBox)*/
-fx-cursor: hand;
-fx-border-color: blue;
-fx-border-width: 5px;

/* Child Node (OK Button)*/
-fx-border-color: red;
-fx-border-width: inherit;
```

The -fx-cursor CSS property is declared in the Node class and is inherited by all nodes by default. The HBox overrides the default value and overrides it to the HAND cursor. Both the OK and Cancel buttons inherit the HAND cursor value for their -fx-cursor from their parent, HBox. When you point your mouse to the area occupied by the HBox and these buttons, your mouse pointer will change to a HAND cursor. You can use the "-fx-cursor: inherit" style on the OK and Cancel buttons to achieve the same functionality you get by default.

Border-related CSS properties are not inherited by nodes by default. The HBox sets its -fx-border-color to blue and -fx-border-width to 5px. The OK button sets its -fx-border-color to red and -fx-border-width to inherit. The inherit value will make the -fx-border-width of the OK button to inherit from its parent (the HBox), which is 5px. Figure 8-3 shows the changes after adding this coding.

Listing 8-6. Inheriting CSS Properties from the Parent Node

```java
// CSSInheritance.java
package com.jdojo.style;

import javafx.application.Application;
import javafx.scene.Scene;
import javafx.scene.control.Button;
import javafx.scene.layout.HBox;
import javafx.stage.Stage;

public class CSSInheritance extends Application {
        public static void main(String[] args) {
                Application.launch(args);
        }
```

```
@Override
public void start(Stage stage) {
        Button okBtn = new Button("OK");
        Button cancelBtn = new Button("Cancel");

        HBox root = new HBox(10); // 10px spacing
        root.getChildren().addAll(okBtn, cancelBtn);

        // Set styles for the OK button and its parent HBox
        root.setStyle(
   "-fx-cursor: hand;-fx-border-color: blue;-fx-border-width: 5px;");
        okBtn.setStyle(
   "-fx-border-color: red;-fx-border-width: inherit;");

        Scene scene = new Scene(root);
        stage.setScene(scene);
        stage.setTitle("CSS Inheritance");
        stage.show();
    }
}
```

Figure 8-3. *A button inheriting its border width and cursor CSS properties from its parent*

■ **Tip** A node inherits -fx-cursor, -fx-text-alignment, and -fx-font CSS properties from its parent by default.

Types of CSS Properties

All values in Java (and in JavaFX as well) have a type. The values of CSS properties set in styles also have types. Each type of value has a different syntax. JavaFX CSS supports the following types:

- inherit
- boolean
- string
- number, integer
- size
- length

- percentage
- angle
- duration
- point
- color-stop
- uri
- effect
- font
- paint
- color

Note that the CSS types have nothing to do with Java types. They can only be used in specifying the values in CSS style sheets or inline styles. The JavaFX runtime takes care of parsing and converting these types to appropriate JavaFX types before assigning them to nodes.

The *inherit* Type

You have seen an example of the use of the inherit type in the previous section. It is used to inherit the value of a CSS property for a node from its parent.

The *boolean* Type

You can specify the boolean type values as true or false. They can also be specified as strings: "true" or "false". The following style sets the -fx-display-caret CSS property of a TextField node to false:

```
.text-field {
        -fx-display-caret: false;
}
```

The *string* Type

String values can be enclosed in single quotes or double quotes. If the string value is enclosed in double quotes, a double quote as part of the value should be escaped, such as \" or \22. Similarly, a single quote as part of the string value enclosed in single quotes must be escaped, such as \' or \27. The following style uses strings to set the skin and font properties. It encloses the string value for the skin property in double quotes and the font family for the font property in single quotes:

```
.my-control {
        -fx-skin: "com.jdojo.MySkin";
        -fx-font: normal bold 20px 'serif';
}
```

▦ **Tip** A string value cannot contain a newline directly. To embed a newline in a string value, use the escape sequence \A or \00000a.

The *number* and *integer* Types

Number values may be represented as integers or real numbers. They are specified using the decimal number format. The following style sets the opacity to 0.60:

```
.my-style {
        -fx-opacity: 0.60;
}
```

The value of a CSS property denoting a size can be specified using a number followed by a unit of length. The unit of length can be px (pixels), mm (millimeters), cm (centimeters), in (inches), pt (points), pc (picas), em, or ex. A size can also be specified using the percentage of a length, for example, the width or height of a node. If a unit of a percentage is specified, it must immediately follow the number, for example, 12px, 2em, 80%:

```
.my-style {
        -fx-font-size: 12px;
        -fx-background-radius: 0.5em;
        -fx-border-width: 5%;
}
```

The *size* Type

A size is a number with units of length or percentage; see the number type earlier.

The length and percentage Types

A length is a number plus one of px, mm, cm, in, pt, pc, em, ex. A percentage is a number plus a "%" sign.

The *angle* Type

An angle is specified using a number and a unit. The unit of an angle can be deg (degrees), rad (radians), grad (gradients), or turn (turns). The following style sets the -fx-rotate CSS property to 45 degrees:

```
.my-style {
        -fx-rotate: 45deg;
}
```

The *duration* Type

A duration is a number plus a duration unit, one of "s" (second), "ms" (millisecond), or "indefinite."

The *point* Type

A point is specified using x and y coordinates. It can be specified using two numbers separated by whitespaces, for example, 0 0, 100 0, 90 67, or in percentage form, for example, 2% 2%. The following style specifies a linear gradient color from the point (0, 0) to (100, 0):

```
.my-style {
        -fx-background-color: linear-gradient(from 0 0 to 100 0, repeat,
            red, blue);
}
```

The *color-stop* Type

A color-stop is used to specify color at a specific distance in linear or radial color gradients. A color-stop consists of a color and a stop distance. The color and the distance are separated by whitespaces. The stop distance may be specified as a percentage, for example, 10%, or as a length, for example, 65px. Some examples of color-stops are white 0%, yellow 50%, and yellow 100px. Please refer to Chapter 7 for more details on how to use color-stops in colors.

The *URI* Type

A URI can be specified using the url(<address>) function. A relative <address> is resolved relative to the location of the CSS file:

```
.image-view {
        -fx-image: url("http://jdojo.com/myimage.png");
}
```

The *effect* Type

Drop shadow and inner shadow effects can be specified for nodes using CSS styles using the dropshadow() and innershadow() CSS functions, respectively. Their signatures are

- dropshadow(<blur-type>, <color>, <radius>, <spread>, <x-offset>, <y-offset>)

- innershadow(<blur-type>, <color>, <radius>, <choke>, <x-offset>, <y-offset>)

The <blur-type> value can be Gaussian, one-pass-box, three-pass-box, or two-pass-box. The color of the shadow is specified in <color>. The <radius> value specifies the radius of the shadow blur kernel between 0.0 and 127.0. The spread/choke of the shadow is specified between 0.0 and 1.0. The last two parameters specify the shadow offsets in pixels in x and y directions. The following styles show how to specify the values for the -fx-effect CSS property:

```
.drop-shadow-1 {
        -fx-effect: dropshadow(gaussian, gray, 10, 0.6, 10, 10);
}

.drop-shadow-2 {
        -fx-effect: dropshadow(one-pass-box, gray, 10, 0.6, 10, 10);
}

.inner-shadow-1 {
        -fx-effect: innershadow(gaussian, gray, 10, 0.6, 10, 10);
}
```

The *font* Type

A font consists of four attributes: family, size, style, and weight. There are two ways to specify the font CSS property:

- Specify the four attributes of a font separately using the four CSS properties: `-fx-font-family`, `-fx-font-size`, `-fx-font-style`, and `-fx-font-weight`.

- Use a shorthand CSS property `-fx-font` to specify all four attributes as one value.

The font family is a string value that can be the actual font family available on the system, for example, `"Arial"`, `"Times"`, or generic family names, for example, `"serif"`, `"sans-serif"`, `"monospace"`.

The font size can be specified in units such as `px`, `em`, `pt`, `in`, and `cm`. If the unit for the font size is omitted, `px` (pixels) is assumed.

The font style can be `normal`, `italic`, or `oblique`.

The font weight can be specified as `normal`, `bold`, `bolder`, `lighter`, 100, 200, 300, 400, 500, 600, 700, 800, or 900.

The following style sets the font attributes separately:

```
.my-font-style {
        -fx-font-family: "serif";
        -fx-font-size: 20px;
        -fx-font-style: normal;
        -fx-font-weight: bolder;
}
```

Another way to specify the font property is to combine all four attributes of the font into one value and use the `-fx-font` CSS property. The syntax for using the `-fx-font` property is

```
-fx-font: <font-style> <font-weight> <font-size> <font-family>;
```

The following style uses the `-fx-font` CSS property to set the font attributes:

```
.my-font-style {
        -fx-font: italic bolder 20px "serif";
}
```

The *paint* and *color* Types

A paint type value specifies a color, for example, the fill color of a rectangle or the background color of a button. You can specify a color value in the following ways:

- Using the linear-gradient() function
- Using the radial-gradient() function
- Using various color values and color functions

Please refer to Chapter 7 for a complete discussion on how to specify gradient colors in string format using the linear-gradient() and radial-gradient() functions. These functions are used to specify color gradients. The following style shows how to use these functions:

```
.my-style {
    -fx-fill: linear-gradient(from 0% 0% to 100% 0%, black 0%, red 100%);
    -fx-background-color: radial-gradient(radius 100%, black, red);
}
```

You can specify a solid color in several ways:

- Using named colors
- Using looked-up colors
- Using the rgb() and rgba() functions
- Using red, green, blue (RGB) hexadecimal notation
- Using the hsb() or hsba() function
- Using color functions: derive() and ladder()

You can use predefined color names to specify the color values, for example, red, blue, green, or aqua:

```
.my-style {
    -fx-background-color: red;
}
```

You can define a color as a CSS property on a node or any of its parents and, later, look it up by name, when you want to use its value. The following styles define a color named my-color and refer to it later:

```
.root {
    my-color: black;
}

.my-style {
    -fx-fill: my-color;
}
```

You can use the rgb(red, green, blue) and the rgba(red, green, blue, alpha) functions to define colors in terms of RGB components:

```
.my-style-1 {
    -fx-fill: rgb(0, 0, 255);
}
```

```
.my-style-2 {
      -fx-fill: rgba(0, 0, 255, 0.5);
}
```

You can specify a color value in the #rrggbb or #rgb format, where rr, gg, and bb are the values for red, green, and blue components, respectively, in hexadecimal format. Note that you need to specify the three components using two digits or one hexadecimal digit. You cannot specify some components in one hexadecimal digit and others in two:

```
.my-style-1 {
      -fx-fill: #0000ff;
}

.my-style-2 {
      -fx-fill: #0bc;
}
```

You can specify a color value in hue, saturation, and brightness (HSB) color components using the hsb(hue, saturation, brightness) or hsba(hue, saturation, brightness, alpha) function:

```
.my-style-1 {
      -fx-fill: hsb(200, 70%, 40%);
}

.my-style-2 {
      -fx-fill: hsba(200, 70%, 40%, 0.30);
}
```

You can compute colors from other colors using the derive() and ladder() functions. The JavaFX default CSS, modena.css, uses this technique. It defines some base colors and derives other colors from the base colors.

The derive function takes two parameters:

```
derive(color, brightness)
```

The derive() function derives a brighter or darker version of the specified color. The brightness value ranges from –100% to 100%. A brightness of –100% means completely black, 0% means no change in brightness, and 100% means completely white. The following style will use a version of red that is 20% darker:

```
.my-style {
      -fx-fill: derive(red, -20%);
}
```

The ladder() function takes a color and one or more color-stops as parameters:

```
ladder(color, color-stop-1, color-stop-2, ...)
```

Think of the ladder() function as creating a gradient using the color-stops and then using the brightness of the specified color to return the color value. If the brightness of the specified color is x%, the color at the x% distance from the beginning of the gradient will be returned. For example, for 0% brightness, the color at the 0.0 end of the gradient is returned; for 40% brightness, the color at the 0.4 end of the gradient is returned.

Consider the following two styles:

```
.root {
        my-base-text-color: red;
}

.my-style {
        -fx-text-fill: ladder(my-base-text-color, white 29%, black 30%);
}
```

The ladder() function will return the color white or black depending on the brightness of the my-base-text-color. If its brightness is 29% or lower, white is returned; otherwise, black is returned. You can specify as many color-stops as you want in the ladder() function to choose from a variety of colors depending on the brightness of the specified color.

You can use this technique to change the color of a JavaFX application on the fly. The default style sheet, modena.css, defines some base colors and uses the derive() and ladder() functions to derive other colors of different brightnesses. You need to redefine the base colors in your style sheet for the root class to make an application-wide color change.

Specifying Background Colors

A node (a Region and a Control) can have multiple background fills, which are specified using three properties:

- -fx-background-color
- -fx-background-radius
- -fx-background-insets

The -fx-background-color property is a list of comma-separated color values. The number of colors in the list determines the number of rectangles that will be painted. You need to specify the radius values for four corners and insets for four sides, for each rectangle, using the other two properties. The number of color values must match the number of radius values and inset values.

The -fx-background-radius property is a list of a comma-separated set of four radius values for the rectangles to be filled. A set of radius values in the list may specify only one value, for example, 10, or four values separated by whitespaces, for example, 10 5 15 20. The radius values are specified for the top-left, top-right, bottom-right, and bottom-left corners in order. If only one radius value is specified, the same radius value is used for all corners.

The -fx-background-insets property is a list of a comma-separated set of four inset values for the rectangles to be filled. A set of inset values in the list may specify only one value, for example, 10, or four values separated by whitespaces, for example, 10 5 15 20. The inset values are specified for the top, right, bottom, and left sides in order. If only one inset value is specified, the same inset value is used for all sides.

Let's look at an example. The following snippet of code creates a Pane, which is a subclass of the Region class:

```
Pane pane = new Pane();
pane.setPrefSize(100, 100);
```

Figure 8-4 shows how the Pane looks when the following three styles are supplied:

```
.my-style-1 {
        -fx-background-color: gray;
        -fx-background-insets: 5;
        -fx-background-radius: 10;
}

.my-style-2 {
        -fx-background-color: gray;
        -fx-background-insets: 0;
        -fx-background-radius: 0;
}

.my-style-3 {
        -fx-background-color: gray;
        -fx-background-insets: 5 10 15 20;
        -fx-background-radius: 10 0 0 5;
}
```

my-style-1   my-style-2   my-style-3

Figure 8-4. *A Pane with three different background fills*

All three styles use a gray fill color, which means that only one rectangle will be drawn. The first style uses a 5px inset on all four sides and a radius of 10px for all corners. The second style uses a 0px inset and a 0px radius, which makes the fill rectangle occupy the entire area of the pane. The third style uses a different inset on each side: 5px on the top, 10px on the right, 15px on the bottom, and 20px on the left. Notice the different unfilled background on each side for the third style. The third style also sets different values for the radius of four corners: 10px for the top left, 0px for the top right, 0px for the bottom right, and 5px for the bottom left. Notice that if the radius of a corner is 0px, the two sides at the corner meet at 90 degrees.

If you apply the following style to the same pane, the background will be filled as shown in Figure 8-5:

```
.my-style-4 {
        -fx-background-color: red, green, blue;
        -fx-background-insets: 5 5 5 5, 10 15 10 10, 15 20 15 15;
        -fx-background-radius: 5 5 5 5, 0 0 10 10, 0 20 5 10;
}
```

Figure 8-5. *A pane with three background fills with different radius and inset values*

The style uses three colors, and, therefore, three background rectangles will be painted. The background rectangles are painted in the order they are specified in the style: red, green, and blue. The inset and radius values are specified in the same order as the colors. The style uses the same value for insets and radii for the red color. You can replace the set of four similar values with one value; that is, 5 5 5 5 in the preceding style can be replaced with 5.

Specifying Borders

A node (a Region and a Control) can have multiple borders through CSS. A border is specified using five properties:

- -fx-border-color
- -fx-border-width
- -fx-border-radius
- -fx-border-insets
- -fx-border-style

Each property consists of a comma-separated list of items. Each item may consist of a set of values, which are separated by whitespaces.

Border Colors

The number of items in the list for the -fx-border-color property determines the number of borders that are painted. The following style will paint one border with the red color:

```
-fx-border-color: red;
```

The following style specifies a set of red, green, blue, and aqua colors to paint the borders on top, right, bottom, and left sides, respectively. Note that it still results in only one border, not four borders, with different colors on four sides:

```
-fx-border-color: red green blue aqua;
```

The following style specifies two sets of border colors:

```
-fx-border-color: red green blue aqua, tan;
```

The first set consists of four colors, red green blue aqua, and the second set consists of only one color, tan. It will result in two borders. The first border will be painted with different colors on four sides; the second border will use the same color on all four sides.

215

■ **Tip** A node may not be rectangular in shape. In that case, only the first border color (and other properties) in the set will be used to paint the entire border.

Border Widths

You can specify the width for borders using the `-fx-border-width` property. You have an option to specify different widths for all four sides of a border. Different border widths are specified for top, right, bottom, and left sides in order. If the unit for the width value is not specified, pixel is used.

The following style specifies one border with all sides painted in red in 2px width:

```
-fx-border-color: red;
-fx-border-width: 2;
```

The following style specifies three borders, as determined by the three sets of colors specified in the `-fx-border-color` property. The first two borders use different border widths of four sides. The third border uses the border width of 3px on all sides:

```
-fx-border-color: red green blue black, tan, aqua;
-fx-border-width: 2 1 2 2, 2 2 2 1, 3;
```

Border Radii

You can specify the radius values for four corners of a border using the `-fx-border-radius` property. You can specify the same radius value for all corners. Different radius values are specified for top-left, top-right, bottom-right, and bottom-left corners in order. If the unit for the radius value is not specified, pixel is used.

The following style specifies one border in red, 2px width, and 5px radii on all four corners:

```
-fx-border-color: red;
-fx-border-width: 2;
-fx-border-radius: 5;
```

The following style specifies three borders. The first two borders use different radius values for four corners. The third border uses the radius value of 0px for all corners:

```
-fx-border-color: red green blue black, tan, aqua;
-fx-border-width: 2 1 2 2, 2 2 2 1, 3;
-fx-border-radius: 5 2 0 2, 0 2 0 1, 0;
```

Border Insets

You can specify the inset values for four sides of a border using the `-fx-border-insets` property. You can specify the same inset value for all sides. Different inset values are specified for top, right, bottom, and left sides in order. If the unit for the inset value is not specified, pixel is used.

The following style specifies one border in red, 2px width, 5px radius, and 20px inset on all four sides:

```
-fx-border-color: red;
-fx-border-width: 2;
-fx-border-radius: 5;
-fx-border-insets: 20;
```

The following style specifies three borders with insets 10px, 20px, and 30px on all sides:

```
-fx-border-color: red green blue black, tan, aqua;
-fx-border-width: 2 1 2 2, 2 2 2 1, 3;
-fx-border-radius: 5 2 0 2, 0 2 0 1, 0;
-fx-border-insets: 10, 20, 30;
```

■ **Tip** An inset is the distance from the side of the node at which the border will be painted. The final location of the border also depends on other properties, for example, -fx-border-width and -fx-border-style.

Border Styles

The -fx-border-style property defines the style of a border. Its value may contain several parts as follows:

```
-fx-border-style: <dash-style> [phase <number>] [<stroke-type>] [line-join <line-join-value>] [line-cap <line-cap-value>]
```

The value for <dash-style> can be none, solid, dotted, dashed, or segments(<number>, <number>...). The value for <stroke-type> can be centered, inside, or outside. The value for <line-join-value> can be miter <number>, bevel, or round. The value for <line-cap-value> can be square, butt, or round.

The simplest border style would be to specify just the value for the <dash-style>:

```
-fx-border-style: solid;
```

The segments() function is used to have a border with a pattern using alternate dashes and gaps:

```
-fx-border-style: segments(dash-length, gap-length, dash-length, ...);
```

The first argument to the function is the length of the dash; the second argument is the length of the gap; and so on. After the last argument, the pattern repeats itself from the beginning. The following style will paint a border with a pattern of a 10px dash, a 5px gap, a 10px dash, and so on:

```
-fx-border-style: segments(10px, 5px);
```

You can pass as many dashes and gap segments to the function as you want. The function expects you to pass an even number of values. If you pass an odd number of values, this will result in values that are concatenated to make them even in number. For example, if you use segments(20px, 10px, 5px), it is the same as if you passed segments(20px, 10px, 5px, 20px, 10px, 5px).

The phase parameter is applicable only when you use the segments() function. The number following the phase parameter specifies the offset into the dashed pattern that corresponds to the beginning of the stroke. Consider the following style:

```
-fx-border-style: segments(20px, 5px) phase 10.0;
```

It specifies the phase parameter as 10.0. The length of the dashing pattern is 25px. The first segment will start at 10px from the beginning of the pattern. That is, the first dash will only be 10px in length. The second segment will be a 5px gap followed by a 20px dash, and so on. The default value for phase is 0.0.

The <stroke-type> has three valid values: centered, inside, and outside. Its value determines where the border is drawn relative to the inset. Assume that you have a 200px by 200px region. Assume that you have specified the top inset as 10px and a top border width of 4px. If <stroke-type> is specified as centered, the border thickness at the top will occupy the area from the 8th pixel to the 12th pixel from the top boundary of the region. For <stroke-type> as inside, the border thickness will occupy the area from the 10th pixel to the 14th pixel. For <stroke-type> as outside, the border thickness at the top will occupy the area from the sixth pixel to the tenth pixel.

You can specify how the two segments of the borders are joined using the line-join parameter. Its value can be miter, bevel, or round. If you specify the value of line-join as miter, you need to pass a miter limit value. If the specified miter limit is less than the miter length, a bevel join is used instead. Miter length is the distance between the inner point and the outer point of a miter join. Miter length is measured in terms of the border width. The miter limit parameter specifies how far the outside edges of two meeting border segments can extend to form a miter join. For example, suppose the miter length is 5 and you specify the miter limit as 4, a bevel join is used; however, if you specify a miter limit greater than 5, a miter join is used. The following style uses a miter limit of 30:

```
-fx-border-style: solid line-join miter 30;
```

The value for the line-cap parameter specifies how the start and end of a border segment are drawn. The valid values are square, butt, and round. The following style specifies a line-cap of round:

```
-fx-border-style: solid line-join bevel 30 line-cap round;
```

Let's look at some examples. Figure 8-6 shows four instances of the Pane class of 100px by 50px, when the following styles are applied to them:

```
.my-style-1 {
        -fx-border-color: black;
        -fx-border-width: 5;
        -fx-border-radius: 0;
        -fx-border-insets: 0;
        -fx-border-style: solid line-join bevel line-cap square;
}

.my-style-2 {
        -fx-border-color: red, black;
        -fx-border-width: 5, 5;
        -fx-border-radius: 0, 0;
        -fx-border-insets: 0, 5;
        -fx-border-style: solid inside, dotted outside;
}
```

```
.my-style-3 {
        -fx-border-color: black, black;
        -fx-border-width: 1, 1;
        -fx-border-radius: 0, 0;
        -fx-border-insets: 0, 5;
        -fx-border-style: solid centered, solid centered;
}

.my-style-4 {
        -fx-border-color: red black red black;
        -fx-border-width: 5;
        -fx-border-radius: 0;
        -fx-border-insets: 0;
        -fx-border-style: solid line-join bevel line-cap round;
}
```

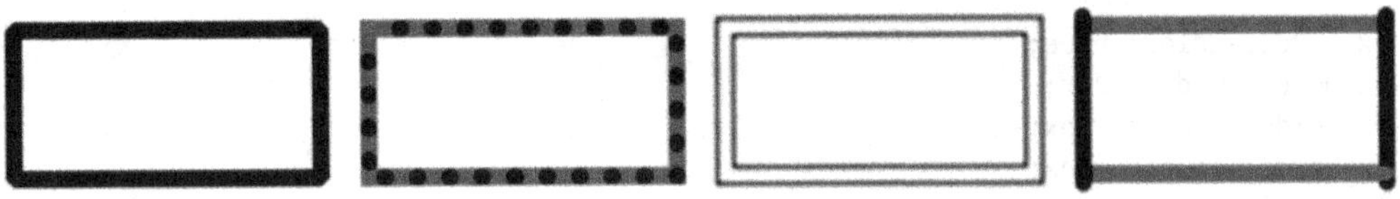

| my-style-1 | my-style-2 | my-style-3 | my-style-4 |

Figure 8-6. *Using border styles*

Notice that the second style achieves overlapping of two borders, one in solid red and one in dotted black, by specifying the appropriate insets and stroke type (inside and outside). Borders are drawn in the order they are specified. It is important that you draw the solid border first in this case; otherwise, you would not see the dotted border. The third one draws two borders, giving it the look of a double border type.

■ **Tip** A Region can also have a background image and a border image specified through CSS. Please refer to the *JavaFX CSS Reference Guide*, which is available online, for more details. Many other CSS styles are supported by nodes in JavaFX. The styles for those nodes will be discussed later in this book.

Understanding Style Selectors

Each style in a style sheet has an associated *selector* that identifies the nodes in the scene graph to which the associated JavaFX CSS property values are applied. JavaFX CSS supports several types of selectors: class selectors, pseudo-class selectors, and ID selectors, among others. Let's look at some of these selector types briefly.

Using Class Selectors

The Node class defines a styleClass variable that is an ObservableList<String>. Its purpose is to maintain a list of JavaFX style class names for a node. Note that the JavaFX class name and the style class name of a node are two different things. A JavaFX class name of a node is a Java class name, for example, javafx. scene.layout.VBox, or simply VBox, which is used to create objects of that class. A style class name of a node is a string name that is used in CSS styling.

You can assign multiple CSS class names to a node. The following snippet of code assigns two style class names, "hbox" and "myhbox", to an HBox:

```
HBox hb = new HBox();
hb.getStyleClass().addAll("hbox", "myhbox");
```

A style class selector applies the associated style to all nodes, which have the same style class name as the name of the selector. A style class selector starts with a period followed by the style class name. Note that the style class names of nodes do not start with a period.

Listing 8-7 shows the content of a style sheet. It has two styles. Both styles use style class selectors because both of them start with a period. The first style class selector is "hbox", which means it will match all nodes with a style class named hbox. The second style uses the style class name as button. Save the style sheet in a file named resources\css\styleclass.css in the CLASSPATH.

Listing 8-7. A Style Sheet with Two Style Class Selectors Named hbox and button

```
.hbox {
        -fx-border-color: blue;
        -fx-border-width: 2px;
        -fx-border-radius: 5px;
        -fx-border-insets: 5px;
        -fx-padding: 10px;
        -fx-spacing: 5px;
        -fx-background-color: lightgray;
        -fx-background-insets: 5px;
}

.button {
        -fx-text-fill: blue;
}
```

Listing 8-8 has the complete program to demonstrate the use of the style class selectors hbox and button. The resulting screen is shown in Figure 8-7.

Listing 8-8. Using Style Class Selectors in Code

```
// StyleClassTest.java
package com.jdojo.style;

import javafx.application.Application;
import javafx.application.Platform;
import javafx.scene.Scene;
import javafx.scene.control.Button;
import javafx.scene.control.Label;
import javafx.scene.control.TextField;
import javafx.scene.layout.HBox;
import javafx.stage.Stage;

public class StyleClassTest extends Application {
        public static void main(String[] args) {
                Application.launch(args);
        }
```

```
@Override
public void start(Stage stage) {
        Label nameLbl = new Label("Name:");
        TextField nameTf = new TextField("");
        Button closeBtn  = new Button("Close");
        closeBtn.setOnAction(e -> Platform.exit());

        HBox root = new HBox();
        root.getChildren().addAll(nameLbl, nameTf, closeBtn);

        // Set the styleClass for the HBox to "hbox"
        root.getStyleClass().add("hbox");

        Scene scene = new Scene(root);
        scene.getStylesheets().add(
                "resources/css/styleclass.css");

        stage.setScene(scene);
        stage.setTitle("Using Style Class Selectors");
        stage.show();
    }
}
```

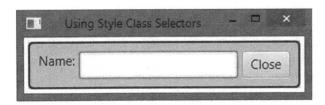

Figure 8-7. *An HBox using border, padding, spacing, and background color from a style sheet*

Notice that you have set the style class name for the HBox (named root in the code) to "hbox", which will apply CSS properties to the HBox from the style with the class selector hbox. The text color of the Close button is blue because of the second style with the style class selector button. You did not set the style class name for the Close button to "button". The Button class adds a style class, which is named "button", to all its instances. This is the reason that the Close button was selected by the button style class selector.

Most of the commonly used controls in JavaFX have a default style class name. You can add more style class names if needed. The default style class names are constructed from the JavaFX class names. The JavaFX class name is converted to lowercase, and a hyphen is inserted in the middle of two words. If the JavaFX class name consists of only one word, the corresponding default style class name is created by just converting it to lowercase. For example, the default style class name is button for Button, label for Label, hyperlink for Hyperlink, text-field for TextField, text-area for TextArea, and check-box for CheckBox.

JavaFX container classes, for example, Region, Pane, HBox, VBox, do not have a default style class name. If you want to style them using style class selectors, you need to add a style class name to them. This is the reason that you had to add a style class name to the HBox that you used in Listing 8-8 to use the style class selector.

■ **Tip** Style class names in JavaFX are case-sensitive.

Sometimes, you might need to know the default style class name of a node to use it in a style sheet. There are three ways to determine the default style class name of a JavaFX node:

- Guess it using the described rules to form the default style class name from the JavaFX class name.

- Use the online *JavaFX CSS Reference Guide* to look up the name.

- Write a small piece of code.

The following snippet of code shows how to print the default style class name for the Button class. Change the name of the JavaFX node class, for example, from Button to TextField, to print the default style class name for other types of nodes:

```
Button btn = new Button();
ObservableList<String> list = btn.getStyleClass();

if (list.isEmpty()) {
        System.out.println("No default style class name");
} else {
        for(String styleClassName : list) {
                System.out.println(styleClassName);
        }
}
```

```
button
```

Class Selector for the *root* Node

The root node of a scene is assigned a style class named "root". You can use the root style class selector for CSS properties that are inherited by other nodes. The root node is the parent of all nodes in a scene graph. Storing CSS properties in the root node is preferred because they can be looked up from any node in the scene graph.

Listing 8-9 shows the content of a style sheet saved in a file resources\css\rootclass.css. The style with the root class selector declares two properties: -fx-cursor and -my-button-color. The -fx-cursor property is inherited by all nodes. If this style sheet is attached to a scene, all nodes will have a HAND cursor unless they override it. The -my-button-color property is a look-up property, which is looked up in the second style to set the text color of buttons.

Listing 8-9. The Content of the Style Sheet with Root As a Style Class Selector

```
.root {
        -fx-cursor: hand;
        -my-button-color: blue;
}
```

```
.button {
        -fx-text-fill: -my-button-color;
}
```

Run the program in Listing 8-10 to see the effects of these changes. Notice that you get a HAND cursor when you move the mouse anywhere in the scene, except over the name text field. This is because the TextField class overrides the -fx-cursor CSS property to set it to the TEXT cursor.

Listing 8-10. Using the Root Style Class Selector

```
// RootClassTest.java
package com.jdojo.style;

import com.jdojo.util.ResourceUtil;
import javafx.application.Application;
import javafx.scene.Scene;
import javafx.scene.control.Button;
import javafx.scene.control.Label;
import javafx.scene.control.TextField;
import javafx.scene.layout.HBox;
import javafx.stage.Stage;

public class RootClassTest extends Application {
        public static void main(String[] args) {
                Application.launch(args);
        }

        @Override
        public void start(Stage stage) {
                Label nameLbl = new Label("Name:");
                TextField nameTf = new TextField("");
                Button closeBtn = new Button("Close");

                HBox root = new HBox();
                root.getChildren().addAll(nameLbl, nameTf, closeBtn);

                Scene scene = new Scene(root);
                /* The root variable is assigned a default style
                        class name "root" */

                   var url =
                       ResourceUtil.getResourceURLStr("css/rootclass.css");
                   scene.getStylesheets().add(url);

                stage.setScene(scene);
                stage.setTitle("Using the root Style Class Selector");
                stage.show();
        }
}
```

Using ID Selectors

The Node class has an id property of the StringProperty type, which can be used to assign a unique id to each node in a scene graph. Maintaining the uniqueness of an id in a scene graph is the responsibility of the developer. It is not an error to set a duplicate id for a node.

You do not use the id property of a node directly in your code, except when you are setting it. It is mainly used for styling nodes using ID selectors. The following snippet of code sets the id property of a Button to "closeBtn":

```
Button b1 = new Button("Close");
b1.setId("closeBtn");
```

An ID selector in a style sheet is preceded by the pound (#) sign. Note that the ID value set for a node does not include the # sign. Listing 8-11 shows the content of a style sheet, which contains two styles, one with a class selector ".button" and one with an ID selector "#closeButton". Save the content of Listing 8-11 in a file called resources\css\idselector.css in the CLASSPATH. Figure 8-8 shows the results after the program is run.

Listing 8-11. A Style Sheet That Uses a Class Selector and an ID Selector

```
.button {
        -fx-text-fill: blue;
}

#closeButton {
        -fx-text-fill: red;
}
```

Figure 8-8. *Buttons using class and ID selectors*

Listing 8-12 presents the program that uses the style sheet in Listing 8-11. The program creates three buttons. It sets the ID for a button to "closeButton". The other two buttons do not have an ID. When the program is run, the Close button's text is in red, whereas the other two have blue text.

Listing 8-12. Using an ID Selector in a Style Sheet

```
// IDSelectorTest.java
package com.jdojo.style;

import com.jdojo.util.ResourceUtil;

import javafx.application.Application;
import javafx.scene.Scene;
import javafx.scene.control.Button;
import javafx.scene.layout.HBox;
import javafx.stage.Stage;
```

```java
public class IDSelectorTest extends Application {
    public static void main(String[] args) {
        Application.launch(args);
    }

    @Override
    public void start(Stage stage) {
        Button openBtn = new Button("Open");
        Button saveBtn = new Button("Save");

        Button closeBtn = new Button("Close");
        closeBtn.setId("closeButton");

        HBox root = new HBox();
        root.getChildren().addAll(openBtn, saveBtn, closeBtn);

        Scene scene = new Scene(root);
        var url = ResourceUtil.getResourceURLStr("css/idselector.css");
        scene.getStylesheets().add(url);

        stage.setScene(scene);
        stage.setTitle("Using ID selectors");
        stage.show();
    }
}
```

Did you notice a conflict in the styles for the Close button? All buttons in JavaFX are assigned a default style class named button, so does the Close button. The Close button also has an ID that matches with the ID style selector. Therefore, both selectors in the style sheet match the Close button. In cases where there are multiple selectors matching a node, JavaFX uses the *specificity of selectors* to determine which selector will be used. In cases where a class selector and an ID selector are used, the ID selector has higher specificity. This is the reason that the ID selector matched the Close button, not the class selector.

■ **Tip** CSS uses complex rules to calculate the specificity of selectors. Please refer to www.w3.org/TR/CSS21/cascade.html#specificity for more details.

Combining ID and Class Selectors

A selector can use the combination of a style class and an ID. In this case, the selector matches all nodes with the specified style class and ID. Consider the following style:

```css
#closeButton.button {
    -fx-text-fill: red;
}
```

The selector #closeButton.button matches all nodes with a closeButton ID and a button style class. You can also reverse the order:

```
.button#closeButton {
        -fx-text-fill: red;
}
```

Now it matches all nodes with a button style class and a closeButton ID.

The Universal Selector

An asterisk (*) is used as a universal selector, which matches any node. The universal selector has the lowest specificity. The following style uses the universal selector to set the text fill property of all nodes to blue:

```
* {
        -fx-text-fill: blue;
}
```

When the universal selector does not appear by itself, it can be ignored. For example, the selectors *.button and .button are the same.

Grouping Multiple Selectors

If the same CSS properties apply to multiple selectors, you have two choices:

- You can use multiple styles by duplicating the property declarations.
- You can group all selectors into one style, separating the selectors by a comma.

Suppose you want to set the button and label classes' text fill color to blue. The following code uses two styles with the duplicate property declarations:

```
.button {
        -fx-text-fill: blue;
}

.label {
        -fx-text-fill: blue;
}
```

The two styles can be combined into one style as follows:

```
.button, .label {
        -fx-text-fill: blue;
}
```

Descendant Selectors

A descendant selector is used to match nodes that are descendants of another node in the scene graph. A descendant selector consists of two or more selectors separated by whitespaces. The following style uses a descendant selector:

```
.hbox .button {
        -fx-text-fill: blue;
}
```

It will select all nodes that have a button style class and are descendants of a node with an hbox style class. The term *descendant* in this context means a child at any level (immediate or nonimmediate).

A descendant selector comes in handy when you want to style parts of JavaFX controls. Many controls in JavaFX consist of subnodes, which are JavaFX nodes. In the *JavaFX CSS Reference Guide*, those subnodes are listed as substructures. For example, a CheckBox consists of a LabeledText (not part of the public API) with a style class name of text and a StackPane with a style class name of box. The box contains another StackPane with the style class name of mark. You can use these pieces of information for the substructure of the CheckBox class to style the subparts. The following styles use descendant selectors to set the text color of all CheckBox instances to blue and the box to a dotted border:

```
.check-box .text {
        -fx-fill: blue;
}

.check-box .box {
        -fx-border-color: black;
        -fx-border-width: 1px;
        -fx-border-style: dotted;
}
```

Child Selectors

A child selector matches a child node. It consists of two or more selectors separated by the greater than sign (>). The following style matches all nodes with a button style class, which are the children of a node with an hbox style class:

```
.hbox > .button {
        -fx-text-fill: blue;
}
```

■ **Tip** CSS supports other types of selectors, for example, sibling selectors and attribute selectors. JavaFX CSS does not reliably support them yet.

State-Based Selectors

State-based selectors are also known as *pseudo-class* selectors. A pseudo-class selector matches nodes based on their current states, for example, matching a node that has focus or matching text input controls that are read-only. A pseudo-class is preceded by a colon and is appended to an existing selector. For example, .button:focused is a pseudo-class selector that matches a node with the button style class name that also has the focus; #openBtn:hover is another pseudo-class selector that matches a node with the ID #openBtn, when the mouse hovers over the node. Listing 8-13 presents the content of a style sheet that has a pseudo-class selector. It changes the text color to red when the mouse hovers over the node. When you add this style sheet to a scene, all buttons will change their text color to red when the mouse hovers over them.

Listing 8-13. A Style Sheet with a Pseudo-class Selector

```
.button:hover {
        -fx-text-fill: red;
}
```

JavaFX CSS does not support the :first-child and :lang pseudo-classes that are supported by CSS. JavaFX does not support *pseudo-elements* that allow you to style the content of nodes (e.g., the first line in a TextArea). Table 8-1 contains a partial list of the pseudo-classes supported by JavaFX CSS. Please refer to the online *JavaFX CSS Reference Guide* for the complete list of pseudo-classes supported by JavaFX CSS.

Table 8-1. *Some Pseudo-classes Supported by JavaFX CSS*

Pseudo-class	Applies to	Description
disabled	Node	It applies when the node is disabled.
focused	Node	It applies when the node has the focus.
hover	Node	It applies when the mouse hovers over the node.
pressed	Node	It applies when the mouse button is clicked over the node.
show-mnemonic	Node	It applies when the mnemonic should be shown.
cancel	Button	It applies when the Button would receive VK_ESC if the event is not consumed.
default	Button	It applies when the Button would receive VK_ENTER if the event is not consumed.
empty	Cell	It applies when the Cell is empty.
filled	Cell	It applies when the Cell is not empty.
selected	Cell, CheckBox	It applies when the node is selected.
determinate	CheckBox	It applies when the CheckBox is in a determinate state.
indeterminate	CheckBox	It applies when the CheckBox is in an indeterminate state.
visited	Hyperlink	It applies when the Hyperlink has been visited.
horizontal	ListView	It applies when the node is horizontal.
vertical	ListView	It applies when the node is vertical.

Using JavaFX Class Names As Selectors

It is allowed, but not recommended, to use the JavaFX class name as a type selector in a style. Consider the following content of a style sheet:

```
HBox {
        -fx-border-color: blue;
        -fx-border-width: 2px;
        -fx-border-insets: 10px;
        -fx-padding: 10px;
}

Button {
        -fx-text-fill: blue;
}
```

Notice that a type selector differs from a class selector in that the former does not start with a period. A class selector is the JavaFX class name of the node without any modification (HBOX and HBox are not the same). If you attach a style sheet with the preceding content to a scene, all HBox instances will have a border, and all Button instances will have blue text.

It is not recommended to use the JavaFX class names as type selectors because the class name may be different when you subclass a JavaFX class. If you depend on the class name in your style sheet, the new classes will not pick up your styles.

Looking Up Nodes in a Scene Graph

You can look up a node in a scene graph by using a selector. Scene and Node classes have a lookup(String selector) method, which returns the reference of the first node found with the specified selector. If no node is found, it returns null. The methods in two classes work a little differently. The method in the Scene class searches the entire scene graph. The method in the Node class searches the node on which it is called and its subnodes. The Node class also has a lookupAll(String selector) method that returns a Set of all Nodes that are matched by the specified selector, including the node on which this method is called and its subnode.

The following snippet of code shows how to use the look-up methods using ID selectors. However, you are not limited to using only ID selectors in these methods. You can use all selectors that are valid in JavaFX:

```
Button b1 = new Button("Close");
b1.setId("closeBtn");
VBox root = new VBox();
root.setId("myvbox");
root.getChildren().addAll(b1);
Scene scene = new Scene(root, 200, 300);
...
Node n1 = scene.lookup("#closeBtn");     // n1 is the reference of b1
Node n2 = root.lookup("#closeBtn");      // n2 is the reference of b1
Node n3 = b1.lookup("#closeBtn");        // n3 is the reference of b1
Node n4 = root.lookup("#myvbox");        // n4 is the reference of root
Node n5 = b1.lookup("#myvbox");          // n5 is null
Set<Node> s = root.lookupAll("#closeBtn"); // s contains the reference of b1
```

Summary

CSS is a language used to describe the presentation of UI elements in a GUI application. It was primarily used in web pages for styling HTML elements and separating presentation from contents and behavior. In a typical web page, the content and presentation are defined using HTML and CSS, respectively.

JavaFX allows you to define the look of JavaFX applications using CSS. You can define UI elements using JavaFX class libraries or FXML and use CSS to define their look.

A CSS rule is also known as a style. A collection of CSS rules is known as a style sheet. Skins are collections of application-specific styles, which define the appearance of an application. Skinning is the process of changing the appearance of an application (or the skin) on the fly. JavaFX does not provide a specific mechanism for skinning. Themes are visual characteristics of an operating system that are reflected in the appearance of UI elements of all applications. JavaFX has no direct support for themes.

You can add multiple style sheets to a JavaFX application. Style sheets are added to a scene or parents. Scene and Parent classes maintain an observable list of string URLs linking to style sheets.

JavaFX 8 through 17 use a default style sheet called Modena. Prior to JavaFX 8, the default style sheet was called Caspian. You can still use the Caspian style sheet as the default in JavaFX 8 using the static method setUserAgentStylesheet(String url) of the Application class. You can refer to the Caspian and Modena style sheets' URLs using the constants named STYLESHEET_CASPIAN and STYLESHEET_MODENA defined in the Application class.

It is common for the visual properties of nodes to come from multiple sources. The JavaFX runtime uses the following priority rules to set the visual properties of a node: inline style (the highest priority), parent style sheets, scene style sheets, values set in the code using the JavaFX API, and user agent style sheets (the lowest priority).

JavaFX offers two types of inheritance for CSS properties: CSS property types and CSS property values. In the first type of inheritance, all CSS properties declared in a JavaFX class are inherited by all its subclasses. In the second type of inheritance, a CSS property for a node may inherit its value from its parent. The parent of a node is the container of the node in the scene graph, not its JavaFX superclass.

Each style in a style sheet has a selector that identifies the nodes in the scene graph to which the style is applied. JavaFX CSS supports several types of selectors: class selectors and most of them work the same way they do in web browsers. You can look up a node in a scene graph by using a selector and the lookup(String selector) method of the Scene and Node classes.

The next chapter will discuss how to handle events in a JavaFX application.

CHAPTER 9

■ ■ ■

Event Handling

In this chapter, you will learn:

- What an event is
- What an event source, an event target, and event type are
- About the event processing mechanism
- How to handle events using event filters and event handlers
- How to handle mouse events, key events, and window events

The examples of this chapter lie in the `com.jdojo.event` package. In order for them to work, you must add a corresponding line to the `module-info.java` file:

```
...
opens com.jdojo.event to javafx.graphics, javafx.base;
...
```

What Is an Event?

In general, the term *event* is used to describe an occurrence of interest. In a GUI application, an event is an occurrence of a user interaction with the application. Clicking the mouse and pressing a key on the keyboard are examples of events in a JavaFX application.

An event in JavaFX is represented by an object of the `javafx.event.Event` class or any of its subclasses. Every event in JavaFX has three properties:

- An event source
- An event target
- An event type

When an event occurs in an application, you typically perform some processing by executing a piece of code. The piece of code that is executed in response to an event is known as an *event handler* or an *event filter*. I will clarify the difference between these shortly. For now, think of both as a piece of code, and I will refer to both of them as event handlers. When you want to handle an event for a UI element, you need to add event handlers to the UI element, for example, a `Window`, a `Scene`, or a `Node`. When the UI element detects the event, it executes your event handlers.

The UI element that calls event handlers is the source of the event for those event handlers. When an event occurs, it passes through a chain of event dispatchers. The source of an event is the current element in the event dispatcher chain. The event source changes as the event passes through one dispatcher to another in the event dispatcher chain.

The event target is the destination of an event. The event target determines the route through which the event travels during its processing. Suppose a mouse click occurs over a Circle node. In this case, the Circle node is the event target of the mouse-clicked event.

The event type describes the type of the event that occurs. Event types are defined in a hierarchical fashion. Each event type has a name and a supertype.

The three properties that are common to all events in JavaFX are represented by objects of three different classes. Specific events define additional event properties; for example, the event class to represent a mouse event adds properties to describe the location of the mouse cursor and the state of the mouse buttons, among others. Table 9-1 lists the classes and interfaces involved in event processing. JavaFX has an event delivery mechanism that defines the details of the occurrence and processing of events. I will discuss all of these in detail in subsequent sections.

Table 9-1. *Classes Involved in Event Processing*

Name	Class/ Interface	Description
Event	Class	An instance of this class represents an event. Several subclasses of the Event class exist to represent specific types of events.
EventTarget	Interface	An instance of this interface represents an event target.
EventType	Class	An instance of this class represents an event type, for example, mouse pressed, mouse released, mouse moved.
EventHandler	Interface	An instance of this interface represents an event handler or an event filter. Its handle() method is called when the event for which it has been registered occurs.

Event Class Hierarchy

Classes representing events in JavaFX are arranged in hierarchical fashion through class inheritance. Figure 9-1 shows a partial class diagram for the Event class. The Event class is at the top of the class hierarchy, and it inherits from java.util.EventObject class, which is not shown in the diagram.

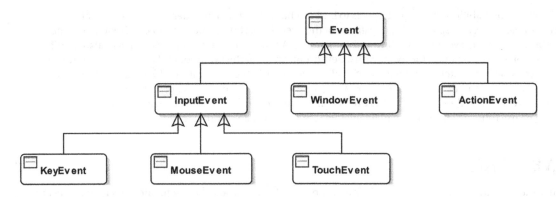

Figure 9-1. *A partial class hierarchy for the* javafx.event.Event *class*

Subclasses of the Event class represent specific types of events. Sometimes, a subclass of the Event class is used to represent a generic event of some kind. For example, the InputEvent class represents a generic event to indicate a user input event, whereas the KeyEvent and MouseEvent classes represent specific input events such as the user input from the keyboard and mouse, respectively. An object of the WindowEvent class represents an event of a window, for example, showing and hiding of the window. An object of the ActionEvent is used to represent several kinds of events denoting some type of action, for example, firing a button or a menu item. Firing of a button may happen if the user clicks it with the mouse, presses some keys, or touches it on the touch screen.

The Event class provides properties and methods that are common to all events. The getSource() method returns an Object, which is the source of the event. The Event class inherits this method from the EventObject class. The getTarget() method returns an instance of the EventTarget interface, which is the target of the event. The getEventType() method returns an object of the EventType class, which indicates the type of the event.

The Event class contains consume() and isConsumed() methods. As noted before, an event travels from one element to another in an event-dispatching chain. Calling the consume() method on an Event object indicates that the event has been consumed and no further processing is required. After the consume() method is called, the event does not travel to the next element in the event processing chain. The isConsumed() method returns true if the consume() method has been called; otherwise, it returns false.

Specific Event subclasses define more properties and methods. For example, the MouseEvent class defines getX() and getY() methods that return the x and y coordinates of the mouse cursor relative to the source of the event. I'll explain the details of the methods in event-specific classes when I discuss them later in this chapter or subsequent chapters.

Event Targets

An *event target* is a UI element (not necessarily just Nodes) that can respond to events. Technically, a UI element that wants to respond to events must implement the EventTarget interface. That is, in JavaFX, implementing the EventTarget interface makes a UI element eligible to be an event target.

The Window, Scene, and Node classes implement the EventTarget interface. This means that all nodes, including windows and scenes, can respond to events. The classes for some UI elements, for example, Tab, TreeItem, and MenuItem, do not inherit from the Node class. They can still respond to events because they implement the EventTarget interface. If you develop a custom UI element, you will need to implement this interface if you want your UI element to respond to events.

The responsibility of an event target is to build a chain of event dispatchers, which is also called the *event route*. An *event dispatcher* is an instance of the EventDispatcher interface. Each dispatcher in the chain can affect the event by handling and consuming. An event dispatcher in the chain can also modify the event properties, substitute the event with a new event, or chain the event route. Typically, an event target route consists of dispatchers associated with all UI elements in the container-child hierarchy. Suppose you have a Circle node placed in an HBox, which is placed in a Scene. The Scene is added to a Stage. If the mouse is clicked on the Circle, the Circle becomes the event target. The Circle builds an event dispatcher chain whose route will be, from head to tail, the Stage, Scene, HBox, and Circle.

Event Types

An instance of the EventType class defines an event type. Why do you need a separate class to define event types? Aren't separate event classes, for example, KeyEvent, MouseEvent, for each event sufficient to define event types? Can't you distinguish one event from another based on the event class? The EventType class is used to further classify the events within an event class. For example, the MouseEvent class only tells us that the user has used the mouse. It does not tell us the details of the mouse use, for example, whether the mouse was pressed, released, dragged, or clicked. The EventType class is used to classify these subevent types of an event. The EventType class is a generic class whose type parameter is defined as follows:

EventType<T extends Event>

Event types are hierarchical. They are hierarchical by implementation, not by class inheritance. Each event type has a name and a supertype. The getName() and getSuperType() methods in the EventType class return the name and supertype of an event type. The constant Event.ANY, which is the same as the constant EventType.ROOT, is the supertype of all events in JavaFX. Figure 9-2 shows a partial list of some event types that have been predefined in some event classes.

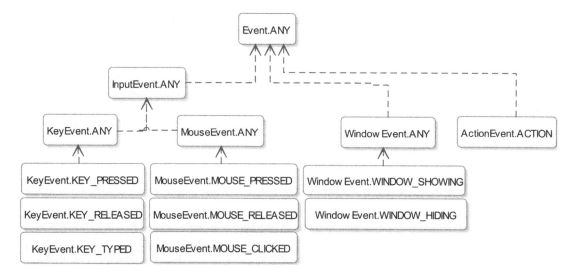

Figure 9-2. *A partial list of predefined event types for some event classes*

Note that the arrows in the diagram do not denote class inheritance. They denote dependencies. For example, the InputEvent.ANY event type depends on the Event.ANY event type, as the latter is the supertype of the former.

An event class, which has subevent types, defines an ANY event type. For example, the MouseEvent class defines an ANY event type that represents a mouse event of any type, for example, mouse released, mouse clicked, mouse moved. MOUSE_PRESSED and MOUSE_RELEASED are other event types defined in the MouseEvent class. The ANY event type in an event class is the supertype of all other event types in the same event class. For example, the MouseEvent.ANY event type is the supertype of MOUSE_RELEASED and MOUSE_PRESSED mouse events.

Event Processing Mechanism

When an event occurs, several steps are performed as part of the event processing:

- Event target selection

- Event route construction

- Event route traversal

Event Target Selection

The first step in the event processing is the selection of the event target. Recall that an event target is the destination node of an event. The event target is selected based on the event type.

For mouse events, the event target is the node at the mouse cursor. Multiple nodes can be available at the mouse cursor. For example, you can have a circle placed over a rectangle. The topmost node at the mouse cursor is selected as the event target.

The event target for key events is the node that has focus. How a node gets the focus depends on the type of the node. For example, a TextField may gain focus by clicking the mouse inside it or using the focus traversal keys such as Tab or Shift + Tab on the Windows format. Shapes such as Circles or Rectangles do not get focus by default. If you want them to receive key events, you can give them focus by calling the requestFocus() method of the Node class.

JavaFX supports touch and gesture events on touch-enabled devices. A touch event is generated by touching a touch screen. Each touch action has a point of contact called a *touch point*. It is possible to touch a touch screen with multiple fingers, resulting in multiple touch points. Each state of a touch point, for example, pressed, released, and so forth, generates a touch event. The location of the touch point determines the target of the touch event. For example, if the location of the touch event is a point within a circle, the circle becomes the target of the touch event. In case of multiple nodes at the touch point, the topmost node is selected as the target.

Users can interact with a JavaFX application using gestures. Typically, a gesture on a touch screen and a track pad consists of multiple touch points with touch actions. Examples of gesture events are rotating, scrolling, swiping, and zooming. A rotating gesture is performed by rotating two fingers around each other. A scrolling gesture is performed by dragging a finger on the touch screen. A swiping gesture is performed by dragging a finger (or multiple fingers) on the touch screen in one direction. A zooming gesture is performed to scale a node by dragging two fingers apart or closer.

The target for gesture events is selected depending on the type of gesture. For direct gestures, for example, gestures performed on touch screens, the topmost node at the center point of all touch points at the start of the gesture is selected as the event target. For indirect gestures, for example, gestures performed on a track pad, the topmost node at the mouse cursor is selected as the event target.

Event Route Construction

An event travels through event dispatchers in an event dispatch chain. The event dispatch chain is the *event route*. The initial and default routes for an event are determined by the event target. The default event route consists of the container-children path starting at the stage to the event target node.

Suppose you have placed a Circle and a Rectangle in an HBox and the HBox is the root node of the Scene of a Stage. When you click the Circle, the Circle becomes the event target. The Circle constructs the default event route, which is the path starting at the stage to the event target (the Circle).

In fact, an event route consists of event dispatchers that are associated with nodes. However, for all practical and understanding purposes, you can think of the event route as the path comprising the nodes. Typically, you do not deal with event dispatchers directly.

Figure 9-3 shows the event route for the mouse-clicked event. The nodes on the event route have been shown in gray background fills. The nodes on the event route are connected by solid lines. Note that the Rectangle that is part of the scene graph is not part of the event path when the Circle is clicked.

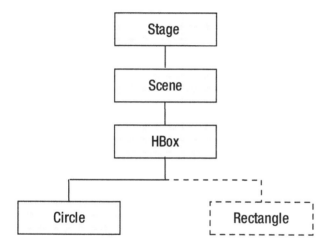

Figure 9-3. *Construction of the default event route for an event*

An event dispatch chain (or event route) has a *head* and a *tail*. In Figure 9-3, the Stage and the Circle are the head and the tail of the event dispatch chain, respectively. The initial event route may be modified as the event processing progresses. Typically, but not necessarily, the event passes through all nodes in its route twice during the event traversal step, as described in the next section.

Event Route Traversal

An event route traversal consists of two phases:

- Capture phase
- Bubbling phase

An event travels through each node in its route twice: once during the capture phase and once during the bubbling phase. You can register event filters and event handlers to a node for specific event types. The event filters and event handlers registered to a node are executed as the event passes through the node during the capture phase and the bubbling phase, respectively. The event filters and handlers are passed in the reference of the current node as the source of the event. As the event travels from one node to another, the event source keeps changing. However, the event target remains the same from the start to the finish of the event route traversal.

During the route traversal, a node can consume the event in event filters or handlers, thus completing the processing of the event. Consuming an event is simply calling the consume() method on the event object. When an event is consumed, the event processing is stopped, even though some of the nodes in the route were not traversed at all.

Event Capture Phase

During the capture phase, an event travels from the head to the tail of its event dispatch chain. Figure 9-4 shows the traveling of a mouse-clicked event for the Circle in our example in the capture phase. The down arrows in the figure denote the direction of the event travel. As the event passes through a node, the registered event filters for the node are executed. Note that the event capture phase executes only event filters, not event handlers, for the current node.

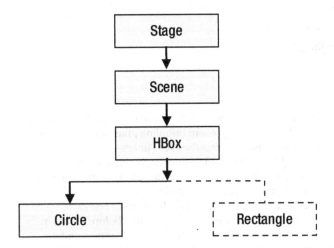

Figure 9-4. *The event capture phase*

In Figure 9-4, the event filters for the Stage, Scene, HBox, and Circle are executed in order, assuming none of the event filters consumes the event.

You can register multiple event filters for a node. If the node consumes the event in one of its event filters, its other event filters, which have not been executed yet, are executed before the event processing stops. Suppose you have registered five event filters for the Scene in our example, and the first event filter that is executed consumes the event. In this case, the other four event filters for the Scene will still be executed. After executing the fifth event filter for the Scene, the event processing will stop, without the event traveling to the remaining nodes (HBox and Circle).

In the event capture phase, you can intercept events (and provide a generic response) that are targeted at the children of a node. For example, you can add event filters for the mouse-clicked event to the Stage in our example to intercept all mouse-clicked events for all its children. You can block events from reaching their targets by consuming the event in event filters for a parent node. For example, if you consume the mouse-clicked event in a filter for the Stage, the event will not reach its target, in our example, the Circle.

Event Bubbling Phase

During the bubbling phase, an event travels from the tail to the head of its event dispatch chain. Figure 9-5 shows the traveling of a mouse-clicked event for the Circle in the bubbling phase.

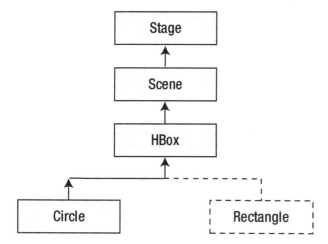

Figure 9-5. *The event bubbling phase*

The up arrows in Figure 9-5 denote the direction of the event travel. As the event passes through a node, the registered event handlers for the node are executed. Note that the event bubbling phase executes event handlers for the current node, whereas the event capture phase executes the event filters.

In our example, the event handlers for the Circle, HBox, Scene, and Stage are executed in order, assuming none of the event filters consumes the event. Note that the event bubbling phase starts at the target of the event and travels up to the topmost parent in the parent-children hierarchy.

You can register multiple event handlers for a node. If the node consumes the event in one of its event handlers, its other event handlers, which have not been executed yet, are executed before the event processing stops. Suppose you have registered five event handlers for the Circle in our example, and the first event handler that is executed consumes the event. In this case, the other four event handlers for the Circle will still be executed. After executing the fifth event handler for the Circle, the event processing will stop, without the event traveling to the remaining nodes (HBox, Scene, and Stage).

Typically, event handlers are registered to target nodes to provide a specific response to events. Sometimes, event handlers are installed on parent nodes to provide a default event response for all its children. If an event target decides to provide a specific response to the event, it can do so by adding event handlers and consuming the event, thus blocking the event from reaching the parent nodes in the event bubbling phase.

Let's look at a trivial example. Suppose you want to display a message box to the user when they click anywhere inside a window. You can register an event handler to the window to display the message box. When the user clicks inside a circle in the window, you want to display a specific message. You can register an event handler to the circle to provide the specific message and consume the event. This will provide a specific event response when the circle is clicked, whereas for other nodes, the window provides a default event response.

Handling Events

Handling an event means executing the application logic in response to the occurrence of the event. The application logic is contained in the event filters and handlers, which are objects of the EventHandler interface, as shown in the following code:

```
public interface EventHandler<T extends Event> extends EventListener
        void handle(T event);
}
```

The EventHandler class is a generic class in the javafx.event package. It extends the EventListener marker interface, which is in the java.util package. The handle() method receives the reference of the event object, for example, the reference of the KeyEvent and MouseEvent, among others.

Both event filters and handlers are objects of the same EventHandler interface. You cannot tell whether an EventHandler object is an event filter or an event handler by just looking at it. In fact, you can register the same EventHandler object as event filters as well as handlers at the same time. The distinction between the two is made when they are registered to a node. Nodes provide different methods to register them. Internally, nodes know whether an EventHandler object was registered as an event filter or a handler. Another distinction between them is made based on the event traversal phase in which they are called. During the event capture phase, the handle() method of registered filters is called, whereas the handle() method of registered handlers is called in the event bubbling phase.

▧ **Tip** In essence, handling an event means writing the application logic for EventHandler objects and registering them to nodes as event filters, handlers, or both.

Creating Event Filters and Handlers

Creating event filters and handlers is as simple as creating objects of the class that implement the EventHandler interface. Using lambda expressions is the best choice for creating the event filters and handlers, as in the following code:

```
EventHandler<MouseEvent> aHandler = e -> /* Event handling code goes here */;
```

I use lambda expressions in this book to create event filters and handlers. If you are not familiar with lambda expressions, I suggest you learn at least the basics so you can understand the event handling code.

The following snippet of code creates a MouseEvent handler. It prints the type of the mouse event that occurs:

```
EventHandler<MouseEvent> mouseEventHandler =
        e -> System.out.println("Mouse event type: " + e.getEventType());
```

Registering Event Filters and Handlers

If you want a node to process events of specific types, you need to register event filters and handlers for those event types to the node. When the event occurs, the handle() method of the registered event filters and handlers for the node is called following the rules discussed in the previous sections. If the node is no longer interested in processing the events, you need to unregister the event filters and handlers from the node. Registering and unregistering event filters and handlers are also known as adding and removing event filters and handlers, respectively.

JavaFX provides two ways to register and unregister event filters and handlers to nodes:

- Using the addEventFilter(), addEventHandler(), removeEventFilter(), and removeEventHandler() methods

- Using the onXXX convenience properties

Using *addXXX( )* and *removeXXX( )* Methods

You can use the addEventFilter() and addEventHandler() methods to register event filters and handlers to nodes, respectively. These methods are defined in the Node class, Scene class, and Window class. Some classes (e.g., MenuItem and TreeItem) can be event targets; however, they are not inherited from the Node class. The classes provide only the addEventHandler() method for event handlers registration, such as

- <T extends Event> void addEventFilter(EventType<T> eventType, EventHandler<? super T> eventFilter)

- <T extends Event> void addEventHandler(EventType<T> eventType, EventHandler<? super T> eventHandler)

These methods have two parameters. The first parameter is the event type, and the second is an object of the EventHandler interface.

You can handle mouse-clicked events for a Circle using the following snippet of code:

```
import javafx.scene.shape.Circle;
import javafx.event.EventHandler;
import javafx.scene.input.MouseEvent;
...
Circle circle = new Circle (100, 100, 50);

// Create a MouseEvent filter
EventHandler<MouseEvent> mouseEventFilter =
        e -> System.out.println("Mouse event filter has been called.");

// Create a MouseEvent handler
EventHandler<MouseEvent> mouseEventHandler =
        e -> System.out.println("Mouse event handler has been called.");

// Register the MouseEvent filter and handler to the Circle
// for mouse-clicked events
circle.addEventFilter(MouseEvent.MOUSE_CLICKED, mouseEventFilter);
circle.addEventHandler(MouseEvent.MOUSE_CLICKED, mouseEventHandler);
```

This code creates two EventHandler objects, which prints a message on the console. At this stage, they are not event filters or handlers. They are just two EventHandler objects. Note that giving the reference variables names and printing messages that use the words filter and handler does not make any difference in their status as filters and handlers. The last two statements register one of the EventHandler objects as an event filter and another as an event handler; both are registered for the mouse-clicked event.

Registering the same EventHandler object as event filters as well as handlers is allowed. The following snippet of code uses one EventHandler object as the filter and handler for the Circle to handle the mouse-clicked event:

```
// Create a MouseEvent EventHandler object
EventHandler<MouseEvent> handler = e ->
    System.out.println("Mouse event filter or handler has been called.");

// Register the same EventHandler object as the MouseEvent filter and handler
// to the Circle for mouse-clicked events
circle.addEventFilter(MouseEvent.MOUSE_CLICKED, handler);
circle.addEventHandler(MouseEvent.MOUSE_CLICKED, handler);
```

■ **Tip** You can add multiple event filters and handlers for a node using the addEventFilter() and addEventHandler() methods. You need to call these methods once for every instance of the event filters and handlers that you want to add.

Listing 9-1 has the complete program to demonstrate the handling of the mouse-clicked events of a Circle object. It uses an event filter and an event handler. Run the program and click inside the circle. When the circle is clicked, the event filter is called first, followed by the event handler. This is evident from the output. The mouse-clicked event occurs every time you click any point inside the circle. If you click outside the circle, the mouse-clicked event still occurs; however, you do not see any output because you have not registered event filters or handlers on the HBox, Scene, and Stage.

Listing 9-1. Registering Event Filters and Handlers

```java
// EventRegistration.java
package com.jdojo.event;

import javafx.application.Application;
import javafx.event.EventHandler;
import javafx.scene.Scene;
import javafx.scene.input.MouseEvent;
import javafx.scene.layout.HBox;
import javafx.scene.paint.Color;
import javafx.scene.shape.Circle;
import javafx.stage.Stage;

public class EventRegistration extends Application {
    public static void main(String[] args) {
        Application.launch(args);
    }

    @Override
    public void start(Stage stage) {
        Circle circle = new Circle (100, 100, 50);
        circle.setFill(Color.CORAL);
```

```
                // Create a MouseEvent filter
                EventHandler<MouseEvent> mouseEventFilter = e ->
                        System.out.println(
                            "Mouse event filter has been called.");

                // Create a MouseEvent handler
                EventHandler<MouseEvent> mouseEventHandler = e ->
                        System.out.println(
                            "Mouse event handler has been called.");

                // Register the MouseEvent filter and handler to
                    // the Circle for mouse-clicked events
                circle.addEventFilter(MouseEvent.MOUSE_CLICKED,
                        mouseEventFilter);
                circle.addEventHandler(MouseEvent.MOUSE_CLICKED,
                        mouseEventHandler);

                HBox root = new HBox();
                root.getChildren().add(circle);
                Scene scene = new Scene(root);
                stage.setScene(scene);
                stage.setTitle("Registering Event Filters and Handlers");
                stage.show();
                stage.sizeToScene();
        }
}
```

```
Mouse event filter has been called.
Mouse event handler has been called.
...
```

To unregister an event filter and an event handler, you need to call the removeEventFilter() and removeEventHandler() methods, respectively:

- `<T extends Event> void removeEventFilter(EventType<T> eventType, EventHandler<? super T> eventFilter)`

- `<T extends Event> void removeEventHandler(EventType<T> eventType, EventHandler<? super T> eventHandler)`

The following snippet of code adds and removes an event filter to a Circle, and, later, it removes them. Note that once an EventHandler is removed from a node, its handle() method is not called when the event occurs:

```
// Create a MouseEvent EventHandler object
EventHandler<MouseEvent> handler = e ->
    System.out.println("Mouse event filter or handler has been called.");

// Register the same EventHandler object as the MouseEvent filter and handler
// to the Circle for mouse-clicked events
circle.addEventFilter(MouseEvent.MOUSE_CLICKED, handler);
circle.addEventHandler(MouseEvent.MOUSE_CLICKED, handler);
```

...

```
// At a later stage, when you are no longer interested in handling the mouse
// clicked event for the Circle, unregister the event filter and handler
circle.removeEventFilter(MouseEvent.MOUSE_CLICKED, handler);
circle.removeEventHandler(MouseEvent.MOUSE_CLICKED, handler);
```

Using *onXXX* Convenience Properties

The Node, Scene, and Window classes contain event properties to store event handlers of some selected event types. The property names use the event type pattern. They are named as onXXX. For example, the onMouseClicked property stores the event handler for the mouse-clicked event type; the onKeyTyped property stores the event handler for the key-typed event; and so on. You can use the setOnXXX() methods of these properties to register event handlers for a node. For example, use the setOnMouseClicked() method to register an event handler for the mouse-clicked event and use the setOnKeyTyped() method to register an event handler for the key-typed event, and so on. The setOnXXX() methods in various classes are known as convenience methods for registering event handlers.

You need to remember some points about the onXXX convenience properties:

- They only support the registration of event handlers, not event filters. If you need to register event filters, use the addEventFilter() method.

- They only support the registration of *one event handler* for a node. Multiple event handlers for a node may be registered using the addEventHandler() method.

- These properties exist only for the commonly used events for a node type. For example, the onMouseClicked property exists in the Node and Scene classes, but not in the Window class; the onShowing property exists in the Window class, but not in the Node and Scene classes.

The program in Listing 9-2 works the same as the program in Listing 9-1. This time, you have used the onMouseClicked property of the Node class to register the mouse-clicked event handler for the circle. Notice that to register the event filter, you have to use the addEventFilter() method as before. Run the program and click inside the circle. You will get the same output you got when running the code in Listing 9-1.

Listing 9-2. Using the Convenience Event Handler Properties

```
// EventHandlerProperties.java
package com.jdojo.event;

import javafx.application.Application;
import javafx.event.EventHandler;
import javafx.scene.Scene;
import javafx.scene.input.MouseEvent;
import javafx.scene.layout.HBox;
import javafx.scene.paint.Color;
import javafx.scene.shape.Circle;
import javafx.stage.Stage;
```

```
public class EventHandlerProperties extends Application {
        public static void main(String[] args) {
                Application.launch(args);
        }

        @Override
        public void start(Stage stage) {
                Circle circle = new Circle (100, 100, 50);
                circle.setFill(Color.CORAL);

                HBox root = new HBox();
                root.getChildren().add(circle);
                Scene scene = new Scene(root);
                stage.setScene(scene);
                stage.setTitle(
                        "Using convenience event handler properties");
                stage.show();
                stage.sizeToScene();

                // Create a MouseEvent filter
                EventHandler<MouseEvent> eventFilter = e ->
                        System.out.println(
                            "Mouse event filter has been called.");

                // Create a MouseEvent handler
                EventHandler<MouseEvent> eventHandler = e ->
                        System.out.println(
                            "Mouse event handler has been called.");

                // Register the filter using the addEventFilter() method
                circle.addEventFilter(MouseEvent.MOUSE_CLICKED,
                        eventFilter);

                // Register the handler using the setter method for
                // the onMouseCicked convenience event property
                circle.setOnMouseClicked(eventHandler);
        }
}
```

The convenience event properties do not provide a separate method to unregister the event handler. Setting the property to null unregisters the event handler that has already been registered:

```
// Register an event handler for the mouse-clicked event
circle.setOnMouseClicked(eventHandler);

...

// Later, when you are no longer interested in processing the mouse-clicked
// event, unregister it.
circle.setOnMouseClicked(null);
```

Classes that define the onXXX event properties also define getOnXXX() getter methods that return the reference of the registered event handler. If no event handler is set, the getter method returns null.

Execution Order of Event Filters and Handlers

There are some execution order rules for event filters and handlers for both similar and different nodes:

- Event filters are called before event handlers. Event filters are executed from the topmost parent to the event target in the parent-child order. Event handlers are executed in the reverse order of the event filters. That is, the execution of the event handlers starts at the event target and moves up in the child-parent order.

- For the same node, event filters and handlers for a specific event type are called before the event filters and handlers for generic types. Suppose you have registered event handlers to a node for MouseEvent.ANY and MouseEvent.MOUSE_CLICKED. Event handlers for both event types are capable of handling mouse-clicked events. When the mouse is clicked on the node, the event handler for the MouseEvent.MOUSE_CLICKED event type is called before the event handler for the MouseEvent.ANY event type. Note that a mouse-pressed event and a mouse-released event occur before a mouse-clicked event occurs. In our example, these events will be handled by the event handler for the MouseEvent.ANY event type.

- The order in which the event filters and handlers for the same event type for a node are executed is not specified. There is one exception to this rule. Event handlers registered to a node using the addEventHandler() method are executed before the event handlers registered using the setOnXXX() convenience methods.

Listing 9-3 demonstrates the execution order of the event filters and handlers for different nodes. The program adds a Circle and a Rectangle to an HBox. The HBox is added to the Scene. An event filter and an event handler are added to the Stage, Scene, HBox, and Circle for the mouse-clicked event. Run the program and click anywhere inside the circle. The output shows the order in which filters and handlers are called. The output contains the event phase, type, target, source, and location. Notice that the source of the event changes as the event travels from one node to another. The location is relative to the event source. Because every node uses its own local coordinate system, the same point, where the mouse is clicked, has different values for (x, y) coordinates relative to different nodes.

Listing 9-3. Execution Order for Event Filters and Handlers

```
// CaptureBubblingOrder.java
package com.jdojo.event;

import javafx.application.Application;
import javafx.event.EventHandler;
import javafx.geometry.Insets;
import javafx.scene.Scene;
import javafx.scene.input.MouseEvent;
import javafx.scene.layout.HBox;
import javafx.scene.paint.Color;
import javafx.scene.shape.Circle;
import javafx.scene.shape.Rectangle;
import javafx.stage.Stage;
import static javafx.scene.input.MouseEvent.MOUSE_CLICKED;
```

If you click the rectangle, you will notice that the output shows the same path for the event through its parents as it did for the circle. The event still passes through the rectangle, which is the event target. However, you do not see any output, because you have not registered any event filters or handlers for the rectangle to output any message. You can click at any point outside the circle and rectangle to see the event target and the event path.

```java
public class CaptureBubblingOrder extends Application {
        public static void main(String[] args) {
                Application.launch(args);
        }

        @Override
        public void start(Stage stage) {
                Circle circle = new Circle (50, 50, 50);
                circle.setFill(Color.CORAL);

                Rectangle rect = new Rectangle(100, 100);
                rect.setFill(Color.TAN);

                HBox root = new HBox();
                root.setPadding(new Insets(20));
                root.setSpacing(20);
                root.getChildren().addAll(circle, rect);

                Scene scene = new Scene(root);

                // Create two EventHandlders
                EventHandler<MouseEvent> filter = e ->
                        handleEvent("Capture", e);
                EventHandler<MouseEvent> handler = e ->
                        handleEvent("Bubbling", e);

                // Register filters
                stage.addEventFilter(MOUSE_CLICKED, filter);
                scene.addEventFilter(MOUSE_CLICKED, filter);
                root.addEventFilter(MOUSE_CLICKED, filter);
                circle.addEventFilter(MOUSE_CLICKED, filter);

                // Register handlers
                stage.addEventHandler(MOUSE_CLICKED, handler);
                scene.addEventHandler(MOUSE_CLICKED, handler);
                root.addEventHandler(MOUSE_CLICKED, handler);
                circle.addEventHandler(MOUSE_CLICKED, handler);

                stage.setScene(scene);
                stage.setTitle(
                        "Event Capture and Bubbling Execution Order");
                stage.show();
        }
```

```
        public void handleEvent(String phase, MouseEvent e) {
                String type = e.getEventType().getName();
                String source = e.getSource().getClass().getSimpleName();
                String target = e.getTarget().getClass().getSimpleName();

                // Get coordinates of the mouse cursor relative to the
                // event source
                double x = e.getX();
                double y = e.getY();

                System.out.println(phase + ": Type=" + type +
                    ", Target=" + target +
                    ", Source=" +  source +
                    ", location(" + x + ", " + y + ")");
        }
}
```

Listing 9-4 demonstrates the execution order of event handlers for a node. It displays a circle. It registers three event handlers for the circle:

- One for the MouseEvent.ANY event type

- One for the MouseEvent.MOUSE_CLICKED event type using the addEventHandler() method

- One for the MouseEvent.MOUSE_CLICKED event type using the setOnMouseClicked() method

Run the program and click inside the circle. The output shows the order in which three event handlers are called. The order will be similar to that presented in the discussion at the beginning of the section.

Listing 9-4. Order of Execution of Event Handlers for a Node

```
// HandlersOrder.java
package com.jdojo.event;

import javafx.application.Application;
import javafx.scene.Scene;
import javafx.scene.input.MouseEvent;
import javafx.scene.layout.HBox;
import javafx.scene.paint.Color;
import javafx.scene.shape.Circle;
import javafx.stage.Stage;

public class HandlersOrder extends Application {
        public static void main(String[] args) {
                Application.launch(args);
        }

        @Override
        public void start(Stage stage) {
                Circle circle = new Circle(50, 50, 50);
                circle.setFill(Color.CORAL);
```

```
                HBox root = new HBox();
                root.getChildren().addAll(circle);
                Scene scene = new Scene(root);

                /* Register three handlers for the circle that can handle
                        mouse-clicked events */
                // This will be called last
                circle.addEventHandler(MouseEvent.ANY, e ->
                        handleAnyMouseEvent(e));

                // This will be called first
                circle.addEventHandler(MouseEvent.MOUSE_CLICKED, e ->
                        handleMouseClicked("addEventHandler()", e));

                // This will be called second
                circle.setOnMouseClicked(e ->
                        handleMouseClicked("setOnMouseClicked()", e));

                stage.setScene(scene);
                stage.setTitle(
                        "Execution Order of Event Handlers of a Node");
                stage.show();
        }

        public void handleMouseClicked(String registrationMethod,
                        MouseEvent e) {
                System.out.println(registrationMethod +
                    ": MOUSE_CLICKED handler detected a mouse click.");
        }

        public void handleAnyMouseEvent(MouseEvent e) {
                // Print a message only for mouse-clicked events,
                // ignoring other mouse events such as mouse-pressed,
                // mouse-released, etc.
                if (e.getEventType() == MouseEvent.MOUSE_CLICKED) {
                    System.out.println(
                                "MouseEvent.ANY handler detected a mouse click.");
                }
        }
}
```

```
addEventHandler(): MOUSE_CLICKED handler detected a mouse click.
setOnMouseClicked(): MOUSE_CLICKED handler detected a mouse click.
MouseEvent.ANY handler detected a mouse click.
```

Consuming Events

An event is consumed by calling its consume() method. The event class contains the method, and it is inherited by all event classes. Typically, the consume() method is called inside the handle() method of the event filters and handlers.

Consuming an event indicates to the event dispatcher that the event processing is complete and that the event should not travel any farther in the event dispatch chain. If an event is consumed in an event filter of a node, the event does not travel to any child node. If an event is consumed in an event handler of a node, the event does not travel to any parent node.

All event filters or handlers for the consuming node are called, irrespective of which filter or handler consumes the event. Suppose you have registered three event handlers for a node and the event handler, which is called first, consumes the event. In this case, the other two event handlers for the node are still called.

If a parent node does not want its child nodes to respond to an event, it can consume the event in its event filter. If a parent node provides a default response to an event in an event handler, a child node can provide a specific response and consume the event, thus suppressing the default response of the parent.

Typically, nodes consume most input events after providing a default response. The rule is that all event filters and handlers of a node are called, even if one of them consumes the event. This makes it possible for developers to execute their event filters and handlers for a node even if the node consumes the event.

The code in Listing 9-5 shows how to consume an event. Figure 9-6 shows the screen when you run the program.

Listing 9-5. Consuming Events

```
// ConsumingEvents.java
package com.jdojo.event;

import javafx.application.Application;
import javafx.event.EventHandler;
import javafx.geometry.Insets;
import javafx.scene.Scene;
import javafx.scene.control.CheckBox;
import javafx.scene.input.MouseEvent;
import static javafx.scene.input.MouseEvent.MOUSE_CLICKED;
import javafx.scene.layout.HBox;
import javafx.scene.paint.Color;
import javafx.scene.shape.Circle;
import javafx.scene.shape.Rectangle;
import javafx.stage.Stage;
```

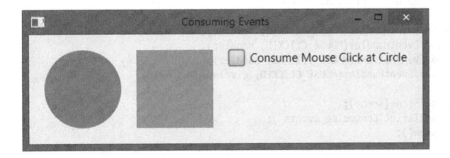

Figure 9-6. *Consuming events*

The program adds a Circle, a Rectangle, and a CheckBox to an HBox. The HBox is added to the scene as the root node. An event handler is added to the Stage, Scene, HBox, and Circle. Notice that you have a different event handler for the Circle, just to keep the program logic simple. When the check box is selected, the event handler for the circle consumes the mouse-clicked event, thus preventing the event from traveling up to the HBox, Scene, and Stage. If the check box is not selected, the mouse-clicked event on the circle travels from the Circle to the HBox, Scene, and Stage. Run the program and, using the mouse, click the different areas of the scene to see the effect. Notice that the mouse-clicked event handlers for the HBox, Scene, and Stage are executed, even if you click a point outside the circle, because they are in the event dispatch chain of the clicked nodes.

```java
public class ConsumingEvents extends Application {
        private CheckBox consumeEventCbx =
                new CheckBox("Consume Mouse Click at Circle");

        public static void main(String[] args) {
                Application.launch(args);
        }

        @Override
        public void start(Stage stage) {
                Circle circle = new Circle (50, 50, 50);
                circle.setFill(Color.CORAL);

                Rectangle rect = new Rectangle(100, 100);
                rect.setFill(Color.TAN);

                HBox root = new HBox();
                root.setPadding(new Insets(20));
                root.setSpacing(20);
                root.getChildren().addAll(circle, rect, consumeEventCbx);

                Scene scene = new Scene(root);

                // Register mouse-clicked event handlers to all nodes,
                // except the rectangle and checkbox
                EventHandler<MouseEvent> handler = e ->
                        handleEvent(e);
                EventHandler<MouseEvent> circleMeHandler = e ->
                        handleEventforCircle(e);

                stage.addEventHandler(MOUSE_CLICKED, handler);
                scene.addEventHandler(MOUSE_CLICKED, handler);
                root.addEventHandler(MOUSE_CLICKED, handler);
                circle.addEventHandler(MOUSE_CLICKED, circleMeHandler);

                stage.setScene(scene);
                stage.setTitle("Consuming Events");
                stage.show();
        }

        public void handleEvent(MouseEvent e) {
                print(e);
        }
```

```
public void handleEventforCircle(MouseEvent e) {
        print(e);
        if (consumeEventCbx.isSelected()) {
                e.consume();
        }
}

public void print(MouseEvent e) {
        String type = e.getEventType().getName();
        String source = e.getSource().getClass().getSimpleName();
        String target = e.getTarget().getClass().getSimpleName();

        // Get coordinates of the mouse cursor relative to the
            // event source
        double x = e.getX();
        double y = e.getY();

        System.out.println("Type=" + type + ", Target=" + target
            ", Source=" +  source +
            ", location(" + x + ", " + y + ")");
    }
}
```

Clicking the check box does not execute the mouse-clicked event handlers for the HBox, Scene, and Stage, whereas clicking the rectangle does. Can you think of a reason for this behavior? The reason is simple. The check box has a default event handler that takes a default action and consumes the event, preventing it from traveling up the event dispatch chain. The rectangle does not consume the event, allowing it to travel up the event dispatch chain.

■ **Tip** Consuming an event by the event target in an event filter has no effect on the execution of any other event filters. However, it prevents the event bubbling phase from happening. Consuming an event in the event handlers of the topmost node, which is the head of the event dispatch chain, has no effect on the event processing at all.

Handling Input Events

An input event indicates a user input (or a user action), for example, clicking the mouse, pressing a key, touching a touch screen, and so forth. JavaFX supports many types of input events. Figure 9-7 shows the class diagram for some of the classes that represent input event. All input event–related classes are in the javafx.scene.input package. The InputEvent class is the superclass of all input event classes. Typically, nodes execute the user-registered input event handlers before taking the default action. If the user event handlers consume the event, nodes do not take the default action. Suppose you register key-typed event handlers for a TextField, which consume the event. When you type a character, the TextField will not add and display it as its content. Therefore, consuming input events for nodes gives you a chance to disable the default behavior of the node. In the next sections, I will discuss mouse and key input events.

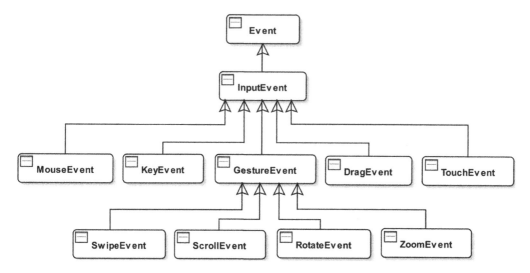

Figure 9-7. *Class hierarchy for some input events*

Handling Mouse Events

An object of the MouseEvent class represents a mouse event. The MouseEvent class defines the following mouse-related event type constants. All constants are of the type EventType<MouseEvent>. The Node class contains the convenience onXXX properties for most of the mouse event types that can be used to add one event handler of a specific mouse event type for a node:

- ANY: It is the supertype of all mouse event types. If a node wants to receive all types of mouse events, you would register handlers for this type. The InputEvent.ANY is the supertype of this event type.

- MOUSE_PRESSED: Pressing a mouse button generates this event. The getButton() method of the MouseEvent class returns the mouse button that is responsible for the event. A mouse button is represented by the NONE, PRIMARY, MIDDLE, and SECONDARY constants defined in the MouseButton enum.

- MOUSE_RELEASED: Releasing a mouse button generates this event. This event is delivered to the same node on which the mouse was pressed. For example, you can press a mouse button on a circle, drag the mouse outside the circle, and release the mouse button. The MOUSE_RELEASED event will be delivered to the circle, not the node on which the mouse button was released.

- MOUSE_CLICKED: This event is generated when a mouse button is clicked on a node. The button should be pressed and released on the same node for this event to occur.

- MOUSE_MOVED: Moving the mouse without pressing any mouse buttons generates this event.

- MOUSE_ENTERED: This event is generated when the mouse enters a node. The event capture and bubbling phases do not take place for this event. That is, event filters and handlers of the parent nodes of the event target of this event are not called.

- MOUSE_ENTERED_TARGET: This event is generated when the mouse enters a node. It is a variant of the MOUSE_ENTERED event type. Unlike the MOUSE_ENTERED event, the event capture and bubbling phases take place for this event.

- MOUSE_EXITED: This event is generated when the mouse leaves a node. The event capture and bubbling phases do not take place for this event, that is, it is delivered only to the target node.

- MOUSE_EXITED_TARGET: This event is generated when the mouse leaves a node. It is a variant of the MOUSE_EXITED event type. Unlike the MOUSE_EXITED event, the event capture and bubbling phases take place for this event.

- DRAG_DETECTED: This event is generated when the mouse is pressed and dragged over a node over a platform-specific distance threshold.

- MOUSE_DRAGGED: Moving the mouse with a pressed mouse button generates this event. This event is delivered to the same node on which the mouse button was pressed, irrespective of the location of the mouse pointer during the drag.

Getting Mouse Location

The MouseEvent class contains methods to give you the location of the mouse when a mouse event occurs. You can obtain the mouse location relative to the coordinate systems of the event source node, the scene, and the screen. The getX() and getY() methods give the (x, y) coordinates of the mouse relative to the event source node. The getSceneX() and getSceneY() methods give the (x, y) coordinates of the mouse relative to the scene to which the node is added. The getScreenX() and getScreenY() methods give the (x, y) coordinates of the mouse relative to the screen to which the node is added.

Listing 9-6 contains the program to show how to use the methods in the MouseEvent class to know the mouse location. It adds a MOUSE_CLICKED event handler to the stage, and the stage can receive the notification when the mouse is clicked anywhere in its area. Run the program and click anywhere in the stage, excluding its title bar if you are running it on the desktop. Each mouse click prints a message describing the source, target, and location of the mouse relative to the source, scene, and screen.

Listing 9-6. Determining the Mouse Location During Mouse Events

```java
// MouseLocation.java
package com.jdojo.event;

import javafx.application.Application;
import javafx.geometry.Insets;
import javafx.scene.Scene;
import javafx.scene.input.MouseEvent;
import javafx.scene.layout.HBox;
import javafx.scene.paint.Color;
import javafx.scene.shape.Circle;
import javafx.scene.shape.Rectangle;
import javafx.stage.Stage;

public class MouseLocation extends Application {
    public static void main(String[] args) {
        Application.launch(args);
    }
```

```
    @Override
    public void start(Stage stage) {
            Circle circle = new Circle (50, 50, 50);
            circle.setFill(Color.CORAL);

            Rectangle rect = new Rectangle(100, 100);
            rect.setFill(Color.TAN);

            HBox root = new HBox();
            root.setPadding(new Insets(20));
            root.setSpacing(20);
            root.getChildren().addAll(circle, rect);

            // Add a MOUSE_CLICKED event handler to the stage
            stage.addEventHandler(MouseEvent.MOUSE_CLICKED, e ->
                    handleMouseMove(e));

            Scene scene = new Scene(root);
            stage.setScene(scene);
            stage.setTitle("Mouse Location");
            stage.show();
    }

    public void handleMouseMove(MouseEvent e) {
            String source = e.getSource().getClass().getSimpleName();
            String target = e.getTarget().getClass().getSimpleName();

            // Mouse location relative to the event source
            double sourceX = e.getX();
            double sourceY = e.getY();

            // Mouse location relative to the scene
            double sceneX = e.getSceneX();
            double sceneY = e.getSceneY();

            // Mouse location relative to the screen
            double screenX = e.getScreenX();
            double screenY = e.getScreenY();

            System.out.println("Source=" +  source +
              ", Target=" + target +
              ", Location:" +
              " source(" + sourceX + ", " + sourceY + ")" +
              ", scene(" + sceneX + ", " + sceneY + ")" +
              ", screen(" + screenX + ", " + screenY + ")");
    }
}
```

Representing Mouse Buttons

Typically, a mouse has three buttons. You will also find some that have only one or two buttons. Some platforms provide ways to simulate the missing mouse buttons. The MouseButton enum in the javafx. scene.input package contains constants to represent mouse buttons. Table 9-2 contains the list of constants defined in the MouseButton enum.

Table 9-2. *Constants for the MouseButton Enum*

MouseButton Enum Constant	Description
NONE	It represents no button.
PRIMARY	It represents the primary button. Usually, it is the left button in the mouse.
MIDDLE	It represents the middle button.
SECONDARY	It represents the secondary button. Usually, it is the right button in the mouse.

The location of the primary and second mouse buttons depends on the mouse configuration. Typically, for right-handed users, the left and right buttons are configured as the primary and secondary buttons, respectively. For the left-handed users, the buttons are configured in the reverse order. If you have a two-button mouse, you do not have a middle button.

State of Mouse Buttons

The MouseEvent object that represents a mouse event contains the state of the mouse buttons at the time the event occurs. The MouseEvent class contains many methods to report the state of mouse buttons. Table 9-3 contains a list of such methods with their descriptions.

Table 9-3. *Methods Related to the State of Mouse Buttons in the MouseEvent Class*

Method	Description
MouseButton getButton()	It returns the mouse button responsible for the mouse event.
int getClickCount()	It returns the number of mouse clicks associated with the mouse event.
boolean isPrimaryButtonDown()	It returns true if the primary button is currently pressed. Otherwise, it returns false.
boolean isMiddleButtonDown()	It returns true if the middle button is currently pressed. Otherwise, it returns false.
boolean isSecondaryButtonDown()	It returns true if the secondary button is currently pressed. Otherwise, it returns false.
boolean isPopupTrigger()	It returns true if the mouse event is the pop-up menu trigger event for the platform. Otherwise, it returns false.
boolean isStillSincePress()	It returns true if the mouse cursor stays within a small area, which is known as the system-provided hysteresis area, between the last mouse-pressed event and the current mouse event.

In many circumstances, the getButton() method may return MouseButton.NONE, for example, when a mouse event is triggered on a touch screen by using the fingers instead of a mouse or when a mouse event, such as a mouse-moved event, is not triggered by a mouse button.

It is important to understand the difference between the getButton() method and other methods, for example, isPrimaryButtonDown(), which returns the pressed state of buttons. The getButton() method returns the button that triggers the event. Not all mouse events are triggered by buttons. For example, a mouse-moved event is triggered when the mouse moves, not by pressing or releasing a button. If a button is not responsible for a mouse event, the getButton() method returns MouseButton.NONE. The isPrimaryButtonDown() method returns true if the primary button is currently pressed, whether or not it triggered the event. For example, when you press the primary button, the mouse-pressed event occurs. The getButton() method will return MouseButton.PRIMARY because this is the button that triggered the mouse-pressed event. The isPrimaryButtonDown() method returns true because this button is pressed when the mouse-pressed event occurs. Suppose you keep the primary button pressed and you press the secondary button. Another mouse-pressed event occurs. However, this time, the getButton() returns MouseButton.SECONDARY, and both isPrimaryButtonDown() and isSecondaryButtonDown() methods return true, because both of these buttons are in the pressed state at the time of the second mouse-pressed event.

A *pop-up* menu, also known as a *context*, *contextual*, or *shortcut* menu, is a menu that gives a user a set of choices that are available in a specific context in an application. For example, when you click the right mouse button in a browser on the Windows platform, a pop-up menu is displayed. Different platforms trigger pop-up menu events differently upon use of a mouse or keyboard. On the Windows platform, typically it is a right mouse click or Shift + F10 key press.

The isPopupTrigger() method returns true if the mouse event is the pop-up menu trigger event for the platform. Otherwise, it returns false. If you perform an action based on the returned value of this method, you need to use it in both mouse-pressed and mouse-released events. Typically, when this method returns true, you let the system display the default pop-up menu.

■ **Tip**   JavaFX provides a *context menu event* that is a specific type of input event. It is represented by the ContextMenuEvent class in the javafx.scene.input package. If you want to handle context menu events, use ContextMenuEvent.

Hysteresis in GUI Applications

Hysteresis is a feature that allows user inputs to be within a range of time or location. The time range within which user inputs are accepted is known as the *hysteresis time*. The area in which user inputs are accepted is known as the *hysteresis area*. Hysteresis time and area are system dependent. For example, modern GUI applications provide features that are invoked by double-clicking a mouse button. A time gap exists between two clicks. If the time gap is within the hysteresis time of the system, two clicks are considered a double-click. Otherwise, they are considered two separate single clicks.

Typically, during a mouse-click event, the mouse is moved by a very tiny distance between the mouse-pressed and mouse-released events. Sometimes, it is important to take into account the distance the mouse is moved during a mouse click. The isStillSincePress() method returns true if the mouse stays in the system-provided hysteresis area since the last mouse-pressed event and the current event. This method is important when you want to consider a mouse-drag action. If this method returns true, you may ignore mouse drags as the mouse movement is still within the hysteresis distance from the point where the mouse was last pressed.

State of Modifier Keys

A modifier key is used to change the normal behavior of other keys. Some examples of modifier keys are Alt, Shift, Ctrl, Meta, Caps Lock, and Num Lock. Not all platforms support all modifier keys. The Meta key is present on Mac, not on Windows. Some systems let you simulate the functionality of a modifier key even if the modifier key is physically not present, for example, you can use the Windows key on Windows to work as the Meta key. The MouseEvent method contains methods to report the pressed state of some of the modifier keys when the mouse event occurs. Table 9-4 lists the methods related to the modifier keys in the MouseEvent class.

Table 9-4. *Methods, Related to the State of Modifier Keys, in the MouseEvent Class*

Method	Description
boolean isAltDown()	It returns true if the Alt key is down for this mouse event. Otherwise, it returns false.
boolean isControlDown()	It returns true if the Ctrl key is down for this mouse event. Otherwise, it returns false.
boolean isMetaDown()	It returns true if the Meta key is down for this mouse event. Otherwise, it returns false.
boolean isShiftDown()	It returns true if the Shift key is down for this mouse event. Otherwise, it returns false.
boolean isShortcutDown()	It returns true if the platform-specific shortcut key is down for this mouse event. Otherwise, it returns false. The shortcut modifier key is the Ctrl key on Windows and Meta key on Mac.

Picking Mouse Events on Bounds

The Node class has a pickOnBounds property to control the way mouse events are picked (or generated) for a node. A node can have any geometric shape, whereas its bounds always define a rectangular area. If the property is set to true, the mouse events are generated for the node if the mouse is on the perimeter or inside of its bounds. If the property is set to false, which is the default value, mouse events are generated for the node if the mouse is on the perimeter or inside of its geometric shape. Some nodes, such as the Text node, have the default value for the pickOnBounds property set to true.

Figure 9-8 shows the perimeter for the geometric shape and bounds of a circle. If the pickOnBounds property for the circle is false, the mouse event will not be generated for the circle if the mouse is one of the four areas in the corners that lie between the perimeter of the geometric shape and bounds.

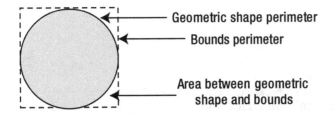

Geometric shape perimeter

Bounds perimeter

Area between geometric
shape and bounds

Figure 9-8. *Difference between the geometric shape and bounds of a circle*

Listing 9-7 contains the program to show the effects of the pickOnBounds property of a Circle node. It displays a window as shown in Figure 9-9. The program adds a Rectangle and a Circle to a Group. Note that the Rectangle is added to the Group before the Circle to keep the former below the latter in Z-order.

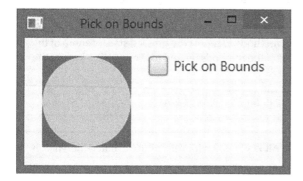

Figure 9-9. *Demonstrating the effects of the pickOnBounds property of a Circle node*

The Rectangle uses red as the fill color, whereas light gray is used as the fill color for the Circle. The area in red is the area between the perimeters of the geometric shape and bounds of the Circle.

You have a check box that controls the pickOnBounds property of the circle. If it is selected, the property is set to true. Otherwise, it is set to false.

When you click the gray area, the Circle always picks up the mouse-clicked event. When you click the red area with the check box unselected, the Rectangle picks up the event. When you click the red area with the check box selected, the Circle picks up the event. The output shows who picks up the mouse-clicked event.

Listing 9-7. Testing the Effects of the pickOnBounds Property for a Circle Node

```java
// PickOnBounds.java
package com.jdojo.event;

import javafx.application.Application;
import javafx.event.ActionEvent;
import javafx.geometry.Insets;
import javafx.scene.Group;
import javafx.scene.Scene;
import javafx.scene.control.CheckBox;
import javafx.scene.input.MouseEvent;
import javafx.scene.layout.HBox;
import javafx.scene.paint.Color;
import javafx.scene.shape.Circle;
import javafx.scene.shape.Rectangle;
import javafx.stage.Stage;

public class PickOnBounds extends Application {
        private CheckBox pickonBoundsCbx = new CheckBox("Pick on Bounds");
        Circle circle = new Circle(50, 50, 50, Color.LIGHTGRAY);
```

```java
public static void main(String[] args) {
        Application.launch(args);
}

@Override
public void start(Stage stage) {
        Rectangle rect = new Rectangle(100, 100);
        rect.setFill(Color.RED);

        Group group = new Group();
        group.getChildren().addAll(rect, circle);

        HBox root = new HBox();
        root.setPadding(new Insets(20));
        root.setSpacing(20);
        root.getChildren().addAll(group, pickonBoundsCbx);

        // Add MOUSE_CLICKED event handlers to the circle and
        // rectangle
        circle.setOnMouseClicked(e -> handleMouseClicked(e));
        rect.setOnMouseClicked(e -> handleMouseClicked(e));

        // Add an Action handler to the checkbox
        pickonBoundsCbx.setOnAction(e -> handleActionEvent(e));

        Scene scene = new Scene(root);
        stage.setScene(scene);
        stage.setTitle("Pick on Bounds");
        stage.show();
}

public void handleMouseClicked(MouseEvent e) {
        String target = e.getTarget().getClass().getSimpleName();
        String type = e.getEventType().getName();
        System.out.println(type + " on " + target);
}

public void handleActionEvent(ActionEvent e) {
        if (pickonBoundsCbx.isSelected()) {
                circle.setPickOnBounds(true);
        } else {
                circle.setPickOnBounds(false);
        }
}
}
```

Mouse Transparency

The Node class has a mouseTransparent property to control whether or not a node and its children receive mouse events. Contrast the pickOnBounds and mouseTransparent properties: the former determines the area of a node that generates mouse events, and the latter determines whether or not a node and its children generate mouse events, irrespective of the value of the former. The former affects only the node on which it is set; the latter affects the node on which it is set and all its children.

The code in Listing 9-8 shows the effects of the mouseTransparent property of a Circle. This is a variant of the program in Listing 9-7. It displays a window that is very similar to the one shown in Figure 9-9. When the check box MouseTransparency is selected, it sets the mouseTransparent property of the circle to true. When the check box is unselected, it sets the mouseTransparent property of the circle to false.

Click the circle, in the gray area, when the check box is selected, and all mouse-clicked events will be delivered to the rectangle. This is because the circle is mouse transparent, and it lets the mouse events pass through. Unselect the check box, and all mouse clicks in the gray area are delivered to the circle. Note that clicking the red area always delivers the event to the rectangle, because the pickOnBounds property for the circle is set to false by default. The output shows the node that receives the mouse-clicked events.

Listing 9-8. Testing the Effects of the mouseTransparent Property for a Circle Node

```
// MouseTransparency.java
package com.jdojo.event;

import javafx.application.Application;
import javafx.event.ActionEvent;
import javafx.geometry.Insets;
import javafx.scene.Group;
import javafx.scene.Scene;
import javafx.scene.control.CheckBox;
import javafx.scene.input.MouseEvent;
import javafx.scene.layout.HBox;
import javafx.scene.paint.Color;
import javafx.scene.shape.Circle;
import javafx.scene.shape.Rectangle;
import javafx.stage.Stage;

public class MouseTransparency extends Application {
        private CheckBox mouseTransparentCbx =
                new CheckBox("Mouse Transparent");
        Circle circle = new Circle(50, 50, 50, Color.LIGHTGRAY);

        public static void main(String[] args) {
                Application.launch(args);
        }

        @Override
        public void start(Stage stage) {
                Rectangle rect = new Rectangle(100, 100);
                rect.setFill(Color.RED);

                Group group = new Group();
                group.getChildren().addAll(rect, circle);
```

```
        HBox root = new HBox();
        root.setPadding(new Insets(20));
        root.setSpacing(20);
        root.getChildren().addAll(group, mouseTransparentCbx);

        // Add MOUSE_CLICKED event handlers to the circle
        // and rectangle
        circle.setOnMouseClicked(e -> handleMouseClicked(e));
        rect.setOnMouseClicked(e -> handleMouseClicked(e));

        // Add an Action handler to the checkbox
        mouseTransparentCbx.setOnAction(e ->
                handleActionEvent(e));

        Scene scene = new Scene(root);
        stage.setScene(scene);
        stage.setTitle("Mouse Transparency");
        stage.show();
    }

    public void handleMouseClicked(MouseEvent e) {
        String target = e.getTarget().getClass().getSimpleName();
        String type = e.getEventType().getName();
        System.out.println(type + " on " + target);
    }

    public void handleActionEvent(ActionEvent e) {
        if (mouseTransparentCbx.isSelected()) {
                circle.setMouseTransparent(true);
        } else {
                circle.setMouseTransparent(false);
        }
    }
}
```

Synthesized Mouse Events

A mouse event can be generated using several types of devices, such as a mouse, track pad, or touch screen. Some actions on a touch screen generate mouse events, which are considered *synthesized mouse events*. The isSynthesized() method of the MouseEvent class returns true if the event is synthesized from using a touch screen. Otherwise, it returns false.

When a finger is dragged on a touch screen, it generates both a scrolling gesture event and a mouse-dragged event. The return value of the isSynthesized() method can be used inside the mouse-dragged event handlers to detect if the event is generated by dragging a finger on a touch screen or by dragging a mouse.

Handling Mouse-Entered and Mouse-Exited Events

Four mouse event types deal with events when the mouse enters or exits a node:

- MOUSE_ENTERED
- MOUSE_EXITED
- MOUSE_ENTERED_TARGET
- MOUSE_EXITED_TARGET

You have two sets of event types for mouse-entered and mouse-exited events. One set contains two types called MOUSE_ENTERED and MOUSE_EXITED, and another set contains MOUSE_ENTERED_TARGET and MOUSE_EXITED_TARGET. They both have something in common, such as when they are triggered. They differ in their delivery mechanisms. I will discuss all of them in this section.

When the mouse enters a node, a MOUSE_ENTERED event is generated. When the mouse leaves a node, a MOUSE_EXITED event is generated. These events do not go through the capture and bubbling phases. That is, they are delivered directly to the target node, not to any of its parent nodes.

▪ **Tip** The MOUSE_ENTERED and MOUSE_EXITED events do not participate in the capture and bubbling phases. However, all event *filters* and *handlers* are executed for the target following the rules for event handling.

The program in Listing 9-9 shows how mouse-entered and mouse-exited events are delivered. The program displays a window as shown in Figure 9-10. It shows a circle with gray fill inside an HBox. Event handlers for mouse-entered and mouse-exited events are added to the HBox and the Circle. Run the program and move the mouse in and out of the circle. When the mouse enters the white area in the window, its MOUSE_ENTERED event is delivered to the HBox. When you move the mouse in and out of the circle, the output shows that the MOUSE_ENTERED and MOUSE_EXITED events are delivered only to the Circle, not to the HBox. Notice that in the output the source and target of these events are always the same, proving that the capture and bubbling phases do not occur for these events. When you move the mouse in and out of the circle, keeping it in the white area, the MOUSE_EXITED event for the HBox does not fire, as the mouse stays on the HBox. To fire the MOUSE_EXITED event on the HBox, you will need to move the mouse outside the scene area, for example, outside the window or over the title bar of the window.

Listing 9-9. Testing Mouse-Entered and Mouse-Exited Events

```java
// MouseEnteredExited.java
package com.jdojo.event;

import javafx.application.Application;
import javafx.geometry.Insets;
import javafx.scene.Scene;
import javafx.scene.input.MouseEvent;
import javafx.scene.layout.HBox;
import javafx.scene.paint.Color;
import javafx.scene.shape.Circle;
import javafx.event.EventHandler;
import javafx.stage.Stage;
import static javafx.scene.input.MouseEvent.MOUSE_ENTERED;
import static javafx.scene.input.MouseEvent.MOUSE_EXITED;
```

```java
public class MouseEnteredExited  extends Application {
        public static void main(String[] args) {
                Application.launch(args);
        }

        @Override
        public void start(Stage stage) {
                Circle circle = new Circle (50, 50, 50);
                circle.setFill(Color.GRAY);

                HBox root = new HBox();
                root.setPadding(new Insets(20));
                root.setSpacing(20);
                root.getChildren().addAll(circle);

                // Create a mouse event handler
                EventHandler<MouseEvent> handler = e -> handle(e);

                // Add mouse-entered and mouse-exited event handlers to
                // the HBox
                root.addEventHandler(MOUSE_ENTERED, handler);
                root.addEventHandler(MOUSE_EXITED, handler);

                // Add mouse-entered and mouse-exited event handlers to
                // the Circle
                circle.addEventHandler(MOUSE_ENTERED, handler);
                circle.addEventHandler(MOUSE_EXITED, handler);

                Scene scene = new Scene(root);
                stage.setScene(scene);
                stage.setTitle("Mouse Entered and Exited Events");
                stage.show();
        }

        public void handle(MouseEvent e) {
                String type = e.getEventType().getName();
                String source = e.getSource().getClass().getSimpleName();
                String target = e.getTarget().getClass().getSimpleName();
                System.out.println("Type=" + type +
                        ", Target=" + target + ", Source=" +  source);
        }
}
```

```
Type=MOUSE_ENTERED, Target=HBox, Source=HBox
Type=MOUSE_ENTERED, Target=Circle, Source=Circle
Type=MOUSE_EXITED, Target=Circle, Source=Circle
Type=MOUSE_ENTERED, Target=Circle, Source=Circle
Type=MOUSE_EXITED, Target=Circle, Source=Circle
Type=MOUSE_EXITED, Target=HBox, Source=HBox
...
```

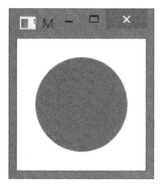

Figure 9-10. *Demonstrating mouse-entered and mouse-exited events*

The MOUSE_ENTERED and MOUSE_EXITED event types provide the functionality needed in most cases. Sometimes, you need these events to go through the normal capture and bubbling phases, so parent nodes can apply filters and provide default responses. The MOUSE_ENTERED_TARGET and MOUSE_EXITED_TARGET event types provide these features. They participate in the event capture and bubbling phases.

The MOUSE_ENTERED and MOUSE_EXITED event types are subtypes of the MOUSE_ENTERED_TARGET and MOUSE_EXITED_TARGET event types. A node interested in the mouse-entered event of its children should add event filters and handlers for the MOUSE_ENTERED_TARGET type. The child node can add MOUSE_ENTERED, MOUSE_ENTERED_TARGET, or both event filters and handlers. When the mouse enters the child node, parent nodes receive the MOUSE_ENTERED_TARGET event. Before the event is delivered to the child node, which is the target node of the event, the event type is changed to the MOUSE_ENTERED type. Therefore, in the same event processing, the target node receives the MOUSE_ENTERED event, whereas all its parent nodes receive the MOUSE_ENTERED_TARGET event. Because the MOUSE_ENTERED event type is a subtype of the MOUSE_ENTERED_TARGET type, either type of event handler on the target can handle this event. The same would apply to the mouse-exited event and its corresponding event types.

Sometimes, inside the parent event handler, it is necessary to distinguish the node that fires the MOUSE_ENTERED_TARGET event. A parent node receives this event when the mouse enters the parent node itself or any of its child nodes. You can check the target node reference, using the getTarget() method of the Event class, for equality with the reference of the parent node, inside the event filters and handlers, to know whether or not the event was fired by the parent.

The program in Listing 9-10 shows how to use the mouse-entered-target and mouse-exited-target events. It adds a Circle and a CheckBox to an HBox. The HBox is added to the Scene. It adds the mouse-entered-target and mouse-exited-target event filters to the HBox and event handlers to the Circle. It also adds mouse-entered and mouse-exited event handlers to the Circle. When the check box is selected, events are consumed by the HBox, so they do not reach the Circle. The following are a few observations when you run the program:

- With the check box unselected, when the mouse enters or leaves the Circle, the HBox receives the MOUSE_ENTERED_TARGET and MOUSE_EXITED_TARGET events. The Circle receives the MOUSE_ENTERED and MOUSE_EXITED events.

- With the check box selected, the HBox receives the MOUSE_ENTERED_TARGET and MOUSE_EXITED_TARGET events and consumes them. The Circle does not receive any events.

- When the mouse enters or leaves the HBox, the white area in the window, the HBox receives the MOUSE_ENTERED and MOUSE_EXITED events, because the HBox is the target of the event.

Play with the application by moving the mouse around, selecting and unselecting the check box. Look at the output to get a feel for how these events are processed.

Listing 9-10. Using the Mouse-Entered-Target and Mouse-Exited-Target Events

```java
// MouseEnteredExitedTarget.java
package com.jdojo.event;

import javafx.application.Application;
import javafx.event.EventHandler;
import javafx.geometry.Insets;
import javafx.scene.Scene;
import javafx.scene.control.CheckBox;
import javafx.scene.input.MouseEvent;
import static javafx.scene.input.MouseEvent.MOUSE_ENTERED;
import static javafx.scene.input.MouseEvent.MOUSE_EXITED;
import static javafx.scene.input.MouseEvent.MOUSE_ENTERED_TARGET;
import static javafx.scene.input.MouseEvent.MOUSE_EXITED_TARGET;
import javafx.scene.layout.HBox;
import javafx.scene.paint.Color;
import javafx.scene.shape.Circle;
import javafx.stage.Stage;

public class MouseEnteredExitedTarget extends Application {
        private CheckBox consumeCbx = new CheckBox("Consume Events");

        public static void main(String[] args) {
                Application.launch(args);
        }

        @Override
        public void start(Stage stage) {
                Circle circle = new Circle(50, 50, 50);
                circle.setFill(Color.GRAY);

                HBox root = new HBox();
                root.setPadding(new Insets(20));
                root.setSpacing(20);
                root.getChildren().addAll(circle, consumeCbx);

                // Create mouse event handlers
                EventHandler<MouseEvent> circleHandler = e ->
                        handleCircle(e);
                EventHandler<MouseEvent> circleTargetHandler = e ->
                        handleCircleTarget(e);
                EventHandler<MouseEvent> hBoxTargetHandler = e ->
                        handleHBoxTarget(e);
```

```
            // Add mouse-entered-target and mouse-exited-target event
            // handlers to HBox
            root.addEventFilter(MOUSE_ENTERED_TARGET,
                    hBoxTargetHandler);
            root.addEventFilter(MOUSE_EXITED_TARGET,
                    hBoxTargetHandler);

            // Add mouse-entered-target and mouse-exited-target event
            // handlers to the Circle
            circle.addEventHandler(MOUSE_ENTERED_TARGET,
                    circleTargetHandler);
            circle.addEventHandler(MOUSE_EXITED_TARGET,
                    circleTargetHandler);

            // Add mouse-entered and mouse-exited event handlers to
            // the Circle
            circle.addEventHandler(MOUSE_ENTERED, circleHandler);
            circle.addEventHandler(MOUSE_EXITED, circleHandler);

            Scene scene = new Scene(root);
            stage.setScene(scene);
            stage.setTitle(
                    "Mouse Entered Target and Exited Target Events");
            stage.show();
    }

    public void handleCircle(MouseEvent e) {
            print(e, "Circle Handler");
    }

    public void handleCircleTarget(MouseEvent e) {
            print(e, "Circle Target Handler");
    }

    public void handleHBoxTarget(MouseEvent e) {
            print(e, "HBox Target Filter");
            if (consumeCbx.isSelected()) {
                e.consume();
                System.out.println(
                        "HBox consumed the " + e.getEventType() + " event");
            }
    }

    public void print(MouseEvent e, String msg) {
            String type = e.getEventType().getName();
            String source = e.getSource().getClass().getSimpleName();
            String target = e.getTarget().getClass().getSimpleName();
            System.out.println(msg + ": Type=" + type +
                                    ", Target=" + target +
                                    ", Source=" + source);
    }
}
```

Handling Key Events

A key event is a type of input event that denotes the occurrence of a keystroke. It is delivered to the node that has focus. An instance of the KeyEvent class, which is declared in the javafx.scene.input package, represents a key event. Key pressed, key released, and key typed are three types of key events. Table 9-5 lists all of the constants in the KeyEvent class, which represent key event types.

Table 9-5. *Constants in the KeyEvent Class to Represent Key Event Types*

Constant	Description
ANY	It is the supertype of other key event types.
KEY_PRESSED	It occurs when a key is pressed.
KEY_RELEASED	It occurs when a key is released.
KEY_TYPED	It occurs when a Unicode character is entered.

■ **Tip** It may not be obvious that shapes, for example, circles or rectangles, can also receive key events. The criterion for a node to receive key events is that the node should have focus. By default, shapes are not part of the focus traversal chain, and mouse clicks do not bring focus to them. Shape nodes can get focus by calling the requestFocus() method.

The key-pressed and key-released events are lower-level events compared to the key-typed event; they occur with a key press and release, respectively, and depend on the platform and keyboard layout.

The key-typed event is a higher-level event. Generally, it does not depend on the platform and keyboard layout. It occurs when a Unicode character is typed. Typically, a key press generates a key-typed event. However, a key release may also generate a key-typed event. For example, when using the Alt key and number pad on Windows, a key-typed event is generated by the release of the Alt key, irrespective of the number of keystrokes entered on the number pad. A key-typed event can also be generated by a series of key presses and releases. For example, the character A is entered by pressing Shift + A, which includes two key presses (Shift and A). In this case, two key presses generate one key-typed event. Not all key presses or releases generate key-typed events. For example, when you press a function key (F1, F2, etc.) or modifier keys (Shift, Ctrl, etc.), no Unicode character is entered, and, hence, no key-typed event is generated.

The KeyEvent class maintains three variables to describe the keys associated with the event: code, text, and character. These variables can be accessed using the getter methods in the KeyEvent class as listed in Table 9-6.

Table 9-6. *Methods in the KeyEvent Class Returning Key Details*

Method	Valid for	Description
KeyCode getCode()	KEY_PRESSED KEY_RELEASED	The KeyCode enum contains a constant to represent all keys on the keyboard. This method returns the KeyCode enum constant that is associated with the key being pressed or released. For the key-typed events, it always returns KeyCode.UNDEFINED, because the key-typed event may not necessarily be triggered by a single keystroke.
String getText()	KEY_PRESSED KEY_RELEASED	It returns a String description of the KeyCode associated with the key-pressed and key-released events. It always returns an empty string for the key-typed events.
String getCharacter()	KEY_TYPED	It returns a character or a sequence of characters associated with a key-typed event as a String. For the key-pressed and key-released events, it always returns KeyEvent.CHAR_UNDEFINED.

It is interesting to note that the return type of the getCharacter() method is String, not char. The design is intentional. Unicode characters outside the basic multilingual plane cannot be represented in one character. Some devices may produce multiple characters using a single keystroke. The return type of String for the getCharacter() method covers these odd cases.

The KeyEvent class contains isAltDown(), isControlDown(), isMetaDown(), isShiftDown(), and isShortcutDown() methods that let you check whether modifier keys are down when a key event occurs.

Handling Key-Pressed and Key-Released Events

Key-pressed and key-released events are handled simply by adding the event filters and handlers to nodes for the KEY_PRESSED and KEY_RELEASED event types. Typically, you use these events to know which keys were pressed or released and to perform an action. For example, you can detect the F1 function key press and display a custom Help window for the node in focus.

The program in Listing 9-11 shows how to handle key-pressed and key-released events. It displays a Label and a TextField. When you run the program, the TextField has focus. Notice the following points when you use keystrokes while running this program:

- Press and release some keys. Output will show the details of events as they occur. A key-released event does not occur for every key-pressed event.

- The mapping between key-pressed and key-released events is not one to one. There may be no key-released event for a key-pressed event (refer to the next item). There may be one key-released event for several key-pressed events. This can happen when you keep a key pressed for a longer period. Sometimes, you do it to type the same character multiple times. Press the A key and hold it for some time and then release it. This will generate several key-pressed events and only one key-released event.

- Press the F1 key. It will display the Help window. Notice that pressing the F1 key does not generate an output for a key-released event, even after you release the key. Can you think of the reason for this? On the key-pressed event, the Help window is displayed, which grabs the focus. The TextField on the main window no longer has focus. Recall that the key events are delivered to the node that has focus, and only one node can have focus in a JavaFX application. Therefore, the key-released event is delivered to the Help window, not the TextField.

Listing 9-11. Handling Key-Pressed and Key-Released Events

```java
// KeyPressedReleased.java
package com.jdojo.event;

import javafx.application.Application;
import javafx.geometry.Insets;
import javafx.scene.Scene;
import javafx.scene.control.Label;
import javafx.scene.control.TextField;
import javafx.scene.input.KeyCode;
import javafx.scene.input.KeyEvent;
import static javafx.scene.input.KeyEvent.KEY_PRESSED;
import javafx.scene.layout.HBox;
import javafx.scene.text.Text;
import javafx.stage.Stage;

public class KeyPressedReleased extends Application {
        public static void main(String[] args) {
                Application.launch(args);
        }

        @Override
        public void start(Stage stage) {
                Label nameLbl = new Label("Name:");
                TextField nameTfl = new TextField();

                HBox root = new HBox();
                root.setPadding(new Insets(20));
                root.setSpacing(20);
                root.getChildren().addAll(nameLbl, nameTfl);

                // Add key pressed and released events to the TextField
                nameTfl.setOnKeyPressed(e -> handle(e));
                nameTfl.setOnKeyReleased(e -> handle(e));

                Scene scene = new Scene(root);
                stage.setScene(scene);
                stage.setTitle("Key Pressed and Released Events");
                stage.show();
        }

        public void handle(KeyEvent e) {
                String type = e.getEventType().getName();
                KeyCode keyCode = e.getCode();
                System.out.println(type + ": Key Code=" +
                   keyCode.getName() +
                   ", Text=" + e.getText());
```

```java
                    // Show the help window when the F1 key is pressed
                    if (e.getEventType() == KEY_PRESSED &&
                                    e.getCode() == KeyCode.F1) {
                        displayHelp();
                        e.consume();
                    }
            }

        public void displayHelp() {
                    Text helpText = new Text("Please enter a name.");
                    HBox root = new HBox();
                    root.setStyle("-fx-background-color: yellow;");
                    root.getChildren().add(helpText);

                    Scene scene = new Scene(root, 200, 100);
                    Stage helpStage = new Stage();
                    helpStage.setScene(scene);
                    helpStage.setTitle("Help");
                    helpStage.show();
            }
}
```

Handling the Key-Typed Event

The key-typed event is used to detect specific keystrokes. You cannot use it to prevent the user from entering certain characters—for this aim, you can use a formatter. We do not explain using formatters at this place, but the setTextFormatter() method description in the API documentation of, for example, the TextField control gives you a starting point if you need to use this kind of functionality.

The program in Listing 9-12 shows a Label and a TextField. It adds a key-typed event handler to the TextField, which prints some information on pressed keys.

Listing 9-12. Using the Key-Typed Event

```java
// KeyTyped.java
package com.jdojo.event;

import javafx.application.Application;
import javafx.geometry.Insets;
import javafx.scene.Scene;
import javafx.scene.control.Label;
import javafx.scene.control.TextField;
import javafx.scene.input.KeyEvent;
import javafx.scene.layout.HBox;
import javafx.stage.Stage;

public class KeyTyped extends Application {
        public static void main(String[] args) {
                Application.launch(args);
        }
```

```
        @Override
        public void start(Stage stage) {
                Label nameLbl = new Label("Name:");
                TextField nameTfl = new TextField();

                HBox root = new HBox();
                root.setPadding(new Insets(20));
                root.setSpacing(20);
                root.getChildren().addAll(nameLbl, nameTfl);

                // Add key-typed event to the TextField
                nameTfl.setOnKeyTyped(e -> handle(e));

                Scene scene = new Scene(root);
                stage.setScene(scene);
                stage.setTitle("Key Typed Event");
                stage.show();
        }

        public void handle(KeyEvent e) {
                String type = e.getEventType().getName();
                System.out.println(type + ": Character=" +
                                e.getCharacter());
        }
}
```

Handling Window Events

A window event occurs when a window is shown, hidden, or closed. An instance of the WindowEvent class in the javafx.stage package represents a window event. Table 9-7 lists the constants in the WindowEvent class.

Table 9-7. *Constants in the* WindowEvent *Class to Represent Window Event Types*

Constant	Description
ANY	It is the supertype of all other window event types.
WINDOW_SHOWING	It occurs just before the window is shown.
WINDOW_SHOWN	It occurs just after the window is shown.
WINDOW_HIDING	It occurs just before the window is hidden.
WINDOW_HIDDEN	It occurs just after the window is hidden.
WINDOW_CLOSE_REQUEST	It occurs when there is an external request to close this window.

The window-showing and window-shown events are straightforward. They occur just before and after the window is shown. Event handlers for the window-showing event should have time-consuming logic, as it will delay showing the window to the user and, hence, degrading the user experience. Initializing some window-level variables is a good example of the kind of code you need to write in this event. Typically, the window-shown event sets the starting direction for the user, for example, setting focus to the first editable field on the window and showing alerts to the user about the tasks that need their attention, among others.

The window-hiding and window-hidden events are counterparts of the window-showing and window-shown events. They occur just before and after the window is hidden.

The window-close-request event occurs when there is an external request to close the window. Using the Close menu from the context menu or the Close icon in the window title bar or pressing the Alt + F4 key combination on Windows is considered an external request to close the window. Note that closing a window programmatically, for example, using the `close()` method of the `Stage` class or `Platform.exit()` method, is not considered an external request. If the window-close-request event is consumed, the window is not closed.

The program in Listing 9-13 shows how to use all window events. You may get a different output than that shown below the code. It adds a check box and two buttons to the primary stage. If the check box is unselected, external requests to close the window are consumed, thus preventing the window from closing. The Close button closes the window. The Hide button hides the primary window and opens a new window, so the user can show the primary window again.

The program adds event handlers to the primary stage for window event types. When the `show()` method on the stage is called, the window-showing and window-shown events are generated. When you click the Hide button, the window-hiding and window-hidden events are generated. When you click the button on the pop-up window to show the primary window, the window-showing and window-shown events are generated again. Try clicking the Close icon on the title bar to generate the window-close-request event. If the Can Close Window check box is not selected, the window is not closed. When you use the Close button to close the window, the window-hiding and window-hidden events are generated, but not the window-close-request event, as it is not an external request to close the window.

Listing 9-13. Using Window Events

```java
// WindowEventApp.java
package com.jdojo.event;

import javafx.application.Application;
import javafx.event.EventType;
import javafx.geometry.Insets;
import javafx.scene.Scene;
import javafx.scene.control.Button;
import javafx.scene.control.CheckBox;
import javafx.scene.layout.HBox;
import javafx.stage.Stage;
import javafx.stage.WindowEvent;
import static javafx.stage.WindowEvent.WINDOW_CLOSE_REQUEST;

public class WindowEventApp  extends Application {
        private CheckBox canCloseCbx = new CheckBox("Can Close Window");

        public static void main(String[] args) {
                Application.launch(args);
        }

        @Override
        public void start(Stage stage) {
                Button closeBtn = new Button("Close");
                closeBtn.setOnAction(e -> stage.close());
```

```java
        Button hideBtn = new Button("Hide");
        hideBtn.setOnAction(e -> {
                showDialog(stage); stage.hide(); });

        HBox root = new HBox();
        root.setPadding(new Insets(20));
        root.setSpacing(20);
        root.getChildren().addAll(
                canCloseCbx, closeBtn, hideBtn);

        // Add window event handlers to the stage
        stage.setOnShowing(e -> handle(e));
        stage.setOnShown(e -> handle(e));
        stage.setOnHiding(e -> handle(e));
        stage.setOnHidden(e -> handle(e));
        stage.setOnCloseRequest(e -> handle(e));

        Scene scene = new Scene(root);
        stage.setScene(scene);
        stage.setTitle("Window Events");
        stage.show();
    }

    public void handle(WindowEvent e) {
        // Consume the event if the CheckBox is not selected
        // thus preventing the user from closing the window
        EventType<WindowEvent> type = e.getEventType();
        if (type == WINDOW_CLOSE_REQUEST &&
                    !canCloseCbx.isSelected()) {
                e.consume();
        }

        System.out.println(type + ": Consumed=" +
                e.isConsumed());
    }

    public void showDialog(Stage mainWindow) {
        Stage popup = new Stage();

        Button closeBtn =
                new Button("Click to Show Main Window");
        closeBtn.setOnAction(e -> {
                popup.close(); mainWindow.show();});

        HBox root = new HBox();
        root.setPadding(new Insets(20));
        root.setSpacing(20);
        root.getChildren().addAll(closeBtn);
```

```
                Scene scene = new Scene(root);
                popup.setScene(scene);
                popup.setTitle("Popup");
                popup.show();
        }
}
```

```
WINDOW_SHOWING: Consumed=false
WINDOW_SHOWN: Consumed=false
WINDOW_HIDING: Consumed=false
WINDOW_HIDDEN: Consumed=false
WINDOW_SHOWING: Consumed=false
WINDOW_SHOWN: Consumed=false
WINDOW_CLOSE_REQUEST: Consumed=true
```

Summary

In general, the term event is used to describe an occurrence of interest. In a GUI application, an event is an occurrence of a user interaction with the application such as clicking the mouse, pressing a key on the keyboard, and so forth. An event in JavaFX is represented by an object of the javafx.event.Event class or any of its subclasses. Every event in JavaFX has three properties: an event source, an event target, and an event type.

When an event occurs in an application, you typically perform some processing by executing a piece of code. The piece of code that is executed in response to an event is known as an event handler or an event filter. When you want to handle an event for a UI element, you need to add event handlers to the UI element, for example, a Window, a Scene, or a Node. When the UI element detects the event, it executes your event handlers.

The UI element that calls event handlers is the source of the event for those event handlers. When an event occurs, it passes through a chain of event dispatchers. The source of an event is the current element in the event dispatcher chain. The event source changes as the event passes through one dispatcher to another in the event dispatcher chain. The event target is the destination of an event, which determines the route the event travels through during its processing. The event type describes the type of the event that occurs. They are defined in a hierarchical fashion. Each event type has a name and a supertype.

When an event occurs, the following three steps are performed in order: event target selection, event route construction, and event route traversal. An event target is the destination node of the event that is selected based on the event type. An event travels through event dispatchers in an event dispatch chain. The event dispatch chain is the event route. The initial and default route for an event is determined by the event target. The default event route consists of the container-children path starting at the stage to the event target node.

An event route traversal consists of two phases: capture and bubbling. An event travels through each node in its route twice: once during the capture phase and once during the bubbling phase. You can register event filters and event handlers to a node for specific event types. The event filters and event handlers registered to a node are executed as the event passes through the node during the capture and the bubbling phases, respectively.

During the route traversal, a node can consume the event in event filters or handlers, thus completing the processing of the event. Consuming an event is simply calling the consume() method on the event object. When an event is consumed, the event processing is stopped, even though some of the nodes in the route were not traversed at all.

The interaction of the user with the UI elements using the mouse, such as clicking, moving, or pressing the mouse, triggers a mouse event. An object of the MouseEvent class represents a mouse event.

A key event denotes the occurrence of a keystroke. It is delivered to the node that has focus. An instance of the KeyEvent class represents a key event. Key pressed, key released, and key typed are three types of key events.

A window event occurs when a window is shown, hidden, or closed. An instance of the WindowEvent class in the javafx.stage package represents a window event.

The next chapter discusses layout panes that are used as containers for other controls and nodes.

CHAPTER 10

■ ■ ■

Understanding Layout Panes

In this chapter, you will learn:

- What a layout pane is

- Classes in JavaFX representing layout panes

- How to add children to layout panes

- Utility classes such as `Insets`, `HPos`, `VPos`, `Side`, `Priority`, etc.

- How to use a `Group` to lay out nodes

- How to work with `Region`s and its properties

- How to use different types of layout panes such as `HBox`, `VBox`, `FlowPane`, `BorderPane`, `StackPane`, `TilePane`, `GridPane`, `AnchorPane`, and `TextFlow`

The examples of this chapter lie in the `com.jdojo.container` package. In order for them to work, you must add a corresponding line to the `module-info.java` file:

```
...
opens com.jdojo.container to javafx.graphics, javafx.base;
...
```

All numbered Java code listings from this chapter are only marked shortly. For the full listings, please go to the download area for this book. Find the listings for this chapter in the `container` folder.

What Is a Layout Pane?

You can use two types of layouts to arrange nodes in a scene graph:

- Static layout

- Dynamic layout

In a static layout, the position and size of nodes are calculated once, and they stay the same as the window is resized. The user interface looks good when the window has the size for which the nodes were originally laid out.

© Kishori Sharan and Peter Späth 2022
K. Sharan and P. Späth, *Learn JavaFX 17*, https://doi.org/10.1007/978-1-4842-7848-2_10

In a dynamic layout, nodes in a scene graph are laid out every time a user action necessitates a change in their position, size, or both. Typically, changing the position or size of one node affects the position and size of all other nodes in the scene graph. The dynamic layout forces the recomputation of the position and size of some or all nodes as the window is resized.

Both static and dynamic layouts have advantages and disadvantages. A static layout gives developers full control on the design of the user interface. It lets you make use of the available space as you see fit. A dynamic layout requires more programming work, and the logic is much more involved. Typically, programming languages supporting a GUI, for example, JavaFX, support dynamic layouts through libraries. Libraries solve most of the use cases for dynamic layouts. If they do not meet your needs, you must do the hard work to roll out your own dynamic layout.

A *layout pane* is a node that contains other nodes, which are known as its children (or child nodes). The responsibility of a layout pane is to lay out its children, whenever needed. A layout pane is also known as a *container* or a *layout container*.

A layout pane has a *layout policy* that controls how the layout pane lays out its children. For example, a layout pane may lay out its children horizontally, vertically, or in any other fashion.

JavaFX contains several layout-related classes, which are the topic of discussion in this chapter. A layout pane performs two things:

- It computes the position (the x and y coordinates) of the node within its parent.
- It computes the size (the width and height) of the node.

For a 3D node, a layout pane also computes the z coordinate of the position and the depth of the size.

The layout policy of a container is a set of rules to compute the position and size of its children. When I discuss containers in this chapter, pay attention to the layout policy of the containers as to how they compute the position and size of their children. A node has three sizes: preferred size, minimum size, and maximum size. Most of the containers attempt to give its children their preferred size. The actual (or current) size of a node may be different from its preferred size. The current size of a node depends on the size of the window, the layout policy of the container, the expanding and shrinking policy for the node, etc.

Layout Pane Classes

JavaFX contains several container classes. Figure 10-1 shows a partial class diagram for the container classes. A container class is a subclass, direct or indirect, of the Parent class.

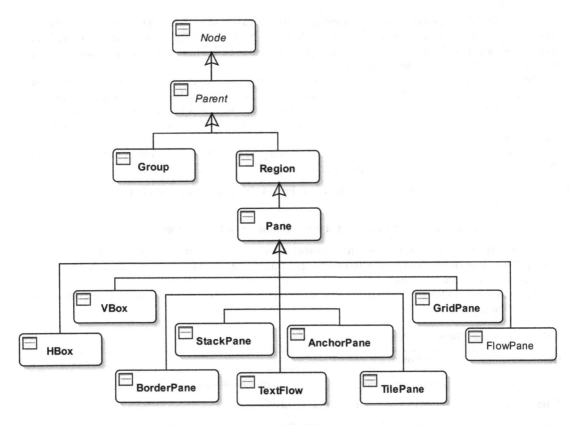

Figure 10-1. *A class diagram for container classes in JavaFX*

A Group lets you apply effects and transformations to all its children collectively. The Group class is in the javafx.scene package.

Subclasses of the Region class are used to lay out children. They can be styled with CSS. The Region class and most of its subclasses are in the javafx.scene.layout package.

It is true that a container needs to be a subclass of the Parent class. However, not all subclasses of the Parent class are containers. For example, the Button class is a subclass of the Parent class; however, it is a control, not a container. A node must be added to a container to be part of a scene graph. The container lays out its children according to its layout policy. If you do not want the container to manage the layout for a node, you need to set the managed property of the node to false. Please refer to Chapter 6 for more details and examples on managed and unmanaged nodes.

A node can be a child node of only one container at a time. If a node is added to a container while it is already the child node of another container, the node is removed from the first container before being added to the second one. Oftentimes, it is necessary to nest containers to create a complex layout. That is, you can add a container to another container as a child node.

The Parent class contains three methods to get the list of children of a container:

- `protected ObservableList<Node> getChildren()`

- `public ObservableList<Node> getChildrenUnmodifiable()`

- `protected <E extends Node> List<E> getManagedChildren()`

The getChildren() method returns a modifiable ObservableList of the child nodes of a container. If you want to add a node to a container, you would add the node to this list. This is the most commonly used method for container classes. We have been using this method to add children to containers such as Group, HBox, VBox, etc., from the very first program.

Notice the protected access for the getChildren() method. If a subclass of the Parent class does not want to be a container, it will keep the access for this method as protected. For example, control-related classes (Button, TextField, etc.) keep this method as protected, so you cannot add child nodes to them. A container class overrides this method and makes it public. For example, the Group and Pane classes expose this method as public.

The getChildrenUnmodifiable() method is declared public in the Parent class. It returns a read-only ObservableList of children. It is useful in two scenarios:

- You need to pass the list of children of a container to a method that should not modify the list.

- You want to know what makes up a control, which is not a container.

The getManagedChildren() method has the protected access. Container classes do not expose it as public. They use it internally to get the list of managed children, during layouts. You will use this method to roll out your own container classes.

Table 10-1 has brief descriptions of the container classes. We will discuss them in detail with examples in subsequent sections.

Table 10-1. *List of Container Classes*

Container Class	Description
Group	A Group applies effects and transformations collectively to all its children.
Pane	It is used for absolute positioning of its children.
HBox	It arranges its children horizontally in a single row.
VBox	It arranges its children vertically in a single column.
FlowPane	It arranges its children horizontally or vertically in rows or columns. If they do not fit in a single row or column, they are wrapped at the specified width or height.
BorderPane	It divides its layout area in the top, right, bottom, left, and center regions and places each of its children in one of the five regions.
StackPane	It arranges its children in a back-to-front stack.
TilePane	It arranges its children in a grid of uniformly sized cells.
GridPane	It arranges its children in a grid of variable-sized cells.
AnchorPane	It arranges its children by anchoring their edges to the edges of the layout area.
TextFlow	It lays out rich text whose content may consist of several Text nodes.

Adding Children to a Layout Pane

A container is meant to contain children. You can add children to a container when you create the container object or after creating it. All container classes provide constructors that take a var-args Node type argument to add the initial set of children. Some containers provide constructors to add an initial set of children and set initial properties for the containers.

You can also add children to a container at any time after the container is created. Containers store their children in an observable list, which can be retrieved using the getChildren() method. Adding a node to a container is as simple as adding a node to that observable list. The following snippet of code shows how to add children to an HBox when it is created and after it is created:

```
// Create two buttons
Button okBtn = new Button("OK");
Button cancelBtn = new Button("Cancel");

// Create an HBox with two buttons as its children
HBox hBox1 = new HBox(okBtn, cancelBtn);

// Create an HBox with two buttons with 20px horizontal spacing between them
double hSpacing = 20;
HBox hBox2 = new HBox(hSpacing, okBtn, cancelBtn);

// Create an empty HBox, and afterwards, add two buttons to it
HBox hBox3 = new HBox();
hBox3.getChildren().addAll(okBtn, cancelBtn);
```

■ **Tip** When you need to add multiple child nodes to a container, use the addAll() method of the ObservableList rather than using the add() method multiple times.

Utility Classes and Enums

While working with layout panes, you will need to use several classes and enums that are related to spacing and directions. These classes and enums are not useful when used stand-alone. They are always used as properties for nodes. This section describes some of these classes and enums.

The Insets Class

The Insets class represents inside offsets in four directions: top, right, bottom, and left, for a rectangular area. It is an immutable class. It has two constructors—one lets you set the same offset for all four directions, and another lets you set different offsets for each direction:

- Insets(double topRightBottomLeft)
- Insets(double top, double right, double bottom, double left)

The Insets class declares a constant, Insets.EMPTY, to represent a zero offset for all four directions. Use the getTop(), getRight(), getBottom(), and getLeft() methods to get the value of the offset in a specific direction.

It is a bit confusing to understand the exact meaning of the term *insets* by looking at the description of the Insets class. Let us discuss its meaning in detail in this section. We talk about insets in the context of two rectangles. An inset is the distance between the same edges (from top to top, from left to left, etc.) of two rectangles. There are four inset values—one for each side of the rectangles. An object of the Insets class stores the four distances. Figure 10-2 shows two rectangles and the insets of the inner rectangle relative to the outer rectangle.

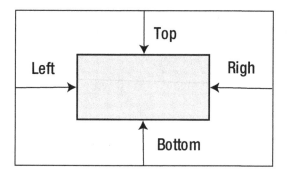

Figure 10-2. *Insets of a rectangular area relative to another rectangular area*

It is possible for two rectangles to overlap instead of one to be contained fully within another. In this case, some inset values may be positive and some negative. Inset values are interpreted relative to a reference rectangle. To interpret an inset value correctly, it is required that you get the position of the reference rectangle, its edge, and the direction in which the inset needs to be measured. The context where the term "insets" is used should make these pieces of information available. In the figure, we can define the same insets relative to the inner or outer rectangle. The inset values would not change. However, the reference rectangle and the direction in which the insets are measured (to determine the sign of the inset values) will change.

Typically, in JavaFX, the term insets and the Insets object are used in four contexts:

- Border insets

- Background insets

- Outsets

- Insets

In the first two contexts, insets mean the distances between the edges of the layout bounds and the inner edge of the border or the inner edge of the background. In these contents, insets are measured inward from the edges of the layout bounds. A negative value for an inset means a distance measured outward from the edges of the layout bounds.

A border stroke or image may fall outside of the layout bounds of a Region. Outsets are the distances between the edges of the layout bounds of a Region and the outer edges of its border. Outsets are also represented as an Insets object.

Javadoc for JavaFX uses the term insets several times to mean the sum of the thickness of the border and the padding measured inward from all edges of the layout bounds. Be careful interpreting the meaning of the term insets when you encounter it in Javadoc.

The HPos Enum

The HPos enum defines three constants: LEFT, CENTER, and RIGHT, to describe the horizontal positioning and alignment.

The VPos Enum

The constants of the VPos enum describe vertical positioning and alignment. It has four constants: TOP, CENTER, BASELINE, and BOTTOM.

The Pos Enum

The constants in the Pos enum describe vertical and horizontal positioning and alignment. It has constants for all combinations of VPos and HPos constants. Constants in Pos enum are BASELINE_CENTER, BASELINE_LEFT, BASELINE_RIGHT, BOTTOM_CENTER, BOTTOM_LEFT, BOTTOM_RIGHT, CENTER, CENTER_LEFT, CENTER_RIGHT, TOP_CENTER, TOP_LEFT, and TOP_RIGHT. It has two methods—getHpos() and getVpos()—that return objects of HPos and VPos enum types, describing the horizontal and vertical positioning and alignment, respectively.

The HorizontalDirection Enum

The HorizontalDirection enum has two constants, LEFT and RIGHT, which denote directions to the left and right, respectively.

The VerticalDirection Enum

The VerticalDirection enum has two constants, UP and DOWN, which denote up and down directions, respectively.

The Orientation Enum

The Orientation enum has two constants, HORIZONTAL and VERTICAL, which denote horizontal and vertical orientations, respectively.

The Side Enum

The Side enum has four constants: TOP, RIGHT, BOTTOM, and LEFT, to denote the four sides of a rectangle.

The Priority Enum

Sometimes, a container may have more or less space available than required to lay out its children using their preferred sizes. The Priority enum is used to denote the priority of a node to grow or shrink when its parent has more or less space. It contains three constants: ALWAYS, NEVER, and SOMETIMES. A node with the ALWAYS priority always grows or shrinks as the available space increases or decreases. A node with NEVER priority never grows or shrinks as the available space increases or decreases. A node with SOMETIMES priority grows or shrinks when there are no other nodes with ALWAYS priority or nodes with ALWAYS priority could not consume all the increased or decreased space.

Understanding Group

A Group has features of a container; for example, it has its own layout policy and coordinate system, and it is a subclass of the Parent class. However, its meaning is best reflected by calling it a *collection of nodes* or a *group*, rather than a *container*. It is used to manipulate a collection of nodes as a single node (or as a group). Transformations, effects, and properties applied to a Group are applied to all nodes in the Group.

A Group has its own layout policy, which does not provide any specific layout to its children, except giving them their preferred size:

- It renders nodes in the order they are added.

- It does not position its children. All children are positioned at (0, 0) by default. You need to write code to position child nodes of a Group. Use the layoutX and layoutY properties of the children nodes to position them within the Group.

- By default, it resizes all its children to their preferred size. The auto-sizing behavior can be disabled by setting its autoSizeChildren property to false. Note that if you disable the auto-sizing property, all nodes, except shapes, will be invisible as their size will be zero, by default.

A Group does not have a size of its own. It is not resizable directly. Its size is the collective bounds of its children. Its bounds change, as the bounds of any or all of its children change. Chapter 6 explains how different types of bounds of a Group are computed.

Creating a Group Object

You can use the no-args constructor to create an empty Group:

```
Group emptyGroup = new Group();
```

Other constructors of the Group class let you add children to the Group. One constructor takes a Collection<Node> as the initial children; another takes a var-args of the Node type.

```
Button smallBtn = new Button("Small Button");
Button bigBtn = new Button("This is a big button");

// Create a Group with two buttons using its var-args constructor
Group group1 = new Group(smallBtn, bigBtn);

List<Node> initialList = new ArrayList<>();
initailList.add(smallBtn);
initailList.add(bigBtn);

// Create a Group with all Nodes in the initialList as its children
Group group2 = new Group(initailList);
```

Rendering Nodes in a Group

Children of a Group are rendered in the order they are added. The following snippet of code, when displayed in a stage, looks as shown in Figure 10-3:

```
Button smallBtn = new Button("Small button");
Button bigBtn = new Button("This is a big button");
Group root = new Group();
root.getChildren().addAll(smallBtn, bigBtn);
Scene scene = new Scene(root);
```

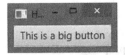

Figure 10-3. *Rendering order of the children in a Group: first smaller and second bigger*

Notice that we have added two buttons to the Group. Only one of the buttons is shown. The smaller button is rendered first because it is the first one in the collection. The bigger button is rendered covering the smaller button. Both buttons exist. One is just hidden under another. If we swap the order in which buttons are added, using the following statement, the resulting screen would be as shown in Figure 10-4. Notice that the left part of the bigger button is covered by the smaller button, and the right part is still showing.

```
// Add the bigger button first
root.getChildren().addAll(bigBtn, smallBtn);
```

Figure 10-4. *Rendering order of the children in a Group: first bigger and second smaller*

■ **Tip**   If you do not want nodes in a Group to overlap, you need to set their positions.

Positioning Nodes in a Group

You can position child nodes in a Group by assigning them absolute positions using the layoutX and layoutY properties of the nodes. Alternatively, you can use the binding API to position them relative to other nodes in the Group.

Listing 10-1 shows how to use the absolute and relative positioning in a Group. Figure 10-5 shows the resulting screen. The program adds two buttons (*OK* and *Cancel*) to the Group. The *OK* button uses absolute positioning; it is placed at (10, 10). The *Cancel* button is placed relative to the *OK* button; its vertical position is the same as the *OK* button; its horizontal position is 10px after the right edge of the *OK* button. Notice the use of the *Fluent Binding API* to accomplish the relative positioning for the *Cancel* button.

Listing 10-1. Laying Out Nodes in a Group

```
// NodesLayoutInGroup.java
// ... full listing in the book's download area.
```

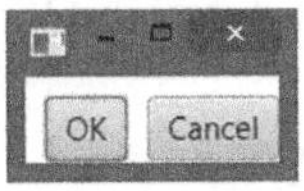

Figure 10-5. *A Group with two buttons using relative positions*

Applying Effects and Transformations to a Group

When you apply effects and transformations to a Group, they are automatically applied to all of its children. Setting a property, for example, the disable or opacity property, on a Group, sets the property on all of its children.

Listing 10-2 shows how to apply effects, transformations, and states to a Group. The program adds two buttons to the Group. It applies a rotation transformation of 10 degrees, a drop shadow effect, and opacity of 80%. Figure 10-6 shows that the transformation, effect, and state applied to the Group are applied to all of its children (two buttons in this case).

Listing 10-2. Applying Effects and Transformations to a Group

```
// GroupEffect.java
// ... full listing in the book's download area.
```

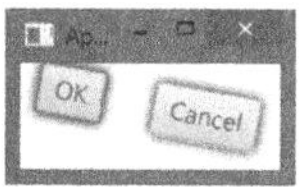

Figure 10-6. *Two buttons in a Group after effects, transformations, and states are applied to the Group*

Styling a Group with CSS

The Group class does not offer much CSS styling. All CSS properties for the Node class are available for the Group class: for example, -fx-cursor, -fx-opacity, -fx-rotate, etc. A Group cannot have its own appearance such as padding, backgrounds, and borders.

Understanding Region

Region is the base class for all layout panes. It can be styled with CSS. Unlike Group, it has its own size. It is resizable. It can have a visual appearance, for example, with padding, multiple backgrounds, and multiple borders. You do not use the Region class directly as a layout pane. If you want to roll out your own layout pane, extend the Pane class, which extends the Region class.

■ **Tip** The Region class is designed to support the CSS3 specification for backgrounds and borders, as they are applicable to JavaFX. The specification for "CSS Backgrounds and Borders Module Level 3" can be found online at www.w3.org/TR/css-backgrounds-3/.

By default, a Region defines a rectangular area. However, it can be changed to any shape. The drawing area of a Region is divided into several parts. Depending on the property settings, a Region may draw outside of its layout bounds. Parts of a Region:

- Backgrounds (fills and images)
- Content area
- Padding

- Borders (strokes and images)
- Margin
- Region insets

Figure 10-7 shows parts of a Region. The margin is not directly supported as of JavaFX 2. You can get the same effect by using Insets for the border.

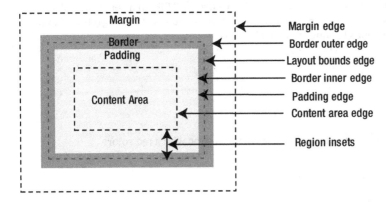

Figure 10-7. *Different parts of a Region*

A region may have a background that is drawn first. The content area is the area where the content of the Region (e.g., controls) is drawn.

The padding is an optional space around the content area. If the padding has a zero width, the padding edge and the content area edge are the same.

The border area is the space around the padding. If the border has a zero width, the border edge and the padding edge are the same.

The margin is the space around the border. The padding and margin are very similar. The only difference between them is that the margin defines the space around the outside edge of the border, whereas the padding defines the space around the inside edge of the border. Margins are supported for controls when they are added to panes, for example, HBox, VBox, etc. However, margins are not directly supported for a Region.

The content area, padding, and borders affect the layout bounds of the Region. You can draw borders outside the layout bounds of a Region, and those borders will not affect the layout bounds of the Region. The margin does not affect the layout bounds of the Region.

The distance between the edge of the layout bounds of the Region and its content area defines the insets for the Region. The Region class computes its insets automatically based on its properties. It has a read-only insets property that you can read to know its insets. Note that a layout container would need to know the area in which to place its children, and they can compute the content area knowing the layout bounds and insets.

■ **Tip** The background fills, background images, border strokes, border images, and content of a Region are drawn in order.

Setting Backgrounds

A Region can have a background that consists of fills, images, or both. A fill consists of a color, radii for four corners, and insets on four sides. Fills are applied in the order they are specified. The color defines the color to be used for painting the background. The radii define the radii to be used for corners; set them to zero if you want rectangular corners. The insets define the distance between the sides of the Region and the outer edges of the background fill. For example, an inset of 10px on top means that a horizontal strip of 10px inside the top edge of the layout bounds will not be painted by the background fill. An inset for the fill may be negative. A negative inset extends the painted area outside of the layout bounds of the Region; and in this case, the drawn area for the Region extends beyond its layout bounds.

The following CSS properties define the background fill for a Region:

- -fx-background-color
- -fx-background-radius
- -fx-background-insets

The following CSS properties fill the entire layout bounds of the Region with a red color:

```
-fx-background-color: red;
-fx-background-insets: 0;
-fx-background-radius: 0;
```

The following CSS properties use two fills:

```
-fx-background-color: lightgray, red;
-fx-background-insets: 0, 4;
-fx-background-radius: 4, 2;
```

The first fill covers the entire Region (see 0px insets) with a light gray color; it uses a 4px radius for all four corners, making the Region look like a rounded rectangle. The second fill covers the Region with a red color; it uses a 4px inset on all four sides, which means that 4px from the edges of the Region are not painted by this fill, and that area will still have the light gray color used by the first fill. A 2px radius for all four corners is used by the second fill.

You can also set the background of a Region in code using Java objects. An instance of the Background class represents the background of a Region. The class defines a Background.EMPTY constant to represent an empty background (no fills and no images).

■ **Tip** A Background object is immutable. It can be safely used as the background of multiple Regions.

A Background object has zero or more fills and images. An instance of the BackgroundFill class represents a fill; an instance of the BackgroundImage class represents an image.

The Region class contains a background property of the ObjectProperty<Background> type. The background of a Region is set using the setBackground(Background bg) method.

The following snippet of code creates a Background object with two BackgroundFill objects. Setting this to a Region produces the same effects of drawing a background with two fills as shown in the preceding snippet of code using the CSS style. Notice that the Insets and CornerRadii classes are used to define the insets and the radius for corners for the fills.

```
import javafx.geometry.Insets;
import javafx.scene.layout.Background;
import javafx.scene.layout.BackgroundFill;
import javafx.scene.layout.CornerRadii;
import javafx.scene.paint.Color;
...
BackgroundFill lightGrayFill =
        new BackgroundFill(Color.LIGHTGRAY,
                                new CornerRadii(4), new Insets(0));

BackgroundFill redFill =
        new BackgroundFill(Color.RED,
                                new CornerRadii(2), new Insets(4));

// Create a Background object with two BackgroundFill objects
Background bg = new Background(lightGrayFill, redFill);
```

The program in Listing 10-3 shows how to set the background for a Pane, which is a Region, using both the CSS properties and the Background object. The resulting screen is shown in Figure 10-8. The getCSSStyledPane() method creates a Pane, adds a background with two fills using CSS, and returns the Pane. The getObjectStyledPane() method creates a Pane, adds a background with two fills using Java classes, and returns the Pane. The start() method adds the two Panes to another Pane and positions them side by side.

Listing 10-3. Using Background Fills As the Background for a Region

```
// BackgroundFillTest.java
// ... full listing in the book's download area.
```

Figure 10-8. *Two Panes having identical backgrounds set: one using CSS and one using Java objects*

The following CSS properties define the background image for a Region:

- -fx-background-image
- -fx-background-repeat
- -fx-background-position
- -fx-background-size

The -fx-background-image property is a CSS URL for the image. The -fx-background-repeat property indicates how the image will be repeated (or not repeated) to cover the drawing area of the Region. The -fx-background-position determines how the image is positioned with the Region. The -fx-background-size property determines the size of the image relative to the Region.

The following CSS properties fill the entire layout bounds of the Region with a red color:

```
-fx-background-image: URL('your_image_url_goes_here');
-fx-background-repeat: space;
-fx-background-position: center;
-fx-background-size: cover;
```

The following snippet of code and the preceding set of the CSS properties will produce identical effects when they are set on a Region:

```
import javafx.scene.image.Image;
import javafx.scene.layout.Background;
import javafx.scene.layout.BackgroundImage;
import javafx.scene.layout.BackgroundPosition;
import javafx.scene.layout.BackgroundRepeat;
import javafx.scene.layout.BackgroundSize;
...
Image image = new Image("your_image_url_goes_here");
BackgroundSize bgSize = new BackgroundSize(100, 100, true, true, false, true);
BackgroundImage bgImage =
    new BackgroundImage(image,
                         BackgroundRepeat.SPACE,
                         BackgroundRepeat.SPACE,
                         BackgroundPosition.DEFAULT,
                         bgSize);

// Create a Background object with an BackgroundImage object
Background bg = new Background(bgImage);
```

Setting Padding

The padding of a Region is the space around its content area. The Region class contains a padding property of the ObjectProperty<Insets> type. You can set separate padding widths for each of the four sides:

```
// Create an HBox
HBox hb = new HBox();

// A uniform padding of 10px around all edges
hb.setPadding(new Insets(10));

// A non-uniform padding: 2px top, 4px right, 6px bottom, and 8px left
hb.setPadding(new Insets(2, 4, 6, 8));
```

Setting Borders

A Region can have a border, which consists of strokes, images, or both. If strokes and images are not present, the border is considered empty. Strokes and images are applied in the order they are specified; all strokes are applied before images. You can set the border by using CSS and by using the Border class in code.

> ■ **Note** We will use the phrases, "the edges of a Region" and "the layout bounds of a Region," in this section, synonymously, which mean the edges of the rectangle defined by the layout bounds of the Region.

A stroke consists of five properties:

- A color

- A style

- A width

- Radii for four corners

- Insets on four sides

The color defines the color to be used for the stroke. You can specify four different colors for the four sides.

The style defines the style for the stroke: for example, solid, dashed, etc. The style also defines the location of the border relative to its insets: for example, inside, outside, or centered. You can specify four different styles for the four sides.

The radii define the radii for corners; set them to zero if you want rectangular corners.

The width of the stroke defines its thickness. You can specify four different widths for the four sides.

The insets of a stroke define the distance from the sides of the layout bounds of the Region where the border is drawn. A positive value for the inset for a side is measured inward from the edge of the Region. A negative value of the inset for a side is measured outward from the edge of the Region. An inset of zero on a side means the edge of the layout bounds itself. It is possible to have positive insets for some sides (e.g., top and bottom) and negative insets for others (e.g., right and left). Figure 10-9 shows the positions of positive and negative insets relative to the layout bounds of a Region. The rectangle in solid lines is the layout bounds of a Region, and the rectangles in dashed lines are the insets lines.

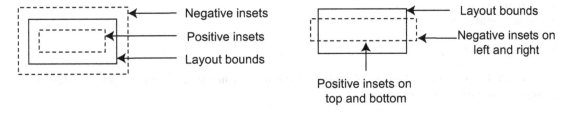

Figure 10-9. *Positions of positive and negative insets relative to the layout bounds*

The border stroke may be drawn inside, outside, or partially inside and partially outside the layout bounds of the Region. To determine the exact position of a stroke relative to the layout bounds, you need to look at its two properties, *insets* and *style*:

- If the style of the stroke is inside, the stroke is drawn inside the insets.

- If the style is outside, it is drawn outside the insets.

- If the style is centered, it is drawn half inside and half outside the insets.

Figure 10-10 shows some examples of the border positions for a Region. The rectangle in dashed lines indicates the layout bounds of the Region. Borders are shown in a light gray color. The label below each Region shows some details of the border properties (e.g., style, insets, and width).

291

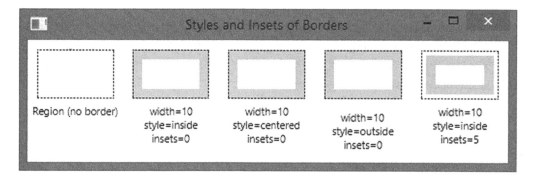

Figure 10-10. *Examples of determining the position of a border based on its style and insets*

The following CSS properties define border strokes for a Region:

- -fx-border-color
- -fx-border-style
- -fx-border-width
- -fx-border-radius
- -fx-border-insets

The following CSS properties draw a border with a stroke of 10px in width and red in color. The outside edge of the border will be the same as the edges of the Region as we have set insets and style as zero and inside, respectively. The border will be rounded on the corners as we have set the radii for all corners to 5px:

```
-fx-border-color: red;
-fx-border-style: solid inside;
-fx-border-width: 10;
-fx-border-insets: 0;
-fx-border-radius: 5;
```

The following CSS properties use two strokes for a border. The first stroke is drawn inside the edges of the Region and the second one outside:

```
-fx-border-color: red, green;
-fx-border-style: solid inside, solid outside;
-fx-border-width: 5, 2 ;
-fx-border-insets: 0, 0;
-fx-border-radius: 0, 0;
```

■ **Tip** The part of the border drawn outside the edges of the Region does not affect its layout bounds. The part of the border drawn outside the edges of the Region is within the layout bounds of the Region. In other words, the border area that falls inside the edges of a Region influences the layout bounds for that Region.

So far, we have discussed the insets for strokes of a border. A border also has *insets* and *outsets*, which are computed automatically based on the properties for its strokes and images. The distance between the edges of the Region and the inner edges of its border, considering all strokes and images that are drawn *inside* the edges of the Region, is known as the *insets of the border*. The distance between the edges of the Region and the outer edges of its border, considering all strokes and images that are drawn *outside* the edges of the Region, is known as the *outsets of the border*. You must be able to differentiate between the insets of a stroke and insets/outsets of a border. The insets of a stroke determine the location where the stroke is drawn, whereas the insets/outsets of a border tell you how far the border extends inside/outside of the edges of the Region. Figure 10-11 shows how the insets and outsets of a border are computed. The dashed line shows the layout bounds of a Region, which has a border with two strokes: one in red and one in green. The following styles, when set on a 150px X 50px Region, result in the border as shown in Figure 10-11:

```
-fx-background-color: white;
-fx-padding: 10;
-fx-border-color: red, green, black;
-fx-border-style: solid inside, solid outside, dashed centered;
-fx-border-width: 10, 8, 1;
-fx-border-insets: 12, -10, 0;
-fx-border-radius: 0, 0, 0;
```

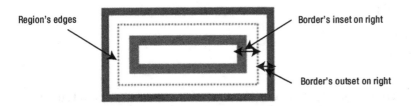

Figure 10-11. *Relationship between insets/outsets of a border and the layout bounds of a Region*

The insets of the border are 22px on all four sides, which is computed (10px + 12px) by adding the 10px width of the red border drawn inside 12px (insets) from the edges of the Region. The outsets of the border are 18px on all four sides, which is computed (8px + 10px) by adding the 8px width of the green border drawn outside 10px (-10 insets) from the edges of the Region.

You can also set the border of a Region in code using Java objects. An instance of the Border class represents the border of a Region. The class defines a Border.EMPTY constant to represent an empty border (no strokes and no images).

■ **Tip**   A Border object is immutable. It can be safely used for multiple Regions.

A Border object has zero or more strokes and images. The Border class provides several constructors that take multiple strokes and images as arguments. The Region class contains a border property of the ObjectProperty<Border> type. The border of a Region is set using the setBorder(Border b) method.

An instance of the BorderStroke class represents a stroke; an instance of the BorderImage class represents an image. The BorderStroke class provides constructors to set the style of the stroke. The following are the two commonly used constructors. The third constructor allows you to set different colors and styles of strokes on four sides.

- BorderStroke(Paint stroke, BorderStrokeStyle style, CornerRadii radii, BorderWidths widths)

- BorderStroke(Paint stroke, BorderStrokeStyle style, CornerRadii radii, BorderWidths widths, Insets insets)

The BorderStrokeStyle class represents the style of a stroke. The BorderWidths class represents widths of a stroke on all four sides of a border. It lets you set the widths as absolute values or as a percentage of the dimensions of the Region. The following snippet of code creates a Border and sets it to a Pane:

```
BorderStrokeStyle style =
    new BorderStrokeStyle(StrokeType.INSIDE,
                StrokeLineJoin.MITER,
                StrokeLineCap.BUTT,
                10,
                0,
                null);
BorderStroke stroke =
    new BorderStroke(Color.GREEN,
                style,
                CornerRadii.EMPTY,
                new BorderWidths(8),
                new Insets(10));
Pane p = new Pane();
p.setPrefSize(100, 50);
Border b = new Border(stroke);
p.setBorder(b);
```

The Border class provides getInsets() and getOutsets() methods that return the insets and outsets for the Border. Both methods return an Insets object. Remember that the insets and outsets for a Border are different from insets of strokes. They are computed automatically based on the insets and styles for strokes and images that a Border has.

You can get all strokes and all images of a Border using its getStrokes() and getImages() methods, which return List<BorderStroke> and List<BorderImage>, respectively. You can compare two Border objects and two BorderStroke objects for equality using their equals() method.

Listing 10-4 demonstrates how to create and set a border to a Pane. It displays a screen with two Panes. One Pane is styled using CSS and another using a Border object. The Panes look similar to the one shown in Figure 10-11. The program prints the insets and outsets for the borders and checks whether both borders are the same or not. Both borders use three strokes. The getCSSStyledPane() method returns a Pane styled with CSS; the getObjectStyledPane() method returns a Pane styled using a Border object.

Listing 10-4. Using Strokes As the Border for a Region

```
// BorderStrokeTest.java
// ... full listing in the book's download area.
```

```
cssBorder insets:Insets [top=22.0, right=22.0, bottom=22.0, left=22.0]
cssBorder outsets:Insets [top=18.0, right=18.0, bottom=18.0, left=18.0]
objectBorder insets:Insets [top=22.0, right=22.0, bottom=22.0, left=22.0]
objectBorder outsets:Insets [top=18.0, right=18.0, bottom=18.0, left=18.0]
Borders are equal.
```

Using an image for a border is not as straightforward as using a stroke. An image defines a rectangular area; so does a Region. A border is drawn around a Region in an area called the border image area. The border area of a Region may be the entire area of the Region; it may be partly or fully inside or outside of the Region. The insets on four edges of the Region define the border image area. To make an image a border around a Region, both the border image area and the image are divided into nine regions: four corners, four sides, and a middle. The border area is divided into nine parts by specifying widths on all four sides, top, right, bottom, and left. The width is the width of the border along those sides. The image is also sliced (divided) into nine regions by specifying the slice width for each side. Figure 10-12 shows a Region, the border image area with its nine regions, an image, and its nine regions (or slices). In the figure, the border image area is the same as the area of the Region.

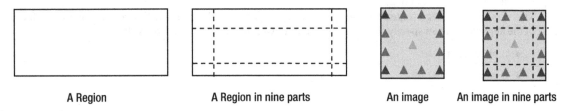

A Region   A Region in nine parts   An image   An image in nine parts

Figure 10-12. *Slicing a Region and an image into nine parts*

■ **Tip**   The border image is not drawn if a Region uses a shape other than a rectangular shape.

Note that the four widths from the edges, while dividing a border area and an image, do not necessarily have to be uniform. For example, you can specify widths as 2px on the top, 10px on the right, 2px on the bottom, and 10px on the left.

After you have divided the border image area and the image into nine regions, you need to specify properties that control the positioning and resizing behavior of the image slices. Each of nine slices of the image has to be positioned and fit inside its corresponding part in the border image area. For example, the image slice in the upper-left corner of the image has to fit in the upper-left corner part of the border image area. The two components, an image slice and its corresponding border image slice, may not be of the same size. You will need to specify how to fill the region in the border image area (scale, repeat, etc.) with the corresponding image slice. Typically, the middle slice of the image is discarded. However, if you want to fill the middle region of the border image area, you can do so with the middle slice of the image.

In Figure 10-12, the boundaries of the Region and the border image area are the same. Figure 10-13 has examples in which the boundaries of the border image area fall inside and outside of the boundary of the Region. It is possible that some regions of the border image area fall outside of the Region and some inside.

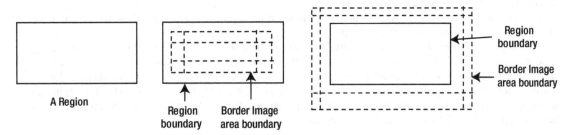

A Region

Region   Border Image
boundary   area boundary

Region
boundary

Border Image
area boundary

Figure 10-13. *Relationship between the area of a Region and the border image area*

The following CSS properties define border images for a Region:

- `-fx-border-image-source`
- `-fx-border-image-repeat`
- `-fx-border-image-slice`
- `-fx-border-image-width`
- `-fx-border-image-insets`

The `-fx-border-image-source` property is a CSS URL for the image. For multiple images, use a comma-separated list of CSS URLs of images.

The `-fx-border-image-repeat` property specifies how a slice of the image will cover the corresponding part of the Region. You can specify the property separately for the x-axis and y-axis. Valid values:

- `no-repeat`
- `repeat`
- `round`
- `space`

The `no-repeat` value specifies that the image slice should be scaled to fill the area without repeating it. The `repeat` value specifies that the image should be repeated (tiled) to fill the area. The `round` value specifies that the image should be repeated (tiled) to fill the area using a whole number of tiles, and if necessary, scale the image to use the whole number of tiles. The `space` value specifies that the image should be repeated (tiled) to fill the area using a whole number of tiles without scaling the image and by distributing the extra space uniformly around the tiles.

The `-fx-border-image-slice` property specifies inward offsets from the top, right, bottom, and left edges of the image to divide it into nine slices. The property can be specified as a number literal or a percentage of the side of the image. If the word fill is present in the value, the middle slice of the image is preserved and is used to fill the middle region of the border image area; otherwise, the middle slice is discarded.

The `-fx-border-image-width` property specifies the inward offsets from four sides of the border image area to divide the border image area into nine regions. Note that we divide the border image area into nine regions, not the Region. The property can be specified as a number literal or a percentage of the side of the border image area.

The `-fx-border-image-insets` property specifies the distance between the edges of the Region and the edges of the border image area on four sides. A positive inset is measured from the edge of the Region toward its center. A negative inset is measured outward from the edge of the Region. In Figure 10-13, the border image area for the Region in the middle has positive insets, whereas the border image area for the Region (third from the left) has negative insets.

Let us look at some examples of using images as a border. In all examples, we will use the image shown in Figure 10-12 as a border for a 200px X 70px Pane.

Listing 10-5 contains the CSS, and Figure 10-14 shows the resulting Panes when the `-fx-border-image-repeat` property is set to `no-repeat`, `repeat`, `space`, and `round`. Notice that we have set the `-fx-border-image-width` and the `-fx-border-image-slice` properties to the same value of 9px. This will cause the corner slices to fit exactly into the corners of the border image area. The middle region of the border image area is not filled because we have not specified the `fill` value for the `-fx-border-image-slice` property. We have used a stroke to draw the boundary of the Pane.

Listing 10-5. Using an Image As a Border Without Filling the Middle Region

```
-fx-border-image-source: url('image_url_goes_here') ;
-fx-border-image-repeat: no-repeat;
-fx-border-image-slice: 9;
-fx-border-image-width: 9;
-fx-border-image-insets: 10;
-fx-border-color: black;
-fx-border-width: 1;
-fx-border-style: dashed inside;
```

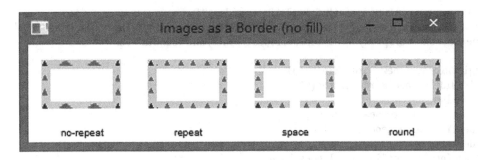

Figure 10-14. *Using different values for repeat without the fill value for the slice property*

Listing 10-6 contains the CSS, which is a slight variation of Listing 10-5. Figure 10-15 shows the resulting Panes. This time, the middle region of the border image area is filled because we have specified the fill value for the -fx-border-image-slice property.

Listing 10-6. Using an Image As a Border Filling the Middle Region

```
-fx-border-image-source: url('image_url_goes_here') ;
-fx-border-image-repeat: no-repeat;
-fx-border-image-slice: 9 fill;
-fx-border-image-width: 9;
-fx-border-image-insets: 10;
-fx-border-color: black;
-fx-border-width: 1;
-fx-border-style: dashed inside;
```

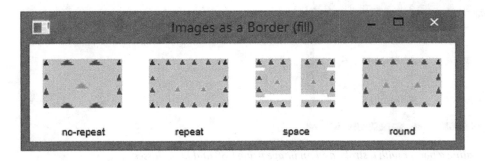

Figure 10-15. *Using different values for repeat with the fill value for the slice property*

The BorderImage class, which is immutable, represents a border image in a Border. All properties for the border image are specified in the constructor:

```
BorderImage(Image image,
            BorderWidths widths,
            Insets insets,
            BorderWidths slices,
            boolean filled,
            BorderRepeat repeatX,
            BorderRepeat repeatY)
```

The BorderRepeat enum contains STRETCH, REPEAT, SPACE, and ROUND constants that are used to indicate how the image slices are repeated in the x and y directions to fill the regions of the border image area. They have the same effect of specifying no-repeat, repeat, space, and round in CSS.

```
BorderWidths regionWidths = new BorderWidths(9);
BorderWidths sliceWidth = new BorderWidths(9);
boolean filled = false;
BorderRepeat repeatX = BorderRepeat.STRETCH;
BorderRepeat repeatY = BorderRepeat.STRETCH;
BorderImage borderImage =
    new BorderImage(new Image("image_url_goes_here"),
                    regionWidths,
                    new Insets(10),
                    sliceWidth,
                    filled,
                    repeatX,
                    repeatY);
```

Listing 10-7 has a program that creates the border using CSS and Java classes. The resulting screen is shown in Figure 10-16. The left and right Panes are decorated with the same borders: one uses CSS and another Java classes.

Listing 10-7. Using Strokes and Images As a Border

```
// BorderImageTest.java
// ... full listing in the book's download area.
```

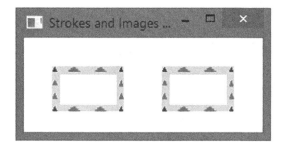

Figure 10-16. *Creating a border with a stroke and an image using CSS and Java classes*

Setting Margins

Setting margins on a Region is not supported directly. Most layout panes support margins for their children. If you want margins for a Region, add it to a layout pane, for example, an HBox, and use the layout pane instead of the Region:

```
Pane p1 = new Pane();
p1.setPrefSize(100, 20);

HBox box = new HBox();

// Set a margin of 10px around all four sides of the Pane
HBox.setMargin(p1, new Insets(10));
box.getChildren().addAll(p1);
```

Now, use box instead of p1 to get the margins around p1.

Understanding Panes

Pane is a subclass of the Region class. It exposes the getChildren() method of the Parent class, which is the superclass of the Region class. This means that instances of the Pane class and its subclasses can add any children.

A Pane provides the following layout features:

- It can be used when absolute positioning is needed. By default, it positions all its children at (0, 0). You need to set the positions of the children explicitly.

- It resizes all resizable children to their preferred sizes.

By default, a Pane has minimum, preferred, and maximum sizes. Its minimum width is the sum of the left and right insets; its minimum height is the sum of the top and bottom insets. Its preferred width is the width required to display all its children at their current x location with their preferred widths; its preferred height is the height required to display all its children at their current y location with their preferred heights. Its maximum width and height are set to Double.MAX_VALUE.

The program in Listing 10-8 shows how to create a Pane, add two Buttons to it, and how to position the Buttons. The resulting screen is shown in Figure 10-17. The Pane uses a border to show the area it occupies in the screen. Try resizing the window, and you will find that the Pane shrinks and expands.

Listing 10-8. Using Panes

```
// PaneTest.java
// ... full listing in the book's download area.
```

Figure 10-17. *A pane with two Buttons*

A Pane lets you set its preferred size:

```
Pane root = new Pane();
root.setPrefSize(300, 200); // 300px wide and 200px tall
```

You can tell the Pane to compute its preferred size based on its children sizes by resetting its preferred width and height to the computed width and height:

```
Pane root = new Pane();

// Set the preferred size to 300px wide and 200px tall
root.setPrefSize(300, 200);

/* Do some processing... */

// Set the default preferred size
root.setPrefSize(Region.USE_COMPUTED_SIZE, Region.USE_COMPUTED_SIZE);
```

■ **Tip** A Pane does not clip its content; its children may be displayed outside its bounds.

Understanding HBox

An HBox lays out its children in a single horizontal row. It lets you set the horizontal spacing between adjacent children, margins for any children, resizing behavior of children, etc. It uses 0px as the default spacing between adjacent children. The default width of the content area and HBox is wide enough to display all its children at their preferred widths, and the default height is the largest of the heights of all its children.

You cannot set the locations for children in an HBox. They are automatically computed by the HBox. You can control the locations of children to some extent by customizing the properties of the HBox and setting constraints on the children.

Creating HBox Objects

Constructors of the HBox class let you create HBox objects with or without specifying the spacing and initial set of children:

```
// Create an empty HBox with the default spacing (0px)
HBox hbox1 = new HBox();

// Create an empty HBox with a 10px spacing
HBox hbox2 = new HBox(10);

// Create an HBox with two Buttons and a 10px spacing
Button okBtn = new Button("OK");
Button cancelBtn = new Button("Cancel");
HBox hbox3 = new HBox(10, okBtn, cancelBtn);
```

The program in Listing 10-9 shows how to use an HBox. It adds a Label, a TextField, and two Buttons to an HBox. Spacing between adjacent children is set to 10px. A padding of 10px is used to maintain a distance between the edges of the HBox and the edges of its children. The resulting window is shown in Figure 10-18.

Listing 10-9. Using the HBox Layout Pane

```
// HBoxTest.java
// ... full listing in the book's download area.
```

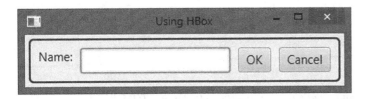

Figure 10-18. *An HBox with a Label, a TextField, and two Buttons*

HBox Properties

The HBox class declares three properties as listed in Table 10-2.

Table 10-2. *Properties Declared in the HBox Class*

Property	Type	Description
alignment	ObjectProperty<Pos>	It specifies the alignment of children relative to the content area of the HBox. The fillHeight property is ignored if the vertical alignment is set to BASELINE. The default value is Pos.TOP_LEFT.
fillHeight	BooleanProperty	It specifies whether the resizable children are resized to fill the full height of the HBox or they are given their preferred heights. This property is ignored, if the vertical alignment is set to BASELINE. The default value is true.
spacing	DoubleProperty	It specifies the horizontal spacing between adjacent children. The default value is zero.

The Alignment Property

Using the alignment property is simple. It specifies how children are aligned within the content area of the HBox. By default, an HBox allocates just enough space for its content to lay out all children at their preferred size. The effect of the alignment property is noticeable when the HBox grows bigger than its preferred size.

The program in Listing 10-10 uses an HBox with two Buttons. It sets the alignment of the HBox to Pos. BOTTOM_RIGHT. It sets the preferred size of the HBox a little bigger than needed to accommodate all its children, so you can see the effect of the alignment. The resulting window is shown in Figure 10-19. When you resize the window, the children stay aligned in the bottom-right area.

Listing 10-10. Using the HBox Alignment Property

```
// HBoxAlignment.java
// ... full listing in the book's download area.
```

Figure 10-19. *An HBox with two Buttons and an alignment property set to Pos.BOTTOM_RIGHT*

The fillHeight Property

The fillHeight property specifies whether the HBox expands its children vertically to fill the height of its content area or keeps them to their preferred height. Note that this property affects only those child nodes that allow for the vertical expansion. For example, by default, the maximum height of a Button is set to its preferred height, and a Button does not become taller than its preferred width in an HBox, even if vertical space is available. If you want a Button to expand vertically, set its maximum height to Double.MAX_VALUE. By default, a TextArea is set to expand. Therefore, a TextArea inside an HBox will become taller as the height of the HBox is increased. If you do not want the resizable children to fill the height of the content area of an HBox, set the fillHeight property to false.

■ **Tip** The preferred height of the content area of an HBox is the largest of the preferred height of its children. Resizable children fill the full height of the content area, provided their maximum height property allows them to expand. Otherwise, they are kept at their preferred height.

The program in Listing 10-11 shows how the fillHeight property affects the height of the children of an HBox. It displays some controls inside an HBox. A TextArea can grow vertically by default. The maximum height of the *Cancel* button is set to Double.MAX_VALUE, so it can grow vertically. A CheckBox is provided to change the value of the fillHeight property of the HBox. The initial window is shown in Figure 10-20. Notice that the Ok button has the preferred height, whereas the *Cancel* button expands vertically to fill the height of the content area as determined by the TextArea. Resize the window to make it taller and change the fillHeight property using the CheckBox; the TextArea and the *Cancel* button expand and shrink vertically.

Listing 10-11. Using the fillHeight Property of an HBox

```
// HBoxFillHeight.java
// ... full listing in the book's download area.
```

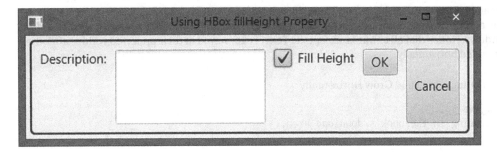

Figure 10-20. *An HBox with some control, where the user can change the fillHeight property*

The Spacing Property

The spacing property specifies the horizontal distance between adjacent children in an HBox. By default, it is set to 0px. It can be set in constructors or using the setSpacing() method.

Setting Constraints for Children in HBox

HBox supports two types of constraints, *hgrow* and *margin*, which can be set on each child node individually. The hgrow constraint specifies whether a child node expands horizontally when additional space is available. The margin constraint specifies space outside the edges of a child node. The HBox class provides setHgrow() and setMargin() static methods to specify these constraints. You can use null with these methods to remove the constraints individually. Use the clearConstraints(Node child) method to remove both constraints for a child node at once.

Letting Children Grow Horizontally

By default, the children in an HBox get their preferred widths. If the HBox is expanded horizontally, its children may get the additional available space, provided their hgrow priority is set to grow. If an HBox is expanded horizontally and none of its children has its hgrow constraint set, the additional space is left unused.

The hgrow priority for a child node is set using the setHgrow() static method of the HBox class by specifying the child node and the priority:

```
HBox root = new HBox(10);
TextField nameFld = new TextField();

// Let the TextField always grow horizontally
root.setHgrow(nameFld, Priority.ALWAYS);
```

To reset the hgrow priority of a child node, use null as the priority:

```
// Stop the TextField from growing horizontally
root.setHgrow(nameFld, null);
```

The program in Listing 10-12 shows how to set the priority of a TextField to Priority.ALWAYS, so it can take all the additional horizontal space when the HBox is expanded. Figure 10-21 shows the initial and expanded windows. Notice that all controls, except the TextField, stayed at their preferred widths, after the window is expanded horizontally.

Listing 10-12. Letting a TextField Grow Horizontally

```
// HBoxHGrow.java
// ... full listing in the book's download area.
```

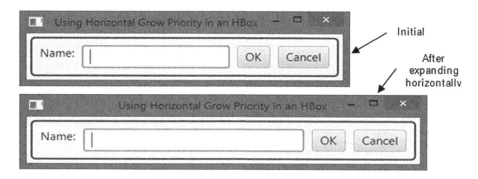

Figure 10-21. *An HBox with a TextField set to always grow horizontally*

Setting Margins for Children

Margins are extra spaces added outside the edges of a node. The following snippet of code shows how to add margins to the children of an HBox:

```
Label nameLbl = new Label("Name:");
TextField nameFld = new TextField();
Button okBtn = new Button("OK");
Button cancelBtn = new Button("Cancel");

HBox hbox = new HBox(nameLbl, nameFld, okBtn, cancelBtn);

// Set a margin for all children:
// 10px top, 2px right, 10px bottom, and 2px left
Insets margin = new Insets(10, 2, 10, 2);
HBox.setMargin(nameLbl, margin);
HBox.setMargin(nameFld, margin);
HBox.setMargin(okBtn, margin);
HBox.setMargin(cancelBtn, margin);
```

You can remove the margin from a child node by setting the margin value to null:

```
// Remove margins for okBtn
HBox.setMargin(okBtn, null);
```

■ **Tip** Be careful when using the `spacing` property of the HBox and the margin constraint on its children. Both will add to the horizontal gap between adjacent children. If you want margins applied, keep the horizontal spacing between children uniform, and set the right and left margins for children to zero.

Understanding VBox

A VBox lays out its children in a single vertical column. It lets you set the vertical spacing between adjacent children, margins for any children, resizing behavior of children, etc. It uses 0px as the default spacing between adjacent children. The default height of the content area of a VBox is tall enough to display all its children at their preferred heights, and the default width is the largest of the widths of all its children.

You cannot set the locations for children in a VBox. They are automatically computed by the VBox. You can control the locations of children to some extent by customizing the properties of the VBox and setting constraints on the children.

Working with a VBox is similar to working with an HBox with a difference that they work in opposite directions. For example, in an HBox, the children fills the height of the content area by default, and in a VBox, children fill the width of the content by default; an HBox lets you set hgrow constraints on a child node, and a VBox lets you set the vgrow constraint.

Creating VBox Objects

Constructors of the VBox class let you create VBox objects with or without specifying the spacing and initial set of children:

```
// Create an empty VBox with the default spacing (0px)
VBox vbox1 = new VBox();

// Create an empty VBox with a 10px spacing
VBox vbox2 = new VBox(10);

// Create a VBox with two Buttons and a 10px spacing
Button okBtn = new Button("OK");
Button cancelBtn = new Button("Cancel");
VBox vbox3 = new VBox(10, okBtn, cancelBtn);
```

The program in Listing 10-13 shows how to use a VBox. It adds a Label, a TextField, and two Buttons to a VBox. Spacing between adjacent children is set to 10px. A padding of 10px is used to maintain a distance between the edges of the VBox and the edges of its children. The resulting window is shown in Figure 10-22.

Listing 10-13. Using the VBox Layout Pane

```
// VBoxTest.java
// ... full listing in the book's download area.
```

Figure 10-22. *A VBox with a Label, a TextField, and two Buttons*

VBox Properties

The VBox class declares three properties as listed in Table 10-3.

Table 10-3. *Properties Declared in the VBox Class*

Property	Type	Description
alignment	ObjectProperty<Pos>	It specifies the alignment of children relative to the content area of the VBox. The default value is Pos.TOP_LEFT.
fillWidth	BooleanProperty	It specifies whether the resizable children are resized to fill the full width of the VBox or they are given their preferred widths. The default value is true.
spacing	DoubleProperty	It specifies the vertical spacing between adjacent children. The default value is zero.

The Alignment Property

Using the alignment property is simple. It specifies how children are aligned within the content area of the VBox. By default, a VBox allocates just enough space for its content to lay out all children at their preferred size. The effect of the alignment property is noticeable when the VBox grows bigger than its preferred size.

The program in Listing 10-14 uses a VBox with two Buttons. It sets the alignment of the VBox to Pos.BOTTOM_RIGHT. It sets the preferred size of the VBox a little bigger than needed to accommodate all its children, so you can see the effect of the alignment. The resulting window is shown in Figure 10-23. When you resize the window, the children stay aligned in the bottom-right area.

Listing 10-14. Using the VBox Alignment Property

```
// VBoxAlignment.java
// ... full listing in the book's download area.
```

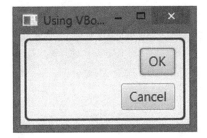

Figure 10-23. *A VBox with two Buttons and an alignment property set to Pos.BOTTOM_RIGHT*

The fillWidth Property

The `fillWidth` property specifies whether the VBox expands its children horizontally to fill the width of its content area or keeps them to their preferred height. Note that this property affects only those child nodes that allow for the horizontal expansion. For example, by default, the maximum width of a Button is set to its preferred width, and a Button does not become wider than its preferred width in a VBox, even if horizontal space is available. If you want a Button to expand horizontally, set its maximum width to Double.MAX_ VALUE. By default, a TextField is set to expand. Therefore, a TextField inside a VBox will become wider as the width of the VBox is increased. If you do not want the resizable children to fill the width of the content area of a VBox, set the `fillWidth` property to false. Run the program in Listing 10-13 and try expanding the window horizontally. The TextField will expand horizontally as the window expands.

■ **Tip**   The preferred width of the content area of a VBox is the largest of the preferred width of its children. Resizable children fill the full width of the content area, provided their maximum width property allows them to expand. Otherwise, they are kept at their preferred width.

It is often needed in a GUI application that you arrange a set of Buttons in a vertical column and make them the same size. You need to add the buttons to a VBox and set the maximum width of all buttons to Double.MAX_VALUE so they can grow to match the width of the widest button in the group. The program in Listing 10-15 shows how to achieve this. Figure 10-24 shows the window.

Listing 10-15. Using the fillWidth Property of a VBox

```
// VBoxFillWidth.java
// ... full listing in the book's download area.
```

Figure 10-24. *A VBox with some control, where the user can change the fillWidth property*

When you expand the VBox horizontally in Listing 10-16, all buttons grow to fill the available extra space. To prevent the buttons from growing when the VBox expands in the horizontal direction, you can add the VBox in an HBox and add the HBox to the scene.

 Tip You can create powerful visual effects by nesting HBox and VBox layout panes. You can also add buttons (or any other types of nodes) in a column in a GridPane to make them the same size. Please refer to the "*Understanding GridPane*" section for more details.

The Spacing Property

The spacing property specifies the vertical distance between adjacent children in a VBox. By default, it is set to 0px. It can be set in the constructors or using the setSpacing() method.

Setting Constraints for Children in VBox

VBox supports two types of constraints, *vgrow* and *margin*, that can be set on each child node individually. The vgrow constraint specifies whether a child node expands vertically when additional space is available. The margin constraint specifies space outside the edges of a child node. The VBox class provides setVgrow() and setMargin() static methods to specify these constraints. You can use null with these methods to remove the constraints individually. Use the clearConstraints(Node child) method to remove both constraints for a child node at once.

Letting Children Grow Vertically

By default, the children in a VBox get their preferred heights. If the VBox is expanded vertically, its children may get the additional available space, provided their vgrow priority is set to grow. If a VBox is expanded vertically and none of its children has its vgrow constraint set, the additional space is left unused.

The vgrow priority for a child node is set using the setVgrow() static method of the VBox class by specifying the child node and the priority:

```
VBox root = new VBox(10);
TextArea desc = new TextArea();
```

```
// Let the TextArea always grow vertically
root.setVgrow(desc, Priority.ALWAYS);
```

To reset the vgrow priority of a child node, use null as the priority:

```
// Stop the TextArea from growing horizontally
root.setVgrow(desc, null);
```

The program in Listing 10-16 shows how to set the priority of a TextArea to Priority.ALWAYS, so it can take all the additional vertical space when the VBox is expanded. Figure 10-25 shows the initial and expanded windows. Notice that the Label stays at its preferred height, after the window is expanded vertically.

Listing 10-16. Letting a TextArea Grow Vertically

```
// VBoxVGrow.java
// ... full listing in the book's download area.
```

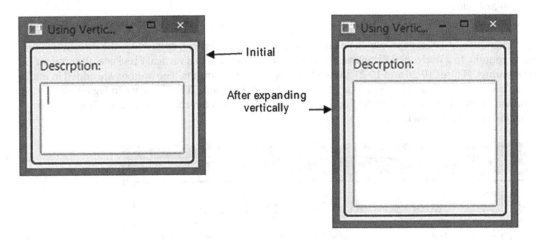

Figure 10-25. *A VBox with a TextArea set to always grow vertically*

Setting Margin for Children

You can set margins for the children of a VBox using its setMargin() static method:

```
Button okBtn = new Button("OK");
Button cancelBtn = new Button("Cancel");
VBox vbox = new VBox(okBtn, cancelBtn);

// Set margins for OK and cancel buttons
Insets margin = new Insets(5);
VBox.setMargin(okBtn, margin);
VBox.setMargin(cancelBtn, margin);
...
// Remove margins for okBtn
VBox.setMargin(okBtn, null);
```

Understanding FlowPane

A FlowPane is a simple layout pane that lays out its children in rows or columns wrapping at a specified width or height. It lets its children flow horizontally or vertically, and hence the name "flow pane." You can specify a preferred wrap length, which is the preferred width for a horizontal flow and the preferred height for a vertical flow, where the content is wrapped. A FlowPane is used in situations where the relative locations of children are not important: for example, displaying a series of pictures or buttons. A FlowPane gives all its children their preferred sizes. Rows and columns may be of different heights and widths. You can customize the vertical alignments of children in rows and the horizontal alignments of children in columns.

■ **Tip** Children in a horizontal FlowPane may be arranged in rows from left to right or right to left, which is controlled by the nodeOrientation property declared in the Node class. The default value for this property is set to NodeOrientation.LEFT_TO_RIGHT. If you want the children to flow right to left, set the property to NodeOrientation.RIGHT_TO_LEFT. This applies to all layout panes that arrange children in rows (e.g., HBox, TilePane, etc.).

The orientation of a FlowPane, which can be set to horizontal or vertical, determines the direction of the flow for its content. In a horizontal FlowPane, the content flows in rows. In a vertical FlowPane, the content flows in columns. Figures 10-26 and 10-27 show a FlowPane with ten buttons. The buttons are added in the order they have been labeled. That is, Button 1 is added before Button 2. The FlowPane in Figure 10-26 has a horizontal orientation, whereas the FlowPane in Figure 10-27 has a vertical orientation. By default, a FlowPane has a horizontal orientation.

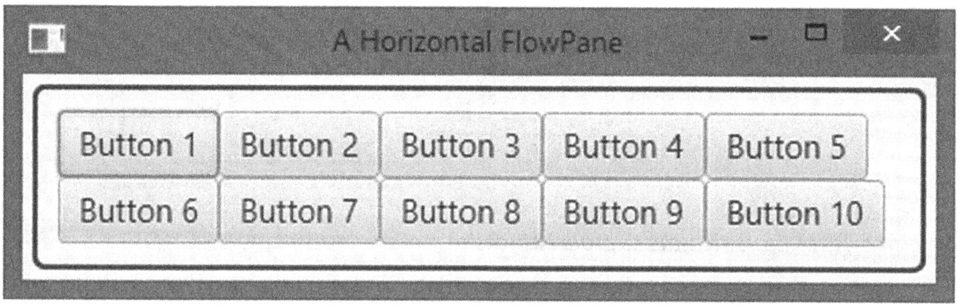

Figure 10-26. *A horizontal flow pane showing ten buttons*

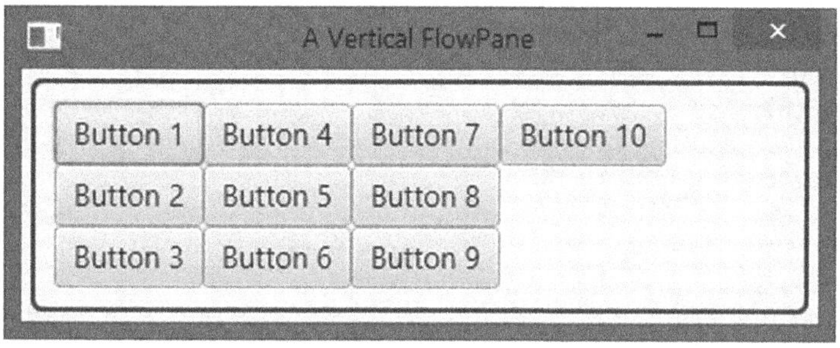

Figure 10-27. *A vertical flow pane showing ten buttons*

Creating FlowPane Objects

The FlowPane class provides several constructors to create FlowPane objects with a specified orientation (horizontal or vertical), a specified horizontal and vertical spacing between children, and a specified initial list of children:

```
// Create an empty horizontal FlowPane with 0px spacing
FlowPane fpane1 = new FlowPane();

// Create an empty vertical FlowPane with 0px spacing
FlowPane fpane2 = new FlowPane(Orientation.VERTICAL);

// Create an empty horizontal FlowPane with 5px horizontal and 10px
// vertical spacing
FlowPane fpane3 = new FlowPane(5, 10);

// Create an empty vertical FlowPane with 5px horizontal and 10px
// vertical spacing
FlowPane fpane4 = new FlowPane(Orientation.VERTICAL, 5, 10);

// Create a horizontal FlowPane with two Buttons and 0px spacing
FlowPane fpane5 =
    new FlowPane(new Button("Button 1"), new Button("Button 2"));
```

The program in Listing 10-17 shows how to create a FlowPane and add children. It adds ten Buttons and uses 5px horizontal and 10px vertical gaps. The window is shown in Figure 10-28.

Listing 10-17. Using a Horizontal FlowPane

```
// FlowPaneTest.java
// ... full listing in the book's download area.
```

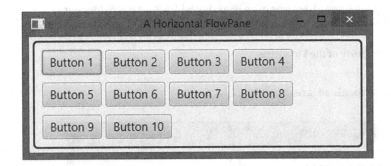

Figure 10-28. *A horizontal pane with ten buttons using 5px hgap and 10px vgap*

FlowPane Properties

Table 10-4 lists several FlowPane class properties that are used to customize the layout of its children.

Table 10-4. *The List of Properties Declared in the FlowPane Class*

Property	Type	Description
alignment	ObjectProperty<Pos>	It specifies the alignment of rows and columns relative to the content area of the FlowPane. The default value is Pos.TOP_LEFT.
rowValignment	ObjectProperty<VPos>	It specifies the vertical alignment of the children within each row in a horizontal FlowPane. It is ignored for a vertical FlowPane.
columnHalignment	ObjectProperty<HPos>	It specifies the horizontal alignment of the children within each column in a vertical FlowPane. It is ignored for a horizontal FlowPane.
hgap, vgap	DoubleProperty	They specify the horizontal and vertical gaps between children. The default is zero.
orientation	ObjectProperty<Orientation>	It specifies the orientation of the FlowPane. It defaults to HORIZONTAL.
prefWrapLength	DoubleProperty	It is the preferred width in a horizontal FlowPane and the preferred height in a vertical FlowPane where the content should wrap. The default is 400.

The Alignment Property

The alignment property of a FlowPane controls the alignment of its content. A Pos value contains a vertical alignment (vpos) and horizontal alignment (hpos). For example, Pos.TOP_LEFT has the vertical alignment as top and horizontal alignment as left. In a horizontal FlowPane, each row is aligned using the hpos value of the alignment, and rows (the entire content) are aligned using the vpos value. In a vertical FlowPane, each column is aligned using the vpos value of the alignment, and the columns (the entire content) are aligned using the hpos value.

The program in Listing 10-18 displays three FlowPanes in an HBox. Each FlowPane has a different alignment. The Text node in each FlowPane displays the alignment used. Figure 10-29 shows the window.

Listing 10-18. Using the Alignment Property of the FlowPane

```
// FlowPaneAlignment.java
// ... full listing in the book's download area.
```

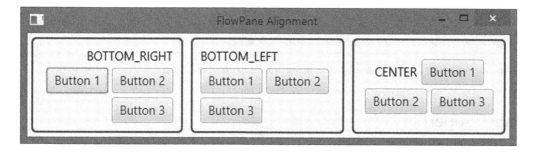

Figure 10-29. *FlowPanes using different alignments for their contents*

The rowValignment and columnHalignment Properties

A FlowPane lays out its children at their preferred sizes. Rows and columns could be of different sizes. You can align children in each row or column using the rowValignment and columnHalignment properties.

In a horizontal FlowPane, children in one row may be of different heights. The height of a row is the largest of the preferred heights of all children in the row. The rowValignment property lets you specify the vertical alignment of children in each row. Its value could be set to one of the constants of the VPos enum: BASELINE, TOP, CENTER, and BOTTOM. If the maximum height value of a child node allows for vertical expansion, the child node will be expanded to fill the height of the row. If the rowValignment property is set to VPos.BASELINE, children are resized to their preferred height instead of expanding to fill the full height of the row.

In a vertical FlowPane, children in one column may be of different widths. The width of a column is the largest of the preferred widths of all children in the column. The columnHalignment property lets you specify the horizontal alignment of children in each column. Its value could be set to one of the constants of the HPos enum: LEFT, RIGHT, and CENTER. If the maximum width value of a child node allows for horizontal expansion, the child node will be expanded to fill the width of the column.

The program in Listing 10-19 creates three FlowPanes and adds them to an HBox. Figure 10-30 shows the window. The first two FlowPanes have horizontal orientations, and the last one has a vertical orientation. The row and column alignments are displayed in the Text node, and the orientations for the FlowPane are displayed in the TextArea node.

Listing 10-19. Using Row and Column Alignments in a FlowPane

```
// FlowPaneRowColAlignment.java
// ... full listing in the book's download area.
```

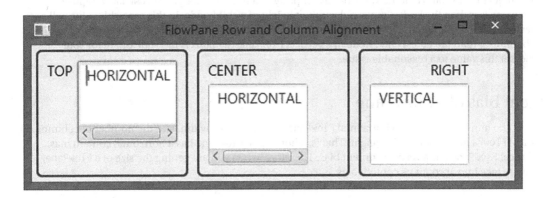

Figure 10-30. *FlowPanes using different row and column alignments*

The hgap and vgap Properties

Using the hgap and vgap properties is straightforward. In a horizontal FlowPane, the hgap property specifies the horizontal spacing between adjacent children in a row, and the vgap property specifies the spacing between adjacent rows. In a vertical FlowPane, the hgap property specifies the horizontal spacing between adjacent columns, and the vgap property specifies the spacing between adjacent children in a column. You can set these properties in the constructors or using the setter methods. We have been using these properties in our examples discussed in this section.

```
// Create a FlowPane with 5px hgap and 10px vgap
FlowPane fpane = new FlowPane(5, 10);
...
// Change the hgap to 15px and vgap to 25px
fpane.setHgap(15);
fpane.setVgap(25);
```

The Orientation Property

The orientation property specifies the flow of content in a FlowPane. If it is set to Orientation.HORIZONTAL, which is the default value, the content flows in rows. If it is set to Orientation.VERTICAL, the content flows in columns. You can specify the orientation in the constructors or using the setter method:

```
// Create a horizontal FlowPane
FlowPane fpane = new FlowPane();
...
// Change the orientation of the FlowPane to vertical
fpane.setOrientation(Orientation.VERTICAL);
```

The prefWrapLength Property

The prefWrapLength property is the preferred width in a horizontal FlowPane or the preferred height in a vertical FlowPane where content should wrap. This is only used to compute the preferred size of the FlowPane. It defaults to 400. Treat the value of this property as a hint to resize your FlowPane. Suppose you set this value to less than the largest preferred width or height of a child node. In this case, this value will not be respected, as a row cannot be shorter than the widest child node in a horizontal FlowPane, or a column cannot be shorter than the tallest child node in a vertical FlowPane. If 400px is too wide or tall for your FlowPane, set this value to a reasonable value.

Content Bias of a FlowPane

Notice that the number of rows in a horizontal FlowPane depends on its width, and the number of columns in a vertical FlowPane depends on its height. That is, a horizontal FlowPane has a horizontal content bias, and a vertical FlowPane has a vertical content bias. Therefore, when you are getting the size of a FlowPane, make sure to take into account its content bias.

Understanding BorderPane

A BorderPane divides its layout area into five regions: top, right, bottom, left, and center. You can place at most one node in each of the five regions. Figure 10-31 shows five Buttons placed in the five regions of the BorderPane—one Button in each region. The Buttons have been labeled the same as their regions in which they are placed. Any of the regions may be null. If a region is null, no space is allocated for it.

Figure 10-31. *Five regions of a BorderPane*

In a typical Windows application, a screen uses the five regions to place its content:

- A menu or a toolbar at the top

- A status bar at the bottom

- A navigation panel on the left

- Additional information on the right

- Main content in the center

A BorderPane satisfies all the layout requirements for a typical Windows-based GUI screen. This is the reason that a BorderPane is most often used as the root node for a scene. Typically, you have more than five nodes in a window. If you have more than one node to place in one of the five regions of a BorderPane, add the nodes to a layout pane, for example, an HBox, a VBox, etc., and then add the layout pane to the desired region of the BorderPane.

A BorderPane uses the following resizing policies for its children:

- The children in the top and bottom regions are resized to their preferred heights. Their widths are extended to fill the available extra horizontal space, provided the maximum widths of the children allow extending their widths beyond their preferred widths.

- The children in the right and left regions are resized to their preferred widths. Their heights are extended to fill the extra vertical space, provided the maximum heights of the children allow extending their heights beyond their preferred heights.

- The child node in the center will fill the rest of the available space in both directions.

Children in a BorderPane may overlap if it is resized to a smaller size than its preferred size. The overlapping rule is based on the order in which the children are added. The children are drawn in the order they are added. This means that a child node may overlap all child nodes added prior to it. Suppose regions are populated in the order of right, center, and left. The left region may overlap the center and right regions, and the center region may overlap the right region.

■ **Tip** You can set the alignments for all children within their regions. You can set the margins for children. As with all layout panes, you can also style a BorderPane with CSS.

Creating BorderPane Objects

The BorderPane class provides constructors to create BorderPane objects with or without children:

```
// Create an empty BorderPane
BorderPane bpane1 = new BorderPane();

// Create a BorderPane with a TextArea in the center
TextArea center = new TextArea();
BorderPane bpane2 = new BorderPane(center);

// Create a BorderPane with a Text node in each of the five regions
Text center = new Text("Center");
Text top = new Text("Top");
Text right = new Text("Right");
Text bottom = new Text("Bottom");
Text left = new Text("Left");
BorderPane bpane3 = new BorderPane(center, top, right, bottom, left);
```

The BorderPane class declares five properties named top, right, bottom, left, and center that store the reference of five children in the five regions. Use the setters for these properties to add a child node to any of the five regions. For example, use the setTop(Node topChild) method to add a child node to the top region. To get the reference of the children in any of the five regions, use the getters for these properties. For example, the getTop() method returns the reference of the child node in the top region.

```
// Create an empty BorderPane and add a text node in each of the five regions
BorderPane bpane = new BorderPane();.
bpane.setTop(new Text("Top"));
bpane.setRight(new Text("Right"));
bpane.setBottom(new Text("Bottom"));
bpane.setLeft(new Text("Left"));
bpane.setCenter(new Text("Center"));
```

■ **Tip** Do not use the ObservableList<Node>, which is returned by the getChildren() method of the BorderPane, to add children to a BorderPane. The children added to this list are ignored. Use the top, right, bottom, left, and center properties instead.

The program in Listing 10-20 shows how to create a BorderPane and add children. It adds children to the right, bottom, and center regions. Two Labels, a TextField, and a TextArea are added to the center region. A VBox with two buttons is added to the right region. A Label to show the status is added to the bottom region. The top and left regions are set to null. The BorderPane is set as the root node for the scene. Figure 10-32 shows the window.

Listing 10-20. Using the BorderPane Layout Pane

```
// BorderPaneTest.java
// ... full listing in the book's download area.
```

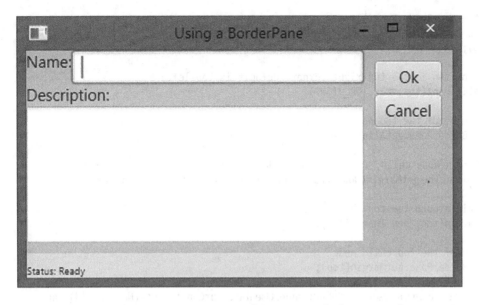

Figure 10-32. *A BorderPane using some controls in its top, right, bottom, and center regions*

BorderPane Properties

The BorderPane class declares five properties: top, right, bottom, left, and center. They are of the ObjectProperty<Node> type. They store the reference of the child nodes in the five regions of the BorderPane. Use the setters of these properties to add children to the BorderPane. Use the getters of properties to get the reference of the child node in any regions.

Recall that not all of the five regions in a BorderPane need to have nodes. If a region does not have a node, no space is allocated for it. Use null to remove a child node from a region. For example, setTop(null) will remove the already added node to the top region. By default, all regions have null nodes as their child nodes.

Setting Constraints for Children in BorderPane

A BorderPane allows you to set alignment and margin constraints on individual children. The alignment for a child node is defined relative to its region. The default alignments:

- Pos.TOP_LEFT for the top child node

- Pos.BOTTOM_LEFT for the bottom child node

- Pos.TOP_LEFT for the left child node

- Pos.TOP_RIGHT for the right child node

- Pos.CENTER for the center child node

Use the setAlignment(Node child, Pos value) static method of the BorderPane class to set the alignment for children. The getAlignment(Node child) static method returns the alignment for a child node:

```
BorderPane root = new BorderPane();
Button top = new Button("OK");
root.setTop(top);

// Place the OK button in the top right corner (default is top left)
BorderPane.setAlignment(top, Pos.TOP_RIGHT);
...
// Get the alignment of the top node
Pos alignment = BorderPane.getAlignment(top);
```

Use the setMargin(Node child, Insets value) static method of the BorderPane class to set the margin for the children. The getMargin(Node child) static method returns the margin for a child node:

```
// Set 10px margin around the top child node
BorderPane.setMargin(top, new Insets(10));
...
// Get the margin of the top child node
Insets margin = BorderPane.getMargin(top);
```

Use null to reset the constraints to the default value. Use the clearConstraints(Node child) static method of the BorderPane to reset all constraints for a child at once:

```
// Clear the alignment and margin constraints for the top child node
BorderPane.clearConstraints(top);
```

Understanding StackPane

A StackPane lays out its children in a stack of nodes. It is simple to use. However, it provides a powerful means to overlay nodes. Children are drawn in the order they are added. That is, the first child node is drawn first; the second child node is drawn next, etc. For example, overlaying text on a shape is as easy as using a StackPane: add the shape as the first child node and the text as the second child node. The shape will be drawn first followed by the text, which makes it seem as if the text is a part of the shape.

Figure 10-33 shows a window with a StackPane set as the root node for its scene. A Rectangle shape and a Text node with text "A Rectangle" are added to the StackPane. The Text is added last, which overlays the Rectangle. The outer border is the border of the StackPane. The dashed inner border is the border of the Rectangle.

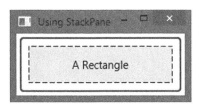

Figure 10-33. *A Text node overlaying a Rectangle in a StackPane*

■ **Tip** You can create very appealing GUI using StackPanes by overlaying different types of nodes. You can overlay text on an image to get an effect as if the text were part of the image. And you can overlay different types of shapes to create a complex shape. Remember that the node that overlays other nodes is added last to the StackPane.

The preferred width of a StackPane is the width of its widest children. Its preferred height is the height of its tallest children. StackPane does clip its content. Therefore, its children may be drawn outside its bounds.

A StackPane resizes its resizable children to fill its content area, provided their maximum size allows them to expand beyond their preferred size. By default, a StackPane aligns all its children to the center of its content area. You can change the alignment for a child node individually or for all children to use the same alignment.

Creating StackPane Objects

The StackPane class provides constructors to create objects with or without children:

```
// Create an empty StackPane
StackPane spane1 = new StackPane();

// Add a Rectangle and a Text to the StackPane
Rectangle rect = new Rectangle(200, 50);
rect.setFill(Color.LAVENDER);
Text text = new Text("A Rectangle");
spane1.getChildren().addAll(rect, text);

// Create a StackPane with a Rectangle and a Text
Rectangle r = new Rectangle(200, 50);
r.setFill(Color.LAVENDER);
StackPane spane2 = new StackPane(r, new Text("A Rectangle"));
```

The program in Listing 10-21 shows how to create a StackPane. It adds a Rectangle and a Text to a StackPane. The Rectangle is added first, and therefore it is overlaid with the Text. Figure 10-33 shows the window.

Listing 10-21. Using StackPane

```
// StackPaneTest.java
// ... full listing in the book's download area.
```

You must add the children to a StackPane in a specific order to create the desired overlay. Children are drawn in the order they exist in the list. The following two statements will not get the same results:

```
// Overlay a Text on a Rectangle
spane1.getChildren().addAll(rect, text);

// Overlay a Rectangle on a Text
spane1.getChildren().addAll(text, rect);
```

If the Text is smaller than the Rectangle, overlaying the Rectangle on the Text will hide the Text. If the Text size is bigger than the Rectangle, the part of the Text outside the Rectangle bounds will be visible.

The program in Listing 10-22 shows how the overlay rules work in a StackPane. The createStackPane() method creates a StackPane with a Rectangle and a Text. It takes the text for the Text node, the opacity of the Rectangle, and a boolean value indicating whether the Rectangle should be added first to the StackPane. The start method creates five StackPanes and adds them to an HBox. Figure 10-34 shows the window.

- In the first StackPane, the text is overlaid on the rectangle. The rectangle is drawn first and the text second. Both are visible.

- In the second StackPane, the rectangle is overlaid on the text. The text is hidden behind the rectangle as the rectangle is drawn over the text and it is bigger than the text.

- In the third StackPane, the rectangle is overlaid on the text. Unlike the second StackPane, the text is visible because we have set the opacity for the rectangle to 0.5, which makes it 50% transparent.

- In the fourth StackPane, the rectangle is overlaid on a big text. The opacity of the rectangle is 100%. Therefore, we see only the part of the text that is outside the bounds of the rectangle.

- In the fifth StackPane, the rectangle is overlaid on a big text. The opacity of the rectangle is 50%. We can see the entire text. The visibility of the text within the bounds of the rectangle is 50% and that of outside the bounds is 100%.

Listing 10-22. Overlaying Rules in a StackPane

```
// StackPaneOverlayTest.java
// ... full listing in the book's download area.
```

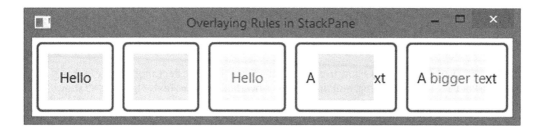

Figure 10-34. *Overlaying a Rectangle on a Text and vice versa*

StackPane Properties

The StackPane class has an alignment property of the ObjectProperty<Pos> type. The property defines the default alignment of all children within the content area of the StackPane. By default, its value is set to Pos.CENTER, which means that all children, by default, are aligned in the center of the content area of the StackPane. This is what we have seen in our previous examples. If you do not want the default alignment for all children, you can change it to any other alignment value. Note that changing the value of the alignment property sets the default alignment for all children.

Individual children may override the default alignment by setting its alignment constraint. We will discuss how to set the alignment constraint on a child node in the next section.

StackPane has several other uses besides overlaying nodes. Whenever you have a requirement to align a node or a collection of nodes in a specific position, try using a StackPane. For example, if you want to display text in the center of your screen, use a StackPane with a Text node as the root node of the scene. The StackPane takes care of keeping the text in the center as the window is resized. Without a StackPane, you will need to use binding to keep the text positioned in the center of the window.

The program in Listing 10-23 uses five StackPanes in an HBox. Each StackPane has a Rectangle overlaid with a Text. The alignment for the StackPane, and hence for all its children, is used as the text for the Text node. Figure 10-35 shows the window. Notice that the Rectangles in StackPanes are bigger than the Texts. Therefore, the Rectangles occupy the entire content area of the StackPanes, and they seem not to be affected by the alignment property.

Listing 10-23. Using the Alignment Property of a StackPane

```
// StackPaneAlignment.java
// ... full listing in the book's download area.
```

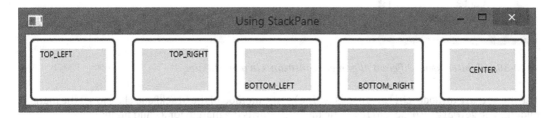

Figure 10-35. *StackPanes using different alignment values*

Setting Constraints for Children

A StackPane allows you to set alignment and margin constraints on individual children. The alignment for a child node is defined relative to the content area of the StackPane.

You should be able to differentiate between the alignment property of a StackPane and the alignment constraint on its children. The alignment property affects all children. Its value is used to align children by default. The alignment constraint on a child node overrides the default alignment value set by the alignment property. The alignment constraint on a child node affects the alignment of only that child node, whereas the alignment property affects all child nodes. When a child node is drawn, JavaFX uses the alignment constraint of the child node for aligning it within the content area of the StackPane. If its alignment constraint is not set, the alignment property of the StackPane is used.

■ **Tip** The default value for the alignment property of StackPane is Pos.CENTER. The default value for the alignment constraint for children is null.

Use the setAlignment(Node child, Pos value) static method of the StackPane class to set the alignment constraints for children. The getAlignment(Node child) static method returns the alignment for a child node, see Listing 10-24 and Figure 10-36.:

```
// Place a Text node in the top left corner of the StackPane
Text topLeft = new Text("top-left");
StackPane.setAlignment(topLeft, Pos.TOP_LEFT);
StackPane root = new StackPane(topLeft);
...
// Get the alignment of the topLeft node
Pos alignment = StackPane.getAlignment(topLeft);
```

Listing 10-24. Using the Alignment Constraints for Children in a StackPane

```
// StackPaneAlignmentConstraint.java
// ... full listing in the book's download area.
```

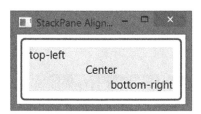

Figure 10-36. *Children using different alignment constraints in a StackPane*

Use the setMargin(Node child, Insets value) static method of the StackPane class to set the margin for children. The getMargin(Node child) static method returns the margin for a child node:

```
// Set 10px margin around the topLeft child node
StackPane.setMargin(topLeft, new Insets(10));
...
// Get the margin of the topLeft child node
Insets margin = StackPane.getMargin(topLeft);
```

Use null to reset the constraints to the default value. Use the clearConstraints(Node child) static method of the StackPane to reset all constraints for a child at once:

```
// Clear the alignment and margin constraints for the topLeft child node
StackPane.clearConstraints(topLeft);
```

After you clear all constraints for a child node, it will use the current value of the alignment property of the StackPane as its alignment and 0px as the margins.

Understanding TilePane

A TilePane lays out its children in a grid of uniformly sized cells, known as tiles. TilePanes work similar to FlowPanes with one difference: in a FlowPane, rows and columns can be of different heights and widths, whereas in a TilePane, all rows have the same heights and all columns have the same widths. The width of the widest child node and the height of the tallest child node are the default widths and heights of all tiles in a TilePane.

The orientation of a TilePane, which can be set to horizontal or vertical, determines the direction of the flow for its content. By default, a TilePane has a horizontal orientation. In a horizontal TilePane, the content flows in rows. The content in rows may flow from left to right (the default) or from right to left. In a vertical TilePane, the content flows in columns. Figures 10-37 and 10-38 show horizontal and vertical TilePanes.

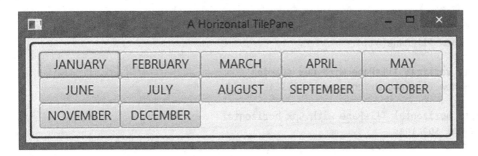

Figure 10-37. *A horizontal TilePane showing months in a year*

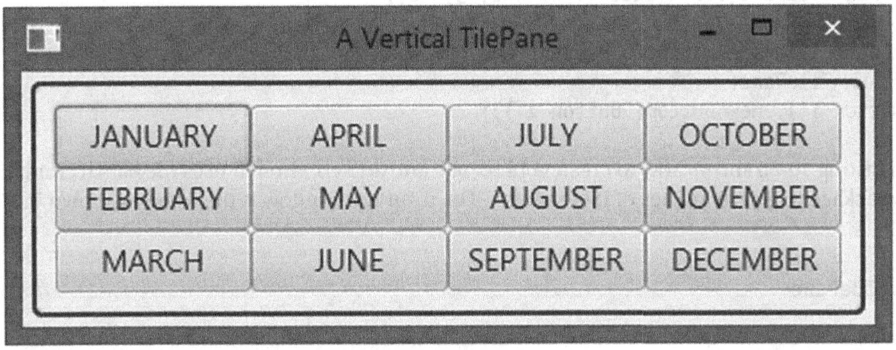

Figure 10-38. *A vertical TilePane showing months in a year*

You can customize the layout in a TilePane using its properties or setting constraints on individual children:

- You can override the default size of tiles.

- You can customize the alignment of the entire content of a TilePane within its content area, which defaults to Pos.TOP_LEFT.

- You can also customize the alignment of each child node within its tile, which defaults to Pos.CENTER.

- You specify the spacing between adjacent rows and columns, which defaults to 0px.

- You can specify the preferred number of columns in a horizontal TilePane and the preferred number of rows in a vertical TilePane. The default values for the preferred number of rows and columns are five.

Creating TilePane Objects

The TilePane class provides several constructors to create TilePane objects with a specified orientation (horizontal or vertical), a specified horizontal and vertical spacing between children, and a specified initial list of children:

```
// Create an empty horizontal TilePane with 0px spacing
TilePane tpane1 = new TilePane();

// Create an empty vertical TilePane with 0px spacing
TilePane tpane2 = new TilePane(Orientation.VERTICAL);

// Create an empty horizontal TilePane with 5px horizontal
// and 10px vertical spacing
TilePane tpane3 = new TilePane(5, 10);

// Create an empty vertical TilePane with 5px horizontal
// and 10px vertical spacing
TilePane tpane4 = new TilePane(Orientation.VERTICAL, 5, 10);

// Create a horizontal TilePane with two Buttons and 0px spacing
TilePane tpane5 = new TilePane(
    new Button("Button 1"), new Button("Button 2"));
```

The program in Listing 10-25 shows how to create a TilePane and add children. It uses the Month enum from the java.time package to get the names of ISO months. The resulting window is the same as shown in Figure 10-37.

Listing 10-25. Using TilePane

```
// TilePaneTest.java
// ... full listing in the book's download area.
```

You can modify the code in Listing 10-25 to get the window in Figure 10-38. You need to specify the orientation of the TilePane as Orientation.VERTICAL and use three as the preferred number of rows:

```
import javafx.geometry.Orientation;
...
double hgap = 5.0;
double vgap = 5.0;
TilePane root = new TilePane(Orientation.VERTICAL, hgap, vgap);
root.setPrefRows(3);
```

TilePane Properties

The TilePane class contains several properties, as listed in Table 10-5, which let you customize the layout of its children.

Table 10-5. *The List of Properties Declared in the TilePane Class*

Property	Type	Description
alignment	ObjectProperty<Pos>	It specifies the alignment of the content of the TilePane relative to its content area. It defaults to Pos.TOP_LEFT.
tileAlignment	ObjectProperty<Pos>	It specifies the default alignment of all children within their tiles. It defaults to Pos.CENTER.
hgap, vgap	DoubleProperty	The hgap property specifies the horizontal gap between adjacent children in a row. The vgap property specifies the vertical gap between adjacent children in a column. The default is zero for both properties.
orientation	ObjectProperty<Orientation>	It specifies the orientation of the TilePane – horizontal or vertical. It defaults to HORIZONTAL.
prefRows	IntegerProperty	It specifies the preferred number of rows for a vertical TilePane. It is ignored for a horizontal TilePane.
prefColumns	IntegerProperty	It specifies the preferred number of columns for a horizontal TilePane. It is ignored for a vertical TilePane.
prefTileWidth	DoubleProperty	It specifies the preferred width of each tile. The default is to use the width of the widest children.
prefTileHeight	DoubleProperty	It specifies the preferred height of each tile. The default is to use the height of the tallest children.
tileHeight	ReadOnlyDoubleProperty	It is a read-only property that stores the actual height of each tile.
tileWidth	ReadOnlyDoubleProperty	It is a read-only property that stores the actual width of each tile.

The Alignment Property

The alignment property of a TilePane controls the alignment of its content within its content area. You can see the effects of this property when the size of the TilePane is bigger than its content. The property works the same way as the alignment property for the FlowPane. Please refer to the description of the alignment property for FlowPane for more details and illustrations.

The tileAlignment Property

The tileAlignment property specifies the default alignment of children within their tiles. Note that this property affects children smaller than the size of tiles. This property affects the default alignment of all children within their tiles. This can be overridden on individual children by setting their alignment constraints. The program in Listing 10-26 shows how to use the tileAlignment property. It shows display windows, as shown in Figure 10-39, with two TilePanes—one has the tileAlignment property set to Pos.CENTER and another Pos.TOP_LEFT.

Listing 10-26. Using the TileAlignment Property of TilePane

```
// TilePaneTileAlignment.java
// ... full listing in the book's download area.
```

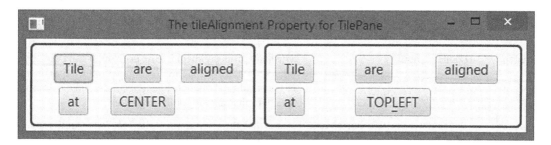

Figure 10-39. *Using the tileAlignment property*

The hgap and vgap Properties

The hgap and vgap properties specify the spacing between adjacent columns and adjacent rows. They default to zero. They can be specified in the constructors or using the setHgap(double hg) and setVgap(double vg) methods of the TilePane.

The Orientation Property

The orientation property specifies the flow of content in a TilePane. If it is set to Orientation.HORIZONTAL, which is the default value, the content flows in rows. If it is set to Orientation.VERTICAL, the content flows in columns. You can specify the orientation in the constructors or using the setter method:

```
// Create a horizontal TilePane
TilePane tpane = new TilePane();
...
// Change the orientation of the TilePane to vertical
tpane.setOrientation(Orientation.VERTICAL);
```

The prefRows and prefColumns Properties

The prefRows property specifies the preferred number of rows for a vertical TilePane. It is ignored for a horizontal TilePane.

The prefColumns specifies the preferred number of columns for a horizontal TilePane. It is ignored for a vertical TilePane.

The default value for prefRows and prefColumns is 5. It is recommended that you use a sensible value for these properties.

Note that these properties are only used to compute the preferred size of the TilePane. If the TilePane is resized to a size other than its preferred size, these values may not reflect the actual number of rows or columns. In Listing 10-26, we have specified three as the preferred number of columns. If you resize the window displayed by Listing 10-26 to a smaller width, you may get only one or two columns, and the number of rows will increase accordingly.

■ **Tip** Recall the prefWrapLength property of the FlowPane that is used to determine the preferred width or height of the FlowPane. The prefRows and prefColumns properties serve the same purpose in a TilePane, as does the prefWrapLength in a FlowPane.

The prefTileWidth and prefTileHeight Properties

A TilePane computes the preferred size of its tiles based on the widest and the tallest children. You can override the computed width and height of tiles using the prefTileWidth and prefTileHeight properties. They default to Region.USE_COMPUTED_SIZE. The TilePane attempts to resize its children to fit in the tile size, provided their minimum and maximum sizes allow them to be resized.

```
// Create a TilePane and set its preferred tile width and height to 40px
TilePane tpane = new TilePane();
tpane.setPrefTileWidth(40);
tpane.setPrefTileHeight(40);
```

The tileWidth and tileHeight Properties

The tileWidth and tileHeight properties specify the actual width and height of each tile. They are read-only properties. If you specify the prefTileWidth and prefTileHeight properties, they return their values. Otherwise, they return the computed size of tiles.

Setting Constraints for Children in TilePane

A TilePane allows you to set alignment and margin constraints on individual children. The alignment for a child node is defined within the tile that contains the child node.

You should be able to differentiate between the three:

- The alignment property of a TilePane

- The tileAlignment property of the TilePane

- The alignment constraint on individual children of the TilePane

The alignment property is used to align the content (all children) within the content area of the TilePane. It affects the content of TilePane as a whole.

The tileAlignment property is used to align all children within their tiles by default. Modifying this property affects all children.

The alignment constraint on a child node is used to align the child node within its tile. It affects only the child node on which it is set. It overrides the default alignment value for the child node that is set using the tileAlignment property of the TilePane.

■ **Tip** The default value for the tileAlignment property of a TilePane is Pos.CENTER. The default value for the alignment constraint for children is null.

Use the setAlignment(Node child, Pos value) static method of the TilePane class to set the alignment constraints for the children. The getAlignment(Node child) static method returns the alignment for a child node:

```
// Place a Text node in the top left corner in a tile
Text topLeft = new Text("top-left");
TilePane.setAlignment(topLeft, Pos.TOP_LEFT);

TilePane root = new TilePane();
root.getChildren().add(topLeft);
...
// Get the alignment of the topLeft node
Pos alignment = TilePane.getAlignment(topLeft);
```

The program in Listing 10-27 adds five buttons to a TilePane. The button labeled "Three" uses a custom tile alignment constraint of Pos.BOTTOM_RIGHT. All other buttons use the default tile alignment, which is Pos.CENTER. Figure 10-40 shows the window.

Listing 10-27. Using the Alignment Constraints for Children in a TilePane

```
// TilePaneAlignmentConstraint.java
// ... full listing in the book's download area.
```

Figure 10-40. *Children using different alignment constraints in a TilePane*

Use the setMargin(Node child, Insets value) static method of the TilePane class to set the margin for children. The getMargin(Node child) static method returns the margin for a child node:

```
// Set 10px margin around the topLeft child node
TilePane.setMargin(topLeft, new Insets(10));
...
// Get the margin of the topLeft child node
Insets margin = TilePane.getMargin(topLeft);
```

Use null to reset the constraints to the default value. Use the clearConstraints(Node child) static method of the TilePane to reset all constraints for a child at once:

```
// Clear the tile alignment and margin constraints for the topLeft child node
TilePane.clearConstraints(topLeft);
```

After you clear all constraints for a child node, it will use the current value of the tileAlignment property of the TilePane as its alignment and 0px as the margins.

Understanding GridPane

GridPane is one of the most powerful layout panes. With power comes complexity. Therefore, it is also a bit complex to learn.

A GridPane lays out its children in a dynamic grid of cells arranged in rows and columns. The grid is dynamic because the number and size of cells in the grid are determined based on the number of children. They depend on the constraints set on children. Each cell in the grid is identified by its position in the column and row. The indexes for columns and rows start at zero. A child node may be placed anywhere in the grid spanning more than one cell. All cells in a row are of the same height. Cells in different rows may have different heights. All cells in a column are of the same width. Cells in different columns may have different widths. By default, a row is tall enough to accommodate the tallest child node in it. A column is wide enough to accommodate the widest child node in it. You can customize the size of each row and column. GridPane also allows for vertical spacing between rows and horizontal spacing between columns.

GridPane does not show the grid lines by default. For debug purposes, you can show the grid lines. Figure 10-41 shows three instances of the GridPane. The first GridPane shows only the grid lines and no child nodes. The second GridPane shows the cell positions, which are identified by row and column indexes. In the figure, (cM, rN) means the cell at the (M+1)th column and the (N+1)th row. For example, (c3, r2) means the cell at the fourth column and the third row. The third GridPane shows six buttons in the grid. Five of the buttons span one row and one column; one of them spans two rows and one column.

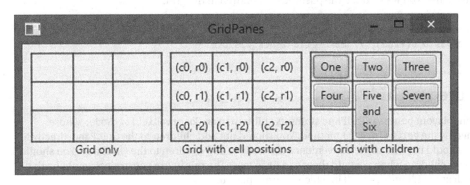

Figure 10-41. *GridPanes with grid only, with cell positions, and with children placed in the grid*

In a GridPane, rows are indexed from top to bottom. The top row has an index of zero. Columns are indexed from left to right or from right to left. If the nodeOrientation property for the GridPane is set to LEFT_TO_RIGHT, the leftmost column has index 0. If it is set to RIGHT_TO_LEFT, the rightmost column has an index of zero. The second grid in Figure 10-41 shows the leftmost column having an index of zero, which means that its nodeOrientation property is set from LEFT_TO_RIGHT.

■ **Tip** A question that is often asked about the GridPane is, "How many cells, and of what sizes, do we need to lay out children in a GridPane?" The answer is simple but sometimes perplexing to beginners. You specify the cell positions and cell spans for the children. GridPane will figure out the number of cells (rows and columns) and their sizes for you. That is, GridPane computes the number of cells and their sizes based on the constraints that you set for the children.

Creating GridPane Objects

The GridPane class contains a no-args constructor. It creates an empty GridPane with 0px spacing between rows and columns, placing the children, which need to be added later, at the top-left corner within its content area:

```
GridPane gpane = new GridPane();
```

Making Grid Lines Visible

The GridPane class contains a gridLinesVisible property of the BooleanProperty type. It controls the visibility of the grid lines. By default, it is set to false, and the grid lines are invisible. It exists for debugging purposes only. Use it when you want to see the positions of children in the grid.

```
GridPane gpane = new GridPane();
gpane.setGridLinesVisible(true); // Make grid lines visible
```

Adding Children to GridPane

Like most of the other layout panes, a GridPane stores its children in an ObservableList<Node> whose reference is returned by the getChildren() method. You should not add children to the GridPane directly to the list. Rather, you should use one of the convenience methods to add children to the GridPane. You should specify constraints for children when you add them to a GridPane. The minimum constraints would be the column and row indexes to identify the cell in which they are placed.

Let us first see the effect of adding the children directly to the observable list of the GridPane. Listing 10-28 contains the program that directly adds three buttons to the list of children of a GridPane. Figure 10-42 shows the window. Notice that the buttons overlap. They are all placed in the same cell (c0, r0). They are drawn in the order they are added to the list.

■ **Tip** In a GridPane, by default, all children are added in the first cell (c0, r0) spanning only one column and one row, thus overlapping each other. They are drawn in the order they are added.

Listing 10-28. Adding Children to the List of Children for a GridPane Directly

```
// GridPaneChildrenList.java
// ... full listing in the book's download area.
```

Figure 10-42. *Three buttons added to the list of children for a GridPane directly*

There are two ways of fixing the problem of overlapping children in Listing 10-28:

- We can set the position in which they are placed, before or after adding them to the list.

- We can use convenience methods of the GridPane class that allow specifying the positions, among other constraints, while adding children to the GridPane.

Setting Positions of Children

You can set the column and row indexes for a child node using one of the following three static methods of the GridPane class:

- `public static void setColumnIndex(Node child, Integer value)`

- `public static void setRowIndex(Node child, Integer value)`

- `public static void setConstraints(Node child,int columnIndex, int rowIndex)`

The program in Listing 10-29 is a modified version of the program in Listing 10-28. It adds the column and row indexes to three buttons, so they are positioned in separate columns in one row. Figure 10-43 shows the window.

Listing 10-29. Setting Positions for Children in a GridPane

```
// GridPaneChildrenPositions.java
// ... full listing in the book's download area.
```

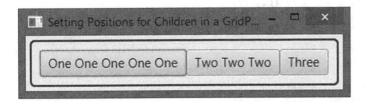

Figure 10-43. *Three buttons added to a GridPane directly and then their position set*

Using Convenience Methods to Add Children

The GridPane class contains the following convenience methods to add children with constraints:

- void add(Node child, int columnIndex, int rowIndex)
- void add(Node child, int columnIndex, int rowIndex, int colspan,int rowspan)
- void addRow(int rowIndex, Node... children)
- void addColumn(int columnIndex, Node... children)

The add() methods let you add a child node specifying the column index, row index, column span, and row span.

The addRow() method adds the specified children in a row identified by the specified rowIndex. Children are added sequentially. If the row already contains children, the specified children are appended sequentially. For example, if the GridPane has no children in the specified row, it will add the first child node at column index 0, the second at column index 1, etc. Suppose the specified row already has two children occupying column indexes 0 and 1. The addRow() method will add children starting at column index 2.

■ **Tip** All children added using the addRow() method span only one cell. Row and column spans for a child node can be modified using the setRowSpan(Node child, Integer value) and setColumnSpan(Node child, Integer value) static methods of the GridPane class. When you modify the row and column spans for a child node, make sure to update row and column indexes of the affected children so they do not overlap.

The addColumn() method adds the specified children sequentially in a column identified by the specified columnIndex. This method adds children to a column the same way the addRow() method adds children to a row.

The following snippet of code creates three GridPanes and adds four buttons to them using three different ways. Figure 10-44 shows one of the GridPanes. All of them will look the same.

```
// Add a child node at a time
GridPane gpane1 = new GridPane();
gpane1.add(new Button("One"), 0, 0);      // (c0, r0)
gpane1.add(new Button("Two"), 1, 0);      // (c1, r0)
gpane1.add(new Button("Three"), 0, 1);    // (c0, r1)
gpane1.add(new Button("Four"), 1, 1);     // (c1, r1)

// Add a row at a time
GridPane gpane2 = new GridPane();
gpane2.addRow(0, new Button("One"), new Button("Two"));
gpane2.addRow(1, new Button("Three"), new Button("Four"));

// Add a column at a time
GridPane gpane3 = new GridPane();
gpane3.addColumn(0, new Button("One"), new Button("Three"));
gpane3.addColumn(1, new Button("Two"), new Button("Four"));
```

Figure 10-44. *A GridPane with four buttons*

Specifying Row and Column Spans

A child node may span more than one row and column, which can be specified using the rowSpan and colSpan constraints. By default, a child node spans one column and one row. These constraints can be specified while adding the child node or later using any of the following methods in the GridPane class:

- void add(Node child, int columnIndex, int rowIndex, int colspan, int rowspan)

- static void setColumnSpan(Node child, Integer value)

- static void setConstraints(Node child, int columnIndex, int rowIndex, int columnspan, int rowspan)

The setConstraints() method is overloaded. Other versions of the method also let you specify the column/row span.

The GridPane class defines a constant named REMAINING that is used for specifying the column/row span. It means that the child node spans the remaining columns or remaining rows.

The following snippet of code adds a Label and a TextField to the first row. It adds a TextArea to the first column of the second row with its colSpan as REMAINING. This makes the TextArea occupy two columns because there are two columns created by the controls added to the first row. Figure 10-45 shows the window.

```
// Create a GridPane and set its background color to lightgray
GridPane root = new GridPane();
root.setGridLinesVisible(true);
root.setStyle("-fx-background-color: lightgray;");

// Add a Label and a TextField to the first row
root.addRow(0, new Label("First Name:"), new TextField());

// Add a TextArea in the second row to span all columns in row 2
TextArea ta = new TextArea();
ta.setPromptText("Enter your resume here");
ta.setPrefColumnCount(10);
ta.setPrefRowCount(3);
root.add(ta, 0, 1, GridPane.REMAINING, 1);
```

Figure 10-45. *A TextArea using GridPane.REMAINING as the colSpan value*

Suppose you add two more children in the first column to occupy the third and fourth columns:

```
// Add a Label and a TextField to the first row
root.addRow(0, new Label("Last Name:"), new TextField());
```

Now, the number of columns has increased from two to four. This will make the TextArea occupy four columns as we set its colSpan as REMAINING. Figure 10-46 shows the new window.

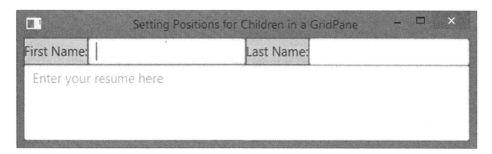

Figure 10-46. *A TextArea using GridPane.REMAINING as the colSpan value*

Creating Forms Using GridPanes

GridPane is best suited for creating forms. Let us build a form using a GridPane. The form will be similar to the one shown in Figure 10-32 that was created using a BorderPane. Our new form will look as shown in Figure 10-47. The figure shows two instances of the window: the form with children (on the left) and the form with grid only (on the right). The form with grid only is shown, so you can visualize the positions and spans of the children within the grid.

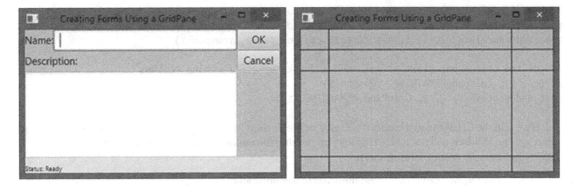

Figure 10-47. *A GridPane with some controls to create a form*

The grid will have three columns and four rows. It has seven children:

- A Label, a TextField, and an *OK* button in the first row
- A Label and a Cancel button in the second row
- A TextArea in the third row
- A Label in the fourth row

The following snippet of code creates all children:

```
// A Label and a TextField
Label nameLbl = new Label("Name:");
TextField nameFld = new TextField();

// A Label and a TextArea
Label descLbl = new Label("Description:");
TextArea descText = new TextArea();
descText.setPrefColumnCount(20);
descText.setPrefRowCount(5);

// Two buttons
Button okBtn = new Button("OK");
Button cancelBtn = new Button("Cancel");
```

All children in the first row span only one cell. The "Description" Label in the second row spans two columns (c0 and c1) and the *Cancel* button only one column. The TextArea in the third row spans two columns (c0 and c1). The Label in the fourth row spans three columns (c0, c1, and c1). The following snippet of code places all children in the grid:

```
// Create a GridPane
GridPane root = new GridPane();

// Add children to the GridPane
root.add(nameLbl, 0, 0, 1, 1);   // (c0, r0, colspan=1, rowspan=1)
root.add(nameFld, 1, 0, 1, 1);   // (c1, r0, colspan=1, rowspan=1)
root.add(descLbl, 0, 1, 3, 1);   // (c0, r1, colspan=3, rowspan=1)
```

```
root.add(descText, 0, 2, 2, 1);  // (c0, r2, colspan=2, rowspan=1)
root.add(okBtn, 2, 0, 1, 1);     // (c2, r0, colspan=1, rowspan=1)
root.add(cancelBtn, 2, 1, 1, 1); // (c2, r1, colspan=1, rowspan=1)

// Let the status bar start at column 0 and take up all remaning columns
// (c0, r3, colspan=REMAININg, rowspan=1)
root.add(statusBar, 0, 3, GridPane.REMAINING, 1);
```

If we add the GridPane to a scene, it will give us the desired look of the form, but not the desired resizing behavior. The children will not resize correctly on resizing the window. We need to specify the correct resizing behavior for some of the children:

- The *OK* and *Cancel* buttons should be of the same size.

- The TextField to enter name should expand horizontally.

- The TextArea to enter the description should expand horizontally and vertically.

- The Label used as the status bar at the bottom should expand horizontally.

Making the *OK* and *Cancel* buttons the same size is easy. By default, a GridPane resizes its children to fill their cells, provided the maximum size of the children allows it. The maximum size of a Button is clamped to its preferred size. We need to set the maximum size of the *OK* button big enough, so it can expand to fill the width of its cell, which would be the same as the preferred width of the widest node in its column (the *Cancel* button):

```
// The max width of the OK button should be big enough, so it can fill the
// width of its cell
okBtn.setMaxWidth(Double.MAX_VALUE);
```

By default, the rows and columns in a GridPane stay at their preferred size when the GridPane is resized. Their horizontal and vertical grow constraints specify how they grow when additional space is available. To let the name, description, and status bar fields grow when the GridPane is expanded, we will set their hgrow and vgrow constraints appropriately:

```
// The name field in the first row should grow horizontally
GridPane.setHgrow(nameFld, Priority.ALWAYS);
```

```
// The description field in the third row should grow vertically
GridPane.setVgrow(descText, Priority.ALWAYS);
```

```
// The status bar in the last row should fill its cell
statusBar.setMaxWidth(Double.MAX_VALUE);
```

When the GridPane is expanded horizontally, the second column, occupied by the name field, grows by taking the extra available width. It makes the description and status bar fields fill the extra width generated in the second column.

When the GridPane is expanded vertically, the third row, occupied by the description field, grows by taking the extra available height. The maximum size of a TextArea is unbounded. That is, it can grow to fill the available space in both directions. The program in Listing 10-30 contains the complete code.

Listing 10-30. Using a GridPane to Create Forms

```
// GridPaneForm.java
// ... full listing in the book's download area.
```

GridPane Properties

The GridPane class contains several properties, as listed in Table 10-6, to customize its layout.

Table 10-6. *The List of Properties Declared in the GridPane Class*

Property	Type	Description
alignment	ObjectProperty<Pos>	It specifies the alignment of the grid (the content of the GridPane) relative to its content area. It defaults to Pos. TOP_LEFT.
gridLinesVisible	BooleanProperty	It is recommend to be used for debug purposes only. It controls whether grid lines are visible or not. It defaults to false.
hgap, vgap	DoubleProperty	They specify the gaps between adjacent columns and rows. The hgap property specifies the horizontal gap between adjacent columns. The vgap property specifies the vertical gap between adjacent rows. They default to zero.

The Alignment Property

The alignment property of a GridPane controls the alignment of its content within its content area. You can see the effects of this property when the size of the GridPane is bigger than its content. The property works the same way as the alignment property for the FlowPane. Please refer to the description of the alignment property for FlowPane for more details and illustrations.

The gridLinesVisible Property

When the gridLinesVisible is set to true, the grid lines in a GridPane are made visible. Otherwise, they are invisible. You should use this feature for debug purposes only:

```
GridPane gpane = new GridPane();
gpane.setGridLinesVisible(true); // Make grid lines visible
```

Sometimes, you may want to show the grid without showing the children to get an idea on how the grid is formed. You can do so by making all children invisible. The GridPane computes the size of the grid for all managed children irrespective of their visibility.

The following snippet of code creates a GridPane and sets the gridLinesVisible property to true. It creates four Buttons, makes them invisible, and adds them to the GridPane. Figure 10-48 shows the window when the GridPane is added to a scene as the root node.

```
GridPane root = new GridPane();

// Make the grid lines visible
root.setGridLinesVisible(true);

// Set the padding to 10px
root.setStyle("-fx-padding: 10;");
```

```
// Make the gridLInes
Button b1 = new Button("One");
Button b2 = new Button("Two");
Button b3 = new Button("Three");
Button b4 = new Button("Four and Five");

// Make all children invisible to see only grid lines
b1.setVisible(false);
b2.setVisible(false);
b3.setVisible(false);
b4.setVisible(false);

// Add children to the GridPane
root.addRow(1, b1, b2);
root.addRow(2, b3, b4);
```

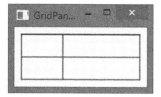

Figure 10-48. *A GridPane showing the grid without children*

The hgap and vgap Properties

You can specify spacing between adjacent columns and rows using the hgap and vgap properties, respectively. By default, they are zero. The program in Listing 10-31 uses these properties of a GridPane. The grid lines are visible to show the gaps clearly. Figure 10-49 shows the window.

Listing 10-31. Using the hgap and vgap Properties of a GridPane

```
// GridPaneHgapVgap.java
// ... full listing in the book's download area.
```

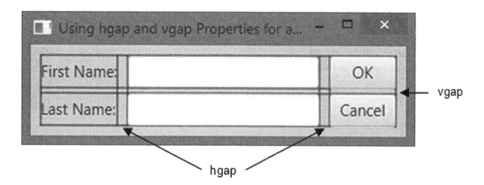

Figure 10-49. *A GridPane using hgap and vgap properties*

Customizing Columns and Rows

You can customize columns and rows in a GridPane using column and row constraints. For example, for a column/row, you can specify

- How the width/height should be computed. Should it be computed based on its content, a fixed width/height, or a percentage of the available width/height?

- Should the children fill the width/height of the column/row?

- Should the column/row grow when the GridPane is resized larger than its preferred width/height?

- How should the children in a column/row be aligned within its layout area (cells)?

An object of the ColumnConstraints class represents constraints for a column, and an object of the RowConstraints class represents constraints for a row. Both classes declare several properties that represent the constraints. Tables 10-7 and 10-8 list the properties with a brief description for the ColumnConstraints and RowConstraints classes.

Table 10-7. *The List of Properties for the ColumnConstraints Class*

Property	Type	Description
fillWidth	BooleanProperty	It specifies whether the children in the column are expanded beyond their preferred width to fill the width of the column. The default value is true.
halignment	ObjectProperty<HPos>	It specifies the default horizontal alignment of the children in a column. Its default value is null. By default, all children in a column are horizontally aligned to HPos.LEFT. An individual child node in the column may override this constraint.
hgrow	ObjectProperty <Priority>	It specifies the horizontal grow priority for the column. This property is used to give additional space to the column when the GridPane is resized larger than its preferred width. If the percentWidth property is set, the value for this property is ignored.
MinWidth, prefWidth, maxWidth	DoubleProperty	They specify the minimum, preferred, and maximum widths of the column. If the percentWidth property is set, the values for these properties are ignored.
		The default values for these properties are set to USE_COMPUTED_SIZE. By default, the minimum width of a column is the largest of the minimum widths of children in the column; the preferred width is the largest of the preferred widths of children in the column; and the maximum width is the smallest of the maximum widths of children in the column.
percentWidth	DoubleProperty	It specifies the width percentage of the column relative to the width of the content area of the GridPane. If it is set to a value greater than zero, the column is resized to have the width that is this percentage of the available width of the GridPane. If this property is set, the minWidth, prefWidth, maxWidth, and hgrow properties are ignored.

Table 10-8. *Properties for the RowConstraints Class*

Property	Type	Description
fillHeight	BooleanProperty	It specifies whether the children in the row are expanded beyond their preferred height to fill the height of the row. The default value is true.
valignment	ObjectProperty<HPos>	It specifies the default vertical alignment of the children in a row. Its default value is null. By default, all children in a row are vertically aligned to VPos.CENTER. An individual child node in the row may override this constraint.
vgrow	ObjectProperty <Priority>	It specifies the vertical grow priority for the row. This property is used to give additional space to the row when the GridPane is resized larger than its preferred height. If the percentHeight property is set, the value for this property is ignored.
MinHeight, prefHeight, maxHeight	DoubleProperty	They specify the minimum, preferred, and maximum heights of the row. If the percentHeight property is set, the values for these properties are ignored.
		The default values for these properties are set to USE_ COMPUTED_SIZE. By default, the minimum height of a row is the largest of the minimum heights of children in the row; the preferred height is the largest of the preferred heights of children in the row; and the maximum height is the smallest of the maximum heights of children in the row.
percentHeight	DoubleProperty	It specifies the height percentage of the row relative to the height of the content area of the GridPane. If it is set to a value greater than zero, the row is resized to have the height that is this percentage of the available height for the GridPane. If this property is set, the minHeight, prefHeight, maxHeight, and vgrow properties are ignored.

The ColumnConstraints and RowConstraints classes provide several constructors to create their objects. Their no-args constructors create their objects with default property values:

```
// Create a ColumnConstraints object with default property values
ColumnConstraints cc1 = new ColumnConstraints();

// Set the percentWidth to 30% and horizontal alignment to center
cc1.setPercentWidth(30);
cc1.setHalignment(HPos.CENTER);
```

If you want to create a fixed width/height column/row, you can use one of the convenience constructors:

```
// Create a ColumnConstraints object with a fixed column width of 100px
ColumnConstraints cc2 = new ColumnConstraints(100);

// Create a RowConstraints object with a fixed row height of 80px
RowConstraints rc2 = new RowConstraints(80);
```

If you want to achieve the same effect of having a fixed width column, you can do so by setting the preferred width to the desired fixed width value and setting the minimum and maximum widths to use the preferred width as shown in the following:

```
// Create a ColumnConstraints object with a fixed column width of 100px
ColumnConstraints cc3 = new ColumnConstraints();
cc3.setPrefWidth(100);
cc3.setMinWidth(Region.USE_PREF_SIZE);
cc3.setMaxWidth(Region.USE_PREF_SIZE);
```

The following snippet of code sets the column width to 30% of the GridPane width and the horizontal alignment for the children in the column as center:

```
ColumnConstraints cc4 = new ColumnConstraints();
cc4.setPercentWidth(30);                    // 30% width
cc4.setHalignment(HPos.CENTER);
```

In a GridPane, the width/height of different columns/rows may be computed differently. Some columns/rows may set the percentage width/height, some fixed sizes, and some may choose to compute their sizes based on their content. The percent size is given the first preference in allocating the space. For example, if two columns set their widths based on percentage and one uses a fixed width, the available width will be allocated first to the two columns using the percentage width, and then to the column using the fixed width.

■ **Tip**　It is possible that the sum of the percentage width/height of all columns/rows exceeds 100. For example, it is permissible to set the percentage width of columns in a GridPane to 30%, 30%, 30%, and 30%. In this case, the percentage value is used as weights, and each of the four columns will be given one-fourth (30/120) of the available width. As another example, if columns use 30%, 30%, 60%, and 60% as the percentage width, they will be treated as weights, allocating them one-sixth (30/180), one-sixth (30/180), one-third (60/180), and one-third (60/180) of the available width, respectively.

A GridPane stores the constraints for columns and rows in ObservableList of ColumnConstraints and RowConstraints. You can obtain the reference of the lists using the getColumnConstraints() and getRowConstraints() methods. The element at a particular index in the list stores the constraints object for the column/row at the same index in the GridPane. The first element in the list, for example, stores the column/row constraints for the first column/row, the second elements for the second column/row, etc. It is possible to set the column/row constraints for some column/row, not for others. In this case, the constraints for the column/row for which the column/row constraints are absent will be computed based on the default values. The following snippet of code creates three ColumnConstraints objects, sets their properties, and adds them to the list of column constraints of a GridPane. Using RowConstraints objects for setting row constraints would use a similar logic.

```
// Set the fixed width to 100px
ColumnConstraints cc1 = new ColumnConstraints(100);

// Set the percent width to 30% and horizontal alignment to center
ColumnConstraints cc2 = new ColumnConstraints();
cc2.setPercentWidth(30);
cc1.setHalignment(HPos.CENTER);
```

```
// Set the percent width to 50%
ColumnConstraints cc3 = new ColumnConstraints();
cc3.setPercentWidth(30);

// Add all column constraints to the column constraints list
GridPane root = new GridPane();
root.getColumnConstraints().addAll(cc1, cc2, cc3);
```

The program in Listing 10-32 uses column and row constraints to customize columns and rows in a GridPane. Figure 10-50 shows the window, after it is resized.

Listing 10-32. Using Column and Row Constraints in a GridPane

```
// GridPaneColRowConstraints.java
// ... full listing in the book's download area.
```

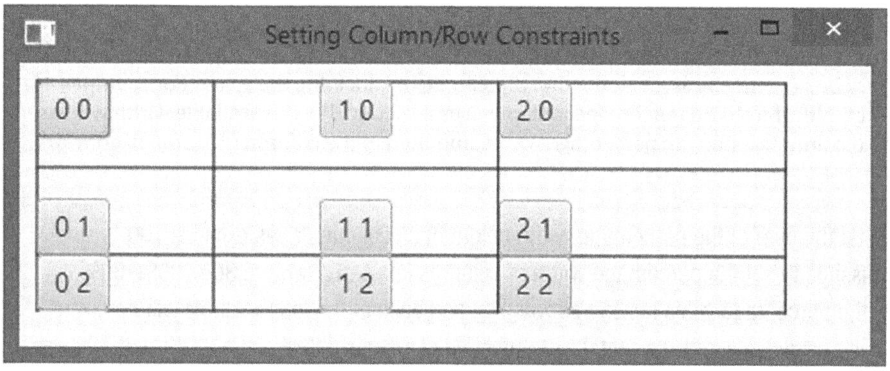

Figure 10-50. *A GridPane using column and row constraints*

The first column width is set to 100px fixed width. Each of the second and third columns is set to occupy 35% of the width. If the needed width (35% + 35% + 100px) is less than the available width, the extra width will be left unused, as has been shown in the figure. The horizontal alignment for the first column is set to center, so all buttons in the first column are horizontally aligned in the center. The buttons in the other two columns use left as the horizontal alignment, which is the default setting. We have three rows. However, the program adds constraints for only the first two rows. The constraints for the third row will be computed based on its content.

When you set column/row constraints, you cannot skip some columns/rows in the middle. That is, you must set the constraints for columns/rows sequentially starting from the first column/row. Setting null for a constraint's object throws a NullPointerException at runtime. If you want to skip setting custom constraints for a row/column in the list, set it to a constraints object that is created using the no-args constructor, which will use the default settings. The following snippet of code sets the column constraints for the first three columns. The second column uses default settings for the constraints:

```
// With 100px fixed width
ColumnConstraints cc1 = new ColumnConstraints(100);

// Use all default settings
ColumnConstraints defaultCc2 = new ColumnConstraints();
```

```
// With 200px fixed width
ColumnConstraints cc3 = new ColumnConstraints(200);

GridPane gpane = new GridPane();
gpane.getColumnConstraints().addAll(cc1, defaultCc2, cc3);
```

■ **Tip** Some column/row constraints set on a column/row can be overridden by children in the column/row individually. Some constraints can be set on children in a column/row and may affect the entire column/row. We will discuss these situations in the next section.

Setting Constraints on Children in GridPane

Table 10-9 lists the constraints that can be set for the children in a GridPane. We have already discussed the column/row index and span constraints. We will discuss the rest in this section. The GridPane class contains two sets of static methods to set these constraints:

- The setConstraints() methods

- The setXxx(Node child, CType cvalue) methods, where Xxx is the constraint name and CType is its type

To remove a constraint for a child node, set it to null.

Table 10-9. *List of Constraints That Can Be Set for the Children in a GridPane*

Constraint	Type	Description
columnIndex	Integer	It is the column index where the layout area of the child node starts. The first column has the index 0. The default value is 0.
rowIndex	Integer	It is the row index where the layout area of the child node starts. The first row has the index 0. The default value is 0.
columnSpan	Integer	It is the number of columns the layout area of a child node spans. The default is 1.
rowSpan	Integer	It is the number of rows the layout area of a child node spans. The default is 1.
halignment	HPos	It specifies the horizontal alignment of the child node within its layout area.
valignment	VPos	It specifies the vertical alignment of the child node within its layout area.
hgrow	Priority	It specifies the horizontal grow priority of the child node.
vgrow	Priority	It specifies the vertical grow priority of the child node.
margin	Insets	It specifies the margin space around the outside of the layout bounds of the child node.

The halignment and valignment Constraints

The `halignment` and `valignment` constraints specify the alignment of a child node within its layout area. They default to `HPos.LEFT` and `VPos.CENTER`. They can be set on the column/row affecting all children. Children may set them individually. The final value applicable to a child node depends on some rules:

- When they are not set for the column/row and not for the child node, the child node will use the default values.

- When they are set for the column/row and not for the child node, the child node will use the value set for the column/row.

- When they are set for the column/row and for the child node, the child node will use the value set for it, not the value set for the column/row. In essence, a child node can override the default value or the value set for the column/row for these constraints.

The program in Listing 10-33 demonstrates the rules mentioned earlier. Figure 10-51 shows the window. The program adds three buttons to a column. The column constraints override the default value of `HPos.LEFT` for the `halignment` constraints for the children and set it to `HPos.RIGHT`. The button labeled "Two" overrides this setting to `HPos.CENTER`. Therefore, all buttons in the column are horizontally aligned to the right, except the button labeled "Two," which is aligned to the center. We set constraints for all three rows. The first and the second rows set `valignment` to `VPos.TOP`. The third row leaves the valignment to the default that is `VPos.CENTER`. The button with the label "One" overrides the `valignment` constraint set on the first row to set it to `VPos.BOTTOM`. Notice that all children follow the preceding three rules to use the `valignment` and `halignment` constraints.

Listing 10-33. Using the halignment and valignment Constraints for Children in a GridPane

```
// GridPaneHValignment.java
// ... full listing in the book's download area.
```

Figure 10-51. *Children overriding the halignment and valignment constraints in a GridPane*

The hgrow and vgrow Constraints

The `hgrow` and `vgrow` constraints specify the horizontal and vertical grow priorities for the entire column and row, even though it can be set for children individually. These constraints can also be set using the `ColumnConstraints` and `RowConstraints` objects for columns and rows. By default, columns and rows do not grow. The final value for these constraints for a column/row is computed using the following rules:

- If the constraints are not set for the column/row and are not set for any children in the column/row, the column/row does not grow if the `GridPane` is resized to a larger width/height than the preferred width/height.

- If the constraints are set for the column/row, the values set in the ColumnConstraints and RowConstraints objects for hgrow and vgrow are used, irrespective of whether the children set these constraints or not.

- If the constraints are not set for the column/row, the maximum values for these constraints set for children in the column/row are used for the entire column/row. Suppose a column has three children and no column constraints have been set for the column. The first child node sets the hgrow to Priority.NEVER; the second to Priority.ALWAYS; and the third to Priority.SOMETIMES. In this case, the maximum of the three priorities would be Priority.ALWAYS, which will be used for the entire column. The ALWAYS priority has the highest value, SOMETIMES the second highest, and NEVER the lowest.

- If a column/row is set to have a fixed or percentage width/height, the hgrow/vgrow constraints will be ignored.

The program in Listing 10-34 demonstrates the preceding rules. Figure 10-52 shows the window when it is expanded horizontally. Notice that the second column grows, but not the first column. The program adds six buttons arranged in two columns. The first column sets the hgrow constraints to Priority.NEVER. The hgrow value set by the column takes priority; the first column does not grow when the GridPane is expanded horizontally. The second column does not use column constraints. The children in this column use three different types of priorities: ALWAYS, NEVER, and SOMETIMES. The maximum of the three priorities is ALWAYS, which makes the second column grow horizontally.

Listing 10-34. Using the hgrow Constraints for Columns and Rows in a GridPane

```
// GridPaneHVgrow.java
// ... full listing in the book's download area.
```

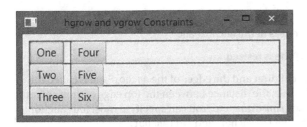

Figure 10-52. Columns and children using the hgrow constraint in a GridPane

The Margin Constraints

Use the setMargin(Node child, Insets value) static method of the GridPane class to set the margin (the space around the layout bounds) for children. The getMargin(Node child) static method returns the margin for a child node:

```
// Set 10px margin around the b1 child node
GridPane.setMargin(b1, new Insets(10));
...
// Get the margin of the b1 child node
Insets margin = GridPane.getMargin(b1);
```

Use null to reset the margin to the default value, which is zero.

Clearing All Constraints

Use the clearConstraints(Node child) static method of the GridPane class to reset all constraints (columnIndex, rowIndex, columnSpan, rowSpan, halignment, valignment, hgrow, vgrow, margin) for a child at once:

```
// Clear all constraints for the b1 child node
GridPane.clearConstraints(b1);
```

Understanding AnchorPane

An AnchorPane lays out its children by anchoring the four edges of its children to its own four edges at a specified distance. Figure 10-53 shows a child node inside an AnchorPane with an anchor distance specified on all four sides.

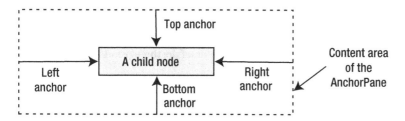

Figure 10-53. *The four side constraints for a child node in an AnchorPane*

An AnchorPane may be used for two purposes:

- For aligning children along one or more edges of the AnchorPane

- For stretching children when the AnchorPane is resized

The specified distance between the edges of the children and the edges of the AnchorPane is called the *anchor* constraint for the sides it is specified. For example, the distance between the top edge of the children and the top edge of the AnchorPane is called topAnchor *constraint*, etc. You can specify at most four anchor constraints for a child node: topAnchor, rightAnchor, bottomAnchor, and leftAnchor.

When you anchor a child node to the two opposite edges (top/bottom or left/right), the children are resized to maintain the specified anchor distance as the AnchorPane is resized.

■ **Tip** The anchor distance is measured from the edges of the content area of the AnchorPane and the edges of the children. That is, if the AnchorPane has a border and padding, the distance is measured from the inner edges of the insets (border + padding).

Creating AnchorPane Objects

You can create an empty AnchorPane using the no-args constructor:

```
AnchorPane apane1 = new AnchorPane();
```

You can also specify the initial list of children for the AnchorPane when you create it, like so:

```
Button okBtn = new Button("OK");
Button cancelBtn = new Button("Cancel");
AnchorPane apane2 = new AnchorPane(okBtn, cancelBtn);
```

You can add children to an AnchorPane after you create it, like so:

```
Button okBtn = new Button("OK");
Button cancelBtn = new Button("Cancel");
AnchorPane apane3 = new AnchorPane();
apane3.getChildren().addAll(okBtn, cancelBtn);
```

You need to keep two points in mind while working with an AnchorPane:

- By default, an AnchorPane places its children at (0, 0). You need to specify anchor constraints for the children to anchor them to one or more edges of the AnchorPane at a specified distance.

- The preferred size of the AnchorPane is computed based on the children preferred sizes and their anchor constraints. It adds the preferred width, left anchor, and right anchor for each child node. The child having maximum of this value determines the preferred width of the AnchorPane. It adds the preferred height, left anchor, and right anchor for each child node. The child having the maximum of this value determines the preferred height of the AnchorPane. It is possible that children will overlap. Children are drawn in the order they are added.

The program in Listing 10-35 adds two buttons to an AnchorPane. One button has a long label and another has a short label. The button with the long label is added first, and, hence, it is drawn first. The second button is drawn second, which overlays the first button as shown in Figure 10-54. The figure shows two views of the window: one when the program is run and another when the window is resized. Both buttons are placed at (0, 0). This program does not take advantage of the anchoring features of the AnchorPane.

Listing 10-35. Using Default Positions in an AnchorPane

```
// AnchorPaneDefaults.java
// ... full listing in the book's download area.
```

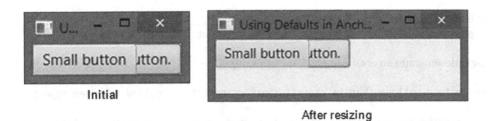

Initial

After resizing

Figure 10-54. *An AnchorPane with two Buttons without having anchor constraints specified*

Setting Constraints for Children in AnchorPane

Table 10-10 lists the constraints that can be set for the children in an AnchorPane. Note that the anchor distance is measured from the edges of the content area of the AnchorPane, not the edges of the layout bounds. Recall that a Region has padding and border insets between the edges of the content area and the layout bounds.

Table 10-10. *The List of Constraints That Can Be Set for the Children in an AnchorPane*

Constraint	Type	Description
topAnchor	Double	It specifies the distance between the top edge of the content area of the AnchorPane and the top edge of the child node.
rightAnchor	Double	It specifies the distance between the right edge of the content area of the AnchorPane and the right edge of the child node.
bottomAnchor	Double	It specifies the distance between the bottom edge of the content area of the AnchorPane and the bottom edge of the child node.
leftAnchor	Double	It specifies the distance between the left edge of the content area of the AnchorPane and the left edge of the child node.

The AnchorPane class contains four static methods that let you set the values for the four anchor constraints. To remove a constraint for a child node, set it to null.

```
// Create a Button and anchor it to top and left edges at 10px from each
Button topLeft = new Button("Top Left");
AnchorPane.setTopAnchor(topLeft, 10.0);  // 10px from the top edge
AnchorPane.setLeftAnchor(topLeft, 10.0); // 10px from the left edge

AnchorPane root = new AnchorPane(topLeft);
```

Use the clearConstraints(Node child) static method to clear the values for all four anchor constraints for a child node.

The setXxxAnchor(Node child, Double value) method takes a Double value as its second parameters. Therefore, you must pass a double value or a Double object to these methods. When you pass a double value, the autoboxing feature of Java will box the value into a Double object for you. A common mistake is to pass an int value:

```
Button b1 = new Button("A button");
AnchorPane.setTopAnchor(b1, 10); // An error: 10 is an int, not a double
```

The preceding code generates an error:

```
Error(18): error: method setTopAnchor in class AnchorPane cannot be applied to given types;
```

The error is generated because we have passed 10 as the second argument. The value 10 is an int literal, which is boxed to an Integer object, not a Double object. Changing 10 to 10D or 10.0 will make it a double value and will fix the error.

The program in Listing 10-36 adds two Buttons to an AnchorPane. The first button has its top and left anchors set. The second button has its bottom and right anchors set. Figure 10-55 shows the window in two states: one when the program is run and another when the window is resized. The initial size of the window is not wide enough to display both buttons, so the buttons overlap. The JavaFX runtime computes the width of the content area of the window based on the preferred size of the bottom-right button, which has the maximum preferred width, and its right anchor value. The figure also shows the window after it is resized. You need to set a sensible preferred size for an AnchorPane, so all children are visible without overlapping.

Listing 10-36. Using an AnchorPane to Align Children to Its Corners

```
// AnchorPaneTest.java
// ... full listing in the book's download area.
```

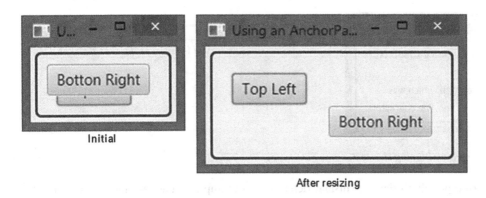

Figure 10-55. Two Buttons in an AnchorPane aligned at top-left and bottom-right corners

When a child node in an AnchorPane is anchored to opposite edges, for example, top/bottom or left/right, the AnchorPane stretches the child node to maintaining the specified anchors.

The program in Listing 10-37 adds a button to an AnchorPane and anchors it to the left and right edges (opposite edges) using an anchor of 10px from each edge. This will make the button stretch when the AnchorPane is resized to a width larger than its preferred width. The button is also anchored to the top edge. Figure 10-56 shows the initial and resized windows.

Listing 10-37. Anchoring Children to Opposite Sides in an AnchorPane

```
// AnchorPaneStretching.java
// ... full listing in the book's download area.
```

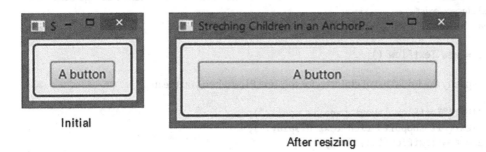

Figure 10-56. An AnchorPane with a Button anchored to opposite sides

Understanding TextFlow

A TextFlow layout pane is designed to display rich text. The rich text is composed of multiple Text nodes. The TextFlow combines the text in all Text nodes to display in a single text flow. A newline character ('\n') in the text of the Text child nodes indicates the start of a new paragraph. The text is wrapped at the width of the TextFlow.

A Text node has its position, size, and wrapping width. However, when it is added to a TextFlow pane, these properties are ignored. Text nodes are placed one after another wrapping them when necessary. A text in a TextFlow may span multiple lines, whereas in a Text node it is displayed in only one line. Figure 10-57 shows a window with a TextFlow as its root node.

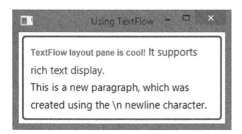

Figure 10-57. *A TextFlow showing rich text*

The TextFlow is especially designed to display rich text using multiple Text nodes. However, you are not limited to adding only Text nodes to a TextFlow. You can add any other nodes to it, for example, Buttons, TextFields, etc. Nodes other than Text nodes are displayed using their preferred sizes.

■ **Tip** You can think of a TextFlow very similar to a FlowPane. Like a FlowPane, a TextFlow lays out its children in a flow from one end to another by treating Text nodes differently. When a Text node is encountered past its width boundary, it breaks the text of the Text node at its width and displays the remaining text in the next line.

Creating TextFlow Objects

Unlike the classes for other layout panes, the TextFlow class is in the javafx.scene.text package where all other text-related classes exist.

You can create an empty TextFlow using the no-args constructor:

```
TextFlow tflow1 = new TextFlow ();
```

You can also specify the initial list of children for the TextFlow when you create it:

```
Text tx1 = new Text("TextFlow layout pane is cool! ");
Text tx2 = new Text("It supports rich text display.");
TextFlow tflow2 = new TextFlow(tx1, tx2);
```

You can add children to a TextFlow after you create it:

```
Text tx1 = new Text("TextFlow layout pane is cool! ");
Text tx2 = new Text("It supports rich text display.");
TextFlow tflow3 = new TextFlow();
tflow3.getChildren().addAll(tx1, tx2);
```

The program in Listing 10-38 shows how to use a TextFlow. It adds three Text nodes to a TextFlow. The text in the third Text node starts with a newline character (\n), which starts a new paragraph. The program sets the preferred width of the TextFlow to 300px and the line spacing to 5px. Figure 10-58 shows the window. When you resize the window, the TextFlow redraws the text wrapping, if necessary, at the new width.

Listing 10-38. Using the TextFlow Layout Pane to Display Rich Text

```
// TextFlowTest.java
// ... full listing in the book's download area.
```

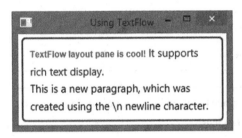

Figure 10-58. *Several Text nodes displayed in a TextFlow as rich text*

A TextFlow also lets you embed nodes other than Text nodes. You can create a form to display text mixed with other types of nodes that users can use. The program in Listing 10-39 embeds a pair of RadioButtons, a TextField, and a Button to a TextFlow to create an online form with text. Users can use these nodes to interact with the form.

Figure 10-59 shows the window. At the time of testing this example, the RadioButtons and TextField nodes did not gain focus using the mouse. Use the Tab key to navigate to these nodes and the spacebar to select a RadioButton.

Listing 10-39. Embedding Nodes Other Than Text Nodes in a TextFlow

```
// TextFlowEmbeddingNodes.java
// ... full listing in the book's download area.
```

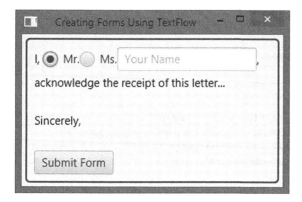

Figure 10-59. *Nodes other than Text nodes embedded in a TextFlow*

TextFlow Properties

The TextFlow class contains two properties, as listed in Table 10-11, to customize its layout.

Table 10-11. *The List of Properties Declared in the TextFlow Class*

Property	Type	Description
lineSpacing	DoubleProperty	It specifies the vertical space between lines. Its default value is 0px.
tabSize	IntegerProperty	The size of a tab stop in spaces.
textAlignment	ObjectProperty <TextAlignment>	It specifies the alignment of the content of the TextFlow. Its value is one of the constants of the TextAlignment enum: LEFT, RIGHT, CENTER, and JUSTIFY. Its default value is LEFT.

The lineSpacing property specifies the vertical space (in pixel) between lines in a TextFlow. We have used it in our previous examples.

```
TextFlow tflow = new TextFlow();
tflow.setLineSpacing(5); // 5px lineSpacing
```

The textAlignment property specifies the alignment of the overall content of the TextFlow. By default, the content is aligned to the left. Figure 10-60 shows the window for the program in Listing 10-39 when the following statement is added after the TextFlow object is created in the program:

```
// Set the textAlignment to CENTER
root.setTextAlignment(TextAlignment.CENTER);
```

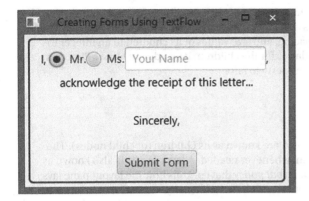

Figure 10-60. *A TextFlow using CENTER as its textAlignment*

Setting Constraints for Children in TextFlow

TextFlow does not allow you to add any constraints to its children, not even a margin.

Snapping to Pixel

Figure 10-61 shows a screen of a device that is five pixels wide and five pixels tall. A circle in the figure represents a pixel. A coordinate (0, 0) is mapped to the upper-left corner of the upper-left pixel. The center of the upper-left pixel maps to the coordinates (0.5, 0.5). All integer coordinates fall in the corners and cracks between the pixels. In the figure, solid lines are drawn through the cracks of pixels and dashed lines through the centers of the pixels.

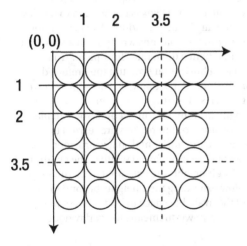

Figure 10-61. *A 5X5 pixel region on the screen*

In JavaFX, coordinates can be specified in floating-point numbers, for example, 0.5, 6.0, etc., which lets you represent any part of a pixel. If the floating-point number is an integer (e.g., 2.0, 3.0, etc.), it will represent corners of the pixel.

353

A Region using floating-point numbers as coordinates will not align exactly at the pixel boundary, and its border may look fuzzy. The Region class contains a snapToPixel property to address this issue. By default, it is set to true, and a Region adjusts the position, spacing, and size values of its children to an integer to match the pixel boundaries, resulting in crisp boundaries for the children. If you do not want a Region to adjust these values to integers, set the snapToPixel property to false.

Summary

A *layout pane* is a node that contains other nodes, which are known as its children (or child nodes). The responsibility of a layout pane is to lay out its children, whenever needed. A layout pane is also known as a *container* or a *layout container*. A layout pane has a *layout policy* that controls how the layout pane lays out its children. For example, a layout pane may lay out its children horizontally, vertically, or in any other fashion. JavaFX contains several layout-related classes. A layout pane computes the position and size of its children. The layout policy of a layout pane is a set of rules to compute the position and size of its children.

Objects of the following classes represent layout panes: HBox, VBox, FlowPane, BorderPane, StackPane, TilePane, GridPane, AnchorPane, and TextFlow. All layout pane classes inherit from the Pane class.

A Group has features of a container; for example, it has its own layout policy and coordinate system, and it is a subclass of the Parent class. However, its meaning is best reflected by calling it a *collection of nodes* or a *group*, rather than a *container*. It is used to manipulate a collection of nodes as a single node (or as a group). Transformations, effects, and properties applied to a Group are applied to all nodes in the Group. A Group has its own layout policy, which does not provide any specific layout to its children, except giving them their preferred size.

An HBox lays out its children in a single horizontal row. It lets you set the horizontal spacing between adjacent children, margins for any children, resizing behavior of children, etc. It uses 0px as the default spacing between adjacent children. The default width of the content area and HBox is wide enough to display all its children at their preferred widths, and the default height is the largest of the heights of all its children.

A VBox lays out its children in a single vertical column. It lets you set the vertical spacing between adjacent children, margins for any children, resizing behavior of children, etc. It uses 0px as the default spacing between adjacent children. The default height of the content area of a VBox is tall enough to display all its children at their preferred heights, and the default width is the largest of the widths of all its children.

A FlowPane is a simple layout pane that lays out its children in rows or columns wrapping at a specified width or height. It lets its children flow horizontally or vertically, and hence the name "flow pane." You can specify a preferred wrap length, which is the preferred width for a horizontal flow and the preferred height for a vertical flow, where the content is wrapped. A FlowPane is used in situations where the relative locations of children are not important, for example, displaying a series of pictures or buttons.

A BorderPane divides its layout area into five regions: top, right, bottom, left, and center. You can place at most one node in each of the five regions. The children in the top and bottom regions are resized to their preferred heights. Their widths are extended to fill the available extra horizontal space, provided the maximum widths of the children allow extending their widths beyond their preferred widths. The children in the right and left regions are resized to their preferred widths. Their heights are extended to fill the extra vertical space, provided the maximum heights of the children allow extending their heights beyond their preferred heights. The child node in the center will fill the rest of the available space in both directions.

A StackPane lays out its children in a stack of nodes. It provides a powerful means to overlay nodes. Children are drawn in the order they are added.

A TilePane lays out its children in a grid of uniformly sized cells, known as tiles. TilePanes work similar to FlowPanes with one difference: in a FlowPane, rows and columns can be of different heights and widths, whereas in a TilePane, all rows have the same heights and all columns have the same widths. The width of the widest child node and the height of the tallest child node are the default widths and heights of all tiles in a TilePane. The orientation of a TilePane, which can be set to horizontal or vertical, determines the direction of the flow for its content. By default, a TilePane has a horizontal orientation.

A GridPane lays out its children in a dynamic grid of cells arranged in rows and columns. The grid is dynamic because the number and size of cells in the grid are determined based on the number of children. They depend on the constraints set on children. Each cell in the grid is identified by its position in the column and row. The indexes for columns and rows start at zero. A child node may be placed anywhere in the grid spanning more than one cell. All cells in a row are of the same height. Cells in different rows may have different heights. All cells in a column are of the same width. Cells in different columns may have different widths. By default, a row is tall enough to accommodate the tallest child node in it. A column is wide enough to accommodate the widest child node in it. You can customize the size of each row and column. GridPane also allows for vertical spacing between rows and horizontal spacing between columns. For debug purposes, you can show the grid lines. Figure 10-41 shows three instances of the GridPane.

An AnchorPane lays out its children by anchoring the four edges of its children to its own four edges at a specified distance. An AnchorPane may be used for aligning children along one or more edges of the AnchorPane or for stretching children when the AnchorPane is resized.

The specified distance between the edges of the children and the edges of the AnchorPane is called the *anchor* constraint for the sides it is specified. When you anchor a child node to the two opposite edges (top/bottom or left/right), the children are resized to maintain the specified anchor distance as the AnchorPane is resized.

A TextFlow layout pane is designed to display rich text. The rich text is composed of multiple Text nodes. The TextFlow combines the text in all Text nodes to display in a single text flow. A newline character ('\n') in the text of the Text child nodes indicates the start of a new paragraph. The text is wrapped at the width of the TextFlow.

■ ■ ■

CHAPTER 11

Model-View-Controller Pattern

In this chapter, you will learn:

- What the model-view-controller pattern is

- What other variants of the model-view-controller pattern are, such as the model-view-presenter pattern

- How to develop a JavaFX application using the model-view-presenter pattern

The examples of this chapter lie in the com.jdojo.mvc package. In order for them to work, you must add the corresponding lines to the module-info.java file:

```
...
opens com.jdojo.mvc to javafx.graphics, javafx.base;
opens com.jdojo.mvc.model to javafx.graphics, javafx.base;
opens com.jdojo.mvc.view to javafx.graphics, javafx.base;
...
```

What Is the Model-View-Controller Pattern?

JavaFX lets you create applications using GUI components. A GUI application performs three tasks: accepts inputs from the user, processes the input, and displays outputs. A GUI application contains two types of code:

- Domain code that deals with domain-specific data and business rules

- Presentation code that deals with manipulating user interface widgets

It is often required that the same data in a specific domain be presented in different forms. For example, you may have a web interface using HTML and a desktop interface using JavaFX to present the same data. For easy maintenance of the application code, it is often necessary to divide the application into two logical modules where one module contains presentation code and another domain code (domain-specific business logic and data). The division is made in such a way that the presentation module can see the domain module, but not vice versa. This type of division supports multiple presentations with the same domain code.

The model-view-controller (MVC) pattern is the oldest and the most popular pattern to model GUI applications to facilitate such a division. The MVC pattern consists of three components: *model*, *view*, and *controller*. Figure 11-1 shows a pictorial view of the MVC components and the interactions among them.

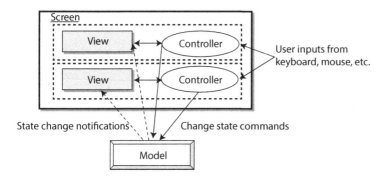

Figure 11-1. *Interaction between participants in the classic MVC pattern*

In MVC, the *model* consists of the domain objects that model the real-world problems. The *view* and *controller* consist of the presentation objects that deal with the presentation such as input, output, and user interactions with GUI elements. The controller accepts the inputs from the users and decides what to do with it. That is, the user interacts with the controller directly. The view displays the output on the screen. Each view is associated with a unique controller and vice versa. Each widget on the screen is a view, which has a corresponding controller. Therefore, there are typically multiple view-controller pairs in a GUI screen. The model is not aware of any specific views and controllers. However, views and controllers are model specific. The controller commands the model to modify its state. The views and model always stay in sync. The model notifies views about changes in its state, so views can display the updated data. The model-to-view interaction is facilitated through an *observer* pattern. Keep in mind that the model is fully unaware of any specific views. The model provides a way for views to subscribe to its state change notifications. Any interested views subscribe to the model to receive state change notifications. The model notifies all views that had subscribed whenever a model's state changes.

What has been described so far about the MVC pattern is the original concept of MVC that was used in developing user interfaces in the Smalltalk-80 language that was created in 1980. There have been many variants of Smalltalk. The concept in MVC that the presentation and domain logic should be separated in a GUI application still holds true. However, in MVC, dividing the responsibilities between three components had issues. Which component, for example, will have the logic to update the attributes of the view, such as changing the view color or disabling it, that depend on the state of the model? Views can have their own states. A list that displays a list of items has the index of the currently selected item. The selected index is the state of the view, not the model. A model may be associated with several views at one time, and it is not the responsibility of the model to store the state of all views.

The issues of which component in MVC has the responsibility of storing the view logic and state led to another variant of MVC called the Application Model MVC (AM-MVC). In AM-MVC, a new component, called *Application Model*, is introduced between the model and the view/controller. Its purpose is to contain the presentation logic and the state, thus solving the issue of which component keeps the presentation logic and the state in the original MVC. The model in MVC is decoupled from the view, and this is also true in AM-MVC. Both use the same observer technique to keep the view and the model in sync. In AM-MVC, the Application Model was supposed to keep the view-related logic but was not allowed to access the view directly. This resulted in bulky and ugly code when the Application Model had to update the view attributes. Figure 11-2 shows a pictorial view of the AM-MVC components and the interactions among them.

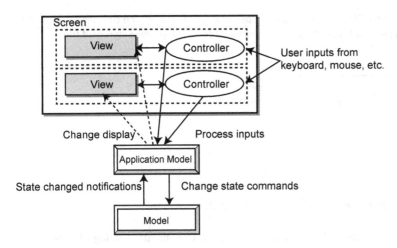

Figure 11-2. *Interaction among participants in the AM-MVC pattern*

Later, modern graphical operating systems like Microsoft Windows and Mac OS offered native widgets, which users can interact with directly. These widgets combined the functions of the view and controller into one. This led to another variant of MVC, called the model-view-presenter (MVP) pattern. Modern widgets also support data binding, which helps keep the view and model in sync with fewer lines of code. Figure 11-3 shows a pictorial view of the MVP components and the interactions among them.

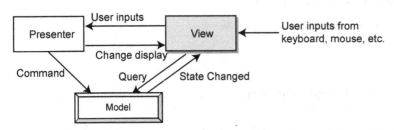

Figure 11-3. *Interactions among participants in the MVP pattern*

In MVC, each widget on the screen is a view, and it has its own unique controller. In MVP, the view is composed of several widgets. The view intercepts the inputs from the user and hands over the control to the presenter. Note that the view does not react to the user inputs. It only intercepts them. The view is also responsible for displaying the data from the model.

The presenter is notified by the view about the user inputs. It determines how to react to the user's input. The presenter is responsible for the presentation logic, manipulating the view, and issuing commands to the model. Once the presenter modifies the model, the view is updated using the observer pattern, as was done in MVC.

The model is responsible for storing domain-specific data and logic. Like MVC, it is independent of any views and presenters. The presenter commands the model to change, and the view updates itself when it receives *state-changed* notifications from the model.

There are some variants of MVP as well. They vary in the responsibility of the view and the presenter. In one variant, the view is responsible for all view-related logic without the help of the presenter. In another variant, the view is responsible for all the simple logic that can be handled declaratively, except when the logic is complex, which is handled by the presenter. In another variant, the presenter handles all view-

359

related logic and manipulates the view. This variant is called *passive view MVP* in which the view is unaware of the model. Figure 11-4 shows a pictorial view of the components in the MVP passive view and the interactions among them.

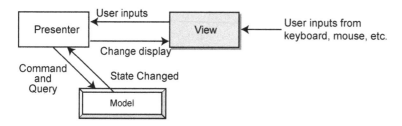

Figure 11-4. *Interactions among the participants in the passive view MVP pattern*

The concept of MVC that the presentation logic should be separated from the domain logic has been around for over 30 years, and it is going to stay in one form or another. All variants of MVC have been attempting to achieve the same function of what the classic MVC did, though in different ways. The variants vary from the classic MVC in the responsibilities of their components. When someone talks about MVC in a GUI application design, make sure you understand which variant of MVC is used and which components perform which tasks.

A Model-View-Presenter Example

This section presents a detailed example that uses the MVP pattern.

The Requirements

For the example here, you will develop a GUI application that will let the user enter the details of a person, validate the data, and save it. The form should contain

- Person ID field: An autogenerated unique noneditable field

- First name field: An editable text field

- Last name field: An editable text field

- Birth date: An editable text field

- Age category: An autocomputed noneditable field based on the birth date

- Save button: A button to save the data

- Close button: A button to close the window

The personal data should be validated against the following rules:

- The first and last names must be at least one character long.

- If a birth date is entered, it must not be a future date.

The Design

Three classes will represent the three components of an MVP:

- Person class
- PersonView and PersonPresenter classes

The Person class represents the model, the PersonView class the view, and the PersonPresenter class the presenter. As required by the MVP pattern, the Person class will be agnostic about the PersonView and the PersonPresenter classes. The PersonView and the PersonPresenter classes will interact with each other, and they will use the Person class directly.

Let's divide the classes related to the model and the view logically by placing them in different Java packages. The com.jdojo.mvc.model package will contain model-related classes, and the com.jdojo.mvc.view package will contain the view-related classes. Figure 11-5 shows the finished window.

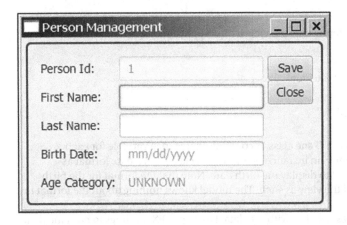

Figure 11-5. *The initial screenshot of the person management window*

The Implementation

The following paragraph describes the implementation of the three layers of the MVP example application.

The Model

Listing 11-1 contains the complete code for the Person class. The Person class contains the code for the domain data and the business rules. In real life, you might want to separate the two into multiple classes. However, for a small application like this, let's keep them in one class.

Listing 11-1. The Person Class Used As the Model

```
// Person.java
// ...find in the book's download area.
```

The Person class declares an AgeCategory enum to represent different ages:

```
public enum AgeCategory {BABY, CHILD, TEEN, ADULT, SENIOR, UNKNOWN};
```

The person ID, first name, last name, and birth date are represented by JavaFX properties. The `personId` property is declared read-only, and it is autogenerated. Relevant setter and getter methods are provided for these properties.

The `isValidBirthDate()` and `isValidPerson()` methods are included to perform domain-specific validations. The `getAgeCategory()` method belongs to the `Person` class as it computes the age category of a person based on their birth date. I have made up some date ranges to divide the age of a person into different categories. You may be tempted to add this method to the view. However, you would then need to duplicate the logic inside this method for each view. The method uses the model data and computes a value. It knows nothing about views, so it belongs to the model, not to the view.

The `save()` method saves the personal data. The save method is trivial; it simply displays a message on the standard output if the personal data are valid. In a real-world application, it would save the data to a database or a file.

The View

The `PersonView` class shown in Listing 11-2 represents the view in this application. It is mainly responsible for displaying the data in the model.

Listing 11-2. The `PersonView` Class Used As the View

```
// PersonView.java
// ...find in the book's download area.
```

The `PersonView` class inherits from the `GridPane` class. It contains an instance variable for each UI component. Its constructor takes the model (an instance of the `Person` class) and a date format as arguments. The date format is the format used to display the birth date. Note that the format for the birth date is view specific, and it should be part of the view as such. The model knows nothing about the format in which the birth date is displayed by views.

The `initFieldData()` method initializes the view with the data. I used JavaFX bindings to bind the data in UI nodes to the model data except for the birth date and age category fields. This method synchronizes the birth date and the age category fields with the model. The `layoutForm()` method lays out the UI nodes in the grid pane. The `bindFieldsToModel()` method binds the person ID, first name, and last name `TextFields` to the corresponding data fields in the model, so they stay in sync. The `syncBirthDate()` method reads the birth date from the model, formats it, and displays it in the view. The `syncAgeCategory()` method synchronizes the age category field, which is computed by the model based on the birth date.

Notice that the view, the `PersonView` class, does not know about the presenter, the `PersonPresenter` class. So how will the view and the presenter communicate? The role of a presenter is mainly to get the user's inputs from the view and act upon them. The presenter will have a reference to the view. It will add event listeners to the view, so it is notified when the data in the view change. In the event handlers, the presenter takes control and processes the inputs. If the application requires a reference to the presenter in the view, you can have that as an argument to the constructor of the view class. Alternatively, you can provide a setter method in the view class to set the presenter.

The Presenter

The `PersonPresenter` class shown in Listing 11-3 represents the presenter in this application. It is mainly responsible for intercepting the new input in the view and processing it. It communicates directly with the model and the view.

Listing 11-3. The `PersonPresenter` Class Used As the Presenter

```
// PersonPresenter.java
// ...find in the book's download area.
```

The constructor of the `PersonPresenter` class takes the model and the view as arguments. The `attachEvents()` method attaches event handlers to the UI components of the view. In this example, you are not interested in intercepting all inputs in the view. But you are interested in the birth date changes and the clicking of the Save and Close buttons. You do not want to detect all edit changes in the birth date field. If you are interested in all changes in the birth date field, you would need to add a change listener for its `text` property. You want to detect changes only when the user is done entering the birth date. For this reason

- You attach a focus listener to the scene and detect if the birth date has lost the focus.

- You attach an action listener to the birth date field, so you intercept the Enter key press while the field has focus.

This validates and refreshes the birth date and age category whenever the birth date field loses focus or the Enter key is pressed while focus is still in the field.

The `handleBirthDateChange()` method handles a change in the birth date field. It validates the birth date format before updating the model. It displays an error message to the user if the birth date is not valid. Finally, it tells the view to update the birth date and age category.

The `saveData()` method is called when the user clicks the Save button, and it commands the model to save the data. The `showError()` method does not belong to the presenter. Here, you added it instead of creating a new view class. It is used to display an error message.

Putting Them Together

Let's put the model, view, and presenter together to use them in an application. The program in Listing 11-4 creates the model, view, and presenter, glues them together, and displays the view in a window as shown in Figure 11-5. Notice that the view must be attached to a scene before the presenter is created. It is required because the presenter attaches a focus change listener to the scene. Creating the presenter before adding the view to the scene will result in a `NullPointerException`.

Listing 11-4. The `PersonApp` Class Uses the Model, View, and Presenter to Create a GUI Application

```
// PersonApp.java
// ...find in the book's download area.
```

Summary

It is often required that the same domain data be presented in different forms. For example, you may have a web interface using HTML and a desktop interface using JavaFX to present the same data. For easy maintenance of the application code, it is often necessary to divide the application into two logical modules where one module contains presentation code and another domain code (domain-specific business logic and data). The division is made in such a way that the presentation module can see the domain module, but not vice versa. This type of division supports multiple presentations with the same domain code. The MVC pattern is the oldest and the most popular pattern to model GUI applications to facilitate such a division. The MVC pattern consists of three components: model, view, and controller.

In MVC, the model consists of the domain objects that model the real-world problems. The view and controller consist of the presentation objects that deal with the presentation such as input, output, and user interactions with GUI elements. The controller accepts the inputs from the users and decides what to do with them. That is, the user interacts with the controller directly. The view displays the output on the screen. Each view is associated with a unique controller and vice versa. Each widget on the screen is a view, which has a corresponding controller. In MVC, dividing the responsibilities between three components created issues. Which component, for example, would have the logic to update the attributes of the view, such as changing the view color or disabling it, that depend on the state of the model?

The issues of which component in MVC has the responsibility of storing the view logic and the state led to another variant of MVC called the Application Model MVC. In AM-MVC, a new component, called the Application Model, was introduced between the model and the view/controller. Its purpose is to contain the presentation logic and the state, thus solving the issue of which component keeps the presentation logic and state in the original MVC.

Later, modern graphical operating systems like Microsoft Windows and Mac OS offered native widgets, which users can interact with directly. These widgets combined the functions of the view and controller into one. This led to another variant of MVC, called the model-view-presenter pattern.

In MVC, each widget on the screen is a view, and it has its unique controller. In MVP, the view is composed of several widgets. The view intercepts the inputs from the user and hands over the control to the presenter. Note that the view does not react to the user's inputs; it only intercepts them. The presenter is notified by the view about the user's inputs and determines how to react to them. The presenter is responsible for the presentation logic, manipulating the view, and issuing commands to the model. Once the presenter modifies the model, the view is updated using the observer pattern, as was done in MVC.

There are some variants of MVP as well. They vary in the responsibility of the view and the presenter. In one variant, the view is responsible for all view-related logic without the help of the presenter. In another variant, the view is responsible for all the simple logic that can be handled declaratively, except when the logic is complex, which is handled by the presenter. In another variant, the presenter handles all view-related logic and manipulates the view. This variant is called passive view MVP, in which the view is unaware of the model.

The next chapter will introduce you to controls that are used to build the view in JavaFX applications.

CHAPTER 12

■ ■ ■

Understanding Controls

In this chapter, you will learn:

- What a control is in Java

- About classes whose instances represent controls in JavaFX

- About controls such as Label, Button, CheckBox, RadioButton, Hyperlink, ChoiceBox, ComboBox, ListView, ColorPicker, DatePicker, TextField, TextArea, and Menu

- How to style controls using a CSS

- How to use the FileChooser and DirectoryChooser dialogs

The examples of this chapter lie in the com.jdojo.control package. In order for them to work, you must add a corresponding line to the module-info.java file:

```
...
opens com.jdojo.control to javafx.graphics, javafx.base;
...
```

There are many controls in JavaFX, and there is a lot to say about controls. For this reason, the example code for the controls is only presented in an abbreviated manner. For the complete listings, please consult the download area for the book.

What Is a Control?

JavaFX lets you create applications using GUI components. An application with a GUI performs three tasks:

- Accepts inputs from the user through input devices such as a keyboard or a mouse

- Processes the inputs (or takes actions based on the input)

- Displays outputs

The UI provides a means to exchange information in terms of input and output between an application and its users. Entering text using a keyboard, selecting a menu item using a mouse, clicking a button, or other actions are examples of providing input to a GUI application. The application displays outputs on a computer monitor using text, charts, dialog boxes, and so forth.

Users interact with a GUI application using graphical elements called *controls* or *widgets*. Buttons, labels, text fields, text area, radio buttons, and check boxes are a few examples of controls. Devices like a keyboard, a mouse, and a touch screen are used to provide input to controls. Controls can also display output to the users. Controls generate events that indicate an occurrence of some kind of interaction between the user and the control. For example, pressing a button using a mouse or a spacebar generates an action event indicating that the user has pressed the button.

JavaFX provides a rich set of easy-to-use controls. Controls are added to layout panes that position and size them. Layout panes were discussed in Chapter 10. This chapter discusses how to use the controls available in JavaFX.

Typically, the MVP pattern (discussed in Chapter 11) is used to develop a GUI application in JavaFX. MVP requires you to have at least three classes and place your business logic in a certain way and in certain classes. Generally, this bloats the application code, although for the right reason. This chapter will focus on the different types of controls, not on learning the MVP pattern. You will embed classes required for MVP patterns into one class to keep the code brief and save a lot of space in this book as well!

Understanding the Control Class Hierarchy

Each control in JavaFX is represented by an instance of a class. If multiple controls share basic features, they inherit from a common base class. Control classes are included in the javafx.scene.control package. A control class is a subclass, direct or indirect, of the Control class, which in turn inherits from the Region. Recall that the Region class inherits from the Parent class. Therefore, technically, a Control is also a Parent. All our discussions about the Parent and Region classes in the previous chapters also apply to all control-related classes.

A Parent can have children. Typically, a control is composed of another node (sometimes, multiple nodes), which is its child node. Control classes do not expose the list of its children through the getChildren() method, and, therefore, you cannot add any children to them.

Control classes expose the list of their internal unmodifiable children through the getChildrenUnmodifiable() method, which returns an ObservableList<Node>. You are not required to know about the internal children of a control to use the control. However, if you need the list of their children, the getChildrenUnmodifiable() method will give you that.

Figure 12-1 shows a class diagram for classes of some commonly used controls. The list of control classes is a lot bigger than the one shown in the class diagram.

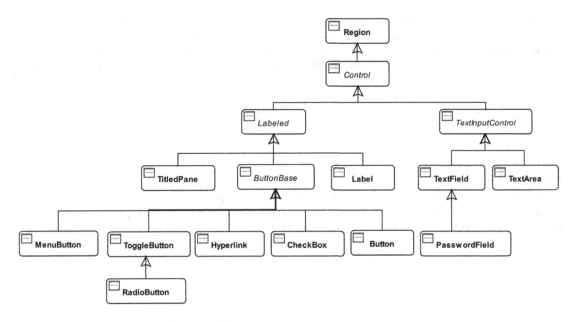

Figure 12-1. *A class diagram for control classes in JavaFX*

The Control class is the base class for all controls. It declares three properties, as shown in Table 12-1, that are common to all controls.

Table 12-1. *Properties Declared in the Control Class*

Property	Type	Description
contextMenu	ObjectProperty<ContextMenu>	Specifies the content menu for the control.
skin	ObjectProperty<Skin<?>>	Specifies the skin for the control.
tooltip	ObjectProperty<Tooltip>	Specifies the tool tip for the control.

The contextMenu property specifies the context menu for the control. A context menu gives a list of choices to the user. Each choice is an action that can be taken on the control in its current state. Some controls have their default context menus. For example, a TextField, when right-clicked, displays a context menu with choices like Undo, Cut, Copy, and Paste. Typically, a context menu is displayed when the user presses a combination of keys (e.g., Shift + F10 on Windows) or clicks the mouse (right-click on Windows) when the control has focus. I will revisit the contextMenu property when I discuss the text input controls.

At the time of this writing, JavaFX doesn't allow access or customization of the default context menu for controls. The contextMenu property is null even if the control has a default context menu. When you set the contextMenu property, it replaces the default context for the control. Note that not all controls have a default context menu, and a context menu is not suitable for all controls. For example, a Button control does not use a context menu.

The visual appearance of a control is known as its *skin*. A skin responds to the state changes in a control by changing its visual appearance. A skin is represented by an instance of the Skin interface. The Control class implements the Skinnable interface, giving all controls the ability to use a skin.

The skin property in the Control class specifies the custom skin for a control. Developing a new skin is not an easy task. For the most part, you can customize the appearance of a control using CSS styles. All controls can be styled using CSS. The Control class implements the Styleable interface, so all controls can be styled. Please refer to Chapter 8 for more details on how to use a CSS. I will discuss some commonly used CSS attributes for some controls in this chapter.

Controls can display a short message called a *tool tip* when the mouse hovers over the control for a short period. An object of the Tooltip class represents a tool tip in JavaFX. The tooltip property in the Control class specifies the tool tip for a control.

Labeled Controls

A labeled control contains a read-only textual content and optionally a graphic as part of its UI. Label, Button, CheckBox, RadioButton, and Hyperlink are some examples of labeled controls in JavaFX. All labeled controls are inherited, directly or indirectly, from the Labeled class, which is declared abstract. The Labeled class inherits from the Control class. Figure 12-2 shows a class diagram for labeled controls. Some of the classes have been left out in the diagram for brevity.

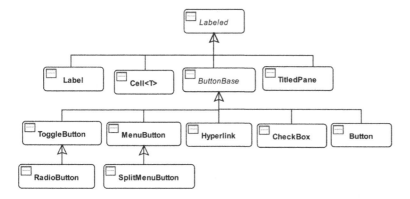

Figure 12-2. *A class diagram for labeled control classes*

The Labeled class declares text and graphic properties to represent the textual and graphic contents, respectively. It declares several other properties to deal with the visual aspects of its contents, for example, alignment, font, padding, and text wrapping. Table 12-2 contains the list of those properties with their brief descriptions. I will discuss some of these properties in the subsequent sections.

Table 12-2. *Properties Declared in the Labeled Class*

Property	Type	Description
alignment	ObjectProperty<Pos>	It specifies the alignment of the content of the control within the content area. Its effect is visible when the content area is bigger than the content (text + graphic). The default value is Pos.CENTER_LEFT.
contentDisplay	ObjectProperty <ContentDisplay>	It specifies positioning of the graphic relative to the text.
ellipsisString	StringProperty	It specifies the string to display for the ellipsis when the text is truncated because the control has a smaller size than the preferred size. The default value is "..." for most locales. Specifying an empty string for this property does not display an ellipsis string in truncated text.
font	ObjectProperty<Font>	It specifies the default font for the text.
graphic	ObjectProperty<Node>	It specifies an optional icon for the control.
graphicTextGap	DoubleProperty	It specifies the amount of text between the graphic and text.
labelPadding	ReadOnlyObjectProperty <Insets>	It is the padding around the content area of the control. By default, it is Insets.EMPTY.
lineSpacing	DoubleProperty	It specifies the space between adjacent lines when the control displays multiple lines.
mnemonicParsing	BooleanProperty	It enables or disables text parsing to detect a mnemonic character. If it is set to true, the text for the control is parsed for an underscore (_) character. The character following the first underscore is added as the mnemonic for the control. Pressing the Alt key on Windows computers highlights mnemonics for all controls.
textAlignment	ObjectProperty <TextAlignment>	It specifies the text alignment within the text bounds for multiline text.
textFill	ObjectProperty<Paint>	It specifies the text color.
textOverrun	ObjectProperty <OverrunStyle>	It specifies how to display the text when the text content exceeds the available space.
text	StringProperty	It specifies the text content.
underline	BooleanProperty	It specifies whether the text content should be underlined.
wrapText	BooleanProperty	It specifies whether the text should be wrapped if the text cannot be displayed in one line.

Positioning Graphic and Text

The contentDisplay property of labeled controls specifies the positioning of the graphic relative to the text. Its value is one of the constants of the ContentDisplay enum: TOP, RIGHT, BOTTOM, LEFT, CENTER, TEXT_ONLY, and GRAPHIC_ONLY. If you do not want to display the text or the graphic, you can use the GRAPHIC_ONLY and TEXT_ONLY values instead of setting the text to an empty string and the graphic to null. Figure 12-3 shows the effects of using different values for the contentDisplay property of a Label. The Label uses Name: as the text and a blue rectangle as the graphic. The value for the contentDisplay property is displayed at the bottom of each instance.

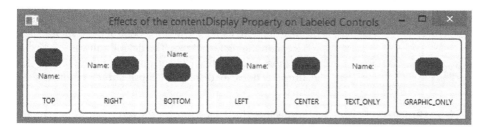

Figure 12-3. *Effects of the* contentDisplay *property on labeled controls*

Understanding Mnemonics and Accelerators

Labeled controls support keyboard *mnemonics*, which is also known as a *keyboard shortcut* or *keyboard indicator*. A mnemonic is a key that sends an ActionEvent to the control. The mnemonic key is often pressed in combination with a modifier key such as an Alt key. The modifier key is platform dependent; however, it is usually an Alt key. For example, suppose you set the C key as a mnemonic for a Close button. When you press Alt + C, the Close button is activated.

Finding the documentation about mnemonics in JavaFX is not easy. It is buried in the documentation for the Labeled and Scene classes. Setting a mnemonic key for a labeled control is easy. You need to precede the mnemonic character with an underscore in the text content and make sure that the mnemonicParsing property for the control is set to true. The first underscore is removed, and the character following it is set as the mnemonic for the control. For some labeled controls, the mnemonic parsing is set to true by default, and for others, you will need to set it.

■ **Tip**   Mnemonics are not supported on all platforms. Mnemonic characters in the text for controls are not underlined, at least on Windows, until the Alt key is pressed.

The following statement will set the C key as the mnemonic for the Close button:

```
// For Button, mnemonic parsing is true by default
Button closeBtn = new Button("_Close");
```

When you press the Alt key, the mnemonic characters for all controls are underlined, and pressing the mnemonic character for any controls will set focus to the control and send it an ActionEvent.

JavaFX provides the following four classes in the javafx.scene.input package to set mnemonics for all types of controls programmatically:

- Mnemonic

- KeyCombination

- KeyCharacterCombination

- KeyCodeCombination

An object of the Mnemonic class represents a mnemonic. An object of the KeyCombination class, which is declared abstract, represents the key combination for a mnemonic. The KeyCharacterCombination and KeyCodeCombination classes are subclasses of the KeyCombination class. Use the former to construct a key combination using a character; use the latter to construct a key combination using a key code. Note that not all keys on the keyboard represent characters. The KeyCodeCombination class lets you create a key combination for any key on the keyboard.

The Mnemonic object is created for a node and is added to a Scene. When the Scene receives an unconsumed key event for the key combination, it sends an ActionEvent to the target node.

The following snippet of code achieves the same result that was achieved using one statement in the preceding example:

```
Button closeBtn = new Button("Close");

// Create a KeyCombination for Alt + C
KeyCombination kc = new KeyCodeCombination(KeyCode.C, KeyCombination.ALT_DOWN);

// Create a Mnemonic object for closeBtn
Mnemonic mnemonic = new Mnemonic(closeBtn, kc);

Scene scene = create a scene...;
scene.addMnemonic(mnemonic); // Add the mnemonic to the scene
```

The KeyCharacterCombination class can also be used to create a key combination for Alt + C:

```
KeyCombination kc = new KeyCharacterCombination("C", KeyCombination.ALT_DOWN);
```

The Scene class supports accelerator keys. An accelerator key, when pressed, executes a Runnable task. Notice the difference between mnemonics and accelerator keys. A mnemonic is associated with a control, and pressing its key combination sends an ActionEvent to the control. An accelerator key is not associated with a control, but rather to a task. The Scene class maintains an ObservableMap<KeyCombination, Runnable>, whose reference can be obtained using the getAccelerators() method.

The following snippet of code adds an accelerator key (Ctrl + X on Windows and Meta + X on Mac) to a Scene, which closes the window associated with the Scene. The SHORTCUT key represents the shortcut key on the platform—Ctrl on Windows and Meta on Mac:

```
Scene scene = create a scene object...;
...
KeyCombination kc = new KeyCodeCombination(KeyCode.X,
                                           KeyCombination.SHORTCUT_DOWN);
Runnable task = () -> scene.getWindow().hide();
scene.getAccelerators().put(kc, task);
```

The program in Listing 12-1 shows how to use mnemonics and accelerator keys. Press Alt + 1 and Alt + 2 to activate Button 1 and Button 2, respectively. Pressing these buttons changes the text for the Label. Pressing the shortcut key + X will close the window.

Listing 12-1. Using Mnemonics and Accelerator Keys

```java
// MnemonicTest.java
package com.jdojo.control;

import javafx.application.Application;
import javafx.scene.Scene;
import javafx.scene.control.Button;
import javafx.scene.control.Label;
import javafx.scene.input.KeyCode;
import javafx.scene.input.KeyCodeCombination;
import javafx.scene.input.KeyCombination;
import javafx.scene.input.Mnemonic;
import javafx.scene.layout.VBox;
import javafx.stage.Stage;

public class MnemonicTest  extends Application {
        public static void main(String[] args) {
                Application.launch(args);
        }

        @Override
        public void start(Stage stage) {
                VBox root = new VBox();
                root.setSpacing(10);
                root.setStyle("-fx-padding: 10;" +
                                "-fx-border-style: solid inside;" +
                                "-fx-border-width: 2;" +
                                "-fx-border-insets: 5;" +
                                "-fx-border-radius: 5;" +
                                "-fx-border-color: blue;");

                Scene scene = new Scene(root);
                Label msg = new Label(
                    "Press Ctrl + X on Windows \nand " +
                    "\nMeta + X on Mac to close the window");
                Label lbl = new Label("Press Alt + 1 or Alt + 2");

                // Use Alt + 1 as the mnemonic for Button 1
                Button btn1 = new Button("Button _1");
                btn1.setOnAction(e -> lbl.setText("Button 1 clicked!"));

                // Use Alt + 2 as the mnemonic key for Button 2
                Button btn2 = new Button("Button 2");
                btn2.setOnAction(e ->
                        lbl.setText("Button 2 clicked!"));
```

```
KeyCombination kc =
        new KeyCodeCombination(KeyCode.DIGIT2,
            KeyCombination.ALT_DOWN);
Mnemonic mnemonic = new Mnemonic(btn2, kc);
scene.addMnemonic(mnemonic);

// Add an accelarator key to the scene
KeyCombination kc4 =
    new KeyCodeCombination(KeyCode.X,
                    KeyCombination.SHORTCUT_DOWN);
Runnable task = () -> scene.getWindow().hide();
scene.getAccelerators().put(kc4, task);

// Add all children to the VBox
root.getChildren().addAll(msg, lbl, btn1, btn2);

stage.setScene(scene);
stage.setTitle("Using Mnemonics and Accelerators");
stage.show();
    }
}
```

Understanding the *Label* Control

An instance of the Label class represents a label control. As the name suggests, a Label is simply a label that is used to identify or describe another component on a screen. It can display a text, an icon, or both. Typically, a Label is placed next to (to the right or left) or at the top of the node it describes.

A Label is not focus traversable. That is, you cannot set the focus to a Label using the Tab key. A Label control does not generate any interesting events that are typically used in an application.

A Label control can also be used to display text in situations where it is acceptable to truncate the text if enough space is not available to display the entire text. Please refer to the API documentation on the textOverrun and ellipsisString properties of the Labeled class for more details on how to control the text truncation behavior in a Label control.

Figure 12-4 shows a window with two Label controls with text First Name: and Last Name:. The Label with the text First Name: is an indicator for the user that they should enter a first name in the field that is placed right next to it. A similar argument goes for the Last Name: Label control.

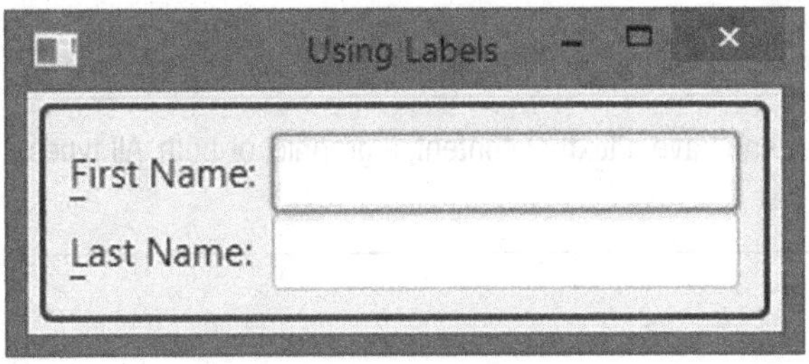

Figure 12-4. A window with two Label controls

The Label class has a very useful labelFor property of ObjectProperty<Node> type. It is set to another node in the scene graph. A Label control can have a mnemonic. Mnemonic parsing for Label controls is set to false by default. When you press the mnemonic key for a Label, the focus is set to the labelFor node for that Label. The following snippet of code creates a TextField and a Label. The Label sets a mnemonic, enables mnemonic parsing, and sets the TextField as its labelFor property. When the Alt + F keys are pressed, focus is moved to the TextField:

```
TextField fNameFld = new TextField();
Label fNameLbl = new Label("_First Name:"); // F is mnemonic
fNameLbl.setLabelFor(fNameFld);
fNameLbl.setMnemonicParsing(true);
```

The program in Listing 12-2 produces the screen shown in Figure 12-4. Press Alt + F and Alt + L to shift focus between the two TextField controls.

Listing 12-2. Using the Label Control

```
// LabelTest.java
// ... find in the book's download area.
```

Understanding Buttons

JavaFX provides three types of controls that represent buttons:

- Buttons to execute commands

- Buttons to make choices

- Buttons to execute commands as well as make choices

All button classes inherit from the ButtonBase class. Please refer to Figure 12-2 for a class diagram. All types of buttons support the ActionEvent. Buttons trigger an ActionEvent when they are activated. A button can be activated in different ways, for example, by using a mouse, a mnemonic, an accelerator key, or other key combinations.

A button that executes a command when activated is known as a *command button*. The Button, Hyperlink, and MenuButton classes represent command buttons. A MenuButton lets the user execute a command from a list of commands. Buttons used for presenting different choices to users are known as *choice buttons*. The ToggleButton, CheckBox, and RadioButton classes represent choice buttons. The third kind of button is a hybrid of the first two kinds. They let users execute a command or make choices. The SplitMenuButton class represents a hybrid button.

■ **Tip** All buttons are labeled controls. Therefore, they can have a textual content, a graphic, or both. All types of buttons are capable of firing an ActionEvent.

Understanding Command Buttons

You have already used command buttons in several instances, for example, a Close button to close a window. In this section, I will discuss buttons that are used as command buttons.

Understanding the Button Control

An instance of the Button class represents a command button. Typically, a Button has text as its label, and an ActionEvent handler is registered to it. The mnemonicParsing property for the Button class is set to true by default.

A Button can be in one of three modes:

- A normal button
- A default button
- A cancel button

For a normal button, its ActionEvent is fired when the button is activated. For a default button, the ActionEvent is fired when the Enter key is pressed and no other node in the scene consumes the key press. For a cancel button, the ActionEvent is fired when the Esc key is pressed and no other node in the scene consumes the key press.

By default, a Button is a normal button. The default and cancel modes are represented by the defaultButton and cancelButton properties. You would set one of these properties to true to make a button a default or cancel button. By default, both properties are set to false.

The following snippet of code creates a normal Button and adds an ActionEvent handler. When the button is activated, for example, by clicking using a mouse, the newDocument() method is called:

```
// A normal button
Button newBtn = new Button("New");
newBtn.setOnAction(e -> newDocument());
```

The following snippet of code creates a default button and adds an ActionEvent handler. When the button is activated, the save() method is called. Note that a default Button is also activated by pressing the Enter key if no other node in the scene consumes the key press:

```
// A default button
Button saveBtn = new Button("Save");
saveBtn.setDefaultButton(true); // Make it a default button
saveBtn.setOnAction(e -> save());
```

The program in Listing 12-3 creates a normal button, a default button, and a cancel button. It adds an ActionEvent listener to all three buttons. Notice that all buttons have a mnemonic (e.g., N for the New button). When the buttons are activated, a message is displayed in a Label. You can activate the buttons by different means:

- Clicking the buttons
- Setting focus to the buttons using the Tab key and pressing the spacebar
- Pressing the Alt key and their mnemonics
- Pressing the Enter key to activate the Save button
- Pressing the Esc key to activate the Cancel button

No matter how you activate the buttons, their `ActionEvent` handler is called. Typically, the `ActionEvent` handler for a button contains the command for the button.

Listing 12-3. Using the `Button` Class to Create Command Buttons

```
// ButtonTest.java
// ... find in the book's download area.
```

■ **Tip**   It is possible to set more than one button in a scene as a default or cancel button. However, only the first one is used. It is poor designing to declare multiple buttons as default and cancel buttons in a scene. By default, JavaFX highlights the default button with a light shade of color to give it a unique look. You can customize the appearance of default and cancel buttons using CSS styles. Setting the same button as a default button and a cancel button is also allowed, but it is a sign of bad design when this is done.

The default CSS style class name for a `Button` is `button`. The `Button` class supports two CSS pseudo-classes: `default` and `cancel`. You can use these pseudo-classes to customize the look for default and cancel buttons. The following CSS style will set the text color for default buttons to blue and cancel buttons to gray:

```
.button:default {
        -fx-text-fill: blue;
}

.button:cancel {
        -fx-text-fill: gray;
}
```

■ **Tip**   You can use CSS styles to create stylish buttons. Please visit the website at `http://fxexperience.com/2011/12/styling-fx-buttons-with-css/` for examples.

Understanding the Hyperlink Control

An instance of the `Hyperlink` class represents a hyperlink control, which looks like a hyperlink in a web page. In a web page, a hyperlink is used to navigate to another web page. However, in JavaFX, an `ActionEvent` is triggered when a `Hyperlink` control is activated, for example, by clicking it, and you are free to perform any action in the `ActionEvent` handler.

A `Hyperlink` control is simply a button styled to look like a hyperlink. By default, mnemonic parsing is off. A `Hyperlink` control can have focus, and by default, it draws a dashed rectangular border when it has focus. When the mouse cursor hovers over a `Hyperlink` control, the cursor changes to a hand, and its text is underlined.

The `Hyperlink` class contains a `visited` property of `BooleanProperty` type. When a `Hyperlink` control is activated for the first time, it is considered "visited," and the `visited` property is set to true automatically. All visited hyperlinks are shown in a different color than the not visited ones. You can also set the `visited` property manually using the `setVisited()` method of the `Hyperlink` class.

The following snippet of code creates a Hyperlink control with the text "JDojo" and adds an ActionEvent handler for the Hyperlink. When the Hyperlink is activated, the www.jdojo.com web page is opened in a WebView, which is another JavaFX control to display a web page. Here, I will use it without any explanation:

```
Hyperlink jdojoLink = new Hyperlink("JDojo");
WebView webview = new WebView();
jdojoLink.setOnAction(e -> webview.getEngine().load("http://www.jdojo.com"));
```

The program in Listing 12-4 adds three Hyperlink controls to the top region of a BorderPane. A WebView control is added in the center region. When you click one of the hyperlinks, the corresponding web page is displayed.

Listing 12-4. Using the Hyperlink Control

```
// HyperlinkTest.java
// ... find in the book's download area.
```

Understanding the *MenuButton* Control

A MenuButton control looks like a button and behaves like a menu. When it is activated (by clicking or other means), it shows a list of options in the form of a pop-up menu. The list of options in the menu is maintained in an ObservableList<MenuItem> whose reference is returned by the getItems() method. To execute a command when a menu option is selected, you need to add the ActionEvent handler to the MenuItems.

The following snippet of code creates a MenuButton with two MenuItems. Each menu item has an ActionEvent handler attached to it. Figure 12-5 shows the MenuButton in two states: not showing and showing.

```
// Create two menu items with an ActionEvent handler.
// Assume that the loadPage() method exists
MenuItem jdojo = new MenuItem("JDojo");
jdojo.setOnAction(e -> loadPage("http://www.jdojo.com"));

MenuItem yahoo = new MenuItem("Yahoo");
yahoo.setOnAction(e -> loadPage("http://www.yahoo.com"));

// Create a MenuButton and the two menu items
MenuButton links = new MenuButton("Visit");
links.getItems().addAll(jdojo, yahoo);
```

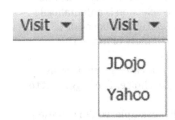

Figure 12-5. *A MenuButton in not showing and showing states*

The MenuButton class declares two properties:

- popupSide
- showing

The popupSide property is of the ObjectProperty<Side> type, and the showing property is of the ReadOnlyBooleanProperty type.

The popupSide property determines which side of the menu should be displayed. Its value is one of the constants in the Side enum: TOP, LEFT, BOTTOM, and RIGHT. The default value is Side.BOTTOM. An arrow in the MenuItem shows the direction set by the popupSide property. The arrow in Figure 12-5 is pointing downward, indicating that the popupSide property is set to Side.BOTTOM. The menu is opened in the direction set in the popupSide property only if space is available to display the menu in that side. If space is not available, the JavaFX runtime will make a smart decision as to which side the menu should be displayed. The value of the showing property is true when the pop-up menu is showing. Otherwise, it is false.

The program in Listing 12-5 creates an application using a MenuButton control that works similar to the one in Listing 12-4 that used a Hyperlink control. Run the application, click the Visit MenuButton at the top right of the window, and select a page to open.

Listing 12-5. Using the MenuButton Control

```
// MenuButtonTest.java
// ... find in the book's download area.
```

Understanding Choice Buttons

JavaFX provides several controls to make one or more selections from a list of available choices:

- ToggleButton
- CheckBox
- RadioButton

■ **Tip** JavaFX also provides ChoiceBox, ComboBox, and ListView controls to allow the user to make a selection from multiple available choices. I will discuss these controls in a separate section.

All three controls are labeled controls, and they help you present multiple choices to the user in different formats. The number of available choices may vary from two to N, where N is a number greater than two.

Selection from the available choices may be mutually exclusive. That is, the user can only make one selection from the list of choices. If the user changes the selection, the previous selection is automatically deselected. For example, the list of gender selection with three choices, Male, Female, and Unknown, is mutually exclusive. The user must select only one of the three choices, not two or more of them. The ToggleButton and RadioButton controls are typically used in this case.

There is a special case of selection where the number of choices is two. In this case, the choices are of boolean type: true or false. Sometimes, it is also referred to as a *Yes/No* or *On/Off* choice. The ToggleButton and CheckBox controls are typically used in this case.

Sometimes, the user can have multiple selections from a list of choices. For example, you may present the user with a list of hobbies to choose zero or more hobbies from the list. The ToggleButton and CheckBox controls are typically used in this case.

Understanding the *ToggleButton* Control

ToggleButton is a two-state button control. The two states are *selected* and *unselected*. Its selected property indicates whether it is selected. The selected property is true when it is in the selected state. Otherwise, it is false. When it is in the selected state, it stays depressed. You can toggle between the selected and unselected states by pressing it, and hence it got the name ToggleButton. For ToggleButtons, mnemonic parsing is enabled by default.

Figure 12-6 shows four toggle buttons with Spring, Summer, Fall, and Winter as their labels. Two of the toggle buttons, Spring and Fall, are selected, and the other two are unselected.

Figure 12-6. *A window showing four toggle buttons*

You create a ToggleButton the same way you create a Button, using the following code:

```
ToggleButton springBtn = new ToggleButton("Spring");
```

A ToggleButton is used to select a choice, not to execute a command. Typically, you do not add ActionEvent handlers to a ToggleButton. Sometimes, you can use a ToggleButton to start or stop an action. For that, you will need to add a ChangeListener for its selected property.

■ **Tip** The ActionEvent handler for a ToggleButton is invoked every time you click it. Notice that the first click selects a ToggleButton, and the second click deselects it. If you select and deselect a ToggleButton, the ActionEvent handler will be called twice.

Toggle buttons may be used in a group from which zero or one ToggleButton can be selected. To add toggle buttons to a group, you need to add them to a ToggleGroup. The ToggleButton class contains a toggleGroup property. To add a ToggleButton to a ToggleGroup, set the toggleGroup property of the ToggleButton to the group. Setting the toggleGroup property to null removes a ToggleButton from the group. The following snippet of code creates four toggle buttons and adds them to a ToggleGroup:

```
ToggleButton springBtn = new ToggleButton("Spring");
ToggleButton summerBtn = new ToggleButton("Summer");
ToggleButton fallBtn = new ToggleButton("Fall");
ToggleButton winterBtn = new ToggleButton("Winter");

// Create a ToggleGroup
ToggleGroup group = new ToggleGroup();

// Add all ToggleButtons to the ToggleGroup
springBtn.setToggleGroup(group);
```

```
summerBtn.setToggleGroup(group);
fallBtn.setToggleGroup(group);
winterBtn.setToggleGroup(group);
```

Each ToggleGroup maintains an ObservableList<Toggle>. Note that Toggle is an interface that is implemented by the ToggleButton class. The getToggles() method of the ToggleGroup class returns the list of Toggles in the group. You can add a ToggleButton to a group by adding it to the list returned by the getToggles() method. The preceding snippet of code may be rewritten as follows:

```
ToggleButton springBtn = new ToggleButton("Spring");
ToggleButton summerBtn = new ToggleButton("Summer");
ToggleButton fallBtn = new ToggleButton("Fall");
ToggleButton winterBtn = new ToggleButton("Winter");

// Create a ToggleGroup
ToggleGroup group = new ToggleGroup();

// Add all ToggleButtons to the ToggleGroup
group.getToggles().addAll(springBtn, summerBtn, fallBtn, winterBtn);
```

The ToggleGroup class contains a selectedToggle property that keeps track of the selected Toggle in the group. The getSelectedToggle() method returns the reference of the Toggle that is selected. If no Toggle is selected in the group, it returns null. Add a ChangeListener to this property if you are interested in tracking the change in selection inside a ToggleGroup.

■ **Tip**   You can select zero or one ToggleButton in a ToggleGroup. Selecting a ToggleButton in a group deselects the already selected ToggleButton. Clicking an already selected ToggleButton in a group deselects it, leaving no ToggleButton in the group selected.

The program in Listing 12-6 adds four toggle buttons to a ToggleGroup. You can select none or at the most one ToggleButton from the group. Figure 12-7 shows two screenshots: one when there is no selection and one when the ToggleButton with the label Summer is selected. The program adds a ChangeListener to the group to track the change in selection and displays the label of the selected ToggleButton in a Label control.

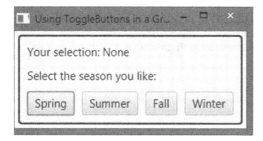 

Figure 12-7. *Four toggle buttons in a ToggleGroup allowing selection of one button at a time*

Listing 12-6. Using Toggle Buttons in a ToggleGroup and Tracking the Selection

```
// ToggleButtonTest.java
// ... find in the book's download area.
```

Understanding the *RadioButton* Control

An instance of the RadioButton class represents a radio button. It inherits from the ToggleButton class. Therefore, it has all of the features of a toggle button. A radio button is rendered differently compared to a toggle button. Like a toggle button, a radio button can be in one of the two states: *selected* and *unselected*. Its selected property indicates its current state. Like a toggle button, its mnemonic parsing is enabled by default. Like a toggle button, it also sends an ActionEvent when it is selected and unselected. Figure 12-8 shows a RadioButton with Summer as its text in selected and unselected states.

In unselected State   In selected State

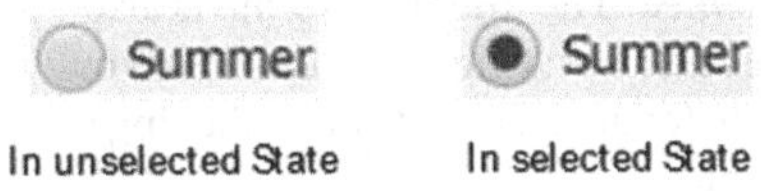

Figure 12-8. *Showing a radio button in selected and unselected states*

There is a significant difference in the use of radio buttons compared to the use of toggle buttons. Recall that when toggle buttons are used in a group, there may not be any selected toggle button in the group. When radio buttons are used in a group, there must be one selected radio button in the group. Unlike a toggle button, clicking a selected radio button in a group does not unselect it. To enforce the rule that one radio button must be selected in a group of radio buttons, one radio button from the group is selected programmatically by default.

■ **Tip**   Radio buttons are used when the user must make a selection from a list of choices. Toggle buttons are used when the user has an option to make one selection or no selection from a list of choices.

The program in Listing 12-7 shows how to use radio buttons inside a ToggleGroup. Figure 12-9 shows the window with the results of running the code. The program is very similar to the previous program that used toggle buttons. With the following code, Summer is set as the default selection:

```
// Select the default season as Summer
summerBtn.setSelected(true);
```

You set the default season in the radio button after you have added the change listener to the group, so the message to display the selected season is updated correctly.

Listing 12-7. Using Radio Buttons in a ToggleGroup and Tracking the Selection

```
// RadioButtonTest.java
// ... find in the book's download area.
```

Figure 12-9. *Four radio buttons in a* `ToggleGroup`

Understanding the *CheckBox* Control

CheckBox is a three-state selection control: *checked, unchecked,* and *undefined.* The undefined state is also known as an *indeterminate* state. A CheckBox supports a selection of three choices: true/false/unknown or yes/no/unknown. Usually, a CheckBox has text as a label, but not a graphic (even though it can). Clicking a CheckBox transitions it from one state to another cycling through three states.

A box is drawn for a CheckBox. In the unchecked state, the box is empty. A tick mark (or a check mark) is present in the box when it is in the checked state. In the undefined state, a horizontal line is present in the box. Figure 12-10 shows a CheckBox labeled Hungry in its three states.

Figure 12-10. *Showing a check box in unchecked, checked, and undefined states*

By default, the CheckBox control supports only two states: *checked* and *unchecked*. The allowIndeterminate property specifies whether the third state (the undefined state) is available for selection. By default, it is set to false:

```
// Create a CheckBox that supports checked and unchecked states only
CheckBox hungryCbx = new CheckBox("Hungry");

// Create a CheckBox and configure it to support three states
CheckBox agreeCbx = new CheckBox("Hungry");
agreeCbx.setAllowIndeterminate(true);
```

The CheckBox class contains selected and indeterminate properties to track its three states. If the indeterminate property is true, it is in the undefined state. If the indeterminate property is false, it is defined and it could be in a checked or unchecked state. If the indeterminate property is false and the selected property is true, it is in a checked state. If the indeterminate property is false and the selected property is false, it is in an unchecked state. Table 12-3 summarizes the rules for determining the state of a check box.

Table 12-3. *Determining the State of a Check Box Based on Its Indeterminate and Selected Properties*

indeterminate	selected	State
false	true	Checked
false	false	Unchecked
true	true/false	Undefined

Sometimes, you may want to detect the state transition in a check box. Because a check box maintains the state information in two properties, you will need to add a ChangeListener to both properties. An ActionEvent is fired when a check box is clicked. You can also use an ActionEvent to detect a state change in a check box. The following snippet of code shows how to use two ChangeListeners to detect a state change in a CheckBox. It is assumed that the changed() method and the rest of the code are part of the same class:

```
// Create a CheckBox to support three states
CheckBox agreeCbx = new CheckBox("I agree");
agreeCbx.setAllowIndeterminate(true);

// Add a ChangeListener to the selected and indeterminate properties
agreeCbx.selectedProperty().addListener(this::changed);
agreeCbx.indeterminateProperty().addListener(this::changed);
...
// A change listener to track the selection in the group
public void changed(ObservableValue<? extends Boolean> observable,
                    Boolean oldValue,
                    Boolean newValue) {
        String state = null;
        if (agreeCbx.isIndeterminate()) {
                state = "Undefined";
        } else if (agreeCbx.isSelected()) {
                state = "Checked";
        } else {
                state = "Unchecked";
        }
        System.out.println(state);
}
```

The program in Listing 12-8 shows how to use CheckBox controls. Figure 12-11 shows the window that results from running this code. The program creates two CheckBox controls. The Hungry CheckBox supports only two states. The I agree CheckBox is configured to support three states. When you change the state for the I agree CheckBox by clicking it, the Label at the top displays the description of the state.

Listing 12-8. Using the CheckBox Control

```
// CheckBoxTest.java
// ... find in the book's download area.
```

Figure 12-11. *Two check boxes: one uses two states and one uses three states*

The default CSS style class name for a CheckBox is check-box. The CheckBox class supports three CSS pseudo-classes: selected, determinate, and indeterminate. The selected pseudo-class applies when the selected property is true. The determinate pseudo-class applies when the indeterminate property is false. The indeterminate pseudo-class applies when the indeterminate property is true.

The CheckBox control contains two substructures: box and mark. You can style them to change their appearance. You can change the background color and border for the box, and you can change the color and shape of the tick mark. Both box and mark are an instance of StackPane. The tick mark is shown giving a shape to the StackPane. You can change the shape for the mark by supplying a different shape in a CSS. By changing the background color of the mark, you change the color of the tick mark. The following CSS will show the box in tan and tick mark in red:

```
.check-box .box {
        -fx-background-color: tan;
}

.check-box:selected .mark {
    -fx-background-color: red;
}
```

Understanding the Hybrid *Button* Control

With our definitions of different button types, a SplitMenuButton falls under the hybrid category. It combines the features of a pop-up menu and a command button. It lets you select an action like a MenuButton control and execute a command like a Button control. The SplitMenuButton class inherits from the MenuButton class.

A SplitMenuButton is divided into two areas: the action area and the menu-open area. When you click in the action area, ActionEvent is fired. The registered ActionEvent handlers execute the command. When the menu-open area is clicked, a menu is shown from which the user will select an action to execute. Mnemonic parsing for SplitMenuButton is enabled by default.

Figure 12-12 shows a SplitMenuButton in two states. The picture on the left shows it in the collapsed state. In the picture on the right, it shows the menu items. Notice the vertical line dividing the control in two halves. The half containing the text Home is the action area. The other half containing the down arrow is the menu-open area.

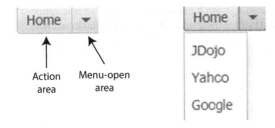

Action area   Menu-open area

Figure 12-12. *A SplitMenuButton in the collapsed and showing states*

You can create a `SplitMenuButton` with menu items or without them using its constructors with the following code:

```
// Create an empty SplitMenuItem
SplitMenuButton splitBtn = new SplitMenuButton();
splitBtn.setText("Home"); // Set the text as "Home"

// Create MenuItems
MenuItem jdojo = new MenuItem("JDojo");
MenuItem yahoo = new MenuItem("Yahoo");
MenuItem google = new MenuItem("Google");

// Add menu items to the MenuButton
splitBtn.getItems().addAll(jdojo, yahoo, google);
```

You need to add an `ActionEvent` handler to execute an action when the `SplitMenuButton` is clicked in the action area:

```
// Add ActionEvent handler when "Home" is clicked
splitBtn.setOnAction(e -> /* Take some action here */);
```

The program in Listing 12-9 shows how to use a `SplitMenuButton`. It adds a `SplitMenuButton` with the text Home and three menu items in the top-right region of a `BorderPane`. A `WebView` is added in the center region. When you click Home, the `www.jdojo.com` web page is opened. When you select a website using the menu by clicking the down arrow, the corresponding website is opened. The program is very similar to the ones you developed earlier using `MenuButton` and `Hyperlink` controls.

Listing 12-9. Using the `SplitMenuButton` Control

```
// SplitMenuButtonTest.java
// ... find in the book's download area.
```

Making Selections from a List of Items

In the previous sections, you have seen how to present users with a list of items, for example, using toggle buttons and radio buttons. Toggle and radio buttons are easier to use because all options are always visible to the users. However, they use a lot of space on the screen. Think about using radio buttons to show the names of all 50 states in the United States to the user. It would take a lot of space. Sometimes, none of the available items in the list is suitable for selection, so you will want to give users a chance to enter a new item that is not in the list.

JavaFX provides some controls that let users select an item(s) from a list of items. They take less space compared to buttons. They provide advanced features to customize their appearance and behaviors. I will discuss the following such controls in subsequent sections:

- ChoiceBox
- ComboBox
- ListView
- ColorPicker
- DatePicker

ChoiceBox lets users select an item from a small list of predefined items. ComboBox is an advanced version of ChoiceBox. It has many features, for example, the ability to be editable or change the appearance of the items in the list, which are not offered in ChoiceBox. ListView provides users an ability to select multiple items from a list of items. Typically, all or more than one item in a ListView is visible to the user all the time. ColorPicker lets users select a color from a standard color palette or define a custom color graphically. DatePicker lets users select a date from a calendar pop-up. Optionally, users can enter a date as text. ComboBox, ColorPicker, and DatePicker have the same superclass ComboBoxBase.

Understanding the *ChoiceBox* Control

ChoiceBox is used to let a user select an item from a small list of items. The items may be any type of objects. ChoiceBox is a parameterized class. The parameter type is the type of the items in its list. If you want to store mixed types of items in a ChoiceBox, you can use its <Object> type, as shown in the following code:

```
// Create a ChoiceBox for any type of items
ChoiceBox<Object> seasons = new ChoiceBox<>();

// Instead create a ChoiceBox for String items
ChoiceBox<String> seasons = new ChoiceBox<>();
```

You can specify the list items while creating a ChoiceBox with the following code:

```
ObservableList<String> seasonList = FXCollections.<String>observableArrayList(
        "Spring", "Summer", "Fall", "Winter");
ChoiceBox<String> seasons = new ChoiceBox<>(seasonList);
```

After you create a ChoiceBox, you can add items to its list of items using the items property, which is of the ObjectProperty<ObservableList<T>> type in which T is the type parameter for the ChoiceBox. The following code will accomplish this:

```
ChoiceBox<String> seasons = new ChoiceBox<>();
seasons.getItems().addAll("Spring", "Summer", "Fall", "Winter");
```

Figure 12-13 shows a choice box in four different states. It has four names of seasons in the list of items. The first picture (labeled #1) shows it in its initial state when there is no selection. The user can open the list of items using the mouse or the keyboard. Clicking anywhere inside the control opens the list of items in a pop-up window, as shown in the picture labeled #2. Pressing the down arrow key when the control has focus also opens the list of items. You can select an item from the list by clicking it or using the up/down arrow and the Enter key. When you select an item, the pop-up window showing the items list is collapsed and the selected item is shown in the control, as shown in the picture labeled #3. The picture labeled #4 shows the control when an item is selected (Spring in this case) and the list items are shown. The pop-up window displays a check mark with the item already selected in the control. Table 12-4 lists the properties declared in the ChoiceBox class.

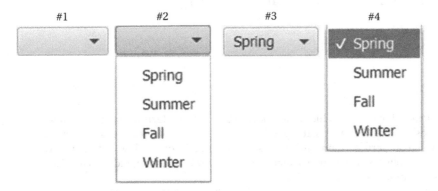

Figure 12-13. *A choice box in different states*

Table 12-4. *Properties Declared in the ChoiceBox Class*

Property	Type	Description
converter	ObjectProperty <StringConverter<T>>	It serves as a converter object whose toString() method is called to get the string representation of the items in the list.
items	ObjectProperty <ObservableList<T>>	It is the list of choices to display in the ChoiceBox.
selectionModel	ObjectProperty <SingleSelectionModel<T>>	It serves as a selection model that keeps track of the selections in a ChoiceBox.
showing	ReadOnlyBooleanProperty	Its true value indicates that the control is showing the list of choices to the user. Its false value indicates that the list of choices is collapsed.
value	ObjectProperty<T>	It is the selected item in the ChoiceBox.

■ **Tip**   You are not limited to showing the items list using the mouse or keyboard. You can show and hide the list programmatically using the show() and hide() methods, respectively.

The value property of the ChoiceBox stores the selected item in the control. Its type is ObjectProperty<T>, where T is the type parameter for the control. If the user has not selected an item, its value is null. The following snippet of code sets the value property:

```
// Create a ChoiceBox for String items
ChoiceBox<String> seasons = new ChoiceBox<String>();
seasons.getItems().addAll("Spring", "Summer", "Fall", "Winter");

// Get the selected value
String selectedValue = seasons.getValue();

// Set a new value
seasons.setValue("Fall");
```

When you set a new value using the setValue() method, the ChoiceBox selects the specified value in the control if the value exists in the list of items. It is possible to set a value that does not exist in the list of items. In that case, the value property contains the newly set item, but the control does not show it. The control keeps showing the previously selected item, if any. When the new item is later added to the list of items, the control shows the item set in the value property.

The ChoiceBox needs to track the selected item and its index in the list of items. It uses a separate object, called the *selection model*, for this purpose. The ChoiceBox class contains a selectionModel property to store the item selection details. ChoiceBox uses an object of the SingleSelectionModel class as its selection model, but you can use your own selection model. The default selection model works in almost all cases. The selection model provides you selection-related functionality:

- It lets you select an item using the index of the item in the list.

- It lets you select the first, next, previous, or last item in the list.

- It lets you clear the selection.

- Its selectedIndex and selectedItem properties track the index and value of the selected item. You can add a ChangeListener to these properties to handle a change in selection in a ChoiceBox. When no item is selected, the selected index is –1, and the selected item is null.

The following snippet of code forces a value in a ChoiceBox by selecting the first item in the list by default:

```
ChoiceBox<String> seasons = new ChoiceBox<>();
seasons.getItems().addAll("Spring", "Summer", "Fall", "Winter", "Fall");

// Select the first item in the list
seasons.getSelectionModel().selectFirst();
```

Use the selectNext() method of the selection model to select the next item from the list. Calling the selectNext() method when the last item is already selected has no effect. Use the selectPrevious() and selectLast() methods to select the previous and the last item in the list, respectively. The select(int index) and select(T item) methods select an item using the index and value of the item, respectively. Note that you can also use the setValue() method of the ChoiceBox to select an item from the list by its value. The clearSelection() method of the selection model clears the current selection, returning the ChoiceBox to a state as if no item had been selected.

The program in Listing 12-10 displays a window as shown in Figure 12-14. It uses a ChoiceBox with a list of four seasons. By default, the program selects the first season from the list. The application forces the user to select one season name by selecting one by default. It adds ChangeListeners to the selectedIndex and selectedItem properties of the selection model. They print the details of the selection change on the standard output. The current selection is shown in a Label control whose text property is bound to the value property of the ChoiceBox. Select a different item from the list and watch the standard output and the window for the details.

Listing 12-10. Using ChoiceBox with a Preselected Item

```
// ChoiceBoxTest.java
// ... find in the book's download area.
```

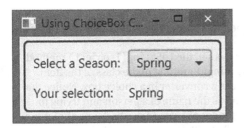

Figure 12-14. *A choice box with a preselected item*

Using Domain Objects in *ChoiceBox*

In the previous example, you used String objects as items in the choice box. You can use any object type as items. ChoiceBox calls the toString() method of every item and displays the returned value in the pop-up list. The following snippet of code creates a choice box and adds four Person objects as its items. Figure 12-15 shows the choice box in the showing state. Notice the items are displayed using the String object returned from the toString() method of the Person class.

```
import com.jdojo.mvc.model.Person;
import javafx.scene.control.ChoiceBox;
...
ChoiceBox<Person> persons = new ChoiceBox<>();
persons.getItems().addAll(new Person("John", "Jacobs", null),
                          new Person("Donna", "Duncan", null),
                          new Person("Layne", "Estes", null),
                          new Person("Mason", "Boyd", null));
```

```
[personId=1, firstName=John, lastName=Jacobs, birthDate=null]

[personId=2, firstName=Donna, lastName=Duncan, birthDate=null]

[personId=3, firstName=Layne, lastName=Estes, birthDate=null]

[personId=4, firstName=Mason, lastName=Boyd, birthDate=null]
```

Figure 12-15. *A choice box showing four Person objects as its list of items*

Typically, the toString() method of an object returns a String that represents the state of the object. It is not meant to provide a customized string representation of the object to be displayed in a choice box. The ChoiceBox class contains a converter property. It is an ObjectProperty of the StringConverter<T> type. A StringConverter<T> object acts as a converter from the object type T to a string and vice versa. The class is declared abstract, as in the following snippet of code:

```
public abstract class StringConverter<T> {
        public abstract String toString(T object);
        public abstract T fromString(String string);
}
```

The toString(T object) method converts the object of type T to a string. The fromString(String string) method converts a string to a T object.

By default, the converter property in a choice box is null. If it is set, the toString(T object) method of the converter is called to get the list of items instead of the toString() method of the class of the item. The PersonStringConverter class shown in Listing 12-11 can act as a converter in a choice box. Notice that you are treating the argument string in the fromString() method as the name of a person and trying to construct a Person object from it. You do not need to implement the fromString() method for a choice box. It will be used in a ComboBox, which I will discuss next. The ChoiceBox will use only the toString(Person p) method.

Listing 12-11. A Person to String Converter

```
// PersonStringConverter.java
package com.jdojo.control;

import com.jdojo.mvc.model.Person;
import javafx.util.StringConverter;

public class PersonStringConverter extends StringConverter<Person> {
        @Override
        public String toString(Person p) {
                return p == null?
                        null : p.getLastName() + ", " + p.getFirstName();
        }

        @Override
        public Person fromString(String string) {
                Person p = null;
                if (string == null) {
                        return p;
                }

                int commaIndex = string.indexOf(",");
                if (commaIndex == -1) {
                        // Treat the string as first name
                        p = new Person(string, null, null);
                } else {
                        // Ignoring string bounds check for brevity
                        String firstName =
                                string.substring(commaIndex + 2);
```

```
                    String lastName = string.substring(
                                0, commaIndex);
                    p = new Person(firstName, lastName, null);
            }
            return p;
        }
}
```

The following snippet of code uses a converter in a ChoiceBox to convert Person objects in its list of items to strings. Figure 12-16 shows the choice box in the showing state.

```
import com.jdojo.mvc.model.Person;
import javafx.scene.control.ChoiceBox;
...
ChoiceBox<Person> persons = new ChoiceBox<>();

// Set a converter to convert a Person object to a String object
persons.setConverter(new PersonStringConverter());

// Add five person objects to the ChoiceBox
persons.getItems().addAll(new Person("John", "Jacobs", null),
                          new Person("Donna", "Duncan", null),
                          new Person("Layne", "Estes", null),
                          new Person("Mason", "Boyd", null));
```

Figure 12-16. *Person objects using a converter in a choice box*

Allowing Nulls in *ChoiceBox*

Sometimes, a choice box may allow the user to select null as a valid choice. This can be achieved by using null as an item in the list of choices, as shown in the following code:

```
ChoiceBox<String> seasons = new ChoiceBox<>();
seasons.getItems().addAll(null, "Spring", "Summer", "Fall", "Winter");
```

The preceding snippet of code produces a choice box as shown in Figure 12-17. Notice that the null item is shown as an empty space.

Figure 12-17. *Null as a choice in a choice box*

It is often required that the null choice be shown as a custom string, for example, "[None]". This can be accomplished using a converter. In the previous section, you used a converter to customize the choices for Person objects. Here, you will use the converter to customize the choice item for null. You can do both in one converter as well. The following snippet of code uses a converter with a ChoiceBox to convert a null choice as "[None]". Figure 12-18 shows the resulting choice box.

```
ChoiceBox<String> seasons = new ChoiceBox<>();
seasons.getItems().addAll(null, "Spring", "Summer", "Fall", "Winter");

// Use a converter to convert null to "[None]"
seasons.setConverter(new StringConverter<String>() {
        @Override
        public String toString(String string) {
                return (string == null) ? "[None]" : string;
        }

        @Override
        public String fromString(String string) {
                return string;
        }
});
```

✓ [None]

Spring

Summer

Fall

Winter

Figure 12-18. *A null choice in a choice box converted as "[None]"*

Using Separators in *ChoiceBox*

Sometimes, you may want to separate choices into separate groups. Suppose you want to show fruits and cooked items in a breakfast menu, and you want to separate one from the other. You would use an instance of the Separator class to achieve this. It appears as a horizontal line in the list of choices. A Separator is not selectable. The following snippet of code creates a choice box with one of its items as a Separator. Figure 12-19 shows the choice box in the showing state.

```
ChoiceBox breakfasts = new ChoiceBox();
breakfasts.getItems().addAll("Apple", "Banana", "Strawberry",
                    new Separator(),
                    "Apple Pie", "Donut", "Hash Brown");
```

Figure 12-19. *A choice box using a separator*

Styling a *ChoiceBox* with CSS

The default CSS style class name for a ChoiceBox is choice-box. The ChoiceBox class supports a showing CSS pseudo-class, which applies when the showing property is true.

The ChoiceBox control contains two substructures: open-button and arrow. You can style them to change their appearance. Both are instances of StackPane. ChoiceBox shows the selected item in a Label. The list of choices is shown in a ContextMenu whose ID is set to choice-box-popup-menu. Each choice is displayed in a menu item whose IDs are set to choice-box-menu-item. The following styles customize the ChoiceBox control. Currently, there is no way to customize the pop-up menu for an individual choice box. The style will affect all instances of the ChoiceBox control at the level (scene or layout pane) at which it is set.

```
/* Set the text color and font size for the selected item in the control */
.choice-box .label {
        -fx-text-fill: blue;
        -fx-font-size: 8pt;
}

/* Set the text color and text font size for choices in the popup list */
#choice-box-menu-item * {
        -fx-text-fill: blue;
        -fx-font-size: 8pt;
}

/* Set background color of the arrow */
.choice-box .arrow {
        -fx-background-color: blue;
}

/* Set the background color for the open-button area */
.choice-box .open-button {
    -fx-background-color: yellow;
}

/* Change the background color of the popup */
#choice-box-popup-menu {
        -fx-background-color: yellow;
}
```

Understanding the *ComboBox* Control

ComboBox is used to let a user select an item from a list of items. You can think of ComboBox as an advanced version of ChoiceBox. ComboBox is highly customizable. The ComboBox class inherits from the ComboBoxBase class, which provides the common functionality for all ComboBox-like controls, such as ComboBox, ColorPicker, and DatePicker. If you want to create a custom control that will allow users to select an item from a pop-up list, you need to inherit your control from the ComboBoxBase class.

The items list in a ComboBox may comprise any type of objects. ComboBox is a parameterized class. The parameter type is the type of the items in the list. If you want to store mixed types of items in a ComboBox, you can use its <Object> type, as in the following code:

```
// Create a ComboBox for any type of items
ComboBox<Object> seasons = new ComboBox<>();

// Instead create a ComboBox for String items
ComboBox<String> seasons = new ComboBox<>();
```

You can specify the list items while creating a ComboBox, as in the following code:

```
ObservableList<String> seasonList = FXCollections.<String>observableArrayList(
    "Spring", "Summer", "Fall", "Winter");
ComboBox<String> seasons = new ComboBox<>(seasonList);
```

After you create a combo box, you can add items to its list of items using the items property, which is of the ObjectProperty<ObservableList<T>> type, in which T is the type parameter for the combo box, as in the following code:

```
ComboBox<String> seasons = new ComboBox<>();
seasons.getItems().addAll("Spring", "Summer", "Fall", "Winter");
```

Like ChoiceBox, ComboBox needs to track the selected item and its index in the list of items. It uses a separate object, called *selection model*, for this purpose. The ComboBox class contains a selectionModel property to store the item selection details. ComboBox uses an object of the SingleSelectionModel class as its selection model. The selection model lets you select an item from the list of items and lets you add ChangeListeners to track changes in index and item selections. Please refer to the section "Understanding the *ChoiceBox* Control" for more details on using a selection model.

Unlike ChoiceBox, ComboBox can be editable. Its editable property specifies whether or not it is editable. By default, it is not editable. When it is editable, it uses a TextField control to show the selected or entered item. The editor property of the ComboBox class stores the reference of the TextField, and it is null if the combo box is not editable, as shown in the following code:

```
ComboBox<String> breakfasts = new ComboBox<>();

// Add some items to choose from
breakfasts.getItems().addAll("Apple", "Banana", "Strawberry");

// By making the control editable, let users enter an item
breakfasts.setEditable(true);
```

ComboBox has a value property that stores the currently selected or entered value. Note that when a user enters a value in an editable combo box, the entered string is converted to the item type T of the combo box. If the item type is not a string, a StringConverter<T> is needed to convert the String value to type T. I will present an example of this shortly.

You can set a prompt text for a combo box that is displayed when the control is editable, it does not have focus, and its value property is null. The prompt text is stored in the promptText property, which is of the StringProperty type, as in the following code:

```
breakfasts.setPromptText("Select/Enter an item"); // Set a prompt text
```

The ComboBox class contains a placeholder property, which stores a Node reference. When the items list is empty or null, the placeholder node is shown in the pop-up area. The following snippet of code sets a Label as a placeholder:

```
Label placeHolder = new Label("List is empty.\nPlease enter an item");
breakfasts.setPlaceholder(placeHolder);
```

The program in Listing 12-12 creates two ComboBox controls: seasons and breakfasts. The combo box having the list of seasons is not editable. The combo box having the list of breakfast items is editable. Figure 12-20 shows the screenshot when the user selected a season and entered a breakfast item, Donut, which is not in the list of breakfast items. A Label control displays the user selection. When you enter a new value in the breakfast combo box, you need to change the focus, press the Enter key, or open the pop-up list to refresh the message Label.

Listing 12-12. Using ComboBox Controls

```
// ComboBoxTest.java
// ... find in the book's download area.
```

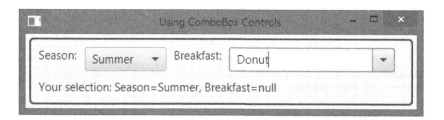

Figure 12-20. *Two ComboBox controls: one noneditable and one editable*

Detecting Value Change in *ComboBox*

Detecting an item change in a noneditable combo box is easily performed by adding a ChangeListener to the selectedIndex or selectedItem property of its selection model. Please refer to the "Understanding the *ChoiceBox* Control" section for more details.

You can still use a ChangeListener for the selectedItem property to detect when the value in an editable combo box changes by selecting from the items list or entering a new value. When you enter a new value, the selectedIndex property does not change because the entered value does not exist in the items list.

Sometimes, you want to perform an action when the value in a combo box changes. You can do so by adding an ActionEvent handler, which is fired when the value changes by any means. You would do this by setting it programmatically, selecting from items list, or entering a new value, as in the following code:

```
ComboBox<String> list = new ComboBox<>();
list.setOnAction(e -> System.out.println("Value changed"));
```

Using Domain Objects in Editable *ComboBox*

In an editable ComboBox<T> where T is something other than String, you must set the converter property to a valid StringConverter<T>. Its toString(T object) method is used to convert the item object to a string to show it in the pop-up list. Its fromString(String s) method is called to convert the entered string to an item object. The value property is updated with the item object converted from the entered string. If the entered string cannot be converted to an item object, the value property is not updated.

The program in Listing 12-13 shows how to use a StringConverter in a combo box, which uses domain objects in its items list. The ComboBox uses Person objects. The PersonStringConverter class, as shown in Listing 12-11, is used as the StringConverter. You can enter a name in the format LastName, FirstName or FirstName in the ComboBox and press the Enter key. The entered name will be converted to a Person object and shown in the Label. The program ignores the error checking in name formatting. For example, if you enter Kishori as the name, it displays null, Kishori in the Label. The program adds a ChangeListener to the selectedItem and selectedIndex properties of the selection model to track the selection change. Notice that when you enter a string in the ComboBox, a change in the selectedIndex property is not reported. An ActionEvent handler for the ComboBox is used to keep the values in the combo box and the text in the Label in sync.

Listing 12-13. Using a StringConverter in a ComboBox

```
// ComboBoxWithConverter.java
// ... find in the book's download area.
```

Customizing the Height of a Pop-Up List

By default, ComboBox shows only ten items in the pop-up list. If the number of items is more than ten, the pop-up list shows a scrollbar. If the number of items is less than ten, the height of the pop-up list is shortened to show only the available items. The visibleRowCount property of the ComboBox controls how many rows are visible in the pop-up list, as in the following code:

```
ComboBox<String> states = new ComboBox<>();
...
// Show five rows in the popup list
states.setVisibleRowCount(5);
```

Using Nodes As Items in *ComboBox*

A combo box has two areas:

- Button area to display the selected item
- Pop-up area to display the items list

Both areas use ListCells to display items. A ListCell is a Cell. A Cell is a Labeled control to display some form of content that may have text, a graphic, or both. The pop-up area is a ListView that contains an instance of ListCell for each item in the list. I will discuss ListView in the next section.

Elements in the items list of a combo box can be of any type, including Node type. It is not recommended to add instances of the Node class directly to the items list. When nodes are used as items, they are added as the graphic to the cells. Scene graphics need to follow the rule that a node cannot be displayed in two places at the same time. That is, a node must be inside one container at a time. When a node from the items list is selected, the node is removed from the pop-up ListView cell and added to the button area. When the pop-up is displayed again, the selected node is not shown in the list as it is already showing in the button area. To avoid this inconsistency in display, avoid using nodes directly as items in a combo box.

Figure 12-21 shows three views of a combo box created using the following snippet of code. Notice that the code adds three instances of HBox, which is a node to the items list. The figure labeled #1 shows the pop-up list when it is opened for the first time, and you see all three items correctly. The figure labeled #2 shows up after the second item is selected, and you see the correct item in the button area. At this time, the second item in the list, an HBox with a rectangle, was removed from the cell in the ListView and added to the cell in the button area. The figure labeled #3 shows the pop-up list when it is open for the second time. At this time, the second item is missing from the list because it is already selected. This problem was discussed in the previous paragraph.

```
Label shapeLbl = new Label("Shape:");
ComboBox<HBox> shapes = new ComboBox<>();
shapes.getItems().addAll(new HBox(new Line(0, 10, 20, 10), new Label("Line")),
                new HBox(new Rectangle(0, 0, 20, 20), new Label("Rectangle")),
                new HBox(new Circle(20, 20, 10), new Label("Circle")));
```

Figure 12-21. *Three views of a combo box with nodes in the items list*

You can fix the display issue that occurs when you use nodes as items. The solution is to add nonnode items in the list and supply a cell factory to create the desired node inside the cell factory. You need to make sure that the nonnode items will provide enough pieces of information to create the node you wanted to insert. The next section explains how to use a cell factory.

Using a Cell Factory in *ComboBox*

The ComboBox class contains a cellFactory property, which is declared as follows:

```
public ObjectProperty<Callback<ListView<T>, ListCell<T>>> cellFactory;
```

Callback is an interface in the javafx.util package. It has a call() method that takes an argument of type P and returns an object of type R, as in the following code:

```
public interface Callback<P,R> {
        public R call(P param);
}
```

The declaration of the cellFactory property states that it stores a Callback object whose call() method receives a ListView<T> and returns a ListCell<T>. Inside the call() method, you create an instance of the ListCell<T> class and override the updateItem(T item, boolean empty) method of the Cell class to populate the cell.

Let's use a cell factory to display nodes in the button area and the pop-up area of a combo box. Listing 12-14 will be our starting point. It declares a StringShapeCell class, which inherits from the ListCell<String> class. You need to update its content in its updateItem() method, which is automatically called. The method receives the item, which in this case is String, and a boolean argument indicating whether the cell is empty. Inside the method, you call the method in the superclass first. You derive a shape from the string argument and set the text and graphic in the cell. The shape is set as the graphic. The getShape() method returns a Shape from a String.

Listing 12-14. A Custom ListCell That Displays a Shape and Its Name

```java
// StringShapeCell.java
package com.jdojo.control;

import javafx.scene.control.ListCell;
import javafx.scene.shape.Circle;
import javafx.scene.shape.Line;
import javafx.scene.shape.Rectangle;
import javafx.scene.shape.Shape;

public class StringShapeCell extends ListCell<String> {
    @Override
    public void updateItem(String item, boolean empty) {
        // Need to call the super first
        super.updateItem(item, empty);

        // Set the text and graphic for the cell
        if (empty) {
            setText(null);
            setGraphic(null);
        } else {
            setText(item);
            Shape shape = this.getShape(item);
            setGraphic(shape);
        }
    }

    public Shape getShape(String shapeType) {
        Shape shape = null;
        switch (shapeType.toLowerCase()) {
            case "line":
                shape = new Line(0, 10, 20, 10);
                break;
            case "rectangle":
                shape = new Rectangle(0, 0, 20, 20);
                break;
            case "circle":
                shape = new Circle(20, 20, 10);
                break;
            default:
                shape = null;
        }
```

```
                return shape;
        }
}
```

The next step is to create a Callback class, as shown in Listing 12-15. The program in this listing is very simple. Its call() method returns an object of the StringShapeCell class. The class will act as a cell factory for ComboBox.

Listing 12-15. A Callback Implementation for Callback<ListView<String>, ListCell<String>>

```java
// ShapeCellFactory.java
package com.jdojo.control;

import javafx.scene.control.ListCell;
import javafx.scene.control.ListView;
import javafx.util.Callback;

public class ShapeCellFactory implements Callback<ListView<String>, ListCell<String>> {
        @Override
        public ListCell<String> call(ListView<String> listview) {
                return new StringShapeCell();
        }
}
```

The program in Listing 12-16 shows how to use a custom cell factory and button cell in a combo box. The program is very simple. It creates a combo box with three String items. It sets an object of the ShapeCellFactory as the cell factory, as in the following code:

```java
// Set the cellFactory property
shapes.setCellFactory(new ShapeCellFactory());
```

Setting the cell factory is not enough in this case. It will only resolve the issue of displaying the shapes in the pop-up area. When you select a shape, it will display the String item, not the shape, in the button area. To make sure, you see the same item in the list for selection, and after you select one, you need to set the buttonCell property, as in the following code:

```java
// Set the buttonCell property
shapes.setButtonCell(new StringShapeCell());
```

Notice the use of the StringShapeCell class in the buttonCell property and ShapeCellFactory class.

Run the program in Listing 12-16. You should be able to select a shape from the list, and the shape should be displayed in the combo box correctly. Figure 12-22 shows three views of the combo box.

Listing 12-16. Using a Cell Factory in a Combo Box

```java
// ComboBoxCellFactory.java
package com.jdojo.control;

import javafx.application.Application;
import javafx.scene.Scene;
import javafx.scene.control.ComboBox;
```

```java
import javafx.scene.control.Label;
import javafx.scene.layout.HBox;
import javafx.stage.Stage;

public class ComboBoxCellFactory extends Application {
        public static void main(String[] args) {
                Application.launch(args);
        }

        @Override
        public void start(Stage stage) {
                Label shapeLbl = new Label("Shape:");
                ComboBox<String> shapes = new ComboBox<>();
                shapes.getItems().addAll("Line", "Rectangle", "Circle");

                // Set the cellFactory property
                shapes.setCellFactory(new ShapeCellFactory());

                // Set the buttonCell property
                shapes.setButtonCell(new StringShapeCell());

                HBox root = new HBox(shapeLbl, shapes);
                root.setStyle("-fx-padding: 10;" +
                                "-fx-border-style: solid inside;" +
                                "-fx-border-width: 2;" +
                                "-fx-border-insets: 5;" +
                                "-fx-border-radius: 5;" +
                                "-fx-border-color: blue;");

                Scene scene = new Scene(root);
                stage.setScene(scene);
                stage.setTitle("Using CellFactory in ComboBox");
                stage.show();
        }
}
```

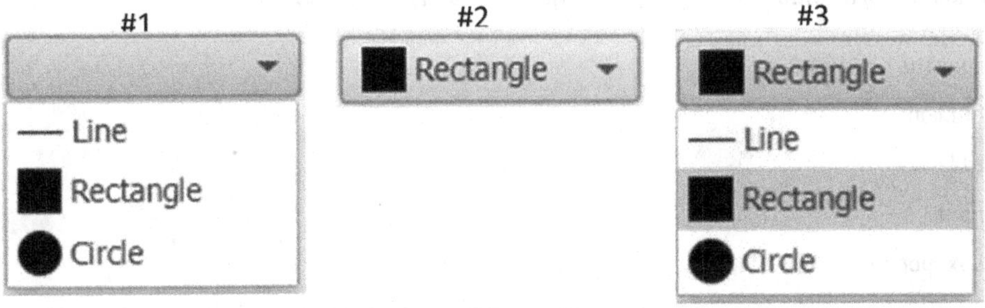

Figure 12-22. *Three views of a combo box with a cell factory*

Using a custom cell factory and button cell in a combo box gives you immense power to customize the look of the pop-up list and the selected item. If using a cell factory looks hard or confusing to you, keep in mind that a cell is a Labeled control, and you are setting the text and graphic in that Labeled control inside the updateItem() method. The Callback interface comes into play because the ComboBox control needs to give you a chance to create a cell when it needs it. Otherwise, you would have to know how many cells to create and when to create them. There is nothing more to it.

The ComboBoxBase class provides four properties that can also be used with ComboBox:

- onShowing
- onShown
- onHiding
- onHidden

These properties are of the type ObjectProperty<EventHandler<Event>>. You can set an event handler to these properties, which will be called before the pop-up list is shown, after it is shown, before it is hidden, and after it is hidden. For example, the onShowing event handlers are handy when you want to customize the pop-up list just before it is shown.

Styling *ComboBox* with CSS

The default CSS style class name for a ComboBox is combo-box. A combo box contains several CSS substructures, as shown in Figure 12-23.

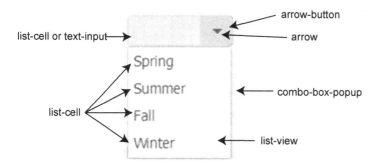

Figure 12-23. *Substructures of a combo box that can be styled separately using CSS*

The CSS names for the substructure are

- arrow-button
- list-cell
- text-input
- combo-box-popup

An arrow-button contains a substructure called arrow. Both arrow-button and arrow are instances of StackPane. The list-cell area represents the ListCell used to show the selected item in a noneditable combo box. The text-input area is the TextField used to show the selected or entered item in an editable combo box. The combo-box-popup is the Popup control that shows the pop-up list when the button is clicked.

It has two substructures: `list-view` and `list-cell`. The `list-view` is the `ListView` control that shows the list of items, and `list-cell` represents each cell in the `ListView`. The following CSS styles customize the appearance of some substructures of `ComboBox`:

```css
/* The ListCell that shows the selected item in a non-editable ComboBox */
.combo-box .list-cell {
        -fx-background-color: yellow;
}

/* The TextField that shows the selected item in an editable ComboBox */
.combo-box .text-input {
        -fx-background-color: yellow;
}

/* Style the arrow button area */
.combo-box .arrow-button {
        -fx-background-color: lightgray;
}

/* Set  the text color in the popup list for ComboBox to blue */
.combo-box-popup .list-view .list-cell {
        -fx-text-fill: blue;
}
```

Understanding the *ListView* Control

`ListView` is used to allow a user to select one item or multiple items from a list of items. Each item in `ListView` is represented by an instance of the `ListCell` class, which can be customized. The items list in a `ListView` may contain any type of objects. `ListView` is a parameterized class. The parameter type is the type of the items in the list. If you want to store mixed types of items in a `ListView`, you can use its <Object> type, as shown in the following code:

```java
// Create a ListView for any type of items
ListView<Object> seasons = new ListView<>();

// Instead create a ListView for String items
ListView<String> seasons = new ListView<>();
```

You can specify the list items while creating a `ListView`, as in the following code:

```java
ObservableList<String> seasonList = FXCollections.<String>observableArrayList(
        "Spring", "Summer", "Fall", "Winter");
ListView<String> seasons = new ListView<>(seasonList);
```

After you create a `ListView`, you can add items to its list of items using the `items` property, which is of the `ObjectProperty<ObservableList<T>>` type in which T is the type parameter for the `ListView`, as in the following code:

```java
ListView<String> seasons = new ListView<>();
seasons.getItems().addAll("Spring", "Summer", "Fall", "Winter");
```

ListView sets its preferred width and height, which are normally not the width and height that you want for your control. It would have helped developers if the control had provided a property such as visibleItemCount. Unfortunately, the ListView API does not support such a property. You need to set them to reasonable values in your code, as follows:

```
// Set preferred width = 100px and height = 120px
seasons.setPrefSize(100, 120);
```

If the space needed to display items is larger than what is available, a vertical, a horizontal, or both scrollbars are automatically added.

The ListView class contains a placeholder property, which stores a Node reference. When the items list is empty or null, the placeholder node is shown in the list area of the ListView. The following snippet of code sets a Label as a placeholder:

```
Label placeHolder = new Label("No seasons available for selection.");
seasons.setPlaceholder(placeHolder);
```

ListView offers a scrolling feature. Use the scrollTo(int index) or scrollTo(T item) method to scroll to a specified index or item in the list. The specified index or item is made visible, if it is not already visible. The ListView class fires a ScrollToEvent when scrolling takes place using the scrollTo() method or by the user. You can set an event handler using the setOnScrollTo() method to handle scrolling.

Each item in a ListView is displayed using an instance of the ListCell class. In essence, a ListCell is a labeled control that is capable of displaying text and a graphic. Several subclasses of ListCell exist to give ListView items a custom look. ListView lets you specify a Callback object as a *cell factory*, which can create custom list cells. A ListView does not need to create as many ListCell objects as the number of items. It can have only as many ListCell objects as the number of visible items on the screen. As items are scrolled, it can reuse the ListCell objects to display different items. Figure 12-24 shows a class diagram for ListCell-related classes.

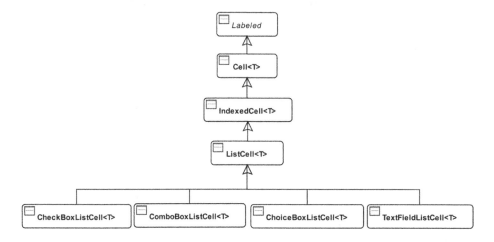

Figure 12-24. *A class diagram for* ListCell*-related classes*

Cells are used as building blocks in different types of controls. For example, ListView, TreeView, and TableView controls use cells in one form or another to display and edit their data. The Cell class is the superclass for all cells. You can override its updateItem(T object, boolean empty) and take full control of how the cell is populated. This method is called automatically by these controls when the item in the cell needs to be updated. The Cell class declares several useful properties: editable, editing, empty, item, and selected. When a Cell is empty, which means it is not associated with any data item, its empty property is true.

The IndexedCell class adds an index property, which is the index of the item in the underlying model. Suppose a ListView uses an ObservableList as a model. The list cell for the second item in the ObservableList will have index 1 (index starts at 0). The cell index facilitates customization of cells based on their indexes, for example, using different colors for cells at odd and even index cells. When a cell is empty, its index is –1.

Orientation of a *ListView*

The items in a ListView may be arranged vertically in a single column (default) or horizontally in a single row. It is controlled by the orientation property, as shown in the following code:

```
// Arrange list of seasons horizontally
seasons.setOrientation(Orientation.HORIZONTAL);
```

Figure 12-25 shows two instances of ListView: one uses vertical orientation and one horizontal orientation. Notice that the odd and even rows or columns have different background colors. This is the default look of the ListView. You can change the appearance using a CSS. Please refer to the "Styling ListView with CSS" section for details.

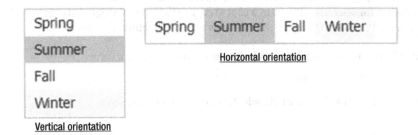

Figure 12-25. *Two instances of* ListView *having the same items but different orientations*

Selection Model in *ListView*

ListView has a selection model that stores the selected state of its items. Its selectionModel property stores the reference of the selection model. By default, it uses an instance of the MultipleSelectionModel class. You can use a custom selection model, however, that is rarely needed. The selection model can be configured to work in two modes:

- Single selection mode
- Multiple selection mode

In single selection mode, only one item can be selected at a time. If an item is selected, the previously selected item is deselected. By default, a ListView supports single selection mode. An item can be selected using a mouse or a keyboard. You can select an item using a mouse click. Using a keyboard to select an item requires that the ListView have focus. You can use the up/down arrow in a vertical ListView and the left/right arrow in a horizontal ListView to select items.

In multiple selection mode, multiple items can be selected at a time. Using only a mouse lets you select only one item at a time. Clicking an item selects the item. Clicking an item with the Shift key pressed selects all contiguous items. Clicking an item with the Ctrl key pressed selects a deselected item and deselects a selected item. You can use the up/down or left/right arrow key to navigate and the Ctrl key with the spacebar or Shift key with the spacebar to select multiple items. If you want a ListView to operate in multiple selection mode, you need to set the selectionMode property of its selection model, as in the following code:

```
// Use multiple selection mode
seasons.getSelectionModel().setSelectionMode(SelectionMode.MULTIPLE);

// Set it back to single selection mode, which is the default for a ListView
seasons.getSelectionModel().setSelectionMode(SelectionMode.SINGLE);
```

The MultipleSelectionModel class inherits from the SelectionModel class, which contains selectedIndex and selectedItem properties.

The selectedIndex property is –1 if there is no selection. In single selection mode, it is the index of the currently selected item. In multiple selection mode, it is the index of the last selected item. In multiple selection mode, use the getSelectedIndices() method that returns a read-only ObservableList<Integer> containing the indexes of all selected items. If you are interested in listening for selection change in a ListView, you can add a ChangeListener to the selectedIndex property or a ListChangeListener to the ObservableList returned by the getSelectedIndices() method.

The selectedItem property is null if there is no selection. In single selection mode, it is the currently selected item. In multiple selection mode, it is the last selected item. In multiple selection mode, use the getSelectedItems() method that returns a read-only ObservableList<T> containing all selected items. If you are interested in listening for selection change in a ListView, you can add a ChangeListener to the selectedItem property or a ListChangeListener to the ObservableList<T> returned by the getSelectedItems() method.

The selection model of ListView contains several methods to select items in different ways:

- The selectAll() method selects all items.

- The selectFirst() and selectLast() methods select the first item and the last item, respectively.

- The selectIndices(int index, int... indices) method selects items at the specified indexes. Indexes outside the valid range are ignored.

- The selectRange(int start, int end) method selects all indexes from the start index (inclusive) to the end index (exclusive).

- The clearSelection() and clearSelection(int index) methods clear all selection and the selection at the specified index, respectively.

The program in Listing 12-17 demonstrates how to use the selection model of a ListView for making selections and listening for selection change events. Figure 12-26 shows the window that results from running this code. Run the application and use a mouse or buttons on the window to select items in the ListView. The selection details are displayed at the bottom.

Listing 12-17. Using a ListView Selection Model

```
// ListViewSelectionModel.java
// ... find in the book's download area.
```

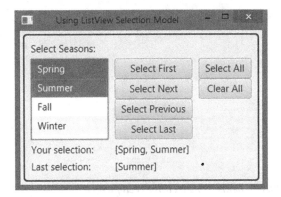

Figure 12-26. *A* ListView *with several buttons to make selections*

Using Cell Factory in *ListView*

Each item in a ListView is displayed in an instance of ListCell, which is a Labeled control. Recall that a Labeled control contains text and a graphic. The ListView class contains a cellFactory property that lets you use custom cells for its items. The property type is ObjectProperty<Callback<ListView<T>,ListCell <T>>>. The reference of the ListView is passed to the call() method of the Callback object, and it returns an instance of the ListCell class. In a large ListView, say 1000 items, the ListCell returned from the cell factory may be reused. The control needs to create only the number of cells that are visible. Upon scrolling, it may reuse the cells that went out of the view to display newly visible items. The updateItem() method of the ListCell receives the reference of the new item.

By default, a ListView calls the toString() method of its items, and it displays the string in its cell. In the updateItem() method of your custom ListCell, you can populate the text and graphic for the cell to display anything you want in the cell based on the item in that cell.

■ **Tip** You used a custom cell factory for the pop-up list of the combo box in the previous section. The pop-up list in a combo box uses a ListView. Therefore, using a custom cell factory in a ListView would be the same as discussed in the earlier combo box section.

The program in Listing 12-18 shows how to use a custom cell factory to display the formatted names of Person items. Figure 12-27 shows the resulting window after running the code. The snippet of code in the program creates and sets a custom cell factory. The updateItem() method of the ListCell formats the name of the Person object and adds a serial number that is the index of the cell plus one.

Listing 12-18. Using a Custom Cell Factory for ListView

```
// ListViewDomainObjects.java
// ... find in the book's download area.
```

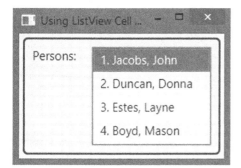

Figure 12-27. *A* ListView *displaying* Person *objects in its list of items using a custom cell factory*

Using Editable *ListView*

The ListView control offers many customizations, and one of them is its ability to let users edit the items. You need to set two properties for a ListView before it can be edited:

- Set the editable property of the ListView to true.

- Set the cellFactory property of the ListView to a cell factory that produces an editable ListCell.

Select a cell and click to start editing. Alternatively, press the spacebar when a cell has focus to start editing. If a ListView is editable and has an editable cell, you can also use the edit(int index) method of the ListView to edit the item in the cell at the specified index.

■ **Tip**   The ListView class contains a read-only editingIndex property. Its value is the index of the item being edited. Its value is −1 if no item is being edited.

JavaFX provides cell factories that let you edit a ListCell using TextField, ChoiceBox, ComboBox, and CheckBox. You can create a custom cell factory to edit cells in some other way. Instances of the TextFieldListCell, ChoiceBoxListCell, ComboBoxListCell, and CheckBoxListCell classes, as list cells in a ListView, provide editing support. These classes are included in the javafx.scene.control.cell package.

Using a *TextField* to Edit *ListView* Items

An instance of the TextFieldListCell is a ListCell that displays an item in a Label when the item is not being edited and in a TextField when the item is being edited. If you want to edit a domain object to a ListView, you will need to use a StringConverter to facilitate the two-way conversion. The forListView() static method of the TextFieldListCell class returns a cell factory configured to be used with String items. The following snippet of code shows how to set a TextField as the cell editor for a ListView:

```
ListView<String> breakfasts = new ListView<>();
...
breakfasts.setEditable(true);
```

```
// Set a TextField as the editor
Callback<ListView<String>, ListCell<String>> cellFactory =
        TextFieldListCell.forListView();
breakfasts.setCellFactory(cellFactory);
```

The following snippet of code shows how to set a TextField as the cell editor with a converter for a ListView that contains Person objects. The converter used in the code was shown in Listing 12-11. The converter object will be used to convert a Person object to a String for displaying and a String to a Person object after editing.

```
ListView<Person> persons = new ListView<>();
...
persons.setEditable(true);

// Set a TextField as the editor.
// Need to use a StringConverter for Person objects.
StringConverter<Person> converter = new PersonStringConverter();
Callback<ListView<Person>, ListCell<Person>> cellFactory
        = TextFieldListCell.forListView(converter);
persons.setCellFactory(cellFactory);
```

The program in Listing 12-19 shows how to edit a ListView item in a TextField. It uses a ListView of domain objects (Person) and a ListView of String objects. After running the program, double-click any items in the two ListViews to start editing. When you are done editing, press the Enter key to commit the changes.

Listing 12-19. Using an Editable ListView

```
// ListViewEditing.java
// ... find in the book's download area.
```

Using a *ChoiceBox*/*ComboBox* to Edit *ListView* Items

An instance of the ChoiceBoxListCell is a ListCell that displays an item in a Label when the item is not being edited and in a ChoiceBox when the item is being edited. If you want to edit a domain object to a ListView, you will need to use a StringConverter to facilitate two-way conversion. You need to supply the list of items to show in the choice box. Use the forListView() static method of the ChoiceBoxListCell class to create a cell factory. The following snippet of code shows how to set a choice box as the cell editor for a ListView:

```
ListView<String> breakfasts = new ListView<>();
...
breakfasts.setEditable(true);

// Set a cell factory to use a ChoiceBox for editing
ObservableList<String> items =
        FXCollections.<String>observableArrayList(
        "Apple", "Banana", "Donut", "Hash Brown");
breakfasts.setCellFactory(ChoiceBoxListCell.forListView(items));
```

The program in Listing 12-20 uses a choice box to edit items in a `ListView`. Double-click an item in a cell to start editing. In edit mode, the cell becomes a choice box. Click the arrow to show the list of items to select. Using a combo box for editing is similar to using a choice box.

Listing 12-20. Using a `ChoiceBox` for Editing Items in a `ListView`

```
// ListViewChoiceBoxEditing.java
// ... find in the book's download area.
```

Using a Check Box to Edit *ListView* Items

The `CheckBoxListCell` class provides the ability to edit a `ListCell` using a check box. It draws a check box in the cell, which can be selected or deselected. Note that the third state, the *indeterminate* state, of the check box is not available for selection while using a check box to edit `ListView` items.

Using a check box to edit `ListView` items is a little different. You need to provide the `CheckBoxListCell` class with an `ObservableValue<Boolean>` object for each item in the `ListView`. Internally, the observable value is bound bidirectionally to the selected state of the check box. When the user selects or deselects an item in the `ListView` using the check box, the corresponding `ObservableValue` object is updated with a true or false value. If you want to know which item is selected, you will need to keep the reference of the `ObservableValue` object.

Let's redo our earlier breakfast example using a check box. The following snippet of code creates a map and adds all items as a key and a corresponding `ObservableValue` item with false value. Using a false value, you want to indicate that the items will be initially deselected:

```
Map<String, ObservableValue<Boolean>> map = new HashMap<>();
map.put("Apple", new SimpleBooleanProperty(false));
map.put("Banana", new SimpleBooleanProperty(false));
map.put("Donut", new SimpleBooleanProperty(false));
map.put("Hash Brown", new SimpleBooleanProperty(false));
```

Now, you create an editable `ListView` with all keys in the map as its items:

```
ListView<String> breakfasts = new ListView<>();
breakfasts.setEditable(true);

// Add all keys from the map as items to the ListView
breakfasts.getItems().addAll(map.keySet());
```

The following snippet of code creates a `Callback` object. Its `call()` method returns the `ObservableValue` object for the specified item passed to the `call()` method. The `CheckBoxListCell` class will call the `call()` method of this object automatically:

```
Callback<String, ObservableValue<Boolean>> itemToBoolean =
    (String item) -> map.get(item);
```

Now it is time to create and set a cell factory for the `ListView`. The `forListView()` static method of the `CheckBoxListCell` class takes a `Callback` object as an argument. If your `ListView` contains domain objects, you can also provide a `StringConverter` to this method, using the following code:

```
// Set the cell factory
breakfasts.setCellFactory(CheckBoxListCell.forListView(itemToBoolean));
```

When the user selects or deselects an item using the check box, the corresponding ObservableValue in the map will be updated. To know whether an item in the ListView is selected, you need to look at the value in the ObservableValue object for that item.

The program in Listing 12-21 shows how to use a check box to edit items in a ListView. Figure 12-28 shows the resulting window after running the code. Select items using a mouse. Pressing the Print Selection button prints the selected items on the standard output.

Listing 12-21. Using a Check Box to Edit ListView Items

```
// ListViewCheckBoxEditing.java
// ... find in the book's download area.
```

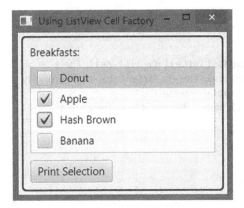

Figure 12-28. *A ListView with a check box for editing its items*

Handling Events While Editing a *ListView*

An editable ListView fires three kinds of events:

- An editStart event when the editing starts

- An editCommit event when the edited value is committed

- An editcancel event when the editing is cancelled

The ListView class defines a ListView.EditEvent<T> static inner class to represent edit-related event objects. Its getIndex() method returns the index of the item that is edited. The getNewValue() method returns the new input value. The getSource() method returns the reference of the ListView firing the event. The ListView class provides onEditStart, onEditCommit, and onEditCancel properties to set the event handlers for these methods.

The following snippet of code adds an editStart event handler to a ListView. The handler prints the index that is being edited and the new item value:

```
ListView<String> breakfasts = new ListView<>();
...
breakfasts.setEditable(true);
breakfasts.setCellFactory(TextFieldListCell.forListView());
```

```
// Add an editStart event handler to the ListView
breakfasts.setOnEditStart(e ->
        System.out.println("Edit Start: Index=" + e.getIndex() +
                           ", item  = " + e.getNewValue()));
```

Listing 12-22 contains a complete program to show how to handle edit-related events in a ListView. Run the program and double-click an item to start editing. After changing the value, press Enter to commit editing or Esc to cancel editing. Edit-related event handlers print messages on the standard output.

Listing 12-22. Handling Edit-Related Events in a ListView

```
// ListViewEditEvents.java
// ... find in the book's download area.
```

Styling *ListView* with CSS

The default CSS style class name for a ListView is list-view, and for ListCell it is list-cell. The ListView class has two CSS pseudo-classes: horizontal and vertical. The -fx-orientation CSS property controls the orientation of the ListView, which can be set to *horizontal* or *vertical*.

You can style a ListView as you style any other controls. Each item is displayed in an instance of ListCell. ListCell provides several CSS pseudo-classes:

- empty
- filled
- selected
- odd
- even

The empty pseudo-class applies when the cell is empty. The filled pseudo-class applies when the cell is not empty. The selected pseudo-class applies when the cell is selected. The odd and even pseudo-classes apply to cells with an odd and even index, respectively. The cell representing the first item is index 0, and it is considered an even cell.

The following CSS styles will highlight even cells with tan and odd cells with light gray:

```
.list-view .list-cell:even {
    -fx-background-color: tan;
}

.list-view .list-cell:odd {
    -fx-background-color: lightgray;
}
```

Developers often ask how to remove the default alternate cell highlighting in a ListView. In the modena.css file, the default background color for all list cells is set to -fx-control-inner-background, which is a CSS-derived color. For all odd list cells, the default color is set to derive(-fx-control-inner-background,-5%). To keep the background color the same for all cells, you need to override the background color of odd list cells as follows:

```
.list-view .list-cell:odd {
    -fx-background-color: -fx-control-inner-background;
}
```

412

This only solves half of the problem; it only takes care of the background colors of the list cells in a normal state inside a ListView. A list cell can be in several states, for example, focused, selected, empty, or filled. To completely address this, you will need to set the appropriate background colors for list cells for all states. Please refer to the modena.css file for a complete list of states that you will need to modify the background colors for list cells.

The ListCell class supports an -fx-cell-size CSS property that is the height of the cells in a vertical ListView and the width of cells in a horizontal ListView.

The list cell could be of the type ListCell, TextFieldListCell, ChoiceBoxListCell, ComboBoxListCell, or CheckBoxListCell. The default CSS style class names for subclasses of ListCell are text-field-list-cell, choice-box-list-cell, combo-box-list-cell, and check-box-list-cell. You can use these style class names to customize their appearance. The following CSS style will show the TextField in an editable ListView in yellow background:

```
.list-view .text-field-list-cell .text-field {
    -fx-background-color: yellow;
}
```

Understanding the *ColorPicker* Control

ColorPicker is a combo box–style control that is especially designed for users to select a color from a standard color palette or create a color using a built-in color dialog. The ColorPicker class inherits from the ComboBoxBase<Color> class. Therefore, all properties declared in the ComboBoxBase class apply to the ColorPicker control as well. I have discussed several of these properties earlier in the "Understanding the *ComboBox* Control" section. If you want to know more about those properties, please refer to that section. For example, the editable, onAction, showing, and value properties work the same way in a ColorPicker as they do in a combo box. A ColorPicker has three parts:

- ColorPicker control
- Color palette
- Custom color dialog

A ColorPicker control consists of several components, as shown in Figure 12-29. You can customize their looks. The color indicator is a rectangle displaying the current color selection. The color label displays the color in text format. If the current selection is one of the standard colors, the label displays the color name. Otherwise, it displays the color value in hex format. Figure 12-30 shows a ColorPicker control and its color palette.

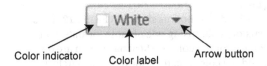

Figure 12-29. *Components of a ColorPicker control*

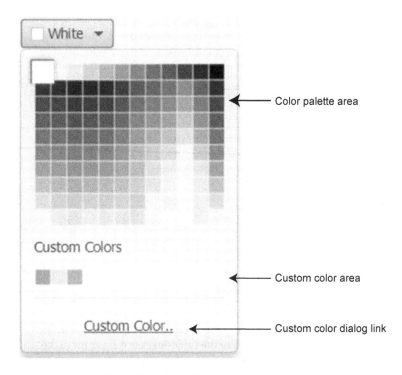

Figure 12-30. ColorPicker *control and its color palette dialog box*

The color palette is shown as a pop-up when you click the arrow button in the control. The color palette consists of three areas:

- A color palette area to show a set of standard colors

- A custom color area showing the list of custom colors

- A hyperlink to open the custom color dialog box

The color palette area shows a set of predefined standard colors. If you click one of the colors, it closes the pop-up and sets the selected color as the value for the ColorPicker control.

The custom color area shows a set of custom colors. When you open this pop-up for the first time, this area is absent. There are two ways to get colors in this area. You can load a set of custom colors, or you can build and save custom colors using the custom color dialog box.

When you click the Custom Color... hyperlink, a custom color dialog box, as shown in Figure 12-31, is displayed. You can use the HSB, RGB, or Web tab to build a custom color using one of these formats. You can also define a new color by selecting a color from the color area or the color vertical bar, which are on the left side of the dialog box. When you click the color area and the color bar, they show a small circle and rectangle to denote the new color. Clicking the Save button selects the custom color in the control and saves it to display later in the custom color area when you open the pop-up again. Clicking the Use button selects the custom color for the control.

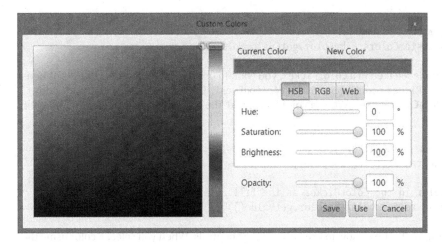

Figure 12-31. *Custom color dialog box of* ColorPicker

Using the *ColorPicker* Control

The ColorPicker class has two constructors. One of them is the default constructor, and the other takes the initial color as an argument. The default constructor uses white as the initial color, as in the following code:

```
// Create a ColorPicker control with an initial color of white
ColorPicker bgColor1 = new ColorPicker();

// Create a ColorPicker control with an initial color of red
ColorPicker bgColor2 = new ColorPicker(Color.RED);
```

The value property of the control stores the currently selected color. Typically, the value property is set when you select a color using the control. However, you can also set it directly in your code, as follows:

```
ColorPicker bgColor = new ColorPicker();
...
// Get the selected color
Color selectedCOlor = bgColor.getValue();

// Set the ColorPicker color to yellow
bgColor.setValue(Color.YELLOW);
```

The getCustomColors() method of the ColorPicker class returns a list of custom colors that you save in the custom color dialog box. Note that custom colors are saved only for the current session and the current ColorPicker control. If you need to, you can save custom colors in a file or database and load them on startup. You will have to write some code to achieve this:

```
ColorPicker bgColor = new ColorPicker();
...
// Load two custom colors
bgColor.getCustomColors().addAll(Color.web("#07FF78"), Color.web("#C2F3A7"));
```

415

```
...
// Get all custom colors
ObservableList<Color> customColors = bgColor.getCustomColors();
```

Typically, when a color is selected in a ColorPicker, you want to use the color for other controls. When a color is selected, the ColorPicker control generates an ActionEvent. The following snippet of code adds an ActionEvent handler to a ColorPicker. When a color is selected, the handler sets the new color as the fill color of a rectangle:

```
ColorPicker bgColor = new ColorPicker();
Rectangle rect = new Rectangle(0, 0, 100, 50);

// Set the selected color in the ColorPicker as the fill color of the Rectangle
bgColor.setOnAction(e -> rect.setFill(bgColor.getValue()));
```

The program in Listing 12-23 shows how to use ColorPicker controls. When you select a color using the ColorPicker, the fill color for the rectangle is updated.

Listing 12-23. Using the ColorPicker Control

```
// ColorPickerTest.java
// ... find in the book's download area.
```

The ColorPicker control supports three looks: combo-box look, button look, and split-button look. The combo-box look is the default look. Figure 12-32 shows a ColorPicker in these three looks, respectively.

Figure 12-32. *Three looks of a* ColorPicker

The ColorPicker class contains two string contents that are the CSS style class name for the button and split-button looks. The constants are

- STYLE_CLASS_BUTTON

- STYLE_CLASS_SPLIT_BUTTON

If you want to change the default look of a ColorPicker, add one of the preceding constants as its style class, as follows:

```
// Use default combo-box look
ColorPicker cp = new ColorPicker(Color.RED);

// Change the look to button
cp.getStyleClass().add(ColorPicker.STYLE_CLASS_BUTTON);

// Change the look to split-button
cp.getStyleClass().add(ColorPicker.STYLE_CLASS_SPLIT_BUTTON);
```

■ **Tip** It is possible to add both STYLE_CLASS_BUTTON and STYLE_CLASS_SPLIT_BUTTON as style classes for a ColorPicker. In such a case, the STYLE_CLASS_BUTTON is used.

Styling *ColorPicker* with CSS

The default CSS style class name for a ColorPicker is color-picker. You can style almost every part of a ColorPicker, for example, color indicator, color label, color palette dialog, and custom color dialog. Please refer to the modena.css file for complete reference.

The -fx-color-label-visible CSS property of the ColorPicker sets whether the color label is visible or not. Its default value is true. The following code makes the color label invisible:

```
.color-picker {
        -fx-color-label-visible: false;
}
```

The color indicator is a rectangle, which has a style class name of picker-color-rect. The color label is a Label, which has a style class name of color-picker-label. The following code shows the color label in blue and sets a 2px thick black stroke around the color indicator rectangle:

```
.color-picker .color-picker-label {
        -fx-text-fill: blue;
}

.color-picker .picker-color .picker-color-rect {
        -fx-stroke: black;
        -fx-stroke-width: 2;
}
```

The style class name for the color palette is color-palette. The following code hides the Custom Colors... hyperlink on the color palette:

```
.color-palette .hyperlink {
        visibility: hidden;
}
```

Understanding the *DatePicker* Control

DatePicker is a combo-box style control. The user can enter a date as text or select a date from a calendar. The calendar is displayed as a pop-up for the control, as shown in Figure 12-33. The DatePicker class inherits from the ComboBoxBase<LocalDate> class. All properties declared in the ComboBoxBase class are also available to the DatePicker control.

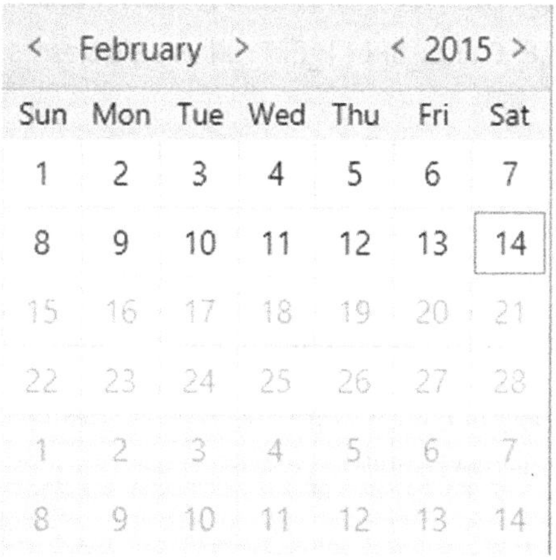

Figure 12-33. *Calendar pop-up for a DatePicker control*

The first row of the pop-up displays the month and year. You can scroll through months and years using the arrows. The second row displays the short names of weeks. The first column displays the week number of the year. By default, the week number column is not displayed. You can use the context menu on the pop-up to display it, or you can set the showWeekNumbers property of the control to show it.

The calendar always displays dates for 42 days. Dates not applicable to the current month are disabled for selection. Each day cell is an instance of the DateCell class. You can provide a cell factory to use your custom cells. You will have an example of using a custom cell factory later.

Right-clicking the first row, week names, week number column, or disabled dates displays the context menu. The context menu also contains a Show Today menu item, which scrolls the calendar to the current date.

Using the *DatePicker* Control

You can create a DatePicker using its default constructor; it uses null as the initial value. You can also pass a LocalDate to another constructor as the initial value, as in the following code:

```
// Create a DatePicker with null as its initial value
DatePicker birthDate1 = new DatePicker();

// Use September 19, 1969 as its initial value
DatePicker birthDate2 = new DatePicker(LocalDate.of(1969, 9, 19));
```

The value property of the control holds the current date in the control. You can use the property to set a date. When the control has a null value, the pop-up shows the dates for the current month. Otherwise, the pop-up shows the dates of the month of the current value, as with the following code:

```
// Get the current value
LocalDate dt = birthDate.getValue();

// Set the current value
birthDate.setValue(LocalDate.of(1969, 9, 19));
```

The DatePicker control provides a TextField to enter a date as text. Its editor property stores the reference of the TextField. The property is read-only. If you do not want users to enter a date, you can set the editable property of the DatePicker to false, as in the following code:

```
DatePicker birthDate = new DatePicker();

// Users cannot enter a date. They must select one from the popup.
birthDate.setEditable(false);
```

The DatePicker has a converter property that uses a StringConverter to convert a LocalDate to a string and vice versa. Its value property stores the date as LocalDate, and its editor displays it as a string, which is the formatted date. When you enter a date as text, the converter converts it to a LocalDate and stores it in the value property. When you pick a date from the calendar pop-up, the converter creates a LocalDate to store in the value property, and it converts it to a string to display in the editor. The default converter uses the default Locale and chronology to format the date. When you enter a date as text, the default converter expects the text in the default Locale and chronology format.

Listing 12-24 contains the code for a LocalDateStringConverter class that is a StringConverter for LocalDate. By default, it formats dates in MM/dd/yyyy format. You can pass a different format in its constructor.

Listing 12-24. A StringConverter to Convert a LocalDate to a String and Vice Versa

```
// LocalDateStringConverter.java
package com.jdojo.control;

import javafx.util.StringConverter;
import java.time.LocalDate;
import java.time.format.DateTimeFormatter;

public class LocalDateStringConverter extends StringConverter<LocalDate> {
        private String pattern = "MM/dd/yyyy";
        private DateTimeFormatter dtFormatter;

        public LocalDateStringConverter() {
                dtFormatter = DateTimeFormatter.ofPattern(pattern);
        }

        public LocalDateStringConverter(String pattern) {
                this.pattern = pattern;
                dtFormatter = DateTimeFormatter.ofPattern(pattern);
        }

        @Override
        public LocalDate fromString(String text) {
                LocalDate date = null;
                if (text != null && !text.trim().isEmpty()) {
                        date = LocalDate.parse(text, dtFormatter);
                }
                return date;
        }
```

```
        @Override
        public String toString(LocalDate date) {
                String text = null;
                if (date != null) {
                        text = dtFormatter.format(date);
                }
                return text;
        }
}
```

To format the date in "MMMM dd, yyyy" format, for example, May 29, 2013, you would create and set the convert as follows:

```
DatePicker birthDate = new DatePicker();
birthDate.setConverter(new LocalDateStringConverter("MMMM dd, yyyy"));
```

You can configure the DatePicker control to work with a specific chronology instead of the default one. The following statement sets the chronology to Thai Buddhist chronology:

```
birthDate.setChronology(ThaiBuddhistChronology.INSTANCE);
```

You can change the default Locale for the current instance of the JVM, and the DatePicker will use the date format and chronology for the default Locale:

```
// Change the default Locale to Canada
Locale.setDefault(Locale.CANADA);
```

Each day cell in the pop-up calendar is an instance of the DateCell class, which is inherited from the Cell<LocalDate> class. The dayCellFactory property of the DatePicker class lets you provide a custom day cell factory. The concept is the same as discussed earlier for providing the cell factory for the ListView control. The following statement creates a day cell factory. It changes the text color of weekend cells to blue and disables all future day cells. If you set this day cell factory to a DatePicker, the pop-up calendar will not let users select a future date because you will have disabled all future day cells:

```
Callback<DatePicker, DateCell> dayCellFactory =
    new Callback<DatePicker, DateCell>() {
        public DateCell call(final DatePicker datePicker) {
            return new DateCell() {
                @Override
                public void updateItem(LocalDate item, boolean empty) {
                    // Must call super
                    super.updateItem(item, empty);
                    // Disable all future date cells
                    if (item.isAfter(LocalDate.now())) {
                        this.setDisable(true);
                    }
                    // Show Weekends in blue
                    DayOfWeek day = DayOfWeek.from(item);
```

```
                if (day == DayOfWeek.SATURDAY ||
                        day == DayOfWeek.SUNDAY) {
                    his.setTextFill(Color.BLUE);
                }
            }
        };
    }
};
```

The following snippet of code sets a custom day cell factory for a birth date DatePicker control. It also makes the control noneditable. The control will force the user to select a nonfuture date from the pop-up calendar:

```
DatePicker birthDate = new DatePicker();

// Set a day cell factory to disable all future day cells
// and show weekends in blue
birthDate.setDayCellFactory(dayCellFactory);

// Users must select a date from the popup calendar
birthDate.setEditable(false);
```

The DatePicker control fires an ActionEvent when its value property changes. The value property may change when a user enters a date, selects a date from the pop-up, or a date is set programmatically, as provided in the following code:

```
// Add an ActionEvent handler
birthDate.setOnAction(e -> System.out.println("Date changed to:" + birthDate.getValue()));
```

Listing 12-25 has a complete program showing how to use a DatePicker control. It uses most of the features of the DatePicker. It displays a window as shown in Figure 12-34. The control is noneditable, forcing the user to select a nonfuture date from the pop-up.

Listing 12-25. Using the DatePicker Control

```
// DatePickerTest.java
// ... find in the book's download area.
```

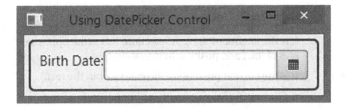

Figure 12-34. A DatePicker control to select a nonfuture date

Styling *DatePicker* with CSS

The default CSS style class name for a DatePicker is date-picker, and for its pop-up, the class name is date-picker-popup. You can style almost every part of a DatePicker, for example, the month-year pane in the top area of the pop-up, day cells, week number cells, and current day cell. Please refer to the modena.css file for complete reference.

The CSS style class name for day cell is day-cell. The day cell for the current date has the style class name as today. The following styles display the current day number in bold and all day numbers in blue:

```
/* Display current day numbers in bolder font */
.date-picker-popup > * > .today {
        -fx-font-weight: bolder;
}

/* Display all day numbers in blue */
.date-picker-popup > * > .day-cell {
    -fx-text-fill: blue;
}
```

Understanding Text Input Controls

JavaFX supports text input controls that let users work with single line or multiple lines of plain text. I will discuss TextField, PasswordField, and TextArea text input controls in this section. All text input controls are inherited from the TextInputControl class. Please refer to Figure 12-1 for a class diagram for the text input controls.

■ **Tip** JavaFX provides a rich text edit control named HTMLEditor. I will discuss HTMLEditor later in this chapter.

The TextInputControl class contains the properties and methods that apply to all types of text input controls. Properties and methods related to the current caret position and movement and text selection are in this class. Subclasses add properties and methods applicable to them. Table 12-5 lists the properties declared in the TextInputControl class.

Table 12-5. *Properties Declared in the TextInputControl Class*

Property	Type	Description
anchor	ReadOnlyIntegerProperty	It is the anchor of the text selection. It is at the opposite end of the caret position in the selection.
caretPosition	ReadOnlyIntegerProperty	It is the current position of the caret within the text.
editable	BooleanProperty	It is true if the control is editable. Otherwise, it is false.
font	ObjectProperty<Font>	It is the default font for the control.
length	ReadOnlyIntegerProperty	It is the number of characters in the control.

(continued)

Table 12-5. (*continued*)

Property	Type	Description
promptText	StringProperty	It is the prompt text. It is displayed in the control when control has no content.
redoable	ReadOnlyBooleanProperty	Tells whether it is possible to redo the latest change.
selectedText	ReadOnlyStringProperty	It is the selected text in the control.
selection	ReadOnlyObjectProperty<IndexRange>	It is the selected text index range.
text	StringProperty	It is the text in the control.
textFormatter	ObjectProperty<TextFormatter<?>>	The currently attached text formatter.
undoable	ReadOnlyBooleanProperty	Tells whether it is possible to undo the latest change.

Positioning and Moving Caret

All text input controls provide a caret. By default, a caret is a blinking vertical line when the control has focus. The current caret position is the target for the next input character from the keyboard. The caret position starts at zero, which is before the first character. Position 1 is after the first character and before the second character and so on. Figure 12-35 shows the caret positions in a text input control that has four characters. The number of characters in the text determines the valid range for the caret position, which is zero to the length of the text. Zero is the only valid caret position if the control does not contain text.

Figure 12-35. *Caret positions in a text input control having four characters*

Several methods take a caret position as an argument. Those methods clamp the argument value to the valid caret position range. Passing a caret position outside the valid range will not throw an exception. For example, if the control has four characters and you want to move the caret to position 10, the caret will be positioned at position 4.

The read-only caretPosition property contains the current caret position. Use the positionCaret(int pos) method to position the caret at the specified pos. The backward() and forward() methods move the caret one character backward and forward, respectively, if there is no selection. If there is a selection, they move the caret position to the beginning and end and clear the selection. The home() and end() methods move the caret before the first character and after the last character, respectively, and clear the selection. The nextWord() method moves the caret to the beginning of the next word and clears the selection. The endOfNextWord() method moves the caret to the end of the next word and clears the selection. The previousWord() method moves the caret to the beginning of the previous word and clears the selection.

Making Text Selection

The TextInputControl class provides a rich API through its properties and methods to deal with text selection. Using the selection API, you can select the entire or partial text and get the selection information.

The selectedText property contains the value of the selected text. Its value is an empty string if there is no selection. The selection property contains an IndexRange that holds the index range of the selection. The getStart() and getEnd() methods of the IndexRange class return the start index and end index of the selection, respectively, and its getLength() method returns the length of the selection. If there is no selection, the lower and upper limits of the range are the same, and they are equal to the caretPosition value.

The anchor and caretPosition properties play a vital role in text selection. The value of these properties defines the selection range. The same value for both properties indicates no selection. Either property may indicate the start or end of the selection range. The anchor value is the caret position when the selection started. You can select characters by moving the caret backward or forward. For example, you can use the left or right arrow key with the Shift key pressed to select a range of characters. If you move the caret forward during the selection process, the anchor value will be less than the caretPosition value. If you move the caret backward during the selection process, the anchor value will be greater than the caretPosition value. Figure 12-36 shows the relation between the anchor and caretPosition values.

Figure 12-36. *Relation between the* anchor *and* caretPosition *properties of a text input control*

In Figure 12-36, the part labeled #1 shows a text input control with the text BLESSINGS. The caretPosition value is 1. The user selects four characters by moving the caret four positions forward, for example, by pressing the Shift key and right arrow key or by dragging the mouse. The selectedText property, as shown in the part labeled #2, is LESS. The anchor value is 1, and the caretPosition value is 5. The selection property has an IndexRange of 1 to 5.

In the part labeled #3, the caretPosition value is 5. The user selects four characters by moving the caret backward as shown in the part labeled #4. The selectedText property, as shown in part labeled #4, is LESS. The anchor value is 5, and the caretPosition value is 1. The selection property has an IndexRange of 1 to 5. Notice that in the parts labeled #2 and #4, the anchor and caretPosition values are different, and the selectedText and selection properties are the same.

Apart from the selection properties, the TextInputControl contains several useful selection-related methods:

- selectAll()
- deselect()
- selectRange(int anchor, int caretPosition)
- selectHome()
- selectEnd()
- extendSelection(int pos)
- selectBackward()
- selectForward()

- `selectPreviousWord()`
- `selectEndOfNextWord()`
- `selectNextWord()`
- `selectPositionCaret(int pos)`
- `replaceSelection(String replacement)`

Notice that you have a `positionCaret(int pos)` method and a `selectPositionCaret(int pos)` method. The former positions the caret at the specified position and clears the selection. The latter moves the caret to the specified pos and extends the selection if one exists. If no selection exists, it forms a selection by the current caret position as the anchor and moving the caret to the specified pos.

The `replaceSelection(String replacement)` method replaces the selected text by the specified replacement. If there is no selection, it clears the selection and inserts the specified replacement at the current caret position.

Modifying the Content

The `text` property of the `TextInputControl` class represents the textual content of text input controls. You can change the content using the `setText(String text)` method and get it using the `getText()` method. The `clear()` method sets the content to an empty string.

The `insertText(int index, String text)` method inserts the specified text at the specified index. It throws an `IndexOutOfBoundsException` if the specified index is outside the valid range (zero to the length of the content). The `appendText(String text)` method appends the specified text to the content. The `deleteText()` method lets you delete a range of characters from the content. You can specify the range as an `IndexRange` object or start and end index. The `deleteNextChar()` and `deletePreviousChar()` methods delete the next and previous character, respectively, from the current caret position if there is no selection. If there is a selection, they delete the selection. They return `true` if the deletion was successful. Otherwise, they return `false`.

The read-only `length` property represents the length of the content. It changes as you modify the content. Practically, the `length` value can be very big. There is no direct way to restrict the number of characters in a text input control. I will cover an example of restricting the length of text shortly.

Cutting, Copying, and Pasting Text

The text input controls support cut, copy, and paste features programmatically, using the mouse and keyboard. To use these features using the mouse and keyboard, use the standard steps supported on your platform. Use the `cut()`, `copy()`, and `paste()` methods to use these features programmatically. The `cut()` method transfers the currently selected text to the clipboard and removes the current selection. The `copy()` method transfers the currently selected text to the clipboard without removing the current selection. The `paste()` method replaces the current selection with the content in the clipboard. If there is no selection, it inserts the clipboard content at the current caret position.

An Example

The program in Listing 12-26 demonstrates how the different properties of text input control change. It displays a window as shown in Figure 12-37. The program uses a `TextField`, which is a text input control, to display one line of text. Each property is displayed in a `Label` by binding the `text` properties to the properties of the `TextField`. After running the program, change the text in the name field, move the caret, and change the selection to see how the properties of the `TextField` change.

Listing 12-26. Using the Properties of Text Input Controls

```
// TextControlProperties.java
// ... find in the book's download area.
```

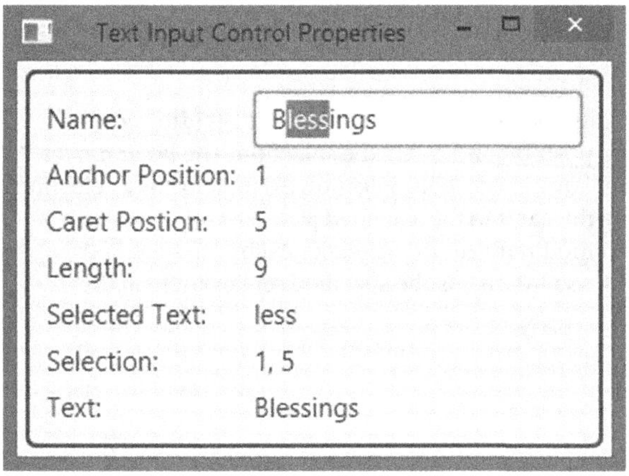

Figure 12-37. *Using properties of text input controls*

Styling *TextInputControl* with CSS

The TextInputControl class introduces a CSS pseudo-class named readonly, which applies when the control is not editable. It adds the following style properties:

- -fx-font
- -fx-text-fill
- -fx-prompt-text-fill
- -fx-highlight-fill
- -fx-highlight-text-fill
- -fx-display-caret

The -fx-font property is inherited from the parent by default. The value for the -fx-display-caret property could be true or false. When it is true, the caret is displayed when the control has focus. Otherwise, the caret is not displayed. Its default value is true. Most of the other properties affect background and text colors.

Understanding the *TextField* Control

TextField is a text input control. It inherits from the TextInputControl class. It lets the user enter a single line of plain text. If you need a control to enter multiline text, use TextArea instead. Newline and tab characters in the text are removed. Figure 12-38 shows a window with two TextFields having the text Layne and Estes.

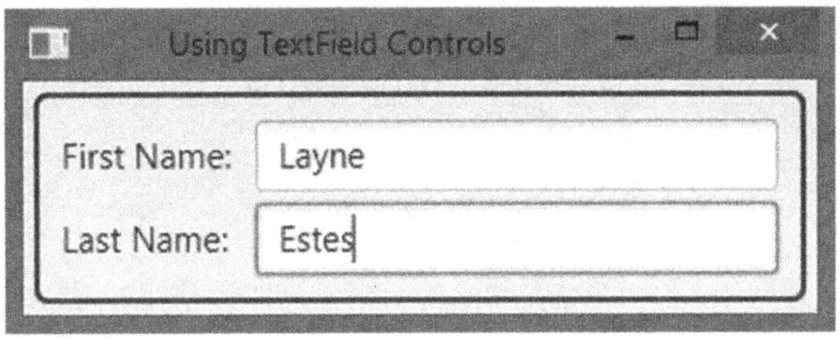

Figure 12-38. *A window with two* TextField *controls*

You can create a TextField with an empty initial text or with a specified initial text, as shown in the following code:

```
// Create a TextField with an empty string as initial text
TextField nameFld1 = new TextField();

// Create a TextField with "Layne Estes" as an initial text
TextField nameFld2 = new TextField("Layne Estes");
```

As I have already mentioned, the text property of the TextField stores the textual content. If you are interested in handling the changes in a TextField, you need to add a ChangeListener to its text property. Most of the time, you will be using its setText(String newText) method to set new text and the getText() method to get the text from it. TextField adds the following properties:

- alignment
- onAction
- prefColumnCount

The alignment property determines the alignment of the text within the TextField area when there is empty space. Its default value is CENTER_LEFT if the node orientation is LEFT_TO_RIGHT and CENTER_RIGHT if the node orientation is RIGHT_TO_LEFT. The onAction property is an ActionEvent handler, which is called when the Enter key is pressed in the TextField, as shown in the following code:

```
TextField nameFld = new TextField();
nameFld.setOnAction(e -> /* Your ActionEvent handler code...*/ );
```

The prefColumnCount property determines the width of the control. By default, its value is 12. A column is wide enough to display an uppercase letter W. If you set its value to 10, the TextField will be wide enough to display ten letter Ws, as shown in the following code:

```
// Set the preferred column count to 10
nameFld.setPrefColumnCount(10);
```

TextField provides a default context menu, as shown in Figure 12-39, that can be displayed by clicking the right mouse button. Menu items are enabled or disabled based on the context. You can replace the default context menu with a custom context menu. Currently, there is no way to customize the default context menu.

Undo

Redo

Cut

Copy

Paste

Delete

Select All

Figure 12-39. *The default context menu for* TextField

The following snippet of code sets a custom context menu for a TextField. It displays a menu item stating that the context menu is disabled. Selecting the menu item does nothing. You will need to add an ActionEvent handler to the menu items in the context menu to perform some action.

```
ContextMenu cm = new ContextMenu();
MenuItem dummyItem = new MenuItem("Context menu is disabled");
cm.getItems().add(dummyItem);

TextField nameFld = new TextField();
nameFld.setContextMenu(cm);
```

The program in Listing 12-27 shows how to use TextField controls. It displays two TextFields. It shows ActionEvent handlers, a custom context menu, and ChangeListeners added to TextFields.

Listing 12-27. Using the TextField Control

```
// TextFieldTest.java
// ... find in the book's download area.
```

Styling *TextField* with CSS

The default CSS style class name for a TextField is text-field. It adds an -fx-alignment property that is the alignment of its text within its content area. There is nothing special that needs to be said about styling TextField.

Understanding the *PasswordField* Control

PasswordField is a text input control. It inherits from TextField and it works much the same as TextField except it masks its text, that is, it does not display the actual characters entered. Rather, it displays an echo character for each character entered. The default echo character is a bullet. Figure 12-40 shows a window with a PasswordField.

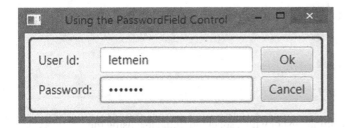

Figure 12-40. *A window using a PasswordField control*

The PasswordField class provides only one constructor, which is a no-args constructor. You can use the setText() and getText() methods to set and get, respectively, the actual text in a PasswordField, as in the following code. Typically, you do not set the password text. The user enters it.

```
// Create a PasswordField
PasswordField passwordFld = new PasswordField();
...
// Get the password text
String passStr = passwordFld.getText();
```

The PasswordField overrides the cut() and copy() methods of the TextInputControl class to make them no-op methods. That is, you cannot transfer the text in a PasswordField to the clipboard using the keyboard shortcuts or the context menu.

The default CSS style class name for a PasswordField is password-field. It has all of the style properties of TextField. It does not add any style properties.

Understanding the *TextArea* Control

TextArea is a text input control. It inherits from the TextInputControl class. It lets the user enter multiline plain text. If you need a control to enter a single line of plain text, use TextField instead. If you want to use rich text, use the HTMLEditor control. Unlike the TextField, newline and tab characters in the text are preserved. A newline character starts a new paragraph in a TextArea. Figure 12-41 shows a window with a TextField and a TextArea. The user can enter a multiline résumé in the TextArea.

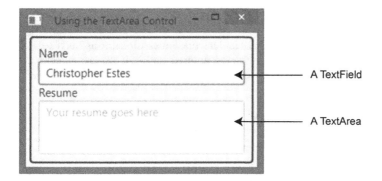

Figure 12-41. *A window with a TextArea control*

You can create a TextArea with an empty initial text or with a specified initial text using the following code:

```
// Create a TextArea with an empty string as its initial text
TextArea resume1 = new TextArea();

// Create a TextArea an initial text
TextArea resume2 = new TextArea("Years of Experience: 19");
```

As already discussed in the previous section, the text property of the TextArea stores the textual content. If you are interested in handling the changes in a TextArea, you need to add a ChangeListener to its text property. Most of the time, you will be using its setText(String newText) method to set new text and its getText() method to get the text from it.

TextArea adds the following properties:

- prefColumnCount
- prefRowCount
- scrollLeft
- scrollTop
- wrapText

The prefColumnCount property determines the width of the control. By default, its value is 32. A column is wide enough to display an uppercase letter W. If you set its value to 80, the TextArea will be wide enough to display 80 letter Ws. The following code accomplishes this:

```
// Set the preferred column count to 80
resume1.setPrefColumnCount(80);
```

The prefRowCount property determines the height of the control. By default, it is 10. The following code sets the row count to 20:

```
// Set the preferred row count to 20
resume.setPrefColumnCount(20);
```

If the text exceeds the number of columns and rows, the horizontal and vertical scroll panes are automatically displayed.

Like TextField, TextArea provides a default context menu. Please refer to the "Understanding Text Input Controls" section for more details on how to customize the default context menu.

The scrollLeft and scrollTop properties are the number of pixels that the text is scrolled to at the top and left. The following code sets it to 30px:

```
// Scroll the resume text by 30px to the top and 30 px to the left
resume.setScrollTop(30);
resume.setScrollLeft(30);
```

By default, TextArea starts a new line when it encounters a newline character in its text. A newline character also creates a new paragraph except for the first paragraph. By default, the text is not wrapped to the next line if it exceeds the width of the control. The wrapText property determines whether the text is wrapped to another line when its run exceeds the width of the control. By default, its value is false. The following code would set the default to true:

```
// Wrap the text if needed
resume.setWrapText(true);
```

The getParagraphs() method of the TextArea class returns an unmodifiable list of all paragraphs in its text. Each element in the list is a paragraph, which is an instance of CharSequence. The returned paragraph does not contain the newline characters. The following snippet of code prints the details, for example, paragraph number, and number of characters, for all paragraphs in the resume TextArea:

```
ObservableList<CharSequence> list = resume.getParagraphs();
int size = list.size();
System.out.println("Paragraph Count:" + size);
for(int i = 0; i < size; i++) {
        CharSequence cs = list.get(i);
        System.out.println("Paragraph #" + (i + 1) + ", Characters=" + cs.length());
        System.out.println(cs);
}
```

The program in Listing 12-28 shows how to use TextArea. It displays a window with a button to print the details of the text in the TextArea.

Listing 12-28. Using TextArea Controls

```
// TextAreaTest.java
// ... find in the book's download area.
```

Styling *TextArea* with CSS

The default CSS style class name for a TextArea is text-area. It does not add any CSS properties to the ones present in its ancestor TextInputControl. It contains scroll-pane and content substructures, which are a ScrollPane and a Region, respectively. The scroll-pane is the scroll pane that appears when its text exceeds its width or height. The content is the region that displays the text.

The following styles set the horizontal and vertical scrollbar policies to always, so the scrollbars should always appear in TextArea. Padding for the content area is set to 10px:

```
.text-area > .scroll-pane {
        -fx-hbar-policy: always;
        -fx-vbar-policy: always;
}

.text-area .content {
        -fx-padding: 10;
}
```

■ **Tip**   At the time of this writing, setting the scrollbar policy for the scroll-pane substructure is ignored by the TextArea.

Showing the Progress of a Task

When you have a long-running task, you need to provide a visual feedback to the user about the progress of the task for a better user experience. JavaFX offers two controls to show the progress:

- ProgressIndicator

- ProgressBar

They differ in the ways they display the progress. The ProgressBar class inherits from the ProgressIndicator class. ProgressIndicator displays the progress in a circular control, whereas ProgressBar uses a horizontal bar. The ProgressBar class does not add any properties or methods. It just uses a different shape for the control. Figure 12-42 shows a ProgressIndicator in indeterminate and determinate states. Figure 12-43 shows a ProgressBar in indeterminate and determinate states. Both figures use the same progress values in the four instances of the determinate states.

Indeterminate   **Determinate**

Figure 12-42. *A ProgressIndicator control in indeterminate and determinate states*

Indeterminate   **Determinate**

Figure 12-43. *A ProgressBar control in indeterminate and determinate states*

The current progress of a task may be determined or not. If the progress cannot be determined, it is said to be in an indeterminate state. If the progress is known, it is said to be in a determinate state. The ProgressIndicator class declares two properties:

- indeterminate
- progress

The indeterminate property is a read-only boolean property. If it returns true, it means it is not possible to determine the progress. A ProgressIndicator in this state is rendered with some kind of repeated animation. The progress property is a double property. Its value indicates the progress between 0% and 100%. A negative value indicates that the progress is indeterminate. A value between 0 and 1.0 indicates a determinate state with a progress between 0% and 100%. A value greater than 1.0 is treated as 1.0 (i.e., 100% progress).

Both classes provide default constructors that create controls in the indeterminate state, as shown in the following code:

```
// Create an indeterminate progress indicator and a progress bar
ProgressIndicator indeterminateInd = new ProgressIndicator();
ProgressBar indeterminateBar = new ProgressBar();
```

The other constructors that take the progress value create controls in the indeterminate or determinate state. If the progress value is negative, they create controls in the indeterminate state. Otherwise, they create controls in the determinate state, as shown in the following code:

```
// Create a determinate progress indicator with 10% progress
ProgressIndicator indeterminateInd = new ProgressIndicator(0.10);
```

```
// Create a determinate progress bar with 70% progress
ProgressBar indeterminateBar = new ProgressBar(0.70);
```

The program in Listing 12-29 shows how to use ProgressIndicator and ProgressBar controls. Clicking the Make Progress button increases the progress by 10%. Clicking the Complete Task button completes the indeterminate tasks by setting their progress to 100%. Typically, the progress properties of these controls are updated by a long-running task when the task progresses to a milestone. You used a button to update the progress property to keep the program logic simple.

Listing 12-29. Using the ProgressIndicator and ProgressBar Controls

```
// ProgressTest.java
// ... find in the book's download area.
```

Styling *ProgressIndicator* with CSS

The default CSS style class name for a ProgressIndicator is progress-indicator. ProgressIndicator supports determinate and indeterminate CSS pseudo-classes. The determinate pseudo-class applies when the indeterminate property is false. The indeterminate pseudo-class applies when the indeterminate property is true.

ProgressIndicator has a CSS style property named -fx-progress-color, which is the color of the progress. The following styles set the progress color to red for the indeterminate progress and blue for determinate progress:

```
.progress-indicator:indeterminate {
        -fx-progress-color: red;
}

.progress-indicator:determinate {
        -fx-progress-color: blue;
}
```

The ProgressIndicator contains four substructures:

- An indicator substructure, which is a StackPane
- A progress substructure, which is a StackPane
- A percentage substructure, which is a Text
- A tick substructure, which is a StackPane

You can style all substructures of a ProgressIndicator. Please refer to the modena.css file for sample code.

Styling *ProgressIndicator* and *ProgressBar* with CSS

The default CSS style class name for a ProgressBar is progress-bar. It supports the CSS style properties:

- -fx-indeterminate-bar-length
- -fx-indeterminate-bar-escape
- -fx-indeterminate-bar-flip
- -fx-indeterminate-bar-animation-time

All properties apply to the bar that shows the indeterminate progress. The default bar length is 60px. Use the -fx-indeterminate-bar-length property to specify a different bar length.

When the -fx-indeterminate-bar-escape property is true, the bar starting edge starts at the starting edge of the track, and the bar trailing edge ends at the ending edge of the track. That is, the bar is displayed beyond the track length. When this property is false, the bar moves within the track length. The default value is true.

The -fx-indeterminate-bar-flip property indicates whether the bar moves only in one direction or both. The default value is true, which means the bar moves in both directions by flipping its direction at the end of each edge.

The -fx-indeterminate-bar-animation-time property is the time in seconds that the bar should take to go from one edge to the other. The default value is 2.

The ProgressBar contains two substructures:

- A track substructure, which is a StackPane
- A bar substructure, which is a region

The following styles modify the background color and radius of the bar and track of the `ProgressBar` control to give it a look as shown in Figure 12-44:

```
.progress-bar .track  {
       -fx-background-color: lightgray;
       -fx-background-radius: 5;
}

.progress-bar .bar  {
       -fx-background-color: blue;
       -fx-background-radius: 5;
}
```

Figure 12-44. *Customizing the bar and track of the* `ProgressBar` *control*

Understanding the *TitledPane* Control

`TitledPane` is a labeled control. The `TitledPane` class inherits from the `Labeled` class. A labeled control can have text and a graphic, so it can have a `TitledPane`. `TitledPane` displays the text as its title. The graphic is shown in the title bar.

Besides text and a graphic, a `TitledPane` has content, which is a `Node`. Typically, a group of controls is placed in a container, and the container is added as the content for the `TitledPane`. `TitledPane` can be in a collapsed or expanded state. In the collapsed state, it displays only the title bar and hides the content. In the expanded state, it displays the title bar and the content. In its title bar, it displays an arrow that indicates whether it is expanded or collapsed. Clicking anywhere in the title bar expands or collapses the content. Figure 12-45 shows a `TitledPane` in both states along with all of its parts.

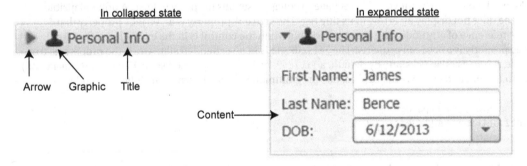

Figure 12-45. *A* `TitledPane` *in the collapsed and expanded states*

Use the default constructor to create a TitledPane without a title and content. You can set them later using the setText() and setContent() methods. Alternatively, you can provide the title and content as arguments to its constructor, using the following code:

```
// Create a TitledPane and set its title and content
TitledPane infoPane1 = new TitledPane();
infoPane1.setText("Personal Info");
infoPane1.setContent(new Label("Here goes the content."));

// Create a TitledPane with a title and content
TitledPane infoPane2 = new TitledPane("Personal Info", new Label("Content"));
```

You can add a graphic to a TitledPane using the setGraphic() method, which is declared in the Labeled class, as shown in the following code:

```
String imageStr = "resources/picture/privacy_icon.png";
URL imageUrl = getClass().getClassLoader().getResource(imageStr);
Image img = new Image(imageUrl.toExternalForm());
ImageView imgView = new ImageView(img);
infoPane2.setGraphic(imgView);
```

The TitledPane class declares four properties:

- animated
- collapsible
- content
- expanded

The animated property is a boolean property that indicates whether collapse and expand actions are animated. By default, it is true and those actions are animated. The collapsible property is a boolean property that indicates whether the TitledPane can collapse. By default, it is set to true and the TitledPane can collapse. If you do not want your TitledPane to collapse, set this property to false. A noncollapsible TitledPane does not display an arrow in its title bar. The content property is an Object property that stores the reference of any node. The content is visible when the control is in the expanded state. The expanded property is a boolean property. The TitledPane is in an expanded state when the property is true. Otherwise, it is in a collapsed state. By default, a TitledPane is in an expanded state. Use the setExpanded() method to expand and collapse the TitledPane programmatically, as shown in the following code:

```
// Set the state to expanded
infoPane2.setExpanded(true);
```

■ **Tip** Add a ChangeListener to its expanded property if you are interested in processing the expanded and collapsed events for a TitledPane.

Typically, TitledPane controls are used in a group in an Accordion control, which displays only one TitledPane from the group in the expanded state at a time to save space. You can also use a stand-alone TitledPane if you want to show controls in groups.

■ **Tip**   Recall that the height of a `TitledPane` changes as it expands and collapses. Do not set its minimum, preferred, and maximum heights in your code. Otherwise, it may result in an unspecified behavior.

The program in Listing 12-30 shows how to use the `TitledPane` control. It displays a window with a TitledPane, which lets the user enter the first name, last name, and birth date of a person.

Listing 12-30. Using the `TitledPane` Control

```
// TitledPaneTest.java
// ... find in the book's download area.
```

Styling *TitledPane* with CSS

The default CSS style class name for a `TitledPane` is `titled-pane`. TitledPane adds two style properties of boolean type:

- `-fx-animated`
- `-fx-collapsible`

The default values for both properties are true. The `-fx-animated` property indicates whether the expanding and collapsing actions are animated. The `-fx-collapsible` property indicates whether the control can be collapsed.

TitledPane supports two CSS pseudo-classes:

- `collapsed`
- `expanded`

The `collapsed` pseudo-class applies when the control is collapsed, and the `expanded` pseudo-class applies when it is expanded.

TitledPane contains two substructures:

- `title`
- `Content`

The `title` substructure is a StackPane that contains the content of the title bar. The `title` substructure contains text and arrow-button substructures. The text substructure is a `Label`, and it holds the title text and the graphic. The arrow-button substructure is a StackPane that contains an arrow substructure, which is also a StackPane. The arrow substructure is an indicator that shows whether the control is in an expanded or collapsed state. The content substructure is a StackPane that contains the content of the control.

Let's look at an example of the effects of applying the four different styles to a `TitledPane` control, as presented in the following code:

```
/* #1 */
.titled-pane > .title  {
        -fx-background-color: lightgray;
        -fx-alignment: center-right;
}
```

437

```
/* #2 */
.titled-pane > .title > .text {
        -fx-font-size: 14px;
        -fx-underline: true;
}

/* #3 */
.titled-pane > .title > .arrow-button > .arrow {
        -fx-background-color: blue;
}

/* #4 */
.titled-pane > .content {
        -fx-background-color: burlywood;
        -fx-padding: 10;
}
```

Style #1 sets the background color of the title to light gray and places the graphic and title at the center right in the title bar. Style #2 changes the font size of the title text to 14px and underlines it. Setting the text color of the title using the -fx-text-fill property does not work at the time of this writing, and setting the -fx-text-fill property on the TitledPane itself affects the text color of the content as well. Style #3 sets the background color of the arrow to blue. Style #4 sets the background color and padding of the content region. Figure 12-46 shows the same window as shown in Figure 12-45 after applying the preceding styles.

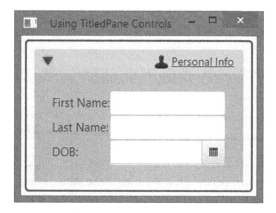

Figure 12-46. *Effects of applying styles to a* TitledPane

Understanding the *Accordion* Control

Accordion is a simple control. It displays a group of TitledPane controls where only one of them is in the expanded state at a time. Figure 12-47 shows a window with an Accordion, which contains three TitledPanes. The General TitledPane is expanded. The Address and Phone TitledPanes are collapsed.

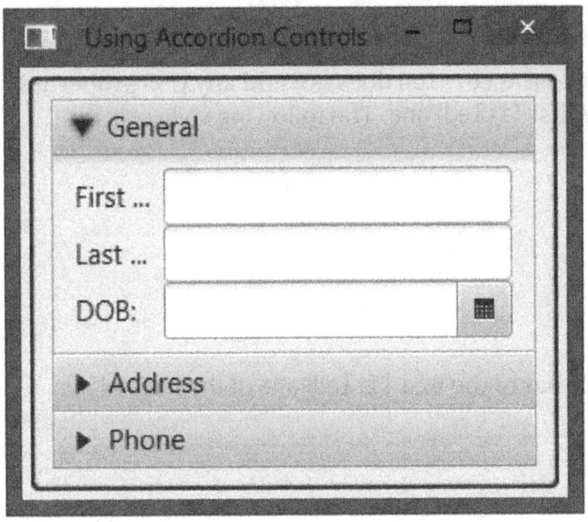

Figure 12-47. An Accordion with three TitledPanes

The Accordion class contains only one constructor (a no-args constructor) to create its object:

```
// Create an Accordian
Accordion root = new Accordion();
```

Accordion stores the list of its TitledPane controls in an ObservableList<TitledPane>. The getPanes() method returns the list of the TitledPane. Use the list to add or remove any TitledPane to the Accordion, as shown in the following code:

```
TitledPane generalPane = new TitledPane();
TitledPane addressPane = new TitledPane();
TitledPane phonePane = new TitledPane();
...
Accordion root = new Accordion();
root.getPanes().addAll(generalPane, addressPane, phonePane);
```

The Accordion class contains an expandedPane property, which stores the reference of the currently expanded TitledPane. By default, an Accordion displays all of its TitledPanes in a collapsed state, and this property is set to null. Click the title bar of a TitledPane or use the setExpandedPane() method to expand a TitledPane. Add a ChangeListener to this property if you are interested in when the expanded TitledPane changes. The program in Listing 12-31 shows how to create and populate an Accordion.

Listing 12-31. Using the Accordion Control

```
// AccordionTest.java
// ... find in the book's download area.
```

Styling *Accordion* with CSS

The default CSS style class name for an Accordion is accordion. Accordion does not add any CSS properties. It contains a first-titled-pane substructure, which is the first TitledPane. The following style sets the background color and insets of the title bar of all TitledPanes:

```
.accordion > .titled-pane > .title {
    -fx-background-color: burlywood;
        -fx-background-insets: 1;
}
```

The following style sets the background color of the title bar of the first TitledPane of the Accordion:

```
.accordion > .first-titled-pane > .title {
    -fx-background-color: derive(red, 80%);
}
```

Understanding the *Pagination* Control

Pagination is used to display a large single content by dividing sections of it into smaller chunks called pages, for example, the results of a search. Figure 12-48 shows a Pagination control. A Pagination control has a page count, which is the number of pages in it. If the number of pages is not known, the page count may be indeterminate. Each page has an index, which starts at zero.

Content for page 3

```
◀  1  2  3  4  5  ▶
       3/5
```

Figure 12-48. A Pagination control

A Pagination control is divided into two areas:

- Content area
- Navigation area

The content area displays the content of the current page. The navigation area contains parts to allow the user to navigate from one page to another. You can navigate between pages sequentially or randomly. The parts of a Pagination control are shown in Figure 12-49.

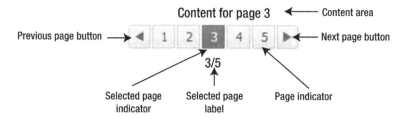

Figure 12-49. Parts of a Pagination control

The previous and next page arrow buttons let the user navigate to the previous and next pages, respectively. The previous page button is disabled when you are on the first page. The next page button is disabled when you are on the last page. Page indicators also let you navigate to a specific page by showing all of the page numbers. By default, page indicators use a tool tip to show the page number, which you have the option to disable using a CSS property. The selected page indicator shows the current page. The selected page label shows the current page selection details.

The Pagination class provides several constructors. They configure the control differently. The default constructor creates a control with an indeterminate page count and zero as the index for the selected page, as in the following code:

```
// Indeterminate page count and first page selected
Pagination pagination1 = new Pagination();
```

When the page count is indeterminate, the page indicator label displays x/..., where x is the current page index plus 1.

You use another constructor to specify a page count, as in the following code:

```
// 5 as the page count and first page selected
Pagination pagination2 = new Pagination(5);
```

You can use yet another constructor to specify the page count and the selected page index, as in the following code:

```
// 5 as the page count and second page selected (page index starts at 0)
Pagination pagination3 = new Pagination(5, 1);
```

The Pagination class declares an INDETERMINATE constant that can be used to specify an indeterminate page count, as in the following code:

```
// Indeterminate page count and second page selected
Pagination pagination4 = new Pagination(Pagination.INDETERMINATE, 1);
```

The Pagination class contains the following properties:

- currentPageIndex
- maxPageIndicatorCount
- pageCount
- pageFactory

The currentPageIndex is an integer property. Its value is the page index of the page to display. The default value is zero. You can specify its value using one of the constructors or using the setCurrentPageIndex() method. If you set its value to less than zero, the first page index, which is zero, is set as its value. If you set its value to greater than the page count minus 1, its value is set to page count minus 1. If you want to know when a new page is displayed, add a ChangeListener to the currentPageIndex property.

The maxPageIndicatorCount is an integer property. It sets the maximum number of page indicators to display. It defaults to ten. Its value remains unchanged if it is set beyond the page count range. If its value is set too high, the value is reduced so that the number of page indicators fits the control. You can set its value using the setMaxPageIndicatorCount() method.

The pageCount is an integer property. It is the number of pages in the Pagination control. Its value must be greater than or equal to one. It defaults to indeterminate. Its value can be set in the constructors or using the setPageCount() method.

The pageFactory is the most important property. It is an object property of the Callback<Integer, Node> type. It is used to generate pages. When a page needs to be displayed, the control calls the call() method of the Callback object passing the page index. The call() method returns a node that is the content of the page. The following snippet of code creates and sets a page factory for a Pagination control. The page factory returns a Label:

```
// Create a Pagination with an indeterminate page count
Pagination pagination = new Pagination();

// Create a page factory that returns a Label
Callback<Integer, Node> factory =
    pageIndex -> new Label("Content for page " + (pageIndex + 1));

// Set the page factory
pagination.setPageFactory(factory);
```

■ **Tip**   The call() method of the page factory should return null if a page index does not exist. The current page does not change when the call() method returns null.

The program in Listing 12-32 shows how to use a Pagination control. It sets the page count to five. The page factory returns a Label with text that shows the page number. It will display a window with a Pagination control similar to the one shown in Figure 12-48.

Listing 12-32. Using the Pagination Control

```
// PaginationTest.java
// ... find in the book's download area.
```

The page indicators may be numeric buttons or bullet buttons. Numeric buttons are used by default. The Pagination class contains a String constant named STYLE_CLASS_BULLET, which is the style class for the control if you want to use bullet buttons. The following snippet of code creates a Pagination control and sets its style class to use bullet buttons as page indicators. Figure 12-50 shows a Pagination control with bullet buttons as page indicators.

```
Pagination pagination = new Pagination(5);

// Use bullet page indicators
pagination.getStyleClass().add(Pagination.STYLE_CLASS_BULLET);
```

Content for page 3

3/5

Figure 12-50. *A Pagination control using bullet buttons as page indicators*

Styling *Pagination* with CSS

The default CSS style class name for a `Pagination` control is `pagination`. `Pagination` adds several CSS properties:

- `-fx-max-page-indicator-count`
- `-fx-arrows-visible`
- `-fx-tooltip-visible`
- `-fx-page-information-visible`
- `-fx-page-information-alignment`

The `-fx-max-page-indicator-count` property specifies the maximum number of page indicators to display. The default value is ten. The `-fx-arrows-visible` property specifies whether the previous and next page buttons are visible. The default value is true. The `-fx-tooltip-visible` property specifies whether a tool tip is displayed when the mouse hovers over a page indicator. The default value is true. The `-fx-page-information-visible` specifies whether the selected page label is visible. The default value is true. The `-fx-page-information-alignment` specifies the location of the selected page label relative to the page indicators. The possible values are top, right, bottom, and left. The default value is bottom, which displays the selected page indicator below the page indicators.

The `Pagination` control has two substructures of the `StackPane` type:

- `page`
- `pagination-control`

The page substructure represents the content area. The `pagination-control` substructure represents the navigation area, and it has the following substructures:

- `left-arrow-button`
- `right-arrow-Button`
- `bullet-button`
- `number-button`
- `page-information`

The `left-arrow-button` and `right-arrow-button` substructures are of the `Button` type. They represent the previous and next page buttons, respectively. The `left-arrow-button` substructure has a `left-arrow` substructure, which is a `StackPane`, and it represents the arrow in the previous page button. The `right-arrow-button` substructure has a `right-arrow` substructure, which is a `StackPane`, and it represents the arrow in the next page button. The `bullet-button` and `number-button` are of the `ToggleButton` type, and they represent the page indicators. The `page-information` substructure is a `Label` that holds the selected page information. The `pagination-control` substructure holds the previous and next page buttons and the page indicators in a substructure called `control-box`, which is an `HBox`.

The following styles make the selected page label invisible, set the page background to light gray, and draw a border around the previous, next, and page indicator buttons. Please refer to the `modena.css` file for more details on how to style a `Pagination` control.

```
.pagination  {
        -fx-page-information-visible: false;
}
```

```
.pagination > .page {
    -fx-background-color: lightgray;
}

.pagination  >  .pagination-control > .control-box {
    -fx-padding: 2;
    -fx-border-style: dashed;
    -fx-border-width: 1;
    -fx-border-radius: 5;
    -fx-border-color: blue;
}
```

Understanding the Tool Tip Control

A tool tip is a pop-up control used to show additional information about a node. It is displayed when a mouse pointer hovers over the node. There is a small delay between when the mouse pointer hovers over a node and when the tool tip for the node is shown. The tool tip is hidden after a small period. It is also hidden when the mouse pointer leaves the control. You should not design a GUI application where the user depends on seeing tool tips for controls, as they may not be shown at all if the mouse pointer never hovers over the controls. Figure 12-51 shows a window with a tool tip, which displays Saves the data text.

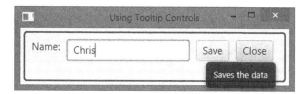

Figure 12-51. *A window showing a tool tip*

A tool tip is represented by an instance of the Tooltip class, which inherits from the PopupControl class. A tool tip can have text and a graphic. You can create a tool tip using its default constructor, which has no text and no graphic. You can also create a tool tip with text using the other constructor, as in the following code:

```
// Create a Tooltip with No text and no graphic
Tooltip tooltip1 = new Tooltip();

// Create a Tooltip with text
Tooltip tooltip2 = new Tooltip("Closes the window");
```

A tool tip needs to be installed for a node using the install() static method of the Tooltip class. Use the uninstall() static method to uninstall a tool tip for a node:

```
Button saveBtn = new Button("Save");
Tooltip tooltip = new Tooltip("Saves the data");

// Install a tooltip
Tooltip.install(saveBtn, tooltip);
...
```

```
// Uninstall the tooltip
Tooltip.uninstall(saveBtn, tooltip);
```

Tool tips are frequently used for UI controls. Therefore, installing tool tips for controls has been made easier. The Control class contains a tooltip property, which is an object property of the Tooltip type. You can use the setTooltip() method of the Control class to set a Tooltip for controls. If a node is not a control, for example, a Circle node, you will need to use the install() method to set a tool tip as shown earlier. The following snippet of code shows how to use the tooltip property for a button:

```
Button saveBtn = new Button("Save");

// Install a tooltip
saveBtn.setTooltip(new Tooltip("Saves the data"));
...
// Uninstall the tooltip
saveBtn.setTooltip(null);
```

■ **Tip** A tool tip can be shared among multiple nodes. A tool tip uses a Label control to display its text and graphic. Internally, all content-related properties set on a tool tip are delegated to the Label control.

The Tooltip class contains several properties:

- text
- graphic
- contentDisplay
- textAlignment
- textOverrun
- wrapText
- graphicTextGap
- font
- activated
- hideDelay
- showDelay
- showDuration

The text property is a String property, which is the text to be displayed in the tool tip. The graphic property is an object property of the Node type. It is an icon for the tool tip. The contentDisplay property is an object property of the ContentDisplay enum type. It specifies the position of the graphic relative to the text. The possible value is one of the constants in the ContentDisplay enum: TOP, RIGHT, BOTTOM, LEFT, CENTER, TEXT_ONLY, and GRAPHIC_ONLY. The default value is LEFT, which places the graphic left to the text.

The following snippet of code uses an icon for a tool tip and places it above the text. The icon is just a Label with X as its text. Figure 12-52 shows how the tool tip looks.

```
// Create and configure the Tooltip
Tooltip closeBtnTip = new Tooltip("Closes the window");
closeBtnTip.setStyle("-fx-background-color: yellow; -fx-text-fill: black;");

// Display the icon above the text
closeBtnTip.setContentDisplay(ContentDisplay.TOP);

Label closeTipIcon = new Label("X");
closeTipIcon.setStyle("-fx-text-fill: red;");
closeBtnTip.setGraphic(closeTipIcon);

// Create a Button and set its Tooltip
Button closeBtn = new Button("Close");
closeBtn.setTooltip(closeBtnTip);
```

Figure 12-52. *Using an icon and placing it at the top of the text in a tool tip*

The textAlignment property is an object property of the TextAlignment enum type. It specifies the text alignment when the text spans multiple lines. The possible value is one of the constants in the TextAlignment enum: LEFT, RIGHT, CENTER, and JUSTIFY.

The textOverrun property is an object property of the OverrunStyle enum type. It specifies the behavior to use when there is not enough space in the tool tip to display the entire text. The default behavior is to use an ellipsis.

The wrapText is a boolean property. It specifies whether text should be wrapped onto another line if its run exceeds the width of the tool tip. The default value is false.

The graphicTextGap property is a double property that specifies the space between the text and graphic in pixel. The default value is four. The font property is an object property of the Font type. It specifies the default font to use for the text. The activated property is a read-only boolean property. It is true when the tool tip is activated. Otherwise, it is false. A tool tip is activated when the mouse moves over a control, and it is shown after it is activated.

The program in Listing 12-33 shows how to create, configure, and set tool tips for controls. After you run the application, place the mouse pointer over the name field, Save button, and Close button. After a short time, their tool tips will be displayed. The tool tip for the Close button looks different from that of the Save button. It uses an icon and different background and text colors.

Listing 12-33. Using the Tooltip Control

```
// TooltipTest.java
// ... find in the book's download area.
```

Styling *Tooltip* with CSS

The default CSS style class name for a Tooltip control is tooltip. Tooltip adds several CSS properties:

- -fx-text-alignment
- -fx-text-overrun
- -fx-wrap-text
- -fx-graphic
- -fx-content-display
- -fx-graphic-text-gap
- -fx-font

All of the CSS properties correspond to the content-related properties in the Tooltip class. Please refer to the previous section for the description of all these properties. The following code sets the background color, text color, and the wrap text properties for Tooltip:

```
.tooltip {
        -fx-background-color: yellow;
        -fx-text-fill: black;
        -fx-wrap-text: true;
}
```

Providing Scrolling Features in Controls

JavaFX provides two controls named ScrollBar and ScrollPane that provide scrolling features to other controls. Typically, these controls are not used alone. They are used to support scrolling in other controls.

Understanding the *ScrollBar* Control

ScrollBar is a basic control that does not provide the scrolling feature by itself. It is represented as a horizontal or vertical bar that lets users choose a value from a range of values. Figure 12-53 shows a horizontal and a vertical scrollbar.

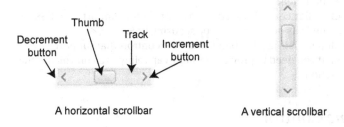

A horizontal scrollbar   A vertical scrollbar

Figure 12-53. Horizontal and vertical scrollbars with their parts

A ScrollBar control consists of four parts:

- An increment button to increase the value
- A decrement button to decrease the value
- A thumb (or knob) to show the current value
- A track where the thumb moves

The increment and decrement buttons in a vertical ScrollBar are on the bottom and top, respectively.

The ScrollBar class provides a default constructor that creates a horizontal scrollbar. You can set its orientation to vertical using the setOrientation() method:

```
// Create a horizontal scroll bar
ScrollBar hsb = new ScrollBar();

// Create a vertical scroll bar
ScrollBar vsb = new ScrollBar();
vsb.setOrientation(Orientation.VERTICAL);
```

The min and max properties represent the range of its value. Its value property is the current value. The default values for min, max, and value properties are 0, 100, and 0, respectively. If you are interested in knowing when the value property changes, you need to add a ChangeListener to it. The following code would set the value properties to 0, 200, and 150:

```
ScrollBar hsb = new ScrollBar();
hsb.setMin(0);
hsb.setMax(200);
hsb.setValue(150);
```

The current value of a scrollbar may be changed in three different ways:

- Programmatically using the setValue(), increment(), and decrement() methods
- By the user dragging the thumb on the track
- By the user clicking the increment and decrement buttons

The blockIncrement and unitIncrement properties specify the amount to adjust the current value when the user clicks the track and the increment or decrement buttons, respectively. Typically, the block increment is set to a larger value than the unit increment.

The default CSS style class name for a ScrollBar control is scroll-bar. ScrollBar supports two CSS pseudo-classes: horizontal and vertical. Some of its properties can be set using CSS.

ScrollBar is rarely used directly by developers. It is used to build complete controls that support scrolling, for example, the ScrollPane control. If you need to provide scrolling capability to a control, use the ScrollPane, which I will discuss in the next section.

Understanding the *ScrollPane* Control

A ScrollPane provides a scrollable view of a node. A ScrollPane consists of a horizontal ScrollBar, a vertical ScrollBar, and a content node. The node for which the ScrollPane provides scrolling is the content node. If you want to provide a scrollable view of multiple nodes, add them to a layout pane, for example, a

GridPane, and then add the layout pane to the ScrollPane as the content node. ScrollPane uses a scroll policy to specify when to show a specific scrollbar. The area through which the content is visible is known as *viewport*. Figure 12-54 shows a ScrollPane with a Label as its content node.

Figure 12-54. *A ScrollPane with a Label as its content node*

■ **Tip** Some of the commonly used controls that need scrolling capability, for example, a TextArea, provide a built-in ScrollPane, which is part of such controls.

You can use the constructors of the ScrollPane class to create an empty ScrollPane or a ScrollPane with a content node, as shown in the following code. You can set the content node later using the setContent() method.

```
Label poemLbl1 = ...
Label poemLbl2 = ...

// Create an empty ScrollPane
ScrollPane sPane1 = new ScrollPane();

// Set the content node for the ScrollPane
sPane1.setContent(poemLbl1);

// Create a ScrollPane with a content node
ScrollPane sPane2 = new ScrollPane(poemLbl2);
```

■ **Tip** The ScrollPane provides the scrolling for its content based on the layout bounds of the content. If the content uses effects or transformation, for example, scaling, you need to wrap the content in a Group and add the Group to the ScrollPane to get proper scrolling.

The ScrollPane class contains several properties, most of which are commonly not used by developers:

- content
- pannable
- fitToHeight
- fitToWidth
- hbarPolicy
- vbarPolicy

- hmin
- hmax
- hvalue
- vmin
- vmax
- vvalue
- prefViewportHeight
- prefViewportWidth
- viewportBounds

The content property is an object property of the Node type, and it specifies the content node. You can scroll the content using the scrollbars or by panning. If you use panning, you need to drag the mouse while left, right, or both buttons are pressed to scroll the content. By default, a ScrollPane is not pannable, and you need to use the scrollbars to scroll through the content. The pannable property is a boolean property that specifies whether the ScrollPane is pannable. Use the setPannable(true) method to make a ScrollPane pannable.

The fitToHeight and fitToWidth properties specify whether the content node is resized to match the height and width of the viewport, respectively. By default, they are false. These properties are ignored if the content node is not resizable. Figure 12-55 shows the same ScrollPane as shown in Figure 12-54 with its fitToHeight and fitToWidth properties set to true. Notice that the Label content node has been resized to fit into the viewport.

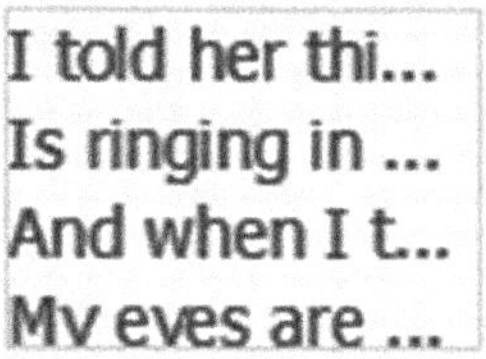

I told her thi...
Is ringing in ...
And when I t...
My eyes are ...

Figure 12-55. *A ScrollPane with fitToHeight and fitToWidth properties set to true*

The hbarPolicy and vbarPolicy properties are object properties of the ScrollPane.ScrollBarPolicy enum type. They specify when to show the horizontal and vertical scrollbars. The possible values are ALWAYS, AS_NEEDED, and NEVER. When the policy is set to ALWAYS, the scrollbar is shown all the time. When the policy is set to AS_NEEDED, the scrollbar is shown when required based on the size of the content. When the policy is set to NEVER, the scrollbar is never shown.

The hmin, hmax, and hvalue properties specify the min, max, and value properties of the horizontal scrollbar, respectively. The vmin, vmax, and vvalue properties specify the min, max, and value properties of the vertical scrollbar, respectively. Typically, you do not set these properties. They change based on the content and as the user scrolls through the content.

The prefViewportHeight and prefViewportWidth are the preferred height and width, respectively, of the viewport that is available to the content node.

The viewportBounds is an object property of the Bounds type. It is the actual bounds of the viewport. The program in Listing 12-34 shows how to use a ScrollPane. It sets a Label with four lines of text as its content. It also makes the ScrollPane pannable. That is, you can drag the mouse clicking its button to scroll through the text.

Listing 12-34. Using ScrollPane

```
// ScrollPaneTest.java
// ... find in the book's download area.
```

The default CSS style class name for a ScrollPane control is scroll-pane. Please refer to the modena.css file for sample styles and the online *JavaFX CSS Reference Guide* for the complete list of CSS properties and pseudo-classes supported by the ScrollPane.

Keeping Things Separate

Sometimes, you may want to place logically related controls side by side horizontally or vertically. For better appearance, controls are grouped using different types of separators. Sometimes, using a border suffices, but sometimes you will use the TitledPane controls. The Separator and SplitPane controls are solely meant for visually separating two controls or two groups of controls.

Understanding the *Separator* Control

A Separator is a horizontal or vertical line that separates two groups of controls. Typically, they are used in menus or combo boxes. Figure 12-56 shows menu items of a restaurant separated by horizontal and vertical separators.

Breakfasts | **Snacks**
Hash Brown | Fries
Hot Cake | Apple

Beverages
Coffee
Tea

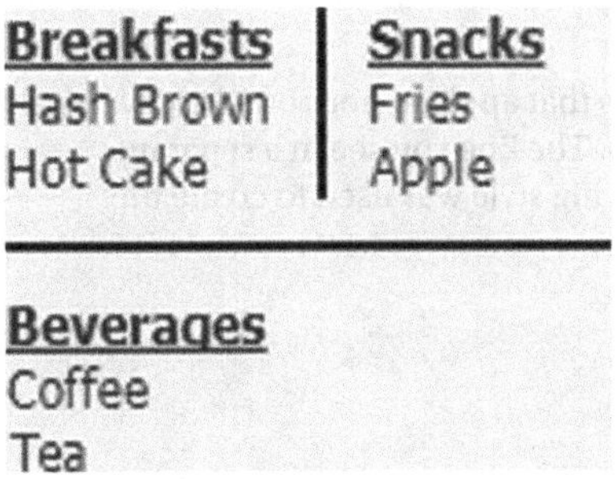

Figure 12-56. Using horizontal and vertical separators

The default constructor creates a horizontal Separator. To create a vertical Separator, you can specify a vertical orientation in the constructor or use the setOrientation() method, as shown in the following code:

```
// Create a horizontal separator
Separator separator1 = new Separator();

// Change the orientation to vertical
separator1.setOrientation(Orientation.VERTICAL);

// Create a vertical separator
Separator separator2 = new Separator(Orientation.VERTICAL);
```

A separator resizes itself to fill the space allocated to it. A horizontal Separator resizes horizontally, and a vertical Separator resizes vertically. Internally, a Separator is a Region. You can change its color and thickness using a CSS.

The Separator class contains three properties:

- orientation
- halignment
- valignment

The orientation property specifies the orientation of the control. The possible values are one of the two constants of the Orientation enum: HORIZONTAL and VERTICAL. The halignment property specifies the horizontal alignment of the separator line within the width of a vertical separator. This property is ignored for a horizontal separator. The possible values are one of the constants of the HPos enum: LEFT, CENTER, and RIGHT. The default value is CENTER. The valignment property specifies the vertical alignment of the separator line within the height of a horizontal separator. This property is ignored for a vertical separator. The possible values are one of the constants of the VPos enum: BASELINE, TOP, CENTER, and BOTTOM. The default value is CENTER.

Styling *Separator* with CSS

The default CSS style class name for a Separator control is separator. Separator contains CSS properties, which correspond to its Java properties:

- -fx-orientation
- -fx-halignment
- -fx-valignment

Separator supports horizontal and vertical CSS pseudo-classes that apply to horizontal and vertical separators, respectively. It contains a line substructure that is a Region. The line you see in a separator is created by specifying the border for the line substructure. The following style was used to create the separators in Figure 12-56:

```
.separator > .line {
    -fx-border-style: solid;
    -fx-border-width: 1;
}
```

You can use an image as a separator. Set the appropriate width or height of the separator and use an image as the background image. The following code assumes that the separator.jpg image file exists in the same directory as the CSS file containing the style. The styles set the preferred height of the horizontal separator and the preferred width of the vertical separator to 10px:

```
.separator {
        -fx-background-image: url("separator.jpg");
        -fx-background-repeat: repeat;
        -fx-background-position: center;
        -fx-background-size: cover;
}

.separator:horizontal {
        -fx-pref-height: 10;
}
```

```
.separator:vertical {
        -fx-pref-width: 10;
}
```

Understanding the *SplitPane* Control

SplitPane arranges multiple nodes by placing them horizontally or vertically separated by a divider. The divider can be dragged by the user, so the node on one side of the divider expands, and the node on the other side shrinks by the same amount. Typically, each node in a SplitPane is a layout pane containing some controls. However, you can use any node, for example, a Button. If you have used Windows Explorer, you are already familiar with using a SplitPane. In a Windows Explorer, the divider separates the tree view and the list view. Using the divider, you can resize the width of the tree view, and the width of the list view resizes with the equal amount in the opposite direction. A resizable HTML frameset works similar to a SplitPane. Figure 12-57 shows a window with a horizontal SplitPane. The SplitPane contains two VBox layout panes; each of them contains a Label and a TextArea. Figure 12-57 shows the divider dragged to the right, so the left VBox gets more width than the right one.

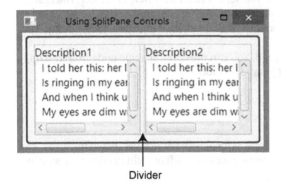

Divider

Figure 12-57. *A window with a horizontal* SplitPane

You can create a SplitPane using the default constructor of the SplitPane class:

```
SplitPane sp = new SplitPane();
```

The getItems() method of the SplitPane class returns the ObservableList<Node> that stores the list of nodes in a SplitPane. Add all your nodes to this list, as shown in the following code:

```
// Create panes
GridPane leftPane = new GridPane();
GridPane centerPane = new GridPane();
GridPane rightPane = new GridPane();

/* Populate the left, center, and right panes with controls here */

// Add panels to the a SplitPane
SplitPane sp = new SplitPane();
sp.getItems().addAll(leftPane, centerPane, rightPane);
```

By default, SplitPane places its nodes horizontally. Its orientation property can be used to specify the orientation:

```
// Place nodes vertically
sp.setOrientation(Orientation.VERTICAL);
```

A divider can be moved between the leftmost and rightmost edges or topmost and bottommost edges provided it does not overlap any other divider. The divider position can be set between 0 and 1. The position 0 means topmost or leftmost. The position 1 means bottommost or rightmost. By default, a divider is placed in the middle with its position set to 0.5. Use either of the following two methods to set the position of a divider:

- setDividerPositions(double... positions)
- setDividerPosition(int dividerIndex, double position)

The setDividerPositions() method takes the positions of multiple dividers. You must provide positions for all dividers from starting up to the one you want to set the positions.

If you want to set the position for a specific divider, use the setDividerPosition() method. The first divider has the index 0. Positions passed in for an index outside the range are ignored.

The getDividerPositions() method returns the positions of all dividers. It returns a double array. The index of dividers matches the index of the array elements.

By default, SplitPane resizes its nodes when it is resized. You can prevent a specific node from resizing with the SplitPane using the setResizableWithParent() static method:

```
// Make node1 non-resizable
SplitPane.setResizableWithParent(node1, false);
```

The program in Listing 12-35 shows how to use SplitPane. It displays a window as shown in Figure 12-57. Run the program and use the mouse to drag the divider to the left or right to adjust the spacing for the left and right nodes.

Listing 12-35. Using SplitPane Controls

```
// SplitPaneTest.java
// ... find in the book's download area.
```

Styling *SplitPane* with CSS

The default CSS style class name for a SplitPane control is split-pane. SplitPane contains -fx-orientation CSS properties, which determine its orientation. The possible values are horizontal and vertical.

SplitPane supports horizontal and vertical CSS pseudo-classes that apply to horizontal and vertical SplitPanes, respectively. The divider is a split-pane-divider substructure of the SplitPane, which is a StackPane. The following code sets a blue background color for dividers, 5px preferred width for dividers in a horizontal SplitPane, and 5px preferred height for dividers in a vertical SplitPane:

```
.split-pane > .split-pane-divider {
    -fx-background-color: blue;
}
```

```
.split-pane:horizontal > .split-pane-divider {
    -fx-pref-width: 5;
}

.split-pane:vertical > .split-pane-divider {
    -fx-pref-height: 5;
}
```

The split-pane-divider substructure contains a grabber substructure, which is a StackPane. Its CSS style class name is horizontal-grabber for a horizontal SplitPane and vertical-grabber for a vertical SplitPane. The grabber is shown in the middle of the divider.

Understanding the *Slider* Control

A Slider lets the user select a numeric value from a numeric range graphically by sliding a thumb (or knob) along a track. A slider can be horizontal or vertical. Figure 12-58 shows a horizontal slider.

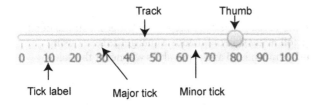

Figure 12-58. *A horizontal* Slider *control and its parts*

A slider has minimum and maximum values that determine the range of the valid selectable values. The thumb of the slider indicates its current value. You can slide the thumb along the track to change the current value. Major and minor tick marks show the location of values along the track. You can also show tick labels. Custom labels are also supported.

The following code creates a Slider control using its default constructor that sets 0, 100, and 0 as the minimum, maximum, and current values, respectively. The default orientation is horizontal.

```
// Create a horizontal slider
Slider s1 = new Slider();
```

Use another constructor to specify the minimum, maximum, and current values:

```
// Create a horizontal slider with the specified min, max, and value
double min = 0.0;
double max = 200.0;
double value = 50.0;
Slider s2 = new Slider(min, max, value);
```

A Slider control contains several properties. I will discuss them by categories.

The orientation property specifies the orientation of the slider:

```
// Create a vertical slider
Slider vs = new Slider();
vs.setOrientation(Orientation.VERTICAL);
```

The following properties are related to the current value and the range of values:

- min
- max
- value
- valueChanging
- snapToTicks

The min, max, and value properties are double properties, and they represent the minimum, maximum, and current values, respectively, of the slider. The current value of the slider can be changed by dragging the thumb on the track or using the setValue() method. The following snippet of code creates a slider and sets its min, max, and value properties to 0, 10, and 3, respectively:

```
Slider scoreSlider = new Slider();
scoreSlider.setMin(0.0);
scoreSlider.setMax(10.0);
scoreSlider.setValue(3.0);
```

Typically, you want to perform an action when the value property of the slider changes. You will need to add a ChangeListener to the value property. The following statement adds a ChangeListener using a lambda expression to the scoreSlider control and prints the old and new values whenever the value property changes:

```
scoreSlider.valueProperty().addListener(
        (ObservableValue<? extends Number> prop, Number oldVal,
            Number newVal) -> {
    System.out.println("Changed from " + oldVal + " to " + newVal);
});
```

The valueChanging property is a boolean property. It is set to true when the user presses the thumb and is set to false when the thumb is released. As the user drags the thumb, the value keeps changing, and the valueChanging property is true. This property helps you avoid repeating an action if you want to take the action only once when the value changes.

The snapToTicks property is a boolean property, which is false by default. It specifies whether the value property of the slider is always aligned with the tick marks. If it is set to false, the value could be anywhere in the min to max range.

Be careful in using the valueChanging property inside a ChangeListener. The listener may be called several times for what the user sees as one change. Expecting that the ChangeListener will be notified when the valueChanging property changes from true to false, you wrap the main logic for the action inside an if statement:

```
if (scoreSlider.isValueChanging()) {
        // Do not perform any action as the value changes
} else {
        // Perform the action as the value has been changed
}
```

The logic works fine when the snapToTicks property is set to true. The ChangeListener for the value property is notified when the valueChanging property changes from true to false only when the snapToTicks property is set to true. Therefore, do not write the preceding logic unless you have set the snapToTicks property to true as well.

The following properties of the Slider class specify the tick spacing:

- majorTickUnit

- minorTickCount

- blockIncrement

The majorTickUnit property is a double property. It specifies the unit of distance between two major ticks. Suppose the min property is set to 0 and the majorTickUnit to 10. The slider will have major ticks at 0, 10, 20, 30, and so forth. An out-of-range value for this property disables the major ticks. The default value for the property is 25.

The minorTickCount property is an integer property. It specifies the number of minor ticks between two major ticks. The default value for the property is 3.

You can change the thumb position by using keys, for example, using left and right arrow keys in a horizontal slider and up and down arrow keys in a vertical slider. The blockIncrement property is a double property. It specifies the amount by which the current value of the slider is adjusted when the thumb is operating by using keys. The default value for the property is 10.

The following properties specify whether the tick marks and tick labels are shown; by default, they are set to false:

- showTickMarks

- showTickLabels

The labelFormatter property is an object property of the StringConverter<Double> type. By default, it is null and the slider uses a default StringConverter that displays the numeric values for the major ticks. The values for the major ticks are passed to the toString() method, and the method is supposed to return a custom label for that value. The following snippet of code creates a slider with custom major tick labels, as shown in Figure 12-59:

```
Slider scoreSlider = new Slider();
scoreSlider.setShowTickLabels(true);
scoreSlider.setShowTickMarks(true);
scoreSlider.setMajorTickUnit(10);
scoreSlider.setMinorTickCount(3);
scoreSlider.setBlockIncrement(20);
scoreSlider.setSnapToTicks(true);

// Set a custom major tick formatter
scoreSlider.setLabelFormatter(new StringConverter<Double>() {
        @Override
        public String toString(Double value) {
                String label = "";
                if (value == 40) {
                        label = "F";
                } else if (value == 70) {
                        label = "C";
                } else if (value == 80) {
                        label = "B";
```

```
            } else if (value == 90) {
                    label = "A";
            }

            return label;
    }

    @Override
    public Double fromString(String string) {
            return null; // Not used
    }
});
```

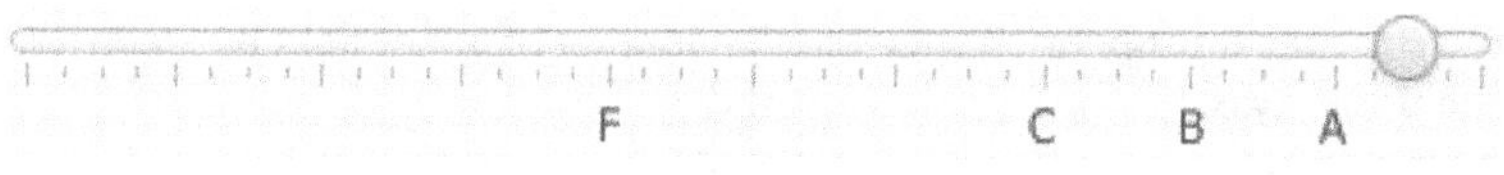

Figure 12-59. *A slider with custom major tick labels*

The program in Listing 12-36 shows how to use Slider controls. It adds a Rectangle, a Label, and three Slider controls to a window. It adds a ChangeListener to the Sliders. Sliders represent red, green, and blue components of a color. When you change the value for a slider, the new color is computed and set as the fill color for the rectangle.

Listing 12-36. Using the Slider Control

```
// SliderTest.java
// ... find in the book's download area.
```

Styling *Slider* with CSS

The default CSS style class name for a Slider control is slider. Slider contains the following CSS properties; each of them corresponds to its Java property in the Slider class:

- -fx-orientation
- -fx-show-tick-labels
- -fx-show-tick-marks
- -fx-major-tick-unit
- -fx-minor-tick-count
- -fx-snap-to-ticks
- -fx-block-increment

Slider supports horizontal and vertical CSS pseudo-classes that apply to horizontal and vertical sliders, respectively. A Slider control contains three substructures that can be styled:

- axis
- track
- thumb

The axis substructure is a NumberAxis. It displays the tick marks and tick labels. The following code sets the tick label color to blue, major tick length to 15px, minor tick length to 5px, major tick color to red, and minor tick color to green:

```
.slider > .axis {
    -fx-tick-label-fill: blue;
    -fx-tick-length: 15px;
    -fx-minor-tick-length: 5px
}

.slider > .axis > .axis-tick-mark {
    -fx-stroke: red;
}

.slider > .axis > .axis-minor-tick-mark {
    -fx-stroke: green;
}
```

The track substructure is a StackPane. The following code changes the background color of track to red:

```
.slider > .track {
    -fx-background-color: red;
}
```

The thumb substructure is a StackPane. The thumb looks circular because it is given a background radius. If you remove the background radius, it will look rectangular, as shown in the following code:

```
.slider .thumb {
    -fx-background-radius: 0;
}
```

You can make an image like a thumb by setting the background of the thumb substructure to an image as follows (assuming that the thumb.jpg image file exists in the same directory as the CSS file containing the style):

```
.slider .thumb {
        -fx-background-image: url("thumb.jpg");
}
```

You can give the thumb any shape using the -fx-shape CSS property. The following code gives the thumb a triangular shape. The triangle is inverted for a horizontal slider and is pointed to the right for a vertical slider. Figure 12-60 shows a horizontal slider with the thumb.

```
/* An inverted triangle */
.slider > .thumb {
      -fx-shape: "M0, 0L10, 0L5, 10 Z";
}

/* A triangle pointing to the right, only if orientation is vertical */
.slider:vertical > .thumb {
      -fx-shape: "M0, 0L10, 5L0, 10 Z";
}
```

Figure 12-60. *A slider with an inverted triangle thumb*

The following code gives the thumb a shape of a triangle placed beside a rectangle. The triangle is inverted for a horizontal slider and is pointed to the right for a vertical slider. Figure 12-61 shows a horizontal slider with the thumb.

```
/* An inverted triangle below a rectangle*/
.slider > .thumb {
      -fx-shape: "M0, 0L10, 0L10, 5L5, 10L0, 5 Z";
}

/* A triangle pointing to the right by the right side of a rectangle */
.slider:vertical > .thumb {
      -fx-shape: "M0, 0L5, 0L10, 5L5, 10L0, 10 Z";
}
```

Figure 12-61. *A slider with a thumb of an inverted triangle below a rectangle*

Understanding Menus

A menu is used to provide a list of actionable items to the user in a compact form. You can also provide the same list of items using a group of buttons, where each button represents an actionable item. It is a matter of preference which one you use: a menu or a group of buttons.

There is a noticeable advantage of using a menu. It uses much less space on the screen, compared to a group of buttons, by folding (or nesting) the group of items under another item. For example, if you have used a file editor, the menu items such as New, Open, Save, and Print are nested under a top-level File menu. A user needs to click the File menu to see the list of items that are available under it. Typically, in cases of a group of buttons, all items are visible to the user all the time, and it is easy for users to know what actions are available. Therefore, there is little trade-off between the amount of space and usability when you decide to use a menu or buttons. Typically, a menu bar is displayed at the top of a window.

■ **Tip** There is another kind of menu, which is called a *context menu* or *pop-up menu*, which is displayed on demand. I will discuss context menus in the next section.

A menu consists of several parts. Figure 12-62 shows a menu and its parts when the Save As submenu is expanded. A menu bar is the topmost part of the menu that holds menus. The menu bar is always visible. File, Edit, Options, and Help are the menu items shown in Figure 12-62. A menu contains menu items and submenus. In Figure 12-62, the File menu contains four menu items: New, Open, Save, and Exit; it contains two separator menu items and one Save As submenu. The Save As submenu contains two menu items: Text and PDF. A menu item is an actionable item. A separator menu item has a horizontal line that separates a group of related menu items from another group of items in a menu. Typically, a menu represents a category of items.

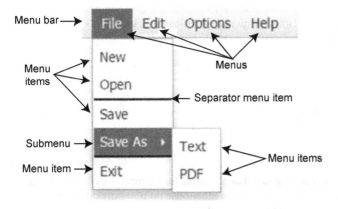

Figure 12-62. *A menu with a menu bar, menus, submenus, separators, and menu items*

Using a menu is a multistep process. The following sections describe the steps in detail. The following is the summary of steps:

1. Create a menu bar and add it to a container.

2. Create menus and add them to the menu bar.

3. Create menu items and add them to the menus.

4. Add ActionEvent handlers to the menu items to perform actions when they are clicked.

Using Menu Bars

A menu bar is a horizontal bar that acts as a container for menus. An instance of the MenuBar class represents a menu bar. You can create a MenuBar using its default constructor:

```
MenuBar menuBar = new MenuBar();
```

MenuBar is a control. Typically, it is added to the top part of a window. If you use a BorderPane as the root for a scene in a window, the top region is the usual place for a MenuBar:

```
// Add the MenuBar to the top region
BorderPane root = new BorderPane();
root.setBottom(menuBar);
```

The MenuBar class contains a useSystemMenuBar property, which is of the boolean type. By default, it is set to false. When set to true, it will use the system menu bar if the platform supports it. For example, Mac supports a system menu bar. If you set this property to true on Mac, the MenuBar will use the system menu bar to display its items:

```
// Let the MenuBar use system menu bar
menuBar.setUseSystemMenuBar(true);
```

A MenuBar itself does not take any space unless you add menus to it. Its size is computed based on the details of the menus it contains. A MenuBar stores all of its menus in an ObservableList of Menu whose reference is returned by its getMenus() method:

```
// Add some menus to the MenuBar
Menu fileMenu = new Menu("File");
Menu editMenu = new Menu("Edit");
menuBar.getMenus().addAll(fileMenu, editMenu);
```

Using Menus

A menu contains a list of actionable items, which are displayed on demand, for example, by clicking it. The list of menu items is hidden when the user selects an item or moves the mouse pointer outside the list. A menu is typically added to a menu bar or another menu as a submenu.

An instance of the Menu class represents a menu. A menu displays text and a graphic. Use the default constructor to create an empty menu, and, later, set the text and graphic:

```
// Create a Menu with an empty string text and no graphic
Menu aMenu = new Menu();

// Set the text and graphic to the Menu
aMenu.setText("Text");
aMenu.setGraphic(new ImageView(new Image("image.jpg")));
```

You can create a menu with its text, or text and a graphic, using other constructors:

```
// Create a File Menu
Menu fileMenu1 = new Menu("File");

// Create a File Menu
Menu fileMenu2 = new Menu("File", new ImageView(new Image("file.jpg")));
```

The Menu class is inherited from the MenuItem class, which is inherited from the Object class. Menu is not a node, and, therefore, it cannot be added to a scene graph directly. You need to add it to a MenuBar. Use the getMenus() method to get the ObservableList<Menu> for the MenuBar and add instances of the Menu class to the list. The following snippet of code adds four Menu instances to a MenuBar:

```
Menu fileMenu = new Menu("File");
Menu editMenu = new Menu("Edit");
Menu optionsMenu = new Menu("Options");
Menu helpMenu = new Menu("Help");

// Add menus to a menu bar
MenuBar menuBar = new MenuBar();
menuBar.getMenus().addAll(fileMenu, editMenu, optionsMenu, helpMenu);
```

When a menu is clicked, typically its list of menu items is displayed, but no action is taken. The Menu class contains the following properties that can be set to handle when its list of options is showing, shown, hiding, and hidden, respectively:

- onShowing
- onShown
- onHiding
- onHidden
- showing

The onShowing event handler is called just before the menu items for the menu is shown. The onShown event handler is called after the menu items are displayed. The onHiding and onHidden event handlers are the counterparts of the onShowing and onShown event handlers, respectively.

Typically, you add an onShowing event handler that enables or disables its menu items based on some criteria. For example, suppose you have an Edit menu with Cut, Copy, and Paste menu items. In the onShowing event handler, you would enable or disable these menu items depending on whether the focus is in a text input control, if the control is enabled, or if the control has selection:

```
editMenu.setOnAction(e -> {/* Enable/disable menu items here */});
```

■ **Tip** Users do not like surprises when using a GUI application. For a better user experience, you should disable menu items instead of making them invisible when they are not applicable. Making them invisible changes the positions of other items, and users have to relocate them.

The showing property is a read-only boolean property. It is set to true when the items in the menu are showing. It is set to false when they are hidden.

The program in Listing 12-37 puts this all together. It creates four menus, a menu bar, adds menus to the menu bar, and adds the menu bar to the top region of a BorderPane. Figure 12-63 shows the menu bar in the window. But you have not seen anything exciting about menus yet! You will need to add menu items to the menus to experience some excitement.

Listing 12-37. Creating a Menu Bar and Adding Menus to It

```java
// MenuTest.java
package com.jdojo.control;

import javafx.application.Application;
import javafx.scene.Scene;
import javafx.scene.control.Menu;
import javafx.scene.control.MenuBar;
import javafx.scene.layout.BorderPane;
import javafx.stage.Stage;

public class MenuTest extends Application {
        public static void main(String[] args) {
                Application.launch(args);
        }

        @Override
        public void start(Stage stage) {
                // Create some menus
                Menu fileMenu = new Menu("File");
                Menu editMenu = new Menu("Edit");
                Menu optionsMenu = new Menu("Options");
                Menu helpMenu = new Menu("Help");

                // Add menus to a menu bar
                MenuBar menuBar = new MenuBar();
                menuBar.getMenus().addAll(
                        fileMenu, editMenu, optionsMenu, helpMenu);

                BorderPane root = new BorderPane();
                root.setTop(menuBar);
                root.setStyle("""
                        -fx-padding: 10;
                  -fx-border-style: solid inside;
                  -fx-border-width: 2;
                  -fx-border-insets: 5;
                  -fx-border-radius: 5;
                  -fx-border-color: blue;""");

                Scene scene = new Scene(root);
                stage.setScene(scene);
                stage.setTitle("Using Menus");
                stage.show();
        }
}
```

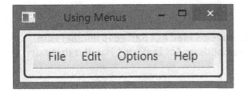

Figure 12-63. *A menu bar with four menus*

Using Menu Items

A menu item is an actionable item in a menu. The action associated with a menu item is performed by the mouse or keys. Menu items can be styled using a CSS.

An instance of the MenuItem class represents a menu item. The MenuItem class is not a node. It is inherited from the Object class and, therefore, cannot be added directly to a scene graph. You need to add it to a menu.

You can add several types of menu items to a menu. Figure 12-64 shows the class diagram for the MenuItem class and its subclasses that represent a specific type of menu item.

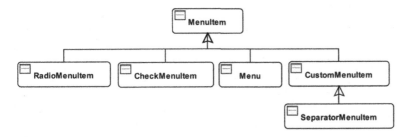

Figure 12-64. *A class diagram for the MenuItem class and its subclasses*

You can use the following types of menu items:

- A MenuItem for an actionable option

- A RadioMenuItem for a group of mutually exclusive options

- A CheckMenuItem for a toggle option

- A Menu, when used as a menu item and acts as a submenu that holds a list of menu items

- A CustomMenuItem for an arbitrary node to be used as a menu item

- A SeparatorMenuItem, which is a CustomMenuItem, to display a separator as a menu item

I will discuss all menu item types in detail in the sections to follow.

465

Using a *MenuItem*

A MenuItem represents an actionable option. When it is clicked, the registered ActionEvent handlers are called. The following snippet of code creates an Exit MenuItem and adds an ActionEvent handler that exits the application:

```
MenuItem exitItem = new MenuItem("Exit");
exitItem.setOnAction(e -> Platform.exit());
```

A MenuItem is added to a menu. A menu stores the reference of its MenuItems in an ObservableList<MenuItem> whose reference can be obtained using the getItems() method:

```
Menu fileMenu = new Menu("File");
fileMenu.getItems().add(exitItem);
```

The MenuItem class contains the following properties that apply to all types of menu items:

- text
- graphic
- disable
- visible
- accelerator
- mnemonicParsing
- onAction
- onMenuValidation
- parentMenu
- parentPopup
- style
- id

The text and graphic properties are the text and graphics for the menu item, respectively, which are of String and Node types. The disable and visible properties are boolean properties. They specify whether the menu item is disabled and visible. The accelerator property is an object property of the KeyCombination type that specifies a key combination that can be used to execute the action associated with the menu item in one keystroke. The following snippet of code creates a Rectangle menu item and sets its accelerator to Alt + R. The accelerator for a menu item is shown next to it, as shown in Figure 12-65, so the user can learn about it by looking at the menu item. The user can activate the Rectangle menu item directly by pressing Alt + R.

```
MenuItem rectItem = new MenuItem("Rectangle");
KeyCombination kr = new KeyCodeCombination(KeyCode.R, KeyCombination.ALT_DOWN);
rectItem.setAccelerator(kr);
```

Rectangle Alt+R

Figure 12-65. *A menu item with an accelerator Alt + R*

The mnemonicParsing property is a boolean property. It enables or disables text parsing to detect a mnemonic character. By default, it is set to true for menu items. If it is set to true, the text for the menu item is parsed for an underscore character. The character following the first underscore is added as the mnemonic for the menu item. Pressing the Alt key on Windows highlights mnemonics for all menu items. Typically, mnemonic characters are shown in an underlined font style. Pressing the key for the mnemonic character activates the menu item.

```
// Create a menu item with x as its mnemonic character
MenuItem exitItem = new MenuItem("E_xit");
```

The onAction property is an ActionEvent handler that is called when the menu item is activated, for example, by clicking it with a mouse or pressing its accelerator key:

```
// Close the application when the Exit menu item is activated
exitItem.setOnAction(e -> Platform.exit());
```

The onMenuValidation property is an event handler that is called when a MenuItem is accessed using its accelerator or when the onShowing event handler for its menu (the parent) is called. For a menu, this handler is called when its menu items are shown.

The parentMenu property is a read-only object property of the Menu type. It is the reference of the Menu, which contains the menu item. Using this property and the items list returned by the getItems() method of the Menu class, you can navigate the menu tree from top to bottom and vice versa.

The parentPopup property is a read-only object property of the ContextMenu type. It is the reference of the ContextMenu in which the menu item appears. It is null for a menu item appearing in a normal menu.

The style and ID properties are included to support styling using a CSS. They represent the CSS style and ID.

Using a *RadioMenuItem*

A RadioMenuItem represents a mutually exclusive option. Typically, you add RadioMenuItem in multiples to a ToggleGroup, so only one item is selected. RadioMenuItem displays a check mark when selected. The following snippet of code creates three instances of RadioMenuItem and adds them to a ToggleGroup. Finally, they are all added to a File Menu. Typically, a RadioMenuItem in a group is selected by default. Figure 12-66 shows the group of RadioMenuItems: once when Rectangle is selected and once when Circle is selected.

```
// Create three RadioMenuItems
RadioMenuItem rectItem = new RadioMenuItem("Rectangle");
RadioMenuItem circleItem = new RadioMenuItem("Circle");
RadioMenuItem ellipseItem = new RadioMenuItem("Ellipse");

// Select the Rantangle option by default
rectItem.setSelected(true);
```

```
// Add them to a ToggleGroup to make them mutually exclusive
ToggleGroup shapeGroup = new ToggleGroup();
shapeGroup.getToggles().addAll(rectItem, circleItem, ellipseItem);

// Add RadioMenuItems to a File Menu
Menu fileMenu = new Menu("File");
fileMenu.getItems().addAll(rectItem, circleItem, ellipseItem);
```

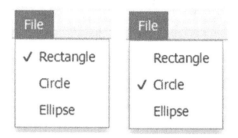

Figure 12-66. *RadioMenuItems in action*

Add an `ActionEvent` handler to the `RadioMenuItem` if you want to perform an action when it is selected. The following snippet of code adds an `ActionEvent` handler to each `RadioMenuItem`, which calls a draw() method:

```
rectItem.setOnAction(e -> draw());
circleItem.setOnAction(e -> draw());
ellipseItem.setOnAction(e -> draw());
```

Using a *CheckMenuItem*

Use a `CheckMenuItem` to represent a boolean menu item that can be toggled between selected and unselected states. Suppose you have an application that draws shapes. You can have a Draw Stroke menu item as a `CheckMenuItem`. When it is selected, a stroke will be drawn for the shape. Otherwise, the shape will not have a stroke, as indicated in the following code. Use an `ActionEvent` handler to be notified when the state of the `CheckMenuItem` is toggled.

```
CheckMenuItem strokeItem = new CheckMenuItem("Draw Stroke");
strokeItem.setOnAction( e -> drawStroke());
```

When a `CheckMenuItem` is selected, a check mark is displayed beside it.

Using a Submenu Item

Notice that the `Menu` class is inherited from the `MenuItem` class. This makes it possible to use a `Menu` in place of a `MenuItem`. Use a `Menu` as a menu item to create a submenu. When the mouse hovers over a submenu, its list of options is displayed.

The following snippet of code creates a MenuBar, adds a File menu, adds New and Open MenuItems and a Save As submenu to the File menu, and adds Text and PDF menu items to the Save As submenu. It produces a menu as shown in Figure 12-67.

```
MenuBar menuBar = new MenuBar();
Menu fileMenu = new Menu("File");
menuBar.getMenus().addAll(fileMenu);

MenuItem newItem = new MenuItem("New");
MenuItem openItem = new MenuItem("Open");
Menu saveAsSubMenu = new Menu("Save As");

// Add menu items to the File menu
fileMenu.getItems().addAll(newItem, openItem, saveAsSubMenu);

MenuItem textItem = new MenuItem("Text");
MenuItem pdfItem = new MenuItem("PDF");
saveAsSubMenu.getItems().addAll(textItem, pdfItem);
```

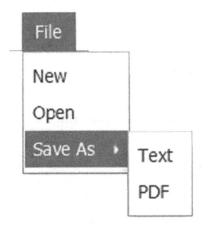

Figure 12-67. *A menu used as a submenu*

Typically, you do not add an ActionEvent handler for a submenu. Rather, you set an event handler to the onShowing property that is called before the list of items for the submenu is displayed. The event handler is used to enable or disable menu items.

Using a *CustomMenuItem*

CustomMenuItem is a simple yet powerful menu item type. It opens the door for all kinds of creativity for designing menu items. It lets you use any node. For example, you can use a Slider, a TextField, or an HBox as a menu item. The CustomMenuItem class contains two properties:

- content
- hideOnClick

The content property is an object property of the Node type. Its value is the node that you want to use as the menu item.

When you click a menu item, all visible menus are hidden, and only top-level menus in the menu bar stay visible. When you use a custom menu item that has controls, you do not want to hide menus when the user clicks it because the user needs to interact with the menu item, for example, to enter or select some data. The hideOnClick property is a boolean property that lets you control this behavior. By default, it is set to true, which means clicking a custom menu hides all showing menus.

The CustomMenuItem class provides several constructors. The default constructor creates a custom menu item setting the content property to null and the hideOnClick property to true, as shown in the following code:

```
// Create a Slider control
Slider slider = new Slider(1, 10, 1);

// Create a custom menu item and set its content and hideOnClick properties
CustomMenuItem cmi1 = new CustomMenuItem();
cmi1.setContent(slider);
cmi1.setHideOnClick(false);

// Create a custom menu item with a Slider content and
// set the hideOnClick property to false
CustomMenuItem cmi2 = new CustomMenuItem(slider);
cmi1.setHideOnClick(false);

// Create a custom menu item with a Slider content and false hideOnClick
CustomMenuItem cmi2 = new CustomMenuItem(slider, false);
```

The following snippet of code produces a menu as shown in Figure 12-68. One of the menu items is a CustomMenuItem, which uses a slider as its content:

```
CheckMenuItem strokeItem = new CheckMenuItem("Draw Stroke");
strokeItem.setSelected(true);

Slider strokeWidthSlider = new Slider(1, 10, 1);
strokeWidthSlider.setShowTickLabels(true);
strokeWidthSlider.setShowTickMarks(true);
strokeWidthSlider.setMajorTickUnit(2);
CustomMenuItem strokeWidthItem = new CustomMenuItem(strokeWidthSlider, false);

Menu optionsMenu = new Menu("Options");
optionsMenu.getItems().addAll(strokeItem, strokeWidthItem);

MenuBar menuBar = new MenuBar();
menuBar.getMenus().add(optionsMenu);
```

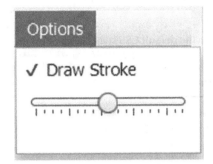

Figure 12-68. *A slider as a custom menu item*

Using a *SeparatorMenuItem*

There is nothing special to discuss about the `SeparatorMenuItem`. It inherits from the `CustomMenuItem`. It uses a horizontal `Separator` control as its `content` and sets the `hideOnClick` to false. It is used to separate menu items belonging to different groups, as shown in the following code. It provides a default constructor:

```
// Create a separator menu item
SeparatorMenuItem smi = SeparatorMenuItem();
```

Putting All Parts of Menus Together

Understanding the parts of menus is easy. However, using them in code is tricky because you have to create all parts separately, add listeners to them, and then assemble them.

The program in Listing 12-38 creates a shape drawing application using menus. It uses all types of menu items. The program displays a window with a `BorderPane` as the root of its scene. The top region contains a menu, and the center region contains a canvas on which shapes are drawn.

Run the application and use the File menu to draw different types of shapes; clicking the Clear menu item clears the canvas. Clicking the Exit menu item closes the application.

Use the Options menu to draw or not to draw the strokes and set the stroke width. Notice that a slider is used as a custom menu item under the Options menu. When you adjust the slider value, the stroke width of the drawn shape is adjusted accordingly. The Draw Stroke menu item is a `CheckMenuItem`. When it is unselected, the slider menu item is disabled, and the shape does not use a stroke.

Listing 12-38. Using Menus in a Shape Drawing Application

```
// MenuItemTest.java
// ... find in the book's download area.
```

Styling Menus Using CSS

There are several components involved in using a menu. Table 12-6 lists the default CSS style class names for components related to menus.

Table 12-6. *CSS Default Style Class Names for Menu-Related Components*

Menu Component	Style Class Name
MenuBar	menu-bar
Menu	menu
MenuItem	menu-item
RadioMenuItem	radio-menu-item
CheckMenuItem	check-menu-item
CustomMenuItem	custom-menu-item
SeparatorMenuItem	separator-menu-item

MenuBar supports an -fx-use-system-menu-bar property, which is set to false by default. It indicates whether to use a system menu for the menu bar. It contains a menu substructure that holds the menus for the menu bar. Menu supports a showing CSS pseudo-class, which applies when the menu is showing. RadioMenuItem and CheckMenuItem support a selected CSS pseudo-class, which applies when the menu items are selected.

You can style several components of menus. Please refer to the modena.css file for the sample styles.

Understanding the *ContextMenu* Control

ContextMenu is a pop-up control that displays a list of menu items on request. It is also known as a *context* or *pop-up* menu. By default, it is hidden. The user has to make a request, usually by right-clicking the mouse button, to show it. It is hidden once a selection is made. The user can dismiss a context menu by pressing the Esc key or clicking outside its bounds.

A context menu has a usability problem. It is difficult for users to know about its existence. Usually, nontechnical users are not accustomed to right-clicking the mouse and making selections. For those users, you can present the same options using toolbars or buttons instead. Sometimes, a text message is included on the screen stating that the user needs to right-click to view or show the context menu.

An object of the ContextMenu class represents a context menu. It stores the reference of its menu items in an ObservableList<MenuItem>. The getItems() method returns the reference of the observable list.

You will use the following three menu items in the examples presented as follows. Note that the menu items in a context menu could be an object of the MenuItem class or its subclasses. For the complete list of menu item types, please refer to the "Understanding Menus" section.

```
MenuItem rectItem = new MenuItem("Rectangle");
MenuItem circleItem = new MenuItem("Circle");
MenuItem ellipseItem = new MenuItem("Ellipse");
```

The default constructor of the ContextMenu class creates an empty menu. You need to add the menu items later:

```
ContextMenu ctxMenu = new ContextMenu();
ctxMenu.getItems().addAll(rectItem, circleItem, ellipseItem);
```

You can use the other constructor to create a context menu with an initial list of menu items:

```
ContextMenu ctxMenu = new ContextMenu(rectItem, circleItem, ellipseItem);
```

Typically, context menus are provided for controls for accessing their commonly used features, for example, Cut, Copy, and Paste features of text input controls. Some controls have default context menus. The control class makes it easy to display a context menu. It has a contextMenu property. You need to set this property to your context menu reference for the control. The following snippet of code sets the context menu for a TextField control:

```
ContextMenu ctxMenu = ...
TextField nameFld = new TextField();
nameFld.setContextMenu(ctxMenu);
```

When you right-click the TextField, your context menu will be displayed instead of the default one.

■ **Tip** Activating an empty context menu does not show anything. If you want to disable the default context menu for a control, set its contextMenu property to an empty ContextMenu.

Nodes that are not controls do not have a contextMenu property. You need to use the show() method of the ContextMenu class to display the context menu for these nodes. The show() method gives you full control of the position where the context menu is displayed. You can use it for controls as well if you want to fine-tune the positioning of the context menu. The show() method is overloaded:

```
void show(Node anchor, double screenX, double screenY)
void show(Node anchor, Side side, double dx, double dy)
```

The first version takes the node for which the context menu is to be displayed with the x and y coordinates relative to the screen. Typically, you display a context menu in the mouse-clicked event where the MouseEvent object provides you the coordinates of the mouse pointer relative to the screen through the getScreenX() and getScreenY() methods.

The following snippet of code shows a context menu for a canvas at (100, 100) relative to the screen coordinate system:

```
Canvas canvas = ...
ctxMenu.show(canvas, 100, 100);
```

The second version lets you fine-tune the position of the context menu relative to the specified anchor node. The side parameter specifies on which side of the anchor node the context menu is displayed. The possible values are one of the constants—TOP, RIGHT, BOTTOM, and LEFT—of the Side enum. The dx and dy parameters specify the x and y coordinates, respectively, relative to the anchor node coordinate system. This version of the show() method requires a little more explanation.

The side parameter has an effect of shifting the x-axis and y-axis of the anchor node. The dx and dy parameters are applied after the axes are shifted. Note that the axes are shifted only for computing the position of the context menu when this version of the method is called. They are not shifted permanently, and the anchor node position does not change at all. Figure 12-69 shows an anchor node and its x- and y-axes for the values of the side parameter. The dx and dy parameters are the x and y coordinates of the point relative to the shifted x-axis and y-axis of the node.

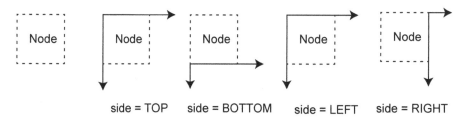

Figure 12-69. Shifting the x-axis and y-axis of the anchor node with the side parameter value

Note that the LEFT and RIGHT values for the side parameter are interpreted based on the node orientation of the anchor node. For a node orientation of RIGHT_TO_LEFT, the LEFT value means the right side of the node.

When you specify TOP, LEFT, or null for the side parameter, the dx and dy parameters are measured relative to the original x- and y-axes of the node. When you specify BOTTOM for the side parameter, the bottom of the node becomes the new x-axis, and the y-axis remains the same. When you specify RIGHT for the side parameter, the right side of the node becomes the new y-axis, and the x-axis remains the same.

The following call to the show() method displays a context menu at the upper-left corner of the anchor node. The value of Side.LEFT or null for the side parameter would display the context menu at the same location:

```
ctxMenu.show(anchor, Side.TOP, 0, 0);
```

The following call to the show() method displays a context menu at the lower-left corner of the anchor node:

```
ctxMenu.show(anchor, Side.BOTTOM, 0, 0);
```

Values for dx and dy can be negative. The following call to the show() method displays a context menu 10px above the upper-left corner of the anchor node:

```
ctxMenu.show(myAnchor, Side.TOP, 0, -10);
```

The hide() method of the ContextMenu class hides the context menu, if it was showing. Typically, the context menu is hidden when you select a menu item. You need to use the hide() method when the context menu uses a custom menu item with the hideOnClick property set to true.

Typically, an ActionEvent handler is added to the menu items of a context menu. The ContextMenu class contains an onAction property, which is an ActionEvent handler. The ActionEvent handler, if set, for a ContextMenu is called every time a menu item is activated. You can use this ActionEvent to execute a follow-up action when a menu item is activated.

The program in Listing 12-39 shows how to use a context menu. It displays a Label and a Canvas. When you right-click the canvas, a context menu with three menu items—Rectangle, Circle, and Ellipse—is displayed. Selecting one of the shapes from the menu items draws the shape on the canvas. The context menu is displayed when the mouse pointer is clicked.

Listing 12-39. Using the ContextMenu Control

```
// ContextMenuTest.java
// ... find in the book's download area.
```

Styling *ContextMenu* with CSS

The default CSS style class name for a ContextMenu is context-menu. Please refer to the modena.css file for sample styles for customizing the appearance of context menus. By default, a context menu uses a drop shadow effect. The following style sets the font size to 8pt and removes the default effect:

```
.context-menu {
        -fx-font-size: 8pt;
        -fx-effect: null;
}
```

Understanding the *ToolBar* Control

ToolBar is used to display a group of nodes, which provide the commonly used action items on a screen. Typically, a ToolBar control contains the commonly used items that are also available through a menu and a context menu.

A ToolBar control can hold many types of nodes. The most commonly used nodes in a ToolBar are buttons and toggle buttons. Separators are used to separate a group of buttons from others. Typically, buttons are kept smaller by using small icons, preferably 16px by 16px in size.

If the items in a toolbar overflow, an overflow button appears to allow users to navigate to the hidden items. A toolbar can have the orientation of horizontal or vertical. A horizontal toolbar arranges the items horizontally in one row. A vertical toolbar arranges the items in one column. Figure 12-70 shows two toolbars: one has no overflow, and one has an overflow. The one with an overflow displays an overflow button (>>). When you click the overflow button, the hidden toolbar items are displayed for selection.

A toolbar with no overflow   A toolbar with an overflow   An overflow button

Figure 12-70. *A horizontal toolbar with three buttons*

You will use the following four ToolBar items in the examples in this chapter:

```
Button rectBtn = new Button("", new Rectangle(0, 0, 16, 16));
Button circleBtn = new Button("", new Circle(0, 0, 8));
Button ellipseBtn = new Button("", new Ellipse(8, 8, 8, 6));
Button exitBtn = new Button("Exit");
```

A ToolBar control stores the reference of items in an ObservableList<Node>. Use the getItems() method to get the reference of the observable list.

The default constructor of the ToolBar class creates an empty toolbar:

```
ToolBar toolBar = new ToolBar();
toolBar.getItems().addAll(circleBtn, ellipseBtn, new Separator(), exitBtn);
```

The ToolBar class provides another constructor that lets you add items:

```
ToolBar toolBar = new ToolBar(
        rectBtn, circleBtn, ellipseBtn,
        new Separator(),
        exitBtn);
```

The orientation property of the ToolBar class specifies its orientation: horizontal or vertical. By default, a toolbar uses the horizontal orientation. The following code sets it to vertical:

```
// Create a ToolBar and set its orientation to VERTICAL
ToolBar toolBar = new ToolBar();
toolBar.setOrientation(Orientation.VERTICAL);
```

■ **Tip** The orientation of a separator in a toolbar is automatically adjusted by the default CSS. It is good practice to provide tool tips for items in a toolbar, as they are small in size and typically do not use text content.

The program in Listing 12-40 shows how to create and use ToolBar controls. It creates a toolbar and adds four items. When you click one of the items with a shape, it draws the shape on a canvas. The Exit item closes the application.

Listing 12-40. Using the ToolBar Control

```
// ToolBarTest.java
// ... find in the book's download area.
```

Styling a Toolbar with CSS

The default CSS style class name for a ToolBar is tool-bar. It contains an -fx-orientation CSS property that specifies its orientation with the possible values of *horizontal* and *vertical*. It supports horizontal and vertical CSS pseudo-classes that apply when its orientation is horizontal and vertical, respectively.

A toolbar uses a container to arrange the items. The container is an HBox for a horizontal orientation and a VBox for a vertical orientation. The CSS style class name for the container is container. You can use all CSS properties for the HBox and VBox for the container. The -fx-spacing CSS property specifies the spacing between two adjacent items in the container. You can set this property for the toolbar or the container. Both of the following styles have the same effect on a horizontal toolbar:

```
.tool-bar {
        -fx-spacing: 2;
}

.tool-bar > .container {
        -fx-spacing: 2;
}
```

A toolbar contains a `tool-bar-overflow-button` substructure to represent the overflow button. It is a StackPane. The `tool-bar-overflow-button` contains an `arrow` substructure to represent the arrow in the overflow button. It is also a StackPane.

Understanding *TabPane* and *Tab*

A window may not have enough space to display all of the pieces of information in one page view. JavaFX provides several controls to break down large content into multiple pages, for example, Accordion and Pagination controls. TabPane and Tab let you present information in a page much better. A Tab represents a page, and a TabPane contains the Tab.

A Tab is not a control. An instance of the Tab class represents a Tab. The Tab class inherits from the Object class. However, the Tab supports some features as controls do, for example, they can be disabled, styled using CSS, and can have context menus and tool tips.

A Tab consists of a title and content. The title consists of text, an optional graphic, and an optional close button to close the tab. The content consists of controls. Typically, controls are added to a layout pane, which is added to the Tab as its content.

Typically, the titles of the Tab in a TabPane are visible. The content area is shared by all Tabs. You need to select a Tab, by clicking its title, to view its content. You can select only one tab at a time in a TabPane. If the titles of all tabs are not visible, a control button is displayed automatically that assists the user in selecting the invisible tabs.

Tabs in a TabPane may be positioned at the top, right, bottom, or left side of the TabPane. By default, they are positioned at the top.

Figure 12-71 shows two instances of a window. The window contains a TabPane with two tabs. In one instance, the General tab is selected, and in another, the Address tab is selected.

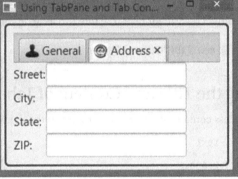

General tab is selected   Address tab is selected

Figure 12-71. *A window with a TabPane, which contains two tabs*

A TabPane is divided into two parts: *header area* and *content area*. The header area displays the titles of tabs; the content area displays the content of the selected tab. The header area is subdivided into the following parts:

- Headers region
- Tab header background
- Control buttons tab
- Tab area

Figure 12-72 shows parts of the header area of a TabPane. The headers region is the entire header area. The tab header background is the area occupied by the titles of the tabs. The control buttons tab contains control buttons that are displayed when the width of the TabPane cannot display all of the tabs. The control buttons tab lets you select the tabs that are currently not visible. The tab area contains a Label and a close button (the X icon next to the tab label). The Label displays the text and icon for a tab. The close button is used to close a selected tab.

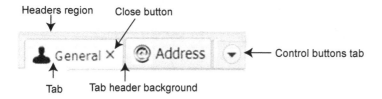

Figure 12-72. *Different parts of the header of a TabPane*

Creating Tabs

You can create a tab using the default constructor of the Tab class with an empty title:

```
Tab tab1 = new Tab();
```

Use the setText() method to set the title text for the tab:

```
tab1.setText("General");
```

The other constructor takes the title text as an argument:

```
Tab tab2 = new Tab("General");
```

Setting the Title and Content of Tabs

The Tab class contains the following properties that let you set the title and content:

- text
- graphic
- closable
- content

The text, graphic, and closable properties specify what appears in the title bar of a tab. The text property specifies a string as the title text. The graphic property specifies a node as the title icon. Notice that the type of the graphic property is Node, so you can use any node as a graphic. Typically, a small icon is set as the graphic. The text property can be set in the constructor or using the setText() method. The following snippet of code creates a tab with text and sets an image as its graphic (assuming the file resources/picture/address_icon.png is included in the package):

```
// Create an ImageView for graphic
String imagePath = "resources/picture/address_icon.png";
URL imageUrl = getClass().getClassLoader().getResource(imagePath);
Image img = new Image(imageUrl.toExternalForm());
ImageView icon = new ImageView(img);

// Create a Tab with "Address" text
Tab addressTab = new Tab("Address");

// Set the graphic
addressTab.setGraphic(icon);
```

The closable property is a boolean property that specifies whether the tab can be closed. If it is set to false, the tab cannot be closed. Closing of tabs is also controlled by the tab-closing policy of the TabPane. If the closable property is set to false, the tab cannot be closed by the user, irrespective of the tab-closing policy of the TabPane. You will learn about tab-closing policy when I discuss the TabPane later.

The content property is a node that specifies the content of the tab. The content of the tab is visible when the tab is selected. Typically, a layout pane with controls is set as the content of a tab. The following snippet of code creates a GridPane, adds some controls, and sets the GridPane as the content of a tab:

```
// Create a GridPane layout pane with some controls
GridPane grid = new GridPane();
grid.addRow(0, new Label("Street:"), streetFld);
grid.addRow(1, new Label("City:"), cityFld);
grid.addRow(2, new Label("State:"), stateFld);
grid.addRow(3, new Label("ZIP:"), zipFld);

Tab addressTab = new Tab("Address");
addressTab.setContent(grid); // Set the content
```

Creating *TabPanes*

The TabPane class provides only one constructor—the default constructor. When you create a TabPane, it has no tabs:

```
TabPane tabPane = new TabPane();
```

Adding Tabs to a *TabPane*

A TabPane stores the references of its tabs in an ObservableList<Tab>. The getTabs() method of the TabPane class returns the reference of the observable list. To add a tab to the TabPane, you need to add it to the observable list. The following snippet of code adds two tabs to a TabPane:

```
Tab generalTab = new Tab("General");
Tab addressTab = new Tab("Address");
...
TabPane tabPane = new TabPane();

// Add the two Tabs to the TabPane
tabPane.getTabs().addAll(generalTab, addressTab);
```

When a tab is not supposed to be part of a TabPane, you need to remove it from the observable list. The TabPane will update its view automatically:

```
// Remove the Address tab
tabPane.getTabs().remove(addressTab);
```

The read-only tabPane property of the Tab class stores the reference of the TabPane that contains the tab. If a tab has not yet been added to a TabPane, its tabPane property is null. Use the getTabPane() method of the Tab class to get the reference of the TabPane.

Putting *TabPanes* and *Tabs* Together

I have covered enough information to allow you to see a TabPane with Tabs in action. Typically, a tab is reused. Inheriting a class from the Tab class helps when reusing a tab. Listings 12-41 and 12-42 create two Tab classes. You will use them as tabs in subsequent examples. The GeneralTab class contains fields to enter the name and birth date of a person. The AddressTab class contains fields to enter an address.

Listing 12-41. A GeneralTab Class That Inherits from the Tab Class

```
// GeneralTab.java
package com.jdojo.control;

import javafx.scene.Node;
import javafx.scene.control.DatePicker;
import javafx.scene.control.Label;
import javafx.scene.control.Tab;
import javafx.scene.control.TextField;
import javafx.scene.layout.GridPane;

public class GeneralTab extends Tab {
        TextField firstNameFld = new TextField();
        TextField lastNameFld = new TextField();
        DatePicker dob = new DatePicker();

        public GeneralTab(String text, Node graphic) {
                this.setText(text);
                this.setGraphic(graphic);
                init();
        }

        public void init() {
                dob.setPrefWidth(200);
                GridPane grid = new GridPane();
                grid.addRow(0, new Label("First Name:"), firstNameFld);
                grid.addRow(1, new Label("Last Name:"), lastNameFld);
                grid.addRow(2, new Label("DOB:"), dob);
                this.setContent(grid);
        }
}
```

Listing 12-42. An AddressTab Class That Inherits from the Tab Class

```java
// AddressTab.java
package com.jdojo.control;

import javafx.scene.Node;
import javafx.scene.control.Label;
import javafx.scene.control.Tab;
import javafx.scene.control.TextField;
import javafx.scene.layout.GridPane;

public class AddressTab extends Tab {
        TextField streetFld = new TextField();
        TextField cityFld = new TextField();
        TextField stateFld = new TextField();
        TextField zipFld = new TextField();

        public AddressTab(String text, Node graphic) {
                this.setText(text);
                this.setGraphic(graphic);
                init();
        }

        public void init() {
                GridPane grid = new GridPane();
                grid.addRow(0, new Label("Street:"), streetFld);
                grid.addRow(1, new Label("City:"), cityFld);
                grid.addRow(2, new Label("State:"), stateFld);
                grid.addRow(3, new Label("ZIP:"), zipFld);
                this.setContent(grid);
        }
}
```

The program in Listing 12-43 creates two tabs. They are instances of the GeneralTab and AddressTab classes. They are added to a TabPane, which is added to the center region of a BorderPane. The program displays a window as shown in Figure 12-71.

Listing 12-43. Using a TabPane and Tabs Together

```java
// TabTest.java
// ... find in the book's download area.
```

Understanding Tab Selection

TabPane supports a single selection model, which allows selecting only one tab at a time. If a tab is selected by the user or programmatically, the previously selected tab is unselected. The Tab class provides the API to allow working with the selection state of an individual tab. The TabPane class provides the API that allows working with the selection of all of its tabs.

The Tab class contains a read-only selected property of the boolean type. It is true when the tab is selected. Otherwise, it is false. Note that it is a property of the Tab, not the TabPane.

Tab lets you add event handlers that are notified when the tab is selected or unselected. The onSelectionChanged property stores the reference of such an event:

```
Tab generalTab = ...
generalTab.setOnSelectionChanged(e -> {
        if (generalTab.isSelected()) {
                System.out.println("General tab has been selected.");
        } else {
                System.out.println("General tab has been unselected.");
        }
});
```

TabPane tracks the selected tab and its index in the list of tabs. It uses a separate object, called *selection model,* for this purpose. The TabPane class contains a selectionModel property to store the tab selection details. The property is an object of the SingleSelectionModel class. You can use your own selection model, which is almost never needed. The selection model provides the selection-related functionalities:

- It lets you select a tab using the index of the tab. The first tab has an index of zero.

- It lets you select the first, next, previous, or last tab in the list.

- It lets you clear the selection. Note that this feature is available, but is not commonly used. A TabPane should always typically have a selected tab.

- The selectedIndex and selectedItem properties track the index and reference of the selected tab. You can add a ChangeListener to these properties to handle a change in tab selection in a TabPane.

By default, a TabPane selects its first tab. The following snippet of code selects the last Tab in a TabPane:

```
tabPane.getSelectionModel().selectLast();
```

Use the selectNext() method of the selection model to select the next tab from the list. Calling this method when the last tab is already selected has no effect.

Use the selectPrevious() and selectLast() methods to select the previous and the last tabs in the list. The select(int index) and select(T item) methods select a tab using the index and reference of the tab.

The program in Listing 12-44 adds two tabs to a TabPane. It adds a selection-changed event handler to both tabs. A ChangeListener is added to the selectedItem property of the selectionModel property of the TabPane. When a selection is made, a detailed message is printed on the standard output. Notice that a message is printed when you run the application because the TabPane selection model selects the first tab by default.

Listing 12-44. Tracking Tab Selection in a TabPane

```
// TabSelection.java
// ... find in the book's download area.
```

Closing Tabs in a *TabPane*

Sometimes, the user needs to add tabs to a TabPane on demand, and they should be able to close tabs as well. For example, all modern web browsers use tabs for browsing and let you open and close tabs. Adding tabs on demand requires some coding in JavaFX. However, closing tabs by the user is built in the Tab and TabPane classes.

Users can close Tabs in a TabPane using the close button that appears in the title bar of Tabs. The tab-closing feature is controlled by the following properties:

- The closable property of the Tab class
- The tabClosingPolicy property of the TabPane class

The closable property of a Tab class specifies whether the tab can be closed. If it is set to false, the tab cannot be closed, irrespective of the value for the tabClosingPolicy. The default value for the property is true. The tabClosingPolicy property specifies how the tab-closing buttons are available. Its value is one of the following constants of the TabPane.TabClosingPolicy enum:

- ALL_TABS
- SELECTED_TAB
- UNAVAILABLE

ALL_TABS means the close button is available for all tabs. That is, any tab can be closed at any time provided the closable property of the tab is true. SELECTED_TAB means the close button appears only for the selected tab. That is, only the selected tab can be closed at any time. This is the default tab-closing policy of a TabPane. UNAVAILABLE means the close button is not available for any tabs. That is, no tabs can be closed by the user, irrespective of their closable properties.

A distinction has to be made between:

- Closing tabs by the user using the close button
- Removing them programmatically by removing them from the observable list of Tabs of the TabPane

Both have the same effect, that Tabs are removed from the TabPane. The discussion in this section applies to closing tabs by the user.

The user action to closing tabs can be vetoed. You can add event handlers for the TAB_CLOSE_REQUEST_ EVENT event for a tab. The event handler is called when the user attempts to close the tab. If the event handler consumes the event, the closing operation is cancelled. You can use the onCloseRequest property of the Tab class to set such an event:

```
Tab myTab = new Tab("My Tab");
myTab.setOnCloseRequest(e -> {
    if (SOME_CONDITION_IS_TRUE) {
        // Cancel the close request
        e.consume();
    }
});
```

A tab also generates a closed event when it is closed by the user. Use the onClosed property of the Tab class to set a closed event handler for a tab. The event handler is typically used to release resources held by the tab:

```
myTab.setOnClosed(e -> {/* Release tab resources here */});
```

The program in Listing 12-45 shows how to use the tab-closing–related properties and events. It displays two tabs in a TabPane. A check box lets you veto the closing of tabs. Unless the check box is selected, an attempt to close tabs is vetoed on the close request event. If you close tabs, you can restore them using the Restore Tabs button. Use the tab-closing policy ChoiceBox to use a different tab-closing policy. For example, if you select UNAVAILABLE as the tab-closing policy, the close buttons will disappear from all tabs. When a tab is closed, a message is printed on the standard output.

Listing 12-45. Using Properties and Events Related to Closing Tabs by Users

```
// TabClosingTest.java
// ... find in the book's download area.
```

Positioning Tabs in a *TabPane*

Tabs in a TabPane may be positioned at the top, right, bottom, or left. The side property of the TabPane specifies the position of tabs. It is set to one of the constants of the Side enum:

- TOP
- RIGHT
- BOTTOM
- LEFT

The default value for the side property is Side.TOP. The following snippet of code creates a TabPane and sets the side property to Side.LEFT to position tabs on the left:

```
TabPane tabPane = new TabPane();
tabPane.setSide(Side.LEFT);
```

▪ **Tip** The actual placement of tabs also uses the node orientation. For example, if the side property is set to Side.LEFT and the node orientation of the TabPane is set to RIGHT_TO_LEFT, the tabs will be positioned on the right side.

The TabPane class contains a rotateGraphic property, which is a boolean property. The property is related to the side property. When the side property is Side.TOP or Side.BOTTOM, the graphics of all tabs in their title bars are in the upright position. By default, when the side property changes to Side.LEFT or Side.RIGHT, the title text is rotated, keeping the graphic upright. The rotateGraphic property specifies whether the graphic is rotated with the text, as shown in the following code. By default, it is set to false.

```
// Rotate the graphic with the text for left and right sides
tabPane.setRotateGraphic(true);
```

Figure 12-73 shows the title bar of a tab in a TabPane with the side property set to TOP and LEFT. Notice the effect on the graphics when the side property is LEFT and the rotateGraphic property is false and true. The rotateGraphic property has no effect when tabs are positioned at the top or bottom.

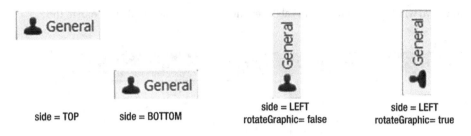

side = TOP	side = BOTTOM	side = LEFT rotateGraphic= false	side = LEFT rotateGraphic= true

Figure 12-73. *Effects of the side and* rotateGraphic *properties of the* TabPane

Sizing Tabs in a *TabPane*

TabPane divides its layout into two parts:

- Header area
- Content area

The header area displays the titles of tabs. The content area displays the content of the selected tab. The size of the content area is automatically computed based on the content of all tabs. TabPane contains the following properties that allow you to set the minimum and maximum sizes of the title bars of tabs:

- tabMinHeight
- tabMaxHeight
- tabMinWidth
- tabMaxWidth

The default values are zero for minimum width and height, and Double.MAX_VALUE for maximum width and height. The default size is computed based on the context of the tab titles. If you want all tab titles to be of a fixed size, set the minimum and maximum width and height to the same value. Note that for the fixed size tabs, the longer text in the title bar will be truncated.

The following snippet of code creates a TabPane and sets the properties, so all tabs are 100px wide and 30px tall:

```
TabPane tabPane = new TabPane();
tabPane.setTabMinHeight(30);
tabPane.setTabMaxHeight(30);
tabPane.setTabMinWidth(100);
tabPane.setTabMaxWidth(100);
```

Using Recessed and Floating *TabPanes*

A TabPane can be in recessed or floating mode. The default mode is recessed mode. In the recessed mode, it *appears* to be fixed. In floating mode, its appearance is changed to make it look like it is floating. In the floating mode, the background color of the header area is removed, and a border around the content area is added. Here is a rule of thumb in deciding which mode to use:

- If you are using a TabPane along with other controls in a window, use floating mode.
- If the TabPane is the only one control on the window, use recessed mode.

485

Figure 12-74 shows two windows with the same TabPane: one in the recessed mode and one in the floating mode.

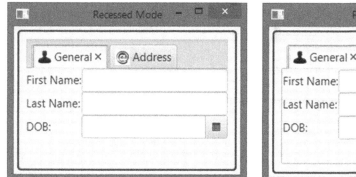 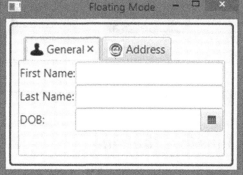

Figure 12-74. *A TabPane in recessed and floating modes*

The floating mode of a TabPane is specified by a style class. The TabPane class contains a STYLE_CLASS_FLOATING constant. If you add this style class to a TabPane, it is in the floating mode. Otherwise, it is in the recessed mode. The following snippet of code shows how to turn the floating mode for a TabPane on and off:

```
TabPane tabPane = new TabPane();

// Turn on the floating mode
tabPane.getStyleClass().add(TabPane.STYLE_CLASS_FLOATING);
...
// Turn off the floating mode
tabPane.getStyleClass().remove(TabPane.STYLE_CLASS_FLOATING);
```

Styling *Tab* and *TabPane* with CSS

The default CSS style class name for a tab and for a TabPane is tab-pane. You can style Tabs directly using the tab style class or using the substructure of TabPane. The latter approach is commonly used.

TabPane supports four CSS pseudo-classes, which correspond to the four values for its side property:

- top
- right
- bottom
- left

You can set the minimum and maximum sizes of the tab titles in a TabPane using the following CSS properties. They correspond to the four properties in the TabPane class. Please refer to the "Sizing Tabs in a *TabPane*" section for a detailed discussion of these properties:

- -fx-tab-min-width
- -fx-tab-max-width

- -fx-tab-min-height
- -fx-tab-max-height

A TabPane divides its layout bounds into two areas: header area and content area. Please refer to Figure 12-72 for the different subparts in the header area. The header area is called the tab-header-area substructure, which contains the following substructures:

- headers-region
- tab-header-background
- control-buttons-tab
- tab

The control-buttons-tab substructure contains a tab-down-button substructure, which contains an arrow substructure. The tab substructure contains tab-label and tab-close-button substructures. The tab-content-area substructure represents the content area of the TabPane. Substructures let you style different parts of TabPane.

The following code removes the background color for the header area as is done when the TabPane is in the floating mode:

```
.tab-pane > .tab-header-area > .tab-header-background {
    -fx-background-color: null;
}
```

The following code shows the text of the selected tab in boldface. Notice the use of the selected pseudo-class for the tab in the selector .tab:selected:

```
.tab-pane > .tab-header-area > .headers-region > .tab:selected
> .tab-container > ,tab-label {
        -fx-font-weight: bold;
}
```

The following code shows Tabs in a TabPane in blue background with 10pt white title text:

```
.tab-pane > .tab-header-area > .headers-region > .tab  {
    -fx-background-color: blue;
}

.tab-pane > .tab-header-area > .headers-region > .tab > .tab-container
> .tab-label {
        -fx-text-fill: white;
        -fx-font-size: 10pt;
}
```

Use the floating style-class for the TabPane when styling it for the floating mode. The following style sets the border color to blue in floating mode:

```
.tab-pane.floating > .tab-content-area {
        -fx-border-color: blue;
}
```

Please refer to the modena.css file for the complete list of styles used for TabPane.

487

Understanding the *HTMLEditor* Control

The HTMLEditor control provides a rich text editing capability to a JavaFX application. It uses HTML as its data model. That is, the formatted text in HTMLEditor is stored in HTML format. An HTMLEditor control can be used for entering formatted text in a business application, for example, product description, or comments. It can also be used to enter email content in an email client application. Figure 12-75 shows a window with an HTMLEditor control.

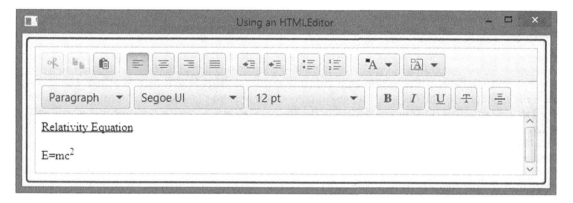

Figure 12-75. *An HTMLEditor control*

An HTMLEditor displays formatting toolbars with it. You cannot hide the toolbars. They can be styled using a CSS. Using the toolbars, you can

- Copy, cut, and paste text using the system clipboard
- Apply text alignment
- Indent text
- Apply bulleted list and numbered list styles
- Set foreground and background colors
- Apply paragraph and heading styles with font family and font size
- Apply formatting styles such as bold, italic, underline, and strikethrough
- Add horizontal rulers

The control supports HTML5. Note that the toolbars do not allow you to apply all kinds of HTML. However, if you load a document that uses those styles, it allows you to edit them. For example, you cannot create an HTML table directly in the control. However, if you load HTML content having HTML tables into the control, you will be able to edit the data in the tables.

The HTMLEditor does not provide an API to load HTML content from a file to save its content to a file. You will have to write your own code to accomplish this.

Creating an *HTMLEditor*

An instance of the HTMLEditor class represents an HTMLEditor control. The class is included in the javafx. scene.web package. Use the default constructor, which is the only constructor provided, to create an HTMLEditor:

```
HTMLEditor editor = new HTMLEditor();
```

Using an *HTMLEditor*

The HTMLEditor class has a very simple API that consists of only three methods:

- getHtmlText()
- setHtmlText(String htmlText)
- print(PrinterJob job)

The getHTMLText() method returns the HTML content as a string. The setHTMLText() method sets the content of the control to the specified HTML string. The print() method prints the content of the control.

The program in Listing 12-46 shows how to use an HTMLEditor. It displays an HTMLEditor, a TextArea, and two Buttons. You can use the buttons to convert text in the HTMLEditor to HTML code and vice versa.

Listing 12-46. Using the HTMLEditor Control

```
// HTMLEditorTest.java
// ... find in the book's download area.
```

Styling *HTMLEditor* with CSS

The default CSS style class name for an HTMLEditor is html-editor. The HTMLEditor uses styles of a Control such as padding, borders, and background color.

You can style each button in the toolbar separately. The following are the list of style class names for the toolbar buttons. The names are self-explanatory, for example, html-editor-align-right and html-editor-hr are the style class names for the toolbar buttons used to right align text and draw a horizontal ruler, respectively.

- html-editor-cut
- html-editor-copy
- html-editor-paste
- html-editor-align-left
- html-editor-align-center
- html-editor-align-right
- html-editor-align-justify
- html-editor-outdent
- html-editor-indent
- html-editor-bullets

- `html-editor-numbers`
- `html-editor-bold`
- `html-editor-italic`
- `html-editor-underline`
- `html-editor-strike`
- `html-editor-hr`

The following code sets a custom image for the Cut button in the toolbar:

```
.html-editor-cut {
      -fx-graphic: url("my_html_editor_cut.jpg");
}
```

Use the `button` and `toggle-button` style class names if you want to apply styles to all toolbar buttons and toggle buttons:

```
/* Set the background colors for all buttons and toggle buttons */
.html-editor .button, .html-editor .toggle-button {
    -fx-background-color: lightblue;
}
```

The `HTMLEditor` shows two `ColorPickers` for users to select the background and foreground colors. Their style class names are `html-editor-background` and `html-editor-foreground`. The following code shows the selected color labels in the `ColorPickers`:

```
.html-editor-background {
    -fx-color-label-visible: true;
}

.html-editor-foreground {
    -fx-color-label-visible: true;
}
```

Choosing Files and Directories

JavaFX provides the `FileChooser` and `DirectoryChooser` classes in the `javafx.stage` package that are used to show file and directory dialogs. The dialogs have a platform-dependent look and feel and cannot be styled using JavaFX. They are *not* controls. I am discussing them in this chapter because they are typically used along with controls. For example, a file or directory dialog is displayed when a button is clicked. On some platforms, for example, some mobile and embedded devices, users may not have access to the file systems. Using these classes to access files and directories on such devices does nothing.

The *FileChooser* Dialog

A `FileChooser` is a standard file dialog. It is used to let the user select files to open or save. Some of its parts, for example, the title, the initial directory, and the list of file extensions, can be specified before opening the dialogs. There are three steps in using a file dialog:

1. Create an object of the FileChooser class.

2. Set the initial properties for the file dialog.

3. Use one of the showXXXDialog() methods to show a specific type of file dialog.

Creating a File Dialog

An instance of the FileChooser class is used to open file dialogs. The class contains a no-args constructor to create its objects:

```
// Create a file dialog
FileChooser fileDialog = new FileChooser();
```

Setting Initial Properties of the Dialog

You can set the following initial properties of the file dialog:

- Title
- initialDirectory
- initialFileName
- Extension filters

The title property of the FileChooser class is a string, which represents the title of the file dialog:

```
// Set the file dialog title
fileDialog.setTitle("Open Resume");
```

The initialDirectory property of the FileChooser class is a File, which represents the initial directory when the file dialog is shown:

```
// Set C:\ as initial directory (on Windows)
fileDialog.setInitialDirectory(new File("C:\\"));
```

The initialFileName property of the FileChooser class is a string that is the initial file name for the file dialog. Typically, it is used for a file save dialog. Its effect depends on the platform if it is used for a file open dialog. For example, it is ignored on Windows:

```
// Set the initial file name
fileDialog.setInitialFileName("untitled.htm");
```

You can set a list of extension filters for a file dialog. Filters are displayed as a drop-down box. One filter is active at a time. The file dialog displays only those files that match the active extension filter. An extension filter is represented by an instance of the ExtensionFilter class, which is an inner static class of the FileChooser class. The getExtensionFilters() method of the FileChooser class returns an ObservableList<FileChooser.ExtensionFilter>. You add the extension filters to the list. An extension filter has two properties: a description and a list of file extension in the form *.<extension>:

```
import static javafx.stage.FileChooser.ExtensionFilter;
...
// Add three extension filters
fileDialog.getExtensionFilters().addAll(
        new ExtensionFilter("HTML Files", "*.htm", "*.html"),
        new ExtensionFilter("Text Files", "*.txt"),
        new ExtensionFilter("All Files", "*.*"));
```

By default, the first extension filter in the list is active when the file dialog is displayed. Use the selectedExtensionFilter property to specify the initial active filter when the file dialog is opened:

```
// Continuing with the above snippet of code, select *.txt filter by default
fileDialog.setSelectedExtensionFilter(
    fileDialog.getExtensionFilters().get(1));
```

The same selectedExtensionFilter property contains the extension filter that is selected by the user when the file dialog is closed.

Showing the Dialog

An instance of the FileChooser class can open three types of file dialogs:

- A file open dialog to select only one file
- A file open dialog to select multiple files
- A file save dialog

The following three methods of the FileChooser class are used to open three types of file dialogs:

- showOpenDialog(Window ownerWindow)
- showOpenMultipleDialog(Window ownerWindow)
- showSaveDialog(Window ownerWindow)

The methods do not return until the file dialog is closed. You can specify null as the owner window. If you specify an owner window, the input to the owner window is blocked when the file dialog is displayed.

The showOpenDialog() and showSaveDialog() methods return a File object, which is the selected file, or null if no file is selected. The showOpenMultipleDialog() method returns a List<File>, which contains all selected files, or null if no files are selected:

```
// Show a file open dialog to select multiple files
List<File> files = fileDialog.showOpenMultipleDialog(primaryStage);
if (files != null) {
        for(File f : files) {
                System.out.println("Selected file :" + f);
        }
} else {
        System.out.println("No files were selected.");
}
```

Use the selectedExtensionFilter property of the FileChooser class to get the selected extension filter at the time the file dialog was closed:

```
import static javafx.stage.FileChooser.ExtensionFilter;
...
// Print the selected extension filter description
ExtensionFilter filter = fileDialog.getSelectedExtensionFilter();
if (filter != null) {
    System.out.println("Selected Filter: " + filter.getDescription());
} else {
        System.out.println("No extension filter selected.");
}
```

Using a File Dialog

The program in Listing 12-47 shows how to use open and save file dialogs. It displays a window with an HTMLEditor and three buttons. Use the Open button to open an HTML file in the editor. Edit the content in the editor. Use the Save button to save the content in the editor to a file. If you chose an existing file in the Save Resume dialog, the content of the file will be overwritten. It is left to the reader as an exercise to enhance the program, so it will prompt the user before overwriting an existing file.

Listing 12-47. Using Open and Save File Dialogs

```
// FileChooserTest.java
// ... find in the book's download area.
```

The *DirectoryChooser* Dialog

Sometimes, you may need to let the user browse a directory from the available file systems on the computer. The DirectoryChooser class lets you display a platform-dependent directory dialog.

The DirectoryChooser class contains two properties:

- title
- initialDirectory

The title property is a string, and it is the title of the directory dialog. The initialDirectory property is a File, and it is the initial directory selected in the dialog when the dialog is shown.

Use the showDialog(Window ownerWindow) method of the DirectoryChooser class to open the directory dialog. When the dialog is opened, you can select at most one directory or close the dialog without selecting a directory. The method returns a File, which is the selected directory, or null if no directory is selected. The method is blocked until the dialog is closed. If an owner window is specified, input to all windows in the owner window chain is blocked when the dialog is shown. You can specify a null owner window.

The following snippet of code shows how to create, configure, and display a directory dialog:

```
DirectoryChooser dirDialog = new DirectoryChooser();

// Configure the properties
dirDialog.setTitle("Select Destination Directory");
dirDialog.setInitialDirectory(new File("c:\\"));
```

```
// Show the directory dialog
File dir = dirDialog.showDialog(null);
if (dir != null) {
        System.out.println("Selected directory: " + dir);
} else {
        System.out.println("No directory was selected.");
}
```

Summary

A user interface is a means to exchange information in terms of input and output between an application and its users. Entering text using a keyboard, selecting a menu item using a mouse, and clicking a button are examples of providing input to a GUI application. The application displays output on a computer monitor using text, charts, and dialog boxes, among others. Users interact with a GUI application using graphical elements called *controls* or *widgets*. Buttons, labels, text fields, text area, radio buttons, and check boxes are a few examples of controls. JavaFX provides a rich set of easy-to-use controls. Controls are added to layout panes that position and size them.

Each control in JavaFX is represented by an instance of a class. Control classes are included in the javafx.scene.control package. A control class in JavaFX is a subclass, direct or indirect, of the Control class, which in turn inherits from the Region class. Recall that the Region class inherits from the Parent class. Therefore, technically, a Control is also a Parent. A Parent can have children. However, control classes do not allow adding children. Typically, a control consists of multiple nodes that are internally maintained. Control classes expose the list of their internal unmodifiable children through the getChildrenUnmodifiable() method, which returns an ObservableList<Node>.

A labeled control contains a read-only textual content and optionally a graphic as part of its user interface. Label, Button, CheckBox, RadioButton, and Hyperlink are some examples of labeled controls in JavaFX. All labeled controls are inherited, directly or indirectly, from the Labeled class that, in turn, inherits from the Control class. The Labeled class contains properties common to all labeled controls, such as content alignment, positioning of text relative to the graphic, and text font.

JavaFX provides button controls that can be used to execute commands, make choices, or both. All button control classes inherit from the ButtonBase class. All types of buttons support the ActionEvent. Buttons trigger an ActionEvent when they are activated. A button can be activated in different ways, for example, by using a mouse, a mnemonic, an accelerator key, or other key combinations. A button that executes a command when activated is known as a command button. The Button, Hyperlink, and MenuButton classes represent command buttons. A MenuButton lets the user execute a command from a list of commands. Buttons used for presenting different choices to users are known as choice buttons. The ToggleButton, CheckBox, and RadioButton classes represent choice buttons. The third kind of button is a hybrid of the first two kinds. They let users execute a command or make choices. The SplitMenuButton class represents a hybrid button.

JavaFX provides controls that let users select an item(s) from a list of items. They take less space compared to buttons. Those controls are ChoiceBox, ComboBox, ListView, ColorPicker, and DatePicker. ChoiceBox lets users select an item from a small list of predefined items. ComboBox is an advanced version of ChoiceBox. It has many features, for example, an ability to be editable or changing the appearance of the items in the list, which are not offered in ChoiceBox. ListView provides users an ability to select multiple items from a list of items. Typically, all or more than one item in a ListView are visible to the user all of the time. ColorPicker lets users select a color from a standard color palette or define a custom color graphically. DatePicker lets users select a date from a calendar pop-up. Optionally, users can enter a date as text. ComboBox, ColorPicker, and DatePicker have the same superclass that is the ComboBoxBase class.

Text input controls let users work with single line or multiple lines of plain text. All text input controls are inherited from the TextInputControl class. There are three types of text input controls: TextField,

PasswordField, and TextArea. TextField lets the user enter a single line of plain text; newlines and tab characters in the text are removed. PasswordField inherits from TextField. It works much the same as TextField, except it masks its text. TextArea lets the user enter multiline plain text. A newline character starts a new paragraph in a TextArea.

For a long-running task, you need to provide visual feedback to the user indicating the progress of the task for a better user experience. The ProgressIndicator and ProgressBar controls are used to show the progress of a task. They differ in the ways they display the progress. The ProgressBar class inherits from the ProgressIndicator class. ProgressIndicator displays the progress in a circular control, whereas ProgressBar uses a horizontal bar.

TitledPane is a labeled control. It displays the text as its title. The graphic is shown in the title bar. Besides text and a graphic, it has content, which is a node. Typically, a group of controls is placed in a container, and the container is added as the content for the TitledPane. TitledPane can be in a collapsed or expanded state. In the collapsed state, it displays only the title bar and hides the content. In the expanded state, it displays the title bar and the content.

Accordion is a control that displays a group of TitledPane controls where only one of them is in the expanded state at a time.

Pagination is a control that is used to display a large single content by dividing it into smaller chunks called pages, for example, the results of a search.

A tool tip is a pop-up control used to show additional information about a node. It is displayed when a mouse pointer hovers over the node. There is a small delay between when the mouse pointer hovers over a node and when the tool tip for the node is shown. The tool tip is hidden after a small period. It is also hidden when the mouse pointer leaves the control. You should not design a GUI application where the user depends on seeing tool tips for controls, as they may not be shown at all if the mouse pointer never hovers over the controls.

The ScrollBar and ScrollPane controls provide scrolling features to other controls. These controls are not used alone. They are always used to support scrolling in other controls.

Sometimes, you want to place logically related controls side by side horizontally or vertically. For better appearance, controls are grouped using different types of separators. The Separator and SplitPane controls are used for visually separating two controls or two groups of controls.

The Slider control lets the user select a numeric value from a numeric range graphically by sliding a thumb (or knob) along a track. A Slider can be horizontal or vertical.

A menu is used to provide a list of actionable items to the user in a compact form. A menu bar is a horizontal bar that acts as a container for menus. An instance of the MenuBar class represents a menu bar. A menu contains a list of actionable items, which are displayed on demand, for example, by clicking it. The list of menu items is hidden when the user selects an item or moves the mouse pointer outside the list. A menu is typically added to a menu bar or another menu as a submenu. An instance of the Menu class represents a menu. A Menu displays text and a graphic. A menu item is an actionable item in a menu. The action associated with a menu item is performed by a mouse or keys. Menu items can be styled using CSS. An instance of the MenuItem class represents a menu item. The MenuItem class is not a node. It is inherited from the Object class and, therefore, cannot be added directly to a scene graph. You need to add it to a Menu.

ContextMenu is a pop-up control that displays a list of menu items on request. It is known as a context or pop-up menu. By default, it is hidden. The user has to make a request, usually by right-clicking the mouse button, to show it. It is hidden once a selection is made. The user can dismiss a context menu by pressing the Esc key or clicking outside its bounds. An object of the ContextMenu class represents a context menu.

ToolBar is used to display a group of nodes, which provide the commonly used action items on a screen. Typically, a ToolBar contains the commonly used items that are also available through a menu and a context menu. A ToolBar can hold many types of nodes. The most commonly used nodes in a ToolBar are buttons and toggle buttons. Separators are used to separate a group of buttons from others. Typically, buttons are kept smaller by using small icons, preferably 16px by 16px in size.

A window may not have enough space to display all of the pieces of information in a one-page view. TabPanes and Tabs let you present information in a page much better. A Tab represents a page, and a TabPane contains the tabs. A Tab is not a control. An instance of the Tab class represents a Tab. The Tab class inherits from the Object class. However, a Tab supports some features as controls do, for example, they can be disabled, styled using CSS, and have context menus and tool tips.

A Tab consists of a title and content. The title consists of text, an optional graphic, and an optional close button to close the tab. The content consists of controls. Typically, the titles of tabs in a TabPane are visible. The content area is shared by all tabs. Tabs in a TabPane may be positioned at the top, right, bottom, or left side of the TabPane. By default, they are positioned at the top.

The HTMLEditor control provides a rich text editing capability to a JavaFX application. It uses HTML as its data model. That is, the formatted text in HTMLEditor is stored in HTML format.

JavaFX provides the FileChooser and DirectoryChooser classes in the javafx.stage package that are used to show file and directory dialogs, respectively. The dialogs have a platform-dependent look and feel and cannot be styled using JavaFX. They are not controls. A FileChooser is a standard file dialog. It is used to let the user select files to open or save. A DirectoryChooser lets the user browse a directory from the available file systems on the machine.

The next chapter will discuss the TableView control that is used to display and edit data in tabular format.

CHAPTER 13

■ ■ ■

Understanding *TableView*

In this chapter, you will learn:

- What a `TableView` is
- How to create a `TableView`
- About adding columns to a `TableView`
- About populating a `TableView` with data
- About showing and hiding and reordering columns in a `TableView`
- About sorting and editing data in a `TableView`
- About adding and deleting rows in a `TableView`
- About resizing columns in a `TableView`
- About styling a `TableView` with CSS

The examples of this chapter lie in the `com.jdojo.control` package. In order for them to work, you must add a corresponding line to the `module-info.java` file:

```
...
opens com.jdojo.control to javafx.graphics, javafx.base;
...
```

Some of the longer listings of this chapter are shown in abbreviated manner. For the complete listings, please consult the download area for the book.

What Is a *TableView*?

`TableView` is a powerful control to display and edit data in a tabular form from a data model. A `TableView` consists of rows and columns. A cell is an intersection of a row and a column. Cells contain the data values. Columns have headers that describe the type of data they contain. Columns can be nested. Resizing and sorting of column data have built-in support. Figure 13-1 shows a `TableView` with four columns that have the header text Id, First Name, Last Name, and Birth Date. It has five rows, with each row containing data for a person. For example, the cell in the fourth row and third column contains the last name Boyd.

Id	First Name	Last Name	Birth Date
1	Ashwin	Sharan	2012-10-11
2	Advik	Sharan	2012-10-11
3	Layne	Estes	2011-12-16
4	Mason	Boyd	2003-04-20
5	Babalu	Sharan	1980-01-10

Figure 13-1. *A TableView showing a list of persons*

TableView is a powerful, but not simple, control. You need to write a few lines of code to use even the simplest TableView that displays some meaningful data to users. There are several classes involved in working with TableView. I will discuss these classes in detail when I discuss the different features of the TableView:

- TableView
- TableColumn
- TableRow
- TableCell
- TablePosition
- TableView.TableViewFocusModel
- TableView.TableViewSelectionModel

The TableView class represents a TableView control. The TableColumn class represents a column in a TableView. Typically, a TableView contains multiple instances of TableColumn. A TableColumn consists of cells, which are instances of the TableCell class. A TableColumn uses two properties to populate cells and render values in them. It uses a cell value factory to extract the value for its cells from the list of items. It uses a cell factory to render data in a cell. You must specify a cell value factory for a TableColumn to see some data in it. A TableColumn uses a default cell factory that knows how to render text and a graphic node.

The TableRow class inherits from the IndexedCell class. An instance of TableRow represents a row in a TableView. You would almost never use this class in an application unless you want to provide a customized implementation for rows. Typically, you customize cells, not rows.

An instance of the TableCell class represents a cell in a TableView. Cells are highly customizable. They display data from the underlying data model for the TableView. They are capable of displaying data as well as graphics.

The TableColumn, TableRow, and TableCell classes contain a tableView property that holds the reference of the TableView that contains them. The tableView property contains null when the TableColumn does not belong to a TableView.

A TablePosition represents the position of a cell. Its getRow() and getColumn() methods return the indexes of the row and column, respectively, to which the cell belongs.

The TableViewFocusModel class is an inner static class of the TableView class. It represents the focus model for the TableView to manage focus for rows and cells.

The TableViewSelectionModel class is an inner static class of the TableView class. It represents the selection model for the TableView to manage selection for rows and cells.

Like ListView and TreeView controls, TableView is virtualized. It creates just enough cells to display the visible content. As you scroll through the content, the cells are recycled. This helps keep the number of nodes in the scene graph to a minimum. Suppose you have 10 columns and 1000 rows in a TableView, and only 10 rows are visible at a time. An inefficient approach would be to create 10,000 cells, one cell for each piece of data. The TableView creates only 100 cells, so it can display ten rows with ten columns. As you scroll through the content, the same 100 cells will be recycled to show the other visible rows. Virtualization makes it possible to use TableView with a large data model without performance penalty for viewing the data in a chunk.

For examples in this chapter, I will use the Person class from Chapter 11 on MVC. The Person class is in the com.jdojo.mvc.model package. Before I start discussing the TableView control in detail, I will introduce a PersonTableUtil class, as shown in Listing 13-1. I will reuse it several times in the examples presented. It has static methods to return an observable list of persona and instances of the TableColumn class to represent columns in a TableView.

Listing 13-1. A PersonTableUtil Utility Class

```java
// PersonTableUtil.java
package com.jdojo.control;

import com.jdojo.mvc.model.Person;
import java.time.LocalDate;
import javafx.collections.FXCollections;
import javafx.collections.ObservableList;
import javafx.scene.control.TableColumn;
import javafx.scene.control.cell.PropertyValueFactory;

public class PersonTableUtil {
    /* Returns an observable list of persons */
    public static ObservableList<Person> getPersonList() {
        Person p1 =
            new Person("Ashwin", "Sharan", LocalDate.of(2012, 10, 11));
        Person p2 =
            new Person("Advik", "Sharan", LocalDate.of(2012, 10, 11));
        Person p3 =
            new Person("Layne", "Estes", LocalDate.of(2011, 12, 16));
        Person p4 =
            new Person("Mason", "Boyd", LocalDate.of(2003, 4, 20));
        Person p5 =
            new Person("Babalu", "Sharan", LocalDate.of(1980, 1, 10));
        return FXCollections.<Person>observableArrayList(p1, p2, p3, p4, p5);
    }

    /* Returns Person Id TableColumn */
    public static TableColumn<Person, Integer> getIdColumn() {
        TableColumn<Person, Integer> personIdCol = new TableColumn<>("Id");
        personIdCol.setCellValueFactory(
                new PropertyValueFactory<>("personId"));
        return personIdCol;
    }

    /* Returns First Name TableColumn */
    public static TableColumn<Person, String> getFirstNameColumn() {
        TableColumn<Person, String> fNameCol =
            new TableColumn<>("First Name");
```

```
        fNameCol.setCellValueFactory(new PropertyValueFactory<>("firstName"));
        return fNameCol;
    }

    /* Returns Last Name TableColumn */
    public static TableColumn<Person, String> getLastNameColumn() {
        TableColumn<Person, String> lastNameCol =
                new TableColumn<>("Last Name");
        lastNameCol.setCellValueFactory(
                new PropertyValueFactory<>("lastName"));
        return lastNameCol;
    }

    /* Returns Birth Date TableColumn */
    public static TableColumn<Person, LocalDate> getBirthDateColumn() {
        TableColumn<Person, LocalDate> bDateCol =
            new TableColumn<>("Birth Date");
        bDateCol.setCellValueFactory(
                new PropertyValueFactory<>("birthDate"));
        return bDateCol;
    }
}
```

Subsequent sections will walk you through the steps to display and edit data in a TableView.

Creating a *TableView*

In the following example, you will use the TableView class to create a TableView control. TableView is a parameterized class, which takes the type of items the TableView contains. Optionally, you can pass the model into its constructor that supplies the data. The constructor creates a TableView without a model. The following statement creates a TableView that will use objects of the Person class as its items:

```
TableView<Person> table = new TableView<>();
```

When you add the preceding TableView to a scene, it displays a placeholder, as shown in Figure 13-2. The placeholder lets you know that you need to add columns to the TableView. There must be at least one visible leaf column in the TableView data.

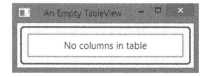

Figure 13-2. *A TableView with no columns and data showing a placeholder*

You would use another constructor of the TableView class to specify the model. It accepts an observable list of items. The following statement passes an observable list of Person objects as the initial data for the TableView:

```
TableView<Person> table = new TableView<>(PersonTableUtil.getPersonList());
```

Adding Columns to a *TableView*

An instance of the TableColumn class represents a column in a TableView. A TableColumn is responsible for displaying and editing the data in its cells. A TableColumn has a header that can display header text, a graphic, or both. You can have a context menu for a TableColumn, which is displayed when the user right-clicks inside the column header. Use the contextMenu property to set a context menu.

The TableColumn<S, T> class is a generic class. The S parameter is the item type, which is of the same type as the parameter of the TableView. The T parameter is the type of data in all cells of the column. For example, an instance of the TableColumn<Person, Integer> may be used to represent a column to display the ID of a Person, which is of int type; an instance of the TableColumn<Person, String> may be used to represent a column to display the *first name* of a person, which is of String type. The following snippet of code creates a TableColumn with First Name as its header text:

```
TableColumn<Person, String> fNameCol = new TableColumn<>("First Name");
```

A TableColumn needs to know how to get the value (or data) for its cells from the model. To populate the cells, you need to set the cellValueFactory property of the TableColumn. If the model for a TableView contains objects of a class that is based on JavaFX properties, you can use an object of the PropertyValueFactory class as the cell value factory, which takes the property name. It reads the property value from the model and populates all of the cells in the column, as in the following code:

```
// Use the firstName property of Person object to populate the column cells
PropertyValueFactory<Person, String> fNameCellValueFactory =
        new PropertyValueFactory<>("firstName");
fNameCol.setCellValueFactory(fNameCellValueFactory);
```

You need to create a TableColumn object for each column in the TableView and set its cell value factory property. The next section will explain what to do if your item class is not based on JavaFX properties, or you want to populate the cells with computed values.

The last step in setting up a TableView is to add TableColumns to its list of columns. A TableView stores references of its columns in an ObservableList<TableColumn> whose reference can be obtained using the getColumns() method of the TableView:

```
// Add the First Name column to the TableView
table.getColumns().add(fNameCol);
```

That is all it takes to use a TableView in its simplest form, which is not so "simple" after all! The program in Listing 13-2 shows how to create a TableView with a model and add columns to it. It uses the PersonTableUtil class to get the list of persons and columns. The program displays a window as shown in Figure 13-3.

Listing 13-2. Using TableView in Its Simplest Form

```
// SimplestTableView.java
package com.jdojo.control;

import com.jdojo.mvc.model.Person;
import javafx.application.Application;
import javafx.scene.Scene;
import javafx.scene.control.TableView;
import javafx.scene.layout.VBox;
import javafx.stage.Stage;
```

```java
public class SimplestTableView extends Application {
        public static void main(String[] args) {
                Application.launch(args);
        }

        @Override
        public void start(Stage stage) {
                // Create a TableView with a list of persons
                TableView<Person> table =
                        new TableView<>(PersonTableUtil.getPersonList());

                // Add columns to the TableView
                table.getColumns().addAll(
                        PersonTableUtil.getIdColumn(),
                        PersonTableUtil.getFirstNameColumn(),
                        PersonTableUtil.getLastNameColumn(),
                        PersonTableUtil.getBirthDateColumn());

                VBox root = new VBox(table);
                root.setStyle("""
                        -fx-padding: 10;
                   -fx-border-style: solid inside;
                   -fx-border-width: 2;
                   -fx-border-insets: 5;
                   -fx-border-radius: 5;
                   -fx-border-color: blue;""");

                Scene scene = new Scene(root);
                stage.setScene(scene);
                stage.setTitle("Simplest TableView");
                stage.show();
        }
}
```

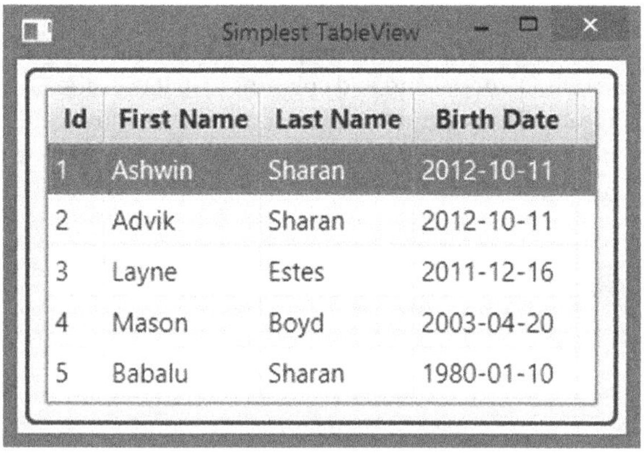

Figure 13-3. *A window with a TableView that displays four columns and five rows*

TableView supports nesting of columns. For example, you can have two columns, First and Last, nested inside a Name column. A TableColumn stores the list of nested columns in an observable list whose reference can be obtained using the getColumns() method of the TableColumn class. The innermost nested columns are known as *leaf columns*. You need to add the cell value factories for the leaf columns. Nested columns only provide visual effects. The following snippet of code creates a TableView and adds an Id column and two leaf columns, First and Last, that are nested in the Name column. The resulting TableView is shown in Figure 13-4. Note that you add the topmost columns to the TableView, not the nested columns. TableView takes care of adding all nested columns for the topmost columns. There is no limit on the level of column nesting.

```
// Create a TableView with data
TableView<Person> table = new TableView<>(PersonTableUtil.getPersonList());

// Create leaf columns - Id, First and Last
TableColumn<Person, String> idCol = new TableColumn<>("Id");
idCol.setCellValueFactory(new PropertyValueFactory<>("personId"));

TableColumn<Person, String> fNameCol = new TableColumn<>("First");
fNameCol.setCellValueFactory(new PropertyValueFactory<>("firstName"));

TableColumn<Person, String> lNameCol = new TableColumn<>("Last");
lNameCol.setCellValueFactory(new PropertyValueFactory<>("lastName"));

// Create Name column and nest First and Last columns in it
TableColumn<Person, String> nameCol = new TableColumn<>("Name");
nameCol.getColumns().addAll(fNameCol, lNameCol);

// Add columns to the TableView
table.getColumns().addAll(idCol, nameCol);
```

Id	Name	
	First	Last
1	Ashwin	Sharan
2	Advik	Sharan
3	Layne	Estes
4	Mason	Boyd
5	Babalu	Sharan

Figure 13-4. *A TableView with nested columns*

The following methods in the TableView class provide information about visible leaf columns:

```
TableColumn<S,?> getVisibleLeafColumn(int columnIndex)
ObservableList<TableColumn<S,?>> getVisibleLeafColumns()
int getVisibleLeafIndex(TableColumn<S,?> column)
```

The getVisibleLeafColumn() method returns the reference of the column for the specified column index. The column index is counted only for the visible leaf column, and the index starts at zero. The getVisibleLeafColumns() method returns an observable list of all visible leaf columns. The getVisibleLeafIndex() method returns the column reference for the specified column index of a visible leaf column.

Customizing *TableView* Placeholder

TableView displays a placeholder when it does not have any visible leaf columns or content. Consider the following snippet of code that creates a TableView and adds columns to it:

```
TableView<Person> table = new TableView<>();
table.getColumns().addAll(PersonTableUtil.getIdColumn(),
                   PersonTableUtil.getFirstNameColumn(),
                   PersonTableUtil.getLastNameColumn(),
                   PersonTableUtil.getBirthDateColumn());
```

Figure 13-5 shows the results of the preceding TableView. Columns and a placeholder are displayed, indicating that the TableView does not have data.

Id	First Name	Last Name	Birth Date
	No content in table		

Figure 13-5. *A TableView control with columns and no data*

You can replace the built-in placeholder using the placeholder property of the TableView. The value for the property is an instance of the Node class. The following statement sets a Label with a generic message as a placeholder:

```
table.setPlaceholder(new Label("No visible columns and/or data exist."));
```

You can set a custom placeholder to inform the user of the specific condition that resulted in showing no data in the TableView. The following statement uses binding to change the placeholder as the conditions change:

```
table.placeholderProperty().bind(
    new When(new SimpleIntegerProperty(0)
                .isEqualTo(table.getVisibleLeafColumns().size()))
        .then(new When(new SimpleIntegerProperty(0)
                        .isEqualTo(table.getItems().size()))
                .then(new Label("No columns and data exist."))
                .otherwise(new Label("No columns exist.")))
        .otherwise(new When(new SimpleIntegerProperty(0)
                        .isEqualTo(table.getItems().size()))
                .then(new Label("No data exist."))
                .otherwise((Label)null)));
```

Populating a *TableColumn* with Data

Cells in a row of a TableView contain data related to an item such as a person, a book, and so forth. Data for some cells in a row may come directly from the attributes of the item or they may be computed.

TableView has an items property of the ObservableList<S> type. The generic type S is the same as the generic type of the TableView. It is the data model for the TableView. Each element in the items list represents a row in the TableView. Adding a new item to the items list adds a new row to the TableView. Deleting an item from the items list deletes the corresponding row from the TableView.

■ **Tip**   Whether updating an item in the items list updates the corresponding data in the TableView depends on how the cell value factory for the column is set up. I will discuss examples of both kinds in this section.

The following snippet of code creates a TableView in which a row represents a Person object. It adds data for two rows:

```
TableView<Person> table = new TableView<>();

Person p1 = new Person("John", "Jacobs", null);
Person p2 = new Person("Donna", "Duncan", null);
table.getItems().addAll(p1, p2);
```

Adding items to a TableView is useless unless you add columns to it. Among several other things, a TableColumn object defines

- Header text and graphic for the column

- A cell value factory to populate the cells in the column

The TableColumn class gives you full control over how cells in a column are populated. The cellValueFactory property of the TableColumn class is responsible for populating cells of the column. A cell value factory is an object of the Callback class, which receives a TableColumn.CellDataFeatures object and returns an ObservableValue.

The CellDataFeatures class is a static inner class of the TableColumn class, which wraps the reference of the TableView, TableColumn, and the item for the row for which the cells of the column are being populated. Use the getTableView(), getTableColumn(), and getValue() methods of the CellDataFeatures class to get the reference of the TableView, TableColumn, and the item for the row, respectively.

When the TableView needs the value for a cell, it calls the call() method of the cell value factory object of the column to which the cell belongs. The call() method is supposed to return the reference of an ObservableValue object, which is monitored for any changes. The returned ObservableValue object may contain any type of object. If it contains a node, the node is displayed as a graphic in the cell. Otherwise, the toString() method of the object is called, and the returned string is displayed in the cell.

The following snippet of code creates a cell value factory using an anonymous class. The factory returns the reference of the firstName property of the Person class. Note that a JavaFX property is an ObservableValue.

```
import static javafx.scene.control.TableColumn.CellDataFeatures;
...
// Create a String column with the header "First Name" for Person object
TableColumn<Person, String> fNameCol = new TableColumn<>("First Name");
```

```
// Create a cell value factory object
Callback<CellDataFeatures<Person, String>, ObservableValue<String>> fNameCellFactory =
  new Callback<CellDataFeatures<Person, String>, ObservableValue<String>>() {
    @Override
    public ObservableValue<String> call(CellDataFeatures<Person,
            String> cellData) {
      Person p = cellData.getValue();
      return p.firstNameProperty();
}};
```

```
// Set the cell value factory
fNameCol.setCellValueFactory(fNameCellFactory);
```

Using a lambda expression to create and set a cell value factory comes in handy. The preceding snippet of code can be written as follows:

```
TableColumn<Person, String> fNameCol = new TableColumn<>("First Name");
fNameCol.setCellValueFactory(cellData ->
    cellData.getValue().firstNameProperty());
```

When a JavaFX property supplies values for cells in a column, creating the cell value factory is easier if you use an object of the PropertyValueFactory class. You need to pass the name of the JavaFX property to its constructor. The following snippet of code does the same as the code shown earlier. You would take this approach to create TableColumn objects inside the utility methods in the PersonTableUtil class.

```
TableColumn<Person, String> fNameCol = new TableColumn<>("First Name");
fNameCol.setCellValueFactory(new PropertyValueFactory<>("firstName"));
```

■ **Tip** Using JavaFX properties as the value supplied for cells has a big advantage. The TableView keeps the value in the property and the cell in sync. Changing the property value in the model automatically updates the value in the cell.

TableColumn also supports POJO (Plain Old Java Object) as items in the TableView. The disadvantage is that when the model is updated, the cell values are not automatically updated. You use the same PropertyValueFactory class to create the cell value factory. The class will look for the public getter and setter methods with the property name you pass. If only the getter method is found, the cell will be read-only. For an xxx property, it tries looking for getXxx() and setXxx() methods using the JavaBeans naming conventions. If the type of xxx is boolean, it also looks for the isXxx() method. If a getter or a setter method is not found, a runtime exception is thrown. The following snippet of code creates a column with the header text Age Category:

```
TableColumn<Person, Person.AgeCategory> ageCategoryCol =
    new TableColumn<>("Age Category");
ageCategoryCol.setCellValueFactory(new PropertyValueFactory<>("ageCategory"));
```

It indicates that the item type is Person and the column type is Person.AgeCategory. It passes ageCategory as the property name into the constructor of the PropertyValueFactory class. First, the class will look for an ageCategory property in the Person class. The Person class does not have this property. Therefore, it will try using the Person class as a POJO for this property. Then it will look for getAgeCategory() and setAgeCategory() methods in the Person class. It finds only the getter method, getAgeCategory(), and hence it will make the column read-only.

The values in the cells of a column do not necessarily have to come from JavaFX or POJO properties. They can be computed using some logic. In such cases, you need to create a custom cell value factory and return a ReadOnlyXxxWrapper object that wraps the computed value. The following snippet of code creates an Age column that displays a computed age in years:

```
TableColumn<Person, String> ageCol = new TableColumn<>("Age");
ageCol.setCellValueFactory(cellData -> {
        Person p = cellData.getValue();
        LocalDate dob = p.getBirthDate();
        String ageInYear = "Unknown";
        if (dob != null) {
                long years = YEARS.between(dob, LocalDate.now());
                if (years == 0) {
                        ageInYear = "< 1 year";
                } else if (years == 1) {
                        ageInYear = years + " year";
                } else {
                        ageInYear = years + " years";
                }
        }
        return new ReadOnlyStringWrapper(ageInYear);
});
```

This completes the different ways of setting the cell value factory for cells of a column in a TableView. The program in Listing 13-3 creates cell value factories for JavaFX properties, a POJO property, and a computed value. It displays a window as shown in Figure 13-6.

Listing 13-3. Setting Cell Value Factories for Columns

```
// TableViewDataTest.java
// ...find in the book's download area
```

Figure 13-6. A TableView having columns for JavaFX properties, POJO properties, and computed values

Cells in a TableView can display text and graphics. If the cell value factory returns an instance of the Node class, which could be an ImageView, the cell displays it as graphic. Otherwise, it displays the string returned from the toString() method of the object. It is possible to display other controls and containers in cells. However, a TableView is not meant for that, and such uses are discouraged. Sometimes, using a specific type of control in a cell, for example, a check box, to show or edit a boolean value provides a better user experience. I will cover such customization of cells shortly.

Using a *Map* As Items in a *TableView*

Sometimes, data in a row for a TableView may not map to a domain object, for example, you may want to display the result set of a dynamic query in a TableView. The items list consists of an observable list of Map. A Map in the list contains values for all columns in the row. You can define a custom cell value factory to extract the data from the Map. The MapValueFactory class is especially designed for this purpose. It is an implementation of the cell value factory, which reads data from a Map for a specified key.

The following snippet of code creates a TableView of Map. It creates an Id column and sets an instance of the MapValueFactory class as its cell value factory specifying the idColumnKey as the key that contains the value for the Id column. It creates a Map and populates the Id column using the idColumnKey. You need to repeat these steps for all columns and rows.

```
TableView<Map> table = new TableView<>();

// Define the column, its cell value factory and add it to the TableView
String idColumnKey = "id";
TableColumn<Map, Integer> idCol = new TableColumn<>("Id");
idCol.setCellValueFactory(new MapValueFactory<>(idColumnKey));
table.getColumns().add(idCol);

// Create and populate a Map an item
Map row1 = new HashMap();
row1.put(idColumnKey, 1);

// Add the Map to the TableView items list
table.getItems().add(row1);
```

The program in Listing 13-4 shows how to use the MapValueFactory as the cell value factory for columns in a TableView. It displays the person's data returned by the getPersonList() method in the PersonTableUtil class.

Listing 13-4. Using MapValueFactory As a Cell Value Factory for Cells in a TableView

```
// TableViewMapDataTest.java
// ...find in the book's download area
```

Showing and Hiding Columns

By default, all columns in a TableView are visible. The TableColumn class has a visible property to set the visibility of a column. If you turn off the visibility of a parent column, a column with nested columns, all of its nested columns will also be invisible:

```
TableColumn<Person, String> idCol = new TableColumn<>("Id");

// Make the Id column invisible
idCol.setVisible(false);
...
// Make the Id column visible
idCol.setVisible(true);
```

Sometimes, you may want to let the user control the visibility of columns. The TableView class has a tableMenuButtonVisible property. If it is set to true, a menu button is displayed in the header area:

```
// Create a TableView
TableView<Person> table = create the TableView here...

// Make the table menu button visible
table.setTableMenuButtonVisible(true);
```

Clicking the menu button displays a list of all leaf columns. Columns are displayed as radio menu items that can be used to toggle their visibility. Figure 13-7 shows a TableView with four columns. Its tableMenuButtonVisible property is set to true. The figure shows a menu with all column names with a check mark. The menu is displayed when the menu button is clicked. The check marks beside the column names indicate that the columns are visible. Clicking the column name toggles its visibility.

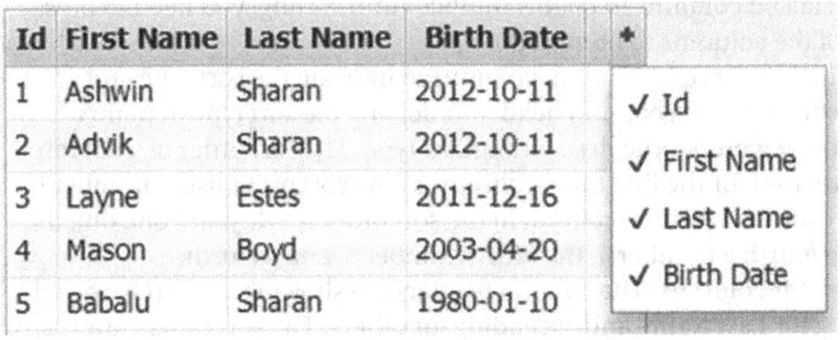

Id	First Name	Last Name	Birth Date	✦
1	Ashwin	Sharan	2012-10-11	✓ Id
2	Advik	Sharan	2012-10-11	✓ First Name
3	Layne	Estes	2011-12-16	✓ Last Name
4	Mason	Boyd	2003-04-20	✓ Birth Date
5	Babalu	Sharan	1980-01-10	

Figure 13-7. A TableView with menu button to toggle the visibility of columns

Reordering Columns in a *TableView*

You can rearrange columns in a TableView in two ways:

- By dragging and dropping columns to a different position
- By changing their positions in the observable list as returned by the getColumns() method of the TableView class

The first option is available by default. The user needs to drag and drop a column at the new position. When a column is reordered, its position in the columns list is changed. The second option will reorder the column directly in the columns list.

There is no easy way to disable the default column-reordering feature. If you want to disable the feature, you would need to add a ChangeListener to the ObservableList returned by the getColumns() method of the TableView. When a change is reported, reset the columns so they are in the original order again.

To enable or disable the column-reordering feature, use the `setReorderable()` method on the columns:

```
table.getColumns().forEach(c -> {
    boolean b = ...; // determine whether column is reorderable
    c.setReorderable(b);
});
```

Sorting Data in a TableView

TableView has built-in support for sorting data in columns. By default, it allows users to sort data by clicking column headers. It also supports sorting data programmatically. You can also disable sorting for a column or all columns in a TableView.

Sorting Data by Users

By default, data in all columns in a TableView can be sorted. Users can sort data in columns by clicking the column headers. The first click sorts the data in ascending order. The second click sorts the data in descending order. The third click removes the column from the sort order list.

By default, single column sorting is enabled. That is, if you click a column, the records in the TableView are sorted based on the data only in the clicked column. To enable multicolumn sorting, you need to press the Shift key while clicking the headers of the columns to be sorted.

TableView displays visual clues in the headers of the sorted columns to indicate the sort type and the sort order. By default, a triangle is displayed in the column header indicating the sort type. It points upward for the ascending sort type and downward for the descending sort type. The sort order of a column is indicated by dots or a number. Dots are used for the first three columns in the sort order list. A number is used for the fourth column onward. For example, the first column in the sort order list displays one dot, the second two dots, the third three dots, the fourth a number 4, the fifth a number 5, and so forth.

Figure 13-8 shows a TableView with four columns. The column headers are showing the sort type and sort orders. The sort types are descending for Last Name and ascending for others. The sort orders are 1, 2, 3, and 4 for Last Name, First Name, Birth Date, and Id, respectively. Notice that dots are used for the sort orders in the first three columns, and a number 4 is used for the Id column because it is fourth on the sort order list. This sorting is achieved by clicking column headers in the following order: Last Name (twice), First Name, Birth Date, and Id.

Id ▲4	First Name ▲	Last Name ▼	Birth Date ▲
2	Advik	Sharan	2012-10-11
1	Ashwin	Sharan	2012-10-11
5	Babalu	Sharan	1980-01-10
3	Layne	Estes	2011-12-16
4	Mason	Boyd	2003-04-20

Figure 13-8. *Column headers showing the sort type and sort order*

Sorting Data Programmatically

Data in columns can be sorted programmatically. The TableView and TableColumn classes provide a very powerful API for sorting. The sorting API consists of several properties and methods in the two classes. Every part and every stage of sorting are customizable. The following sections describe the API with examples.

Making a Column Sortable

The sortable property of a TableColumn determines whether the column is sortable. By default, it is set to true. Set it to false to disable the sorting for a column:

```
// Disable sorting for fNameCol column
fNameCol.setSortable(false);
```

Specifying the Sort Type of a Column

A TableColumn has a sort type, which can be ascending or descending. It is specified through the sortType property. The ASCENDING and DESCENDING constants of TableColumn.SortType enum represent the ascending and descending, respectively, sort types for columns. The default value for the sortType property is TableColumn.SortType.ASCENDING. The DESCENDING constant is set as follows:

```
// Set the sort type for fNameCol column to descending
fNameCol.setSortType(TableColumn.SortType.DESCENDING);
```

Specifying the *Comparator* for a Column

A TableColumn uses a Comparator to sort its data. You can specify the Comparator for a TableColumn using its comparator property. The comparator is passed in the objects in two cells being compared. A TableColumn uses a default Comparator, which is represented by the constant TableColumn.DEFAULT_COMPARATOR. The default comparator compares data in two cells using the following rules:

- It checks for null values. The null values are sorted first. If both cells have null, they are considered equal.

- If the first value being compared is an instance of the Comparable interface, it calls the compareTo() method of the first object passing the second object as an argument to the method.

- If neither of the preceding two conditions are true, it converts the two objects into strings calling their toString() methods and uses a Comparator to compare the two String values.

In most cases, the default comparator is sufficient. The following snippet of code uses a custom comparator for a String column that compares only the first characters of the cell data:

```
TableColumn<Person, String> fNameCol = new TableColumn<>("First Name");
...
// Set a custom comparator
fNameCol.setComparator((String n1, String n2) -> {
        if (n1 == null && n2 == null) {
                return 0;
        }
```

```
        if (n1 == null) {
                return -1;
        }

        if (n2 == null) {
                return 1;
        }

        String c1 = n1.isEmpty()? n1:String.valueOf(n1.charAt(0));
        String c2 = n2.isEmpty()? n2:String.valueOf(n2.charAt(0));
        return c1.compareTo(c2);
});
```

Specifying the Sort Node for a Column

The TableColumn class contains a sortNode property, which specifies a node to display a visual clue in the column header about the current sort type and sort order for the column. The node is rotated by 180 degrees when the sort type is ascending. The node is invisible when the column is not part of the sort. By default, it is null and the TableColumn provides a triangle as the sort node.

Specifying the Sort Order of Columns

The TableView class contains several properties that are used in sorting. To sort columns, you need to add them to the sort order list of the TableView. The sortOrder property specifies the sort order. It is an ObservableList of TableColumn. The order of a TableColumn in the list specifies the order of the column in the sort. Rows are sorted based on the first column in the list. If values in two rows in the column are equal, the second column in the sort order list is used to determine the sort order of the two rows and so on.

The following snippet of code adds two columns to a TableView and specifies their sort order. Notice that both columns will be sorted in ascending order, which is the default sort type. If you want to sort them in descending order, set their sortType property as follows:

```
// Create a TableView with data
TableView<Person> table = new TableView<>(PersonTableUtil.getPersonList());

TableColumn<Person, String> lNameCol = PersonTableUtil.getLastNameColumn();
TableColumn<Person, String> fNameCol = PersonTableUtil.getFirstNameColumn();

// Add columns to the TableView
table.getColumns().addAll(lNameCol, fNameCol );

// Add columns to the sort order to sort by last name followed by first name
table.getSortOrder().addAll(lNameCol, fNameCol);
```

The sortOrder property of the TableView is monitored for changes. If it is modified, the TableView is sorted immediately based on the new sort order. Adding a column to a sort order list does not guarantee inclusion of the column in sorting. The column must also be sortable to be included in sorting. The sortType property of the TableColumn is also monitored for changes. Changing the sort type of a column, which is in the sort order list, resorts the TableView data immediately.

Getting the Comparator for a *TableView*

TableView contains a read-only comparator property, which is a Comparator based on the current sort order list. You rarely need to use this Comparator in your code. If you pass two TableView items to the compare() method of the Comparator, it will return a negative integer, zero, or a positive integer indicating that the first item is less than, equal to, or greater than the second item, respectively.

Recall that TableColumn also has a comparator property, which is used to specify how to determine the order of values in the cells of the TableColumn. The comparator property of the TableView combines the comparator properties of all TableColumns in its sort order list.

Specifying the Sort Policy

A TableView has a sort policy to specify how the sorting is performed. It is a Callback object. The TableView is passed in as an argument to the call() method. The method returns true if the sorting succeeds. It returns false or null if the sorting fails.

The TableView class contains a DEFAULT_SORT_POLICY constant, which is used as a default sort policy for a TableView. It sorts the items list of the TableView using its comparator property. Specify a sort policy to take full charge of the sorting algorithm. The call() method of the sort policy Callback object will perform the sorting of the items of the TableView.

As a trivial example, setting the sort policy to null will disable the sorting, as no sorting will be performed when sorting is requested by the user or program:

```
TableView<Person> table = ...

// Disable sorting for the TableView
table.setSortPolicy(null);
```

Sometimes, it is useful to disable sorting temporarily for performance reasons. Suppose you have a sorted TableView with a large number of items, and you want to make several changes to the sort order list. Every change in the sort order list will trigger a sort on the items. In this case, you may disable the sorting by setting the sort policy to null, make all your changes, and enable the sorting by restoring the original sort policy. A change in the sort policy triggers an immediate sort. This technique will sort the items only once:

```
TableView<Person> table = ...
...
// Store the current sort policy
Callback<TableView<Person>, Boolean> currentSortPolicy =
    table.getSortPolicy();

// Disable the sorting
table.setSortPolicy(null)

// Make all changes that might need or trigger sorting
...

// Restore the sort policy that will sort the data once immediately
table.setSortPolicy(currentSortPolicy);
```

Sorting Data Manually

TableView contains a sort() method that sorts the items in the TableView using the current sort order list. You may call this method to sort items after adding a number of items to a TableView. This method is automatically called when the sort type of a column, the sort order, or sort policy changes.

Handling Sorting Event

TableView fires a SortEvent when it receives a request for sorting and just before it applies the sorting algorithm to its items. Add a SortEvent listener to perform any action before the actual sorting is performed:

```
TableView<Person> table = ...
table.setOnSort(e -> {/* Code to handle the sort event */});
```

If the SortEvent is consumed, the sorting is aborted. If you want to disable sorting for a TableView, consume the SortEvent as follows:

```
// Disable sorting for the TableView
table.setOnSort(e -> e.consume());
```

Disabling Sorting for a TableView

There are several ways you can disable sorting for a TableView:

- Setting the sortable property for a TableColumn disables sorting only for that column. If you set the sortable property to false for all columns in a TableView, the sorting for the TableView is disabled.

- You can set the sort policy for the TableView to null.

- You can consume the SortEvent for the TableView.

- Technically, it is possible, though not recommended, to override the sort() method of the TableView class and provide an empty body for the method.

The best way to disable sorting partially or completely for a TableView is to disable sorting for some or all of its columns.

Customizing Data Rendering in Cells

A cell in a TableColumn is an instance of the TableCell class, which displays the data in the cell. A TableCell is a Labeled control, which is capable of displaying text, a graphic, or both.

You can specify a cell factory for a TableColumn. The job of a cell factory is to render the data in the cell. The TableColumn class contains a cellFactory property, which is a Callback object. Its call() method is passed in the reference of the TableColumn to which the cell belongs. The method returns an instance of TableCell. The updateItem() method of the TableCell is overridden to provide the custom rendering of the cell data.

TableColumn uses a default cell factory if its cellFactory property is not specified. The default cell factory displays the cell data depending on the type of the data. If the cell data comprise a node, the data are displayed in the graphic property of the cell. Otherwise, the toString() method of the cell data is called, and the returned string is displayed in the text property of the cell.

Up to this point, you have been using a list of Person objects as the data model in the examples for displaying data in a TableView. The Birth Date column is formatted as yyyy-mm-dd, which is the default ISO date format returned by the toString() method of the LocalDate class. If you would like to format birth dates in the mm/dd/yyyy format, you can achieve this by setting a custom cell factory for the Birth Date column:

```
TableColumn<Person, LocalDate> birthDateCol = ...;
birthDateCol.setCellFactory (col -> {
    TableCell<Person, LocalDate> cell =
        new TableCell<Person, LocalDate>() {
          @Override
          public void updateItem(LocalDate item, boolean empty) {
              super.updateItem(item, empty);

              // Cleanup the cell before populating it
              this.setText(null);
              this.setGraphic(null);

              if (!empty) {
                  // Format the birth date in mm/dd/yyyy format
                  String formattedDob =
                      DateTimeFormatter.ofPattern("MM/dd/yyyy").
                          format(item);
                  this.setText(formattedDob);
              }
          }
    };
    return cell;
});
```

You can also use the preceding technique to display images in cells. In the updateItem() method, create an ImageView object for the image and display it using the setGraphic() method of the TableCell. TableCell contains tableColumn, tableRow, and tableView properties that store the references of its TableColumn, TableRow, and TableView, respectively. These properties are useful to access the item in the data model that represents the row for the cell.

If you replace the if statement in the preceding snippet of code with the following code, the Birth Date column displays the birth date and age category, for example, 10/11/2012 (BABY):

```
if (!empty) {
    String formattedDob =
        DateTimeFormatter.ofPattern("MM/dd/yyyy").format(item);

    if (this.getTableRow() != null ) {
        // Get the Person item for this cell
        int rowIndex = this.getTableRow().getIndex();
        Person p = this.getTableView().getItems().get(rowIndex);
        String ageCategory = p.getAgeCategory().toString();

        // Display birth date and age category together
        this.setText(formattedDob + " (" + ageCategory + ")" );
    }
}
```

The following are subclasses of `TableCell` that render cell data in different ways. For example, a `CheckBoxTableCell` renders cell data in a check box, and a `ProgressBarTableCell` renders a number using a progress bar:

- `CheckBoxTableCell`

- `ChoiceBoxTableCell`

- `ComboBoxTableCell`

- `ProgressBarTableCell`

- `TextFieldTableCell`

The following snippet of code creates a column labeled Baby? and sets a cell factory to display the value in a `CheckBoxTableCell`. The `forTableColumn(TableColumn<S, Boolean> col)` method of the `CheckBoxTableCell` class returns a `Callback` object that is used as a cell factory:

```
// Create a "Baby?" column
TableColumn<Person, Boolean> babyCol = new TableColumn<>("Baby?");
babyCol.setCellValueFactory(cellData -> {
        Person p = cellData.getValue();
        Boolean v =  (p.getAgeCategory() == Person.AgeCategory.BABY);
        return new ReadOnlyBooleanWrapper(v);
});

// Set a cell factory that will use a CheckBox to render the value
babyCol.setCellFactory(CheckBoxTableCell.<Person>forTableColumn(babyCol));
```

Please explore the API documentation for other subclasses of the `TableCell` and how to use them. For example, you can display a combo box with a list of choices in the cells of a column. Users can select one of the choices as the cell data.

Listing 13-5 has a complete program to show how to use custom cell factories. It displays a window as shown in Figure 13-9. The program uses a cell factory to format the birth date in mm/dd/yyyy format and a cell factory to display whether a person is a baby using a check box.

Listing 13-5. Using a Custom Cell Factory for a TableColumn

```
// TableViewCellFactoryTest.java
// ...find in the book's download area
```

Figure 13-9. *Using custom cell factories to format data in cells and display cell data in check boxes*

Selecting Cells and Rows in a *TableView*

TableView has a selection model represented by its property selectionModel. A selection model is an instance of the TableViewSelectionModel class, which is an inner static class of the TableView class. The selection model supports cell-level and row-level selection. It also supports two selection modes: single and multiple. In the single selection mode, only one cell or row can be selected at a time. In the multiple selection mode, multiple cells or rows can be selected. By default, single-row selection is enabled. You can enable multirow selection, as follows:

```
TableView<Person> table = ...

// Turn on multiple-selection mode for the TableView
TableViewSelectionModel<Person> tsm = table.getSelectionModel();
tsm.setSelectionMode(SelectionMode.MULTIPLE);
```

The cell-level selection can be enabled by setting the cellSelectionEnabled property of the selection model to true, as in the following snippet of code. When the property is set to true, the TableView is put in cell-level selection mode, and you cannot select an entire row. If multiple selection mode is enabled, you can still select all cells in a row. However, the row itself is not reported as selected as the TableView is in the cell-level selection mode. By default, cell-level selection mode is false.

```
// Enable cell-level selection
tsm.setCellSelectionEnabled(true);
```

The selection model provides information about the selected cells and rows. The isSelected(int rowIndex) method returns true if the row at the specified rowIndex is selected. Use the isSelected(int rowIndex, TableColumn<S,?> column) method to know if a cell at the specified rowIndex and column is selected. The selection model provides several methods to select cells and rows and get the report of selected cells and rows:

- The selectAll() method selects all cells or rows.

- The select() method is overloaded. It selects a row, a row for an item, and a cell.

- The isEmpty() method returns true if there is no selection. Otherwise, it returns false.

- The getSelectedCells() method returns a read-only ObservableList<TablePosition> that is the list of currently selected cells. The list changes as the selection in the TableView changes.

- The getSelectedIndices() method returns a read-only ObservableList<Integer> that is the list of currently selected indexes. The list changes as the selection in the TableView changes. If row-level selection is enabled, an item in the list is the row index of the selected row. If cell-level selection is enabled, an item in the list is the row index of the row in which one or more cells are selected.

- The getSelectedItems() method returns a read-only ObservableList<S> where S is the generic type of the TableView. The list contains all items for which the corresponding row or cells have been selected.

- The clearAndSelect() method is overloaded. It lets you clear all selections before selecting a row or a cell.

- The clearSelection() method is overloaded. It lets you clear selections for a row, a cell, or the entire TableView.

It is often a requirement to make some changes or take an action when a cell or row selection changes in a TableView. For example, a TableView may act as a master list in a master-detail data view. When the user selects a row in the master list, you want to refresh the data in the detail view. If you are interested in handling the selection change event, you need to add a ListChangeListener to one of the ObservableLists returned by the preceding listed methods that reports on the selected cells or rows. The following snippet of code adds a ListChangeListener to the ObservableList returned by the getSelectedIndices() method to track the row selection change in a TableView:

```
TableView<Person> table = ...
TableViewSelectionModel<Person> tsm = table.getSelectionModel();
ObservableList<Integer> list = tsm.getSelectedIndices();

// Add a ListChangeListener
list.addListener((ListChangeListener.Change<? extends Integer> change) -> {
        System.out.println("Row selection has changed");
});
```

Editing Data in a *TableView*

A cell in a TableView can be edited. An editable cell switches between editing and nonediting modes. In editing mode, cell data can be modified by the user. For a cell to enter editing mode, the TableView, TableColumn, and TableCell must be editable. All three of them have an editable property, which can be set to true using the setEditable(true) method. By default, TableColumn and TableCell are editable. To make cells editable in a TableView, you need to make the TableView editable:

```
TableView<Person> table = ...
table.setEditable(true);
```

The TableColumn class supports three types of events:

- onEditStart
- onEditCommit
- onEditCancel

The onEditStart event is fired when a cell in the column enters editing mode. The onEditCommit event is fired when the user successfully commits the editing, for example, by pressing the Enter key in a TextField. The onEditCancel event is fired when the user cancels the editing, for example, by pressing the Esc key in a TextField.

The events are represented by an object of the TableColumn.CellEditEvent class. The event object encapsulates the old and new values in the cell, the row object from the items list of the TableView, TableColumn, TablePosition indicating the cell position where the editing is happening, and the reference of the TableView. Use the methods of the CellEditEvent class to get these values.

Making a TableView editable does not let you edit its cell data. You need to do a little more plumbing before you can edit data in cells. Cell-editing capability is provided through specialized implementation of the TableCell class. The JavaFX library provides a few of these implementations. Set the cell factory for a column to use one of the following implementations of the TableCell to edit cell data:

- CheckBoxTableCell
- ChoiceBoxTableCell
- ComboBoxTableCell
- TextFieldTableCell

Editing Data Using a Check Box

A CheckBoxTableCell renders a check box inside the cell. Typically, it is used to represent a boolean value in a column. The class provides a way to map other types of values to a boolean value using a Callback object. The check box is selected if the value is true. Otherwise, it is unselected. Bidirectional binding is used to bind the selected property of the check box and the underlying ObservableValue. If the user changes the selection, the underlying data are updated and vice versa.

You do not have a boolean property in the Person class. You must create a boolean column by providing a cell value factory, as shown in the following code. If a Person is a baby, the cell value factory returns true. Otherwise, it returns false.

```
TableColumn<Person, Boolean> babyCol = new TableColumn<>("Baby?");
babyCol.setCellValueFactory(cellData -> {
        Person p = cellData.getValue();
        Boolean v = (p.getAgeCategory() == Person.AgeCategory.BABY);
        return new ReadOnlyBooleanWrapper(v);
});
```

Getting a cell factory to use CheckBoxTableCell is easy. Use the forTableColumn() static method to get a cell factory for the column:

```
// Set a CheckBoxTableCell to display the value
babyCol.setCellFactory(CheckBoxTableCell.<Person>forTableColumn(babyCol));
```

A CheckBoxTableCell does not fire the cell-editing events. The selected property of the check box is bound to the ObservableValue representing the data in the cell. If you are interested in tracking the selection change event, you need to add a ChangeListener to the data for the cell.

Editing Data Using a Choice Box

A ChoiceBoxTableCell renders a choice box with a specified list of values inside the cell. The type of values in the list must match the type of the TableColumn. The data in a ChoiceBoxTableCell are displayed in a Label when the cell is not being edited. A ChoiceBox is used when the cell is being edited.

The Person class does not have a gender property. You want to add a Gender column to a TableView<Person>, which can be edited using a choice box. The following snippet of code creates the TableColumn and sets a cell value factory, which sets all cells to an empty string. You would set the cell value factory to use the gender property of the Person class if you had one.

```
// Gender is a String, editable, ComboBox column
TableColumn<Person, String> genderCol = new TableColumn<>("Gender");

// Use an appropriate cell value factory.
// For now, set all cells to an empty string
genderCol.setCellValueFactory(cellData -> new ReadOnlyStringWrapper(""));
```

You can create a cell factory that uses a choice box for editing data in cells using the forTableColumn() static method of the ChoiceBoxTableCell class. You need to specify the list of items to be displayed in the choice box:

```
// Set a cell factory, so it can be edited using a ChoiceBox
genderCol.setCellFactory(
        ChoiceBoxBoxTableCell.<Person, String>forTableColumn(
                "Male", "Female")
);
```

When an item is selected in the choice box, the item is set to the underlying data model. For example, if a column is based on a property in the domain object, the selected item will be set to the property. You can set an onEditCommit event handler that is fired when the user selects an item. The following snippet of code adds such a handler for the Gender column that prints a message on the standard output:

```
// Add an onEditCommit handler
genderCol.setOnEditCommit(e -> {
        int row = e.getTablePosition().getRow();
        Person person = e.getRowValue();
        System.out.println("Gender changed (" + person.getFirstName() +
                " " + person.getLastName() + ")" + " at row " + (row + 1) +
            ". New value = " + e.getNewValue());
});
```

Clicking a selected cell puts the cell into editing mode. Double-clicking an unselected cell puts the cell into editing mode. Changing the focus to another cell or selecting an item from the list puts the editing cell into nonediting mode, and the current value is displayed in a Label.

Editing Data Using a Combo Box

A ComboBoxTableCell renders a combo box with a specified list of values inside the cells. It works similar to a ChoiceBoxTableCell. Please refer to the section "Editing Data Using a Choice Box" for more details.

Editing Data Using a *TextField*

A TextFieldTableCell renders a TextField inside the cell when the cell is being edited where the user can modify the data. It renders the cell data in a Label when the cell is not being edited.

Clicking a selected cell or double-clicking an unselected cell puts the cell into editing mode, which displays the cell data in a TextField. Once the cell is in editing mode, you need to click in the TextField (one more click!) to put the caret in the TextField so you can make changes. Notice that you need a minimum of three clicks to edit a cell, which is a pain for those users who have to edit a lot of data. Let's hope that the designers of the TableView API will make data editing less cumbersome in future releases.

If you are in the middle of editing a cell data, press the Esc key to cancel editing, which will return the cell to nonediting mode and reverts to the old data in the cell. Pressing the Enter key commits the data to the underlying data model if the TableColumn is based on a Writable ObservableValue.

If you are editing a cell using a TextFieldTableCell, moving the focus to another cell, for example, by clicking another cell, cancels the editing and puts the old value back in the cell. This is not what a user expects. At present, there is no easy solution for this problem. You will have to create a subclass of TableCell and add a focus change listener, so you can commit the data when the TextField loses focus.

Use the forTableColumn() static method of the TextFieldTableCell class to get a cell factory that uses a TextField to edit cell data. The following snippet of code shows how to do it for a First Name String column:

```
TableColumn<Person, String> fNameCol = new TableColumn<>("First Name");
fNameCol.setCellFactory(TextFieldTableCell.<Person>forTableColumn());
```

Sometimes, you need to edit nonstring data using a TextField, for example, for a date. The date may be represented as an object of the LocalDate class in the model. You may want to display it in a TextField as a formatted string. When the user edits the date, you want to commit the data to the model as a LocalDate. The TextFieldTableCell class supports this kind of object-to-string and vice versa conversion through a StringConverter. The following snippet of code sets a cell factory for a Birth Date column with a StringConverter, which converts a string to a LocalDate and vice versa. The column type is LocalDate. By default, the LocalDateStringConverter assumes a date format of mm/dd/yyyy.

```
TableColumn<Person, LocalDate> birthDateCol = new TableColumn<>("Birth Date");
LocalDateStringConverter converter = new LocalDateStringConverter();
birthDateCol.setCellFactory(
    TextFieldTableCell.<Person, LocalDate>forTableColumn(converter));
```

The program in Listing 13-6 shows how to edit data in a TableView using different types of controls. The TableView contains Id, First Name, Last Name, Birth Date, Baby, and Gender columns. The Id column is noneditable. The First Name, Last Name, and Birth Date columns use TextFieldTableCell, so they can be edited using a TextField. The Baby column is a noneditable computed field and is not backed by the data model. It uses CheckBoxTableCell to render its values. The Gender column is an editable computed field. It is not backed by the data model. It uses a ComboBoxTableCell that presents the user a list of values (Male and Female) in editing mode. When the user selects a value, the value is not saved to the data model. It stays in the cell. An onEditCommit event handler is added that prints the gender selection on the standard output. The program displays a window as shown in Figure 13-10, where it can be seen that you have already selected a gender value for all persons. The Birth Date value for the fifth row is being edited.

Listing 13-6. Editing Data in a `TableView`

```
// TableViewEditing.java
// ...find in the book's download area
```

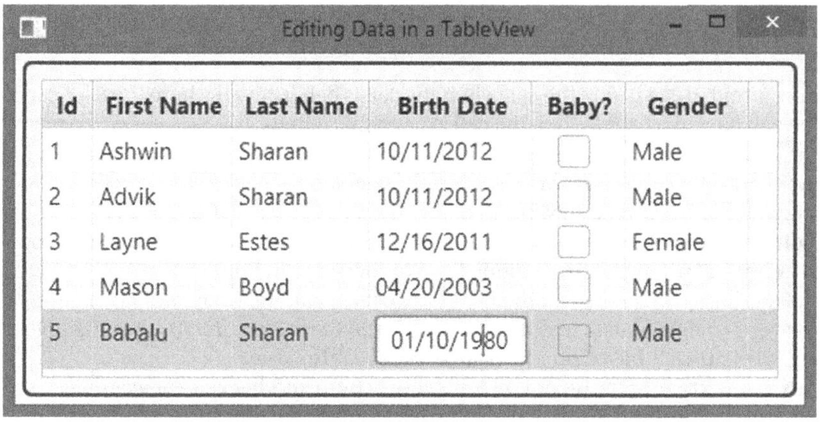

Figure 13-10. *A `TableView` with a cell in editing mode*

Editing Data in TableCell Using Any Control

In the previous section, I discussed editing data in cells of a `TableView` using different controls, for example, `TextField`, `CheckBox`, and `ChoiceBox`. You can subclass `TableCell` to use any control to edit cell data. For example, you may want to use a `DatePicker` to select a date in cells of a date column or `RadioButtons` to select from multiple options. The possibilities are endless.

You need to override four methods of the `TableCell` class:

- `startEdit()`
- `commitEdit()`
- `cancelEdit()`
- `updateItem()`

The `startEdit()` method for the cell transitions from nonediting mode to editing mode. Typically, you set the control of your choice in the `graphic` property of the cell with the current data.

The `commitEdit()` method is called when the user action, for example, pressing the Enter key in a `TextField`, indicates that the user is done modifying the cell data and the data need to be saved in the underlying data model. Typically, you do not need to override this method as the modified data are committed to the data model if the `TableColumn` is based on a `Writable ObservableValue`.

The `cancelEdit()` method is called when the user action, for example, pressing the Esc key in a `TextField`, indicates that the user wants to cancel the editing process. When the editing process is cancelled, the cell returns to nonediting mode. You need to override this method and revert the cell data to their old values.

The `updateItem()` method is called when the cell needs to be rendered again. Depending on the editing mode, you need to set the text and graphic properties of the cell appropriately.

Now let's develop a DatePickerTableCell class that inherits from the TableCell class. You can use instances of DatePickerTableCell when you want to edit cells of a TableColumn using a DatePicker control. The TableColumn must be of LocalDate. Listing 13-7 has the complete code for the DatePickerTableCell class.

Listing 13-7. The DatePickerTableCell Class to Allow Editing Table Cells Using a DatePicker Control

```
// DatePickerTableCell.java
// ...find in the book's download area
```

The DatePickerTableCell class supports a StringConverter and the editable property value for the DatePicker. You can pass them to the constructors or the forTableColumn() methods. It creates a DatePicker control when the startEdit() method is called for the first time. A ChangeListener is added that commits the data when a new date is entered or selected. Several versions of the forTableColumn() static methods are provided that return cell factories. The following snippet of code shows how to use the DatePickerTableCell class:

```
TableColumn<Person, LocalDate> birthDateCol = ...

// Set a cell factory for birthDateCol. The date format is mm/dd/yyyy
// and the DatePicker is editable.
birthDateCol.setCellFactory(DatePickerTableCell.<Person>forTableColumn());

// Set a cell factory for birthDateCol. The date format is "Month day, year"
// and and the DatePicker is non-editable
StringConverter converter = new LocalDateStringConverter("MMMM dd, yyyy");
birthDateCol.setCellFactory(DatePickerTableCell.<Person>forTableColumn(
    converter, false));
```

The program in Listing 13-8 uses DatePickerTableCell to edit data in the cells of a Birth Date column. Run the application and then double-click a cell in the Birth Date column. The cell will display a DatePicker control. You cannot edit the date in the DatePicker, as it is noneditable. You will need to select a date from the pop-up calendar.

Listing 13-8. Using DatePickerTableCell to Edit a Date in Cells

```
// CustomTableCellTest.java
// ...find in the book's download area
```

Adding and Deleting Rows in a *TableView*

Adding and deleting rows in a TableView are easy. Note that each row in a TableView is backed by an item in the items list. Adding a row is as simple as adding an item in the items list. When you add an item to the items list, a new row appears in the TableView at the same index as the index of the added item in the items list. If the TableView is sorted, it may need to be resorted after adding a new row. Call the sort() method of the TableView to resort the rows after adding a new row.

You can delete a row by removing its item from the items list. An application provides a way for the user to indicate the rows that should be deleted. Typically, the user selects one or more rows to delete. Other options are to add a Delete button to each row or to provide a Delete check box to each row. Clicking the Delete button should delete the row. Selecting the Delete check box for a row indicates that the row is marked for deletion.

The program in Listing 13-9 shows how to add and delete rows to a TableView. It displays a window with three sections:

- The Add Person form at the top has three fields to add person details and an Add button. Enter the details for a person and click the Add button to add a record to the TableView. Error checking is skipped in the code.

- In the middle, you have two buttons. One button is used to restore the default rows in the TableView. Another button deletes the selected rows.

- At the bottom, a TableView is displayed with some rows. The multirow selection is enabled. Use the Ctrl or Shift key with the mouse to select multiple rows.

Listing 13-9. Adding and Deleting Rows in a TableView

```
// TableViewAddDeleteRows.java
// ...find in the book's download area
```

Most of the logic in the code is simple. The deleteSelectedRows() method implements the logic to delete the selected rows. When you remove an item from the items list, the selection model does not remove its index. Suppose the first row is selected. If you remove the first item from the items list, the second row, which becomes the first row, is selected. To make sure that this does not happen, you clear the selection for the row before you remove it from the items list. You delete rows from last to first (higher index to lower index) because when you delete an item from the list, all of the items after the deleted items will have different indexes. Suppose you have selected rows at indexes 1 and 2. Deleting a row at index 1 first changes the index of the index 2 to 1. Performing deletion from last to first takes care of this issue.

Scrolling in a *TableView*

TableView automatically provides vertical and horizontal scrollbars when rows or columns fall beyond the available space. Users can use the scrollbars to scroll to a specific row or column. Sometimes, you need programmatic support for scrolling. For example, when you append a row to a TableView, you may want the row visible to the user by scrolling it to the view. The TableView class contains four methods that can be used to scroll to a specific row or column:

- scrollTo(int rowIndex)
- scrollTo(S item)
- scrollToColumn(TableColumn<S,?> column)
- scrollToColumnIndex(int columnIndex)

The scrollTo() method scrolls the row with the specified index or item to the view. The scrollToColumn() and scrollToColumnIndex() methods scroll to the specified column and columnIndex, respectively.

TableView fires a ScrollToEvent when there is a request to scroll to a row or column using one of the abovementioned scrolling methods. The ScrollToEvent class contains a getScrollTarget() method that returns the row index or the column reference depending on the scroll type:

```
TableView<Person> table = ...

// Add a ScrollToEvent for row scrolling
table.setOnScrollTo(e -> {
```

```
        int rowIndex = e.getScrollTarget();
        System.out.println("Scrolled to row " + rowIndex);
});

// Add a ScrollToEvent for column scrolling
table.setOnScrollToColumn(e -> {
        TableColumn<Person, ?> column = e.getScrollTarget();
        System.out.println("Scrolled to column " + column.getText());
});
```

■ **Tip** The ScrollToEvent is not fired when the user scrolls through the rows and columns. It is fired when you call one of the four scrolling-related methods of the TableView class.

Resizing a *TableColumn*

Whether a TableColumn is resizable by the user is specified by its resizable property. By default, a TableColumn is resizable. How a column in a TableView is resized is specified by the columnResizePolicy property of the TableView. The property is a Callback object. Its call() method takes an object of the ResizeFeatures class, which is a static inner class of the TableView class. The ResizeFeatures object encapsulates the delta by which the column is resized, the TableColumn being resized, and the TableView. The call() method returns true if the column was resized by the delta amount successfully. Otherwise, it returns false.

The TableView class provides two built-in resize policies as constants:

- CONSTRAINED_RESIZE_POLICY

- UNCONSTRAINED_RESIZE_POLICY

CONSTRAINED_RESIZE_POLICY ensures that the sum of the width of all visible leaf columns is equal to the width of the TableView. Resizing a column adjusts the width of all columns to the right of the resized column. When the column width is increased, the width of the rightmost column is decreased up to its minimum width. If the increased width is still not compensated, the width of the second rightmost column is decreased up to its minimum width and so on. When all columns to the right have their minimum widths, the column width cannot be increased any more. The same rule applies in the opposite direction when a column is resized to decrease its width.

When the width of a column is increased, UNCONSTRAINED_RESIZE_POLICY shifts all columns to its right by the amount the width is increased. When the width is decreased, columns to the right are shifted to the left by the same amount. If a column has nested columns, resizing the column evenly distributes the delta among the immediate children columns. This is the default column resize policy for a TableView:

```
TableView<Person> table = ...;

// Set the column resize policy to constrained resize policy
table.setColumnResizePolicy(TableView.CONSTRAINED_RESIZE_POLICY);
```

You can also create a custom column resize policy. The following snippet of code will serve as a template. You will need to write the logic to consume the delta, which is the difference between the new and old width of the column:

```
TableView<Person> table = new TableView<>(PersonTableUtil.getPersonList());
table.setColumnResizePolicy(resizeFeatures -> {
    boolean consumedDelta = false; double delta = resizeFeatures.getDelta();
    TableColumn<Person, ?> column = resizeFeatures.getColumn();
    TableView<Person> tableView = resizeFeatures.getTable();

    // Adjust the delta here...

    return consumedDelta;
});
```

You can disable column resizing by setting a trivial callback that does nothing. Its call() simply returns true indicating that it has consumed the delta:

```
// Disable column resizing
table.setColumnResizePolicy(resizeFeatures -> true);
```

Styling a *TableView* with CSS

You can style a TableView and all its parts, for example, column headers, cells, placeholder, and so forth. Applying a CSS to TableView is very complex and broad in scope. This section covers a brief overview of CSS styling for TableView. The default CSS style class name for a TableView is table-view. The default CSS style classes for a cell, a row, and a column header are table-cell, table-row-cell, and column-header, respectively:

```
/* Set the font for the cells */
.table-row-cell {
        -fx-font-size: 10pt;
        -fx-font-family: Arial;
}

/* Set the font size and text color for column headers */
.table-view .column-header .label{
        -fx-font-size: 10pt;
        -fx-text-fill: blue;
}
```

TableView supports the following CSS pseudo-classes:

- cell-selection
- row-selection

The cell-selection pseudo-class is applied when the cell-level selection is enabled, whereas the row-selection pseudo-class is applied for row-level selection. The constrained-resize pseudo-class is applied when the column resize policy is CONSTRAINED_RESIZE_POLICY.

Alternate rows in a TableView are highlighted by default. The following code removes the alternate row highlighting. It sets the white background color for all rows:

```
.table-row-cell {
    -fx-background-color: white;
}
```

```
.table-row-cell .table-cell {
        -fx-border-width: 0.25px;
        -fx-border-color: transparent gray gray transparent;
}
```

TableView shows empty rows to fill its available height. The following code removes the empty rows. In fact, it makes them appear as removed:

```
.table-row-cell:empty {
        -fx-background-color: transparent;
}

.table-row-cell:empty .table-cell {
        -fx-border-width: 0px;
}
```

TableView contains several substructures that can be styled separately:

- column-resize-line
- column-overlay
- placeholder
- column-header-background

The column-resize-line substructure is a Region and is shown when the user tries to resize a column. The column-overlay substructure is a Region and is shown as an overlay for the column being moved. The placeholder substructure is a StackPane and is shown when the TableView does not have columns or data, as in the following code:

```
/* Make the text in the placeholder red and bold */
.table-view .placeholder .label {
        -fx-text-fill: red;
        -fx-font-weight: bold;
}
```

The column-header-background substructure is a StackPane, and it is the area behind the column headers. It contains several substructures. Its filler substructure, which is a Region, is the area between the rightmost column and the right edge of the TableView in the header area. Its show-hide-columns-button substructure, which is a StackPane, is the area that shows the menu button to display the list of columns to show and hide. Please refer to the modena.css file and the *JavaFX CSS Reference Guide* for a complete list of properties of TableView that can be styled. The following code sets the filler background to white:

```
/* Set the filler background to white*/
.table-view .column-header-background .filler {
        -fx-background-color: white;
}
```

Summary

TableView is a control that is used to display and edit data in a tabular form. A TableView consists of rows and columns. The intersection of a row and a column is called a cell. Cells contain the data values. Columns have headers that describe the type of data they contain. Columns can be nested. Resizing and sorting of column data have built-in support. The following classes are used to work with a TableView control: TableView, TableColumn, TableRow, TableCell, TablePosition, TableView.TableViewFocusModel, and TableView.TableViewSelectionModel. The TableView class represents a TableView control. The TableColumn class represents a column in a TableView. Typically, a TableView contains multiple instances of TableColumn. A TableColumn consists of cells, which are instances of the TableCell class. A TableColumn is responsible for displaying and editing the data in its cells. A TableColumn has a header that can display header text, a graphic, or both. You can have a context menu for a TableColumn, which is displayed when the user right-clicks inside the column header. Use the contextMenu property to set a context menu.

The TableRow class inherits from the IndexedCell class. An instance of TableRow represents a row in a TableView. You almost never use this class in your application unless you want to provide a customized implementation for rows. Typically, you customize cells, not rows.

An instance of the TableCell class represents a cell in a TableView. Cells are highly customizable. They display data from the underlying data model for the TableView. They are capable of displaying data as well as graphics. Cells in a row of a TableView contain data related to an item such as a person, a book, and so forth. Data for some cells in a row may come directly from the attributes of the item, or they may be computed.

TableView has an items property of the ObservableList<S> type. The generic type S is the same as the generic type of the TableView. It is the data model for the TableView. Each element in the items list represents a row in the TableView. Adding a new item to the items list adds a new row to the TableView. Deleting an item from the items list deletes the corresponding row from the TableView.

The TableColumn, TableRow, and TableCell classes contain a tableView property that holds the reference of the TableView that contains them. The tableView property contains null when the TableColumn does not belong to a TableView.

A TablePosition represents the position of a cell. Its getRow() and getColumn() methods return the indexes of rows and columns, respectively, to which the cell belongs.

The TableViewFocusModel class is an inner static class of the TableView class. It represents the focus model for the TableView to manage focus for rows and cells.

The TableViewSelectionModel class is an inner static class of the TableView class. It represents the selection model for the TableView to manage selection for rows and cells.

By default, all columns in a TableView are visible. The TableColumn class has a visible property to set the visibility of a column. If you turn off the visibility of a parent column, a column with nested columns, all of its nested columns will be invisible.

You can rearrange columns in a TableView in two ways: by dragging and dropping columns to a different position or by changing their positions in the observable list of returned by the getColumns() method of the TableView class. The first option is available by default.

TableView has built-in support for sorting data in columns. By default, it allows users to sort data by clicking column headers. It also supports sorting data programmatically. You can also disable sorting for a column or all columns in a TableView.

TableView supports customization at several levels. It lets you customize the rendering of columns, for example, you can display data in a column using a check box, a combo box, or a TextField. You can also style a TableView using CSS.

The next chapter will discuss 2D shapes and how they can be added to a scene.

■ **Tip** The TreeView and TreeTableView chapters from the previous edition were omitted in this book. The handling of those controls is very similar to table views, and the chapters were quite large, so in order to keep this edition at a reasonable extent there is just a concise introduction to tree controls in the appendix.

CHAPTER 14

■ ■ ■

Understanding 2D Shapes

In this chapter, you will learn:

- What 2D shapes are and how they are represented in JavaFX
- How to draw 2D shapes
- How to draw complex shapes using the Path class
- How to draw shapes using the Scalable Vector Graphics (SVG)
- How to combine shapes to build another shape
- How to use strokes for a shape
- How to style shapes using Cascading Style Sheets (CSS)

The examples of this chapter lie in the com.jdojo.shape package. In order for them to work, you must add a corresponding line to the module-info.java file:

```
...
opens com.jdojo.shape to javafx.graphics, javafx.base;
...
```

What Are 2D Shapes?

Any shape that can be drawn in a two-dimensional plane is called a 2D shape. JavaFX offers a variety of nodes to draw different types of shapes (lines, circles, rectangles, etc.). You can add shapes to a scene graph.

Shapes can be two-dimensional or three-dimensional. In this chapter, I will discuss 2D shapes. Chapter 16 discusses 3D shapes.

All shape classes are in the javafx.scene.shape package. Classes representing 2D shapes are inherited from the abstract Shape class as shown in Figure 14-1.

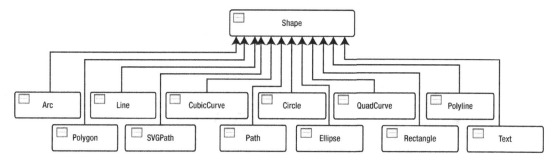

Figure 14-1. *A class diagram for classes representing 2D shapes*

A shape has a size and a position, which are defined by their properties. For example, the width and height properties define the size of a rectangle, the radius property defines the size of a circle, the x and y properties define the position of the upper-left corner of a rectangle, the centerX and centerY properties define the center of a circle, etc.

Shapes are not resized by their parents during layout. The size of a shape changes only when its size-related properties are changed. You may find a phrase like "JavaFX shapes are nonresizable." It means shapes are nonresizable by their parent during layout. They can be resized only by changing their properties.

Shapes have an interior and a stroke. The properties for defining the interior and stroke of a shape are declared in the Shape class. The fill property specifies the color to fill the interior of the shape. The default fill is Color.BLACK. The stroke property specifies the color for the outline stroke, which is null by default, except for Line, Polyline, and Path, which have Color.BLACK as the default stroke. The strokeWidth property specifies the width of the outline, which is 1.0px by default. The Shape class contains other stroke-related properties that I will discuss in the section "Understanding the Stroke of a Shape."

The Shape class contains a smooth property, which is true by default. Its true value indicates that an antialiasing hint should be used to render the shape. If it is set to false, the antialiasing hint will not be used, which may result in the edges of shapes being not crisp.

The program in Listing 14-1 creates two circles. The first circle has a light gray fill and no stroke, which is the default. The second circle has a yellow fill and a 2.0px wide black stroke. Figure 14-2 shows the two circles.

Listing 14-1. Using fill and stroke Properties of the Shape Class

```java
// ShapeTest.java
package com.jdojo.shape;

import javafx.application.Application;
import javafx.scene.Scene;
import javafx.scene.layout.HBox;
import javafx.scene.paint.Color;
import javafx.scene.shape.Circle;
import javafx.stage.Stage;

public class ShapeTest extends Application {
    public static void main(String[] args) {
        Application.launch(args);
    }
```

```java
@Override
public void start(Stage stage) {
    // Create a circle with a light gray fill and no stroke
    Circle c1 = new Circle(40, 40, 40);
    c1.setFill(Color.LIGHTGRAY);

    // Create a circle with an yellow fill and a black stroke
    // of 2.0px
    Circle c2 = new Circle(40, 40, 40);
    c2.setFill(Color.YELLOW);
    c2.setStroke(Color.BLACK);
    c2.setStrokeWidth(2.0);

    HBox root = new HBox(c1, c2);
    root.setSpacing(10);
    root.setStyle("""
        -fx-padding: 10;
        -fx-border-style: solid inside;
        -fx-border-width: 2;
        -fx-border-insets: 5;
        -fx-border-radius: 5;
        -fx-border-color: blue;""");

    Scene scene = new Scene(root);
    stage.setScene(scene);
    stage.setTitle("Using Shapes");
    stage.show();
}
}
```

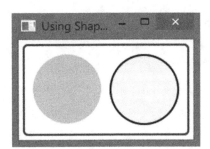

Figure 14-2. *Two circles with different fills and strokes*

Drawing 2D Shapes

The following sections describe in detail how to use the JavaFX classes representing 2D shapes to draw those shapes.

Drawing Lines

An instance of the Line class represents a line node. A Line has no interior. By default, its fill property is set to null. Setting fill has no effects. The default stroke is Color.BLACK, and the default strokeWidth is 1.0. The Line class contains four double properties:

- startX

- startY

- endX

- endY

The Line represents a line segment between (startX, startY) and (endX, endY) points. The Line class has a no-args constructor, which defaults all its four properties to zero resulting in a line from (0, 0) to (0, 0), which represents a point. Another constructor takes values for startX, startY, endX, and endY. After you create a Line, you can change its location and length by changing any of the four properties.

The program in Listing 14-2 creates some Lines and sets their stroke and strokeWidth properties. The first Line will appear as a point. Figure 14-3 shows the line.

Listing 14-2. Using the Line Class to Create Line Nodes

```java
// LineTest.java
package com.jdojo.shape;

import javafx.application.Application;
import javafx.scene.Scene;
import javafx.scene.layout.HBox;
import javafx.scene.paint.Color;
import javafx.scene.shape.Line;
import javafx.stage.Stage;

public class LineTest extends Application {
        public static void main(String[] args) {
            Application.launch(args);
        }

        @Override
        public void start(Stage stage) {
            // It will be just a point at (0, 0)
            Line line1 = new Line();

            Line line2 = new Line(0, 0, 50, 0);
            line2.setStrokeWidth(1.0);

            Line line3 = new Line(0, 50, 50, 0);
            line3.setStrokeWidth(2.0);
            line3.setStroke(Color.RED);

            Line line4 = new Line(0, 0, 50, 50);
            line4.setStrokeWidth(5.0);
            line4.setStroke(Color.BLUE);
```

```
            HBox root = new HBox(line1, line2, line3, line4);
            root.setSpacing(10);
            root.setStyle("""
                -fx-padding: 10;
                -fx-border-style: solid inside;
                -fx-border-width: 2;
                -fx-border-insets: 5;
                -fx-border-radius: 5;
                -fx-border-color: blue;""");

            Scene scene = new Scene(root);
            stage.setScene(scene);
            stage.setTitle("Using Lines");
            stage.show();
        }
    }
```

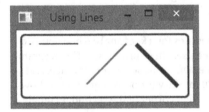

Figure 14-3. *Using line nodes*

Drawing Rectangles

An instance of the Rectangle class represents a rectangle node. The class uses six properties to define the rectangle:

- x

- y

- width

- height

- arcWidth

- arcHeight

The x and y properties are the x and y coordinates of the upper-left corner of the rectangle in the local coordinate system of the node. The width and height properties are the width and height of the rectangle, respectively. Specify the same width and height to draw a square.

By default, the corners of a rectangle are sharp. A rectangle can have rounded corners by specifying the arcWidth and arcHeight properties. You can think of one of the quadrants of an ellipse positioned at the four corners to make them round. The arcWidth and arcHeight properties are the horizontal and vertical diameters of the ellipse. By default, their values are zero, which makes a rectangle have sharp corners.

Figure 14-4 shows two rectangles—one with sharp corners and one with rounded corners. The ellipse is shown to illustrate the relationship between the arcWidth and arcHeight properties for a rounded rectangle.

A rectangle with
sharp corners

A rounded rectangle

Figure 14-4. *Rectangles with sharp and rounded corners*

The Rectangle class contains several constructors. They take various properties as arguments. The default values for x, y, width, height, arcWidth, and arcHeight properties are zero. The constructors are

- Rectangle()

- Rectangle(double width, double height)

- Rectangle(double x, double y, double width, double height)

- Rectangle(double width, double height, Paint fill)

You will not see effects of specifying the values for the x and y properties for a Rectangle when you add it to most of the layout panes as they place their children at (0, 0). A Pane uses these properties. The program in Listing 14-3 adds two rectangles to a Pane. The first rectangle uses the default values of zero for the x and y properties. The second rectangle specifies 120 for the x property and 20 for the y property. Figure 14-5 shows the positions of the two rectangles inside the Pane. Notice that the upper-left corner of the second rectangle (on the right) is at (120, 20).

Listing 14-3. Using the Rectangle Class to Create Rectangle Nodes

```java
// RectangleTest.java
package com.jdojo.shape;

import javafx.application.Application;
import javafx.scene.Scene;
import javafx.scene.layout.Pane;
import javafx.scene.paint.Color;
import javafx.scene.shape.Rectangle;
import javafx.stage.Stage;

public class RectangleTest extends Application {
    public static void main(String[] args) {
        Application.launch(args);
    }

    @Override
    public void start(Stage stage) {
        // x=0, y=0, width=100, height=50, fill=LIGHTGRAY, stroke=null
        Rectangle rect1 = new Rectangle(100, 50, Color.LIGHTGRAY);

        // x=120, y=20, width=100, height=50, fill=WHITE, stroke=BLACK
        Rectangle rect2 = new Rectangle(120, 20, 100, 50);
        rect2.setFill(Color.WHITE);
```

```
        rect2.setStroke(Color.BLACK);
        rect2.setArcWidth(10);
        rect2.setArcHeight(10);

        Pane root = new Pane();
        root.getChildren().addAll(rect1, rect2);
        Scene scene = new Scene(root);
        stage.setScene(scene);
        stage.setTitle("Using Rectangles");
        stage.show();
    }
}
```

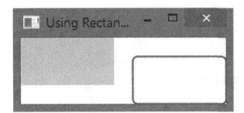

Figure 14-5. *Rectangles inside a Pane, which uses the x and y properties to position them*

Drawing Circles

An instance of the Circle class represents a circle node. The class uses three properties to define the circle:

- centerX
- centerY
- radius

The centerX and centerY properties are the x and y coordinates of the center of the circle in the local coordinate system of the node. The radius property is the radius of the circle. The default values for these properties are zero.

The Circle class contains several constructors:

- Circle()
- Circle(double radius)
- Circle(double centerX, double centerY, double radius)
- Circle(double centerX, double centerY, double radius, Paint fill)
- Circle(double radius, Paint fill)

The program in Listing 14-4 adds two circles to an HBox. Notice that the HBox does not use centerX and centerY properties of the circles. Add them to a Pane to see the effects. Figure 14-6 shows the two circles.

Listing 14-4. Using the Circle Class to Create Circle Nodes

```
// CircleTest.java
package com.jdojo.shape;

import javafx.application.Application;
import javafx.scene.Scene;
import javafx.scene.layout.HBox;
import javafx.scene.paint.Color;
import javafx.scene.shape.Circle;
import javafx.stage.Stage;

public class CircleTest extends Application {
        public static void main(String[] args) {
            Application.launch(args);
        }

        @Override
        public void start(Stage stage) {
            // centerX=0, centerY=0, radius=40, fill=LIGHTGRAY,
            // stroke=null
            Circle c1 = new Circle(0, 0, 40);
            c1.setFill(Color.LIGHTGRAY);

            // centerX=10, centerY=10, radius=40. fill=YELLOW,
            // stroke=BLACK
            Circle c2 = new Circle(10, 10, 40, Color.YELLOW);
            c2.setStroke(Color.BLACK);
            c2.setStrokeWidth(2.0);

            HBox root = new HBox(c1, c2);
            root.setSpacing(10);
            root.setStyle("""
               -fx-padding: 10;
               -fx-border-style: solid inside;
               -fx-border-width: 2;
               -fx-border-insets: 5;
               -fx-border-radius: 5;
               -fx-border-color: blue;""");

            Scene scene = new Scene(root);
            stage.setScene(scene);
            stage.setTitle("Using Circle");
            stage.show();
        }
}
```

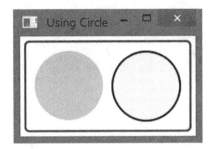

Figure 14-6. *Using circle nodes*

Drawing Ellipses

An instance of the Ellipse class represents an ellipse node. The class uses four properties to define the ellipse:

- centerX
- centerY
- radiusX
- radiusY

The centerX and centerY properties are the x and y coordinates of the center of the circle in the local coordinate system of the node. The radiusX and radiusY are the radii of the ellipse in the horizontal and vertical directions. The default values for these properties are zero. A circle is a special case of an ellipse when radiusX and radiusY are the same.

The Ellipse class contains several constructors:

- Ellipse()
- Ellipse(double radiusX, double radiusY)
- Ellipse(double centerX, double centerY, double radiusX, double radiusY)

The program in Listing 14-5 creates three instances of the Ellipse class. The third instance draws a circle as the program sets the same value for the radiusX and radiusY properties. Figure 14-7 shows the three ellipses.

Listing 14-5. Using the Ellipse Class to Create Ellipse Nodes

```
// EllipseTest.java
package com.jdojo.shape;

import javafx.application.Application;
import javafx.scene.Scene;
import javafx.scene.layout.HBox;
import javafx.scene.paint.Color;
import javafx.scene.shape.Ellipse;
import javafx.stage.Stage;
```

```java
public class EllipseTest extends Application {
        public static void main(String[] args) {
            Application.launch(args);
        }

        @Override
        public void start(Stage stage) {
            Ellipse e1 = new Ellipse(50, 30);
            e1.setFill(Color.LIGHTGRAY);

            Ellipse e2 = new Ellipse(60, 30);
            e2.setFill(Color.YELLOW);
            e2.setStroke(Color.BLACK);
            e2.setStrokeWidth(2.0);

            // Draw a circle using the Ellipse class (radiusX=radiusY=30)
            Ellipse e3 = new Ellipse(30, 30);
            e3.setFill(Color.YELLOW);
            e3.setStroke(Color.BLACK);
            e3.setStrokeWidth(2.0);

            HBox root = new HBox(e1, e2, e3);
            root.setSpacing(10);
            root.setStyle("""
               -fx-padding: 10;
               -fx-border-style: solid inside;
               -fx-border-width: 2;
               -fx-border-insets: 5;
               -fx-border-radius: 5;
               -fx-border-color: blue;""");

            Scene scene = new Scene(root);
            stage.setScene(scene);
            stage.setTitle("Using Ellipses");
            stage.show();
        }
}
```

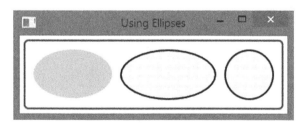

Figure 14-7. *Using ellipse nodes*

Drawing Polygons

An instance of the Polygon class represents a polygon node. The class does not define any public properties. It lets you draw a polygon using an array of (x, y) coordinates defining the vertices of the polygon. Using the Polygon class, you can draw any type of geometric shape that is created using connected lines (triangles, pentagons, hexagons, parallelograms, etc.).

The Polygon class contains two constructors:

- `Polygon()`

- `Polygon(double... points)`

The no-args constructor creates an empty polygon. You need add the (x, y) coordinates of the vertices of the shape. The polygon will draw a line from the first vertex to the second vertex, from the second to the third, and so on. Finally, the shape is closed by drawing a line from the last vertex to the first vertex.

The Polygon class stores the coordinates of the vertices in an ObservableList<Double>. You can get the reference of the observable list using the getPoints() method. Notice that it stores the coordinates in a list of Double, which is simply a number. It is your job to pass the numbers in pairs, so they can be used as (x, y) coordinates of vertices. If you pass an odd number of numbers, no shape is created. The following snippet of code creates two triangles—one passes the coordinates of the vertices in the constructor, and another adds them to the observable list later. Both triangles are geometrically the same:

```
// Create an empty triangle and add vertices later
Polygon triangle1 = new Polygon();
triangle1.getPoints().addAll(50.0, 0.0,
                     0.0, 100.0,
                     100.0, 100.0);

// Create a triangle with vertices
Polygon triangle2 = new Polygon(50.0, 0.0,
                     0.0, 100.0,
                     100.0, 100.0);
```

The program in Listing 14-6 creates a triangle, a parallelogram, and a hexagon using the Polygon class as shown in Figure 14-8.

Listing 14-6. Using the Polygon Class to Create a Triangle, a Parallelogram, and a Hexagon

```
// PolygonTest.java
package com.jdojo.shape;

import javafx.application.Application;
import javafx.scene.Scene;
import javafx.scene.layout.HBox;
import javafx.scene.paint.Color;
import javafx.scene.shape.Polygon;
import javafx.stage.Stage;

public class PolygonTest extends Application {
    public static void main(String[] args) {
        Application.launch(args);
    }
```

```java
@Override
public void start(Stage stage) {
    Polygon triangle1 = new Polygon();
    triangle1.getPoints().addAll(50.0, 0.0,
        0.0, 50.0,
        100.0, 50.0);
    triangle1.setFill(Color.WHITE);
    triangle1.setStroke(Color.RED);

    Polygon parallelogram = new Polygon();
    parallelogram.getPoints().addAll(
        30.0, 0.0,
        130.0, 0.0,
        100.00, 50.0,
        0.0, 50.0);
    parallelogram.setFill(Color.YELLOW);
    parallelogram.setStroke(Color.BLACK);

    Polygon hexagon = new Polygon(
        100.0, 0.0,
        120.0, 20.0,
        120.0, 40.0,
        100.0, 60.0,
        80.0, 40.0,
        80.0, 20.0);
    hexagon.setFill(Color.WHITE);
    hexagon.setStroke(Color.BLACK);

    HBox root = new HBox(triangle1, parallelogram, hexagon);
    root.setSpacing(10);
    root.setStyle("""
        -fx-padding: 10;
        -fx-border-style: solid inside;
        -fx-border-width: 2;
        -fx-border-insets: 5;
        -fx-border-radius: 5;
        -fx-border-color: blue;""");

    Scene scene = new Scene(root);
    stage.setScene(scene);
    stage.setTitle("Using Polygons");
    stage.show();
}
}
```

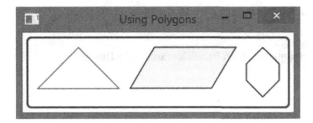

Figure 14-8. *Using polygon nodes*

Drawing Polylines

A polyline is similar to a polygon, except that it does not draw a line between the last and first points. That is, a polyline is an open polygon. However, the `fill` color is used to fill the entire shape as if the shape was closed.

An instance of the `Polyline` class represents a polyline node. The class does not define any public properties. It lets you draw a polyline using an array of (x, y) coordinates defining the vertices of the polyline. Using the `Polyline` class, you can draw any type of geometric shape that is created using connected lines (triangles, pentagons, hexagons, parallelograms, etc.).

The `Polyline` class contains two constructors:

- `Polyline()`
- `Polyline(double... points)`

The no-args constructor creates an empty polyline. You need add (x, y) coordinates of the vertices of the shape. The polygon will draw a line from the first vertex to the second vertex, from the second to the third, and so on. Unlike a `Polygon`, the shape is not closed automatically. If you want to close the shape, you need to add the coordinates of the first vertex as the last pair of numbers.

If you want to add coordinates of vertices later, add them to the `ObservableList<Double>` returned by the `getPoints()` method of the `Polyline` class. The following snippet of code creates two triangles with the same geometrical properties using different methods. Notice that the first and the last pairs of numbers are the same in order to close the triangle:

```
// Create an empty triangle and add vertices later
Polygon triangle1 = new Polygon();
triangle1.getPoints().addAll(
    50.0, 0.0,
    0.0, 100.0,
    100.0, 100.0,
    50.0, 0.0);

// Create a triangle with vertices
Polygon triangle2 = new Polygon(
    50.0, 0.0,
    0.0, 100.0,
    100.0, 100.0,
    50.0, 0.0);
```

The program in Listing 14-7 creates a triangle, an open parallelogram, and a hexagon using the Polyline class as shown in Figure 14-9.

Listing 14-7. Using the Polyline Class to Create a Triangle, an Open Parallelogram, and a Hexagon

```java
// PolylineTest.java
package com.jdojo.shape;

import javafx.application.Application;
import javafx.scene.Scene;
import javafx.scene.layout.HBox;
import javafx.scene.paint.Color;
import javafx.scene.shape.Polyline;
import javafx.stage.Stage;

public class PolylineTest extends Application {
    public static void main(String[] args) {
        Application.launch(args);
    }

    @Override
    public void start(Stage stage) {
        Polyline triangle1 = new Polyline();
        triangle1.getPoints().addAll(
            50.0, 0.0,
            0.0, 50.0,
            100.0, 50.0,
            50.0, 0.0);
        triangle1.setFill(Color.WHITE);
        triangle1.setStroke(Color.RED);

        // Create an open parallelogram
        Polyline parallelogram = new Polyline();
        parallelogram.getPoints().addAll(
            30.0, 0.0,
            130.0, 0.0,
            100.00, 50.0,
            0.0, 50.0);
        parallelogram.setFill(Color.YELLOW);
        parallelogram.setStroke(Color.BLACK);

        Polyline hexagon = new Polyline(
            100.0, 0.0,
            120.0, 20.0,
            120.0, 40.0,
            100.0, 60.0,
            80.0, 40.0,
            80.0, 20.0,
            100.0, 0.0);
        hexagon.setFill(Color.WHITE);
        hexagon.setStroke(Color.BLACK);
```

```
        HBox root = new HBox(triangle1, parallelogram, hexagon);
        root.setSpacing(10);
        root.setStyle("""
            -fx-padding: 10;
            -fx-border-style: solid inside;
            -fx-border-width: 2;
            -fx-border-insets: 5;
            -fx-border-radius: 5;
            -fx-border-color: blue;""");

        Scene scene = new Scene(root);
        stage.setScene(scene);
        stage.setTitle("Using Polylines");
        stage.show();
    }
}
```

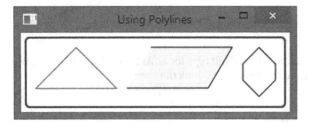

Figure 14-9. *Using polyline nodes*

Drawing Arcs

An instance of the Arc class represents a sector of an ellipse. The class uses seven properties to define the ellipse:

- centerX
- centerY
- radiusX
- radiusY
- startAngle
- length
- type

The first four properties define an ellipse. Please refer to the section "Drawing Ellipses" for how to define an ellipse. The last three properties define a sector of the ellipse that is the Arc node. The startAngle property specifies the start angle of the section in degrees measured counterclockwise from the positive x-axis. It defines the beginning of the arc. The length is an angle in degrees measured counterclockwise from the start angle to define the end of the sector. If the length property is set to 360, the Arc is a full ellipse. Figure 14-10 illustrates the properties.

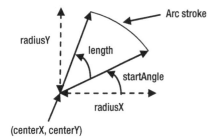

Figure 14-10. *Properties defining an Arc*

The type property specifies the way the Arc is closed. It is one of the constants, OPEN, CHORD, and ROUND, defined in the ArcType enum:

- The ArcType.OPEN does not close the arc.

- The ArcType.CHORD closes the arc by joining the starting and ending points by a straight line.

- The ArcType.ROUND closes the arc by joining the starting and ending points to the center of the ellipse.

Figure 14-11 shows the three closure types for an arc. The default type for an Arc is ArcType.OPEN. If you do not apply a stroke to an Arc, both ArcType.OPEN and ArcType.CHORD look the same.

Figure 14-11. *Closure types of an arc*

The Arc class contains two constructors:

- Arc()

- Arc(double centerX, double centerY, double radiusX, double radiusY, double startAngle, double length)

The program in Listing 14-8 shows how to create Arc nodes. The resulting window is shown in Figure 14-12.

Listing 14-8. Using the Arc Class to Create Arcs, Which Are Sectors of Ellipses

```
// ArcTest.java
package com.jdojo.shape;

import javafx.application.Application;
import javafx.scene.Scene;
import javafx.scene.layout.HBox;
import javafx.scene.paint.Color;
```

```java
import javafx.scene.shape.Arc;
import javafx.scene.shape.ArcType;
import javafx.stage.Stage;

public class ArcTest extends Application {
        public static void main(String[] args) {
            Application.launch(args);
        }

        @Override
        public void start(Stage stage) {
            // An OPEN arc with a fill
            Arc arc1 = new Arc(0, 0, 50, 100, 0, 90);
            arc1.setFill(Color.LIGHTGRAY);

            // An OPEN arc with no fill and a stroke
            Arc arc2 = new Arc(0, 0, 50, 100, 0, 90);
            arc2.setFill(Color.TRANSPARENT);
            arc2.setStroke(Color.BLACK);

            // A CHORD arc with no fill and a stroke
            Arc arc3 = new Arc(0, 0, 50, 100, 0, 90);
            arc3.setFill(Color.TRANSPARENT);
            arc3.setStroke(Color.BLACK);
            arc3.setType(ArcType.CHORD);

            // A ROUND arc with no fill and a stroke
            Arc arc4 = new Arc(0, 0, 50, 100, 0, 90);
            arc4.setFill(Color.TRANSPARENT);
            arc4.setStroke(Color.BLACK);
            arc4.setType(ArcType.ROUND);

            // A ROUND arc with a gray fill and a stroke
            Arc arc5 = new Arc(0, 0, 50, 100, 0, 90);
            arc5.setFill(Color.GRAY);
            arc5.setStroke(Color.BLACK);
            arc5.setType(ArcType.ROUND);

            HBox root = new HBox(arc1, arc2, arc3, arc4, arc5);
            root.setSpacing(10);
            root.setStyle("""
               -fx-padding: 10;
               -fx-border-style: solid inside;
               -fx-border-width: 2;
               -fx-border-insets: 5;
               -fx-border-radius: 5;
               -fx-border-color: blue;""");
```

```
        Scene scene = new Scene(root);
        stage.setScene(scene);
        stage.setTitle("Using Arcs");
        stage.show();
    }
}
```

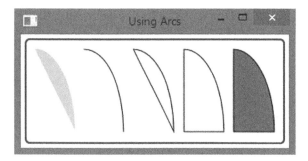

Figure 14-12. *Using Arc nodes*

Drawing Quadratic Curves

Bezier curves are used in computer graphics to draw smooth curves. An instance of the QuadCurve class represents a quadratic Bezier curve segment intersecting two specified points using a specified Bezier control point. The QuadCurve class contains six properties to specify the three points:

- startX

- startY

- controlX

- controlY

- endX

- endY

The QuadCurve class contains two constructors:

- QuadCurve()

- QuadCurve(double startX, double startY, double controlX, double controlY, double endX, double endY)

The program in Listing 14-9 draws the same quadratic Bezier curve twice—once with a stroke and a transparent fill and once with no stroke and a light gray fill. Figure 14-13 shows the two curves.

Listing 14-9. Using the QuadCurve Class to Draw Quadratic BezierCurve

```java
// QuadCurveTest.java
package com.jdojo.shape;

import javafx.application.Application;
import javafx.scene.Scene;
import javafx.scene.layout.HBox;
import javafx.scene.paint.Color;
import javafx.scene.shape.QuadCurve;
import javafx.stage.Stage;

public class QuadCurveTest extends Application {
    public static void main(String[] args) {
        Application.launch(args);
    }

    @Override
    public void start(Stage stage) {
        QuadCurve qc1 = new QuadCurve(0, 100, 20, 0, 150, 100);
        qc1.setFill(Color.TRANSPARENT);
        qc1.setStroke(Color.BLACK);

        QuadCurve qc2 = new QuadCurve(0, 100, 20, 0, 150, 100);
        qc2.setFill(Color.LIGHTGRAY);

        HBox root = new HBox(qc1, qc2);
        root.setSpacing(10);
        root.setStyle("""
           -fx-padding: 10;
           -fx-border-style: solid inside;
           -fx-border-width: 2;
           -fx-border-insets: 5;
           -fx-border-radius: 5;
           -fx-border-color: blue;""");

        Scene scene = new Scene(root);
        stage.setScene(scene);
        stage.setTitle("Using QuadCurves");
        stage.show();
    }
}
```

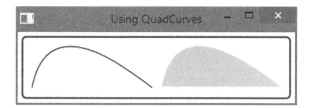

Figure 14-13. *Using quadratic Bezier curves*

Drawing Cubic Curves

An instance of the CubicCurve class represents a cubic Bezier curve segment intersecting two specified points using two specified Bezier control points. Please refer to the Wikipedia article at http://en.wikipedia.org/wiki/Bezier_curves for a detailed explanation and demonstration of Bezier curves. The CubicCurve class contains eight properties to specify the four points:

- startX
- startY
- controlX1
- controlY1
- controlX2
- controlY2
- endX
- endY

The CubicCurve class contains two constructors:

- CubicCurve()
- CubicCurve(double startX, double startY, double controlX1, double controlY1, double controlX2, double controlY2, double endX, double endY)

The program in Listing 14-10 draws the same cubic Bezier curve twice—once with a stroke and a transparent fill and once with no stroke and a light gray fill. Figure 14-14 shows the two curves.

Listing 14-10. Using the CubicCurve Class to Draw a Cubic Bezier Curve

```
// CubicCurveTest.java
package com.jdojo.shape;

import javafx.application.Application;
import javafx.scene.Scene;
import javafx.scene.layout.HBox;
import javafx.scene.paint.Color;
import javafx.scene.shape.CubicCurve;
import javafx.stage.Stage;
```

```java
public class CubicCurveTest extends Application {
    public static void main(String[] args) {
        Application.launch(args);
    }

    @Override
    public void start(Stage stage) {
        CubicCurve cc1 = new CubicCurve(0, 50, 20, 0, 50, 80, 50, 0);
        cc1.setFill(Color.TRANSPARENT);
        cc1.setStroke(Color.BLACK);

        CubicCurve cc2 = new CubicCurve(0, 50, 20, 0, 50, 80, 50, 0);
        cc2.setFill(Color.LIGHTGRAY);

        HBox root = new HBox(cc1, cc2);
        root.setSpacing(10);
        root.setStyle("""
            -fx-padding: 10;
            -fx-border-style: solid inside;
            -fx-border-width: 2;
            -fx-border-insets: 5;
            -fx-border-radius: 5;
            -fx-border-color: blue;""");

        Scene scene = new Scene(root);
        stage.setScene(scene);
        stage.setTitle("Using CubicCurves");
        stage.show();
    }
}
```

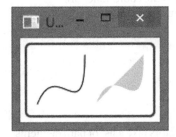

Figure 14-14. *Using cubic Bezier curves*

Building Complex Shapes Using the Path Class

I discussed several shape classes in the previous sections. They are used to draw simple shapes. It is not convenient to use them for complex shapes. You can draw complex shapes using the Path class. An instance of the Path class defines the path (outline) of a shape. A path consists of one or more subpaths. A subpath consists of one or more path elements. Each subpath has a starting point and an ending point.

A path element is an instance of the PathElement abstract class. The following subclasses of the PathElement class exist to represent a specific type of path elements:

- MoveTo

- LineTo

- HLineTo

- VLineTo

- ArcTo

- QuadCurveTo

- CubicCurveTo

- ClosePath

Before you see an example, let us outline the process of creating a shape using the Path class. The process is similar to drawing a shape on a paper with a pencil. First, you place the pencil on the paper. You can restate it, "You move the pencil to a point on the paper." Regardless of what shape you want to draw, moving the pencil to a point must be the first step. Now, you start moving your pencil to draw a path element (e.g., a horizontal line). The starting point of the current path element is the same as the ending point of the previous path element. Keep drawing as many path elements as needed (e.g., a vertical line, an arc, and a quadratic Bezier curve). At the end, you can end the last path element at the same point where you started or somewhere else.

The coordinates defining a PathElement can be absolute or relative. By default, coordinates are absolute. It is specified by the absolute property of the PathElement class. If it is true, which is the default, the coordinates are absolute. If it is false, the coordinates are relative. The absolute coordinates are measured relative to the local coordinate system of the node. Relative coordinates are measured treating the ending point of the previous PathElement as the origin.

The Path class contains three constructors:

- Path()

- Path(Collection<? extends PathElement> elements)

- Path(PathElement... elements)

The no-args constructor creates an empty shape. The other two constructors take a list of path elements as arguments. A Path stores path elements in an ObservableList<PathElement>. You can get the reference of the list using the getElements() method. You can modify the list of path elements to modify the shape. The following snippet of code shows two ways of creating shapes using the Path class:

```
// Pass the path elements to the constructor
Path shape1 = new Path(pathElement1, pathElement2, pathElement3);

// Create an empty path and add path elements to the elements list
Path shape2 = new Path();
shape2.getElements().addAll(pathElement1, pathElement2, pathElement3);
```

■ **Tip** An instance of the PathElement may be added as a path element to Path objects simultaneously. A Path uses the same fill and stroke for all its path elements.

The MoveTo Path Element

A MoveTo path element is used to make the specified x and y coordinates as the current point. It has the effect of lifting and placing the pencil at the specified point on the paper. The first path element of a Path object must be a MoveTo element, and it must not use relative coordinates. The MoveTo class defines two double properties that are the x and y coordinates of the point:

- x

- y

The MoveTo class contains two constructors. The no-args constructor sets the current point to (0.0, 0.0). The other constructor takes the x and y coordinates of the current point as arguments:

```
// Create a MoveTo path element to move the current point to (0.0, 0.0)
MoveTo mt1 = new MoveTo();

// Create a MoveTo path element to move the current point to (10.0, 10.0)
MoveTo mt2 = new MoveTo(10.0, 10.0);
```

■ **Tip** A path must start with a MoveTo path element. You can have multiple MoveTo path elements in a path. A subsequent MoveTo element denotes the starting point of a new subpath.

The LineTo Path Element

A LineTo path element draws a straight line from the current point to the specified point. It contains two double properties that are the x and y coordinates of the end of the line:

- x

- y

The LineTo class contains two constructors. The no-args constructor sets the end of the line to (0.0, 0.0). The other constructor takes the x and y coordinates of the end of the line as arguments:

```
// Create a LineTo path element with its end at (0.0, 0.0)
LineTo lt1 = new LineTo();

// Create a LineTo path element with its end at (10.0, 10.0)
LineTo lt2 = new LineTo(10.0, 10.0);
```

With the knowledge of the MoveTo and LineTo path elements, you can construct shapes that are made of lines only. The following snippet of code creates a triangle as shown in Figure 14-15. The figure shows the triangle and its path elements. The arrows show the flow of the drawing. Notice that the drawing starts at (0.0) using the first MoveTo path element.

```
Path triangle = new Path(
    new MoveTo(0, 0),
    new LineTo(0, 50),
    new LineTo(50, 50),
    new LineTo(0, 0));
```

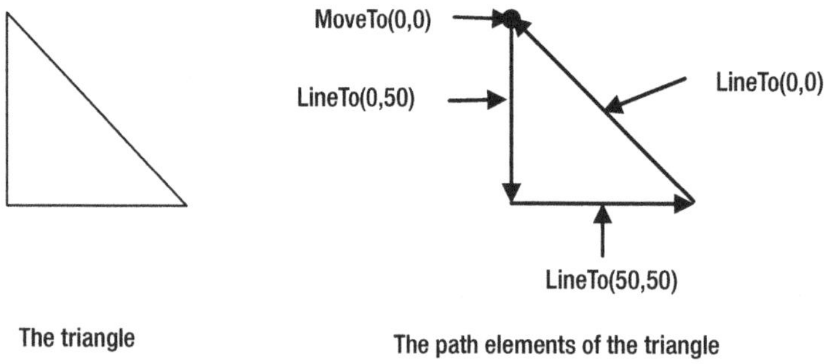

The triangle   The path elements of the triangle

Figure 14-15. *Creating a triangle using the MoveTo and LineTo path elements*

The ClosePath path element closes a path by drawing a straight line from the current point to the starting point of the path. If multiple MoveTo path elements exist in a path, a ClosePath draws a straight line from the current point to the point identified by the last MoveTo. You can rewrite the path for the previous triangle example using a ClosePath:

```
Path triangle = new Path(
    new MoveTo(0, 0),
    new LineTo(0, 50),
    new LineTo(50, 50),
    new ClosePath());
```

The program in Listing 14-11 creates two Path nodes: one triangle and one with two inverted triangles to give it a look of a star as shown in Figure 14-16. In the second shape, each triangle is created as a subpath—each subpath starting with a MoveTo element. Notice the two uses of the ClosePath elements. Each ClosePath closes its subpath.

Listing 14-11. Using the Path Class to Create a Triangle and a Star

```
// PathTest.java
package com.jdojo.shape;

import javafx.application.Application;
import javafx.scene.Scene;
import javafx.scene.layout.HBox;
import javafx.scene.shape.ClosePath;
import javafx.scene.shape.LineTo;
```

```java
import javafx.scene.shape.MoveTo;
import javafx.scene.shape.Path;
import javafx.stage.Stage;

public class PathTest extends Application {
        public static void main(String[] args) {
            Application.launch(args);
        }

        @Override
        public void start(Stage stage) {
            Path triangle = new Path(
                new MoveTo(0, 0),
                new LineTo(0, 50),
                new LineTo(50, 50),
                new ClosePath());

            Path star = new Path();
            star.getElements().addAll(
                new MoveTo(30, 0),
                new LineTo(0, 30),
                new LineTo(60, 30),
                new ClosePath(),/* new LineTo(30, 0), */
                new MoveTo(0, 10),
                new LineTo(60, 10),
                new LineTo(30, 40),
                new ClosePath() /*new LineTo(0, 10)*/);

            HBox root = new HBox(triangle, star);
            root.setSpacing(10);
            root.setStyle("""
                -fx-padding: 10;
                -fx-border-style: solid inside;
                -fx-border-width: 2;
                -fx-border-insets: 5;
                -fx-border-radius: 5;
                -fx-border-color: blue;""");

            Scene scene = new Scene(root);
            stage.setScene(scene);
            stage.setTitle("Using Paths");
            stage.show();
        }
}
```

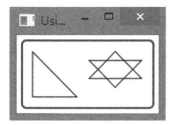

Figure 14-16. *Shapes based on path elements*

The HLineTo and VLineTo Path Elements

The HLineTo path element draws a horizontal line from the current point to the specified x coordinate. The y coordinate of the ending point of the line is the same as the y coordinate of the current point. The x property of the HLineTo class specifies the x coordinate of the ending point:

```
// Create an horizontal line from the current point (x, y) to (50, y)
HLineTo hlt = new HLineTo(50);
```

The VLineTo path element draws a vertical line from the current point to the specified y coordinate. The x coordinate of the ending point of the line is the same as the x coordinate of the current point. The y property of the VLineTo class specifies the y coordinate of the ending point:

```
// Create a vertical line from the current point (x, y) to (x, 50)
VLineTo vlt = new VLineTo(50);
```

■ **Tip** The LineTo path element is the generic version of HLineTo and VLineTo.

The following snippet of code creates the same triangle as discussed in the previous section. This time, you use HLineTo and VLineTo path elements to draw the base and height sides of the triangle instead of the LineTo path elements:

```
Path triangle = new Path(
    new MoveTo(0, 0),
    new VLineTo(50),
    new HLineTo(50),
    new ClosePath());
```

The ArcTo Path Element

An ArcTo path element defines a segment of ellipse connecting the current point and the specified point. It contains the following properties:

- radiusX

- radiusY

- x

- y

- XAxisRotation

- largeArcFlag

- sweepFlag

The radiusX and radiusY properties specify the horizontal and vertical radii of the ellipse. The x and y properties specify the x and y coordinates of the ending point of the arc. Note that the starting point of the arc is the current point of the path.

The XAxisRotation property specifies the rotation of the x-axis of the ellipse in degrees. Note that the rotation is for the x-axis of the ellipse from which the arc is obtained, not the x-axis of the coordinate system of the node. A positive value rotates the x-axis counterclockwise.

The largeArcFlag and sweepFlag properties are Boolean type, and by default, they are set to false. Their uses need a detailed explanation. Two ellipses can pass through two given points as shown in Figure 14-17 giving us four arcs to connect the two points.

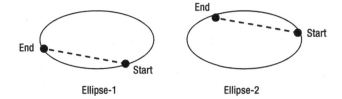

Figure 14-17. *Effects of the largeArcFlag and sweepFlag properties on an ArcTo path element*

Figure 14-17 shows starting and ending points labeled Start and End, respectively. Two points on an ellipse can be traversed through the larger arc or smaller arc. If the largeArcFlag is true, the larger arc is used. Otherwise, the smaller arc is used.

When it is decided that the larger or smaller arc is used, you still have two choices: which ellipse of the two possible ellipses will be used? This is determined by the sweepFlag property. Try drawing the arc from the starting point to the ending point using two selected arcs—the two larger arcs or the two smaller arcs. For one arc, the traversal will be clockwise and for the other counterclockwise. If the sweepFlag is true, the ellipse with the clockwise traversal is used. If the sweepFlag is false, the ellipse with the counterclockwise traversal is used. Table 14-1 shows which type of arc from which ellipse will be used based on the two properties.

Table 14-1. *Choosing the Arc Segment and the Ellipse Based on the largeArcFlag and sweepFlag Properties*

largeArcFlag	sweepFlag	Arc Type	Ellipse
true	true	Larger	Ellipse-2
true	false	Larger	Ellipse-1
false	true	Smaller	Ellipse-1
false	false	Smaller	Ellipse-2

The program in Listing 14-12 uses an ArcTo path element to build a Path object. The program lets the user change properties of the ArcTo path element. Run the program and change largeArcFlag, sweepFlag, and other properties to see how they affect the ArcTo path element.

Listing 14-12. Using ArcTo Path Elements

```java
// ArcToTest.java
package com.jdojo.shape;

import javafx.application.Application;
import javafx.scene.Scene;
import javafx.scene.control.CheckBox;
import javafx.scene.control.Label;
import javafx.scene.control.Slider;
import javafx.scene.layout.BorderPane;
import javafx.scene.layout.GridPane;
import javafx.scene.shape.ArcTo;
import javafx.scene.shape.HLineTo;
import javafx.scene.shape.MoveTo;
import javafx.scene.shape.Path;
import javafx.scene.shape.VLineTo;
import javafx.stage.Stage;

public class ArcToTest extends Application {
    private ArcTo arcTo;

    public static void main(String[] args) {
        Application.launch(args);
    }

    @Override
    public void start(Stage stage) {
        // Create the ArcTo path element
        arcTo = new ArcTo();

        // Use the arcTo element to build a Path
        Path path = new Path(
            new MoveTo(0, 0),
            new VLineTo(100),
```

```
            new HLineTo(100),
            new VLineTo(50),
            arcTo);

        BorderPane root = new BorderPane();
        root.setTop(this.getTopPane());
        root.setCenter(path);
        root.setStyle("""
            -fx-padding: 10;
            -fx-border-style: solid inside;
            -fx-border-width: 2;
            -fx-border-insets: 5;
            -fx-border-radius: 5;
            -fx-border-color: blue;""");

        Scene scene = new Scene(root);
        stage.setScene(scene);
        stage.setTitle("Using ArcTo Path Elements");
        stage.show();
    }

    private GridPane getTopPane() {
        CheckBox largeArcFlagCbx = new CheckBox("largeArcFlag");
        CheckBox sweepFlagCbx = new CheckBox("sweepFlag");
        Slider xRotationSlider = new Slider(0, 360, 0);
        xRotationSlider.setPrefWidth(300);
        xRotationSlider.setBlockIncrement(30);
        xRotationSlider.setShowTickMarks(true);
        xRotationSlider.setShowTickLabels(true);

        Slider radiusXSlider = new Slider(100, 300, 100);
        radiusXSlider.setBlockIncrement(10);
        radiusXSlider.setShowTickMarks(true);
        radiusXSlider.setShowTickLabels(true);

        Slider radiusYSlider = new Slider(100, 300, 100);
        radiusYSlider.setBlockIncrement(10);
        radiusYSlider.setShowTickMarks(true);
        radiusYSlider.setShowTickLabels(true);

        // Bind ArcTo properties to the control data
        arcTo.largeArcFlagProperty().bind(
                largeArcFlagCbx.selectedProperty());
        arcTo.sweepFlagProperty().bind(
                sweepFlagCbx.selectedProperty());
        arcTo.XaxisRotationProperty().bind(
                xRotationSlider.valueProperty());
        arcTo.radiusXProperty().bind(
                radiusXSlider.valueProperty());
        arcTo.radiusYProperty().bind(
                radiusYSlider.valueProperty());
```

```
        GridPane pane = new GridPane();
        pane.setHgap(5);
        pane.setVgap(10);
        pane.addRow(0, largeArcFlagCbx, sweepFlagCbx);
        pane.addRow(1, new Label("XAxisRotation"), xRotationSlider);
        pane.addRow(2, new Label("radiusX"), radiusXSlider);
        pane.addRow(3, new Label("radiusY"), radiusYSlider);

        return pane;
    }
}
```

The QuadCurveTo Path Element

An instance of the QuadCurveTo class draws a quadratic Bezier curve from the current point to the specified ending point (x, y) using the specified control point (controlX, controlY). It contains four properties to specify the ending and control points.

- x

- y

- controlX

- controlY

The x and y properties specify the x and y coordinates of the ending point. The controlX and controlY properties specify the x and y coordinates of the control point.

The QuadCurveTo class contains two constructors:

- QuadCurveTo()

- QuadCurveTo(double controlX, double controlY, double x, double y)

The following snippet of code uses a QuadCurveTo with the (10, 100) control point and (0, 0) ending point. Figure 14-18 shows the resulting path.

```
Path path = new Path(
    new MoveTo(0, 0),
    new VLineTo(100),
    new HLineTo(100),
    new VLineTo(50),
    new QuadCurveTo(10, 100, 0, 0));
```

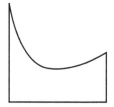

Figure 14-18. *Using a QuadCurveTo path element*

The CubicCurveTo Path Element

An instance of the CubicCurveTo class draws a cubic Bezier curve from the current point to the specified ending point (x, y) using the specified control points (controlX1, controlY1) and (controlX2, controlY2). It contains six properties to specify the ending and control points:

- x

- y

- controlX1

- controlY1

- controlX2

- controlY2

The x and y properties specify the x and y coordinates of the ending point. The controlX1 and controlY1 properties specify the x and y coordinates of the first control point. The controlX2 and controlY2 properties specify the x and y coordinates of the second control point.

The CubicCurveTo class contains two constructors:

- CubicCurveTo()

- CubicCurveTo(double controlX1, double controlY1, double controlX2, double controlY2, double x, double y)

The following snippet of code uses a CubicCurveTo with the (10, 100) and (40, 80) as control points and (0, 0) as the ending point. Figure 14-19 shows the resulting path.

```
Path path = new Path(
    new MoveTo(0, 0),
    new VLineTo(100),
    new HLineTo(100),
    new VLineTo(50),
    new CubicCurveTo(10, 100, 40, 80, 0, 0));
```

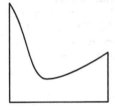

Figure 14-19. *Using a QuadCurveTo path element*

The ClosePath Path Element

The ClosePath path element closes the current subpath. Note that a Path may consist of multiple subpaths, and, therefore, it is possible to have multiple ClosePath elements in a Path. A ClosePath element draws a straight line from the current point to the initial point of the current subpath and ends the subpath. A ClosePath element may be followed by a MoveTo element, and in that case, the MoveTo element is the starting point of the next subpath. If a ClosePath element is followed by a path element other than a MoveTo element, the next subpath starts at the starting point of the subpath that was closed by the ClosePath element.

The following snippet of code creates a Path object, which uses two subpaths. Each subpath draws a triangle. The subpaths are closed using ClosePath elements. Figure 14-20 shows the resulting shape.

```
Path p1 = new Path(
    new MoveTo(50, 0),
    new LineTo(0, 50),
    new LineTo(100, 50),
    new ClosePath(),
    new MoveTo(90, 15),
    new LineTo(40, 65),
    new LineTo(140, 65),
    new ClosePath());
p1.setFill(Color.LIGHTGRAY);
```

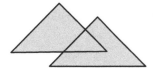

Figure 14-20. *A shape using two subpaths and a ClosePath element*

The Fill Rule for a Path

A Path can be used to draw very complex shapes. Sometimes, it is hard to determine whether a point is inside or outside the shape. The Path class contains a fillRule property that is used to determine whether a point is inside a shape. Its value could be one of the constants of the FillRule enum: NON_ZERO and EVEN_ODD. If a point is inside the shape, it will be rendered using the fill color. Figure 14-21 shows two triangles created by a Path and a point in the area common to both triangles. I will discuss whether the point is considered inside the shape.

Figure 14-21. *A shape made of two triangular subpaths*

The direction of the stroke is the vital factor in determining whether a point is inside a shape. The shape in Figure 14-21 can be drawn using strokes in different directions. Figure 14-22 shows two of them. In Shape-1, both triangles use counterclockwise strokes. In Shape-2, one triangle uses a counterclockwise stroke, and another uses a clockwise stroke.

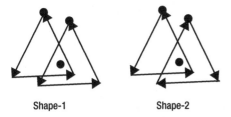

Shape-1   Shape-2

Figure 14-22. *A shape made of two triangular subpaths using different stroke directions*

The fill rule of a Path draws rays from the point to infinity, so they can intersect all path segments. In the NON_ZERO fill rule, if the number of path segments intersected by rays is equal in counterclockwise and clockwise directions, the point is outside the shape. Otherwise, the point is inside the shape. You can understand this rule by using a counter, which starts with zero. Add one to the counter for every ray intersecting a path segment in the counterclockwise direction. Subtract one from the counter for every ray intersecting a path segment in the clockwise direction. At the end, if the counter is nonzero, the point is inside; otherwise, the point is outside. Figure 14-23 shows the same two paths made of two triangular subpaths with their counter values when the NON_ZERO fill rule is applied. The rays drawn from the point are shown in dashed lines. The point in the first shape scores six (a nonzero value), and it is inside the path. The point in the second shape scores zero, and it is outside the path.

Like the NON_ZERO fill rule, the EVEN_ODD fill rule also draws rays from a point in all directions extending to infinity, so all path segments are intersected. It counts the number of intersections between the rays and the path segments. If the number is odd, the point is inside the path. Otherwise, the point is outside the path. If you set the fillRule property to EVEN_ODD for the two shapes shown in Figure 14-23, the point is outside the path for both shapes because the number of intersections between rays and path segments is six (an even number) in both cases. The default value for the fillRule property of a Path is FillRule.NON_ZERO.

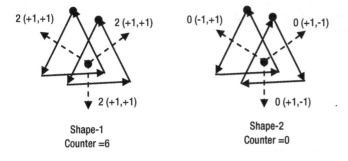

Shape-1
Counter =6

Shape-2
Counter =0

Figure 14-23. *Applying the NON_ZERO fill rule to two triangular subpaths*

The program in Listing 14-13 is an implementation of the examples discussed in this section. It draws four paths: the first two (counting from the left) with NON_ZERO fill rules and the last two with EVEN_ODD fill rules. Figure 14-24 shows the paths. The first and third paths use a counterclockwise stroke for drawing both triangular subpaths. The second and fourth paths are drawn using a counterclockwise stroke for one triangle and a clockwise stroke for another.

Listing 14-13. Using Fill Rules for Paths

```java
// PathFillRule.java
package com.jdojo.shape;

import javafx.application.Application;
import javafx.scene.Scene;
import javafx.scene.layout.HBox;
import javafx.scene.paint.Color;
import javafx.scene.shape.FillRule;
import javafx.scene.shape.LineTo;
import javafx.scene.shape.MoveTo;
import javafx.scene.shape.Path;
import javafx.scene.shape.PathElement;
import javafx.stage.Stage;

public class PathFillRule extends Application {
      public static void main(String[] args) {
          Application.launch(args);
      }

      @Override
      public void start(Stage stage) {
          // Both triangles use a counterclockwise stroke
          PathElement[] pathElements1 = {
             new MoveTo(50, 0),
             new LineTo(0, 50),
             new LineTo(100, 50),
             new LineTo(50, 0),
             new MoveTo(90, 15),
             new LineTo(40, 65),
             new LineTo(140, 65),
             new LineTo(90, 15)};

          // One triangle uses a clockwise stroke and
          // another uses a counterclockwise stroke
          PathElement[] pathElements2 = {
             new MoveTo(50, 0),
             new LineTo(0, 50),
             new LineTo(100, 50),
             new LineTo(50, 0),
             new MoveTo(90, 15),
             new LineTo(140, 65),
             new LineTo(40, 65),
             new LineTo(90, 15)};

          /* Using the NON-ZERO fill rule by default */
          Path p1 = new Path(pathElements1);
          p1.setFill(Color.LIGHTGRAY);
```

```
        Path p2 = new Path(pathElements2);
        p2.setFill(Color.LIGHTGRAY);

        /* Using the EVEN_ODD fill rule */
        Path p3 = new Path(pathElements1);
        p3.setFill(Color.LIGHTGRAY);
        p3.setFillRule(FillRule.EVEN_ODD);

        Path p4 = new Path(pathElements2);
        p4.setFill(Color.LIGHTGRAY);
        p4.setFillRule(FillRule.EVEN_ODD);

        HBox root = new HBox(p1, p2, p3, p4);
        root.setSpacing(10);
        root.setStyle("""
            -fx-padding: 10;
            -fx-border-style: solid inside;
            -fx-border-width: 2;
            -fx-border-insets: 5;
            -fx-border-radius: 5;
            -fx-border-color: blue;""");

        Scene scene = new Scene(root);
        stage.setScene(scene);
        stage.setTitle("Using Fill Rules for Paths");
        stage.show();
    }
}
```

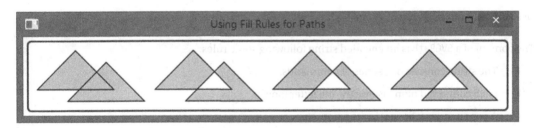

Figure 14-24. *Paths using different fill rules*

Drawing Scalable Vector Graphics

An instance of the SVGPath class draws a shape from path data in an encoded string. You can find the SVG specification at www.w3.org/TR/SVG. You can find the detailed rules of constructing the path data in string format at www.w3.org/TR/SVG/paths.html. JavaFX partially supports SVG specification.

The SVGPath class contains a no-args constructor to create its object:

```
// Create a SVGPath object
SVGPath sp = new SVGPath();
```

The SVGPath class contains two properties:

- content
- fillRule

The content property defines the encoded string for the SVG path. The fillRule property specifies the fill rule for the interior of the shape, which could be FillRule.NON_ZERO or FillRule.EVEN_ODD. The default value for the fillRule property is FillRule.NON_ZERO. Please refer to the section "The Fill Rule for a Path" for more details on fill rules. Fill rules for a Path and a SVGPath work the same.

The following snippet of code sets "M50, 0 L0, 50 L100, 50 Z" encoded string as the content for a SVGPath object to draw a triangle as shown in Figure 14-25:

```
SVGPath sp2 = new SVGPath();
sp2.setContent("M50, 0 L0, 50 L100, 50 Z");
sp2.setFill(Color.LIGHTGRAY);
sp2.setStroke(Color.BLACK);
```

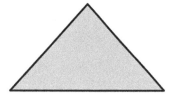

Figure 14-25. *A triangle using a SVGPath*

The content of a SVGPath is an encoded string following some rules:

- The string consists of a series of commands.
- Each command name is exactly one letter long.
- A command is followed by its parameters.
- Parameter values for a command are separated by a comma or a space. For example, "M50, 0 L0, 50 L100, 50 Z" and "M50 0 L0 50 L100 50 Z" represent the same path. For readability, you will use a comma to separate two values.
- You do not need to add spaces before or after the command character. For example, "M50 0 L0 50 L100 50 Z" can be rewritten as "M50 0L0 50L100 50Z".

Let us consider the SVG content used in the previous example:

```
M50, 0 L0, 50 L100, 50 Z
```

The content consists of four commands:

- M50, 0

- L0, 50

- L100, 50

- Z

Comparing the SVG path commands with the Path API, the first command is "MoveTo (50, 0)"; the second command is "LineTo(0, 50)"; the third command is "LineTo(100, 50)"; and the fourth command is "ClosePath".

■ **Tip**   The command name in SVGPath content is the first letter of the classes representing path elements in a Path object. For example, an absolute MoveTo in the Path API becomes M in SVGPath content, an absolute LineTo becomes L, and so on.

The parameters for the commands are coordinates, which can be absolute or relative. When the command name is in uppercase (e.g., M), its parameters are considered absolute. When the command name is in lowercase (e.g., m), its parameters are considered relative. The "closepath" command is Z or z. Because the "closepath" command does not take any parameters, both uppercase and lowercase versions behave the same.

Consider the content of two SVG paths:

- M50, 0 L0, 50 L100, 50 Z

- M50, 0 l0, 50 l100, 50 Z

The first path uses absolute coordinates. The second path uses absolute and relative coordinates. Like a Path, a SVGPath must start with a "moveTo" command, which must use absolute coordinates. If a SVGPath starts with a relative "moveTo" command (e.g., "m 50, 0"), its parameters are treated as absolute coordinates. In the foregoing SVG paths, you can start the string with "m50, 0", and the result will be the same.

The previous two SVG paths will draw two different triangles, as shown in Figure 14-26, even though both use the same parameters. The first path draws the triangle on the left, and the second one draws the triangle on the right. The commands in the second path are interpreted as follows:

- Move to (50, 0).

- Draw a line from the current point (50, 0) to (50, 50). The ending point (50, 50) is derived by adding the x and y coordinates of the current point to the relative "lineto" command (l) parameters. The ending point becomes (50, 50).

- Draw a line from the current point (50, 50) to (150, 100). Again, the coordinates of the ending point are derived by adding the x and y coordinates of the current point (50, 50) to the command parameter "l100, 50" (the first character in "l100, 50" is the lowercase L, not the digit 1).

- Then close the path (Z).

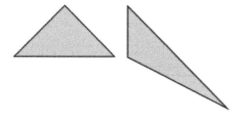

Figure 14-26. *Using absolute and relative coordinates in SVG paths*

Table 14-2 lists the commands used in the content of the SVGPath objects. It also lists the equivalent classes used in the Path API. The table lists the command, which uses absolute coordinates. The relative versions of the commands use lowercase letters. The plus sign (+) in the parameter column indicates that multiple parameters may be used.

Table 14-2. *List of SVG Path Commands*

Command	Parameter	Command Name	Path API Class
M	(x, y)+	moveto	MoveTo
L	(x, y)+	lineto	LineTo
H	x+	lineto	HLineTo
V	y+	lineto	VLineTo
A	(rx, ry, x-axis-rotation, large-arc-flag, sweep-flag, x, y)+	arcto	ArcTo
Q	(x1, y1, x, y)+	Quadratic Bezier curveto	QuadCurveTo
T	(x, y)+	Shorthand/smooth quadratic Bezier curveto	QuadCurveTo
C	(x1, y1, x2, y2, x, y)+	curveto	CubicCurveTo
S	(x2, y2, x, y)+	Shorthand/smooth curveto	CubicCurveTo
Z	None	closePath	ClosePath

The "moveTo" Command

The "moveTo" command M starts a new subpath at the specified (x, y) coordinates. It may be followed by one or multiple pairs of coordinates. The first pair of coordinates is considered the x and y coordinates of the point, which the command will make the current point. Each additional pair is treated as a parameter for a "lineto" command. If the "moveTo" command is relative, the "lineto" command will be relative. If the "moveTo" command is absolute, the "lineto" command will be absolute. For example, the following two SVG paths are the same:

```
M50, 0 L0, 50 L100, 50 Z
M50, 0, 0, 50, 100, 50 Z
```

The "lineto" Commands

There are three "lineto" commands: L, H, and V. They are used to draw straight lines.

The command L is used to draw a straight line from the current point to the specified (x, y) point. If you specify multiple pairs of (x, y) coordinates, it draws a polyline. The final pair of the (x, y) coordinate becomes the new current point. The following SVG paths will draw the same triangle. The first one uses two L commands, and the second one uses only one:

- M50, 0 L0, 50 L100, 50 L50, 0

- M50, 0 L0, 50, 100, 50, 50, 0

The H and V commands are used to draw horizontal and vertical lines from the current point. The command H draws a horizontal line from the current point (cx, cy) to (x, cy). The command V draws a vertical line from the current point (cx, cy) to (cx, y). You can pass multiple parameters to them. The final parameter value defines the current point. For example, "M0, 0H200, 100 V50Z" will draw a line from (0, 0) to (200, 0), from (200, 0) to (100, 0). The second command will make (100, 0) as the current point. The third command will draw a vertical line from (100, 0) to (100, 50). The z command will draw a line from (100, 50) to (0, 0). The following snippet of code draws a SVG path as shown in Figure 14-27:

```
SVGPath p1 = new SVGPath();
p1.setContent("M0, 0H-50, 50, 0 V-50, 50, 0, -25 L25, 0");
p1.setFill(Color.LIGHTGRAY);
p1.setStroke(Color.BLACK);
```

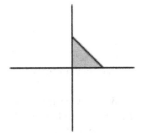

Figure 14-27. *Using multiple parameters to "lineto" commands*

The "arcto" Command

The "arcto" command A draws an elliptical arc from the current point to the specified (x, y) point. It uses rx and ry as the radii along x-axis and y-axis. The x-axis-rotation is a rotation angle in degrees for the x-axis of the ellipse. The large-arc-flag and sweep-flag are the flags used to select one arc out of four possible arcs. Use 0 and 1 for flag values, where 1 means true and 0 means false. Please refer to the section "The ArcTo Path Element" for a detailed explanation of all its parameters. You can pass multiple arcs parameters, and in that case, the ending point of an arc becomes the current point for the subsequent arc. The following snippet of code draws two SVG paths with arcs. The first path uses one parameter for the "arcTo" command, and the second path uses two parameters. Figure 14-28 shows the paths.

```
SVGPath p1 = new SVGPath();
```

```
// rx=150, ry=50, x-axis-rotation=0, large-arc-flag=0,
// sweep-flag 0, x=-50, y=50
p1.setContent("M0, 0 A150, 50, 0, 0, 0, -50, 50 Z");
p1.setFill(Color.LIGHTGRAY);
p1.setStroke(Color.BLACK);

// Use multiple arcs in one "arcTo" command
SVGPath p2 = new SVGPath();

// rx1=150, ry1=50, x-axis-rotation1=0, large-arc-flag1=0,
// sweep-flag1=0, x1=-50, y1=50
// rx2=150, ry2=10, x-axis-rotation2=0, large-arc-flag2=0,
// sweep-flag2=0, x2=10, y2=10
p2.setContent("M0, 0 A150 50 0 0 0 -50 50, 150 10 0 0 0 10 10 Z");
p2.setFill(Color.LIGHTGRAY);
p2.setStroke(Color.BLACK);
```

Figure 14-28. *Using "arcTo" commands to draw elliptical arc paths*

The "Quadratic Bezier curveto" Command

Both commands Q and T are used to draw quadratic Bezier curves.

The command Q draws a quadratic Bezier curve from the current point to the specified (x, y) point using the specified (x1, y1) as the control point.

The command T draws a quadratic Bezier curve from the current point to the specified (x, y) point using a control point that is the reflection of the control point on the previous command. The current point is used as the control point if there was no previous command or the previous command was not Q, q, T, or t.

The command Q takes the control point as parameters, whereas the command T assumes the control point. The following snippet of code uses the commands Q and T to draw quadratic Bezier curves as shown in Figure 14-29:

```
SVGPath p1 = new SVGPath();
p1.setContent("M0, 50 Q50, 0, 100, 50");
p1.setFill(Color.LIGHTGRAY);
p1.setStroke(Color.BLACK);

SVGPath p2 = new SVGPath();
p2.setContent("M0, 50 Q50, 0, 100, 50 T200, 50");
p2.setFill(Color.LIGHTGRAY);
p2.setStroke(Color.BLACK);
```

Figure 14-29. *Using Q and T commands to draw quadratic Bezier curves*

The "Cubic Bezier curveto" Command

The commands C and S are used to draw cubic Bezier curves.

The command C draws a cubic Bezier curve from the current point to the specified point (x, y) using the specified control points (x1, y1) and (x2, y2).

The command S draws a cubic Bezier curve from the current point to the specified point (x, y). It assumes the first control point to be the reflection of the second control point on the previous command. The current point is used as the first control point if there was no previous command or the previous command was not C, c, S, or s. The specified point (x2, y2) is the second control point. Multiple sets of coordinates draw a polybezier.

The following snippet of code uses the commands C and S to draw cubic Bezier curves as shown in Figure 14-30. The second path uses the command S to use the reflection of the second control point of the previous command C as its first control point:

```
SVGPath p1 = new SVGPath();
p1.setContent("M0, 0 C0, -100, 100, 100, 0");
p1.setFill(Color.LIGHTGRAY);
p1.setStroke(Color.BLACK);

SVGPath p2 = new SVGPath();
p2.setContent("M0, 0 C0, -100, 100, 100, 0 S200 100 200, 0");
p2.setFill(Color.LIGHTGRAY);
p2.setStroke(Color.BLACK);
```

Figure 14-30. *Using C and S commands to draw cubic Bezier curves*

The "closepath" Command

The "closepath" commands Z and z draw a straight line from the current point to the starting point of the current subpath and end the subpath. Both uppercase and lowercase versions of the command work the same.

Combining Shapes

The Shape class provides three static methods that let you perform union, intersection, and subtraction of shapes:

- union(Shape shape1, Shape shape2)
- intersect(Shape shape1, Shape shape2)
- subtract(Shape shape1, Shape shape2)

The methods return a new Shape instance. They operate on the areas of the input shapes. If a shape does not have a fill and a stroke, its area is zero. The new shape has a stroke and a fill. The union() method combines the areas of two shapes. The intersect() method uses the common areas between the shapes to create the new shape. The subtract() method creates a new shape by subtracting the specified second shape from the first shape.

The program in Listing 14-14 combines two circles using the union, intersection, and subtraction operations. Figure 14-31 shows the resulting shapes.

Listing 14-14. Combining Shapes to Create New Shapes

```
// CombiningShapesTest.java
package com.jdojo.shape;

import javafx.application.Application;
import javafx.scene.Scene;
import javafx.scene.layout.HBox;
import javafx.scene.paint.Color;
import javafx.scene.shape.Circle;
import javafx.scene.shape.Shape;
import javafx.stage.Stage;

public class CombiningShapesTest extends Application {
    public static void main(String[] args) {
        Application.launch(args);
    }

    @Override
    public void start(Stage stage) {
        Circle c1 = new Circle (0, 0, 20);
        Circle c2 = new Circle (15, 0, 20);

        Shape union = Shape.union(c1, c2);
        union.setStroke(Color.BLACK);
        union.setFill(Color.LIGHTGRAY);

        Shape intersection = Shape.intersect(c1, c2);
        intersection.setStroke(Color.BLACK);
        intersection.setFill(Color.LIGHTGRAY);

        Shape subtraction = Shape.subtract(c1, c2);
        subtraction.setStroke(Color.BLACK);
        subtraction.setFill(Color.LIGHTGRAY);
```

```
        HBox root = new HBox(union, intersection, subtraction);
        root.setSpacing(20);
        root.setStyle("""
            -fx-padding: 10;
            -fx-border-style: solid inside;
            -fx-border-width: 2;
            -fx-border-insets: 5;
            -fx-border-radius: 5;
            -fx-border-color: blue;""");

        Scene scene = new Scene(root);
        stage.setScene(scene);
        stage.setTitle("Combining Shapes");
        stage.show();
    }
}
```

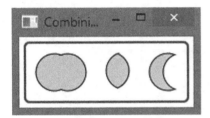

Figure 14-31. *Shapes created by combining two circles*

Understanding the Stroke of a Shape

Stroking is the process of painting the outline of a shape. Sometimes, the outline of a shape is also known as stroke. The Shape class contains several properties to define the appearance of the stroke of a shape:

- stroke
- strokeWidth
- strokeType
- strokeLineCap
- strokeLineJoin
- strokeMiterLimit
- strokeDashOffset

The stroke property specifies the color of the stroke. The default stroke is set to null for all shapes except Line, Path, and Polyline, which have Color.BLACK as their default stroke.

The strokeWidth property specifies the width of the stroke. It is 1.0px by default.

The stroke is painted along the boundary of a shape. The strokeType property specifies the distribution of the width of the stroke on the boundary. Its value is one of the three constants, CENTERED, INSIDE, and OUTSIDE, of the StrokeType enum. The default value is CENTERED. The CENTERED stroke type draws a half of the stroke width outside and half inside the boundary. The INSIDE stroke type draws the stroke inside the boundary. The OUTSIDE stroke draws the stroke outside the boundary. The stroke width of a shape is included in its layout bounds.

The program in Listing 14-15 creates four rectangles as shown in Figure 14-32. All rectangles have the same width and height (50px and 50px). The first rectangle, counting from the left, has no stroke, and it has layout bounds of 50px X 50px. The second rectangle uses a stroke of width 4px and an INSIDE stroke type. The INSIDE stroke type is drawn inside the width and height boundary, and the rectangle has the layout bounds of 50px X 50px. The third rectangle uses a stroke width 4px and a CENTERED stroke type, which is the default. The stroke is drawn 2px inside the boundary and 2px outside the boundary. The 2px outside stroke is added to the dimensions of all four making the layout bounds to 54px X 54px. The fourth rectangle uses a 4px stroke width and an OUTSIDE stroke type. The entire stroke width falls outside the width and height of the rectangle making the layouts to 58px X 58px.

Listing 14-15. Effects of Applying Different Stroke Types on a Rectangle

```java
// StrokeTypeTest.java
package com.jdojo.shape;

import javafx.application.Application;
import javafx.geometry.Pos;
import javafx.scene.Scene;
import javafx.scene.layout.HBox;
import javafx.scene.paint.Color;
import javafx.scene.shape.Rectangle;
import javafx.scene.shape.StrokeType;
import javafx.stage.Stage;

public class StrokeTypeTest extends Application {
        public static void main(String[] args) {
            Application.launch(args);
        }

        @Override
        public void start(Stage stage) {
            Rectangle r1 = new Rectangle(50, 50);
            r1.setFill(Color.LIGHTGRAY);

            Rectangle r2 = new Rectangle(50, 50);
            r2.setFill(Color.LIGHTGRAY);
            r2.setStroke(Color.BLACK);
            r2.setStrokeWidth(4);
            r2.setStrokeType(StrokeType.INSIDE);

            Rectangle r3 = new Rectangle(50, 50);
            r3.setFill(Color.LIGHTGRAY);
            r3.setStroke(Color.BLACK);
            r3.setStrokeWidth(4);
```

```
Rectangle r4 = new Rectangle(50, 50);
r4.setFill(Color.LIGHTGRAY);
r4.setStroke(Color.BLACK);
r4.setStrokeWidth(4);
r4.setStrokeType(StrokeType.OUTSIDE);

HBox root = new HBox(r1, r2, r3, r4);
root.setAlignment(Pos.CENTER);
root.setSpacing(10);
root.setStyle("""
    -fx-padding: 10;
    -fx-border-style: solid inside;
    -fx-border-width: 2;
    -fx-border-insets: 5;
    -fx-border-radius: 5;
    -fx-border-color: blue;""");

Scene scene = new Scene(root);
stage.setScene(scene);
stage.setTitle("Using Different Stroke Types for Shapes");
stage.show();
    }
}
```

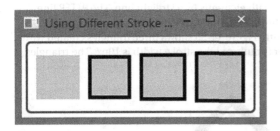

Figure 14-32. *Rectangles using different types of strokes*

The strokeLineCap property specifies the ending decoration of a stroke for unclosed subpaths and dash segments. Its value is one of the constants of the StrokeLineCap enum: BUTT, SQUARE, and ROUND. The default is BUTT. The BUTT line cap adds no decoration to the end of a subpath; the stroke starts and ends exactly at the starting and ending points. The SQUARE line cap extends the end by half the stroke width. The ROUND line cap adds a round cap to the end. The round cap uses a radius equal to half the stroke width. Figure 14-33 shows three lines, which are unclosed subpaths. All lines are 100px wide using 10px stroke width. The figure shows the strokeLineCap they use. The width of the layout bounds of the line using the BUTT line cap remains 100px. However, for other two lines, the width of the layout bounds increases to 110px—increasing by 10px at both ends.

573

BUTT

SQUARE

ROUND

Figure 14-33. *Different line cap styles for strokes*

Note that the strokeLineCap properties are applied to the ends of a line segment of *unclosed* subpaths. Figure 14-34 shows three triangles created by unclosed subpaths. They use different stroke line caps. The SVG path data "M50, 0L0, 50 M0, 50 L100, 50 M100, 50 L50, 0" was used to draw the triangles. The fill was set to null and the stroke width to 10px.

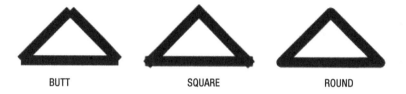

BUTT   SQUARE   ROUND

Figure 14-34. *Triangles using unclosed subpaths using different stroke line caps*

The strokeLineJoin property specifies how two successive path elements of a subpath are joined. Its value is one of the constants of the StrokeLineJoin enum: BEVEL, MITER, and ROUND. The default is MITER. The BEVEL line join connects the outer corners of path elements by a straight line. The MITER line join extends the outer edges of two path elements until they meet. The ROUND line join connects two path elements by rounding their corners by half the stroke width. Figure 14-35 shows three triangles created with the SVG path data "M50, 0L0, 50 L100, 50 Z". The fill color is null, and the stroke width is 10px. The triangles use different line joins as shown in the figure.

BEVEL   MITER   ROUND

Figure 14-35. *Triangles using different stroke line join types*

A MITER line join joins two path elements by extending their outer edges. If the path elements meet at a smaller angle, the length of the join may become very big. You can limit the length of the join using the strokeMiterLimit property. It specifies the ratio of the miter length and the stroke width. The miter length is the distance between the most inside point and the most outside point of the join. If the two path elements cannot meet by extending their outer edges within this limit, a BEVEL join is used instead. The default value is 10.0. That is, by default, the miter length may be up to ten times the stroke width.

The following snippet of code creates two triangles as shown in Figure 14-36. Both use a MITER line join by default. The first triangle uses 2.0 as the miter limit. The second triangle uses the default miter limit, which is 10.0. The stroke width is 10px. The first triangle tries to join the corners by extending two lines up to 20px, which is computed by multiplying the 10px stroke width by the miter limit of 2.0. The corners cannot be joined using the MITER join within 20px, so a BEVEL join is used.

```
SVGPath t1 = new SVGPath();
t1.setContent("M50, 0L0, 50 L100, 50 Z");
t1.setStrokeWidth(10);
t1.setFill(null);
t1.setStroke(Color.BLACK);
t1.setStrokeMiterLimit(2.0);

SVGPath t2 = new SVGPath();
t2.setContent("M50, 0L0, 50 L100, 50 Z");
t2.setStrokeWidth(10);
t2.setFill(null);
t2.setStroke(Color.BLACK);
```

Figure 14-36. *Triangles using different stroke miter limits*

By default, the stroke draws a solid outline. You can also have a dashed outline. You need to provide a dashing pattern and a dash offset. The dashing pattern is an array of double that is stored in an ObservableList<Double>. You can get the reference of the list using the getStrokeDashArray() method of the Shape class. The elements of the list specify a pattern of dashes and gaps. The first element is the dash length, the second gap, the third dash length, the fourth gap, and so on. The dashing pattern is repeated to draw the outline. The strokeDashOffset property specifies the offset in the dashing pattern where the stroke begins.

The following snippet of code creates two instances of Polygon as shown in Figure 14-37. Both use the same dashing patterns but a different dash offset. The first one uses the dash offset of 0.0, which is the default. The stroke of the first rectangle starts with a 15.0px dash, which is the first element of the dashing pattern, which can be seen in the dashed line drawn from the (0, 0) to (100, 0). The second Polygon uses a dash offset of 20.0, which means the stroke will start 20.0px inside the dashing pattern. The first two elements 15.0 and 3.0 are inside the dash offset 20.0. Therefore, the stroke for the second Polygon starts at the third element, which is a 5.0px dash.

```
Polygon p1 = new Polygon(0, 0, 100, 0, 100, 50, 0, 50, 0, 0);
p1.setFill(null);
p1.setStroke(Color.BLACK);
p1.getStrokeDashArray().addAll(15.0, 5.0, 5.0, 5.0);

Polygon p2 = new Polygon(0, 0, 100, 0, 100, 50, 0, 50, 0, 0);
p2.setFill(null);
p2.setStroke(Color.BLACK);
p2.getStrokeDashArray().addAll(15.0, 5.0, 5.0, 5.0);
p2.setStrokeDashOffset(20.0);
```

Figure 14-37. *Two polygons using dashing patterns for their outline*

Styling Shapes with CSS

All shapes do not have a default style class name. If you want to apply styles to shapes using CSS, you need to add style class names to them. All shapes can use the following CSS properties:

- `-fx-fill`
- `-fx-smooth`
- `-fx-stroke`
- `-fx-stroke-type`
- `-fx-stroke-dash-array`
- `-fx-stroke-dash-offset`
- `-fx-stroke-line-cap`
- `-fx-stroke-line-join`
- `-fx-stroke-miter-limit`
- `-fx-stroke-width`

All CSS properties correspond to the properties in the Shape class, which I have discussed at length in the previous section. Rectangle supports two additional CSS properties to specify arc width and height for rounded rectangles:

- `-fx-arc-height`
- `-fx-arc-width`

The following snippet of code creates a Rectangle and adds *rectangle* as its style class name:

```
Rectangle r1 = new Rectangle(200, 50);
r1.getStyleClass().add("rectangle");
```

The following style will produce a rectangle as shown in Figure 14-38:

```
.rectangle {
        -fx-fill: lightgray;
        -fx-stroke: black;
        -fx-stroke-width: 4;
        -fx-stroke-dash-array: 15 5 5 10;
        -fx-stroke-dash-offset: 20;
        -fx-stroke-line-cap: round;
        -fx-stroke-line-join: bevel;
}
```

Figure 14-38. *Applying CSS styles to a rectangle*

Summary

Any shape that can be drawn in a two-dimensional plane is called a 2D shape. JavaFX offers various nodes to draw different types of shapes (lines, circles, rectangles, etc.). You can add shapes to a scene graph. All shape classes are in the javafx.scene.shape package. Classes representing 2D shapes are inherited from the abstract Shape class. A shape can have a stroke that defines the outline of the shape. A shape may have a fill.

An instance of the Line class represents a line node. A Line has no interior. By default, its fill property is set to null. Setting fill has no effect. The default stroke is Color.BLACK, and the default strokeWidth is 1.0.

An instance of the Rectangle class represents a rectangle node. The class uses six properties to define the rectangle: x, y, width, height, arcWidth, and arcHeight. The x and y properties are the x and y coordinates of the upper-left corner of the rectangle in the local coordinate system of the node. The width and height properties are the width and height of the rectangle, respectively. Specify the same width and height to draw a square. By default, the corners of a rectangle are sharp. A rectangle can have rounded corners by specifying the arcWidth and arcHeight properties.

An instance of the Circle class represents a circle node. The class uses three properties to define the circle: centerX, centerY, and radius. The centerX and centerY properties are the x and y coordinates of the center of the circle in the local coordinate system of the node. The radius property is the radius of the circle. The default values for these properties are zero.

An instance of the Ellipse class represents an ellipse node. The class uses four properties to define the ellipse: centerX, centerY, radiusX, radiusY. The centerX and centerY properties are the x and y coordinates of the center of the circle in the local coordinate system of the node. The radiusX and radiusY are the radii of the ellipse in the horizontal and vertical directions. The default values for these properties are zero. A circle is a special case of an ellipse when radiusX and radiusY are the same.

An instance of the Polygon class represents a polygon node. The class does not define any public properties. It lets you draw a polygon using an array of (x, y) coordinates defining the vertices of the polygon. Using the Polygon class, you can draw any type of geometric shape that is created using connected lines (triangles, pentagon, hexagon, parallelogram, etc.).

A polyline is similar to a polygon, except that it does not draw a line between the last and first points. That is, a polyline is an open polygon. However, the fill color is used to fill the entire shape as if the shape was closed. An instance of the Polyline class represents a polyline node.

An instance of the Arc class represents a sector of an ellipse. The class uses seven properties to define the ellipse: centerX, centerY, radiusX, radiusY, startAngle, length, and type. The first four properties define an ellipse. The last three properties define a sector of the ellipse that is the Arc node. The startAngle property specifies the start angle of the section in degrees measured counterclockwise from the positive x-axis. It defines the beginning of the arc. The length is an angle in degrees measured counterclockwise from the start angle to define the end of the sector. If the length property is set to 360, the Arc is a full ellipse.

Bezier curves are used in computer graphics to draw smooth curves. An instance of the QuadCurve class represents a quadratic Bezier curve segment intersecting two specified points using a specified Bezier control point.

An instance of the CubicCurve class represents a cubic Bezier curve segment intersecting two specified points using two specified Bezier control points.

You can draw complex shapes using the Path class. An instance of the Path class defines the path (outline) of a shape. A path consists of one or more subpaths. A subpath consists of one or more path elements. Each subpath has a starting point and an ending point. A path element is an instance of the PathElement abstract class. Several subclasses of the PathElement class exist to represent a specific type of path elements; those classes are MoveTo, LineTo, HLineTo, VLineTo, ArcTo, QuadCurveTo, CubicCurveTo, and ClosePath.

JavaFX partially supports SVG specification. An instance of the SVGPath class draws a shape from path data in an encoded string.

JavaFX lets you create a shape by combining multiple shapes. The Shape class provides three static methods named union(), intersect(), and subtract() that let you perform union, intersection, and subtraction of two shapes that are passed as the arguments to these methods. The methods return a new Shape instance. They operate on the areas of the input shapes. If a shape does not have a fill and a stroke, its area is zero. The new shape has a stroke and a fill. The union() method combines the areas of two shapes. The intersect() method uses the common areas between the shapes to create the new shape. The subtract() method creates a new shape by subtracting the specified second shape from the first shape.

Stroking is the process of painting the outline of a shape. Sometimes, the outline of a shape is also known as stroke. The Shape class contains several properties such as stroke, strokeWidth, and so on to define the appearance of the stroke of a shape.

JavaFX lets you style 2D shapes with CSS.

The next chapter will discuss how to handle text drawing.

■ ■ ■

CHAPTER 15

Understanding Text Nodes

In this chapter, you will learn:

- What a Text node is and how to create it
- The coordinate system used for drawing Text nodes
- How to display multiline text in a Text node
- How to set fonts for a Text node
- How to access installed fonts and how to install custom fonts
- How to set the fill and stroke for Text nodes
- How to apply decoration such as underline and strikethrough to Text nodes
- How to apply font smoothing
- How to style Text nodes using CSS

The examples of this chapter lie in the com.jdojo.shape package. In order for them to work, you must add a corresponding line to the module-info.java file:

```
...
opens com.jdojo.shape to javafx.graphics, javafx.base;
...
```

What Is a Text Node?

A text node is an instance of the Text class that is used to render text. The Text class contains several properties to customize the appearance of text. The Text class and all its related classes—for example, the Font class, the TextAlignment enum, the FontWeight enum, etc.—are in the javafx.scene.text package.

The Text class inherits from the Shape class. That is, a Text is a Shape, which allows you to use all properties and methods of the Shape class on a Text node. For example, you can apply a fill color and a stroke to a Text node. Because Text is a node, you can use features of the Node class: for example, applying effects and transformations. You can also set text alignment, font family, font size, text wrapping style, etc., on a Text node.

Figure 15-1 shows three text nodes. The first one (from the left) is a simple text node. The second one uses bold text in a bigger font size. The third one uses the Reflection effect, a bigger font size, a stroke, and a fill.

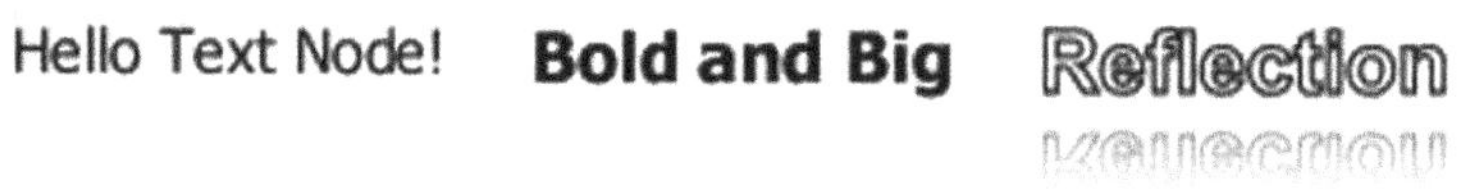

Hello Text Node!   **Bold and Big**   Reflection

Figure 15-1. *A window showing three Text nodes*

Creating a Text Node

An instance of the Text class represents a Text node. A Text node contains text and properties to render the text. You can create a Text node using one of the constructors of the Text class:

- Text()
- Text(String text)
- Text(double x, double y, String text)

The no-args constructor creates a Text node with an empty string as its text. Other constructors let you specify the text and position the node.

The text property of the Text class specifies the text (or content) of the Text node. The x and y properties specify the x and y coordinates of the text origin, which are described in the next section.

```
// Create an empty Text Node and later set its text
Text t1 = new Text();
t1.setText("Hello from the Text node!");

// Create a Text Node with initial text
Text t2 = new Text("Hello from the Text node!");

// Create a Text Node with initial text and position
Text t3 = new Text(50, 50, "Hello from the Text node!");
```

■ **Tip**   The width and height of a text node are automatically determined by its font. By default, a Text node uses a system default font to render its text.

The program in Listing 15-1 creates three Text nodes, sets their different properties, and adds them to an HBox. The Text nodes are displayed as shown in Figure 15-1.

Listing 15-1. Creating Text Nodes

```
// TextTest.java
package com.jdojo.shape;

import javafx.application.Application;
import javafx.scene.Scene;
import javafx.scene.effect.Reflection;
import javafx.scene.layout.HBox;
import javafx.scene.paint.Color;
```

```
import javafx.scene.text.Font;
import javafx.scene.text.FontWeight;
import javafx.scene.text.Text;
import javafx.stage.Stage;

public class TextTest extends Application {
        public static void main(String[] args) {
                Application.launch(args);
        }

        @Override
        public void start(Stage stage) {
                Text t1 = new Text("Hello Text Node!");

                Text t2 = new Text("Bold and Big");
                t2.setFont(Font.font("Tahoma", FontWeight.BOLD, 16));

                Text t3 = new Text("Reflection");
                t3.setEffect(new Reflection());
                t3.setStroke(Color.BLACK);
                t3.setFill(Color.WHITE);
                t3.setFont(Font.font("Arial", FontWeight.BOLD, 20));

                HBox root = new HBox(t1, t2, t3);
                root.setSpacing(20);
                root.setStyle("""
                        -fx-padding: 10;
                    -fx-border-style: solid inside;
                    -fx-border-width: 2;
                    -fx-border-insets: 5;
                    -fx-border-radius: 5;
                    -fx-border-color: blue;""");

                Scene scene = new Scene(root);
                stage.setScene(scene);
                stage.setTitle("Using Text Nodes");
                stage.show();
        }
}
```

Understanding the Text Origin

Apart from the local and parent coordinate system, a Text node has an additional coordinate system. It is the coordinate system used for drawing the text. Three properties of the Text class define the text coordinate system:

- x

- y

- textOrigin

The x and y properties define the x and y coordinates of the text origin. The textOrigin property is of type VPos. Its value could be VPos.BASELINE, VPos.TOP, VPos.CENTER, and VPos.BOTTOM. The default is VPos. BASELINE. It defines where the x-axis of the text coordinate system lies within the text height. Figure 15-2 shows the local and text coordinate systems of a text node. The local coordinate axes are in solid lines. The text coordinate axes are in dashed lines.

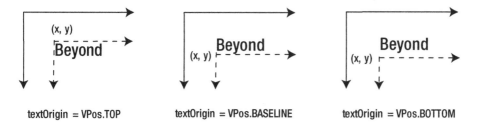

textOrigin = VPos.TOP   textOrigin = VPos.BASELINE   textOrigin = VPos.BOTTOM

Figure 15-2. *Effects of the textOrigin property on the vertical location of text drawing*

When the textOrigin is VPos.TOP, the x-axis of the text coordinate system is aligned with the top of the text. That is, the y property of the Text node is the distance between the x-axis of the local coordinate system and the top of the displayed text. A font places its characters on a line called the *baseline*. The VPos.BASELINE aligns the x-axis of the text coordinate system with the baseline of the font. Note that some characters (e.g., g, y, j, p, etc.) are extended below the baseline. The VPos.BOTTOM aligns the x-axis of the text coordinate system with the bottom of the displayed text accounting for the descent for the font. The VPos.CENTER (not shown in the figure) aligns the x-axis of the text coordinate system in the middle of the displayed text, accounting for the ascent and descent for the font.

■ **Tip**   The Text class contains a read-only baselineOffset property. Its value is the vertical distance between the top and baseline of the text. It is equal to the max ascent of the font.

Most of the time, you need not worry about the textOrigin property of the Text node, except when you need to align it vertically relative to another node. Listing 15-2 shows how to center a Text node horizontally and vertically in a scene. To center the node vertically, you must set the textOrigin property to VPos. TOP. The text is displayed as shown in Figure 15-3. If you do not set the textOrigin property, its y-axis is aligned with its baseline, and it appears above the centerline of the scene.

Listing 15-2. Centering a Text Node in a Scene

```java
// TextCentering.java
package com.jdojo.shape;

import javafx.application.Application;
import javafx.geometry.VPos;
import javafx.scene.Group;
import javafx.scene.Scene;
import javafx.scene.text.Text;
import javafx.stage.Stage;
```

```java
public class TextCentering extends Application {
        public static void main(String[] args) {
                Application.launch(args);
        }

        @Override
        public void start(Stage stage) {
                Text msg = new Text("A Centered Text Node");

                // Must set the textOrigian to VPos.TOP to center
                // the text node vertcially within the scene
                msg.setTextOrigin(VPos.TOP);

                Group root = new Group();
                root.getChildren().addAll(msg);
                Scene scene = new Scene(root, 200, 50);
                msg.layoutXProperty().bind(
                        scene.widthProperty().subtract(
                    msg.layoutBoundsProperty().get().getWidth()).
                        divide(2));
                msg.layoutYProperty().bind(
                        scene.heightProperty().subtract(
                    msg.layoutBoundsProperty().get().getHeight()).
                        divide(2));

                stage.setTitle("Centering a Text Node in a Scene");
                stage.setScene(scene);
                stage.sizeToScene();
                stage.show();
        }
}
```

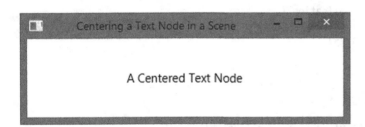

Figure 15-3. *A Text node centered in a scene*

583

Displaying Multiline Text

A Text node is capable of displaying multiple lines of text. It creates a new line in two cases:

- A newline character "\n" in the text creates a new line causing the characters following the newline to wrap to the next line.

- The Text class contains a wrappingWidth property, which is 0.0 by default. Its value is specified in pixels, not characters. If it is greater than zero, the text in each line is wrapped to at the specified value.

The lineSpacing property specifies the vertical spacing in pixels between two lines. It is 0.0 by default. The textAlignment property specifies the horizontal alignment of the text lines in the bounding box. The widest line defines the width of the bounding box. Its value has no effect in a single-line Text node. Its value can be one of the constants of the TextAlignment enum: LEFT, RIGHT, CENTER, and JUSTIFY. The default is TextAlignment.LEFT.

The program in Listing 15-3 creates three multiline Text nodes as shown in Figure 15-4. The text for all nodes is the same. The text contains three newline characters. The first node uses the default LEFT text alignment and a line spacing of 5px. The second node uses RIGHT text alignment with the default line spacing of 0px. The third node uses a wrappingWidth of 100px. A new line is created at 100px as well as a newline character "\n".

Listing 15-3. Using Multiline Text Nodes

```java
// MultilineText.java
package com.jdojo.shape;

import javafx.application.Application;
import javafx.scene.Scene;
import javafx.scene.layout.HBox;
import javafx.scene.text.Text;
import javafx.scene.text.TextAlignment;
import javafx.stage.Stage;

public class MultilineText extends Application {
        public static void main(String[] args) {
                Application.launch(args);
        }

        @Override
        public void start(Stage stage) {
                String text = """
                        Strange fits of passion have I known:
                    And I will dare to tell,
                    But in the lover's ear alone,
                    What once to me befell.""".stripIndent();

                Text t1 = new Text(text);
                t1.setLineSpacing(5);

                Text t2 = new Text(text);
                t2.setTextAlignment(TextAlignment.RIGHT);
```

```
        Text t3 = new Text(text);
        t3.setWrappingWidth(100);

        HBox root = new HBox(t1, t2, t3);
        root.setSpacing(20);
        root.setStyle("""
                -fx-padding: 10;
            -fx-border-style: solid inside;
            -fx-border-width: 2;
            -fx-border-insets: 5;
            -fx-border-radius: 5;
             -fx-border-color: blue;""");

        Scene scene = new Scene(root);
        stage.setScene(scene);
        stage.setTitle("Using Multiline Text Nodes");
        stage.show();
    }
}
```

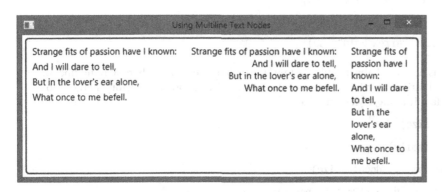

Figure 15-4. *Multiline Text nodes*

Setting Text Fonts

The font property of the Text class defines the font for the text. The default font used is from the "System" font family with the "Regular" style. The size of the default font is dependent on the platform and the desktop settings of the user.

A font has a *family* and a *family name*. A font family is also known as a *typeface*. A font family defines shapes (or glyphs) for characters. The same characters appear differently when displayed using fonts belonging to different font families. Variants of a font are created by applying styles. Each variant of the font has a name that consists of the family name and the style names. For example, "Arial" is a family name of a font, whereas "Arial Regular," "Arial Bold," and "Arial Bold Italic" are names of the variants of the "Arial" font.

Creating Fonts

An instance of the Font class represents a font. The Font class provides two constructors:

- Font(double size)
- Font(String name, double size)

The first constructor creates a Font object of the specified size that belongs to the "System" font family. The second one creates a Font object of the specified full name of the font and the specified size. The size of the font is specified in points. The following snippet of code creates some font objects of the "Arial" family. The getFamily(), getName(), and getSize() methods of the Font class return the family name, full name, and size of the font, respectively.

```
// Arial Plain
Font f1 = new Font("Arial", 10);

// Arial Italic
Font f2 = new Font("Arial Italic", 10);

// Arial Bold Italic
Font f3 = new Font("Arial Bold Italic", 10);

// Arial Narrow Bold
Font f4 = new Font("Arial Narrow Bold", 30);
```

If the full font name is not found, the default "System" font will be created. It is hard to remember or know the full names for all variants of a font. To address this, the Font class provides factory methods to create fonts using a font family name, styles, and size:

- font(double size)
- font(String family)
- font(String family, double size)
- font(String family, FontPosture posture, double size)
- font(String family, FontWeight weight, double size)
- font(String family, FontWeight weight, FontPosture posture, double size)

The font() methods let you specify the family name, font weight, font posture, and font size. If only the family name is provided, the default font size is used, which depends on the platform and the desktop setting of the user.

The font weight specifies how bold the font is. Its value is one of the constants of the FontWeight enum: THIN, EXTRA_LIGHT, LIGHT, NORMAL, MEDIUM, SEMI_BOLD, BOLD, EXTRA_BOLD, BLACK. The constant THIN represents the thinnest font and the constant BLACK the thickest font.

The posture of a font specifies whether it is italicized. It is represented by one of the two constants of the FontPosture enum: REGULAR and ITALIC.

The following snippet of code creates fonts using the factory methods of the Font class:

```
// Arial Regular
Font f1 = Font.font("Arial", 10);

// Arial Bold
```

```java
Font f2 = Font.font("Arial", FontWeight.BOLD, 10);

// Arial Bold Italic
Font f3 = Font.font("Arial", FontWeight.BOLD, FontPosture.ITALIC, 10);

// Arial THIN
Font f4 = Font.font("Arial", FontWeight.THIN, 30);
```

■ **Tip**   Use the getDefault() static method of the Font class to get the system default font.

The program in Listing 15-4 creates Text nodes and sets their font property. The first Text node uses the default font. Figure 15-5 shows the Text nodes. The text for the Text nodes is the String returned from the toString() method of their Font objects.

Listing 15-4. Setting Fonts for Text Nodes

```java
// TextFontTest.java
package com.jdojo.shape;

import javafx.application.Application;
import javafx.scene.Scene;
import javafx.scene.layout.VBox;
import javafx.scene.text.Font;
import javafx.scene.text.FontPosture;
import javafx.scene.text.FontWeight;
import javafx.scene.text.Text;
import javafx.stage.Stage;

public class TextFontTest extends Application {
        public static void main(String[] args) {
                Application.launch(args);
        }

        @Override
        public void start(Stage stage) {
                Text t1 = new Text();
                t1.setText(t1.getFont().toString());

                Text t2 = new Text();
                t2.setFont(Font.font("Arial", 12));
                t2.setText(t2.getFont().toString());

                Text t3 = new Text();
                t3.setFont(Font.font("Arial", FontWeight.BLACK, 12));
                t3.setText(t2.getFont().toString());
```

```
            Text t4 = new Text();
            t4.setFont(Font.font(
                    "Arial", FontWeight.THIN, FontPosture.ITALIC, 12));
            t4.setText(t2.getFont().toString());

            VBox root = new VBox(t1, t2, t3, t4);
            root.setSpacing(10);
            root.setStyle("""
                    -fx-padding: 10;
                -fx-border-style: solid inside;
                -fx-border-width: 2;
                -fx-border-insets: 5;
                -fx-border-radius: 5;
                -fx-border-color: blue;""");

            Scene scene = new Scene(root);
            stage.setScene(scene);
            stage.setTitle("Setting Fonts for Text Nodes");
            stage.show();
        }
}
```

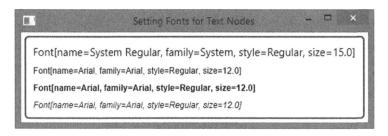

Figure 15-5. *Text nodes using variants of the "Arial" font family*

Accessing Installed Fonts

You can get the list of installed fonts on your machine. You can get the list of font family names, full font names, and full font names for a specified family name for all installed fonts. The following static methods in the Font class provide these lists:

- List<String> getFamilies()

- List<String> getFontNames()

- List<String> getFontNames(String family)

The following snippet of code prints the family names of all installed fonts on a machine. The output was generated on Windows. A partial output is shown:

```
// Print the family names of all installed fonts
for(String familyName: Font.getFamilies()) {
        System.out.println(familyName);
}
```

```
Agency FB
Algerian
Arial
Arial Black
Arial Narrow
Arial Rounded MT Bold
```

...

The following snippet of code prints the full names of all installed fonts on a machine. The output was generated on Windows. A partial output is shown:

```
// Print the full names of all installed fonts
for(String fullName: Font.getFontNames()) {
        System.out.println(fullName);
}
```

```
Agency FB
Agency FB Bold
Algerian
Arial
Arial Black
Arial Bold
Arial Bold Italic
Arial Italic
Arial Narrow
Arial Narrow Bold
Arial Narrow Bold Italic
More output goes here...
```

The following snippet of code prints the full names of all installed fonts for the "Times New Roman" family:

```
// Print the full names of "Times New Roman" family
for(String fullName: Font.getFontNames("Times New Roman")) {
        System.out.println(fullName);
}
```

```
Times New Roman
Times New Roman Bold
Times New Roman Bold Italic
Times New Roman Italic
```

Using Custom Fonts

You can load custom fonts from external sources: for example, from a file from the local file system or from a URL. The loadFont() static method in the Font class loads a custom font:

- loadFont(InputStream in, double size)

- loadFont(String urlStr, double size)

Upon successfully loading of the custom font, the loadFont() method registers the font with the JavaFX graphics engine, so a font can be created using the constructors and factory methods of the Font class. The method also creates a Font object of the specified size and returns it. Therefore, the size parameter exists for loading the font and creating its object in the same method call. If the method cannot load the font, it returns null.

The program in Listing 15-5 shows how to load a custom font from a local file system. The font file name is *4starfac.ttf*. This is just an example—you can specify any font you like. The file is assumed to be in the CLASSPATH under the *resources\font* directory. After the font is loaded successfully, it is set for the first Text node. A new Font object is created for its family name and set for the second Text node. If the font file does not exist or the font cannot be loaded, an appropriate error message is displayed in the window. Figure 15-6 shows the window when the font is loaded successfully.

Listing 15-5. Loading and Using Custom Fonts Using the Font Class

```java
// TextCustomFont.java
package com.jdojo.shape;

import java.net.URL;
import javafx.application.Application;
import javafx.scene.Scene;
import javafx.scene.layout.HBox;
import javafx.scene.text.Font;
import javafx.scene.text.FontPosture;
import javafx.scene.text.FontWeight;
import javafx.scene.text.Text;
import javafx.stage.Stage;

public class TextCustomFont extends Application {
    public static void main(String[] args) {
        Application.launch(args);
    }

    @Override
    public void start(Stage stage) {
        Text t1 = new Text();
        t1.setLineSpacing(10);

        Text t2 = new Text("Another Text node");

        // Load the custom font
        String fontFile =
                "resources/font/4starfac.ttf";
        URL url =
```

```java
            this.getClass().getClassLoader().
            getResource(fontFile);
if (url != null) {
    String urlStr = url.toExternalForm();
    Font customFont = Font.loadFont(urlStr, 16);
    if (customFont != null ) {
        // Set the custom font  for the first
                // Text node
        t1.setFont(customFont);

        // Set the text and line spacing
        t1.setText(
                "Hello from the custom font!!! \n" +
                "Font Family: " +
            customFont.getFamily());

        // Create an object of the custom font and
                // use it
        Font font2 =
                    Font.font(customFont.getFamily(),
                            FontWeight.BOLD,
                FontPosture.ITALIC,
                            24);

            // Set the custom font for the second
                    // Text node
            t2.setFont(font2);
    } else {
        t1.setText(
                "Could not load the custom font from " +
                urlStr);
    }
} else {
        t1.setText(
                "Could not find the custom font file " +
            fontFile +
                " in CLASSPATH. Used the default font.");
}

HBox root = new HBox(t1, t2);
root.setSpacing(20);
root.setStyle("""
        -fx-padding: 10;
    -fx-border-style: solid inside;
    -fx-border-width: 2;
    -fx-border-insets: 5;
    -fx-border-radius: 5;
    -fx-border-color: blue;""");
```

```
                    Scene scene = new Scene(root);
                    stage.setScene(scene);
                    stage.setTitle("Loading and Using Custom Font");
                    stage.show();
            }
    }
```

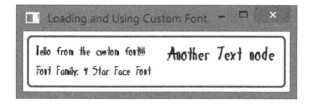

Figure 15-6. *Text nodes using custom fonts*

Setting Text Fill and Stroke

A Text node is a shape. Like a shape, it can have a fill and a stroke. By default, a Text node has a null stroke and a Color.BLACK fill. The Text class inherits properties and methods for setting its stroke and fill from the Shape class. I have discussed them at length in Chapter 14.

The program in Listing 15-6 shows how to set a stroke and a fill for Text nodes. Figure 15-7 shows two Text nodes. The first one uses a red stroke and a white fill. The second one uses a black stroke and white fill. The stroke style for the second one uses a dashed line.

Listing 15-6. Using Stroke and Fill for Text Nodes

```
// TextFillAndStroke.java
package com.jdojo.shape;

import javafx.application.Application;
import javafx.scene.Scene;
import javafx.scene.layout.HBox;
import javafx.scene.paint.Color;
import javafx.scene.text.Font;
import javafx.scene.text.Text;
import javafx.stage.Stage;

public class TextFillAndStroke extends Application {
        public static void main(String[] args) {
                Application.launch(args);
        }

        @Override
        public void start(Stage stage) {
                Text t1 = new Text("Stroke and fill!");
                t1.setStroke(Color.RED);
```

```java
            t1.setFill(Color.WHITE);
            t1.setFont(new Font(36));

            Text t2 = new Text("Dashed Stroke!");
            t2.setStroke(Color.BLACK);
            t2.setFill(Color.WHITE);
            t2.setFont(new Font(36));
            t2.getStrokeDashArray().addAll(5.0, 5.0);

            HBox root = new HBox(t1, t2);
            root.setSpacing(20);
            root.setStyle("""
                    -fx-padding: 10;
                -fx-border-style: solid inside;
                -fx-border-width: 2;
                -fx-border-insets: 5;
                -fx-border-radius: 5;
                -fx-border-color: blue;""");

            Scene scene = new Scene(root);
            stage.setScene(scene);
            stage.setTitle("Using Stroke and Fill for Text Nodes");
            stage.show();
        }
}
```

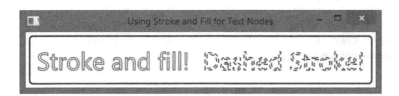

Figure 15-7. *Text nodes using strokes and fills*

Applying Text Decorations

The Text class contains two boolean properties to apply text decorations to its text:

- strikethrough
- underline

By default, both properties are set to `false`. If the `strikethrough` is set to true, a line is drawn through each line of text. If the `underline` is set to true, a line is drawn below each line of text. The following snippet of code uses the decorations for Text nodes. The nodes are shown in Figure 15-8.

```
Text t1 = new Text("It uses the \nunderline decoration.");
t1.setUnderline(true);

Text t2 = new Text("It uses the \nstrikethrough decoration.");
t2.setStrikethrough(true);
```

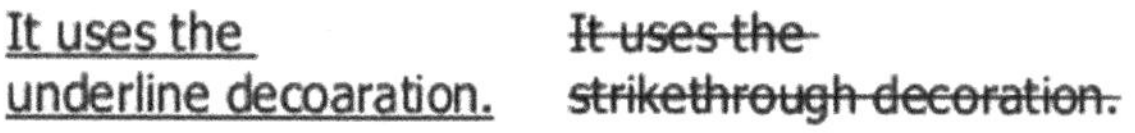

<u>It uses the</u> <s>It uses the</s>
<u>underline decoaration.</u> <s>strikethrough decoration.</s>

Figure 15-8. *Text nodes using the underline and strikethrough decorations*

Applying Font Smoothing

The Text class contains a `fontSmoothingType` property, which can be used to apply a gray or LCD font smoothing. Its value is one of the constants of the `FontSmoothingType` enum: GRAY and LCD. The default smoothing type is `fontSmoothingType.GRAY`. The LCD smoothing type is used as a hint. The following snippet of code creates two Text nodes: one uses LCD and one GRAY font smoothing type. The Text nodes have been shown in Figure 15-9.

```
Text t1 = new Text("Hello world in LCD.");
t1.setFontSmoothingType(FontSmoothingType.LCD);

Text t2 = new Text("Hello world in GRAY.");
t2.setFontSmoothingType(FontSmoothingType.GRAY);
```

Hello world in LCD.   Hello world in GRAY.

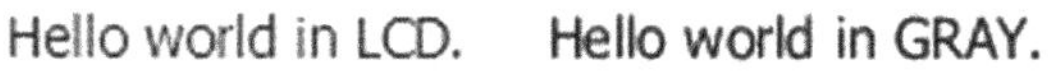

Figure 15-9. *Text nodes using LCD and GRAY font smoothing types*

Styling a Text Node with CSS

A Text node does not have a default CSS style class name. In addition to all CSS properties of the Shape, a Text node supports the following CSS properties:

- `-fx-font`
- `-fx-font-smoothing-type`
- `-fx-text-origin`
- `-fx-text-alignment`
- `-fx-strikethrough`
- `-fx-underline`

I have discussed all properties in the previous sections. The -fx-font property is inherited from the parent. If the parent does not set the property, the default system font is used. The valid values for the -fx-font-smoothing-type property are lcd and gray. The valid values for the -fx-text-origin property are baseline, top, and bottom. Let us create a style named *my-text* as follows. It sets a font and a linear gradient fill. The fill starts as a light gray color and ends as black:

```
.my-text {
        -fx-font: 36 Arial;
        -fx-fill: linear-gradient(from 0% 0% to 100% 0%,
                                    lightgray 0%, black 100%);
        -fx-font-smoothing-type: lcd;
        -fx-underline: true;
}
```

The following snippet of code creates a Text node and sets its style class name to *my-text*. Figure 15-10 shows the Text node with its styles applied to it.

```
Text t1 = new Text("Styling Text Nodes!");
t1.getStyleClass().add("my-text");
```

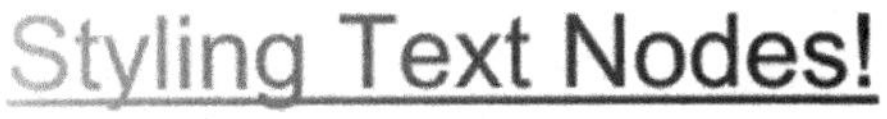

Styling Text Nodes!

Figure 15-10. *A Text node using CSS styles*

Summary

A text node is an instance of the Text class that is used to render text. The Text class contains several properties to customize the appearance of text. The Text class and all its related classes are in the javafx. scene.text package. The Text class inherits from the Shape class. That is, a Text is a Shape, which allows you to use all properties and methods of the Shape class on a Text node. A Text node is capable of displaying multiple lines of text.

A Text node contains text and properties to render the text. You can create a Text node using one of the three constructors of the Text class. You can specify the text or text and position of the text while creating the node. The no-args constructor creates a text node with an empty text and is located at (0, 0).

The no-args constructor creates a Text node with an empty string as its text. Other constructors let you specify the text and position the node. The width and height of a text node are automatically determined by its font. By default, a Text node uses a system default font to render its text.

Apart from the local and parent coordinate system, a Text node has an additional coordinate system. It is the coordinate system used for drawing the text. The x, y, and textOrigin properties of the Text class define the text coordinate system. The x and y properties define the x and y coordinates of the text origin. The textOrigin property is of type VPos. Its value could be VPos.BASELINE, VPos.TOP, VPos.CENTER, and VPos.BOTTOM. The default is VPos.BASELINE. It defines where the x-axis of the text coordinate system lies within the text height.

The font property of the Text class defines the font for the text. The default font used is from the "System" font family with the "Regular" style. The size of the default font is dependent on the platform and the desktop settings of the user. An instance of the Font class represents a font. The Font class contains several static methods that let you access the installed fonts on your computer and load custom fonts from font files.

A Text node is a shape. Like a shape, it can have a fill and a stroke. By default, a Text node has a null stroke and a Color.BLACK fill.

The strikethrough and underline properties of the Text class let you apply decorations to the text. By default, both properties are set to false.

The Text class contains a fontSmoothingType property, which can be used to apply a gray or LCD font smoothing. Its value is one of the constants of the FontSmoothingType enum: GRAY and LCD. The default smoothing type is fontSmoothingType.GRAY. The LCD smoothing type is used as a hint.

You can style Text nodes using CSS. Setting font, text alignment, font smoothing, and decorations are supported through CSS.

The next chapter will discuss how to draw 3D shapes in JavaFX.

CHAPTER 16

■ ■ ■

Understanding 3D Shapes

In this chapter, you will learn:

- About 3D shapes and the classes representing 3D shapes in JavaFX
- How to check whether your machine supports 3D
- About the 3D coordinate system used in JavaFX
- About the rendering order of nodes
- How to draw predefined 3D shapes
- About the different types of cameras and how to use them to render scenes
- How to use light sources to view 3D objects in scenes
- How to create and use subscenes
- How to draw user-defined 3D shapes in JavaFX

The examples of this chapter lie in the com.jdojo.shape3d package. In order for them to work, you must add a corresponding line to the module-info.java file:

```
...
opens com.jdojo.shape3d to javafx.graphics, javafx.base;
...
```

What Are 3D Shapes?

Any shape, drawn in a three-dimensional space, having three dimensions (length, width, and depth) is known as a 3D shape. Cubes, spheres, and pyramids are examples.

JavaFX offers real 3D shapes as nodes. It provides two types of 3D shapes:

- Predefined shapes
- User-defined shapes

Box, sphere, and cylinder are three predefined 3D shapes that you can readily use in your JavaFX applications. You can also create any type of 3D shapes using a triangle mesh.

Figure 16-1 shows a class diagram of classes representing JavaFX 3D shapes. The 3D shape classes are in the javafx.scene.shape package. The Box, Sphere, and Cylinder classes represent the three predefined shapes. The MeshView class represents a user-defined 3D shape in a scene.

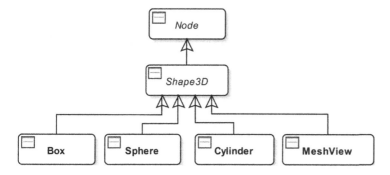

Figure 16-1. *A class diagram for classes representing 3D shapes*

The 3D visualization in JavaFX is accomplished using lights and cameras. Lights and cameras are also nodes, which are added to the scene. You add 3D nodes to a scene, light it with lights, and view it using a camera. The positions of lights and cameras in the space determine the lighted and viewable areas of the scene. Figure 16-2 shows a 3D box, which is created using an instance of the Box class.

Figure 16-2. *An example of a 3D box shape*

Checking Support for 3D

JavaFX 3D support is a conditional feature. If it is not supported on your platform, you get a warning message on the console when you run a program that attempts to use 3D features. Run the program in Listing 16-1 to check if your machine supports JavaFX 3D. The program will print a message stating whether the 3D support is available.

Listing 16-1. Checking JavaFX 3D Support on Your Machine

```
// Check3DSupport.java
package com.jdojo.shape3d;

import javafx.application.ConditionalFeature;
import javafx.application.Platform;

public class Check3DSupport {
    public static void main(String[] args) {
        boolean supported =
                Platform.isSupported(ConditionalFeature.SCENE3D);
        if (supported) {
```

```
            System.out.println("3D is supported on your machine.");
        } else {
            System.out.println("3D is not supported on your machine.");
        }
    }
}
```

The 3D Coordinate System

A point in the 3D space is represented by (x, y, z) coordinates. A 3D object has three dimensions: x, y, and z. Figure 16-3 shows the 3D coordinate system used in JavaFX.

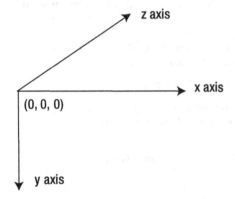

Figure 16-3. *The 3D coordinate system used in JavaFX*

The positive direction of the x-axis points to the right from the origin; the positive direction of the y-axis points down; the positive direction of the z-axis points into the screen (away from the viewer). The negative directions on the axes, which are not shown, extend in the opposite directions at the origin.

Rendering Order of Nodes

Suppose you are looking at two overlapping objects at a distance. The object closer to you always overlaps the object farther from you, irrespective of the sequence in which they appeared in the view. When dealing with 3D objects in JavaFX, you would like them to appear the same way.

In JavaFX, by default, nodes are rendered in the order they are added to the scene graph. Consider the following snippet of code:

```
Rectangle r1 = new Rectangle(0, 0, 100, 100);
Rectangle r2 = new Rectangle(50, 50, 100, 100);
Group group = new Group(r1, r2);
```

Two rectangles are added to a group. The rectangle r1 is rendered first followed by rectangle r2. The overlapping area will show only the area of r2, not r1. If the group was created as new Group(r2, r1), the rectangle r2 will be rendered first followed with rectangle r1. The overlapping area will show the area of r1, not r2. Let us add the z coordinates for the two rectangles as follows:

```
Rectangle r1 = new Rectangle(0, 0, 100, 100);
r1.setTranslateZ(10);

Rectangle r2 = new Rectangle(50, 50, 100, 100);
r2.setTranslateZ(50);

Group group = new Group(r1, r2);
```

The foregoing snippet of code will produce the same effect as before. The rectangle r1 will be rendered first followed by the rectangle r2. The z values for the rectangles are ignored. In this case, you would like to render the rectangle r1 last as it is closer to the viewer (z=10 is closer than z=50).

The previous rendering behavior is not desirable in a 3D space. You expect the 3D objects to appear the same way as they would appear in a real world. You need to do two things two achieve this.

- When creating a Scene object, specify that it needs to have a depth buffer.

- Specify in the nodes that their z coordinate values should be used during rendering. That is, they need to be rendered according to their depth (the distance from the viewer).

When you create a Scene object, you need to specify the depthBuffer flag, which is set to false by default:

```
// Create a Scene object with depthBuffer set to true
double width = 300;
double height = 200;
boolean depthBuffer = true;
Scene scene = new Scene(root, width, height, depthBuffer);
```

The depthBuffer flag for a scene cannot be changed after the scene is created. You can check whether a scene has a depthBuffer using the isDepthBuffer() method of the Scene object.

The Node class contains a depthTest property, which is available for all nodes in JavaFX. Its value is one of the constants of the javafx.scene.DepthTest enum:

- ENABLE

- DISABLE

- INHERIT

The ENABLE value for the depthTest indicates that the z coordinate values should be taken into account when the node is rendered. When the depth testing is enabled for a node, its z coordinate is compared with all other nodes with depth testing enabled, before rendering.

The DISABLE value indicates that the nodes are rendered in the order they are added to the scene graph.

The INHERIT value indicates that the depthTest property for a node is inherited from its parent. If a node has a null parent, it is the same as ENABLE.

The program in Listing 16-2 demonstrates the concepts of using the depth buffer for a scene and the depth test for nodes. It adds two rectangles to a group. The rectangles are filled with red and green colors. The z coordinates for the red and green rectangles are 400px and 300px, respectively. The green rectangle is added to the group first. However, it is rendered first as it is closer to the viewer. You have added a camera to the scene, which is needed to view objects having depth (the z coordinate). The CheckBox is used to enable and disable the depth test for the rectangles. When the depth test is disabled, the rectangles are rendered in the order they are added to the group: the green rectangle followed with the red rectangle. Figure 16-4 shows rectangles in both states.

Listing 16-2. Enabling/Disabling the DepthTest Property for Nodes

```java
// DepthTestCheck.java
package com.jdojo.shape3d;

import javafx.application.Application;
import javafx.scene.Group;
import javafx.scene.PerspectiveCamera;
import javafx.scene.Scene;
import javafx.scene.control.CheckBox;
import javafx.scene.layout.BorderPane;
import javafx.scene.paint.Color;
import javafx.scene.shape.Rectangle;
import javafx.scene.DepthTest;
import javafx.stage.Stage;

public class DepthTestCheck  extends Application {
        public static void main(String[] args) {
                Application.launch(args);
        }

        @Override
        public void start(Stage stage) {
                // Create two rectangles and add then to a Group
                Rectangle red = new Rectangle(100, 100);
                red.setFill(Color.RED);
                red.setTranslateX(100);
                red.setTranslateY(100);
                red.setTranslateZ(400);

                Rectangle green = new Rectangle(100, 100);
                green.setFill(Color.GREEN);
                green.setTranslateX(150);
                green.setTranslateY(150);
                green.setTranslateZ(300);

                Group center = new Group(green, red);

                CheckBox depthTestCbx =
                        new CheckBox("DepthTest for Rectangles");
                depthTestCbx.setSelected(true);
                depthTestCbx.selectedProperty().addListener(
                    (prop, oldValue, newValue) -> {
```

```
                    if (newValue) {
                        red.setDepthTest(DepthTest.ENABLE);
                        green.setDepthTest(DepthTest.ENABLE);
                    }
                    else {
                        red.setDepthTest(DepthTest.DISABLE);
                        green.setDepthTest(DepthTest.DISABLE);
                    }
            });

            // Create a BorderPane as the root node for the scene.
            // Need to set the background transparent, so the camera
            // can view the rectangles behind the surface of the
            // BorderPane
            BorderPane root = new BorderPane();
            root.setStyle("-fx-background-color: transparent;");
            root.setTop(depthTestCbx);
            root.setCenter(center);

            // Create a scene with depthBuffer enabled
            Scene scene = new Scene(root, 200, 200, true);

            // Need to set a camera to look into the 3D space of
            // the scene
            scene.setCamera(new PerspectiveCamera());

            stage.setScene(scene);
            stage.setTitle("Depth Test");
            stage.show();
        }
}
```

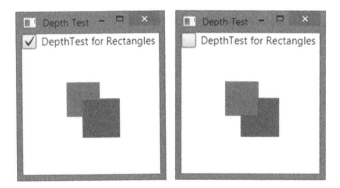

Figure 16-4. *Effects of the depthTest property on rendering nodes*

Using Predefined 3D Shapes

JavaFX 8 provides the following three built-in 3D geometric shapes:

- Box
- Sphere
- Cylinder

The shapes are represented by instances of the Box, Sphere, and Cylinder classes. The classes inherit from the Shape3D class, which contains three properties that are common to all types of 3D shapes:

- Material
- Draw mode
- Cull face

I will discuss these properties in detail in subsequent sections. If you do not specify these properties for a shape, reasonable defaults are provided.

The properties specific to a shape type are defined in the specific class defining the shape. For example, properties for a box are defined in the Box class. All shapes are nodes. Therefore, you can apply transformations to them. You can position them at any point in the 3D space using the translateX, translateY, and translateZ transformations.

■ **Tip** The center of a 3D shape is located at the origin of the local coordinate system of the shape.

A Box is defined by the following three properties:

- width
- height
- depth

The Box class contains two constructors:

- Box()
- Box(double width, double height, double depth)

The no-args constructor creates a Box with width, height, and depth of 2.0 each. The other constructor lets you specify the dimensions of the Box. The center of the Box is located at the origin of its local coordinate system:

```
// Create a Box with width=10, height=20, and depth=50
Box box = new Box(10, 20, 50);
```

A Sphere is defined by only one property named radius. The Sphere class contains three constructors:

- Sphere()
- Sphere(double radius)
- Sphere(double radius, int divisions)

The no-args constructor creates a sphere of radius 1.0.

The second constructor lets you specify the `radius` of the sphere.

The third constructor lets you specify the `radius` and `divisions`. A 3D sphere is made up of many divisions, which are constructed from connected triangles. The value of the number of divisions defines the resolution of the sphere. The higher the number of divisions, the smoother the sphere looks. By default, a value of 64 is used for the `divisions`. The value of `divisions` cannot be less than 1.

```
// Create a Sphere with radius =50
Sphere sphere = new Sphere(50);
```

A `Cylinder` is defined by two properties:

- `radius`
- `height`

The `radius` of the cylinder is measured on the XZ plane. The axis of the cylinder is measured along the y-axis. The `height` of the cylinder is measured along its axis. The `Cylinder` class contains three constructors:

- `Cylinder()`
- `Cylinder(double radius, double height)`
- `Cylinder(double radius, double height, int divisions)`

The no-args constructor creates a `Cylinder` with a 1.0 `radius` and a 2.0 `height`.

The second constructor lets you specify the `radius` and `height` properties.

The third constructor lets you specify the number of `divisions`, which defines the resolution of the cylinder. The higher the number of divisions, the smoother the cylinder looks. Its default value is 64 (the documentation specifies 15 here, which is wrong) along the x-axis and z-axis each. Its value cannot be less than 3. If a value less than 3 is specified, a value of 3 is used. Note that the number of divisions does not apply along the y-axis. Suppose the number of divisions is 10. It means that the vertical surface of the cylinder is created using 10 triangles. The height of the triangle will extend the entire height of the cylinder. The base of the cylinder will be created using 10 triangles as well.

```
// Create a cylinder with radius=40 and height=120
Cylinder cylinder = new Cylinder(40, 120);
```

The program in Listing 16-3 shows how to create 3D shapes. Figure 16-5 shows the shapes.

Listing 16-3. Creating 3D Primitive Shapes: Box, Sphere, and Cylinder

```java
// PreDefinedShapes.java
package com.jdojo.shape3d;

import javafx.application.Application;
import javafx.scene.Group;
import javafx.scene.PerspectiveCamera;
import javafx.scene.PointLight;
import javafx.scene.Scene;
import javafx.scene.shape.Box;
import javafx.scene.shape.Cylinder;
import javafx.scene.shape.Sphere;
import javafx.stage.Stage;
```

```java
public class PreDefinedShapes extends Application {
        public static void main(String[] args) {
                Application.launch(args);
        }

        @Override
        public void start(Stage stage) {
                // Create a Box
                Box box = new Box(100, 100, 100);
                box.setTranslateX(150);
                box.setTranslateY(0);
                box.setTranslateZ(400);

                // Create a Sphere
                Sphere sphere = new Sphere(50);
                sphere.setTranslateX(300);
                sphere.setTranslateY(-5);
                sphere.setTranslateZ(400);

                // Create a cylinder
                Cylinder cylinder = new Cylinder(40, 120);
                cylinder.setTranslateX(500);
                cylinder.setTranslateY(-25);
                cylinder.setTranslateZ(600);

                // Create a light
                PointLight light = new PointLight();
                light.setTranslateX(350);
                light.setTranslateY(100);
                light.setTranslateZ(300);

                // Add shapes and a light to the group
                Group root = new Group(box, sphere, cylinder, light);

                // Create a Scene with depth buffer enabled
                Scene scene = new Scene(root, 300, 100, true);

                // Set a camera to view the 3D shapes
                PerspectiveCamera camera = new PerspectiveCamera(false);
                camera.setTranslateX(100);
                camera.setTranslateY(-50);
                camera.setTranslateZ(300);
                scene.setCamera(camera);

                stage.setScene(scene);
                stage.setTitle(
                        "Using 3D Shapes: Box, Sphere and Cylinder");
                stage.show();
        }
}
```

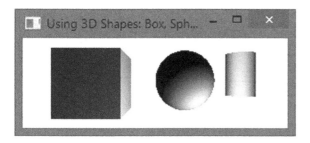

Figure 16-5. *Primitive 3D shapes: a box, a sphere, and a cylinder*

The program creates the three shapes and positions them in the space. It creates a light, which is an instance of the PointLight, and positions it in the space. Note that a light is also a Node. The light is used to light the 3D shapes. All shapes and the light are added to a group, which is added to the scene.

To view the shapes, you need to add a camera to the scene. The program adds a PerspectiveCamera to the scene. Note that you need to position the camera as its position and orientation in the space determine what you see. The origin of the local coordinate system of the camera is located at the center of the scene. Try resizing the window after you run the program. You will notice that the view of the shapes changes as you resize the window. It happens because the center of the scene is changing when you resize the window, which in turn repositions the camera, resulting in the change in the view.

Specifying the Shape Material

A material is used for rendering the surface of shapes. You can specify the material for the surface of 3D objects using the material property, which is defined in the Shape3D class. The material property is an instance of the abstract class Material. JavaFX provides the PhongMaterial class as the only concrete implementation of Material. Both classes are in the javafx.scene.paint package. An instance of the PhongMaterial class represents Phong shaded material. Phong shaded material is based on Phong shading and the Phong reflection model (also known as Phong illumination and Phong lighting), which were developed at the University of Utah by Bui Tuong Phong as part of his Ph.D. dissertation in 1973. A complete discussion of the Phong model is beyond the scope of this book. The model provides an empirical formula to compute the color of a pixel on the geometric surface in terms of the following properties defined in the PhongMaterial class:

- diffuseColor
- diffuseMap
- specularColor
- specularMap
- selfIlluminationMap
- specularPower
- bumpMap

The PhongMaterial class contains three constructors:

- PhongMaterial()

- PhongMaterial(Color diffuseColor)

- PhongMaterial(Color diffuseColor, Image diffuseMap, Image specularMap, Image bumpMap, Image selfIlluminationMap)

The no-args constructor creates a PhongMaterial with the diffuse color as Color.WHITE. The other two constructors are used to create a PhongMaterial with the specified properties.

When you do not provide a material for a 3D shape, a default material with a diffuse color of Color. LIGHTGRAY is used for rendering the shape. All shapes in our previous example in Listing 16-3 used the default material.

The following snippet of code creates a Box, creates a PhongMaterial with tan diffuse color, and sets the material to the box:

```
Box box = new Box(100, 100, 100);
PhongMaterial material = new PhongMaterial();
material.setDiffuseColor(Color.TAN);
box.setMaterial(material);
```

You can use an Image as the diffuse map to have texture for the material, as shown in the following code:

```
Box boxWithTexture = new Box(100, 100, 100);
PhongMaterial textureMaterial = new PhongMaterial();
Image randomness = new Image("resources/picture/randomness.jpg");
textureMaterial.setDiffuseMap(randomness);
boxWithTexture.setMaterial(textureMaterial);
```

The program in Listing 16-4 shows how to create and set material for shapes. It creates two boxes. It sets the diffuse color for one box and the diffuse map for the other. The image used for the diffuse map provides the texture for the surface of the second box. The two boxes look as shown in Figure 16-6.

Listing 16-4. Using the Diffuse Color and Diffuse Map to Create PhongMaterial

```
// MaterialTest.java
package com.jdojo.shape3d;

import com.jdojo.util.ResourceUtil;

import javafx.application.Application;
import javafx.scene.Group;
import javafx.scene.PerspectiveCamera;
import javafx.scene.PointLight;
import javafx.scene.Scene;
import javafx.scene.image.Image;
import javafx.scene.paint.Color;
import javafx.scene.paint.PhongMaterial;
import javafx.scene.shape.Box;
import javafx.stage.Stage;
```

```
public class MaterialTest extends Application {
        public static void main(String[] args) {
                Application.launch(args);
        }

        @Override
        public void start(Stage stage) {
                // Create a Box
                Box box = new Box(100, 100, 100);

                // Set the material for the box
                PhongMaterial material = new PhongMaterial();
                material.setDiffuseColor(Color.TAN);
                box.setMaterial(material);

                // Place the box in the space
                box.setTranslateX(250);
                box.setTranslateY(0);
                box.setTranslateZ(400);

                // Create a Box with texture
                Box boxWithTexture = new Box(100, 100, 100);
                PhongMaterial textureMaterial = new PhongMaterial();
                    Image randomness =
                        new Image(ResourceUtil.getResourceURLStr(
                            "picture/randomness.jpg"));
                textureMaterial.setDiffuseMap(randomness);
                boxWithTexture.setMaterial(textureMaterial);

                // Place the box in the space
                boxWithTexture.setTranslateX(450);
                boxWithTexture.setTranslateY(-5);
                boxWithTexture.setTranslateZ(400);

                PointLight light = new PointLight();
                light.setTranslateX(250);
                light.setTranslateY(100);
                light.setTranslateZ(300);

                Group root = new Group(box, boxWithTexture);

                // Create a Scene with depth buffer enabled
                Scene scene = new Scene(root, 300, 100, true);

                // Set a camera to view the 3D shapes
                PerspectiveCamera camera = new PerspectiveCamera(false);
                camera.setTranslateX(200);
                camera.setTranslateY(-50);
                camera.setTranslateZ(325);
                scene.setCamera(camera);
```

```
        stage.setScene(scene);
        stage.setTitle(
                "Using Material Color and Texture for 3D Surface");
        stage.show();
    }
}
```

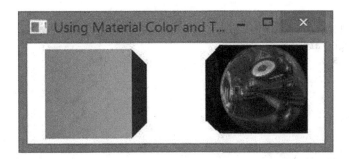

Figure 16-6. *Two boxes: one with a tan diffuse color and one with texture using a diffuse map*

Specifying the Draw Mode of Shapes

A 3D shape surface consists of many connected polygons made up of triangles. For example, a Box is made up of 12 triangles—each side of the Box using two triangles. The drawMode property in the Shape3D class specifies how the surface of 3D shapes is rendered. Its value is one of the constants of the DrawMode enum:

- DrawMode.FILL
- DrawMode.LINE

The DrawMode.FILL is the default, and it fills the interior of the triangles. The DrawMode.LINE draws only the outline of the triangles. That is, it draws only lines connecting the vertices of the consecutive triangles.

```
// Create a Box with outline only
Box box = new Box(100, 100, 100);
box.setDrawMode(DrawMode.LINE);
```

The program in Listing 16-5 shows how to draw only the outline of 3D shapes. Figure 16-7 shows the shapes. The program is similar to the one shown in Listing 16-3. The program sets the drawMode property of all shapes to DrawMode.LINE. The program specifies the divisions of creating the Sphere and Cylinder. Change the value for divisions to a lesser value. You will notice that the number of triangles used to create the shapes decreases, making the shape less smooth.

Listing 16-5. Drawing Only Lines for 3D Shapes

```
// DrawModeTest.java
package com.jdojo.shape3d;

import javafx.application.Application;
import javafx.scene.Group;
```

609

```java
import javafx.scene.PerspectiveCamera;
import javafx.scene.PointLight;
import javafx.scene.Scene;
import javafx.scene.shape.Box;
import javafx.scene.shape.Cylinder;
import javafx.scene.shape.DrawMode;
import javafx.scene.shape.Sphere;
import javafx.stage.Stage;

public class DrawModeTest extends Application {
        public static void main(String[] args) {
                Application.launch(args);
        }

        @Override
        public void start(Stage stage) {
                // Create a Box
                Box box = new Box(100, 100, 100);
                box.setDrawMode(DrawMode.LINE);
                box.setTranslateX(150);
                box.setTranslateY(0);
                box.setTranslateZ(400);

                // Create a Sphere: radius = 50, divisions=20
                Sphere sphere = new Sphere(50, 20);
                sphere.setDrawMode(DrawMode.LINE);
                sphere.setTranslateX(300);
                sphere.setTranslateY(-5);
                sphere.setTranslateZ(400);

                // Create a cylinder: radius=40, height=120, divisions=5
                Cylinder cylinder = new Cylinder(40, 120, 5);
                cylinder.setDrawMode(DrawMode.LINE);
                cylinder.setTranslateX(500);
                cylinder.setTranslateY(-25);
                cylinder.setTranslateZ(600);

                PointLight light = new PointLight();
                light.setTranslateX(350);
                light.setTranslateY(100);
                light.setTranslateZ(300);

                Group root = new Group(box, sphere, cylinder, light);

                // Create a Scene with depth buffer enabled
                Scene scene = new Scene(root, 300, 100, true);

                // Set a camera to view the 3D shapes
                PerspectiveCamera camera = new PerspectiveCamera(false);
                camera.setTranslateX(100);
                camera.setTranslateY(-50);
```

```
        camera.setTranslateZ(300);
        scene.setCamera(camera);

        stage.setScene(scene);
        stage.setTitle("Drawing Only Lines");
        stage.show();
    }
}
```

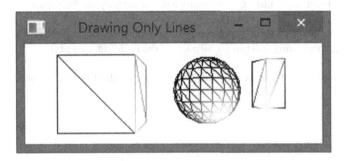

Figure 16-7. *Drawing the outline of 3D shapes*

Specifying the Face Culling for Shapes

A 3D object is never visible entirely. For example, you can never see an entire building at once. When you change the viewing angle, you see different parts of the building. If you face the front of the building, you see only the front part of the building. Standing in front, if you move to the right, you see the front and right sides of the building.

The surface of 3D objects is made of connected triangles. Each triangle has two faces: the exterior face and the interior face. You see the exterior face of the triangles when you look at the 3D objects. Not all triangles are visible all the time. Whether a triangle is visible depends on the position of the camera. There is a simple rule to determine the visibility of triangles making up the surface of a 3D object. Draw a line coming out from the plane of the triangle, and the line is perpendicular to the plane of a triangle. Draw another line from the point where the first line intersects the plane of the triangle to the viewer. If the angle between two lines is greater than 90 degrees, the face of the triangle is not visible to the view. Otherwise, the face of the triangle is visible to the viewer. Note that not both faces of a triangle are visible at the same time.

Face culling is a technique of rendering 3D geometry based on the principle that the nonvisible parts of an object should not be rendered. For example, if you are facing a building from the front, there is no need to render the sides, top, and bottom of the building, as you cannot see them.

■ **Tip** Face culling is used in 3D rendering to enhance performance.

611

The Shape3D class contains a cullFace property that specifies the type of culling applied in rendering the shape. Its value is one of the constants of the CullFace enum:

- BACK

- FRONT

- NONE

The CullFace.BACK specifies that all triangles that cannot be seen through the camera in its current position should be culled (i.e., not rendered). That is, all triangles whose exterior faces are not facing the camera should be culled. If you are facing the front of a building, this setting will render only the front part of the building. This is the default.

The CullFace.FRONT specifies that all triangles whose exterior faces are facing the camera should be culled. If you are facing the front of a building, this setting will render all parts of the building, except the front part.

The CullFace.NONE specifies that no face culling should be applied. That is, all triangles making up the shape should be rendered:

```
// Create a Box with no face culling
Box box = new Box(100, 100, 100);
Box.setCullFace(CullFace.NONE);
```

It is easy to see the effect of face culling when you draw the shape using the drawMode as DrawMode.LINE. I will draw only nonculled triangles. Figure 16-8 shows the same Box using three different face cullings. The first Box (from left) uses the back-face culling, the second front-face culling, and the third one uses no culling. Notice that the first picture of the Box shows the front, right, and top faces, whereas these faces are culled in the second Box. In the second picture, you see the back, left, and bottom faces. Note that when you use front-face culling, you see the interior faces of the triangles as the exterior faces are hidden from the view.

CullFace.BACK   CullFace.FRONT   CullFace.NONE

Figure 16-8. *A box using different cullFace properties*

Using Cameras

Cameras are used to render the scene. Two types of cameras are available:

- Perspective camera

- Parallel camera

The names of the cameras suggest the projection type they use to render the scene. Cameras in JavaFX are nodes. They can be added to the scene graph and positioned like other nodes.

The abstract base class Camera represents a camera. Two concrete subclasses of the Camera class exist: PerspectiveCamera and ParallelCamera. The three classes are in the javafx.scene package.

A PerspectiveCamera defines the viewing volume for a perspective projection, which is a truncated right pyramid as shown in Figure 16-9. The camera projects the objects contained within the near and far clipping planes onto the projection plane. Therefore, any objects outside the clipping planes are not visible.

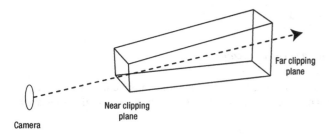

Figure 16-9. *The viewing volume of a perspective camera defined by the near clip and far clip planes*

The content that the camera will project onto the projection plane is defined by two properties in the Camera class:

- nearClip
- farClip

The nearClip is the distance between the camera and the near clipping plane. Objects closer to the camera than the nearClip are not rendered. The default value is 0.1.

The farClip is the distance between the camera and the far clipping plane. Objects farther from the camera than the farClip are not rendered. The default value is 100.

The PerspectiveCamera class contains two constructors:

- PerspectiveCamera()
- PerspectiveCamera(boolean fixedEyeAtCameraZero)

The no-args constructor creates a PerspectiveCamera with the fixedEyeAtCameraZero flag set to false, which makes it behave more or less like a parallel camera where the objects in the scene at Z=0 stay the same size when the scene is resized. The second constructor lets you specify this flag. If you want to view 3D objects with real 3D effects, you need to set this flag to true. Setting this flag to true will adjust the size of the projected images of the 3D objects as the scene is resized. Making the scene smaller will make the objects look smaller as well.

```
// Create a perspective camera for viewing 3D objects
PerspectiveCamera camera = new PerspectiveCamera(true);
```

The PerspectiveCamera class declares two additional properties:

- fieldOfView
- verticalFieldOfView

The fieldOfView is measured in degrees, and it is the view angle of the camera. Its default value is 30 degrees.

The verticalFieldOfView property specifies whether the fieldOfView property applies to the vertical dimension of the projection plane. By default, its value is true. Figure 16-10 depicts the camera, its view angle, and field of view.

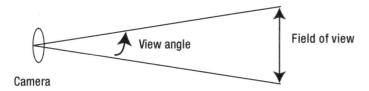

Figure 16-10. *The view angle and field of view for a perspective camera*

An instance of the ParallelCamera specifies the viewing volume for a parallel projection, which is a rectangular box. The ParallelCamera class does not declare any additional properties. It contains a no-args constructor:

```
ParallelCamera camera = new ParallelCamera();
```

You can set a camera for a scene using the setCamera() method of the Scene class:

```
Scene scene = create a scene....
PerspectiveCamera camera = new PerspectiveCamera(true);
scene.setCamera(camera);
```

Because a camera is a node, you can add it to the scene graph:

```
PerspectiveCamera camera = new PerspectiveCamera(true);
Group group = new Group(camera);
```

You can move and rotate the camera as you move and rotate nodes. To move it to a different position, use the translateX, translateY, and translateZ properties. To rotate, use the Rotate transformation.

The program in Listing 16-6 uses a PerspectiveCamera to view a Box. You have used two lights: one to light the front and the top faces and one to light the bottom face of the box. The camera is animated by rotating it indefinitely along the x-axis. As the camera rotates, it brings different parts of the box into the view. You can see the effect of the two lights when the bottom of the box comes into the view. The bottom is shown in green, whereas the top and front are in red.

Listing 16-6. Using a PerspectiveCamera As a Node

```
// CameraTest.java
package com.jdojo.shape3d;

import javafx.animation.Animation;
import javafx.animation.RotateTransition;
import javafx.application.Application;
import javafx.scene.Group;
import javafx.scene.PerspectiveCamera;
import javafx.scene.PointLight;
import javafx.scene.Scene;
import javafx.scene.paint.Color;
import javafx.scene.shape.Box;
```

```
import javafx.scene.shape.CullFace;
import javafx.scene.transform.Rotate;
import javafx.stage.Stage;
import javafx.util.Duration;

public class CameraTest extends Application {
        public static void main(String[] args) {
                Application.launch(args);
        }

        @Override
        public void start(Stage stage) {
                Box box = new Box(100, 100, 100);
                box.setCullFace(CullFace.NONE);
                box.setTranslateX(250);
                box.setTranslateY(100);
                box.setTranslateZ(400);

                PerspectiveCamera camera = new PerspectiveCamera(false);
                camera.setTranslateX(100);
                camera.setTranslateY(-50);
                camera.setTranslateZ(300);

                // Add a Rotation animation to the camera
                RotateTransition rt =
                        new RotateTransition(Duration.seconds(2), camera);
                rt.setCycleCount(Animation.INDEFINITE);
                rt.setFromAngle(0);
                rt.setToAngle(90);
                rt.setAutoReverse(true);
                rt.setAxis(Rotate.X_AXIS);
                rt.play();

                PointLight redLight = new PointLight();
                redLight.setColor(Color.RED);
                redLight.setTranslateX(250);
                redLight.setTranslateY(-100);
                redLight.setTranslateZ(250);

                PointLight greenLight = new PointLight();
                greenLight.setColor(Color.GREEN);
                greenLight.setTranslateX(250);
                greenLight.setTranslateY(300);
                greenLight.setTranslateZ(300);

                Group root = new Group(box, redLight, greenLight);
                root.setRotationAxis(Rotate.X_AXIS);
                root.setRotate(30);

                Scene scene = new Scene(root, 500, 300, true);
                scene.setCamera(camera);
```

```
                    stage.setScene(scene);
                    stage.setTitle("Using camaras");
                    stage.show();
        }
}
```

Using Light Sources

Similar to the real world, you need a light source to view the 3D objects in a scene. An instance of the abstract base class LightBase represents a light source. Its two concrete subclasses, AmbientLight and PointLight, represent an ambient light and a point light. Light source classes are in the javafx.scene package. The LightBase class inherits from the Node class. Therefore, a light source is a node, and it can be added to the scene graph as any other nodes.

A light source has three properties: light color, on/off switch, and a list of affected nodes. The LightBase class basically contains the following two properties:

- color

- lightOn

The color specifies the color of the light. The lightOn specifies whether the light is on. The getScope() method of the LightBase class returns an ObservableList<Node>, which is the hierarchical list of nodes affected by this light source. If the list is empty, the scope of the light source is universe, which means that it affects all nodes in the scene. The latter however does not affect nodes that are part of the exclusion scope; see the API documentation for details.

An instance of the AmbientLight class represents an ambient light source. An ambient light is a nondirectional light that seems to come from all directions. Its intensity is constant on the surface of the affected shapes.

```
// Create a red ambient light
AmbientLight redLight = new AmbientLight(Color.RED);
```

An instance of the PointLight class represents a point light source. A point light source is a fixed point in space and radiates lights equally in all directions. The intensity of a point light decreases as the distance of the lighted point increases from the light source.

```
// Create a Add the point light to a group
PointLight redLight = new PointLight(Color.RED);
redLight.setTranslateX(250);
redLight.setTranslateY(-100);
redLight.setTranslateZ(290);
Group group = new Group(node1, node2, redLight);
```

Creating Subscenes

A scene can use only one camera. Sometimes, you may want to view different parts of a scene using multiple cameras. JavaFX introduces the concept as subscenes. A subscene is a container for a scene graph. It can have its own width, height, fill color, depth buffer, antialiasing flag, and camera. An instance of the SubScene class represents a subscene. The SubScene inherits from the Node class. Therefore, a subscene can be used wherever a node can be used. A subscene can be used to separate 2D and 3D nodes in an application. You can use a camera for the subscene to view 3D objects that will not affect the 2D nodes in the other part of the main scene. The following snippet of code creates a SubScene and sets a camera to it:

```
SubScene ss = new SubScene(root, 200, 200, true, SceneAntialiasing.BALANCED);
PerspectiveCamera camera = new PerspectiveCamera(false);
ss.setCamera(camera);
```

■ **Tip** If a SubScene contains Shape3D nodes having a light node, a head light with a PointLight with Color.WHITE light source is provided. The head light is positioned at the camera position.

The program in Listing 16-7 shows how to use subscenes. The getSubScene() method creates a SubScene with a Box, a PerspectiveCamera, and a PointLight. An animation is set up to rotate the camera along the specified axis. The start() method creates two subscenes and adds them to an HBox. One subscene swings the camera along the y-axis and another along the x-axis. The HBox is added to the main scene.

Listing 16-7. Using Subscenes

```java
// SubSceneTest.java
package com.jdojo.shape3d;

import javafx.animation.Animation;
import javafx.animation.RotateTransition;
import javafx.application.Application;
import javafx.geometry.Point3D;
import javafx.scene.Group;
import javafx.scene.PerspectiveCamera;
import javafx.scene.PointLight;
import javafx.scene.Scene;
import javafx.scene.SceneAntialiasing;
import javafx.scene.SubScene;
import javafx.scene.layout.HBox;
import javafx.scene.paint.Color;
import javafx.scene.shape.Box;
import javafx.scene.shape.CullFace;
import javafx.scene.transform.Rotate;
import javafx.stage.Stage;
import javafx.util.Duration;
```

```java
public class SubSceneTest extends Application {
        public static void main(String[] args) {
                Application.launch(args);
        }

        @Override
        public void start(Stage stage) {
                SubScene ySwing = getSubScene(Rotate.Y_AXIS);
                SubScene xSwing = getSubScene(Rotate.X_AXIS);
                HBox root = new HBox(20, ySwing, xSwing);
                Scene scene = new Scene(root, 500, 300, true);
                stage.setScene(scene);
                stage.setTitle("Using Sub-Scenes");
                stage.show();
        }

        private SubScene getSubScene(Point3D rotationAxis) {
                Box box = new Box(100, 100, 100);
                box.setCullFace(CullFace.NONE);
                box.setTranslateX(250);
                box.setTranslateY(100);
                box.setTranslateZ(400);

                PerspectiveCamera camera = new PerspectiveCamera(false);
                camera.setTranslateX(100);
                camera.setTranslateY(-50);
                camera.setTranslateZ(300);

                // Add a Rotation animation to the camera
                RotateTransition rt =
                        new RotateTransition(Duration.seconds(2), camera);
                rt.setCycleCount(Animation.INDEFINITE);
                rt.setFromAngle(-10);
                rt.setToAngle(10);
                rt.setAutoReverse(true);
                rt.setAxis(rotationAxis);
                rt.play();

                PointLight redLight = new PointLight(Color.RED);
                redLight.setTranslateX(250);
                redLight.setTranslateY(-100);
                redLight.setTranslateZ(290);

                // If you remove the redLight from the following group,
                // a default head light will be provided by the SubScene.
                Group root = new Group(box, redLight);
                root.setRotationAxis(Rotate.X_AXIS);
                root.setRotate(30);
```

```
        SubScene ss =
                new SubScene(root, 200, 200, true,
                                SceneAntialiasing.BALANCED);
        ss.setCamera(camera);
        return ss;
    }
}
```

Creating User-Defined Shapes

JavaFX lets you define a 3D shape using a mesh of polygons. An instance of the abstract Mesh class represents the mesh data. The TriangleMesh class is a concrete subclass of the Mesh class. A TriangleMesh represents a 3D surface consisting of a mesh of triangles.

■ **Tip** In 3D modeling, a mesh of different types of polygons can be used to construct a 3D object. JavaFX supports only a mesh of triangles.

An instance of the MeshView class represents a 3D surface. The data for constructing a MeshView is specified as an instance of the Mesh.

Supplying the mesh data by hand is not an easy task. The problem is complicated by the way you need to specify the data. I will make it easier by demonstrating the mesh usage from a very simple use case to a more complex one.

A TriangleMesh needs to supply data for three aspects of a 3D object:

- Points
- Texture coordinates
- Faces

■ **Note** If you have not worked with 3D objects using a mesh of triangles before, the explanation may seem a little complex. You need to be patient and learn a step at a time to understand the process of creating a 3D object using a mesh of triangles.

Points are the vertices of the triangles in the mesh. You need to specify the (x, y, z) coordinates of vertices in an array. Suppose v0, v1, v2, v3, v4, and so on are the points in 3D space that represent the vertices of the triangles in a mesh. Points in a TriangleMesh are specified as an array of floats.

The texture of a 3D surface is provided as an image that is a 2D object. Texture coordinates are points in a 2D plane, which are mapped to the vertices of triangles. You need to think of the triangles in a mesh unwrapped and placed onto a 2D plane. Overlay the image that supplies the surface texture for the 3D shape onto the same 2D plane. Map the vertices of the triangles to the 2D coordinates of the image to get a pair of (u, v) coordinates for each vertex in the mesh. The array of such (u, v) coordinates is the texture coordinate. Suppose t0, t1, t2, t3, t4, and so on are the texture coordinates.

Faces are the planes created by joining the three edges of the triangles. Each triangle has two faces: a front face and a back face. A face is specified in terms of indexes in the points and texture coordinates arrays. A face is specified as v0, t0, v1, t1, v2, t2, and so on, where v1 is the index of the vertex in the points array and t1 is the index of the vertex in the texture coordinates array.

Consider the box shown in Figure 16-11.

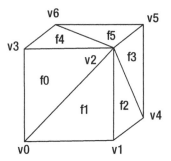

Figure 16-11. *A box made of 12 triangles*

A box consists of six sides. Each side is a rectangle. Each rectangle consists of two triangles. Each triangle has two faces: a front face and a back face. A box has eight vertices. You have named vertices as v0, v1, v2, and so on, and the faces as f0, f1, f2, and so on in the figure. You do not see the numberings for the vertices and faces that are not visible in the current orientation of the box. Each vertex is defined by a triple (x, y, z), which is the coordinate of the vertex in the 3D space. When you use the term *vertex v1*, you, technically, mean its coordinates (x1, y1, z1) for the vertex.

To create a mesh of triangles, you need to specify all vertices making up the 3D object. In the case of a box, you need to specify the eight vertices. In the `TriangleMesh` class, the vertices are known as `points`, and they are specified as an observable array of `float`. The following pseudo-code creates the array of vertices. The first array is for understanding purposes only. The actual array specifies the coordinates of the vertices:

```
// For understanding purpose only
float[] points = {
    v0,
    v1,
    v2,
    ...
    v7};
```

```
// The actual array contain (x, y, z) coordinates of all vertices
float[] points = {
    x0, y0, z0, // v0
    x1, y1, z1, // v1
    x2, y2, z2, // v2
    ...
    x7, y7, z7  // v7
};
```

In the `points` array, the indexes 0 to 2 contain coordinates of the first vertex, indexes 3 to 5 contain the coordinates of the second vertex, and so on. How do you number the vertices? That is, which vertex is #1 and which one is #2, and so on? There is no rule to specify the order to vertices. It is all up to you how you number them. JavaFX cares about only one thing: you must include all vertices making up the shape in the `points` array. You are done with generating the `points` array. You will use it later.

Now, you need to create an array containing coordinates of 2D points. Creating this array is a little tricky. Beginners have hard time understanding this. Consider the figure shown in Figure 16-12.

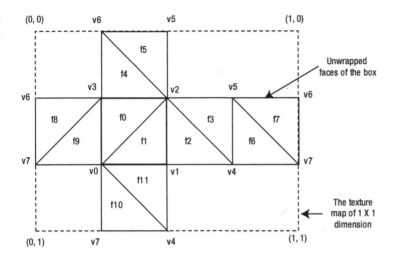

Figure 16-12. *Surface of a box mapped onto a 2D plane*

Figures 16-11 and 16-12 are two views of the surface of the same box. Figure 16-12 mapped the surface from the 3D space to a 2D plane. Think of the box as a 3D object made of 12 triangular pieces of paper. Figure 16-11 shows those 12 pieces of paper put together as a 3D box, whereas Figure 16-12 shows the same pieces of paper put side by side on the floor (a 2D plane).

■ **Tip** It is up to you to decide how you want to map the surface of a 3D object into a 2D plane. For example, in Figure 16-12, you could have also mapped the bottom side of the box into the lower, left, or top of the unit square.

Think of an image that you want to use as the texture for your box. The image will not have the third dimension (z dimension). The image needs to be applied on the surface of the box. JavaFX needs to know how the vertices on the box are mapped to the points on the image. You provide this information in terms of mapping of box vertices to the points on the image.

Now, think of a unit square (a 1 x 1 square) that represents the texture image. Overlay the unit square on the unwrapped faces of the box. The unit square is shown in dotted outline in Figure 16-12. The upper-left corner of the square has the coordinates (0, 0); the lower-left corner has the coordinates (0, 1); the upper-right corner has the coordinates (1, 0); the lower-right corner has the coordinates (1, 1).

In Figure 16-12, when you opened the surface of the box to put it onto a 2D plane, some of the vertices had to be split into multiple vertices. The box has eight vertices. The mapped box into the 2D plane has 14 vertices. The figure shows some of the vertices having the same number as those vertices representing the same vertex in the 3D box. Each vertex mapped into 2D plane (in Figure 16-12) becomes an element in the `texture coordinates` array. Figure 16-13 shows those 14 texture points; they are numbered as t0, t1, t2, and so on. You can number the vertices of the box onto the 2D plane in any order you want. The x and y coordinates of a texture point will be between 0 and 1. The actual mapping of these coordinates to the actual image size is performed by JavaFX. For example, (0.25, 0.) may be used for the coordinates of the vertex t9 and (0.25, 0.25) for the vertex t10.

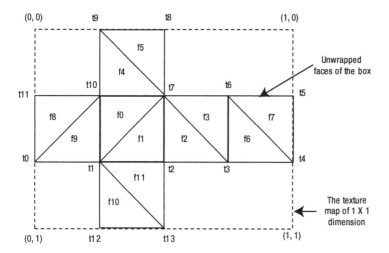

Figure 16-13. *A box surface mapped onto a 2D plane with texture coordinates*

You can create the `texture coordinates` array as shown in the following code. Like the `points` array, the following is the pseudo-code. The first array is for understanding the concept, and the second array is the actual one that is used in code:

```
// For understanding purpose-only
float[] texCoords = {
    t0,
    t1,
    t2,
    ...
    t14};
```

```
// The actual texture coordinates of vertices
float[] texCoords = {
    x0, y0, // t0
    x1, y1, // t1
    x2, y2, // t2
    ...
    x13, y13 // t13
};
```

The third piece of information that you need to specify is an array of faces. Note that each triangle has two faces. In our figures, you have shown only the front faces of the triangles. Specifying faces is the most confusing step in creating a `TriangleMesh` object. A face is specified using the `points` array and `texture coordinates` array. You use the indexes of the vertices in the `point` array and the indexes of the texture points in the `texture coordinates` array to specify a face. A face is specified using six integers in the following formats:

```
iv0, it0, iv1, it1, iv2, it2
```

Here

- iv0 is the index of the vertex v0 in the points array, and it0 is the index of the point t0 in the texture coordinates array.

- iv1 and it1 are the indexes of the vertex v1 and point t1 in the points and texture coordinates arrays.

- iv2 and it2 are the indexes of the vertex v2 and point t2 in the points and texture coordinates arrays.

Figure 16-14 shows only two triangles, which make up the front side of the box.

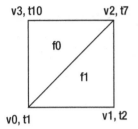

Figure 16-14. *Two triangles of the box with their vertices in points and texture coordinates arrays*

Figure 16-14 is the superimposition of the figures shown in Figures 16-12 and 16-13. The figure shows the vertex number and their corresponding texture coordinate point number. To specify the f0 in the faces array, you can specify the vertices of the triangle in two ways, counterclockwise and clockwise:

```
ivo, it1, iv2, it7, iv3, it10 (Counterclockwise)
ivo, it1, iv3, it10, iv2, it7 (Clockwise)
```

The starting vertex does not matter in specifying a face. You can start with any vertex and go in a clockwise or a counterclockwise direction. When the vertices for a face are specified in the counterclockwise direction, it is considered the front face. Otherwise, it is considered the back face. The following series of numbers will specify the face f1 in our figure:

```
ivo, it1, iv1, it2, iv2, it7 (Counterclockwise: front-face)
ivo, it1, iv2, it7, iv1, it2 (Clockwise: back-face)
```

To determine whether you are specifying the front face or back face, apply the following rules as illustrated in Figure 16-15:

- Draw a line perpendicular to the surface of the triangle going outward.

- Imagine you are looking into the surface by aligning your view along the line.

- Try traversing the vertices in counterclockwise. The sequence of vertices will give you a front face. If you traverse the vertices clockwise, the sequence will give you a back face.

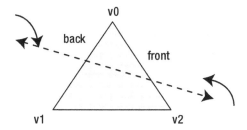

Figure 16-15. *Winding order of vertices of a triangle*

The following pseudo-code illustrates how to create an int array for specifying faces. The int values are the array indexes from the points and texture coordinates arrays:

```
int[] faces = new int[] {
ivo, it1, iv2, it7, iv3, it10, // f0: front-face
ivo, it1, iv3, it10, iv2, it7, // f0: back-face
ivo, it1, iv1, it2, iv2, it7,  // f1: front-face
ivo, it1, iv2, it7, iv1, it2   // f1: back-face
...
};
```

Once you have the points, texture coordinates, and faces arrays, you can construct a TriangleMesh object as follows:

```
TriangleMesh mesh = new TriangleMesh();
mesh.getPoints().addAll(points);
mesh.getTexCoords().addAll(texCoords);
mesh.getFaces().addAll(faces);
```

A TriangleMesh provides the data for constructing a user-defined 3D object. A MeshView object creates the surface for the object with a specified TriangleMesh:

```
// Create a MeshView
MeshView meshView = new MeshView();
meshView.setMesh(mesh);
```

Once you have a MeshView object, you need to add it to a scene graph to view it. You can view it the same way you have been viewing the predefined 3D shapes Boxes, Spheres, and Cylinders.

In the next few sections, you will create 3D objects using a TriangleMesh. You will start with the simplest 3D object, which is a triangle.

Creating a 3D Triangle

You may argue that a triangle is a 2D shape, not a 3D shape. It is agreed that a triangle is a 2D shape. You will create a triangle in a 3D space using a TriangleMesh. The triangle will have two faces. This example is chosen because it is the simplest shape you can create with a mesh of triangles. In the case of a triangle, the mesh consists of only one triangle. Figure 16-16 shows a triangle in the 3D space and its vertices mapped into a 2D plane.

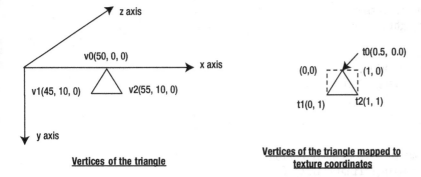

Figure 16-16. *Vertices of a triangle in the 3D space and mapped onto a 2D plane*

The triangle can be created using a mesh of one triangle. Let us create the points array for the TriangleMesh object:

```
float[] points = {50, 0, 0,  // v0 (iv0 = 0)
           45, 10, 0, // v1 (iv1 = 1)
           55, 10, 0  // v2 (iv2 = 2)
};
```

The second part of the figure, shown on the right, maps the vertices of the triangle to a unit square. You can create the texture coordinates array as follows:

```
float[] texCoords = {0.5f, 0.5f,  // t0 (it0 = 0)
    0.0f, 1.0f,  // t1 (it1 = 1)
    1.0f, 1.0f   // t2 (it2 = 2)
};
```

Using the points and texture coordinates arrays, you can specify the faces array as follows:

```
int[] faces = {
    0, 0, 2, 2, 1, 1,  // iv0, it0, iv2, it2, iv1, it1 (front face)
    0, 0, 1, 1, 2, 2   // iv0, it0, iv1, it1, iv2, it2 back face
};
```

Listing 16-8 contains the complete program to create a triangle using a TriangleMesh. It adds two different lights to light the two faces of the triangle. An animation rotates the camera, so you can view both sides of the triangle in different colors. The createMeshView() method has the coordinate values and logic to create the MeshView.

Listing 16-8. Creating a Triangle Using a TriangleMesh

```
// TriangleWithAMesh.java
package com.jdojo.shape3d;

import javafx.animation.Animation;
import javafx.animation.RotateTransition;
import javafx.application.Application;
import javafx.scene.Group;
```

```java
import javafx.scene.PerspectiveCamera;
import javafx.scene.PointLight;
import javafx.scene.Scene;
import javafx.scene.paint.Color;
import javafx.scene.shape.MeshView;
import javafx.scene.shape.TriangleMesh;
import javafx.scene.transform.Rotate;
import javafx.stage.Stage;
import javafx.util.Duration;

public class TriangleWithAMesh extends Application {
        public static void main(String[] args) {
                Application.launch(args);
        }

        @Override
        public void start(Stage stage) {
                // Create a MeshView and position it in the space
                MeshView meshView = this.createMeshView();
                meshView.setTranslateX(250);
                meshView.setTranslateY(100);
                meshView.setTranslateZ(400);

                // Scale the Meshview to make it look bigger
                meshView.setScaleX(10.0);
                meshView.setScaleY(10.0);
                meshView.setScaleZ(10.0);

                PerspectiveCamera camera = new PerspectiveCamera(false);
                camera.setTranslateX(100);
                camera.setTranslateY(-50);
                camera.setTranslateZ(300);

                // Add a Rotation animation to the camera
                RotateTransition rt =
                        new RotateTransition(Duration.seconds(2), camera);
                rt.setCycleCount(Animation.INDEFINITE);
                rt.setFromAngle(-30);
                rt.setToAngle(30);
                rt.setAutoReverse(true);
                rt.setAxis(Rotate.Y_AXIS);
                rt.play();

                // Front light is red
                PointLight redLight = new PointLight();
                redLight.setColor(Color.RED);
                redLight.setTranslateX(250);
                redLight.setTranslateY(150);
                redLight.setTranslateZ(300);

                // Back light is green
```

```
            PointLight greenLight = new PointLight();
            greenLight.setColor(Color.GREEN);
            greenLight.setTranslateX(200);
            greenLight.setTranslateY(150);
            greenLight.setTranslateZ(450);

            Group root = new Group(meshView, redLight, greenLight);

            // Rotate the triangle with its lights to 90 degrees
            root.setRotationAxis(Rotate.Y_AXIS);
            root.setRotate(90);

            Scene scene = new Scene(root, 400, 300, true);
            scene.setCamera(camera);
            stage.setScene(scene);
            stage.setTitle(
                    "Creating a Triangle using a TriangleMesh");
            stage.show();
    }

    public MeshView createMeshView() {
            float[] points = {50, 0, 0,   // v0 (iv0 = 0)
                            45, 10, 0, // v1 (iv1 = 1)
                            55, 10, 0  // v2 (iv2 = 2)
                            };

            float[] texCoords = { 0.5f, 0.5f, // t0 (it0 = 0)
                            0.0f, 1.0f, // t1 (it1 = 1)
                            1.0f, 1.0f  // t2 (it2 = 2)
                            };

            int[] faces = {
                0, 0, 2, 2, 1, 1, // iv0, it0, iv2, it2, iv1, it1
                                        // (front face)
                0, 0, 1, 1, 2, 2  // iv0, it0, iv1, it1, iv2, it2
                                        // (back face)
            };

            // Create a TriangleMesh
            TriangleMesh mesh = new TriangleMesh();
            mesh.getPoints().addAll(points);
            mesh.getTexCoords().addAll(texCoords);
            mesh.getFaces().addAll(faces);

            // Create a MeshView
            MeshView meshView = new MeshView();
            meshView.setMesh(mesh);

            return meshView;
    }
}
```

627

Creating a 3D Rectangle

In this section, you will create a rectangle using a mesh of two triangles. This will give us an opportunity to use what you have learned so far. Figure 16-17 shows a rectangle in the 3D space and its vertices mapped into a 2D plane.

Vertices of the rectangle   **Vertices of the rectangle mapped to texture coordinates**

Figure 16-17. *Vertices of a rectangle in the 3D space and mapped into a 2D plane*

The rectangle consists of two triangles. Both triangles have two faces. In the figure, I have shown only two faces f0 and f1. The following is the points array for the four vertices of the rectangle:

```
float[] points = {
    50, 0, 0,  // v0 (iv0 = 0)
    50, 10, 0, // v1 (iv1 = 1)
    60, 10, 0, // v2 (iv2 = 2)
    60, 0, 0   // v3 (iv3 = 3)
};
```

The texture coordinates array can be constructed as follows:

```
float[] texCoords = {
    0.0f, 0.0f,  // t0 (it0 = 0)
    0.0f, 1.0f,  // t1 (it1 = 1)
    1.0f, 1.0f,  // t2 (it2 = 2)
    1.0f, 0.0f   // t3 (it3 = 3)
};
```

You will specify the four faces as follows:

```
int[] faces =
    { 0, 0, 3, 3, 1, 1,  // iv0, it0, iv3, it3, iv1, it1 (f0 front face)
      0, 0, 1, 1, 3, 3,  // iv0, it0, iv1, it1, iv3, it3 (f0 back face)
      1, 1, 3, 3, 2, 2,  // iv1, it1, iv3, it3, iv2, it2 (f1 front face)
      1, 1, 2, 2, 3, 3   // iv1, it1, iv2, it2, iv3, it3 (f1 back face)
    };
```

If you plug the aforementioned three arrays into the createMeshView() method in Listing 16-8, you will get a rotating rectangle.

Creating a Tetrahedron

Now, you are prepared to create a little complex 3D object. You will create a tetrahedron. Figure 16-18 shows the top view of a tetrahedron.

Figure 16-18. *A tetrahedron*

A tetrahedron consists of four triangles. It has four vertices. Three triangles meet at a point. Figure 16-19 shows the two views of the tetrahedron. On the left, you have numbered the four vertices as v0, v1, v2, and v3 and four faces as f0, f1, f2, and f3. Note that the face f3 is the face of the triangle at the base, and it is not visible from the top view. The second view has unwrapped the four triangles giving rise to eight vertices on the 2D plane. The dotted rectangle is the unit square into which the eight vertices will be mapped.

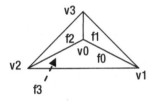 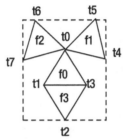

Vertices of the tetrahedron

Vertices of the tetrahedron mapped
to texture coordinates

Figure 16-19. *Vertices of a tetrahedron in the 3D space and mapped into a 2D plane*

You can create the points, faces, and texture coordinates arrays as follows:

```
float[] points = {10, 10, 10, // v0 (iv0 = 0)
            20, 20, 0,  // v1 (iv1 = 1)
            0, 20, 0,   // v2 (iv2 = 2)
            10, 20, 20  // v3 (iv3 = 3)
        };
```

```
float[] texCoords = {
        0.50f, 0.33f, // t0 (it0 = 0)
        0.25f, 0.75f, // t1 (it1 = 1)
        0.50f, 1.00f, // t2 (it2 = 2)
        0.66f, 0.66f, // t3 (it3 = 3)
        1.00f, 0.35f, // t4 (it4 = 4)
        0.90f, 0.00f, // t5 (it5 = 5)
        0.10f, 0.00f, // t6 (it6 = 6)
        0.00f, 0.35f  // t7 (it7 = 7)
};
```

```
int[] faces = {
        0, 0, 2, 1, 1, 3, // f0 front-face
        0, 0, 1, 3, 2, 1, // f0 back-face
        0, 0, 1, 4, 3, 5, // f1 front-face
        0, 0, 3, 5, 1, 4, // f1 back-face
        0, 0, 3, 6, 2, 7, // f2 front-face
        0, 0, 2, 7, 3, 6, // f2 back-face
        1, 3, 3, 2, 2, 1, // f3 front-face
        1, 3, 2, 1, 3, 2  // f3 back-face
};
```

Listing 16-9 contains a complete program to show how to construct a tetrahedron using a TriangleMesh. The tetrahedron is rotated along the y-axis, so you can view two of its vertical faces. Figure 16-20 shows the window with the tetrahedron.

Listing 16-9. Creating a Tetrahedron Using a TriangleMesh

```java
// Tetrahedron.java
package com.jdojo.shape3d;

import javafx.application.Application;
import javafx.scene.Group;
import javafx.scene.PerspectiveCamera;
import javafx.scene.PointLight;
import javafx.scene.Scene;
import javafx.scene.paint.Color;
import javafx.scene.shape.MeshView;
import javafx.scene.shape.TriangleMesh;
import javafx.scene.transform.Rotate;
import javafx.stage.Stage;

public class Tetrahedron extends Application {
        public static void main(String[] args) {
                Application.launch(args);
        }

        @Override
        public void start(Stage stage) {
                MeshView meshView = this.createMeshView();
                meshView.setTranslateX(250);
                meshView.setTranslateY(50);
                meshView.setTranslateZ(400);

                meshView.setScaleX(10.0);
                meshView.setScaleY(20.0);
                meshView.setScaleZ(10.0);

                PerspectiveCamera camera = new PerspectiveCamera(false);
                camera.setTranslateX(100);
                camera.setTranslateY(0);
                camera.setTranslateZ(100);
```

```
            PointLight redLight = new PointLight();
            redLight.setColor(Color.RED);
            redLight.setTranslateX(250);
            redLight.setTranslateY(-100);
            redLight.setTranslateZ(250);

            Group root = new Group(meshView, redLight);
            root.setRotationAxis(Rotate.Y_AXIS);
            root.setRotate(45);

            Scene scene = new Scene(root, 200, 150, true);
            scene.setCamera(camera);
            stage.setScene(scene);
            stage.setTitle("A Tetrahedron using a TriangleMesh");
            stage.show();
    }

    public MeshView createMeshView() {
            float[] points = {10, 10, 10, // v0 (iv0 = 0)
                        20, 20, 0,  // v1 (iv1 = 1)
                        0, 20, 0,   // v2 (iv2 = 2)
                        10, 20, 20  // v3 (iv3 = 3)
                   };

            float[] texCoords = {
                    0.50f, 0.33f, // t0 (it0 = 0)
                    0.25f, 0.75f, // t1 (it1 = 1)
                    0.50f, 1.00f, // t2 (it2 = 2)
                    0.66f, 0.66f, // t3 (it3 = 3)
                    1.00f, 0.35f, // t4 (it4 = 4)
                    0.90f, 0.00f, // t5 (it5 = 5)
                    0.10f, 0.00f, // t6 (it6 = 6)
                    0.00f, 0.35f  // t7 (it7 = 7)
            };

            int[] faces = {
                    0, 0, 2, 1, 1, 3, // f0 front-face
                    0, 0, 1, 3, 2, 1, // f0 back-face
                    0, 0, 1, 4, 3, 5, // f1 front-face
                    0, 0, 3, 5, 1, 4, // f1 back-face
                    0, 0, 3, 6, 2, 7, // f2 front-face
                    0, 0, 2, 7, 3, 6, // f2 back-face
                    1, 3, 3, 2, 2, 1, // f3 front-face
                    1, 3, 2, 1, 3, 2, // f3 back-face
            };

            TriangleMesh mesh = new TriangleMesh();
            mesh.getPoints().addAll(points);
            mesh.getTexCoords().addAll(texCoords);
            mesh.getFaces().addAll(faces);
```

```
            MeshView meshView = new MeshView();
            meshView.setMesh(mesh);

            return meshView;
        }
}
```

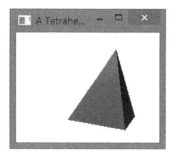

Figure 16-20. *A tetrahedron using a TriangleMesh*

Summary

Any shape, drawn in a three-dimensional space, having three dimensions (length, width, and depth) is known as a 3D shape such as cubes, spheres, pyramids, and so on. JavaFX provides 3D shapes as nodes. It offers two types of 3D shapes: predefined shapes and user-defined shapes.

Box, sphere, and cylinder are three predefined 3D shapes that you can readily use in your JavaFX applications. You can create any type of 3D shapes using a triangle mesh. The Box, Sphere, and Cylinder classes represent the three predefined shapes. The MeshView class represents a user-defined 3D shape in a scene. The 3D shape classes are in the javafx.scene.shape package.

JavaFX 3D support is a conditional feature. If it is not supported on your platform, you get a warning message on the console when you run a program that attempts to use 3D features. The method Platform. isSupported(ConditionalFeature.SCENE3D) returns true if 3D is supported on your platform.

When dealing with 3D objects in JavaFX, you would like the object closer to you to overlap the object farther from you. In JavaFX, by default, nodes are rendered in the order they are added to the scene graph. In order for 3D shapes to appear as they would appear in the real world, you need to specify two things. First, when you create a Scene object, specify that it needs to have a depth buffer, and, second, specify that the nodes' z coordinate values should be used when they are rendered.

Cameras are used to render the scene. Cameras in JavaFX are nodes. They can be added to the scene graph and positioned like other nodes. Perspective camera and parallel camera are two types of cameras used in JavaFX, and they are represented by the PerspectiveCamera and ParallelCamera classes. A perspective camera defines the viewing volume for a perspective projection, which is a truncated right pyramid. The camera projects the objects contained within the near and far clipping planes onto the projection plane. Therefore, any objects outside the clipping planes are not visible. A parallel camera specifies the viewing volume for a parallel projection, which is a rectangular box.

Similar to the real world, you need a light source to view the 3D objects in a scene. An instance of the abstract base class LightBase represents a light source. Its two concrete subclasses, AmbientLight and PointLight, represent an ambient light and a point light.

A scene can use only one camera. Sometimes, you may want to view different parts of a scene using multiple cameras. JavaFX includes the concept of subscenes. A subscene is a container for a scene graph. It can have its own width, height, fill color, depth buffer, antialiasing flag, and camera. An instance of the SubScene class represents a subscene. The SubScene inherits from the Node class.

The next chapter will discuss how to apply different types of effects to nodes in a scene graph.

CHAPTER 17

■ ■ ■

Applying Effects

In this chapter, you will learn:

- What an effect is
- How to chain effects
- What different types of effects are
- How to use perspective transformation effects

The examples of this chapter lie in the com.jdojo.effect package. In order for them to work, you must add a corresponding line to the module-info.java file:

```
...
opens com.jdojo.effect to javafx.graphics, javafx.base;
...
```

What Is an Effect?

An effect is a filter that accepts one or more graphical inputs, applies an algorithm on the inputs, and produces an output. Typically, effects are applied to nodes to create visually appealing user interfaces. Examples of effects are shadow, blur, warp, glow, reflection, blending, and different types of lighting, among others. The JavaFX library provides several effect-related classes. Effects are conditional features. They are applied to nodes and will be ignored if they are not available on a platform. Figure 17-1 shows four Text nodes using the drop shadow, blur, glow, and bloom effects.

Figure 17-1. Text nodes with different effects

The Node class contains an effect property that specifies the effect applied to the node. By default, it is null. The following snippet of code applies a drop shadow effect to a Text node:

```
Text t1 = new Text("Drop Shadow");
t1.setFont(Font.font(24));
t1.setEffect(new DropShadow());
```

An instance of the Effect class represents an effect. The Effect class is the abstract base for all effect classes. All effect classes are included in the javafx.scene.effect package.

The program in Listing 17-1 creates Text nodes and applies effects to them. These nodes are the ones shown in Figure 17-1. I will explain the different types of effects and their usages in subsequent sections.

Listing 17-1. Applying Effects to Nodes

```
// EffectTest.java
package com.jdojo.effect;

import javafx.application.Application;
import javafx.scene.Scene;
import javafx.scene.effect.Bloom;
import javafx.scene.effect.BoxBlur;
import javafx.scene.effect.DropShadow;
import javafx.scene.effect.Glow;
import javafx.scene.layout.HBox;
import javafx.scene.layout.StackPane;
import javafx.scene.paint.Color;
import javafx.scene.shape.Rectangle;
import javafx.scene.text.Font;
import javafx.scene.text.FontWeight;
import javafx.scene.text.Text;
import javafx.stage.Stage;

public class EffectTest extends Application {
        public static void main(String[] args) {
                Application.launch(args);
        }

        @Override
        public void start(Stage stage) {
                Text t1 = new Text("Drop Shadow!");
                t1.setFont(Font.font(24));
                t1.setEffect(new DropShadow());

                Text t2 = new Text("Blur!");
                t2.setFont(Font.font(24));
                t2.setEffect(new BoxBlur());

                Text t3 = new Text("Glow!");
                t3.setFont(Font.font(24));
                t3.setEffect(new Glow());
```

```
Text t4 = new Text("Bloom!");
t4.setFont(Font.font("Arial", FontWeight.BOLD, 24));
t4.setFill(Color.WHITE);
t4.setEffect(new Bloom(0.10));

// Stack the Text node with bloom effect over a
    // Reactangle
Rectangle rect = new Rectangle(100, 30, Color.GREEN);
StackPane spane = new StackPane(rect, t4);

HBox root = new HBox(t1, t2, t3, spane);
root.setSpacing(20);
root.setStyle("""
        -fx-padding: 10;
    -fx-border-style: solid inside;
    -fx-border-width: 2;
    -fx-border-insets: 5;
    -fx-border-radius: 5;
    -fx-border-color: blue;""");

Scene scene = new Scene(root);
stage.setScene(scene);
stage.setTitle("Applying Effects");
stage.show();
    }
}
```

■ **Tip** An effect applied to a Group is applied to all its children. It is also possible to chain multiple effects where the output of one effect becomes the input for the next effect in the chain. The layout bounds of a node are not affected by the effects applied to it. However, the local bounds and bounds in the parent are affected by the effects.

Chaining Effects

Some effects can be chained with other effects when they are applied in sequence. The output of the first effect becomes the input for the second effect and so on, as shown in Figure 17-2.

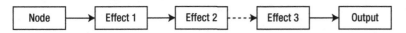

Figure 17-2. *A chain of effects applied on a node*

Effect classes that allow chaining contain an input property to specify the effect that precedes it. If the input is null, the effect is applied to the node on which this effect is set instead of being applied to the preceding input effect. By default, the input is null. The following snippet of code creates two chains of effects on Text nodes, as shown in Figure 17-3:

```
// Effect Chain: Text >> Reflection >> Shadow
DropShadow dsEffect = new DropShadow();
dsEffect.setInput(new Reflection());
Text t1 = new Text("Reflection and Shadow");
t1.setEffect(dsEffect);

// Effect Chain: Text >> Shadow >> Reflection
Reflection reflection = new Reflection();
reflection.setInput(new DropShadow());
Text t2 = new Text("Shadow and Reflection");
t2.setEffect(reflection);
```

Figure 17-3. *Chaining a DropShadow effect with a Reflection effect*

In Figure 17-3, a Reflection effect followed by a DropShadow is applied to the text on the left; a DropShadow followed by a Reflection effect is applied to the text on the right. Notice the sequence of effects makes a difference in the output. The second chain of effects produces a taller output as the reflection also includes the shadow.

If an effect allows chaining, it will have an input property. In subsequent sections, I will list the input property for the effect classes, but not discuss it.

Shadowing Effects

A shadowing effect draws a shadow and applies it to an input. JavaFX supports three types of shadowing effects:

- DropShadow
- InnerShadow
- Shadow

The *DropShadow* Effect

The DropShadow effect draws a shadow (a blurred image) behind the input, so the input seems to be raised. It gives the input a 3D look. The input can be a node or an effect in a chain of effects.

An instance of the DropShadow class represents a DropShadow effect. The size, location, color, and quality of the effect are controlled by several properties of the DropShadow class:

- offsetX
- offsetY
- color
- blurType
- radius
- spread
- width
- height
- input

The DropShadow class contains several constructors that let you specify the initial values for the properties:

- DropShadow()
- DropShadow(BlurType blurType, Color color, double radius, double spread, double offsetX, double offsetY)
- DropShadow(double radius, Color color)
- DropShadow(double radius, double offsetX, double offsetY, Color color)

The offsetX and offsetY properties control the position of the shadow in pixels relative to the input. By default, their values are zero. The positive values of offsetX and offsetY move the shadow in the positive x-axis and y-axis directions, respectively. The negative values move the shadow in the reverse directions.

The following snippet of code creates a DropShadow object with the offsetX and offsetY of 10px. The third rectangle from the left in Figure 17-4 shows the rectangle with the effect using the same rectangle with a DropShadow effect and different x and y offsets. For the fourth from the left rectangle, the shadow is positioned at the lower-right corner of the rectangle as the rectangle size (50, 25) matches the offsets (50, 25).

```
DropShadow dsEffect = new DropShadow();
dsEffect.setOffsetX(10);
dsEffect.setOffsetY(10);

Rectangle rect = new Rectangle(50, 25, Color.LIGHTGRAY);
rect.setEffect(dsEffect);
```

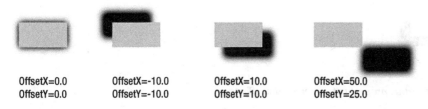

| OffsetX=0.0 | OffsetX=-10.0 | OffsetX=10.0 | OffsetX=50.0 |
| OffsetY=0.0 | OffsetY=-10.0 | OffsetY=10.0 | OffsetY=25.0 |

***Figure 17-4.** Effects of the offsetX and offsetY properties on a DropShadow effect*

The color property specifies the color of the shadow. By default, it is Color.BLACK. The following code would set the color to red:

```
DropShadow dsEffect = new DropShadow();
dsEffect.setColor(Color.RED);
```

The blurring in the shadow can be achieved using different algorithms. The blurType property specifies the type of blurring algorithm for the shadow. Its value is one of the following constants of the BlurType enum:

- ONE_PASS_BOX
- TWO_PASS_BOX
- THREE_PASS_BOX
- GAUSSIAN

The ONE_PASS_BOX uses a single pass of the box filter to blur the shadow. The TWO_PASS_BOX uses two passes of the box filter to blur the shadow. The THREE_PASS_BOX uses three passes of the box filter to blur the shadow. The GAUSSIAN uses a Gaussian blur kernel to blur the shadow. The blur quality of the shadow is the least in ONE_PASS_BOX and the best in GAUSSIAN. The default is THREE_PASS_BOX, which is very close to GAUSSIAN in quality. The following snippet of code sets the GAUSSIAN blur type:

```
DropShadow dsEffect = new DropShadow();
dsEffect.setBlurType(BlurType.GAUSSIAN);
```

The radius property specifies the distance the shadow is spread on each side of the source pixel. If the radius is zero, the shadow has sharp edges. Its value can be between 0 and 127. The default value is 10. The blurring outside the shadow region is achieved by blending the shadow color and the background color. The blur color fades out over the radius distance from the edges.

Figure 17-5 shows a rectangle twice with a DropShadow effect. The one on the left uses the radius of 0.0, which results in sharp edges of the shadow. The one on the right uses the default radius of 10.0 that spreads the shadow 10px around the edges. The following snippet of code produces the first rectangle in the figure that has sharp edges of the shadow:

```
DropShadow dsEffect = new DropShadow();
dsEffect.setOffsetX(10);
dsEffect.setOffsetY(10);
dsEffect.setRadius(0);

Rectangle rect = new Rectangle(50, 25, Color.LIGHTGRAY);
rect.setEffect(dsEffect);
```

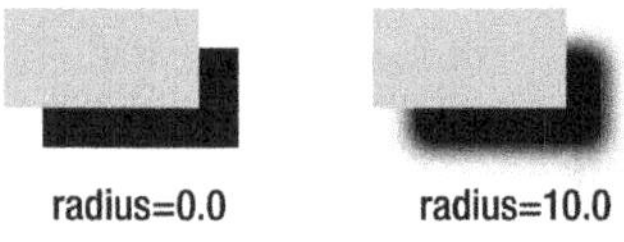

radius=0.0   radius=10.0

Figure 17-5. *Effects of the radius property of a DropShadow effect*

The spread property specifies the portion of the radius, which has the same color as the shadow. The color for the remaining portion of the radius is determined by the blur algorithm. Its value is between 0.0 and 1.0. The default is 0.0.

Suppose you have a DropShadow with a radius 10.0 and a spread value of 0.60 and the shadow color is black. In this case, the blur color will be black up to 6px around the source pixel. It will start fading out from the seventh pixel to the tenth pixel. If you specify the spread value as 1.0, there would be no blurring of the shadow. Figure 17-6 shows three rectangles with a DropShadow using a radius of 10.0. The three DropShadow effects use different spread values. The spread of 0.0 blurs fully along the radius. The spread of 0.50 spreads the shadow color in the first half of the radius and blurs the second half. The spread of 1.0 spreads the shadow color fully along the radius, and there is no blurring. The following snippet of code produces the middle rectangle in Figure 17-6:

```
DropShadow dsEfefct = new DropShadow();
dsEfefct.setOffsetX(10);
dsEfefct.setOffsetY(10);
dsEfefct.setRadius(10);
dsEfefct.setSpread(.50);

Rectangle rect = new Rectangle(50, 25, Color.LIGHTGRAY);
rect.setEffect(dsEfefct);
```

spread=0.0   spread=0.5   spread=1.0

Figure 17-6. Effects of the spread property of a DropShadow effect

The width and height properties specify the horizontal and vertical distances, respectively, from the source pixel up to where the shadow color is spread. Their values are between 0 and 255. Setting their values is equivalent to setting the radius property, so they are equal to (2 * radius + 1). Their default value is 21.0. When you change the radius, the width and height properties are adjusted using the formula if they are not bound. However, setting the width and height changes the radius value, so the average of the width and height is equal to (2 * radius + 1). Figure 17-7 shows four rectangles with DropShadow effects. Their width and height properties were set as shown under each rectangle. Their radius properties were adjusted automatically. The fourth from the left rectangle was produced using the following snippet of code:

```
DropShadow dsEffect = new DropShadow();
dsEffect.setOffsetX(10);
dsEffect.setOffsetY(10);
dsEffect.setWidth(20);
dsEffect.setHeight(20);

Rectangle rect = new Rectangle(50, 25, Color.LIGHTGRAY);
rect.setEffect(dsEffect);
```

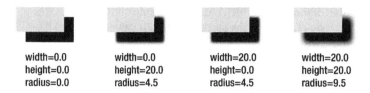

width=0.0	width=0.0	width=20.0	width=20.0
height=0.0	height=20.0	height=0.0	height=20.0
radius=0.0	radius=4.5	radius=4.5	radius=9.5

Figure 17-7. *Effects of setting the width and height of a* DropShadow

The program in Listing 17-2 lets you experiment with properties of the DropShadow effect. It displays a window as shown in Figure 17-8. Change the properties to see their effects in action.

Listing 17-2. Experimenting with DropShadow Properties

```
// DropShadowTest.java
// ...find in the book's download area.
```

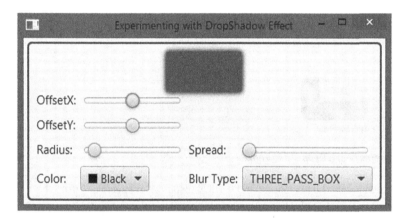

Figure 17-8. *A window that allows you to change the properties of a* DropShadow *effect at runtime*

The *InnerShadow* Effect

The InnerShadow effect works very similar to the DropShadow effect. It draws a shadow (a blurred image) of an input inside the edges of the input, so the input seems to have depth or a 3D look. The input can be a node or an effect in a chain of effects.

An instance of the InnerShadow class represents an InnerShadow effect. The size, location, color, and quality of the effect are controlled by several properties of the InnerShadow class:

- offsetX
- offsetY
- color
- blurType
- radius

- choke
- width
- height
- input

The number of properties of the InnerShadow class is equal to that for the DropShadow class. The spread property in the DropShadow class is replaced by the choke property in the InnerShadow class, which works similar to the spread property in the DropShadow class. Please refer to the previous section "The *DropShadow* Effect" for a detailed description and examples of these properties.

The DropShadow class contains several constructors that let you specify the initial values for the properties:

- InnerShadow()
- InnerShadow(BlurType blurType, Color color, double radius, double choke, double offsetX, double offsetY)
- InnerShadow(double radius, Color color)
- InnerShadow(double radius, double offsetX, double offsetY, Color color)

The program in Listing 17-3 creates a Text node and two Rectangle nodes. An InnerShadow is applied to all three nodes. Figure 17-9 shows the results for these nodes. Notice that the shadow is not spread outside the edges of the nodes. You need to set the offsetX and offsetY properties to see a noticeable effect.

Listing 17-3. Using the InnerShadow Class

```
// InnerShadowTest.java
// ...find in the book's download area.
```

Figure 17-9. A Text and two Rectangle nodes using InnerShadow effects

The *Shadow* Effect

The Shadow effect creates a shadow with blurry edges of its input. Unlike DropShadow and InnerShadow, it modifies the original input itself to convert it into a shadow. Typically, a Shadow effect is combined with the original input to create a higher-level shadowing effect:

- You can apply a Shadow effect with a light color to a node and superimpose it on a duplicate of the original node to create a glow effect.

- You can create a Shadow effect with a dark color and place it behind the original node to create a DropShadow effect.

An instance of the Shadow class represents a Shadow effect. The size, color, and quality of the effect are controlled by several properties of the Shadow class:

- color
- blurType
- radius
- width
- height
- input

These properties work the same way they work in the DropShadow. Please refer to the section "The *DropShadow* Effect" for a detailed description and examples of these properties.

The Shadow class contains several constructors that let you specify the initial values for the properties:

- Shadow()
- Shadow(BlurType blurType, Color color, double radius)
- Shadow(double radius, Color color)

The program in Listing 17-4 demonstrates how to use the Shadow effect. It creates three Text nodes. A shadow is applied to all three nodes. The output of the first shadow is displayed. The output of the second shadow is superimposed on the original node to achieve a glow effect. The output of the third shadow is placed behind its original node to achieve a DropShadow effect. Figure 17-10 shows these three nodes.

Listing 17-4. Using a Shadow Effect and Creating High-Level Effects

```
// ShadowTest.java
// ...find in the book's download area.
```

Figure 17-10. *Applying a shadow to a Text node and creating Glow and DropShadow effects*

Blurring Effects

A blurring effect produces a blurred version of an input. JavaFX lets you apply different types of blurring effects, which differ in the algorithms used to create these effects.

The *BoxBlur* Effect

The BoxBlur effect uses a box filter kernel to produce a blurring effect. An instance of the BoxBlur class represents a BoxBlur effect. The size and quality of the effect can be configured using these properties of the class:

- width
- height
- iterations
- input

The width and height properties specify the horizontal and vertical size of the effect, respectively. Imagine a box defined by the width and height centered on a pixel of the input. The color information of the pixel is spread within the box during the blurring process. The values of these properties are between 0.0 and 255.0. The default values are 5.0. A value of less than or equal to 1.0 does not produce the blurring effect in the corresponding direction.

The iterations property specifies the number of times the blurring effect is applied. A higher value produces a better quality blur. Its value can be between zero and three. The default is one. The value of three produces the blur quality comparable to the Gaussian blur, discussed in the next section. The value of zero produces no blur at all.

The BoxBlur class contains two constructors:

- BoxBlur()
- BoxBlur(double width, double height, int iterations)

The no-args constructor creates a BoxBlur object with the width and height of 5.0 pixels and iterations of 1. The other constructor lets you specify the initial value for the width, height, and iterations properties, as in the following section of code:

```
// Create a BoxBlur with defaults: width=5.0, height=5.0, iterations=1
BoxBlur bb1 = new BoxBlur();

// Create a BoxBlur with width=10.0, height=10.0, iterations=3
BoxBlur bb2 = new BoxBlur(10, 10, 3);
```

The following snippet of code creates four Text nodes and applies BoxBlur effects of various qualities. Figure 17-11 shows the results of these Text nodes. Notice that the last Text node does not have any blur effect as the iterations property is set to zero.

```
Text t1 = new Text("Box Blur");
t1.setFont(Font.font(24));
t1.setEffect(new BoxBlur(5, 10, 1));
```

```
Text t2 = new Text("Box Blur");
t2.setFont(Font.font(24));
t2.setEffect(new BoxBlur(10, 5, 2));

Text t3 = new Text("Box Blur");
t3.setFont(Font.font(24));
t3.setEffect(new BoxBlur(5, 5, 3));

Text t4 = new Text("Box Blur");
t4.setFont(Font.font(24));
t4.setEffect(new BoxBlur(5, 5, 0)); // Zero iterations = No blurring
```

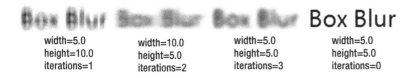

width=5.0	width=10.0	width=5.0	width=5.0
height=10.0	height=5.0	height=5.0	height=5.0
iterations=1	iterations=2	iterations=3	iterations=0

Figure 17-11. *Text nodes with BoxBlur effects of varying qualities*

The *GaussianBlur* Effect

The GaussianBlur effect uses a Gaussian convolution kernel to produce a blurring effect. An instance of the GaussianBlur class represents a GaussianBlur effect. The effect can be configured using two properties of the class:

- radius
- input

The radius property controls the distribution of the blur in pixels from the source pixel. The greater this value, the more the blur effect. Its value can be between 0.0 and 63.0. The default value is 10.0. A radius of 0 pixels produces no blur effect.

The GaussianBlur class contains two constructors:

- GaussianBlur()
- GaussianBlur(double radius)

The no-args constructor creates a GaussianBlur object with a default radius of 10.0px. The other constructor lets you specify the initial value for the radius, as in the following code:

```
// Create a GaussianBlur with a 10.0 pixels radius
GaussianBlur gb1 = new GaussianBlur();

// Create a GaussianBlur with a 20.0 pixels radius
GaussianBlur gb2 = new GaussianBlur(20);
```

The following snippet of code creates four Text nodes and applies GaussianBlur effects of different radius values. Figure 17-12 shows the results of these Text nodes. Notice that the last Text node does not have any blur effect as the radius property is set to zero.

```
Text t1 = new Text("Gaussian Blur");
t1.setFont(Font.font(24));
t1.setEffect(new GaussianBlur(5));

Text t2 = new Text("Gaussian Blur");
t2.setFont(Font.font(24));
t2.setEffect(new GaussianBlur(10));

Text t3 = new Text("Gaussian Blur");
t3.setFont(Font.font(24));
t3.setEffect(new GaussianBlur(15));

Text t4 = new Text("Gaussian Blur");
t4.setFont(Font.font(24));
t4.setEffect(new GaussianBlur(0)); // radius = 0 means no blur
```

radius=5.0   radius=10.0   radius=15.0   radius=0.0

Figure 17-12. *Text nodes with GaussianBlur effects of varying sizes*

The *MotionBlur* Effect

The MotionBlur effect produces a blurring effect by motion. The input looks as if you are seeing it while it is moving. A Gaussian convolution kernel is used with a specified angle to produce the effect. An instance of the MotionBlur class represents a MotionBlur effect. The effect can be configured using the three properties of the class:

- radius

- angle

- input

The radius and input properties work the same as respective properties for the GaussianBlur class, as described in the previous section. The angle property specifies the angle of the motion in degrees. By default, the angle is zero.

The MotionBlur class contains two constructors:

- MotionBlur()

- MotionBlur(double angle, double radius)

The no-args constructor creates a MotionBlur object with a default radius of 10.0px and an angle of 0.0 degrees. The other constructor lets you specify the initial value for the angle and radius, as shown in the following code:

```
// Create a MotionBlur with a 0.0 degrees angle and a 10.0 pixels radius
MotionBlur mb1 = new MotionBlur();
```

```
// Create a MotionBlur with a 30.0 degrees angle and a 20.0 pixels radius
MotionBlur mb1 = new MotionBlur(30.0, 20.0);
```

The program in Listing 17-5 shows how to use the MotionBlur effect on a Text node, with the results shown in Figure 17-13. The two sliders let you change the radius and angle properties.

Listing 17-5. Using the MotionBlur Effect on a Text Node

```
// MotionBlurTest.java
// ...find in the book's download area.
```

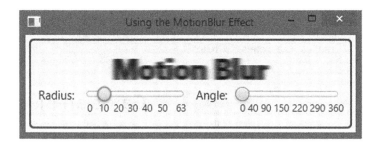

Figure 17-13. *Text nodes with GaussianBlur effects of varying sizes*

The *Bloom* Effect

The Bloom effect adds a glow to the pixels of its input that have a luminosity greater than or equal to a specified limit. Note that not all pixels in a Bloom effect are made to glow.

An instance of the Bloom class represents a Bloom effect. It contains two properties:

- threshold
- input

The threshold property is a number between 0.0 and 1.0. Its default value is 0.30. All pixels in the input having a luminosity greater than or equal to the threshold property are made to glow. The brightness of a pixel is determined by its luminosity. A pixel with a luminosity of 0.0 is not bright at all. A pixel with a luminosity of 1.0 is 100% bright. By default, all pixels having a luminosity greater than or equal to 0.3 are made to glow. A threshold of 0.0 makes all of the pixels glow. A threshold of 1.0 makes almost no pixels glow.

The Bloom class contains two constructors:

- Bloom()
- Bloom(double threshold)

The no-args constructor creates a Bloom object with a default threshold of 0.30. The other constructor lets you specify the threshold value, as shown in the following code:

```
// Create a Bloom with threshold 0.30
Bloom b1 = new Bloom();
```

```
// Create a Bloom with threshold 0.10 - more pixels will glow.
Bloom b2 = new Bloom(0.10);
```

Figure 17-14 shows four Text nodes with Bloom effects that have different threshold values. A Text node is laid over a rectangle using a StackPane. Notice that the lower the threshold value, the higher the blooming effect. The following snippet of code creates the first Text node and Rectangle pair from the left in Figure 17-14:

```
Text t1 = new Text("Bloom");
t1.setFill(Color.YELLOW);
t1.setFont(Font.font(null, FontWeight.BOLD, 24));
t1.setEffect(new Bloom(0.10));
Rectangle r1 = new Rectangle(100, 50, Color.GREEN);
StackPane sp1 = new StackPane(r1, t1);
```

threshold=0.1   threshold=0.3   threshold=0.7   threshold=1.0

Figure 17-14. *Text nodes with Bloom effects*

The *Glow* Effect

The Glow effect makes the bright pixels of the input brighter. An instance of the Glow class represents a Glow effect. It contains two properties:

- level
- input

The level property specifies the intensity of the Glow effect. It is a number between 0.0 and 1.0, and its default value is 0.30. A level of 0.0 adds no glow, and a level of 1.0 adds the maximum glow.

The Glow class contains two constructors:

- Glow()
- Glow(double level)

The no-args constructor creates a Glow object with a default level of 0.30. The other constructor lets you specify the level value, as shown in the following code:

```
// Create a Glow with level 0.30
Glow g1 = new Glow();

// Create a Glow with level 0.90 - more glow.
Glow g2 = new Glow(0.90);
```

Figure 17-15 shows four Text nodes with Glow effects with different level values. A Text node is laid over a rectangle using a StackPane. Notice that the higher the level value, the higher the glowing effect. The following snippet of code creates the first Text node and Rectangle pair from the left in Figure 17-15:

```
Text t1 = new Text("Glow");
t1.setFill(Color.YELLOW);
t1.setFont(Font.font(null, FontWeight.BOLD, 24));
t1.setEffect(new Glow(0.10));
Rectangle r1 = new Rectangle(100, 50, Color.GREEN);
StackPane sp1 = new StackPane(r1, t1);
```

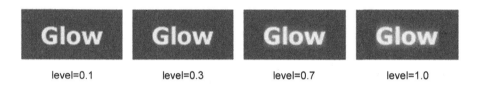

| level=0.1 | level=0.3 | level=0.7 | level=1.0 |

Figure 17-15. *Text nodes with Glow effects*

The *Reflection* Effect

The Reflection effect adds a reflection of the input below the input. An instance of the Reflection class represents a reflection effect. The position, size, and opacity of the reflection are controlled by various properties:

- topOffset
- fraction
- topOpacity
- bottomOpacity
- input

The topOffset specifies the distance in pixels between the bottom of the input and the top of the reflection. By default, it is 0.0. The fraction property specifies the fraction of the input height that is visible in the reflection. It is measured from the bottom. Its value can be between 0.0 and 1.0. A value of 0.0 means no reflection. A value of 1.0 means the entire input is visible in the reflection. A value of 0.25 means 25% of the input from the bottom is visible in the reflection. The default value is 0.75. The topOpacity and bottomOpacity properties specify the opacity of the reflection at its top and bottom extremes. Their values can be between 0.0 and 1.0. The default value is 0.50 for the topOpacity and 0.0 for the bottomOpacity.

The Reflection class contains two constructors:

- Reflection()
- Reflection(double topOffset, double fraction, double topOpacity, double bottomOpacity)

The no-args constructor creates a Reflection object with the default initial values for its properties. The other constructor lets you specify the initial values for the properties, as shown in the following code:

```
// Create a Reflection with default values
Reflection g1 = new Reflection();

// Create a Reflection with topOffset=2.0, fraction=0.90,
// topOpacity=1.0, and bottomOpacity=1.0
Reflection g2 = new Reflection(2.0, 0.90, 1.0, 1.0);
```

Figure 17-16 shows four Text nodes with Reflection effects configured differently. The following snippet of code creates the second Text node from the left, which shows the full input as the reflection:

```
Text t2 = new Text("Chatar");
t2.setFont(Font.font(null, FontWeight.BOLD, 24));
t2.setEffect(new Reflection(0.0, 1.0, 1.0, 1.0));
```

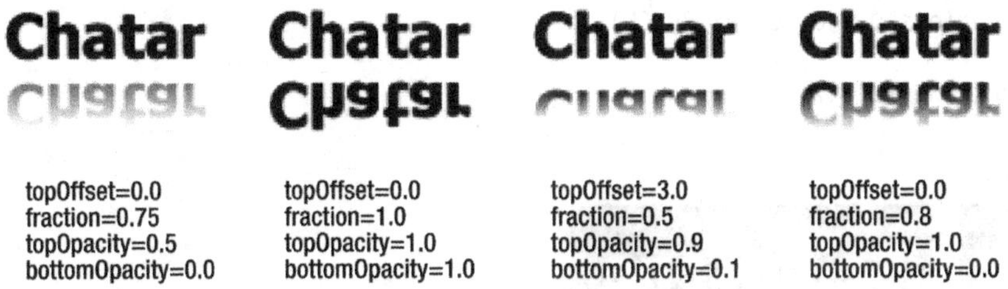

Chatar ᴄⴑᑯᒋᴦᵒᴸ	**Chatar** **ᴄⴑᑯᒋᴦᵒᴸ**	**Chatar** ᴄⴑᑯᒋᴦᵒᴸ	**Chatar** ᴄⴑᑯᒋᴦᵒᴸ
topOffset=0.0 fraction=0.75 topOpacity=0.5 bottomOpacity=0.0	topOffset=0.0 fraction=1.0 topOpacity=1.0 bottomOpacity=1.0	topOffset=3.0 fraction=0.5 topOpacity=0.9 bottomOpacity=0.1	topOffset=0.0 fraction=0.8 topOpacity=1.0 bottomOpacity=0.0

Figure 17-16. *Text nodes with Reflection effects*

The *SepiaTone* Effect

Sepia is a reddish-brown color. Sepia toning is performed on black-and-white photographic prints to give them a warmer tone. An instance of the SepiaTone class represents a SepiaTone effect. It contains two properties:

- level
- input

The level property specifies the intensity of the SepiaTone effect. It is a number between 0.0 and 1.0. Its default value is 1.0. A level of 0.0 adds no sepia toning, and a level of 1.0 adds the maximum sepia toning.

The SepiaTone class contains two constructors:

- SepiaTone ()
- SepiaTone (double level)

The no-args constructor creates a SepiaTone object with a default level of 1.0. The other constructor lets you specify the level value, as shown in the following code:

```
// Create a SepiaTone with level 1.0
SepiaTone g1 = new SepiaTone ();
```

651

```
// Create a SepiaTone with level 0.50
SepiaTone g2 = new SepiaTone(0.50);
```

The following snippet of code creates two Text nodes with the results shown in Figure 17-17. Notice that the higher the level value, the higher the sepia toning effect:

```
Text t1 = new Text("SepiaTone");
t1.setFill(Color.WHITE);
t1.setFont(Font.font(null, FontWeight.BOLD, 24));
1.setEffect(new SepiaTone(0.50));
Rectangle r1 = new Rectangle(150, 50, Color.BLACK);
r1.setOpacity(0.50);
StackPane sp1 = new StackPane(r1, t1);

Text t2 = new Text("SepiaTone");
t2.setFill(Color.WHITE);
t2.setFont(Font.font(null, FontWeight.BOLD, 24));
t2.setEffect(new SepiaTone(1.0));
Rectangle r2 = new Rectangle(150, 50, Color.BLACK);
r2.setOpacity(0.50);
StackPane sp2 = new StackPane(r2, t2);
```

level=0.5   level=1.0

Figure 17-17. *Text nodes with SepiaTone effects*

The *DisplacementMap* Effect

The DisplacementMap effect shifts each pixel in the input to produce an output. The name has two parts: "Displacement" and "Map." The first part implies that the effect displaces the pixels in the input. The second part implies that the displacement is based on a map that provides a displacement factor for each pixel in the output.

An instance of the DisplacementMap class represents a DisplacementMap. The class contains several properties to configure the effect:

- mapData
- scaleX
- scaleY
- offsetX

- offsetY

- wrap

- input

The mapData property is an instance of the FloatMap class. A FloatMap is a data structure that stores up to four values for each point in a rectangular area represented by its width and height properties. For example, you can use a FloatMap to store four components of the color (red, green, blue, and alpha) for each pixel in a two-dimensional rectangle. Each of the four values associated with a pair of numbers in the FloatMap is said to be in a band numbered 0, 1, 2, and 3. The actual meaning of the values in each band is context dependent. The following code provides an example of setting the FloatMap width and height:

```
// Create a FloatMap (width = 100, height = 50)
FloatMap map = new FloatMap(100, 50);
```

Now you need to populate the FloatMap with band values for each pair of numbers. You can use one of the following methods of the FloatMap class to populate it with the data:

- setSample(int x, int y, int band, float value)

- setSamples(int x, int y, float s0)

- setSamples(int x, int y, float s0, float s1)

- setSamples(int x, int y, float s0, float s1, float s2)

- setSamples(int x, int y, float s0, float s1, float s2, float s3)

The setSample() method sets the specified value in the specified band for the specified (x, y) location. The setSamples() methods sets the specified values in the bands determined by the positions of the values in the method call. That is, the first value is set for band 0, the second value for band 1, and so forth:

```
// Set 0,50f for band 0 and band 1 for each point in the map
for (int i = 0; i < 100; i++) {
        for (int j = 0; j < 50; j++) {
                map.setSamples(i, j, 0.50f, 0.50f);
        }
}
```

The DisplacementMap class requires that you set the mapData property to a FloatMap that contains values for band 0 and band 1 for each pixel in the output.

The scaleX, scaleY, offsetX, and offsetY are double properties. They are used in the equation (described shortly) to compute the displacement of the pixels. The scaleX and scaleY properties have 1.0 as their default values. The offsetX and offsetY properties have 0.0 as their default values.

The following equation is used to compute the pixel at (x, y) coordinates in the output. The abbreviations dst and src in the equation represent the destination and source, respectively:

```
dst[x,y] = src[x + (offsetX + scaleX * mapData[x,y][0]) * srcWidth,
            y + (offsetY + scaleY * mapData[x,y][1]) * srcHeight]
```

If the preceding equation looks very complex, don't be intimidated. In fact, the equation is very simple once you read the explanation that follows. The mapData[x,y][0] and mapData[x,y][1] parts in the equation refer to the values at band 0 and band 1, respectively, in the FloatMap for the location at (x, y).

Suppose you want to get the pixel for the (x, y) coordinates in the output, that is, you want to know which pixel from the input will be moved to (x, y) in the output. First, make sure you get the starting point right. To repeat, the equation starts with a point (x, y) in the output and finds the pixel at (x1, y1) in the input that will move to (x, y) in the output.

■ **Tip**   Many will get the equation wrong by thinking that you start with a pixel in the input and then find its location in the output. This is not true. The equation works the other way around. It picks a point (x, y) in the output and then finds which pixel in the input will move to this point.

The following are the steps to fully explain the equation:

- You want to find the pixel in the input that will be moved to the point (x, y) in the output.

- Get the values (band 0 and band 1) from the mapData for (x, y).

- Multiply the mapData values by the scale (scaleX for x coordinate and scaleY for y coordinate).

- Add the corresponding offset values to the values computed in the previous step.

- Multiply the previous step values with the corresponding dimensions of the input. This gives you the offset values along the x and y coordinate axes from the output (x, y) from where the pixels in the input will be moving to the (x, y) in the output.

- Add the values in the previous step to the x and y coordinates of the point in the output. Suppose these values are (x1, y1). The pixel at (x1, y1) in the input moves to the point (x, y) in the output.

If you still have problem understanding the pixel-shifting logic, you can break the preceding equation into two parts:

```
x1 = x + (offsetX + scaleX * mapData[x,y][0]) * srcWidth
y1 = y + (offsetY + scaleY * mapData[x,y][1]) * srcHeight
```

You can read these equations as "The pixel at (x, y) in the output is obtained by moving the pixel at (x1, y1) in the input to (x, y)."

If you leave the scale and offset values to their default

- Use a positive value in band 0 to move the input pixels to the left.

- Use a negative value in band 0 to move the input pixels to the right.

- Use a positive value in band 1 to move the input pixels up.

- Use a negative value in band 1 to move the input pixels down.

The program in Listing 17-6 creates a Text node and adds a DisplacementMap effect to the node. In the mapData, it sets values, so all pixels in the top half of the input are moved to the right by 1 pixel, and all pixels in the bottom half of the input are moved to the left by 1 pixel. The Text node will look like the one shown in Figure 17-18.

Listing 17-6. Using the `DisplacementMap` Effect

```
// DisplacementmapTest.java
// ...find in the book's download area.
```

Figure 17-18. *A Text node with a DisplacementMap effect*

The `DisplacementMap` class contains a `wrap` property, which is set to false by default. A pixel in the output is a pixel in the input that is moved to a new location. The location of the pixel in the input that needs to move to a new location is computed by the equation. It is possible that for some locations in the output, you do not have available pixels in the input. Suppose you have a 100px wide by 50px tall rectangle, and you apply a `DisplacementMap` effect to move all pixels to the left by 50px. The points at x = 75 in the output will get the pixel at x = 125 in the input. The input is only 100px wide. Therefore, for all points x > 50 in the output, you will not have available pixels in the input. If the `wrap` property is set to true, when the locations of the pixels in the input to be moved are outside the input bounds, the locations are computed by taking their modulus with the corresponding dimension (width along the x-axis and height along the y-axis) of the input. In the example, x = 125 will be reduced to 125 % 100, which is 25, and the pixels at x = 25 in the input will be moved to x = 75 in the output. If the `wrap` property is false, the pixels in the output are left transparent.

Figure 17-19 shows two `Text` nodes with `DisplacementMap` effects. Pixels in both nodes are moved 100px to the left. The `Text` node at the top has the `wrap` property set to false, whereas the `Text` node at the bottom has the `wrap` property set to true. Notice that the output for the bottom node is filled by wrapping the input. The program in Listing 17-7 is used to apply the wrapping effects.

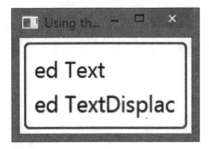

Figure 17-19. *Effects of using the wrap property in DisplacementMap*

Listing 17-7. Using the `wrap` Property in the `DisplacementMap` Effect

```
// DisplacementMapWrap.java
// ...find in the book's download area.
```

The *ColorInput* Effect

The ColorInput effect is a simple effect that fills (floods) a rectangular region with a specified paint. Typically, it is used as an input to another effect.

An instance of the ColorInput class represents the ColorInput effect. The class contains five properties that define the location, size, and the paint for the rectangular region:

- x

- y

- width

- height

- paint

Creating a ColorInput object is similar to creating a rectangle filled with the paint of the ColorInput. The x and y properties specify the location of the upper-left corner of the rectangular region in the local coordinate system. The width and height properties specify the size of the rectangular region. The default value for x, y, width, and height is 0.0. The paint property specifies the fill paint. The default value for paint is Color.RED.

You can use the following constructors to create an object of the ColorInput class:

- ColorInput()

- ColorInput(double x, double y, double width, double height, Paint paint)

The following snippet of code creates a ColorInput effect and applies it to a rectangle. The rectangle with the effect applied is shown in Figure 17-20. Note that when you apply the ColorInput effect to a node, all you see is the rectangular area generated by the ColorInput effect. As stated earlier, the ColorInput effect is not applied directly on nodes. Rather, it is used as an input to another effect.

```
ColorInput effect = new ColorInput();
effect.setWidth(100);
effect.setHeight(50);
effect.setPaint(Color.LIGHTGRAY);

// Size of the Rectangle does not matter to the rectangular area
// of the ColorInput
Rectangle r1 = new Rectangle(100, 50);
r1.setEffect(effect);
```

Figure 17-20. *A ColorInput effect applied to a rectangle*

The *ColorAdjust* Effect

The ColorAdjust effect adjusts the hue, saturation, brightness, and contrast of pixels by the specified delta amount. Typically, the effect is used on an ImageView node to adjust the color of an image.

An instance of the ColorAdjust class represents the ColorAdjust effect. The class contains five properties that define the location, size, and the paint for the rectangular region:

- hue
- saturation
- brightness
- contrast
- input

The hue, saturation, brightness, and contrast properties specify the delta amount by which these components are adjusted for all pixels. They range from –1.0 to 1.0. Their default values are 0.0.

The program in Listing 17-8 shows how to use the ColorAdjust effect on an image. It displays an image and four sliders to change the properties of the ColorAdjust effect. Adjust their values using the sliders to see the effects. If the program does not find the image, it prints a message and displays a Text node overlaying a rectangle in a StackPane, and the effect is applied to the StackPane.

Listing 17-8. Using the ColorAdjust Effect to Adjust the Color of Pixels in an Image

```
// ColorAdjustTest.java
// ...find in the book's download area.
```

The *ImageInput* Effect

The ImageInput effect works like the ColorInput effect. It passes the given image as an input to another effect. The given image is not modified by this effect. Typically, it is used as an input to another effect, not as an effect directly applied to a node.

An instance of the ImageInput class represents the ImageInput effect. The class contains three properties that define the location and the source of the image:

- x
- y
- source

The x and y properties specify the location of the upper-left corner of the image in the local coordinate system of the content node on which the effect is finally applied. Their default values are 0.0. The source property specifies the Image object to be used.

You can use the following constructors to create an object of the ColorInput class:

- ImageInput()
- ImageInput(Image source)
- ImageInput(Image source, double x, double y)

The program in Listing 17-9 shows how to use the ImageInput effect. It passes an ImageInput as an input to a DropShadow effect, which is applied on a rectangle, as shown in Figure 17-21.

Listing 17-9. Using an ImageInput Effect As an Input to a DropShadow Effect

```
// ImageInputTest.java
// ...find in the book's download area.
```

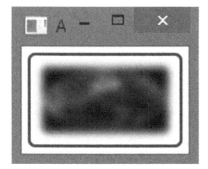

Figure 17-21. *An ImageInput effect with a DropShadow effect applied to a rectangle*

The *Blend* Effect

Blending combines two pixels at the same location from two inputs to produce one composite pixel in the output. The Blend effect takes two input effects and blends the overlapping pixels of the inputs to produce an output. The blending of two inputs is controlled by a blending mode.

An instance of the Blend class represents the Blend effect. The class contains properties to specify the

- topInput
- bottomInput
- mode
- opacity

The topInput and bottomInput properties specify the top and bottom effects, respectively. They are null by default. The mode property specifies the blending mode, which is one of the constants defined in the BlendMode enum. The default is BlendMode.SRC_OVER. JavaFX provides 17 predefined blending modes. Table 17-1 lists all of the constants in the BlendMode enum with a brief description of each. All blending modes use the SRC_OVER rules to blend the alpha components. The opacity property specifies the opacity to be applied to the top input before the blending is applied. The opacity is 1.0 by default.

Table 17-1. *The Constants in the* BlendMode *Enum with Their Descriptions*

BlendMode Enum Constant	Description
ADD	It adds the color (red, green, and blue) and alpha values for the pixels in the top and bottom inputs to get the new component value.
MULTIPLY	It multiplies the color components from two inputs.
DIFFERENCE	It subtracts the darker color components from any inputs from the lighter color components of the other input to get the resulting color components.
RED	It replaces the red component of the bottom input with the red component of the top input, leaving all other color components unaffected.
BLUE	It replaces the blue component of the bottom input with the blue component of the top input, leaving all other color components unaffected.
GREEN	It replaces the green component of the bottom input with the green component of the top input, leaving all other color components unaffected.
EXCLUSION	It multiplies the color components of the two inputs and doubles the result. The value thus obtained is subtracted from the sum of the color components of the bottom input to get the resulting color component.
COLOR_BURN	It divides the inverse of the bottom input color components by the top input color components and inverts the result.
COLOR_DODGE	It divides the bottom input color components by the inverse of the top input color.
LIGHTEN	It uses the lighter of the color components from the two inputs.
DARKEN	It uses the darker of the color components from the two inputs.
SCREEN	It inverts the color components from both inputs, multiplies them, and inverts the result.
OVERLAY	Depending on the bottom input color, it multiplies or screens the input color components.
HARD_LIGHT	Depending on the top input color, it multiplies or screens the input color components.
SOFT_LIGHT	Depending on the top input color, it darkens or lightens the input color components.
SRC_ATOP	It keeps the bottom input for the nonoverlapping area and the top input for the overlapping area.
SRC_OVER	The top input is drawn over the bottom input. Therefore, the overlapping area shows the top input.

The program in Listing 17-10 creates two ColorInput effects of the same size. Their x and y properties are set in such a way that they overlap. These two effects are used as top and bottom inputs to the Blend effect. A combo box and a slider are provided to select the blending mode and the opacity of the top input. Figure 17-22 shows the window that results from running this code. Run the program and try selecting different blending modes to see the Blend effect in action.

Listing 17-10. Using the Blend Effect

```
// BlendTest.java
// ...find in the book's download area.
```

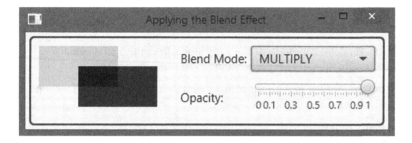

Figure 17-22. The Blend effect

The *Lighting* Effect

The Lighting effect, as the name suggests, simulates a light source shining on a specified node in a scene to give the node a 3D look. A Lighting effect uses a light source, which is an instance of the Light class, to produce the effect. Different types of configurable lights are available. If you do not specify a light source, the effect uses a default light source.

An instance of the Lighting class represents a Lighting effect. The class contains two constructors:

- Lighting()
- Lighting(Light light)

The no-args constructor uses a default light source. The other constructor lets you specify a light source.

Applying a Lighting effect to a node may be a simple or complex task depending on the type of effect you want to achieve. Let's look at a simple example. The following snippet of code applies a Lighting effect to a Text node to give it a 3D look, as shown in Figure 17-23:

```
// Create a Text Node
Text text = new Text("Chatar");
text.setFill(Color.RED);
text.setFont(Font.font(null, FontWeight.BOLD, 72));
HBox.setMargin(text, new Insets(10));

// Set a Lighting effect to the Text node
text.setEffect(new Lighting());
```

Chatar

Figure 17-23. A Text node with a Lighting effect using the default for the light source

In the preceding example, adding the Lighting effect is as simple as creating an object of the Lighting class and setting it as the effect for the Text node. I will discuss some complex Lighting effects later. The Lighting class contains several properties to configure the effect:

- contentInput
- surfaceScale
- bumpInput
- diffuseConstant
- specularConstant
- specularExponent
- light

If you use a chain of effects, the contentInput property specifies the input effect to the Lighting effect. This property is named as input in all other effects discussed earlier. I will not discuss this property further in this section. Please refer to the section "Chaining Effects" for more details on how to use this property.

Customizing the Surface Texture

The surfaceScale and bumpInput properties are used to provide texture to a 2D surface to make it look like a 3D surface. Pixels, based on their opacity, look high or low to give the surface a texture. Transparent pixels appear low, and opaque pixels appear raised.

The surfaceScale property lets you control the surface roughness. Its value ranges from 0.0 to 10.0. The default is 1.5. For a higher surfaceScale, the surface appears rougher, giving it a more 3D look.

You can pass an Effect as an input to the Lighting effect using its bumpInput property. The opacity of the pixels in the bumpInput is used to obtain the height of the pixels of the lighted surface, and then the surfaceScale is applied to increase the roughness. If bumpInput is null, the opacity of the pixels from the node on which the effect is applied is used to generate the roughness of the surface. By default, a Shadow effect with a radius of 10 is used as the bumpInput. You can use an ImageInput, a blur effect, or any other effect as the bumpInput for a Lighting effect.

The program in Listing 17-11 displays a Text node with a Lighting effect. The bumpInput is set to null. It provides a check box to set a GaussianBlur effect as the bumpInput and a slider to adjust the surfaceScale value. Figure 17-24 shows two screenshots: one without a bump input and another with a bump input. Notice the difference in the surface texture.

Listing 17-11. Using the surfaceScale and bumpInput Properties

```
// SurfaceTexture.java
// ...find in the book's download area.
```

Figure 17-24. *The effects of* surfaceScale *and* bumpInput *on a* Lighting *effect on a* Text *node*

Understanding Reflection Types

When light falls on an opaque surface, part of light is absorbed, part is transmitted, and some is reflected. A 3D look is achieved by showing part of the surface brighter and part shadowy. You see the reflected light from the surface. The 3D look varies depending on the light source and the way the node surface reflects the light. The structure of the surface at the microscopic level defines the details of the reflection, such as the intensity and directions. Among several reflection types, two types are worth mentioning at this point: diffuse reflection and specular reflection.

In a *diffuse* reflection, the surface reflects an incident ray of light at many angles. That is, a diffuse reflection scatters a ray of light by reflecting it in all directions. A perfect diffuse reflection reflects light equally in all directions. The surface using a diffuse reflection appears to be equally bright from all directions. This does not mean that the entire diffuse surface is visible. The visibility of an area on a diffuse surface depends on the direction of the light and the orientation of the surface. The brightness of the surface depends on the surface type itself and the intensity of the light. Typically, a rough surface, for example, clothing, paper, or plastered walls, reflects light using a diffuse reflection. Surfaces may appear smooth to the eyes, for example, paper or clothing, but they are rough at the microscopic level, and they reflect light diffusively.

In a *specular* reflection, the surface reflects a ray of light in exactly one direction. That is, there is a single reflected ray for one incident ray. A smooth surface at the microscopic level, for example, mirrors or polished marbles, produces a specular reflection. Some smooth surfaces may not be 100% smooth at the microscopic level, and they may reflect part of the light diffusively as well. Specular reflection produces a brighter surface compared to diffuse reflection. Figure 17-25 depicts the ways light is reflected in diffuse and specular reflections.

Figure 17-25. *Diffuse and specular reflection types*

Three properties of the Lighting class are used to control the size and intensity of the reflection:

- diffuseConstant
- specularConstant
- specularExponent

These properties are of the double type. The diffuseConstant is used for diffuse reflection. The specularConstant and specularExponent are used for specular reflection. The diffuseConstant property specifies a multiplier for the diffuse reflection intensity. Its value ranges from 0.0 to 2.0 with a default of 1.0. A higher value makes the surface brighter. The specularConstant property specifies the fraction of the light to which the specular reflection applies. Its value ranges from 0.0 to 2.0 with a default value of 0.30. A higher value means a bigger-sized specular highlight. The specularExponent specifies the shininess of the surface. A higher value means a more intense reflection and the surface looks shinier. The specularExponent ranges from 0.0 to 40.0 with a default value of 20.0.

Listing 17-12 contains the code for a utility class that binds the properties of the Lighting class to some controls that will be used to control the properties in the examples discussed later.

Listing 17-12. A Utility Class That Creates a Set of Controls Bound to the Properties of a Lighting Instance

```
// LightingUtil.java
// ...find in the book's download area.
```

The program in Listing 17-13 uses the utility class to bind the properties of a Lighting effect to UI controls. It displays a window as shown in Figure 17-26. Change the reflection properties using the sliders to see their effects.

Listing 17-13. Controlling Reflection's Details

```
// ReflectionTypeTest.java
// ...find in the book's download area.
```

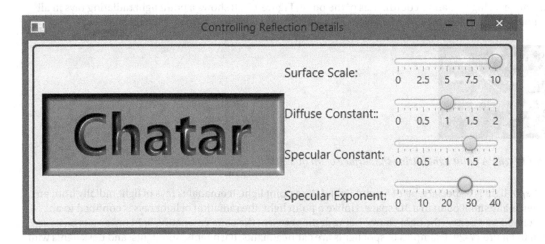

Figure 17-26. *Effects of reflection properties on lighting nodes*

Understanding the Light Source

JavaFX provides three built-in light sources: distant light, point light, and spot light. A *distant* light is also known as a *directional* or *linear* light. A distant light source emanates parallel rays of light in a *specific direction* on the entire surface uniformly. The sun is a perfect example of a distant light source for the lighted surface of an object on the earth. The light source is so distant from the lighted object that the rays are almost parallel. A distant light source lights a surface uniformly, irrespective of its distance from the surface. This does not mean that the entire object is lighted. For example, when you stand in sunlight, not all parts of your body are lighted. However, the lighted part of your body has uniform light. The lighted part of an object depends on the direction distant light source of the light. Figure 17-27 shows a distant light hitting some part of the surface of an object. Notice that the rays of light are seen, not the light source itself, because, for a distant light, only the direction of the light is important, not the distance of the light source from the lighted object.

Figure 17-27. *A distant light hitting the surface of an object*

A *point* light source emanates rays of light in all directions from an infinitesimally small point in a 3D space. Theoretically, the light source has no dimension. It emanates light uniformly in all directions. Therefore, unlike the distant light, the direction of the point light source relative to the lighted object is immaterial. Bare light bulbs, stars (excluding the sun, which serves like a distant light), and candlelight are examples of point light sources. The intensity of a point light hitting a surface decreases with the square of the distance between the surface and the point light source. If a point light is very close to the surface, it creates a hotspot, which is a very bright point on the surface. To avoid hotspots, you need to move the light source a little away from the surface. A point light source is defined at a specific point in a 3D space, for example, using x, y, and z coordinates of the point. Figure 17-28 shows a point light radiating rays in all directions. The point on the object surface closest to the light will be illuminated the most.

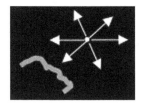

Figure 17-28. *A point light hitting the surface of an object*

A *spot* light is a special type of a point light. Like a point light, it emanates rays of light radially from an infinitesimally small point in a 3D space. Unlike a point light, the radiation of light rays is confined to an area defined by a cone—the light source being at the vertex of the cone emanating light toward its base, as shown in Figure 17-29. Examples of spot lights are car headlights, flashlights, spotlights, and desk lights with lampshades. A spot light is aimed at a point on the surface, which is the point on the surface where the cone axis is located. The cone axis is the line joining the vertex of the cone to the center of the base of the cone. In Figure 17-29, the cone axis is shown with a dashed arrow. The effect of a spot light is defined by the position of the vertex of the cone, the cone angle, and the rotation of the cone. The rotation of the cone determines the point on the surface that is intersected by the cone axis. The angle of the cone controls the area of the lighted area. The intensity of a spot light is highest along the cone axis. You can simulate a distant light using a spot light if you pull the spot light "far" back, so the rays of light reaching the surface are parallel.

Figure 17-29. *A spot light hitting the surface of an object*

A light source is an instance of the abstract Light class. A light has a color, which is specified by using the color property of the Light class. For example, using a red color Light will make a Text node with a white fill look red.

There are three subclasses of the Light class to represent specific types of light source. The subclasses are static inner classes of the Light class:

- Light.Distant
- Light.Point
- Light.Spot

A class diagram for classes representing light sources is shown in Figure 17-30. The Light.Spot class inherits from the Light.Point class. Classes define properties to configure the specific type of light sources.

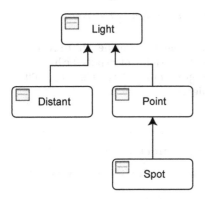

Figure 17-30. *A class diagram for classes representing a light source*

■ **Tip**   When you do not provide a light source for a lighting effect, a distant light is used, which is an instance of the Light.Distant class.

665

Using a Distant Light Source

An instance of the Light.Distant class represents a distant light source. The class contains two properties to specify the direction of the light source:

- azimuth

- elevation

Both properties are of the double type. Their values are specified in degrees. Both properties are used together to position the light source in a 3D space in a specific direction. By default, their values are 45 degrees. They do not have maximum and minimum values. Their values are computed using modulo 360. For example, an azimuth value of 400 is effectively 40 (400 modulo 360 = 40).

The azimuth property specifies the direction angle in the XY plane. A positive value is measured clockwise, and a negative value is measured counterclockwise. A 0 value for the azimuth is located at the 3 o'clock position, 90 at 6 o'clock, 180 at 9 o'clock, 270 at 12 o'clock, and 360 at 3 o'clock. An azimuth of –90 will be located at 12 o'clock. Figure 17-31 shows the location of the distant light in the XY plane for different azimuth values.

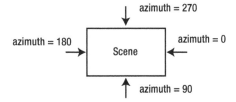

Figure 17-31. *Determining the direction of the distant light in the XY plane using the azimuth value*

The elevation property specifies the direction angle of the light source in the YZ plane. The elevation property values of 0 and 180 make the light source stay on the XY plane. An elevation of 90 puts the light source in front of the scene, and the entire scene is lighted. An elevation greater than 180 and less than 360 puts the light source behind the scene making it appear dark (without light).

The Light.Distant class contains two constructors:

- Light.Distant()

- Light.Distant(double azimuth, double elevation, Color color)

The no-args constructor uses 45.0 degrees for azimuth and elevation and Color.WHITE as the light color. The other constructor lets you specify these properties.

The program in Listing 17-14 shows how to use a Light.Distant light. It displays a window that lets you set the direction for a distant light shining on a rectangle and a Text node. Figure 17-32 shows an example of a text and rectangle with a distant light.

Listing 17-14. Using a Distant Light Source

```
// DistantLightTest.java
// ...find in the book's download area.
```

Figure 17-32. *A distant light lighting a Text node and a rectangle*

Using a Point Light Source

An instance of the Light.Point class represents a point light source. The class contains three properties to specify the position of the light source in space: x, y, and z. The x, y, and z properties are the x, y, and z coordinates of the point where the point light is located in the space. If you set the z property to 0.0, the light source will be in the plane of the scene showing as a very tiny bright point lighting a very small area. As the z value increases, the light source moves away from the scene plane, lighting more area on the scene. A negative value of z will move the light source behind the scene, leaving it with no light, and the scene will look completely dark.

The Light.Point class contains two constructors:

- Light.Point()
- Light.Point(double x, double y, double z, Color color)

The no-args constructor places the point light at (0, 0, 0) and uses a Color.WHITE color for the light. The other constructor lets you specify the location and the color of the light source.

The program in Listing 17-15 shows how to use a Light.Point light. It displays a window with sliders at the bottom to change the location of the point light source. As the point light source moves away from the scene, some area on the scene will be brighter than the other area. Figure 17-33 shows an example of a Text node overlaid on a rectangle being lighted by a point light.

Listing 17-15. Using a Point Light Source

```
// PointLightTest.java
// ...find in the book's download area.
```

Figure 17-33. *A point light lighting a Text node and a rectangle*

Using a Spot Light Source

An instance of the Light.Spot class represents a spot light source. The class inherits from the Light.Point class. The inherited properties (x, y, and z) from the Light.Point class specify the location of the light source, which coincides with the vertex of the cone. The Light.Spot class contains four properties to specify the position of the light source in space:

- pointsAtX
- pointsAtY
- pointsAtZ
- specularExponent

The pointsAtX, pointsAtY, and pointsAtZ properties specify a point in the space to set the direction of the light. A line starting from (x, y, z) and going toward (pointsAtX, pointsAtY, pointsAtZ) is the cone axis, which is also the direction of the light. By default, they are set to 0.0. The specularExponent property defines the focus of the light (the width of the cone), which ranges from 0.0 to 4.0. The default is 1.0. The higher the value for the specularExponent, the narrower the cone is and the more focused light will be on the scene.

The Light.Spot class contains two constructors:

- Light.Spot()
- Light.Spot(double x, double y, double z, double specularExponent, Color color)

The no-args constructor places the light at (0, 0, 0) and uses a Color.WHITE color for the light. Because the default values for pointsAtX, pointsAtY, and pointsAtZ are 0.0, the light does not have a direction. The other constructor lets you specify the location and the color of the light source. The cone axis will pass from the specified (x, y, x) to (0, 0, 0).

The program in Listing 17-16 shows how to use a Light.Spot light. It displays a window that lets you configure the location, direction, and focus of the light using sliders at the bottom. Figure 17-34 shows an example of a Light.Spot light focused almost in the middle of the rectangle.

Listing 17-16. Using a Spot Light Source

```
// SpotLightTest.java
// ...find in the book's download area.
```

Figure 17-34. *A spot light lighting a Text node and a rectangle*

The *PerspectiveTransform* Effect

A PerspectiveTransform effect gives a 2D node a 3D look by mapping the corners to different locations. The straight lines in the original nodes remain straight. However, parallel lines in the original nodes may not necessarily remain parallel.

An instance of the PerspectiveTransform class represents a PerspectiveTransform effect. The class contains eight properties to specify the x and y coordinates of four corners:

- ulx
- uly
- urx
- ury
- lrx
- lry
- llx
- lly

The first letter in the property names (u or l) indicates upper and lower. The second letter in the property names (l or r) indicates left and right. The last letter in the property names (x or y) indicates the x or y coordinate of a corner. For example, urx indicates the x coordinate of the upper-right corner.

■ **Tip** The PerspectiveTransform class also contains an input property to specify the input effect to it in a chain of effects.

The PerspectiveTransform class contains two constructors:

- PerspectiveTransform()
- PerspectiveTransform(double ulx, double uly, double urx, double ury, double lrx, double lry, double llx, double lly)

The no-args constructor creates a PerspectiveTransform object with all new corners at (0, 0). If you set the object as an effect to a node, the node will be reduced to a point, and you will not be able to see the node. The other constructor lets you specify the new coordinates for the four corners of the node.

The program in Listing 17-17 creates two sets of a Text node and a rectangle. It adds two sets to two different groups. It applies a PerspectiveTransform effect on the second group. Both groups are shown in Figure 17-35. The group on the left shows the original nodes; the group on the right has the effect applied to it.

Listing 17-17. Using the PerspectiveTransform Effect

```
// PerspectiveTransformTest.java
// ...find in the book's download area.
```

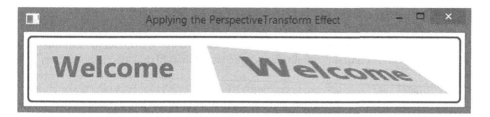

Figure 17-35. *Text and* `Rectangle` *nodes with a* `PerspectiveTransform` *effect*

Summary

An effect is a filter that accepts one or more graphical inputs, applies an algorithm on the inputs, and produces an output. Typically, effects are applied to nodes to create visually appealing user interfaces. Examples of effects are shadow, blur, warp, glow, reflection, blending, and different types of lighting. The JavaFX library provides several effect-related classes. Effect is a conditional feature. Effects applied to nodes will be ignored if it is not available on a platform. The `Node` class contains an `effect` property that specifies the effect applied to the node. By default, it is `null`. An instance of the `Effect` class represents an effect. The `Effect` class is the abstract base for all effect classes. All effect classes are included in the `javafx.scene.effect` package.

Some effects can be chained with other effects. The effects are applied in sequence. The output of the first effect becomes the input for the second effect and so on. Effect classes that allow chaining contain an `input` property to specify the effect that precedes it. If the `input` property is `null`, the effect is applied to the node on which this effect is set. By default, the `input` property is `null`.

A shadowing effect draws a shadow and applies it to an input. JavaFX supports three types of shadowing effects: `DropShadow`, `InnerShadow`, and `Shadow`.

A blurring effect produces a blurred version of an input. JavaFX lets you apply different types of blurring effects, which differ in the algorithms they use to create the effect. Three types of blurring effects are `BoxBlur`, `GaussianBlur`, and `MotionBlur`.

The `Bloom` effect adds glow to the pixels of its input that have a luminosity greater than or equal to a specified limit. Note that not all pixels in a `Bloom` effect are made to glow. An instance of the `Bloom` class represents a `Bloom` effect.

The `Glow` effect makes the bright pixels of the input brighter. An instance of the `Glow` class represents a `Glow` effect.

The `Reflection` effect adds a reflection of the input below the input. An instance of the `Reflection` class represents a `reflection` effect.

Sepia is a reddish-brown color. Sepia toning is performed on black-and-white photographic prints to give them a warmer tone. An instance of the `SepiaTone` class represents a `SepiaTone` effect.

The `DisplacementMap` effect shifts each pixel in the input to produce an output. The name has two parts: Displacement and Map. The first part implies that the effect displaces the pixels in the input. The second part implies that the displacement is based on a map that provides a displacement factor for each pixel in the output. An instance of the `DisplacementMap` class represents a `DisplacementMap`.

The `ColorInput` effect is a simple effect that fills (floods) a rectangular region with a specified paint. Typically, it is used as an input to another effect. An instance of the `ColorInput` class represents the `ColorInput` effect.

The `ImageInput` effect works like the `ColorInput` effect. It passes the given image as an input to another effect. The given image is not modified by this effect. Typically, it is used as an input to another effect, not as an effect directly applied to a node. An instance of the `ImageInput` class represents the `ImageInput` effect.

Blending combines two pixels at the same location from two inputs to produce one composite pixel in the output. The Blend effect takes two input effects and blends the overlapping pixels of the inputs to produce an output. The blending of two inputs is controlled by a blending mode. JavaFX provides 17 predefined blending modes. An instance of the Blend class represents the Blend effect.

The Lighting effect, as the name suggests, simulates a light source shining on a specified node in a scene to give the node a 3D look. A Lighting effect uses a light source, which is an instance of the Light class, to produce the effect.

A PerspectiveTransform effect gives a 2D node a 3D look by mapping the corners to different locations. The straight lines in the original nodes remain straight. However, parallel lines in the original nodes may not necessarily remain parallel. An instance of the PerspectiveTransform class represents a PerspectiveTransform effect.

The next chapter will discuss how to apply different types of transformations to nodes.

CHAPTER 18

■ ■ ■

Understanding Transformations

In this chapter, you will learn:

- What a transformation is
- What are translation, rotation, scale, and shear transformations and how to apply them to nodes
- How to apply multiple transformations to a node

The examples of this chapter lie in the com.jdojo.transform package. In order for them to work correctly, you must add a corresponding line to the module-info.java file:

```
...
opens com.jdojo.transform to javafx.graphics, javafx.base;
...
```

What Is a Transformation?

A transformation is a mapping of points in a coordinate space to points in the same coordinate space, preserving a set of geometric properties. Several types of transformations can be applied to points in a coordinate space. JavaFX supports the following types of transformation:

- Translation
- Rotation
- Shear
- Scale
- Affine

An instance of the abstract Transform class represents a transformation in JavaFX. The Transform class contains common methods and properties used by all types of transformations on nodes. It contains factory methods to create specific types of transformations. Figure 18-1 shows a class diagram for the classes representing different types of transformations. The name of the class matches with the type of transformation the class provides. All classes are in the javafx.scene.transform package.

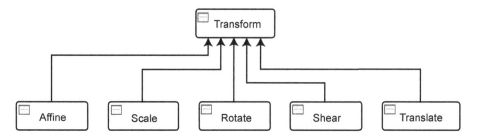

Figure 18-1. *A class diagram for transform-related classes*

An affine transformation is the generalized transformation that preserves the number and uniqueness of points, the straightness of lines, and the properties points exhibit if lying in planes. The parallel lines (and planes) remain parallel after the transformation. It may not preserve the angles between lines or the distances between points. However, the ratios of distances between points on a straight line are preserved. Translation, scale, homothetic transformation, similarity transformation, reflection, rotation, shear, and so on are examples of the affine transformation.

An instance of the Affine class represents an affine transformation. The class is not easy to use for beginners. Its use requires advanced knowledge of mathematics such as the matrix. If you need a specific type of transformation, use the specific subclasses such as Translate, Shear, and so on, rather than using the generalized Affine class. You can also combine multiple individual transformations to create a more complex one. We will not discuss this class in this book.

Using transformations is easy. However, sometimes it might appear confusing because there are multiple ways to create and apply them.

There are two ways to create a Transform instance:

- Use one of the factory methods of the Transform class—for example, the translate() method for creating a Translate object, the rotate() method to create a Rotate object, etc.

- Use the specific class to create a specific type of transform—for example, the Translate class for a translation, the Rotate class for a rotation, etc.

Both of the following Translate objects represent the same translation:

```
double tx = 20.0;
double ty = 10.0;

// Using the factory method in the Transform class
Translate translate1 = Transform.translate(tx, ty);

// Using the Translate class constructor
Translate translate2 = new Translate(tx, ty);
```

There are two ways to apply a transformation to a node:

- Use the specific properties in the Node class. For example, use the translateX, translateY, and translateZ properties of the Node class to apply a translation to a node. Note that you cannot apply a shear transformation this way.

- Use the transforms sequence of a node. The getTransforms() method of the Node class returns an ObservableList<Transform>. Populate this list with all the Transform objects. The Transforms will be applied in sequence. You can apply a shear transformation only using this method.

The two methods of applying Transforms work somewhat differently. We will discuss the differences when we discuss the specific types of transformation. Sometimes, it is possible to use both of the foregoing methods to apply transformations, and in that case, the transformations in the transforms sequence are applied before the transformation set on the properties of the node.

The following snippet of code applies three transformations to a rectangle: shear, scale, and translation:

```
Rectangle rect = new Rectangle(100, 50, Color.LIGHTGRAY);
// Apply transforms using the transforms sequence of the Rectangle
Transform shear = Transform.shear(2.0, 1.2);
Transform scale = Transform.scale(1.1, 1.2);
rect.getTransforms().addAll(shear, scale);
// Apply a translation using the translatex and translateY
// properties of the Node class
rect.setTranslateX(10);
rect.setTranslateY(10);
```

The shear and scale are applied using the transforms sequence. The translation is applied using the translateX and translateY properties of the Node class. The transformations in the transforms sequence, shear and scale, are applied in sequence followed by the translation.

The Translation Transformation

A translation moves every point of a node by a fixed distance in a specified direction relative to its parent coordinate system. It is achieved by shifting the origin of the local coordinate system of the node to a new location. Computing the new locations of points is easy—just add a triplet of numbers to the coordinates of each point in a 3D space. In a 2D space, add a pair of numbers to the coordinates of each point.

Suppose you want to apply translation to a 3D coordinate space by (tx, ty, tz). If a point had coordinates (x, y, z) before the translation, after the translation its coordinates would be $(x + tx, y + ty, z + tz)$.

Figure 18-2 shows an example of a translation transformation. Axes before the transformations are shown in solid lines. Axes after the transformations are shown in dashed lines. Note that the coordinates of the point P remain the same $(4, 3)$ in the translated coordinate spaces. However, the coordinates of the point relative to the original coordinate space change after the transformation. The point in the original coordinate space is shown in a solid black fill color, and in the transformed coordinate space, it is shown without a fill color. The origin of the coordinate system $(0, 0)$ has been shifted to $(3, 2)$. The coordinates of the point P (the shifted point) in the original coordinate space become $(7, 5)$, which is computed as $(4+3, 3+2)$.

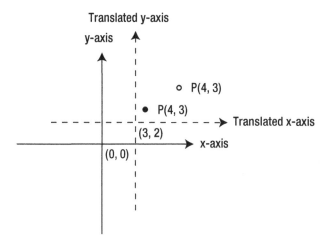

Figure 18-2. *An example of a translation transformation*

An instance of the Translate class represents a translation. It contains three properties:

- x

- y

- z

The properties specify the x, y, and z coordinates of the new origin of the local coordinate system of the node after translation. The default values for the properties are 0.0.

The Translate class provides three constructors:

- Translate()

- Translate(double x, double y)

- Translate(double x, double y, double z)

The no-args constructor creates a Translate object with the default values for the x, y, and z properties, which, in essence, represents no translation. The other two constructors let you specify the translation distance along the three axes. A transformation to a Group is applied to all the nodes in the Group.

Compare the use of the layoutX and layoutY properties of the Node class with the translateX and translateY properties. The layoutX and layoutY properties position the node in its local coordinate system without transforming the local coordinate system, whereas the translateX and translateY properties transform the local coordinate system of the node by shifting the origin. Typically, layoutX and layoutY are used to place a node in a scene, whereas translation is used for moving a node in an animation. If you set both properties for a node, its local coordinate system will be transformed using the translation, and, then, the node will be placed in the new coordinate system using its layoutX and layoutY properties.

The program in Listing 18-1 creates three rectangles. By default, they are placed at (0, 0). It applies a translation to the second and third rectangles. Figure 18-3 shows the rectangles after the translation.

Listing 18-1. Applying Translations to Nodes

```java
// TranslateTest.java
package com.jdojo.transform;

import javafx.application.Application;
import javafx.scene.Scene;
import javafx.scene.layout.Pane;
import javafx.scene.paint.Color;
import javafx.scene.shape.Rectangle;
import javafx.scene.transform.Translate;
import javafx.stage.Stage;

public class TranslateTest extends Application {
    public static void main(String[] args) {
        Application.launch(args);
    }

    @Override
    public void start(Stage stage) {
        Rectangle rect1 =
                new Rectangle(100, 50, Color.LIGHTGRAY);
        rect1.setStroke(Color.BLACK);

        Rectangle rect2 = new Rectangle(100, 50, Color.YELLOW);
        rect2.setStroke(Color.BLACK);

        Rectangle rect3 =
                new Rectangle(100, 50, Color.STEELBLUE);
        rect3.setStroke(Color.BLACK);

        // Apply a translation on rect2 using the transforms
            // sequence
        Translate translate1 = new Translate(50, 10);
        rect2.getTransforms().addAll(translate1);

        // Apply a translation on rect3 using the translateX
        // and translateY properties
        rect3.setTranslateX(180);
        rect3.setTranslateY(20);

        Pane root = new Pane(rect1, rect2, rect3);
        root.setPrefSize(300, 80);
        Scene scene = new Scene(root);
        stage.setScene(scene);
        stage.setTitle(
                "Applying the Translation Transformation");
        stage.show();
    }
}
```

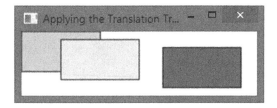

Figure 18-3. *Rectangles with translations*

The Rotation Transformation

In a rotation transformation, the axes are rotated around a pivot point in the coordinate space, and the coordinates of points are mapped to the new axes. Figure 18-4 shows the axes of a coordinate system in a 2D plane rotated by an angle of 30 degrees. The axis of rotation is the z-axis. The origin of the original coordinate system is used as the pivot point of rotation. The original axes are shown in solid lines and the rotated axes in dashed lines. The point P in the original coordinate system is shown in a black fill and in the rotated coordinate system with no fill.

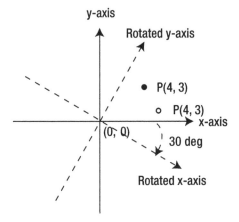

Figure 18-4. *An example of a rotation transformation*

An instance of the Rotate class represents a rotation transformation. It contains five properties to describe the rotation:

- angle
- axis
- pivotX
- pivotY
- pivotZ

The angle property, specifies the angle of rotation in degrees. The default is 0.0 degrees. A positive value for the angle is measured clockwise.

The axis property specifies the axis of rotation at the pivot point. Its value can be one of the constants, X_AXIS, Y_AXIS, and Z_AXIS, defined in the Rotate class. The default axis of rotation is Rotate.Z_AXIS.

The pivotX, pivotY, and pivotZ properties are the x, y, and z coordinates of the pivot point. The default values for the properties are 0.0.

The Rotate class contains several constructors:

- Rotate()

- Rotate(double angle)

- Rotate(double angle, double pivotX, double pivotY)

- Rotate(double angle, double pivotX, double pivotY, double pivotZ)

- Rotate(double angle, double pivotX, double pivotY, double pivotZ, Point3D axis)

- Rotate(double angle, Point3D axis)

The no-args constructor creates an identity rotation, which does not have any effect on the transformed node. The other constructors let you specify the details.

The program in Listing 18-2 creates two rectangles and places them at the same location. The opacity of the second rectangle is set to 0.5, so we can see through it. The coordinate system of the second rectangle is rotated by 30 degrees in the clockwise direction using the origin as the pivot point. Figure 18-5 shows the rotated rectangle.

Listing 18-2. Using a Rotation Transformation

```java
// RotateTest.java
package com.jdojo.transform;

import javafx.application.Application;
import javafx.scene.Scene;
import javafx.scene.layout.Pane;
import javafx.scene.paint.Color;
import javafx.scene.shape.Rectangle;
import javafx.scene.transform.Rotate;
import javafx.stage.Stage;

public class RotateTest extends Application {
        public static void main(String[] args) {
                Application.launch(args);
        }

        @Override
        public void start(Stage stage) {
                Rectangle rect1 =
                        new Rectangle(100, 50, Color.LIGHTGRAY);
                rect1.setStroke(Color.BLACK);

                Rectangle rect2 =
                        new Rectangle(100, 50, Color.LIGHTGRAY);
                rect2.setStroke(Color.BLACK);
                rect2.setOpacity(0.5);
```

```
                    // Apply a rotation on rect2. The rotation angle is
                        // 30 degree clockwise
                    // (0, 0) is the pivot point
                    Rotate rotate = new Rotate(30, 0, 0);
                    rect2.getTransforms().addAll(rotate);

                    Pane root = new Pane(rect1, rect2);
                    root.setPrefSize(300, 80);
                    Scene scene = new Scene(root);
                    stage.setScene(scene);
                    stage.setTitle("Applying the Rotation Transformation");
                    stage.show();
        }
}
```

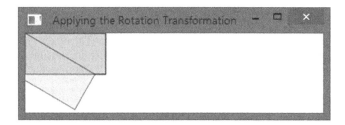

Figure 18-5. *A Rectangle using a rotation transformation*

It is easy to visualize the effect of a rotation when the pivot point is the origin of the local coordinate system of the node, and the upper-left corner of a node is located at the origin as well. Let us consider the following snippet of code that rotates a rectangle as shown in Figure 18-6:

```
Rectangle rect1 = new Rectangle(100, 50, Color.LIGHTGRAY);
rect1.setY(20);
rect1.setStroke(Color.BLACK);
Rectangle rect2 = new Rectangle(100, 50, Color.LIGHTGRAY);
rect2.setY(20);
rect2.setStroke(Color.BLACK);
rect2.setOpacity(0.5);
// Apply a rotation on rect2. The rotation angle is 30 degree anticlockwise
// (100, 0) is the pivot point.
Rotate rotate = new Rotate(-30, 100, 0);
rect2.getTransforms().addAll(rotate);
```

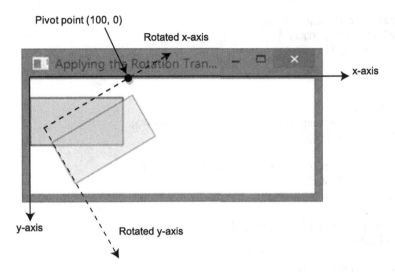

Figure 18-6. *Rotating a Rectangle using a pivot point other than the origin of its local coordinate system*

The coordinates of the upper left of the rectangles are set to (0, 20). A point at (100, 0) is used as the pivot point to rotate the second rectangle. The pivot point is located on the x-axis of the rectangle. The coordinate system of the second rectangle is pinned at (100, 0) and, then, rotated by 30 degrees in the anticlockwise direction. Notice that the second rectangle maintains its location (0, 20) in the rotated coordinate space.

You can also apply a rotation to a node using the rotate and rotationAxis properties of the Node class. The rotate property specifies the angle of rotation in degrees. The rotationAxis property specifies the axis of rotation. The center of the untransformed layout bounds of the node is used as the pivot point.

■ **Tip**   The default pivot point used in a transforms sequence is the origin of the local coordinate system of the node, whereas the rotate property of the Node class uses the center of the untransformed layout bounds of the node as the pivot point.

The program in Listing 18-3 creates two rectangles similar to the ones in Listing 18-2. It uses the rotate property of the Node class to rotate the rectangle by 30 degrees. Figure 18-7 shows the rotated rectangle. Compare the rotated rectangles in Figures 18-5 and 18-7. The former uses the origin of the local coordinate system as the pivot point, and the latter uses the center of the rectangle as the pivot point.

Listing 18-3. Using the rotate Property of the Node Class to Rotate a Rectangle

```java
// RotatePropertyTest.java
package com.jdojo.transform;

import javafx.application.Application;
import javafx.scene.Scene;
import javafx.scene.layout.Pane;
import javafx.scene.paint.Color;
import javafx.scene.shape.Rectangle;
import javafx.stage.Stage;
```

```
public class RotatePropertyTest extends Application {
        public static void main(String[] args) {
                Application.launch(args);
        }

        @Override
        public void start(Stage stage) {
                Rectangle rect1 = new Rectangle(100, 50, Color.LIGHTGRAY);
                rect1.setStroke(Color.BLACK);

                Rectangle rect2 = new Rectangle(100, 50, Color.LIGHTGRAY);
                rect2.setStroke(Color.BLACK);
                rect2.setOpacity(0.5);

                // Use the rotate property of the node class
                rect2.setRotate(30);

                Pane root = new Pane(rect1, rect2);
                root.setPrefSize(300, 80);
                Scene scene = new Scene(root);
                stage.setScene(scene);
                stage.setTitle("Applying the Rotation Transformation");
                stage.show();
        }
}
```

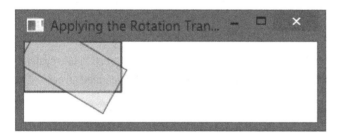

Figure 18-7. *A Rectangle rotated using the rotate property of the Node class*

The Scale Transformation

A scale transformation scales the unit of measurement along axes of a coordinate system by a scale factor. This causes the dimensions of a node to change (stretch or shrink) by the specified scale factors along axes. The dimension along an axis is multiplied by the scale factor along that axis. The transformation is applied at a pivot point whose coordinates remain the same after the transformation.

An instance of the Scale class represents a scale transformation. It contains the following six properties to describe the transformation:

- x
- y

- z
- pivotX
- pivotY
- pivotZ

The x, y, and z properties specify the scale factors along the x-axis, y-axis, and z-axis. They are 1.0 by default.

The pivotX, pivotY, and pivotZ properties are the x, y, and z coordinates of the pivot point. The default values for the properties are 0.0.

The Scale class contains several constructors:

- Scale()
- Scale(double x, double y)
- Scale(double x, double y, double z)
- Scale(double x, double y, double pivotX, double pivotY)
- Scale(double x, double y, double z, double pivotX, double pivotY, double pivotZ)

The no-args constructor creates an identity scale transformation, which does not have any effect on the transformed node. The other constructors let you specify the scale factors and the pivot point.

You can use an object of the Scale class or the scaleX, scaleY, and scaleZ properties of the Node class to apply a scale transformation. By default, the pivot point used by the Scale class is at (0, 0, 0). The properties of the Node class use the center of the node as the pivot point.

The program in Listing 18-4 creates two rectangles. Both are placed at the same location. One of them is scaled and the other not. The opacity of the not scaled rectangle is set to 0.5, so we can see through it. Figure 18-8 shows the rectangles. The scaled rectangle is smaller. The coordinate system of the second rectangle is scaled by 0.5 along the x-axis and 0.50 along the y-axis. The scaleX and scaleY properties are used to apply the transformation, which uses the center of the rectangles as the pivot point making the rectangles shrink, but keeping it at the same location.

Listing 18-4. Using Scale Transformations

```java
// ScaleTest.java
package com.jdojo.transform;

import javafx.application.Application;

import javafx.scene.Scene;
import javafx.scene.layout.Pane;
import javafx.scene.paint.Color;
import javafx.scene.shape.Rectangle;
import javafx.stage.Stage;

public class ScaleTest extends Application {
        public static void main(String[] args) {
                Application.launch(args);
        }
```

```
        @Override
        public void start(Stage stage) {
                Rectangle rect1 =
                        new Rectangle(100, 50, Color.LIGHTGRAY);
                rect1.setStroke(Color.BLACK);
                rect1.setOpacity(0.5);

                Rectangle rect2 =
                        new Rectangle(100, 50, Color.LIGHTGRAY);
                rect2.setStroke(Color.BLACK);

                // Apply a scale on rect2. Center of the Rectangle is
                    // the pivot point.
                rect2.setScaleX(0.5);
                rect2.setScaleY(0.5);

                Pane root = new Pane(rect1, rect2);
                root.setPrefSize(150, 60);
                Scene scene = new Scene(root);
                stage.setScene(scene);
                stage.setTitle("Applying the Scale Transformation");
                stage.show();
        }
}
```

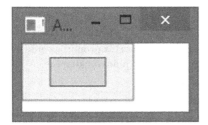

Figure 18-8. *Two Rectangles using scale transformations*

If the pivot point is not the center of the node, the scale transformation may move the node. The program in Listing 18-5 creates two rectangles. Both are placed at the same location. One of them is scaled and the other not. The opacity of the not scaled rectangle is set to 0.5, so we can see through it. Figure 18-9 shows the rectangles. The scaled rectangle is smaller. A Scale object with the transforms sequence is used to apply the transformation, which uses the upper-left corner of the rectangle as the pivot point making the rectangle shrink, but moving it to the left to keep the coordinates of its upper-left corner the same (150, 0) in the transformed coordinate system. The scaled rectangle shrinks by half (scale factor = 0.50) in both directions and moves half the distance to the left.

Listing 18-5. Using Scale Transformations

```
// ScalePivotPointTest.java
package com.jdojo.transform;
import javafx.application.Application;
```

```java
import javafx.scene.Scene;
import javafx.scene.layout.Pane;
import javafx.scene.paint.Color;
import javafx.scene.shape.Rectangle;

import javafx.scene.transform.Scale;
import javafx.stage.Stage;

public class ScalePivotPointTest extends Application {
        public static void main(String[] args) {
                Application.launch(args);
        }

        @Override
        public void start(Stage stage) {
                Rectangle rect1 =
                        new Rectangle(100, 50, Color.LIGHTGRAY);
                rect1.setX(150);
                rect1.setStroke(Color.BLACK);
                rect1.setOpacity(0.5);

                Rectangle rect2 =
                        new Rectangle(100, 50, Color.LIGHTGRAY);
                rect2.setX(150);
                rect2.setStroke(Color.BLACK);

                // Apply a scale on rect2. The origin of the local
                    // coordinate system of rect4 is the pivot point
                Scale scale = new Scale(0.5, 0.5);
                rect2.getTransforms().addAll(scale);

                Pane root = new Pane(rect1, rect2);
                root.setPrefSize(300, 60);
                Scene scene = new Scene(root);
                stage.setScene(scene);
                stage.setTitle("Applying the Scale Transformation");
                stage.show();
        }
}
```

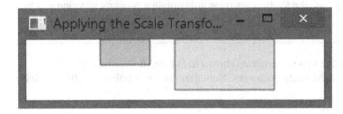

Figure 18-9. *Two Rectangles using scale transformations*

The Shear Transformation

A shear transformation rotates axes of the local coordinate system of the node around a pivot point, so the axes are no longer perpendicular. A rectangular node becomes a parallelogram after the transformation.

An instance of the Shear class represents a shear transformation. It contains four properties to describe the transformation:

- x
- y
- pivotX
- pivotY

The x property specifies a multiplier by which the coordinates of points are shifted along the positive x-axis by a factor of the y coordinate of the point. The default is 0.0.

The y property specifies a multiplier by which the coordinates of points are shifted along the positive y-axis by a factor of the x coordinate of the point. The default is 0.0.

The pivotX and pivotY properties are the x and y coordinates of the pivot point about which the shear occurs. The default values for them are 0.0. The pivot point is not shifted by the shear. By default, the pivot point is the origin of the untransformed coordinate system.

Suppose you have a point (x1, y1) inside a node, and by the shear transformation, the point is shifted to (x2, y2). You can use the following formula to compute (x2, y2):

```
x2 = pivotX + (x1 - pivotX) + x * (y1 - pivotY)
y2 = pivotY + (y1 - pivotY) + y * (x1 - pivotX)
```

All coordinates (x1, y1, x2, and y2) in the previous formula are in the untransformed local coordinate system of the node. Notice that if (x1, y1) is the pivot point, the foregoing formula computes the shifted point (x2, y2), which is the same as (x1, y1). That is, the pivot point is not shifted.

The Shear class contains several constructors:

- Shear()
- Shear(double x, double y)
- Shear(double x, double y, double pivotX, double pivotY)

The no-args constructor creates an identity shear transformation, which does not have any effect on the transformed node. The other constructors let you specify the shear multipliers and the pivot point.

■ **Tip** You can apply a shear transformation to a node using only a Shear object in the transforms sequence. Unlike for other types of transformations, the Node class does not contain a property allowing you to apply shear transformation.

The program in Listing 18-6 applies a Shear to a rectangle as shown in Figure 18-10. The original rectangle is also shown. A multiplier of 0.5 is used along both axes. Note that the pivot point is (0, 0), which is the default.

Listing 18-6. Using the Shear Transformation

```java
// ShearTest.java
package com.jdojo.transform;

import javafx.application.Application;
import javafx.scene.Group;
import javafx.scene.Scene;
import javafx.scene.paint.Color;
import javafx.scene.shape.Rectangle;
import javafx.scene.transform.Shear;
import javafx.stage.Stage;

public class ShearTest extends Application {
        public static void main(String[] args) {
                Application.launch(args);
        }

        @Override
        public void start(Stage stage) {
                Rectangle rect1 =
                        new Rectangle(100, 50, Color.LIGHTGRAY);
                rect1.setStroke(Color.BLACK);

                Rectangle rect2 =
                        new Rectangle(100, 50, Color.LIGHTGRAY);
                rect2.setStroke(Color.BLACK);
                rect2.setOpacity(0.5);

                // Apply a shear on rect2. The x and y multipliers are
                    // 0.5 and (0, 0) is the pivot point.
                Shear shear = new Shear(0.5, 0.5);
                rect2.getTransforms().addAll(shear);

                Group root = new Group(rect1, rect2);
                Scene scene = new Scene(root);
                stage.setScene(scene);
                stage.setTitle("Applying the Shear Transformation");
                stage.show();
        }
}
```

687

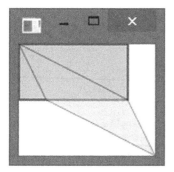

Figure 18-10. *A Rectangle with a shear transformation using (0, 0) as the pivot point*

Let us use a pivot point other than (0, 0) for a Shear transformation. Consider the following snippet of code:

```
Rectangle rect1 = new Rectangle(100, 50, Color.LIGHTGRAY);
rect1.setX(100);
rect1.setStroke(Color.BLACK);
Rectangle rect2 = new Rectangle(100, 50, Color.LIGHTGRAY);
rect2.setX(100);
rect2.setStroke(Color.BLACK);
rect2.setOpacity(0.5);

// Apply a shear on rect2. The x and y multipliers are 0.5 and
// (100, 50) is the pivot point.
Shear shear = new Shear(0.5, 0.5, 100, 50);
rect2.getTransforms().addAll(shear);
```

The code is similar to the one shown in Listing 18-6. The upper-left corners of the rectangles are placed at (100, 0), so we can see the sheared rectangle fully. We have used (100, 50), which is the lower-left corner of the rectangle, as the pivot point. Figure 18-11 shows the transformed rectangle. Notice that the transformation did not shift the pivot point.

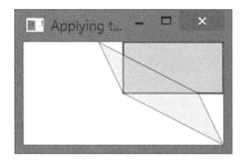

Figure 18-11. *A Rectangle with a shear transformation using (100, 50) as the pivot point*

Let us apply our formula to validate the coordinates of the upper-right corner, which is originally at (200, 0) relative to the untransformed coordinate system of the rectangle:

```
x1 = 200
y1 = 0
pivotX = 100
pivotY = 50
x = 0.5
y = 0.5

x2 = pivotX + (x1 - pivotX) + x * (y1 - pivotY)
   = 100 + (200 - 100) + 0.5 * (0 - 50)
   = 175

y2 = pivotY + (y1 - pivotY) + y * (x1 - pivotX)
   = 50 + (0 -50) + 0.5 * (200 - 100)
   = 50
```

Therefore, (175, 50) is the shifted location of the upper-right corner in the untransformed coordinate system of the rectangle.

Applying Multiple Transformations

You can apply multiple transformations to a node. As mentioned previously, the transformations in the transforms sequence are applied before the transformation set on the properties of the node. When properties of the Node class are used, translation, rotation, and scale are applied in sequence. When the transforms sequence is used, transformations are applied in the order they are stored in the sequence.

The program in Listing 18-7 creates three rectangles and positions them at the same location. It applies multiple transformations to the second and third rectangles in different order. Figure 18-12 shows the result. The first rectangle is shown at its original position, as we did not apply any transformation to it. Notice that two rectangles ended up at different locations. If you change the order of the transformation for the third rectangle as shown next, both rectangles will overlap:

```
rect3.getTransforms().addAll(
    new Translate(100, 0),
    new Rotate(30, 50, 25),
    new Scale(1.2, 1.2, 50, 25));
```

Listing 18-7. Using Multiple Transformations on a Node

```
// MultipleTransformations.java
package com.jdojo.transform;

import javafx.application.Application;
import javafx.scene.Group;
import javafx.scene.Scene;
import javafx.scene.layout.Pane;
import javafx.scene.paint.Color;
import javafx.scene.shape.Rectangle;
import javafx.scene.transform.Rotate;
```

```java
import javafx.scene.transform.Scale;
import javafx.scene.transform.Translate;
import javafx.stage.Stage;

public class MultipleTransformations extends Application {
        public static void main(String[] args) {
                Application.launch(args);
        }

        @Override
        public void start(Stage stage) {
                Rectangle rect1 =
                        new Rectangle(100, 50, Color.LIGHTGRAY);
                rect1.setStroke(Color.BLACK);

                Rectangle rect2 =
                        new Rectangle(100, 50, Color.LIGHTGRAY);
                rect2.setStroke(Color.BLACK);
                rect2.setOpacity(0.5);

                Rectangle rect3 =
                        new Rectangle(100, 50, Color.LIGHTCYAN);
                rect3.setStroke(Color.BLACK);
                rect3.setOpacity(0.5);

                // apply transformations to rect2
                rect2.setTranslateX(100);
                rect2.setTranslateY(0);
                rect2.setRotate(30);
                rect2.setScaleX(1.2);
                rect2.setScaleY(1.2);

                // Apply the same transformation as on rect2, but in a
                    // different order
                rect3.getTransforms().addAll(
                        new Scale(1.2, 1.2, 50, 25),
                  new Rotate(30, 50, 25),
                  new Translate(100, 0));

                Group root = new Group(rect1, rect2, rect3);
                Scene scene = new Scene(root);
                stage.setScene(scene);
                stage.setTitle("Applying Multiple Transformations");
                stage.show();
        }
}
```

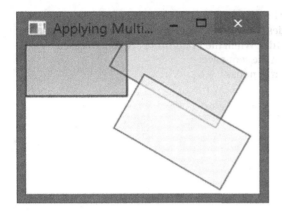

Figure 18-12. *Rectangles with multiple transformations*

Summary

A transformation is a mapping of points in a coordinate space to points in the same coordinate space, preserving a set of geometric properties. Several types of transformations can be applied to points in a coordinate space. JavaFX supports the following types of transformation: translation, rotation, shear, scale, and affine.

An instance of the abstract Transform class represents a transformation in JavaFX. The Transform class contains common methods and properties used by all types of transformations on nodes. It contains factory methods to create specific types of transformations. All transformation classes are in the javafx.scene.transform package.

An affine transformation is the generalized transformation that preserves the number and uniqueness of points, the straightness of lines, and the properties points exhibit if lying on planes. The parallel lines (and planes) remain parallel after the transformation. The affine transformation may not preserve the angles between lines and the distances between points. However, the ratios of distances between points on a straight line are preserved. Translation, scale, homothetic transformation, similarity transformation, reflection, rotation, and shear are examples of the affine transformation. An instance of the Affine class represents an affine transformation.

There are two ways to apply a transformation to a node: using the specific properties in the Node class and using the transforms sequence of a node.

A translation moves every point of a node by a fixed distance in a specified direction relative to its parent coordinate system. It is achieved by shifting the origin of the local coordinate system of the node to a new location. An instance of the Translate class represents a translation.

In a rotation transformation, the axes are rotated around a pivot point in the coordinate space, and the coordinates of points are mapped to the new axes. An instance of the Rotate class represents a rotation transformation.

A scale transformation scales the unit of measurement along axes of a coordinate system by a scale factor. This causes the dimensions of a node to change (stretch or shrink) by the specified scale factors along axes. The dimension along an axis is multiplied by the scale factor along that axis. The transformation is applied at a pivot point whose coordinates remain the same after the transformation. An instance of the Scale class represents a scale transformation.

A shear transformation rotates axes of the local coordinate system of the node around a pivot point, so the axes are no longer perpendicular. A rectangular node becomes a parallelogram after the transformation. An instance of the Shear class represents a shear transformation.

You can apply multiple transformations to a node. The transformations in the `transforms` sequence are applied before the transformation set on the properties of the node. When properties of the Node class are used, translation, rotation, and scale are applied in order. When the `transforms` sequence is used, transformations are applied in the order they are stored in the sequence.

The next chapter will discuss how to apply animation to nodes.

■ ■ ■

CHAPTER 19

Understanding Animation

In this chapter, you will learn:

- What animation is in JavaFX

- About classes in JavaFX that are used in performing animation in JavaFX

- How to perform a timeline animation and how to set up cue points on a timeline animation

- How to control animation such as playing, reversing, pausing, and stopping

- How to perform animation using transitions

- About different types of interpolators and their roles in animation

The examples of this chapter lie in the com.jdojo.animation package. In order for them to work, you must add a corresponding line to the module-info.java file:

```
...
opens com.jdojo.animation to javafx.graphics, javafx.base;
...
```

What Is Animation?

In the real world, *animation* implies some kind of motion, which is generated by displaying images in quick succession. For example, when you watch a movie, you are watching images, which change so quickly that you get an illusion of motion.

In JavaFX, animation is defined as changing the property of a node over time. If the property that changes determines the location of the node, the animation in JavaFX will produce an illusion of motion as found in movies. Not all animations have to involve motion; for example, changing the fill property of a shape over time is an animation in JavaFX that does not involve motion.

To understand how animation is performed, it is important to understand some key concepts:

- Timeline

- Key frame

- Key value

- Interpolator

Animation is performed over a period of time. A *timeline* denotes the progression of time during animation with an associated key frame at a given instant. A *key frame* represents the state of the node being animated at a specific instant on the timeline. A key frame has associated key values. A *key value* represents the value of a property of the node along with an interpolator to be used.

Suppose you want to move a circle in a scene from left to right horizontally in ten seconds. Figure 19-1 shows the circle at some positions. The thick horizontal line represents a timeline. Circles with a solid outline represent the key frames at specific instants on the timeline. The key values associated with key frames are shown at the top line. For example, the value for the translateX property of the circle for the key frame at the fifth second is 500, which is shown as tx=500 in the figure.

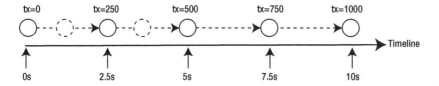

Figure 19-1. *Animating a circle along a horizontal line using a timeline*

The developer provides timelines, key frames, and key values. In this example, there are five key frames. If JavaFX shows only five key frames at the five respective instants, the animation will look jerky. To provide a smooth animation, JavaFX needs to interpolate the position of the circle at any instant on the timeline. That is, JavaFX needs to create intermediate key frames between two consecutive provided key frames. JavaFX does this with the help of an *interpolator*. By default, it uses a *linear interpolator*, which changes the property being animated linearly with time. That is, if the time on the timeline passes x%, the value of the property will be x% between the initial and final target values. Circles with the dashed outline are created by JavaFX using an interpolator.

Understanding Animation Classes

Classes providing animation in JavaFX are in the javafx.animation package, except the Duration class, which is in the javafx.util package. Figure 19-2 shows a class diagram for most of the animation-related classes.

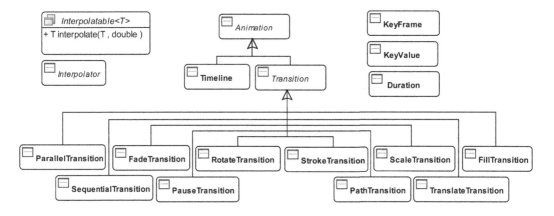

Figure 19-2. *A class diagram for core classes used in animation*

The abstract Animation class represents an Animation. It contains common properties and methods used by all types of animation.

JavaFX supports two types of animations:

- Timeline animations

- Transitions

In a timeline animation, you create a timeline and add key frames to it. JavaFX creates the intermediate key frames using an interpolator. An instance of the Timeline class represents a timeline animation. This type of animation requires a little more code, but it gives you more control.

Several types of animations are commonly performed (moving a node along a path, changing the opacity of a node over time, etc.). These types of animations are known as transitions. They are performed using an internal timeline. An instance of the Transition class represents a transition animation. Several subclasses of the Transition class exist to support specific types of transitions. For example, the FadeTransition class implements a fading effect animation by changing the opacity of a node over time. You create an instance of the Transition class (typically, an instance of one of its subclasses) and specify the initial and final values for the property to be animated and the duration for the animation. JavaFX takes care of creating the timeline and performing the animation. This type of animation is easier to use.

Sometimes, you may want to perform multiple transitions sequentially or simultaneously. The SequentialTransition and ParallelTransition classes let you perform a set of transitions sequentially and simultaneously, respectively.

Understanding Utility Classes

Before discussing the details of JavaFX animation, I will discuss a few utility classes that are used in implementing animations. The following sections will discuss those classes.

Understanding the Duration Class

The Duration class is in the javafx.util package. It represents a duration of time in milliseconds, seconds, minutes, and hours. It is an immutable class. A Duration represents the amount of time for each cycle of an animation. A Duration can represent a positive or negative duration.

You can create a Duration object in three ways:

- Using the constructor

- Using factory methods

- Using the valueOf() method from a duration in String format

The constructor takes the amount of time in milliseconds:

```
Duration tenMillis = new Duration(10);
```

Factory methods create Duration objects for different units of time. They are millis(), seconds(), minutes(), and hours():

```
Duration tenMillis = Duration.millis(10);
Duration tenSeconds = Duration.seconds(10);
Duration tenMinutes = Duration.minutes(10);
Duration tenHours = Duration.hours(10);
```

The valueOf() static method takes a String argument containing the duration of time and returns a Duration object. The format of the argument is "number[ms|s|m|h]", where number is the amount of time, and ms, s, m, and h denote milliseconds, seconds, minutes, and hours, respectively.

```
Duration tenMillis = Duration.valueOf("10.0ms");
Duration tenMillisNeg = Duration.valueOf("-10.0ms");
```

You can also represent a duration of an unknown amount of time and an indefinite time using the UNKNOWN and INDEFINITE constants of the Duration class, respectively. You can use the isIndefinite() and isUnknown() methods to check if a duration represents an indefinite or unknown amount of time. The class declares two more constants, ONE and ZERO, that represent durations of one millisecond and zero (no time), respectively.

The Duration class provides several methods to manipulate durations (adding a duration to another duration, dividing and multiplying a duration by a number, comparing two durations, etc.). Listing 19-1 shows how to use the Duration class.

Listing 19-1. Using the Duration Class

```java
// DurationTest.java
package com.jdojo.animation;

import javafx.util.Duration;

public class DurationTest {
    public static void main(String[] args) {
        Duration d1 = Duration.seconds(30.0);
        Duration d2 = Duration.minutes(1.5);
        Duration d3 = Duration.valueOf("35.25ms");
        System.out.println("d1  = " + d1);
        System.out.println("d2  = " + d2);
        System.out.println("d3  = " + d3);

        System.out.println("d1.toMillis() = " + d1.toMillis());
        System.out.println("d1.toSeconds() = " + d1.toSeconds());
        System.out.println("d1.toMinutes() = " + d1.toMinutes());
        System.out.println("d1.toHours() = " + d1.toHours());

        System.out.println("Negation of d1  = " + d1.negate());
        System.out.println("d1 + d2 = " + d1.add(d2));
        System.out.println("d1 / 2.0 = " + d1.divide(2.0));

        Duration inf = Duration.millis(1.0/0.0);
        Duration unknown = Duration.millis(0.0/0.0);
        System.out.println("inf.isIndefinite() = " +
                inf.isIndefinite());
        System.out.println("unknown.isUnknown() = " +
                unknown.isUnknown());
    }
}
```

```
d1  = 30000.0 ms
d2  = 90000.0 ms
d3  = 35.25 ms
d1.toMillis() = 30000.0
d1.toSeconds() = 30.0
d1.toMinutes() = 0.5
d1.toHours() = 0.008333333333333333
Negation of d1  = -30000.0 ms
d1 + d2 = 120000.0 ms
d1 / 2.0 = 15000.0 ms
inf.isIndefinite() = true
unknown.isUnknown() = true
```

Understanding the KeyValue Class

An instance of the KeyValue class represents a key value that is interpolated for a particular interval during animation. It encapsulates three things:

- A target

- An end value for the target

- An interpolator

The target is a WritableValue, which qualifies all JavaFX properties to be a target. The end value is the value for the target at the end of the interval. The interpolator is used to compute the intermediate key frames.

A key frame contains one or more key values, and it defines a specific point on a timeline. Figure 19-3 shows an interval on a timeline. The interval is defined by two instants: *instant1* and *instant2*. Both instants have an associated key frame; each key frame contains a key value. An animation may progress forward or backward on the timeline. When an interval starts, the end value of the target is taken from the key value of the end key frame of the interval, and its interpolator is used to compute the intermediate key frames. Suppose, in the figure, the animation is progressing in the forward direction and instant1 occurs before instant2. From instant1 to instant2, the interpolator of the key-value2 will be used to compute the key frames for the interval. If the animation is progressing in the backward direction, the interpolator of the key-value1 will be used to compute the intermediate key frames from instant2 to instant1.

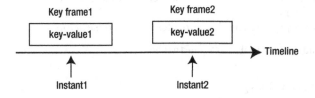

Figure 19-3. *Key frames at two instants on a timeline*

The KeyValue class is immutable. It provides two constructors:

- KeyValue(WritableValue<T> target, T endValue)

- KeyValue(WritableValue<T> target, T endValue, Interpolator interpolator)

The Interpolator.LINEAR is used as the default interpolator that interpolates the animated property linearly with time. I will discuss different types of interpolators later.

The following snippet of code creates a Text object and two KeyValue objects. The translateX property is the target. 0 and 100 are the end values for the target. The default interpolator is used:

```
Text msg = new Text("JavaFX animation is cool!");
KeyValue initKeyValue = new KeyValue(msg.translateXProperty(), 0.0);
KeyValue endKeyValue = new KeyValue(msg.translateXProperty(), 100.0);
```

The following snippet of code is similar to the one shown earlier. It uses the Interpolator.EASE_BOTH interpolator, which slows down the animation in the start and toward the end:

```
Text msg = new Text("JavaFX animation is cool!");
KeyValue initKeyValue = new KeyValue(msg.translateXProperty(), 0.0,
    Interpolator.EASE_BOTH);
KeyValue endKeyValue = new KeyValue(msg.translateXProperty(), 100.0,
    Interpolator.EASE_BOTH);
```

Understanding the KeyFrame Class

A key frame defines the target state of a node at a specified point on the timeline. The target state is defined by the key values associated with the key frame.

A key frame encapsulates four things:

- An instant on the timeline
- A set of KeyValues
- A name
- An ActionEvent handler

The instant on the timeline with which the key frame is associated is defined by a Duration, which is an offset of the key frame on the timeline.

The set of KeyValues defines the end value of the target for the key frame.

A key frame may optionally have a name that can be used as a cue point to jump to the instant defined by it during an animation. The getCuePoints() method of the Animation class returns a Map of cue points on the Timeline.

Optionally, you can attach an ActionEvent handler to a KeyFrame. The ActionEvent handler is called when the time for the key frame arrives during animation.

An instance of the KeyFrame class represents a key frame. The class provides several constructors:

- KeyFrame(Duration time, EventHandler<ActionEvent> onFinished,
  KeyValue... values)

- KeyFrame(Duration time, KeyValue... values)

- KeyFrame(Duration time, String name, EventHandler<ActionEvent>
  onFinished, Collection<KeyValue> values)

- KeyFrame(Duration time, String name, EventHandler<ActionEvent>
  onFinished, KeyValue... values)

- KeyFrame(Duration time, String name, KeyValue... values)

The following snippet of code creates two instances of KeyFrame that specify the translateX property of a Text node at zero seconds and three seconds on a timeline:

```
Text msg = new Text("JavaFX animation is cool!");
KeyValue initKeyValue = new KeyValue(msg.translateXProperty(), 0.0);
KeyValue endKeyValue = new KeyValue(msg.translateXProperty(), 100.0);

KeyFrame initFrame = new KeyFrame(Duration.ZERO, initKeyValue);
KeyFrame endFrame = new KeyFrame(Duration.seconds(3), endKeyValue);
```

Understanding the Timeline Animation

A timeline animation is used for animating any properties of a node. An instance of the Timeline class represents a timeline animation. Using a timeline animation involves the following steps:

- Construct key frames.
- Create a Timeline object with key frames.
- Set the animation properties.
- Use the play() method to run the animation.

You can add key frames to a Timeline at the time of creating it or after. The Timeline instance keeps all key frames in an ObservableList<KeyFrame> object. The getKeyFrames() method returns the list. You can modify the list of key frames at any time. If the timeline animation is already running, you need to stop and restart it to pick up the modified list of key frames.

The Timeline class contains several constructors:

- Timeline()
- Timeline(double targetFramerate)
- Timeline(double targetFramerate, KeyFrame... keyFrames)
- Timeline(KeyFrame... keyFrames)

The no-args constructor creates a Timeline with no key frames with animation running at the optimum rate. Other constructors let you specify the target frame rate for the animation, which is the number of frames per second, and the key frames.

Note that the order in which the key frames are added to a Timeline is not important. Timeline will order them based on their time offset.

The program in Listing 19-2 starts a timeline animation that scrolls a text horizontally from right to left across the scene forever. Figure 19-4 shows a screenshot of the animation.

Listing 19-2. Scrolling Text Using a Timeline Animation

```
// ScrollingText.java
// ...find in the book's download area.
```

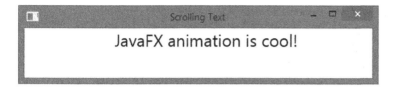

Figure 19-4. *Scrolling text using a timeline animation*

The logic to perform the animation is in the start() method. The method starts with creating a Text object, a Pane with the Text object, and setting up a scene for the stage. After showing the stage, it sets up an animation.

It gets the width of the scene and the Text object:

```
double sceneWidth = scene.getWidth();
double msgWidth = msg.getLayoutBounds().getWidth();
```

Two key frames are created: one for time = 0 seconds and one for time = 3 seconds. The animation uses the translateX property of the Text object to change its horizontal position to make it scroll. At zero seconds, the Text is positioned at the scene width, so it is invisible. At three seconds, it is placed to the left of the scene at a distance equal to its length, so again it is invisible:

```
KeyValue initKeyValue = new KeyValue(msg.translateXProperty(), sceneWidth);
KeyFrame initFrame = new KeyFrame(Duration.ZERO, initKeyValue);

KeyValue endKeyValue = new KeyValue(msg.translateXProperty(), -1.0 * msgWidth);
KeyFrame endFrame = new KeyFrame(Duration.seconds(3), endKeyValue);
```

A Timeline object is created with two key frames:

```
Timeline timeline = new Timeline(initFrame, endFrame);
```

By default, the animation will run only one time. That is, the Text will scroll from right to left once, and the animation will stop. You can set the cycle count for an animation, which is the number of times the animation needs to run. You run the animation forever by setting the cycle count to Timeline.INDEFINITE:

```
timeline.setCycleCount(Timeline.INDEFINITE);
```

Finally, the animation is started by calling the play() method:

```
timeline.play();
```

Our example has a flaw. The scrolling of the text does not update its initial horizontal position when the width of the scene changes. You can rectify this problem by updating the initial key frame whenever the scene width changes. Append the following statement to the start() method of Listing 19-2. It adds a ChangeListener for the scene width that updates key frames and restarts the animation:

```
scene.widthProperty().addListener( (prop, oldValue , newValue) -> {
        KeyValue kv = new KeyValue(msg.translateXProperty(),
            scene.getWidth());
        KeyFrame kf = new KeyFrame(Duration.ZERO, kv);
        timeline.stop();
```

```
        timeline.getKeyFrames().clear();
        timeline.getKeyFrames().addAll(kf, endFrame);
        timeline.play();
});
```

It is possible to create a Timeline animation with only one key frame. The key frame is treated as the last key frame. The Timeline synthesizes an initial key frame (for time = 0 seconds) using the current values for the WritableValue being animated. To see the effect, let us replace the statement

```
Timeline timeline = new Timeline(initFrame, endFrame);
```

in Listing 19-2 with the following:

```
Timeline timeline = new Timeline(endFrame);
```

The Timeline will create an initial key frame with the current value of the translateX property of the Text object, which is 0.0. This time, the Text scrolls differently. The scrolling starts by placing the Text at 0.0 and scrolling it to the left, so it goes beyond the scene.

Controlling an Animation

The Animation class contains properties and methods that can be used to control animation in various ways. The following sections will explain those properties and methods and how to use them to control animation.

Playing an Animation

The Animation class contains four methods to play an animation:

- play()
- playFrom(Duration time)
- playFrom(String cuePoint)
- playFromStart()

The play() method plays an animation from its current position. If the animation was never started or stopped, it will play from the beginning. If the animation was paused, it will play from the position where it was paused. You can use the jumpTo(Duration time) and jumpTo(String cuePoint) methods to set the current position of the animation to a specific duration or a cue point, before calling the play() method. Calling the play() method is asynchronous. The animation may not start immediately. Calling the play() method while animation is running has no effect.

The playFrom() method plays an animation from the specified duration or the specified cue point. Calling this method is equivalent to setting the current position using the jumpTo() method and then calling the play() method.

The playFromStart() method plays the animation from the beginning (duration = 0).

Delaying the Start of an Animation

You can specify a delay in starting the animation using the delay property. The value is specified in Duration. By default, it is zero milliseconds:

```
Timeline timeline = ...

// Delay the start of the animation by 2 seconds
timeline.setDelay(Duration.seconds(2));

// Play the animation
timeline.play();
```

Stopping an Animation

Use the stop() method to stop a running animation. The method has no effect if the animation is not running. The animation may not stop immediately when the method is called as the method executes asynchronously. The method resets the current position to the beginning. That is, calling play() after stop() will play the animation from the beginning:

```
Timeline timeline = ...
...
timeline.play();
...
timeline.stop();
```

Pausing an Animation

Use the pause() method to pause an animation. Calling this method when animation is not running has no effect. This method executes asynchronously. Calling the play() method when the animation is paused plays it from the current position. If you want to play the animation from the start, call the playFromStart() method.

Knowing the State of an Animation

An animation can be one of the following three states:

- Running
- Paused
- Stopped

The three states are represented by RUNNING, STOPPED, and PAUSED constants of the Animation.Status enum. You do not change the state of an animation directly. It is changed by calling one of the methods of the Animation class. The class contains a read-only status property that can be used to know the state of the animation at any time:

```
Timeline timeline = ...
...
Animation.Status status = timeline.getStatus();
switch(status) {
        case RUNNING:
                System.out.println("Running");
                break;
        case STOPPED:
                System.out.println("Stopped");
                break;
        case PAUSED:
                System.out.println("Paused");
                break;
}
```

Looping an Animation

An animation can cycle multiple times, even indefinitely. The cycleCount property specifies the number of cycles in an animation, which defaults to one. If you want to run the animation in an infinite loop, specify Animation.INDEFINITE as the cycleCount. The cycleCount must be set to a value greater than zero. If the cycleCount is changed while the animation is running, the animation must be stopped and restarted to pick up the new value:

```
Timeline timeline1 = ...
Timeline1.setCycleCount(Timeline.INDEFINITE); // Run the animation forever

Timeline timeline2 = ...
Timeline2.setCycleCount(2); // Run the animation for two cycles
```

Auto Reversing an Animation

By default, an animation runs only in the forward direction. For example, our scrolling text animation scrolled the text from right to left in one cycle. In the next cycle, the scrolling occurs again from right to left.

Using the autoReverse property, you can define whether the animation is performed in the reverse direction for alternating cycles. By default, it is set to false. Set it to true to reverse the direction of the animation:

```
Timeline timeline = ...
timeline.setAutoReverse(true); // Reverse direction on alternating cycles
```

If you change the autoReverse, you need to stop and restart the animation for the new value to take effect.

Attaching an onFinished Action

You can execute an `ActionEvent` handler when an animation finishes. Stopping the animation or terminating the application while the animation is running will not execute the handler. You can specify the handler in the `onFinished` property of the `Animation` class. The following snippet of code sets the `onFinished` property to an `ActionEvent` handler that prints a message on the standard output:

```
Timeline timeline = ...
timeline.setOnFinished(e -> System.out.print("Animation finished."));
```

Note that an animation with an `Animation.INDEFINITE` cycle count will not finish, and attaching such an action to the animation will never execute.

Knowing the Duration of an Animation

An animation involves two types of durations:

- Duration to play one cycle of the animation

- Duration to play all cycles of the animation

These durations are not set directly. They are set using other properties of the animation (cycle count, key frames, etc.).

The duration for one cycle is set using key frames. The key frame with the maximum duration determines the duration for one cycle when the animation is played at the rate 1.0. The read-only `cycleDuration` property of the `Animation` class reports the duration for one cycle.

The total duration for an animation is reported by the read-only `totalDuration` property. It is equal to `cycleCount * cycleDuration`. If the `cycleCount` is set to `Animation.INDEFINITE`, the `totalDuration` is reported as `Duration.INDEFINITE`.

Note that the actual duration for an animation depends on its play rate represented by the `rate` property. Because the play rate can be changed while animation is running, there is no easy way to compute the actual duration of an animation.

Adjusting the Speed of an Animation

The `rate` property of the `Animation` class specifies the direction and the speed for the animation. The sign of its value indicates the direction. The magnitude of the value indicates the speed. A positive value indicates the play in the forward direction. A negative value indicates the play in the backward direction. A value of 1.0 is considered the normal rate of play, a value of 2.0 double the normal rate, 0.50 half the normal rate, and so on. A rate of 0.0 stops the play.

It is possible to invert the `rate` of a running animation. In that case, the animation is played in the reverse direction from the current position for the duration that has already elapsed. Note that you cannot start an animation using a negative `rate`. An animation with a negative `rate` will not start. You can change the `rate` to be negative only when the animation has played for a while.

```
Timeline timeline = ...

// Play the animation at double the normal rate
Timeline.setRate(2.0);
...
```

```
timeline.play();
...
// Invert the rate of the play
timeline.setRate(-1.0 * timeline.getRate());
```

The read-only currentRate property indicates the current rate (the direction and speed) at which the animation is playing. The values for the rate and currentRate properties may not be equal. The rate property indicates the rate at which the animation is expected to play when it runs, whereas the currentRate indicates the rate at which the animation is being played. When the animation is stopped or paused, the currentRate value is 0.0. If the animation reverses its direction automatically, the currentRate will report a different direction during reversal; for example, if the rate is 1.0, the currentRate reports 1.0 for the forward play cycle and –1.0 for the reverse play cycle.

Understanding Cue Points

You can set up cue points on a timeline. Cue points are named instants on the timeline. An animation can jump to a cue point using the jumpTo(String cuePoint) method. An animation maintains an Observable Map<String,Duration> of cue points. The key in the map is the name of the cue points, and the values are the corresponding duration on the timeline. Use the getCuePoints() method to get the reference of the cue points map.

There are two ways to add cue points to a timeline:

- Giving a name to the KeyFrame you add to a timeline that adds a cue point in the cue point map

- Adding name-duration pairs to the map returned by the getCuePoints() method of the Animation class

---

■ **Tip** Every animation has two predefined cue points: "start" and "end." They are set at the start and end of the animation. The two cue points do not appear in the map returned by the getCuePoints() method.

The following snippet of code creates a KeyFrame with a name "midway." When it is added to a timeline, a cue point named "midway" will be added to the timeline automatically. You can jump to this KeyFrame using jumpTo("midway").

```
// Create a KeyFrame with name "midway"
KeyValue midKeyValue = ...
KeyFrame midFrame = new KeyFrame(Duration.seconds(5), "midway", midKeyValue);
```

The following snippet of code adds two cue points directly to the cue point map of a timeline:

```
Timeline timeline = ...
timeline.getCuePoints().put("3 seconds", Duration.seconds(3));
timeline.getCuePoints().put("7 seconds", Duration.seconds(7));
```

The program in Listing 19-3 shows how to add and use cue points on a timeline. It adds a KeyFrame with a "midway" name, which automatically becomes a cue point. It adds two cue points, "3 seconds" and "7 seconds," directly to the cue point map. The list of available cue points is shown in a ListView on the left side of the screen. A Text object scrolls with a cycle duration of ten seconds. The program displays a window as shown in Figure 19-5. Select a cue point from the list, and the animation will start playing from that point.

Listing 19-3. Using Cue Points in Animation

```
// CuePointTest.java
// ...find in the book's download area.
```

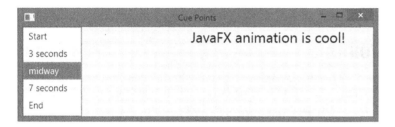

Figure 19-5. *Scrolling text with the list of cue points*

Understanding Transitions

In the previous sections, you saw animations using a timeline that involved setting up key frames on the timeline. Using timeline animation is not easy in all cases. Consider moving a node in a circular path. Creating key frames and setting up a timeline to move the node on the circular path are not easy. JavaFX contains a number of classes (known as *transitions*) that let you animate nodes using predefined properties.

All transition classes inherit from the Transition class, which, in turn, inherits from the Animation class. All methods and properties in the Animation class are also available for use in creating transitions. The transition classes take care of creating the key frames and setting up the timeline. You need to specify the node, duration for the animation, and end values that are interpolated. Special transition classes are available to combine multiple animations that may run sequentially or in parallel.

The Transition class contains an interpolator property that specifies the interpolator to be used during animation. By default, it uses Interpolator.EASE_BOTH, which starts the animation slowly, accelerates it, and slows it down toward the end.

Understanding the Fade Transition

An instance of the FadeTransition class represents a fade-in or fade-out effect for a node by gradually increasing or decreasing the opacity of the node over the specified duration. The class defines the following properties to specify the animation:

- duration

- node

- fromValue

- toValue

- byValue

The duration property specifies the duration for one cycle of the animation.

The node property specifies the node whose opacity property is changed.

The fromValue property specifies the initial value for the opacity. If it is not specified, the current opacity of the node is used.

The toValue property specifies the opacity end value. The opacity of the node is updated between the initial value and the toValue for one cycle of the animation.

The byValue property lets you specify the opacity end value differently using the formula

```
opacity_end_value = opacity_initial_value + byValue
```

The byValue lets you set the opacity end value by incrementing or decrementing the initial value by an offset. If both toValue and byValue are specified, the toValue is used.

Suppose you want to set the initial and end opacity of a node between 1.0 and 0.5 in an animation. You can achieve it by setting the fromValue and toValue to 1.0 and 0.50 or by setting fromValue and byValue to 1.0 and –0.50.

The valid opacity value for a node is between 0.0 and 1.0. It is possible to set FadeTransition properties to exceed the range. The transition takes care of clamping the actual value in the range.

The following snippet of code sets up a fade-out animation for a Rectangle by changing its opacity from 1.0 to 0.20 in two seconds:

```
Rectangle rect = new Rectangle(200, 50, Color.RED);
FadeTransition fadeInOut = new FadeTransition(Duration.seconds(2), rect);
fadeInOut.setFromValue(1.0);
fadeInOut.setToValue(.20);
fadeInOut.play();
```

The program in Listing 19-4 creates a fade-out and fade-in effect in an infinite loop for a Rectangle.

Listing 19-4. Creating a Fading Effect Using the FadeTransition Class

```
// FadeTest.java

package com.jdojo.animation;

import javafx.animation.FadeTransition;
import javafx.application.Application;
import javafx.scene.Scene;
import javafx.scene.layout.HBox;
import javafx.scene.paint.Color;
import javafx.scene.shape.Rectangle;
import javafx.stage.Stage;
import javafx.util.Duration;

public class FadeTest extends Application {
        public static void main(String[] args) {
                Application.launch(args);
        }

        @Override
```

```
public void start(Stage stage) {
        Rectangle rect = new Rectangle(200, 50, Color.RED);
        HBox root = new HBox(rect);
        Scene scene = new Scene(root);
        stage.setScene(scene);
        stage.setTitle("Fade-in and Fade-out");
        stage.show();

        // Set up a fade-in and fade-out animation for the
            // rectangle
        FadeTransition fadeInOut =
                new FadeTransition(Duration.seconds(2), rect);
        fadeInOut.setFromValue(1.0);
        fadeInOut.setToValue(.20);
        fadeInOut.setCycleCount(FadeTransition.INDEFINITE);
        fadeInOut.setAutoReverse(true);
        fadeInOut.play();
    }
}
```

Understanding the Fill Transition

An instance of the FillTransition class represents a fill transition for a shape by gradually transitioning the fill property of the shape between the specified range and duration. The class defines the following properties to specify the animation:

- duration
- shape
- fromValue
- toValue

The duration property specifies the duration for one cycle of the animation.

The shape property specifies the Shape whose fill property is changed.

The fromValue property specifies the initial fill color. If it is not specified, the current fill of the shape is used.

The toValue property specifies the fill end value.

The fill of the shape is updated between the initial value and the toValue for one cycle of the animation. The fill property in the Shape class is defined as a Paint. However, the fromValue and toValue are of the type Color. That is, the fill transition works for two Colors, not two Paints.

The following snippet of code sets up a fill transition for a Rectangle by changing its fill from blue violet to azure in two seconds:

```
FillTransition fillTransition = new FillTransition(Duration.seconds(2), rect);
fillTransition.setFromValue(Color.BLUEVIOLET);
fillTransition.setToValue(Color.AZURE);
fillTransition.play();
```

The program in Listing 19-5 creates a fill transition to change the fill color of a Rectangle from blue violet to azure in two seconds in an infinite loop.

Listing 19-5. Creating a Fill Transition Using the FillTransition Class

```
// FillTest.java
// ...find in the book's download area.
```

Understanding the Stroke Transition

An instance of the StrokeTransition class represents a stroke transition for a shape by gradually transitioning the stroke property of the shape between the specified range and duration. The stroke transition works the same as the fill transition, except that it interpolates the stroke property of the shape rather than the fill property. The StrokeTransition class contains the same properties as the FillTransition class. Please refer to the section "Understanding the Fill Transition" for more details. The following snippet of code starts animating the stroke of a Rectangle in an infinite loop. The stroke changes from red to blue in a cycle duration of two seconds:

```
Rectangle rect = new Rectangle(200, 50, Color.WHITE);
StrokeTransition strokeTransition =
    new StrokeTransition(Duration.seconds(2), rect);
strokeTransition.setFromValue(Color.RED);
strokeTransition.setToValue(Color.BLUE);
strokeTransition.setCycleCount(StrokeTransition.INDEFINITE);
strokeTransition.setAutoReverse(true);
strokeTransition.play();
```

Understanding the Translate Transition

An instance of the TranslateTransition class represents a translate transition for a node by gradually changing the translateX, translateY, and translateZ properties of the node over the specified duration. The class defines the following properties to specify the animation:

- duration
- node
- fromX
- fromY
- fromZ
- toX
- toY
- toZ
- byX
- byY
- byZ

The duration property specifies the duration for one cycle of the animation.

The node property specifies the node whose translateX, translateY, and translateZ properties are changed.

The initial location of the node is defined by the (fromX, fromY, fromZ) value. If it is not specified, the current (translateX, translateY, translateZ) value of the node is used as the initial location.

The (toX, toY, toZ) value specifies the end location.

The (byX, byY, byZ) value lets you specify the end location using the following formula:

```
translateX_end_value = translateX_initial_value + byX
translateY_end_value = translateY_initial_value + byY
translateZ_end_value = translateZ_initial_value + byZ
```

If both (toX, toY, toZ) and (byX, byY, byZ) values are specified, the former is used.

The program in Listing 19-6 creates a translate transition in an infinite loop for a Text object by scrolling it across the width of the scene. The program in Listing 19-2 created the same animation using a Timeline object with one difference. They use different interpolators. By default, timeline-based animations use the Interpolator.LINEAR interpolator, whereas transition-based animation uses the Interpolator.EASE_BOTH interpolator. When you run the program in Listing 19-6, the text starts scrolling slow in the beginning and end, whereas in Listing 19-2, the text scrolls with a uniform speed all the time.

Listing 19-6. Creating a Translate Transition Using the TranslateTransition Class

```
// TranslateTest.java
// ...find in the book's download area.
```

Understanding the Rotate Transition

An instance of the RotateTransition class represents a rotation transition for a node by gradually changing its rotate property over the specified duration. The rotation is performed around the center of the node along the specified axis. The class defines the following properties to specify the animation:

- duration
- node
- axis
- fromAngle
- toAngle
- byAngle

The duration property specifies the duration for one cycle of the animation.

The node property specifies the node whose rotate property is changed.

The axis property specifies the axis of rotation. If it is unspecified, the value for the rotationAxis property, which defaults to Rotate.Z_AXIS, for the node is used. The possible values are Rotate.X_AXIS, Rotate.Y_AXIS, and Rotate.Z_AXIS.

The initial angle for the rotation is specified by the fromAngle property. If it is unspecified, the value for the rotate property of the node is used as the initial angle.

The toAngle specifies the end rotation angle.

The byAngle lets you specify the end rotation angle using the following formula:

```
rotation_end_value = rotation_initial_value + byAngle
```

If both toAngle and byAngle values are specified, the former is used. All angles are specified in degrees. Zero degrees correspond to the 3 o'clock position. Positive values for angles are measured clockwise.

The program in Listing 19-7 creates a rotate transition in an infinite loop for a Rectangle. It rotates the Rectangle in clockwise and counterclockwise directions in alternate cycles.

Listing 19-7. Creating a Rotate Transition Using the RotateTransition Class

```
// RotateTest.java
// ...find in the book's download area.
```

Understanding the Scale Transition

An instance of the ScaleTransition class represents a scale transition for a node by gradually changing its scaleX, scaleY, and scaleZ properties over the specified duration. The class defines the following properties to specify the animation:

- duration
- node
- fromX
- fromY
- fromZ
- toX
- toY
- toZ
- byX
- byY
- byZ

The duration property specifies the duration for one cycle of the animation.

The node property specifies the node whose scaleX, scaleY, and scaleZ properties are changed.

The initial scale of the node is defined by the (fromX, fromY, fromZ) value. If it is not specified, the current (scaleX, scaleY, scaleZ) value of the node is used as the initial scale.

The (toX, toY, toZ) value specifies the end scale.

The (byX, byY, byZ) value lets you specify the end scale using the following formula:

```
scaleX_end_value = scaleX_initial_value + byX
scaleY_end_value = scaleY_initial_value + byY
scaleZ_end_value = scaleZ_initial_value + byZ
```

If both (toX, toY, toZ) and (byX, byY, byZ) values are specified, the former is used.

The program in Listing 19-8 creates a scale transition in an infinite loop for a Rectangle by changing its width and height between 100% and 20% of their original values in two seconds.

Listing 19-8. Creating a Scale Transition Using the ScaleTransition Class

```
// ScaleTest.java
// ...find in the book's download area.
```

Understanding the Path Transition

An instance of the PathTransition class represents a path transition for a node by gradually changing its translateX and translateY properties to move it along a path over the specified duration. The path is defined by the outline of a Shape. The class defines the following properties to specify the animation:

- duration
- node
- path
- orientation

The duration property specifies the duration for one cycle of the animation.

The node property specifies the node whose rotate property is changed.

The path property defines the path along which the node is moved. It is a Shape. You can use an Arc, a Circle, a Rectangle, an Ellipse, a Path, a SVGPath, and so on as the path.

The moving node may maintain the same upright position, or it may be rotated to keep it perpendicular to the tangent of the path at any point along the path. The orientation property specifies the upright position of the node along the path. Its value is one of the constants (NONE and ORTHOGONAL_TO_TANGENT) of the PathTransition.OrientationType enum. The default is NONE, which maintains the same upright position. The ORTHOGONAL_TO_TANGENT value keeps the node perpendicular to the tangent of the path at any point. Figure 19-6 shows the positions of a Rectangle moving along a Circle using a PathTransition. Notice the way the Rectangle is rotated along the path when the ORTHOGONAL_TO_TANGENT orientation is used.

NONE   ORTHOGONAL_TO_TANGENT

Figure 19-6. *Effect of using the orientation property of the PathTransition class*

You can specify the duration, path, and node for the path transition using the properties of the PathTransition class or in the constructors. The class contains the following constructors:

- PathTransition()
- PathTransition(Duration duration, Shape path)
- PathTransition(Duration duration, Shape path, Node node)

The program in Listing 19-9 creates a path transition in an infinite loop for a Rectangle. It moves the Rectangle along a circular path defined by the outline of a Circle.

Listing 19-9. Creating a Path Transition Using the PathTransition Class

```
// PathTest.java
// ...find in the book's download area.
```

Understanding the Pause Transition

An instance of the PauseTransition class represents a pause transition. It causes a delay of the specified duration. Its use is not obvious. It is not used alone. Typically, it is used in a sequential transition to insert a pause between two transitions. It defines a duration property to specify the duration of the delay.

A pause transition is also useful if you want to execute an ActionEvent handler after a specified duration when a transition is finished. You can achieve this by setting its onFinished property, which is defined in the Animation class.

```
// Create a pause transition of 400 milliseconds that is the default duration
PauseTransition pt1 = new PauseTransition();

// Change the duration to 10 seconds
pt1.setDuration(Duration.seconds(10));

// Create a pause transition of 5 seconds
PauseTransition pt2 = new PauseTransition(Duration.seconds(5));
```

If you change the duration of a running pause transition, you need to stop and restart the transition to pick up the new duration. You will have an example when I discuss the sequential transition.

Understanding the Sequential Transition

An instance of the SequentialTransition class represents a sequential transition. It executes a list of animations in sequential order. The list of animations may contain timeline-based animations, transition-based animations, or both.

The SequentialTransition class contains a node property that is used as the node for animations in the list if the animation does not specify a node. If all animations specify a node, this property is not used.

A SequentialTransition maintains the animations in an ObservableList<Animation>. The getChildren() method returns the reference of the list.

The following snippet of code creates a fade transition, a pause transition, and a path transition. Three transitions are added to a sequential transition. When the sequential transition is played, it will play the fade transition, pause transition, and the path transition in sequence:

```
FadeTransition fadeTransition = ...
PauseTransition pauseTransition = ...
PathTransition pathTransition = ...

SequentialTransition st = new SequentialTransition();
st.getChildren().addAll(fadeTransition, pauseTransition, pathTransition);
st.play();
```

■ **Tip** The SequentialTransition class contains constructors that let you specify the list of animations and node.

The program in Listing 19-10 creates a scale transition, a fill transition, a pause transition, and a path transition, which are added to a sequential transition. The sequential transition runs in an infinite loop. When the program runs

- It scales up the rectangle to double its size, and then down to the original size.

- It changes the fill color of the rectangle from red to blue and then back to red.

- It pauses for 200 milliseconds and then prints a message on the standard output.

- It moves the rectangle along the outline of a circle.

- The foregoing sequence of animations is repeated indefinitely.

Listing 19-10. Creating a Sequential Transition Using the SequentialTransition Class

```
// SequentialTest.java
// ...find in the book's download area.
```

Understanding the Parallel Transition

An instance of the ParallelTransition class represents a parallel transition. It executes a list of animations simultaneously. The list of animations may contain timeline-based animations, transition-based animations, or both.

The ParallelTransition class contains a node property that is used as the node for animations in the list if the animation does not specify a node. If all animations specify a node, this property is not used.

A ParallelTransition maintains the animations in an ObservableList<Animation>. The getChildren() method returns the reference of the list.

The following snippet of code creates a fade transition and a path transition. The transitions are added to a parallel transition. When the sequential transition is played, it will apply the fading effect and move the node at the same time:

```
FadeTransition fadeTransition = ...
PathTransition pathTransition = ...

ParallelTransition pt = new ParallelTransition();
pt.getChildren().addAll(fadeTransition, pathTransition);
pt.play();
```

■ **Tip** The ParallelTransition class contains constructors that let you specify the list of animations and node.

The program in Listing 19-11 creates a fade transition and a rotate transition. It adds them to a parallel transition. When the program is run, the rectangle rotates and fades in/out at the same time.

Listing 19-11. Creating a Parallel Transition Using the ParallelTransition Class

```
// ParallelTest.java
// ...find in the book's download area.
```

Understanding Interpolators

An interpolator is an instance of the abstract Interpolator class. An interpolator plays an important role in an animation. Its job is to compute the key values for the intermediate key frames during animation. Implementing a custom interpolator is easy. You need to subclass the Interpolator class and override its curve() method. The curve() method is passed the time elapsed for the current interval. The time is normalized between 0.0 and 1.0. The start and end of the interval have the value of 0.0 and 1.0, respectively. The value passed to the method would be 0.50 when half of the interval time has elapsed. The return value of the method indicates the fraction of change in the animated property.

The following interpolator is known as a linear interpolator whose curve() method returns the passed in argument value:

```
Interpolator linearInterpolator = new Interpolator() {
        @Override
        protected double curve(double timeFraction) {
                return timeFraction;
        }
};
```

The linear interpolator mandates that the percentage of change in the animated property is the same as the progression of the time for the interval.

Once you have a custom interpolator, you can use it in constructing key values for key frames in a timeline-based animation. For a transition-based animation, you can use it as the interpolator property of the transition classes.

The animation API calls the interpolate() method of the Interpolator. If the animated property is an instance of Number, it returns

```
startValue + (endValue - startValue) * curve(timeFraction)
```

Otherwise, if the animated property is an instance of the Interpolatable, it delegates the interpolation work to the interpolate() method of the Interpolatable. Otherwise, the interpolator defaults to a discrete interpolator by returning 1.0 when the time fraction is 1.0, and 0.0 otherwise.

JavaFX provides some standard interpolators that are commonly used in animations. They are available as constants in the Interpolator class or as its static methods:

- Linear interpolator
- Discrete interpolator
- Ease-in interpolator
- Ease-out interpolator
- Ease-both interpolator
- Spline interpolator
- Tangent interpolator

Understanding the Linear Interpolator

The Interpolator.LINEAR constant represents a linear interpolator. It interpolates the value of the animated property of a node linearly with time. The percentage change in the property for an interval is the same as the percentage of the time passed.

Understanding the Discrete Interpolator

The Interpolator.DISCRETE constant represents a discrete interpolator. A discrete interpolator jumps from one key frame to the next, providing no intermediate key frame. The curve() method of the interpolator returns 1.0 when the time fraction is 1.0, and 0.0 otherwise. That is, the animated property value stays at its initial value for the entire duration of the interval. It jumps to the end value at the end of the interval. The program in Listing 19-12 uses discrete interpolators for all key frames. When you run the program, it moves text jumping from a key frame to another. Compare this example with the scrolling text example, which used a linear interpolator. The scrolling text example moved the text smoothly, whereas this example created a jerk in the movement.

Listing 19-12. Using a Discrete Interpolator to Animate Hopping Text

```
// HoppingText.java
// ...find in the book's download area.
```

Understanding the Ease-In Interpolator

The Interpolator.EASE_IN constant represents an ease-in interpolator. It starts the animation slowly for the first 20% of the time interval and accelerates afterward.

Understanding the Ease-Out Interpolator

The Interpolator.EASE_OUT constant represents an ease-out interpolator. It plays animation at a constant speed up to 80% of the time interval and slows down afterward.

Understanding the Ease-Both Interpolator

The Interpolator.EASE_BOTH constant represents an ease-both interpolator. Its plays the animation slower in the first 20% and the last 20% of the time interval and maintains a constant speed otherwise.

Understanding the Spline Interpolator

The Interpolator.SPLINE(double x1, double y1, double x2, double y2) static method returns a spline interpolator. It uses a cubic spline shape to compute the speed of the animation at any point in the interval. The parameters (x1, y1) and (x2, y2) define the control points of the cubic spline shape with (0, 0) and (1, 1) as implicit anchor points. The values of the parameters are between 0.0 and 1.0.

The slope at a given point on the cubic spline shape defines the acceleration at that point. A slope approaching the horizontal line indicates deceleration, whereas a slope approaching the vertical line indicates acceleration. For example, using (0, 0, 1, 1) as the parameters to the SPLINE method creates an interpolator with a constant speed, whereas the parameters (0.5, 0, 0.5, 1.0) will create an interpolator that accelerates in the first half and decelerates in the second half. Please refer to www.w3.org/TR/SMIL/smil-animation.html#animationNS-OverviewSpline for more details.

Understanding the Tangent Interpolator

The Interpolator.TANGENT static method returns a tangent interpolator, which defines the behavior of an animation before and after a key frame. All other interpolators interpolate data between two key frames. If you specify a tangent interpolator for a key frame, it is used to interpolate data before and after the key frame. The animation curve is defined in terms of a tangent, which is known as in-tangent, at a specified duration before the key frame and a tangent, which is called an out-tangent, at a specified duration after the key frame. This interpolator is used only in timeline-based animations as it affects two intervals.

The TANGENT static method is overloaded:

- Interpolator TANGENT(Duration t1, double v1, Duration t2, double v2)

- Interpolator TANGENT(Duration t, double v)

In the first version, the parameters t1 and t2 are the duration before and after the key frame, respectively. The parameters v1 and v2 are the in-tangent and out-tangent values. That is, v1 is the tangent value at duration t1, and v2 is the tangent value at duration t2. The second version specifies the same value for both pairs.

Summary

In JavaFX, animation is defined as changing the property of a node over time. If the property that changes determines the location of the node, the animation in JavaFX will produce an illusion of motion. Not all animations have to involve motion; for example, changing the fill property of a Shape over time is an animation in JavaFX that does not involve motion.

Animation is performed over a period of time. A *timeline* denotes the progression of time during animation with an associated key frame at a given instant. A *key frame* represents the state of the node being animated at a specific instant on the timeline. A key frame has associated key values. A *key value* represents the value of a property of the node along with an interpolator to be used.

A timeline animation is used for animating any properties of a node. An instance of the Timeline class represents a timeline animation. Using a timeline animation involves the following steps: constructing key frames, creating a Timeline object with key frames, setting the animation properties, and using the play() method to run the animation. You can add key frames to a Timeline at the time of creating it or after. The Timeline instance keeps all key frames in an ObservableList<KeyFrame> object. The getKeyFrames() method returns the list. You can modify the list of key frames at any time. If the timeline animation is already running, you need to stop and restart it to pick up the modified list of key frames.

The Animation class contains several properties and methods to control animation such as playing, reversing, pausing, and stopping.

You can set up cue points on a timeline. Cue points are named instants on the timeline. An animation can jump to a cue point using the jumpTo(String cuePoint) method.

Using timeline animation is not easy in all cases. JavaFX contains a number of classes (known as *transitions*) that let you animate nodes using predefined properties. All transition classes inherit from the Transition class, which, in turn, inherits from the Animation class. The transition classes take care of creating the key frames and setting up the timeline. You need to specify the node, duration for the animation, and end values that are interpolated. Special transition classes are available to combine multiple animations that may run sequentially or in parallel. The `Transition` class contains an `interpolator` property that specifies the interpolator to be used during animation. By default, it uses `Interpolator.EASE_BOTH`, which starts the animation slowly, accelerates it, and slows it down toward the end.

An interpolator is an instance of the abstract `Interpolator` class. Its job is to compute the key values for the intermediate key frames during animation. JavaFX provides several built-in interpolators such as linear, discrete, ease-in, and ease-out. You can also implement a custom interpolator easily. You need to subclass the `Interpolator` class and override its `curve()` method. The `curve()` method is passed the time elapsed for the current interval. The time is normalized between 0.0 and 1.0. The return value of the method indicates the fraction of change in the animated property.

The next chapter will discuss how to incorporate different types of charts in a JavaFX application.

CHAPTER 20

■ ■ ■

Understanding Charts

In this chapter, you will learn:

- What a chart is
- What the Chart API is in JavaFX
- How to create different types of charts using the Chart API
- How to style charts with CSS

The examples of this chapter lie in the com.jdojo.chart package. In order for them to work, you must add a corresponding line to the module-info.java file:

```
...
opens com.jdojo.chart to javafx.graphics, javafx.base;
...
```

What Is a Chart?

A chart is a graphical representation of data. Charts provide an easier way to analyze large volume of data visually. Typically, they are used for monitoring and reporting purposes. Different types of charts exist. They differ in the way they represent the data. Not all types of charts are suitable for analyzing all types of data. For example, a line chart is suitable for understanding the comparative trend in data, whereas a bar chart is suitable for comparing data in different categories.

JavaFX supports charts, which can be integrated in a Java application by writing few lines of code. It contains a comprehensive, extensible Chart API that provides built-in support for several types of charts.

Understanding the Chart API

The Chart API consists of a number of predefined classes in the javafx.scene.chart package. Figure 20-1 shows a class diagram for classes representing different types of charts.

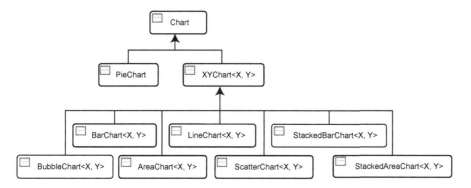

Figure 20-1. *A class diagram for the classes representing charts in JavaFX*

The abstract Chart is the base class for all charts. It inherits the Node class. Charts can be added to a scene graph. They can also be styled with CSS as any other nodes. I will discuss styling charts in the sections that discuss specific types of charts. The Chart class contains properties and methods common to all types of charts.

JavaFX divides charts into two categories:

- Charts having no axis

- Charts having an x-axis and a y-axis

The PieChart class falls into the first category. It has no axis, and it is used to draw a pie chart.

The XYChart class falls into the second category. It is the abstract base class for all charts having two axes. Its subclasses, for example, LineChart, BarChart, etc., represent specific types of charts.

Every chart in JavaFX has three parts:

- A title

- A legend

- Content (or data)

Different types of charts define their data differently. The Chart class contains the following properties that are common to all types of charts:

- title

- titleSide

- legend

- legendSide

- legendVisible

- animated

The title property specifies the title for a chart. The titleSide property specifies the location of the title. By default, the title is placed above the chart content. Its value is one of the constants of the Side enum: TOP (default), RIGHT, BOTTOM, and LEFT.

Typically, a chart uses different types of symbols to represent data in different categories. A legend lists symbols with their descriptions. The legend property is a Node, and it specifies the legend for the chart. By default, a legend is placed below the chart content. The legendSide property specifies the location of the legend, which is one of the constants of the Side enum: TOP, RIGHT, BOTTOM (default), and LEFT. The legendVisible property specifies whether the legend is visible. By default, it is visible.

The animated property specifies whether the change in the content of the chart is shown with some type of animation. By default, it is true.

Styling Charts with CSS

You can style all types of charts. The Chart class defines properties common to all types of charts. The default CSS style-class name for a chart is *chart*. You can specify the legendSide, legendVisible, and titleSide properties for all charts in a CSS as shown:

```
.chart {
        -fx-legend-side: top;
        -fx-legend-visible: true;
        -fx-title-side: bottom;
}
```

Every chart defines two substructures:

- chart-title
- chart-content

The chart-title is a Label, and the chart-content is a Pane. The following styles set the background color for all charts to yellow and the title font to Arial 16px bold:

```
.chart-content {
        -fx-background-color: yellow;
}

.chart-title {
        -fx-font-family: "Arial";
        -fx-font-size: 16px;
        -fx-font-weight: bold;
}
```

The default style-class name for legends is *chart-legend*. The following style sets the legend background color to light gray:

```
.chart-legend {
        -fx-background-color: lightgray;
}
```

Every legend has two substructures:

- chart-legend-item
- chart-legend-item-symbol

The `chart-legend-item` is a `Label`, and it represents the text in the legend. The `chart-legend-item-symbol` is a `Node`, and it represents the symbol next to the label, which is a circle by default. The following style sets the font size for the labels in legends to 10px and the legend symbols to an arrow:

```
.chart-legend-item {
        -fx-font-size: 16px;
}

.chart-legend-item-symbol {
        -fx-shape: "M0 -3.5 v7 l 4 -3.5z";
}
```

■ **Note**   Many examples in this chapter use external resources such as CSS files. You will need to make sure the `ResourceUtil` class points to the `resources` directory (part of the sources bundle provided with the book). Download the sources from `www.apress.com/source-code`.

Data Used in Chart Examples

I will discuss different types of charts shortly. Charts will use data from Table 20-1, which has the actual and estimated population of some countries in the world. The data has been taken from the report published by the United Nations at `www.un.org`. The population values have been rounded.

Table 20-1. *Current and Estimated Populations (in Millions) of Some Countries in the World*

	1950	2000	2050	2100	2150	2200	2250	2300
China	555	1275	1395	1182	1149	1201	1247	1285
India	358	1017	1531	1458	1308	1304	1342	1372
Brazil	54	172	233	212	202	208	216	223
UK	50	59	66	64	66	69	71	73
USA	158	285	409	437	453	470	483	493

Understanding the PieChart

A pie chart consists of a circle divided into sectors of different central angles. Typically, a pie is circular. The sectors are also known as *pie pieces* or *pie slices*. Each sector in the circle represents a quantity of some kind. The central angle of the area of a sector is proportional to the quantity it represents. Figure 20-2 shows a pie chart that displays the population of five countries in the year 2000.

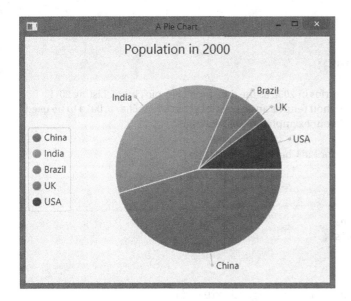

Figure 20-2. *A pie chart showing the population of five countries in 2000*

An instance of the PieChart class represents a pie chart. The class contains two constructors:

- PieChart()
- PieChart(ObservableList<PieChart.Data> data)

The no-args constructor creates a pie chart with no content. You can add the content later using its data property. The second constructor creates a pie chart with the specified data as its content.

```
// Create an empty pie chart
PieChart chart = new PieChart();
```

A slice in a pie chart is specified as an instance of the PieChart.Data class. A slice has a name (or a label) and a pie value represented by the name and pieValue properties of the PieChart.Data class, respectively. The following statement creates a slice for a pie chart. The slice name is "China," and the pie value is 1275:

```
PieChart.Data chinaSlice = new PieChart.Data("China", 1275);
```

The content of a pie chart (all slices) is specified in an ObservableList<PieChart.Data>. The following snippet of code creates an ObservableList<PieChart.Data> and adds three pie slices to it:

```
ObservableList<PieChart.Data> chartData = FXCollections.observableArrayList();
chartData.add(new PieChart.Data("China", 1275));
chartData.add(new PieChart.Data("India", 1017));
chartData.add(new PieChart.Data("Brazil", 172));
```

Now, you can use the second constructor to create a pie chart by specifying the chart content:

```
// Create a pie chart with content
PieChart charts = new PieChart(chartData);
```

You will use populations of different countries in 2050 as the data for all our pie charts. Listing 20-1 contains a utility class. Its getChartData() method returns an ObservableList of PieChart.Data to be used as data for a pie chart. You will use this class in our examples in this section.

Listing 20-1. A Utility Class to Generate Data for Pie Charts

```
// PieChartUtil.java
package com.jdojo.chart;

import javafx.collections.FXCollections;
import javafx.collections.ObservableList;
import javafx.scene.chart.PieChart;

public class PieChartUtil {
        public static ObservableList<PieChart.Data> getChartData() {
                ObservableList<PieChart.Data> data =
                        FXCollections. observableArrayList();
                data.add(new PieChart.Data("China", 1275));
                data.add(new PieChart.Data("India", 1017));
                data.add(new PieChart.Data("Brazil", 172));
                data.add(new PieChart.Data("UK", 59));
                data.add(new PieChart.Data("USA", 285));
                return data;
        }
}
```

The PieChart class contains several properties:

- data

- startAngle

- clockwise

- labelsVisible

- labelLineLength

The data property specifies the content for the chart in an ObservableList<PieChart.Data>.

The startAngle property specifies the angle in degrees to start the first pie slice. By default, it is zero degrees, which corresponds to a three o'clock position. A positive startAngle is measured anticlockwise. For example, a 90-degree startAngle will start at the 12 o'clock position.

The clockwise property specifies whether the slices are placed clockwise starting at the startAngle. By default, it is true.

The labelsVisible property specifies whether the labels for slices are visible. Labels for slices are displayed close to the slice, and they are placed outside the slices. The label for a slice is specified using the name property of the PieChart.Data class. In Figure 20-2, "China," "India," "Brazil," etc., are labels for slices.

Labels and slices are connected through straight lines. The labelLineLength property specifies the length of those lines. Its default value is 20.0 pixels.

The program in Listing 20-2 uses a pie chart to display the population for five countries in 2000. The program creates an empty pie chart and sets its title. The legend is placed on the left side. Later, it sets the data for the chart. The data is generated in the getChartData() method, which returns an ObservableList<PieChart.Data> containing the name of the countries as the labels for pie slices and their populations as pie values. The program displays a window as shown in Figure 20-2.

Listing 20-2. Using the PieChart Class to Create a Pie Chart

```java
// PieChartTest.java
package com.jdojo.chart;

import javafx.application.Application;
import javafx.collections.ObservableList;
import javafx.geometry.Side;
import javafx.scene.Scene;
import javafx.scene.chart.PieChart;
import javafx.scene.layout.StackPane;
import javafx.stage.Stage;

public class PieChartTest extends Application {
        public static void main(String[] args) {
                Application.launch(args);
        }

        @Override
        public void start(Stage stage) {
                PieChart chart = new PieChart();
                chart.setTitle("Population in 2000");

                // Place the legend on the left side
                chart.setLegendSide(Side.LEFT);

                // Set the data for the chart
                ObservableList<PieChart.Data> chartData =
                        PieChartUtil.getChartData();
                chart.setData(chartData);

                StackPane root = new StackPane(chart);
                Scene scene = new Scene(root);

                stage.setScene(scene);
                stage.setTitle("A Pie Chart");
                stage.show();
        }
}
```

Customizing Pie Slices

Each pie slice data is represented by a Node. The reference to the Node can be obtained using the getNode() method of the PieChart.Data class. The Node is created when the slices are added to the pie chart. Therefore, you must call the getNode() method on the PieChart.Data representing the slice after adding it to the chart. Otherwise, it returns null. The program in Listing 20-3 customizes all pie slices of a pie chart to add a tool tip to them. The tool tip shows the slice name, pie value, and percent pie value. The addSliceTooltip() method contains the logic to accessing the slice Nodes and adding the tool tips. You can customize pie slices to animate them, let the user drag them out from the pie using the mouse, etc. See Figure 20-3.

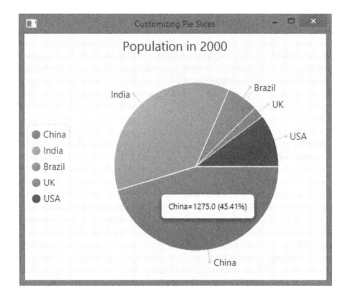

Figure 20-3. *A pie slice showing a tool tip with its pie value and percentage of the total pie*

Listing 20-3. Adding Tool Tips to Pie Slices

```
// PieSliceTest.java
// ...find in the book's download area.
```

Styling the PieChart with CSS

All properties, except the data property, defined in the PieChart class, can be styled using CSS as shown in the following:

```
.chart {
        -fx-clockwise: false;
        -fx-pie-label-visible: true;
        -fx-label-line-length: 10;
        -fx-start-angle: 90;
}
```

Four style classes are added to each pie slice added to a pie chart:

- `chart-pie`
- `data<i>`
- `default-color<j>`
- `negative`

The `<i>` in the style-class name `data<i>` is the slice index. The first slice has the class `data0`, the second `data1`, the third `data2`, etc.

The `<j>` in the style-class name `default-color<j>` is the color index of the series. In a pie chart, you can think of each slice as a series. The default CSS (Modena.css) defines eight series colors. If your pie slice has more than eight slices, the slice color will be repeated. The concept of series in a chart will be more evident when I discuss two-axis charts in the next section.

The *negative* style class is added only when the data for the slice is negative.

Define a style for a *chart-pie* style-class name if you want that style to apply to all pie slices. The following style will set a white border with 2px of background insets for all pie slices. It will show a wider gap between two slices as you have set 2px insets:

```
.chart-pie {
        -fx-border-color: white;
        -fx-background-insets: 2;
}
```

You can define colors for pie slices using the following styles. It defines colors for only five slices. Slices beyond the sixth one will use default colors:

```
.chart-pie.default-color0 {-fx-pie-color: red;}
.chart-pie.default-color1 {-fx-pie-color: green;}
.chart-pie.default-color2 {-fx-pie-color: blue;}
.chart-pie.default-color3 {-fx-pie-color: yellow;}
.chart-pie.default-color4 {-fx-pie-color: tan;}
```

Using More Than Eight Series Colors

It is quite possible that you will have more than eight series (slices in a pie chart) in a chart, and you do not want to repeat the colors for the series. The technique is discussed for a pie chart. However, it can be used for a two-axis chart as well.

Suppose you want to use a pie that will display populations of ten countries. If you use the code for this pie chart, the colors for the ninth and tenth slices will be the same as the colors for the first and second slices, respectively. First, you need to define the colors for the ninth and tenth slices as shown in Listing 20-4.

Listing 20-4. Additional Series Colors

```
/* additional_series_colors.css */
.chart-pie.default-color8 {
        -fx-pie-color: gold;
}
```

```
.chart-pie.default-color9 {
        -fx-pie-color: khaki;
}
```

The pie slices and the legend symbols will be assigned style-class names such as default-color0, default-color2... default-color7. You need to identify the nodes for the slices and legend symbols associated with data items with an index greater than seven and replace their default-color<j> style-class name with the new ones. For example, for the ninth and tenth slices, the style-class names are default-color0 and default-color1 as the color series number is assigned as (dataIndex % 8). You will replace them with default-color9 and default-color10.

The program in Listing 20-5 shows how to change the colors for the slices and legend symbols. It adds ten slices to a pie chart. The setSeriesColorStyles() method replaces the style-class names for the slice nodes for the ninth and tenth slices and for their associated legend symbols. Figure 20-4 shows the pie chart. Notice the colors for "Germany" and "Indonesia" are gold and khaki as set in the CSS. Comment the last statement in the start() method, which is a call to the setSeriesColorStyles(), and you will find that the colors for "Germany" and "Indonesia" will be the same as the colors for "China" and "India."

Listing 20-5. A Pie Chart Using Color Series Up to Index 10

```
// PieChartExtraColor.java
// ...find in the book's download area.
```

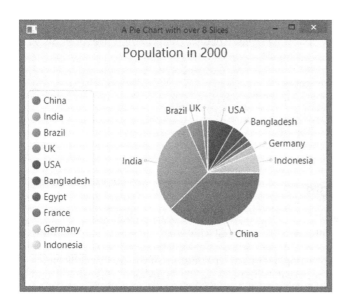

Figure 20-4. A pie chart using over eight slice colors

Using Background Images for Pie Slices

You can also use a background image in a pie slice. The following style defines the background image for the first pie slice:

```
.chart-pie.data0 {
        -fx-background-image: url("china_flag.jpg");
}
```

Listing 20-6 contains the content of a CSS file named pie_slice.css. It defines styles that specify the background images used for pie slices, the preferred size of the legend symbols, and the length of the line joining the pie slices and their labels.

Listing 20-6. A CSS for Customizing Pie Slices

```
// pie_slice.css
/* Set a background image for pie slices */
.chart-pie.data0 {-fx-background-image: url("china_flag.jpg");}
.chart-pie.data1 {-fx-background-image: url("india_flag.jpg");}
.chart-pie.data2 {-fx-background-image: url("brazil_flag.jpg");}
.chart-pie.data3 {-fx-background-image: url("uk_flag.jpg");}
.chart-pie.data4 {-fx-background-image: url("usa_flag.jpg");}

/* Set the preferred size for legend symbols */
.chart-legend-item-symbol {
        -fx-pref-width: 100;
        -fx-pref-height: 30;
}

.chart {
        -fx-label-line-length: 10;
}
```

The program in Listing 20-7 creates a pie chart. It uses the same data as you have been using in our previous examples. The difference is that it sets a CSS defined in a *pie_slice.css* file:

```
// Set a CSS for the scene
scene.getStylesheets().addAll("resources/css/pie_slice.css");
```

The resulting window is shown in Figure 20-5. Notice that slices and legend symbols show the flags of the countries. It is important to keep in mind that you have matched the index of the chart data and the index in the CSS file to match countries and their flags.

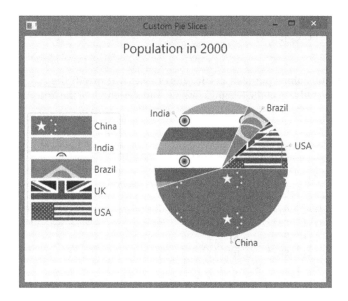

Figure 20-5. *A pie chart using a background image for its slices*

■ **Tip**   It is also possible to style the shape of the line joining the pie slices and their labels, labels for the pie slices, and the legend symbols in a pie chart.

Listing 20-7. Using Pie Slices with a Background Image

```
// PieChartCustomSlice.java
// ...find in the book's download area.
```

Understanding the XYChart

An instance of a concrete subclass of the abstract XYChart<X,Y> class defines a two-axis chart. The generic type parameters X and Y are the data types of values plotted along the x-axis and y-axis, respectively.

Representing Axes in an XYChart

An instance of a concrete subclass of the abstract Axis<T> class defines an axis in the XYChart. Figure 20-6 shows a class diagram for the classes representing axes.

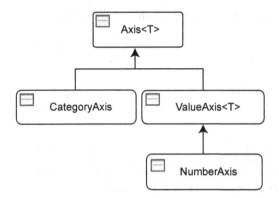

Figure 20-6. *A class diagram for classes representing axes in an XYChart*

The abstract Axis<T> class is the base class for all classes representing axes. The generic parameter T is the type of the values plotted along the axis, for example, String, Number, etc. An axis displays ticks and tick labels. The Axis<T> class contains properties to customize the ticks and tick labels. An axis can have a label, which is specified in the label property.

The concrete subclasses CategoryAxis and NumberAxis are used for plotting String and Number data values along an axis, respectively. They contain properties specific to the data values. For example, NumberAxis inherits ValueAxis<T>'s lowerBound and upperBound properties, which specify the lower and upper bounds of the data plotted on the axis. By default, the range of the data on an axis is automatically determined based on the data. You can turn off this feature by setting the autoRanging property in the Axis<T> class to false. The following snippet of code creates an instance of the CategoryAxis and NumberAxis and sets their labels:

```
CategoryAxis xAxis = new CategoryAxis();
xAxis.setLabel("Country");
NumberAxis yAxis = new NumberAxis();
yAxis.setLabel("Population (in millions)");
```

■ **Tip** Use a CategoryAxis to plot String values along an axis, and use a NumberAxis to plot numeric values along an axis.

Adding Data to an XYChart

Data in an XYChart represents points in the 2D plane defined by the x-axis and y-axis. A point in a 2D plane is specified using the x and y coordinates, which are values along the x-axis and y-axis, respectively. The data in an XYChart is specified as an ObservableList of named series. A series consists of multiple data items, which are points in the 2D plane. How the points are rendered depends on the chart type. For example, a scatter chart shows a symbol for a point, whereas a bar chart shows a bar for a point.

An instance of the nested static `XYChart.Data<X,Y>` class represents a data item in a series. The class defines the following properties:

- XValue
- YValue
- extraValue
- node

The XValue and YValue are the values for the data item along the x-axis and y-axis, respectively. Their data types need to match the data type of the x-axis and y-axis for the chart. The `extraValue` is an `Object`, which can be used to store any additional information for the data item. Its use depends on the chart type. If the chart does not use this value, you can use it for any other purpose: for example, to store the tool tip value for the data item. The `node` specifies the node to be rendered for the data item in the chart. By default, the chart will create a suitable node depending on the chart type.

Suppose both axes of an XYChart plot numeric values. The following snippet of code creates some data items for the chart. The data items are the population of China in 1950, 2000, and 2050:

```
XYChart.Data<Number, Number> data1 = new XYChart.Data<>(1950, 555);
XYChart.Data<Number, Number> data2 = new XYChart.Data<>(2000, 1275);
XYChart.Data<Number, Number> data3 = new XYChart.Data<>(2050, 1395);
```

An instance of the nested static `XYChart.Series<X,Y>` class represents a series of data items. The class defines the following properties:

- name
- data
- chart
- node

The name is the name of the series. The `data` is an `ObservableList` of `XYChart.Data<X,Y>`. The chart is a read-only reference to the chart to which the series belong. The node is a `Node` to display for this series. A default node is automatically created based on the chart type. The following snippet of code creates a series, sets its name, and adds data items to it:

```
XYChart.Series<Number, Number> seriesChina = new XYChart.Series<>();
seriesChina.setName("China");
seriesChina.getData().addAll(data1, data2, data3);
```

The data property of the XYChart class represents the data for the chart. It is an `ObservableList` of `XYChart.Series` class. The following snippet of code creates and adds the data for an XYChart chart assuming the data series `seriesIndia` and `seriesUSA` exist:

```
XYChart<Number, Number> chart = ...
chart.getData().addAll(seriesChina, seriesIndia, seriesUSA);
```

How the data items for a series are displayed depends on the specific chart type. Every chart type has a way to distinguish one series from another.

You will reuse the same series of data items representing the population of some countries in some years several times. Listing 20-8 has code for a utility class. The class consists of two static methods that generate and return XYChart data. The getCountrySeries() method returns the list of series that plots the years along the x-axis and the corresponding populations along the y-axis. The getYearSeries() method returns a list of series that plots the countries along the x-axis and the corresponding populations along the y-axis. You will be calling these methods to get data for our XYCharts in subsequent sections.

Listing 20-8. A Utility Class to Generate Data Used in XYCharts

```java
// XYChartDataUtil.java
// ...abbreviated, find the full listing in the book's download area.
package com.jdojo.chart;

import javafx.collections.FXCollections;
import javafx.collections.ObservableList;
import javafx.scene.chart.XYChart;

@SuppressWarnings("unchecked")
public class XYChartDataUtil {
    public static
    ObservableList<XYChart.Series<Number, Number>> getCountrySeries() {
        XYChart.Series<Number, Number> seriesChina =
            new XYChart.Series<>();
        seriesChina.setName("China");
        seriesChina.getData().addAll(
            new XYChart.Data<>(1950, 555),
            new XYChart.Data<>(2000, 1275),
            ...
        );

        ...
        ObservableList<XYChart.Series<Number, Number>> data =
          FXCollections.<XYChart.Series<Number, Number>>observableArrayList();
        data.addAll(seriesChina, seriesIndia, seriesUSA);
        return data;
    }

    ...
}
```

Understanding the BarChart

A bar chart renders the data items as horizontal or vertical rectangular bars. The lengths of the bars are proportional to the value of the data items.

An instance of the BarChart class represents a bar chart. In a bar chart, one axis must be a CategoryAxis and the other a ValueAxis/NumberAxis. The bars are drawn vertically or horizontally, depending on whether the CategoryAxis is the x-axis or the y-axis.

The BarChart contains two properties to control the distance between two bars in a category and the distance between two categories:

- barGap
- categoryGap

The default value is 4 pixels for the barGap and 10 pixels for the categoryGap.

The BarChart class contains three constructors to create bar charts by specifying axes, data, and gap between two categories:

- BarChart(Axis<X> xAxis, Axis<Y> yAxis)
- BarChart(Axis<X> xAxis, Axis<Y> yAxis, ObservableList<XYChart. Series<X,Y>> data)
- BarChart(Axis<X> xAxis, Axis<Y> yAxis, ObservableList<XYChart. Series<X,Y>> data, double categoryGap)

Notice that you must specify at least the axes when you create a bar chart. The following snippet of code creates two axes and a bar chart with those axes:

```
CategoryAxis xAxis = new CategoryAxis();
xAxis.setLabel("Country");

NumberAxis yAxis = new NumberAxis();
yAxis.setLabel("Population (in millions)");

// Create a bar chart
BarChart<String, Number> chart = new BarChart<>(xAxis, yAxis);
```

The bars in the chart will appear vertically as the category axis is added as the x-axis. You can populate the chart with data using its setData() method:

```
// Set the data for the chart
chart.setData(XYChartDataUtil.getYearSeries());
```

The program in Listing 20-9 shows how to create and populate a vertical bar chart as shown in Figure 20-7.

Listing 20-9. Creating a Vertical Bar Chart

```
// VerticalBarChart.java
// ...find in the book's download area.
```

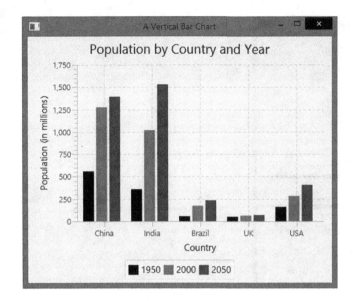

Figure 20-7. *A vertical bar chart*

The program in Listing 20-10 shows how to create and populate a horizontal bar chart as shown in Figure 20-8. The program needs to supply data to the chart in an ObservableList of XYChart. Series<Number,String>. The getYearSeries() method in the XYChartDataUtil class returns XYChart. Series<String,Number>. The getChartData() method in the program converts the series data from <String,Number> to <Number,String> format as needed to create a horizontal bar chart.

Listing 20-10. Creating a Horizontal Bar Chart

```
// HorizontalBarChart.java
// ...find in the book's download area.
```

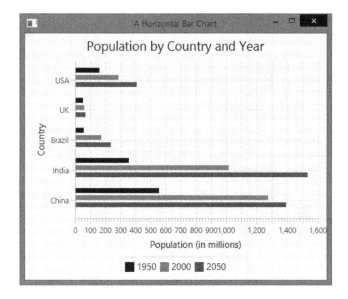

Figure 20-8. *A horizontal bar chart*

■ **Tip**   Each bar in a bar chart is represented with a node. The user can interact with the bars in a bar chart, by adding event handlers to the nodes representing the data items. Please refer to the section on the pie chart for an example in which you added tool tips for the pie slices.

Styling the BarChart with CSS

By default, a BarChart is given style-class names: *chart* and *bar-chart*.

The following style sets the default values for the barGap and categoryGap properties for all bar charts to 0px and 20px. The bars in the same category will be placed next to each other:

```
.bar-chart {
        -fx-bar-gap: 0;
        -fx-category-gap: 20;
}
```

You can customize the appearance of the bars for each series or each data item in a series. Each data item in a BarChart is represented by a node. The node gets five default style-class names:

- chart-bar
- series<i>
- data<j>
- default-color<k>
- negative

In series<i>, <i> is the series index. For example, the first series is given the style-class name as series0, the second as series1, etc.

In data<j>, <j> is the index of the data item within a series. For example, the first data item in each series gets a style-class name as data0, the second as data1, etc.

In default-color<k>, <k> is the series color index. For example, each data item in the first series will get a style-class name as default-color0, in the second series default-color1, etc. The default CS defines only eight series colors. The value for <k> is equal to (i%8), where i is the series index. That is, series colors will repeat if you have more than eight series in a bar chart. Please refer to the pie chart section on how to use unique colors for series with index greater than eight. The logic will be similar to the one used for a pie chart, with a difference that, this time, you will be looking up the bar-legend-symbol within a series instead of a pie-legend-symbol.

The negative class is added if the data value is negative.

Each legend item in a bar chart is given the following style-class names:

- chart-bar
- series<i>
- bar-legend-symbol
- default-color<j>

In series<i>, <i> is the series index. In default-color<j>, <j> is the color index of the series. The legend color will repeat, as the bar colors do, if the number of series exceeds eight.

The following style defines the color of the bars for all data items in series with series indices 0, 8, 16, 24, etc., as blue:

```
.chart-bar.default-color0 {
        -fx-bar-fill: blue;
}
```

Understanding the StackedBarChart

A stacked bar chart is a variation of the bar chart. In a stacked bar chart, the bars in a category are stacked. Except for the placement of the bars, it works the same way as the bar chart.

An instance of the StackedBarChart class represents a stacked bar chart. The bars can be placed horizontally or vertically. If the x-axis is a CategoryAxis, the bars are placed vertically. Otherwise, they are placed horizontally. Like the BarChart, one of the axes must be a CategoryAxis and the other a ValueAxis/NumberAxis.

The StackedBarChart class contains a categoryGap property that defines the gap between bars in adjacent categories. The default gap is 10px. Unlike the BarChart class, the StackedBarChart class does not contain a barGap property, as the bars in one category are always stacked.

The constructors of the StackedBarChart class are similar to the ones for the BarChart class. They let you specify the axes, chart data, and category gap.

There is one notable difference in creating the CategoryAxis for the BarChart and the StackedBarChart. The BarChart reads the category values from the data, whereas you must explicitly add all category values to the CategoryAxis for a StackedBarChart:

```
CategoryAxis xAxis = new CategoryAxis();
xAxis.setLabel("Country");
```

```
// Must set the categories in a StackedBarChart explicitly. Otherwise,
// the chart will not show bars.
xAxis.getCategories().addAll("China," "India," "Brazil," "UK," "USA");

NumberAxis yAxis = new NumberAxis();
yAxis.setLabel("Population (in millions)");

StackedBarChart<String, Number> chart = new StackedBarChart<>(xAxis, yAxis);
```

The program in Listing 20-11 shows how to create a vertical stacked bar chart. The chart is shown in Figure 20-9. To create a horizontal stacked bar chart, use a CategoryAxis as the y-axis.

Listing 20-11. Creating a Vertical Stacked Bar Chart

```
// VerticalStackedBarChart.java
// ...find in the book's download area.
```

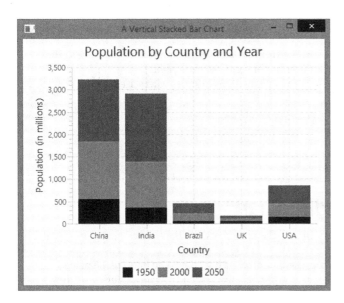

Figure 20-9. *A vertical stacked bar chart*

Styling the StackedBarChart with CSS

By default, a StackedBarChart is given style-class names: *chart* and *stacked-bar-chart.*
The following style sets the default value for the categoryGap properties for all stacked bar charts to 20px. The bars in a category will be placed next to each other:

```
.stacked-bar-chart {
      -fx-category-gap: 20;
}
```

In a stacked bar chart, the style-class names assigned to the nodes representing bars and legend items are the same as that of a bar chart. Please refer to the section *"Styling the BarChart with CSS"* for more details.

Understanding the ScatterChart

A bar chart renders the data items as symbols. All data items in a series use the same symbol. The location of the symbol for a data item is determined by the values on the data item along the x-axis and y-axis.

An instance of the ScatterChart class represents a scatter chart. You can use any type of Axis for the x-axis and y-axis. The class does not define any additional properties. It contains constructors that allow you to create a scatter chart by specifying axes and data:

- ScatterChart(Axis<X> xAxis, Axis<Y> yAxis)

- ScatterChart(Axis<X> xAxis, Axis<Y> yAxis, ObservableList<XYChart.Series<X,Y>> data)

Recall that the autoRanging for an Axis is set to true by default. If you are using numeric values in a scatter chart, make sure to set the autoRanging to false. It is important to set the range of the numeric values appropriately to get uniformly distributed points in the chart. Otherwise, the points may be located densely in a small area, and it will be hard to read the chart.

The program in Listing 20-12 shows how to create and populate a scatter chart as shown in Figure 20-10. Both axes are numeric axes. The x-axis is customized. The autoRanging is set to false; reasonable lower and upper bounds are set. The tick unit is set to 50. If you do not customize these properties, the ScatterChart will automatically determine them, and the chart data will be hard to read:

```
NumberAxis xAxis = new NumberAxis();
xAxis.setLabel("Year");
xAxis.setAutoRanging(false);
xAxis.setLowerBound(1900);
xAxis.setUpperBound(2300);
xAxis.setTickUnit(50);
```

Listing 20-12. Creating a Scatter Chart

```
// ScatterChartTest.java
package com.jdojo.chart;

import javafx.application.Application;
import javafx.collections.ObservableList;
import javafx.scene.Scene;
import javafx.scene.chart.NumberAxis;
import javafx.scene.chart.ScatterChart;
import javafx.scene.chart.XYChart;
import javafx.scene.layout.StackPane;
import javafx.stage.Stage;

public class ScatterChartTest extends Application {
    public static void main(String[] args) {
        Application.launch(args);
    }
```

```
@Override
public void start(Stage stage) {
        NumberAxis xAxis = new NumberAxis();
        xAxis.setLabel("Year");

        // Customize the x-axis, so points are scattered uniformly
        xAxis.setAutoRanging(false);
        xAxis.setLowerBound(1900);
        xAxis.setUpperBound(2300);
        xAxis.setTickUnit(50);

        NumberAxis yAxis = new NumberAxis();
        yAxis.setLabel("Population (in millions)");

        ScatterChart<Number,Number> chart =
                new ScatterChart<>(xAxis, yAxis);
        chart.setTitle("Population by Year and Country");

        // Set the data for the chart
        ObservableList<XYChart.Series<Number,Number>> chartData =
            XYChartDataUtil.getCountrySeries();
        chart.setData(chartData);

        StackPane root = new StackPane(chart);
        Scene scene = new Scene(root);
        stage.setScene(scene);
        stage.setTitle("A Scatter Chart");
        stage.show();
    }
}
```

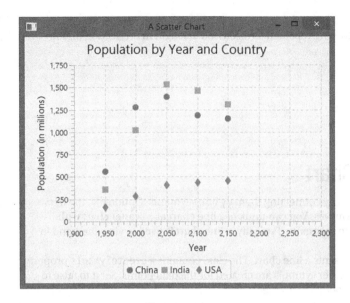

Figure 20-10. *A scatter chart*

■ **Tip** You can use the node property for data items to specify symbols in a ScatterChart.

Styling the ScatterChart with CSS

The ScatterChart is not assigned any additional style-class name other than *chart*.

You can customize the appearance of the symbols for each series or each data item in a series. Each data item in a ScatterChart is represented by a node. The node gets five default style-class names:

- chart-symbol
- series<i>
- data<j>
- default-color<k>
- negative

Please refer to the section "Styling the BarChart with CSS" for more details on the meanings of <i>, <j>, and <k> in these style-class names.

Each legend item in a scatter chart is given the following style-class names:

- chart-symbol
- series<i>
- data<j>
- default-color<k>

The following style will display the data items in the first series as triangles filled in blue. Note that only eight color series are defined. After that, colors are repeated as discussed at length in the section on the pie chart.

```
.chart-symbol.default-color0 {
        -fx-background-color: blue;
        -fx-shape: "M5, 0L10, 5L0, 5z";
}
```

Understanding the LineChart

A line chart displays the data items in a series by connecting them by line segments. Optionally, the data points themselves may be represented by symbols. You can think of a line chart as a scatter chart with symbols in a series connected by straight line segments. Typically, a line chart is used to view the trend in data change over time or in a category.

An instance of the LineChart class represents a line chart. The class contains a createSymbols property, which is set to true by default. It controls whether symbols are created for the data points. Set it to false to show only straight lines connecting the data points in a series.

The LineChart class contains two constructors to create line charts by specifying axes and data:

- LineChart(Axis<X> xAxis, Axis<Y> yAxis)

- LineChart(Axis<X> xAxis, Axis<Y> yAxis, ObservableList<XYChart.Series<X,Y>> data)

The program in Listing 20-13 shows how to create and populate a line chart as shown in Figure 20-11. The program is the same as for using the scatter chart, except that it uses the LineChart class. The chart displays circles as symbols for data items. You can remove the symbols by using the following statement, after you create the line chart:

```
// Do not create the symbols for the data items
chart.setCreateSymbols(false);
```

Listing 20-13. Creating a Line Chart

```
// LineChartTest.java
// ...find in the book's download area.
```

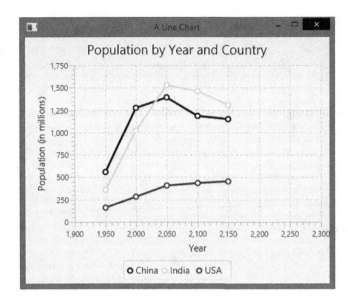

Figure 20-11. *A line chart*

Styling the LineChart with CSS

The LineChart is not assigned any additional style-class name other than *chart*. The following style specifies that the LineChart should not create symbols:

```
.chart {
        -fx-create-symbols: false;
}
```

The LineChart creates a Path node to show the lines connecting all data points for a series. A line for a series is assigned the following style-class names:

- chart-series-line
- series<i>
- default-color<j>

Here, <i> is the series index, and <j> is the color index of the series.

If the createSymbols property is set to true, a symbol is created for each data point. Each symbol node is assigned the following style-class names:

- chart-line-symbol
- series<i>
- data<j>
- default-color<k>

Here, <i> is the series index, <j> is the data item index within a series, and <k> is the color index of the series.

743

Each series is assigned a legend item, which gets the following style-class names:

- `chart-line-symbol`
- `series<i>`
- `default-color<j>`

The following styles set the line stroke for the color index 0 of the series to blue. The symbol for the series is also shown in blue:

```
.chart-series-line.default-color0 {
    -fx-stroke: blue;
}

.chart-line-symbol.default-color0 {
    -fx-background-color: blue, white;
}
```

Understanding the BubbleChart

A bubble chart is very similar to a scatter chart, except that it has the ability to represent three values for a data point. A bubble is used to represent a data item in a series. You can set the radius of the bubble to represent the third value for the data point.

An instance of the BubbleChart class represents a bubble chart. The class does not define any new properties. A bubble chart uses the extraValue property of the XYChart.Data class to get the radius of the bubble. The bubble is an ellipse whose radii are scaled based on the scale used for the axes. Bubbles look more like a circle (or less stretched on one direction) if the scales for the x-axis and y-axis are almost equal.

■ **Tip** The bubble radius is set by default, which is scaled using the scale factor of the axes. You may not see the bubbles if the scale factors for axes are very small. To see the bubbles, set the extraValue in data items to a high value or use higher scale factors along the axes.

The BubbleChart class defines two constructors:

- `BubbleChart(Axis<X> xAxis, Axis<Y> yAxis)`
- `BubbleChart(Axis<X> xAxis, Axis<Y> yAxis, ObservableList<XYChart.Series<X,Y>> data)`

The program in Listing 20-14 shows how to create a bubble chart as shown in Figure 20-12. The chart data is passed to the setBubbleRadius() method, which explicitly sets the extraValue for all data points to 20px. If you want to use the radii of bubbles to represent another dimension of data, you can set the extraValue accordingly.

Listing 20-14. Creating a Bubble Chart

```
// BubbleChartTest.java
// ...find in the book's download area.
```

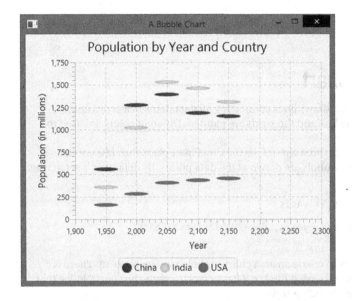

Figure 20-12. *A bubble chart*

Styling the BubbleChart with CSS

The BubbleChart is not assigned any additional style-class name other than *chart.*

You can customize the appearance of the bubbles for each series or each data item in a series. Each data item in a BubbleChart is represented by a node. The node gets four default style-class names:

- chart-bubble
- series<i>
- data<j>
- default-color<k>

Here, <i> is the series index, <j> is the data item index within a series, and <k> is the color index of the series.

Each series is assigned a legend item, which gets the following style-class names:

- chart-bubble
- series<i>
- bubble-legend-symbol
- default-color<k>

Here, <i> and <k> have the same meanings as described earlier.

The following style sets the fill color for the series color index 0 to blue. The bubbles and legend symbols for the data items in the first series will be displayed in blue. The color will repeat for series indices 8, 16, 24, etc.

```
.chart-bubble.default-color0 {
        -fx-bubble-fill: blue;
}
```

Understanding the AreaChart

The area chart is a variation of the line chart. It draws lines connecting all data items in a series and, additionally, fills the area between where the line and the x-axis are painted. Different colors are used to paint areas for different series.

An instance of the AreaChart represents an area chart. Like the LineChart class, the class contains a createSymbols property to control whether symbols are drawn at the data points. By default, it is set to true. The class contains two constructors:

- AreaChart(Axis<X> xAxis, Axis<Y> yAxis)

- AreaChart(Axis<X> xAxis, Axis<Y> yAxis, ObservableList<XYChart.Series<X,Y>> data)

The program in Listing 20-15 shows how to create an area chart as shown in Figure 20-13. There is nothing new in the program, except that you have used the AreaChart class to create the chart. Notice that the area for a series overlays the area for the preceding series.

Listing 20-15. Creating an Area Chart

```
// AreaChartTest.java
// ...find in the book's download area.
```

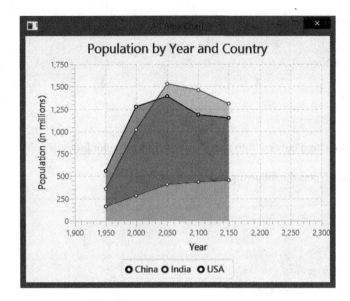

Figure 20-13. *An area chart*

Styling the AreaChart with CSS

The AreaChart is not assigned any additional style-class name other than *chart*. The following style specifies that the AreaChart should not create symbols for representing the data points:

```
.chart {
        -fx-create-symbols: false;
}
```

Each series in an AreaChart is represented by a Group containing two Path nodes. One Path represents the line segment connecting all data points in the series, and another Path represents the area covered by the series. The Path node representing the line segment for a series is assigned the following style-class names:

- chart-series-area-line

- series<i>

- default-color<j>

Here, <i> is the series index, and <j> is the color index of the series.
The Path node representing the area for a series is assigned the following style-class names:

- chart-series-area-fill

- series<i>

- default-color<j>

Here, <i> is the series index, and <j> is the color index of the series.

If the `createSymbols` property is set to true, a symbol is created for each data point. Each symbol node is assigned the following style-class names:

- `chart-area-symbol`
- `series<i>`
- `data<j>`
- `default-color<k>`

Here, `<i>` is the series index, `<j>` is the data item index within a series, and `<k>` is the color index of the series.

Each series is assigned a legend item, which gets the following style-class names:

- `chart-area-symbol`
- `series<i>`
- `area-legend-symbol`
- `default-color<j>`

Here, `<i>` is the series index, and `<j>` is the color index of the series.

The following style sets the area fill color for the color index 0 for the series to blue with 20% opacity. Make sure to set transparent colors for the area fills as areas overlap in an `AreaChart`:

```
.chart-series-area-fill.default-color0 {
        -fx-fill: rgba(0, 0, 255, 0.20);
}
```

The following styles set the blue as the color for symbols, line segment, and legend symbol for the color index 0 for the series:

```
/* Data point symbols color */
.chart-area-symbol.default-color0. {
        -fx-background-color: blue, white;
}

/* Series line segment color */
.chart-series-area-line.default-color0 {
        -fx-stroke: blue;
}

/* Series legend symbol color */
.area-legend-symbol.default-color0 {
        -fx-background-color: blue, white;
}
```

Understanding the StackedAreaChart

The stacked area chart is a variation of the area chart. It plots data items by painting an area for each series. Unlike the area chart, areas for series do not overlap; they are stacked.

An instance of the StackedAreaChart represents a stacked area chart. Like the AreaChart class, the class contains a createSymbols property. The class contains two constructors:

- StackedAreaChart(Axis<X> xAxis, Axis<Y> yAxis)
- StackedAreaChart(Axis<X> xAxis, Axis<Y> yAxis, ObservableList<XYChart.
  Series<X,Y>> data)

The program in Listing 20-16 shows how to create a stacked area chart as shown in Figure 20-14. The program is the same as the one that created an AreaChart, except that you have used the StackedAreaChart class to create the chart.

Listing 20-16. Creating a Stacked Area Chart

```
// StackedAreaChartTest.java
// ...find in the book's download area.
```

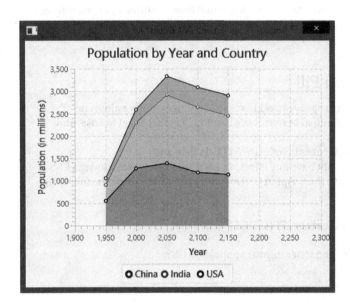

Figure 20-14. A stacked area chart

Styling the StackedAreaChart with CSS

Styling a StackedAreaChart is the same as styling an AreaChart. Please refer to the section "Styling the AreaChart with CSS" for more details.

Customizing XYChart Appearance

You have seen how to apply chart-specific CSS styles to customize the appearance of charts. In this section, you will look at some more ways to customize the XYChart plot and axes. The XYChart class contains several boolean properties to change the chart plot appearance:

- `alternativeColumnFillVisible`
- `alternativeRowFillVisible`
- `horizontalGridLinesVisible`
- `verticalGridLinesVisible`
- `horizontalZeroLineVisible`
- `verticalZeroLineVisible`

The chart area is divided into a grid of columns and rows. Horizontal lines are drawn passing through major ticks on the y-axis making up rows. Vertical lines are drawn passing through major ticks on the x-axis making up columns.

Setting Alternate Row/Column Fill

The `alternativeColumnFillVisible` and `alternativeRowFillVisible` control whether alternate columns and rows in the grid are filled. By default, `alternativeColumnFillVisible` is set to false, and `alternativeRowFillVisible` is set to true.

As of the time of this writing, setting the `alternativeColumnFillVisible` and `alternativeRowFillVisible` properties does not have any effects in JavaFX 8, which uses Modena CSS by default. There are two solutions. You can use the Caspian CSS for your application using the following statement:

```
Application.setUserAgentStylesheet(Application.STYLESHEET_CASPIAN);
```

The other solution is to include the following styles in your application CSS:

```
.chart-alternative-column-fill {
        -fx-fill: #eeeeee;
        -fx-stroke: transparent;
        -fx-stroke-width: 0;
}

.chart-alternative-row-fill {
        -fx-fill: #eeeeee;
        -fx-stroke: transparent;
        -fx-stroke-width: 0;
}
```

These styles are taken from Caspian CSS. These styles set the `fill` and `stroke` properties to `null` in Modena CSS.

Showing Zero Line Axes

The axes for a chart may not include zero lines. Whether zero lines are included depends on the lower and upper bounds represented by the axes. The horizontalZeroLineVisible and verticalZeroLineVisible control whether zero lines should be visible. By default, they are visible. Note that the zero line for an axis is visible only when the axis has both positive and negative data to plot. If you have negative and positive values along the y-axis, an additional horizontal axis will appear indicating the zero value along the y-axis. The same rule applies for values along the x-axis. If the range for an axis is set explicitly using its lower and upper bounds, the visibility of the zero line depends on whether zero falls in the range.

Showing Grid Lines

The horizontalGridLinesVisible and verticalGridLinesVisible specify whether the horizontal and vertical grid lines are visible. By default, both are set to true.

Formatting Numeric Tick Labels

Sometimes, you may want to format the values displayed on a numeric axis. You want to format the labels for the numeric axis for different reasons:

- You want to add prefixes or suffixes to the tick labels. For example, you may want to display a number 100 as $100 or 100M.

- You may be supplying the chart scaled data to get an appropriate scale value for the axis. For example, for the actual value 100, you may be supplying 10 to the chart. In this case, you would like to display the actual value 100 for the label.

The ValueAxis class contains a tickLabelFormatter property, which is a StringConverter, and it is used to format tick labels. By default, tick labels for a numeric axis are formatted using a default formatter. The default formatter is an instance of the static inner class NumberAxis.DefaultFormatter.

In our examples of XYChart, you had set the label for the y-axis to "Population (in millions)" to indicate that the tick values on the axis are in millions. You can use a label formatter to append "M" to the tick values to indicate the same meaning. The following snippet of code will accomplish this:

```
NumberAxis yAxis = new NumberAxis();
yAxis.setLabel("Population");

// Use a formatter for tick labels on y-axis to append
// M (for millions) to the population value
yAxis.setTickLabelFormatter(new StringConverter<Number>() {
        @Override
        public String toString(Number value) {
                // Append M to the value
                return Math.round(value.doubleValue()) + "M";
        }

        @Override
        public Number fromString(String value) {
                // Strip M from the value
```

751

```
                value = value.replaceAll("M", "");
                return Double.parseDouble(value);
        }
});
```

The NumberAxis.DefaultFormatter works better for adding a prefix or suffix to tick labels. This formatter is kept in sync with the autoRanging property for the axis. You can pass a prefix and a suffix to the constructor. The following snippet of code accomplishes the same thing as the preceding snippet of code:

```
NumberAxis yAxis = new NumberAxis();
yAxis.setLabel("Population");
yAxis.setTickLabelFormatter(new NumberAxis.DefaultFormatter(yAxis, null, "M"));
```

You can customize several visual aspects of an Axis. Please refer to the API documentation for the Axis class and its subclasses for more details.

The program in Listing 20-17 shows how to customize a line chart. The chart is shown in Figure 20-15. It formats the tick labels on the y-axis to append "M" to the label value. It hides the grid lines and shows the alternate column fills.

Listing 20-17. Formatting Tick Labels and Customizing Chart Plot

```
// CustomizingCharts.java
// ...find in the book's download area.
```

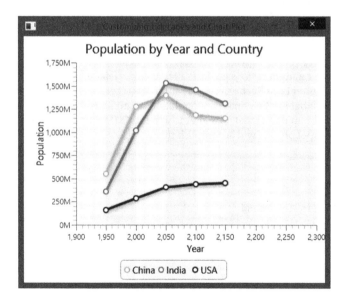

Figure 20-15. *A line chart with formatted tick labels and customized plot*

Summary

A chart is a graphical representation of data. Charts provide an easier way to analyze a large volume of data visually. Typically, they are used for reporting purposes. Different types of charts exist. They differ in the way they represent the data. Not all types of charts are suitable for analyzing all types of data. For example, a line chart is suitable for understanding the comparative trend in data, whereas a bar chart is suitable for comparing data in different categories.

JavaFX supports charts, which can be integrated in a Java application by writing a few lines of code. It contains a comprehensive, extensible Chart API that provides built-in support for several types of charts. The Chart API consists of a number of predefined classes in the javafx.scene.chart package. Few of those classes are Chart, XYChart, PieChart, BarChart, and LineChart.

The abstract Chart is the base class for all charts. It inherits the Node class. Charts can be added to a scene graph. They can also be styled with CSS as any other nodes. Every chart in JavaFX has three parts: a title, a legend, and data. Different types of charts define their data differently. The Chart class contains the properties to deal with the title and legend.

A chart can be animated. The animated property in the Chart class specifies whether the change in the content of the chart is shown with some type of animation. By default, it is true.

A pie chart consists of a circle divided into sectors of different central angles. Typically, a pie is circular. The sectors are also known as *pie pieces* or *pie slices*. Each sector in the circle represents a quantity of some kind. The central angle of the area of a sector is proportional to the quantity it represents. An instance of the PieChart class represents a pie chart.

A bar chart renders the data items as horizontal or vertical rectangular bars. The lengths of the bars are proportional to the value of the data items. An instance of the BarChart class represents a bar chart.

A stacked bar chart is a variation of the bar chart. In a stacked bar chart, the bars in a category are stacked. Except for the placement of the bars, it works the same way as the bar chart. An instance of the StackedBarChart class represents a stacked bar chart.

A scatter chart renders the data items as symbols. All data items in a series use the same symbol. The location of the symbol for a data item is determined by the values on the data item along the x-axis and y-axis. An instance of the ScatterChart class represents a scatter chart.

A line chart displays the data items in a series by connecting them by line segments. Optionally, the data points themselves may be represented by symbols. You can think of a line chart as a scatter chart with symbols in a series connected by straight line segments. Typically, a line chart is used to view the trend in data change over time or in a category. An instance of the LineChart class represents a line chart.

A bubble chart is very similar to a scatter chart, except that it has the ability to represent three values for a data point. A bubble is used to represent a data item in a series. You can set the radius of the bubble to represent the third value for the data point. An instance of the BubbleChart class represents a bubble chart.

The area chart is a variation of the line chart. It draws lines connecting all data items in a series and, additionally, fills the area between where the line and the x-axis are painted. Different colors are used to paint areas for different series. An instance of the AreaChart represents an area chart.

The stacked area chart is a variation of the area chart. It plots data items by painting an area for each series. Unlike the area chart, areas for series do not overlap; they are stacked. An instance of the StackedAreaChart represents a stacked area chart.

Besides using CSS to customize the appearance of charts, the Chart API provides several properties and methods to customize charts' appearance such as adding alternate row/column fills, showing zero line axes, showing grid lines, and formatting numeric tick labels.

The next chapter will discuss how to work with images in JavaFX using the Image API.

CHAPTER 21

■ ■ ■

Understanding the Image API

In this chapter, you will learn:

- What the Image API is
- How to load an image
- How to view an image in an `ImageView` node
- How to perform image operations such as reading/writing pixels, creating an image from scratch, and saving the image to the file system
- How to take the snapshot of nodes and scenes

The examples of this chapter lie in the `com.jdojo.image` package. In order for them to work, you must add a corresponding line to the `module-info.java` file:

```
...
opens com.jdojo.image to javafx.graphics, javafx.base;
...
```

What Is the Image API?

JavaFX provides the Image API that lets you load and display images and read/write raw image pixels. A class diagram for the classes in the Image API is shown in Figure 21-1. All classes are in the `javafx.scene.image` package. The API lets you

- Load an image in memory
- Display an image as a node in a scene graph
- Read pixels from an image
- Write pixels to an image
- Convert a node in a scene graph to an image and save it to the local file system

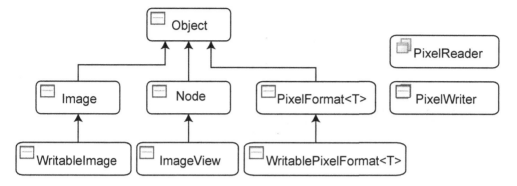

Figure 21-1. *A class diagram for classes in the Image API*

An instance of the Image class represents an image in memory. You can construct an image in a JavaFX application by supplying pixels to a WritableImage instance.

An ImageView is a Node. It is used to display an Image in a scene graph. If you want to display an image in an application, you need to load the image in an Image and display the Image in an ImageView.

Images are constructed from pixels. Data for pixels in an image may be stored in different formats. A PixelFormat defines how the data for a pixel for a given format is stored. A WritablePixelFormat represents a destination format to write pixels with full pixel color information.

The PixelReader and PixelWriter interfaces define methods to read from an Image and write data to a WritableImage. Besides an Image, you can read pixels from and write pixels to any surface that contains pixels.

I will cover examples of using these classes in the sections to follow.

Loading an Image

An instance of the Image class is an in-memory representation of an image. The class supports BMP, PNG, JPEG, and GIF image formats. It loads an image from a source, which can be specified as a string URL or an InputStream. It can also scale the original image while loading.

The Image class contains several constructors that let you specify the properties for the loaded image:

- Image(InputStream is)

- Image(InputStream is, double requestedWidth, double requestedHeight, boolean preserveRatio, boolean smooth)

- Image(String url)

- Image(String url, boolean backgroundLoading)

- Image(String url, double requestedWidth, double requestedHeight, boolean preserveRatio, boolean smooth)

- Image(String url, double requestedWidth, double requestedHeight, boolean preserveRatio, boolean smooth, boolean backgroundLoading)

There is no ambiguity of the source of the image if an InputStream is specified as the source. If a string URL is specified as the source, it could be a valid URL or a valid path in the CLASSPATH. If the specified URL is not a valid URL, it is used as a path, and the image source will be searched on the path in the CLASSPATH:

```
// Load an image from local machine using an InputStream
String sourcePath = "C:\\mypicture.png";
Image img = new Image(new FileInputStream(sourcePath));

// Load an image from an URL
Image img = new Image("http://jdojo.com/wp-content/uploads/2013/03/randomness.jpg");

// Load an image from the CLASSPATH. The image is located in the resources.picture package
Image img = new Image("resources/picture/randomness.jpg");
```

In the preceding statement, the specified URL resources/picture/randomness.jpg is not a valid URL. The Image class will treat it as a path expecting it to exist in the CLASSPATH. It treats the resource. picture as a package and the randomness.jpg as a resource in that package.

■ **Tip**   Make sure to add valid URLs if you want to test the code snippets in this chapter. Either you make sure you use relative URLs like resources/picture/randomness.jpg that are in the CLASSPATH or specify absolute URLs like http://path/to/my/server/resources/picture/randomness.jpg or file:// some/absolute/path/resources/picture/randomness.jpg .

Specifying the Image-Loading Properties

Some constructors let you specify some image-loading properties to control the quality of the image and the loading process:

- requestedWidth
- requestedHeight
- preserveRatio
- smooth
- backgroundLoading

The requestedWidth and requestedHeight properties specify the scaled width and height of the image. By default, an image is loaded in its original size.

The preserveRatio property specifies whether to preserve the aspect ratio of the image while scaling. By default, it is false.

The smooth property specifies the quality of the filtering algorithm to be used in scaling. By default, it is false. If it is set to true, a better quality filtering algorithm is used, which slows down the image-loading process a bit.

The backgroundLoading property specifies whether to load the image asynchronously. By default, the property is set to false, and the image is loaded synchronously. The loading process starts when the Image object is created. If this property is set to true, the image is loaded asynchronously in a background thread.

Reading the Loaded Image Properties

The Image class contains the following read-only properties:

- width
- height
- progress
- error
- exception

The width and height properties are the width and height of the loaded image, respectively. They are zero if the image failed to load.

The progress property indicates the progress in loading the image data. It is useful to know the progress when the backgroundLoading property is set to true. Its value is between 0.0 and 1.0 where 0.0 indicates 0% loading and 1.0 indicates 100% loading. When the backgroundLoading property is set to false (the default), its value is 1.0. You can add a ChangeListener to the progress property to know the progress in image loading. You may display a text as a placeholder for an image while it is loading and update the text with the current progress in the ChangeListener:

```
// Load an image in the background
String imagePath = "resources/picture/randomness.jpg";
Boolean backgroundLoading = true;
Image image = new Image(imagePath, backgroundLoading);

// Print the loading progress on the standard output
image.progressProperty().addListener((prop, oldValue, newValue) -> {
        System.out.println("Loading:" +
                Math.round(newValue.doubleValue() * 100.0) + "%");
});
```

The error property indicates whether an error occurred while loading the image. If it is true, the exception property specifies the Exception that caused the error. At the time of this writing, TIFF image format is not supported on Windows. The following snippet of code attempts to load a TIFF image on Windows XP, and it produces an error. The code contains an error handling logic that adds a ChangeListener to the error property if backgroundLoading is true. Otherwise, it checks for the value of the error property:

```
String imagePath = "resources/picture/test.tif";
Boolean backgroundLoading = false;
Image image = new Image(imagePath, backgroundLoading);

// Add a ChangeListener to the error property for background loading and
// check its value for non-background loading
if (image.isBackgroundLoading()) {
    image.errorProperty().addListener((prop, oldValue, newValue) -> {
            if (newValue) {
                System.out.println(
                        "An error occurred while loading the image.\n" +
                        "Error message: " +
                        image.getException().getMessage());
```

```
        }
    });
}
else if (image.isError()) {
    System.out.println("An error occurred while loading the image.\n" +
                "Error message: " +
                        image.getException().getMessage());
}
```

```
An error occurred while loading the image.
Error message: No loader for image data
```

Viewing an Image

An instance of the ImageView class is used to display an image loaded in an Image object. The ImageView class inherits from the Node class, which makes an ImageView suitable to be added to a scene graph. The class contains several constructors:

- ImageView()
- ImageView(Image image)
- ImageView(String url)

The no-args constructor creates an ImageView without an image. Use the image property to set an image. The second constructor accepts the reference of an Image. The third constructor lets you specify the URL of the image source. Internally, it creates an Image using the specified URL:

```
// Create an empty ImageView and set an Image for it later
ImageView imageView = new ImageView();
imageView.setImage(new Image("resources/picture/randomness.jpg"));

// Create an ImageView with an Image
ImageView imageView = new ImageView(new Image("resources/picture/randomness.jpg"));

// Create an ImageView with the URL of the image source
ImageView imageView = new ImageView("resources/picture/randomness.jpg");
```

The program in Listing 21-1 shows how to display an image in a scene. It loads an image in an Image object. The image is scaled without preserving the aspect ratio. The Image object is added to an ImageView, which is added to an HBox. Figure 21-2 shows the window.

Listing 21-1. Displaying an Image in an ImageView Node

```
// ImageTest.java
package com.jdojo.image;

import com.jdojo.util.ResourceUtil;
```

```java
import javafx.application.Application;
import javafx.scene.Scene;
import javafx.scene.image.Image;
import javafx.scene.image.ImageView;
import javafx.scene.layout.HBox;
import javafx.stage.Stage;

public class ImageTest extends Application {
        public static void main(String[] args) {
                Application.launch(args);
        }

        @Override
        public void start(Stage stage) {
            String imagePath =
                    ResourceUtil.getResourceURLStr("picture/randomness.jpg");
            // Scale the image to 200 X 100
            double requestedWidth = 200;
            double requestedHeight = 100;
            boolean preserveRatio = false;
            boolean smooth = true;
            Image image = new Image(imagePath,
                                requestedWidth,
                                requestedHeight,
                                preserveRatio,
                                smooth);
            ImageView imageView = new ImageView(image);

            HBox root = new HBox(imageView);
            Scene scene = new Scene(root);
            stage.setScene(scene);
            stage.setTitle("Displaying an Image");
            stage.show();
        }
}
```

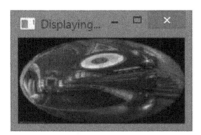

Figure 21-2. *A window with an image*

Multiple Views of an Image

An Image loads an image in memory from its source. You can have multiple views of the same Image. An ImageView provides one of the views.

You have an option to resize the original image while loading, displaying, or at both times. Which option you choose to resize an image depends on the requirement at hand:

- Resizing an image in an Image object resizes the image permanently in memory, and all views of the image will use the resized image. Once an Image is resized, its size cannot be altered. You may want to reduce the size of an image in an Image object to save memory.

- Resizing an image in an ImageView resizes the image only for this view. You can resize the view of an image in an ImageView even after the image has been displayed.

We have already discussed how to resize an image in an Image object. In this section, we will discuss resizing an image in an ImageView.

Similar to the Image class, the ImageView class contains the following four properties to control the resizing of view of an image:

- fitWidth
- fitHeight
- preserveRatio
- smooth

The fitWidth and fitHeight properties specify the resized width and height of the image, respectively. By default, they are zero, which means that the ImageView will use the width and height of the loaded image in the Image.

The preserveRatio property specifies whether to preserve the aspect ratio of the image while resizing. By default, it is false.

The smooth property specifies the quality of the filtering algorithm to be used in resizing. Its default value is platform dependent. If it is set to true, a better quality filtering algorithm is used.

The program in Listing 21-2 loads an image in an Image object in original size. It creates three ImageView objects of the Image specifying different sizes. Figure 21-3 shows the three images. The image shows a junk school bus and a junk car. The image is used with a permission from Richard Castillo (www. digitizedchaos.com).

Listing 21-2. Displaying the Same Image in Different ImageView in Different Sizes

```
// MultipleImageViews.java
// ...find in the book's download area.
```

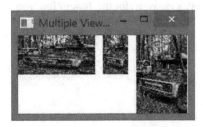

Figure 21-3. *Three views of the same image*

Viewing an Image in a Viewport

A viewport is a rectangular region to view part of a graphics. It is common to use scrollbars in conjunction with a viewport. As the scrollbars are scrolled, the viewport shows different parts of the graphics.

An ImageView lets you define a viewport for an image. In JavaFX, a viewport is an instance of the javafx.geometry.Rectangle2D object. A Rectangle2D is immutable. It is defined in terms of four properties: minX, minY, width, and height. The (minX, minY) value defines the location of the upper-left corner of the rectangle. The width and height properties specify its size. You must specify all properties in the constructor:

```
// Create a viewport located at (0, 0) and of size 200 X 100
Rectangle2D viewport = new Rectangle2D(0, 0, 200,100);
```

The ImageView class contains a viewport property, which provides a viewport into the image displayed in the ImageView. The viewport defines a rectangular region in the image. The ImageView shows only the region of the image that falls inside the viewport. The location of the viewport is defined relative to the image, not the ImageView. By default, the viewport of an ImageView is null, and the ImageView shows the whole image.

The following snippet of code loads an image in its original size in an Image. The Image is set as the source for an ImageView. A viewport 200 X 100 in size is set for the ImageView. The viewport is located at (0, 0). This shows in the ImageView the top-left 200 X 100 region of the image:

```
String imagePath = "resources/picture/school_bus.jpg";
Image image = new Image(imagePath);
imageView = new ImageView(image);
Rectangle2D viewport = new Rectangle2D(0, 0, 200, 100);
imageView.setViewport(viewport);
```

The following snippet of code will change the viewport to show the 200 X 100 lower-right region of the image:

```
double minX = image.getWidth() - 200;
double minY = image.getHeight() - 100;
Rectangle2D viewport2 = new Rectangle2D(minX, minY, 200, 100);
imageView.setViewport(viewport2);
```

■ **Tip** The Rectangle2D class is immutable. Therefore, you need to create a new viewport every time you want to move the viewport into the image.

The program in Listing 21-3 loads an image into an ImageView. It sets a viewport for the ImageView. You can drag the mouse, while pressing the left, right, or both buttons, to scroll to the different parts of the image into the view.

Listing 21-3. Using a Viewport to View Part of an Image

```
// ImageViewPort.java
// ...find in the book's download area.
```

The program declares a few class and instance variables. The VIEWPORT_WIDTH and VIEWPORT_HEIGHT are constants holding the width and height of the viewport. The startX and startY instance variables will hold the x and y coordinates of the mouse when the mouse is pressed or dragged. The ImageView instance variable holds the reference of the ImageView. We need this reference in the mouse-dragged event handler.

The starting part of the start() method is simple. It creates an Image, an ImageView, and sets a viewport for the ImageView. Then, it sets the mouse-pressed and mouse-dragged event handlers to the ImageView:

```
// Set the mouse pressed and mouse dragged event handlers
imageView.setOnMousePressed(this::handleMousePressed);
imageView.setOnMouseDragged(this::handleMouseDragged);
```

In the handleMousePressed() method, we store the coordinates of the mouse in the startX and startY instance variables. The coordinates are relative to the ImageView:

```
startX = e.getX();
startY = e.getY();
```

The handleMousePressed() method computes the new location of the viewport inside the image because of the mouse drag and sets a new viewport at the new location. First, it computes the dragged distance for the mouse along the x-axis and y-axis:

```
// How far the mouse was dragged
double draggedDistanceX = e.getX() - startX;
double draggedDistanceY = e.getY() - startY;
```

You reset the startX and startY values to the mouse location that triggered the current mouse-dragged event. This is important to get the correct dragged distance when the user keeps the mouse pressed, drags it, stops without releasing the mouse, and drags it again:

```
// Reset the starting point for the next drag
// if the user keeps the mouse pressed and drags again
startX = e.getX();
startY = e.getY();
```

You compute the new location of the upper-left corner of the viewport. You always have a viewport in the ImageView. The new viewport will be located at the dragged distance from the old location:

```
// Get the minX and minY of the current viewport
double curMinX = imageView.getViewport().getMinX();
double curMinY = imageView.getViewport().getMinY();

// Move the new viewport by the dragged distance
double newMinX = curMinX + draggedDistanceX;
double newMinY = curMinY + draggedDistanceY;
```

It is fine to place the viewport outside the region of the image. The viewport simply displays an empty area when it falls outside the image area. To restrict the viewport inside the image area, we clamp the location of the viewport:

```
// Make sure the viewport does not fall outside the image area
newMinX = clamp(newMinX, O, imageView.getImage().getWidth() - VIEWPORT_WIDTH);
newMinY = clamp(newMinY, O, imageView.getImage().getHeight() - VIEWPORT_HEIGHT);
```

Finally, we set a new viewport using the new location:

```
// Set a new viewport
imageView.setViewport(new Rectangle2D(newMinX, newMinY, VIEWPORT_WIDTH, VIEWPORT_HEIGHT));
```

■ **Tip** It is possible to scale or rotate the ImageView and set a viewport to view the region of the image defined by the viewport.

Understanding Image Operations

JavaFX supports reading pixels from an image, writing pixels to an image, and creating a snapshot of the scene. It supports creating an Image from scratch. If an image is writable, you can also modify the image in memory and save it to the file system. The image API provides access to each pixel in the image. It supports reading and writing one pixel or a chunk of pixels at a time. This section will discuss operations supported by the Image API with simple examples.

Pixel Formats

The Image API in JavaFX gives you access to each pixel in an image. A pixel stores information about its color (red, green, blue) and opacity (alpha). The pixel information can be stored in several formats.

An instance the PixelFormat<T extends Buffer> represents the layout of data for a pixel. You need to know the pixel format when you read the pixels from an image. You need to specify the pixel format when you write pixels to an image. The WritablePixelFormat class inherits from the PixelFormat class, and its instance represents a pixel format that can store full color information. An instance of the WritablePixelFormat class is used when writing pixels to an image.

Both class PixelFormat and its subclass WritablePixelFormat are abstract. The PixelFormat class provides several static methods to obtain instances to PixelFormat and WritablePixelFormat abstract classes. Before we discuss how to get an instance of the PixelFormat, let us discuss types of storage formats available for storing the pixel data.

A PixelFormat has a type that specifies the storage format for a single pixel. The constants of the PixelFormat.Type enum represent different types of storage formats:

- BYTE_RGB

- BYTE_BGRA

- BYTE_BGRA_PRE

- BYTE_INDEXED

- INT_ARGB

- INT_ARGB_PRE

In the BYTE_RGB format, the pixels are assumed opaque. The pixels are stored in adjacent bytes as red, green, and blue, in order.

In the BYTE_BGRA format, pixels are stored in adjacent bytes as blue, green, red, and alpha in order. The color values (red, green, and blue) are not pre-multiplied with the alpha value.

The BYTE_BGRA_PRE type format is similar to BYTE_BGRA, except that in BYTE_BGRA_PRE the stored color component values are pre-multiplied by the alpha value.

In the BYTE_INDEXED format, a pixel is as a single byte. A separate lookup list of colors is provided. The single byte value for the pixel is used as an index in the lookup list to get the color value for the pixel.

In the INT_ARGB format, each pixel is stored in a 32-bit integer. Bytes from the most significant byte (MSB) to the least significant byte (LSB) store alpha, red, green, and blue values. The color values (red, green, and blue) are not pre-multiplied with the alpha value. The following snippet of code shows how to extract components from a pixel value in this format:

```
int pixelValue = get the value for a pixel...
int alpha = (pixelValue >> 24) & 0xff;
int red   = (pixelValue >> 16) & 0xff;
int green = (pixelValue >>  8) & 0xff;
int blue  = pixelValue & 0xff;
```

The INT_ARGB_PRE format is similar to the INT_ARGB format, except that INT_ARGB_PRE stores the color values (red, green, and blue) pre-multiplied with the alpha value.

Typically, you need to create a WritablePixelFormat when you write pixels to create a new image. When you read pixels from an image, the pixel reader will provide you a PixelFormat instance that will tell you how the color information in the pixels are stored. The following snippet of code creates some instances of the WritablePixelFormat class:

```
import javafx.scene.image.PixelFormat;
import javafx.scene.image.WritablePixelFormat;
import java.nio.ByteBuffer;
import java.nio.IntBuffer;
...
// BYTE_BGRA Format type
WritablePixelFormat<ByteBuffer> format1 = PixelFormat.getByteBgraInstance();

// BYTE_BGRA_PRE Format type
WritablePixelFormat<ByteBuffer> format2 =
    PixelFormat.getByteBgraPreInstance();

// INT_ARGB Format type
WritablePixelFormat<IntBuffer> format3 = PixelFormat.getIntArgbInstance();

// INT_ARGB_PRE Format type
WritablePixelFormat<IntBuffer> format4 = PixelFormat.getIntArgbPreInstance();
```

Pixel format classes are not useful without pixel information. After all, they describe the layout of information in a pixel! We will use these classes when we read and write image pixels in the sections to follow. Their use will be obvious in the examples.

Reading Pixels from an Image

An instance of the PixelReader interface is used to read pixels from an image. Use the getPixelReader() method of the Image class to obtain a PixelReader. The PixelReader interface contains the following methods:

- int getArgb(int x, int y)

- Color getColor(int x, int y)

- Void getPixels(int x, int y, int w, int h,
  WritablePixelFormat<ByteBuffer> pixelformat, byte[] buffer, int offset,
  int scanlineStride)

- void getPixels(int x, int y, int w, int h,
  WritablePixelFormat<IntBuffer> pixelformat, int[] buffer, int offset,
  int scanlineStride)

- <T extends Buffer> void getPixels(int x, int y, int w, int h,
  WritablePixelFormat<T> pixelformat, T buffer, int scanlineStride)

- PixelFormat getPixelFormat()

The PixelReader interface contains methods to read one pixel or multiple pixels at a time. Use the getArgb() and getColor() methods to read the pixel at the specified (x, y) coordinate. Use the getPixels() method to read pixels in bulk. Use the getPixelFormat() method to get the PixelFormat that best describes the storage format for the pixels in the source.

The getPixelReader() method of the Image class returns a PixelReader only if the image is readable. Otherwise, it returns null. An image may not be readable if it is not fully loaded yet, it had an error during loading, or its format does not support reading pixels:

```
Image image = new Image("file://.../resources/picture/ksharan.jpg");

// Get the pixel reader
PixelReader pixelReader = image.getPixelReader();
if (pixelReader == null) {
        System.out.println("Cannot read pixels from the image");
} else {
        // Read image pixels
}
```

Once you have a PixelReader, you can read pixels invoking one of its methods. The program in Listing 21-4 shows how to read pixels from an image. The code is self-explanatory:

- The start() method creates an Image. The Image is loaded synchronously.

- The logic to read the pixels is in the readPixelsInfo() method. The method receives a fully loaded Image. It uses the getColor() method of the PixelReader to get the pixel at a specified location. It prints the colors for all pixels. At the end, it prints the pixel format, which is BYTE_RGB.

Listing 21-4. Reading Pixels from an Image

```
// ReadPixelInfo.java
// ...find in the book's download area.
```

```
Color at (0, 0) = 0xb5bb41ff
Color at (1, 0) = 0xb0b53dff
...
Color at (233, 287) = 0x718806ff
Color at (234, 287) = 0x798e0bff
Pixel format type: BYTE_RGB
```

Reading pixels in bulk is a little more difficult than reading one pixel at a time. The difficulty arises from the setup information that you have to provide to the getPixels() method. We will repeat the preceding example by reading all pixels in bulk using the following method of the PixelReader:

```
void getPixels(int x, int y,
               int width, int height,
               WritablePixelFormat<ByteBuffer> pixelformat,
               byte[] buffer,
               int offset,
               int scanlineStride)
```

The method reads the pixels from rows in order. The pixels in the first row are read, then the pixels from the second row, and so on. It is important that you understand the meaning of all parameters to the method.

The method reads the pixels of a rectangular region in the source.

The x and y coordinates of the upper-left corner of the rectangular region are specified in the x and y arguments.

The width and height arguments specify the width and height of the rectangular region.

The pixelformat specifies the format of the pixel that should be used to store the read pixels in the specified buffer.

The buffer is a byte array in which the PixelReader will store the read pixels. The length of the array must be big enough to store all read pixels.

The offset specifies the starting index in the buffer array to store the first pixel data. Its value of zero indicates that the data for the first pixel will start at index 0 in the buffer.

The scanlineStride specifies the distance between the start of one row of data in the buffer and the start of the next row of data. Suppose you have two pixels in a row, and you want to read in the BYTE_BGRA format taking 4 bytes for a pixel. One row of data can be stored in 8 bytes. If you specify 8 as the argument value, the data for the next row will start in the buffer just after the data for the previous row data ends. If you specify the argument value 10, the last 2 bytes will be empty for each row of data. The first row pixels will be stored from index 0 to 7. The indexes 8 and 9 will be empty (or not written). Indexes 10 to 17 will store pixel data for the second row leaving indexes 18 and 19 empty. You may want to specify a bigger value for the argument than needed to store one row of pixel data if you want to fill the empty slots with your own values later. Specifying a value less than needed will overwrite part of the data in the previous row.

The following snippet of code shows how to read all pixels from an image in a byte array, in BYTE_BGRA format:

```
Image image = ...
PixelReader pixelReader = image.getPixelReader();

int x = 0;
int y = 0;
int width = (int)image.getWidth();
int height = (int)image.getHeight();
int offset = 0;
```

```
int scanlineStride = width * 4;
byte[] buffer = new byte[width * height * 4];

// Get a WritablePixelFormat for the BYTE_BGRA format type
WritablePixelFormat<ByteBuffer> pixelFormat = PixelFormat.getByteBgraInstance();

// Read all pixels at once
pixelReader.getPixels(x, y,
                width, height,
                pixelFormat,
                buffer,
                offset,
                scanlineStride);
```

The x and y coordinates of the upper-left corner of the rectangular region to be read are set to zero. The width and height of the region are set to the width and height of the image. This sets up the arguments to read the entire image.

You want to read the pixel data into the buffer starting at index 0, so you set the offset argument to 0.

You want to read the pixel data in BYTE_BGRA format type, which takes 4 bytes to store data for one pixel. We have set the scanlineStride argument value, which is the length of a row data, to width * 4, so a row data starts at the next index from where the previous row data ended.

You get an instance of the WritablePixelFormat to read the data in the BYTE_BGRA format type. Finally, we call the getPixels() method of the PixelReader to read the pixel data. The buffer will be filled with the pixel data when the getPixels() method returns.

■ **Tip**   Setting the value for the scanlineStride argument and the length of the buffer array depends on the pixelFormat argument. Other versions of the getPixels() method allow reading pixel data in different formats.

The program in Listing 21-5 has the complete source code to read pixels in bulk. After reading all pixels, it decodes the color components in the byte array for the pixel at (0, 0). It reads the pixel at (0, 0) using the getColor() method. The pixel data at (0, 0) obtained through both methods are printed on the standard output.

Listing 21-5. Reading Pixels from an Image in Bulk

```
// BulkPixelReading.java
// ...find in the book's download area.
```

```
red=181, green=187, blue=65, alpha=255
red=181, green=187, blue=65, alpha=255
```

Writing Pixels to an Image

You can write pixels to an image or any surface that supports writing pixels. For example, you can write pixels to a WritableImage and a Canvas.

■ **Tip**   An Image is a read-only pixel surface. You can read pixels from an Image. However, you cannot write pixels to an Image. If you want to write to an image or create an image from scratch, use a WritableImage.

An instance of the PixelWriter interface is used to write pixels to a surface. A PixelWriter is provided by the writable surface. For example, you can use the getPixelWriter() method of the Canvas and WritableImage to obtain a PixelWriter for them.

The PixelWriter interface contains methods to write pixels to a surface and obtain the pixel format supported by the surface:

- PixelFormat getPixelFormat()

- void setArgb(int x, int y, int argb)

- void setColor(int x, int y, Color c)

- void setPixels(int x, int y, int w, int h, PixelFormat<ByteBuffer> pixelformat, byte[] buffer, int offset, int scanlineStride)

- void setPixels(int x, int y, int w, int h, PixelFormat<IntBuffer> pixelformat, int[] buffer, int offset, int scanlineStride)

- <T extends Buffer> void setPixels(int x, int y, int w, int h, PixelFormat<T> pixelformat, T buffer, int scanlineStride)

- void setPixels(int dstx, int dsty, int w, int h, PixelReader reader, int srcx, int srcy)

The getPixelFormat() method returns the pixel format in which the pixels can be written to the surface. The setArgb() and setColor() methods allow for writing one pixel at the specified (x, y) location in the destination surface. The setArgb() method accepts the pixel data in an integer in the INT_ARGB format, whereas the setColor() method accepts a Color object. The setPixels() methods allow for bulk pixel writing.

You can use an instance of the WritableImage to create an image from scratch. The class contains three constructors:

- WritableImage(int width, int height)

- WritableImage(PixelReader reader, int width, int height)

- WritableImage(PixelReader reader, int x, int y, int width, int height)

The first constructor creates an empty image of the specified width and height:

```
// Create a new empty image of 200 X 100
WritableImage newImage = new WritableImage(200, 100);
```

The second constructor creates an image of the specified width and height. The specified reader is used to fill the image with pixels. An ArrayIndexOutOfBoundsException is thrown if the reader reads from a surface that does not have the necessary number of rows and columns to fill the new image. Use this constructor to copy the whole or part of an image. The following snippet of code creates a copy of an image:

```
String imagePath = "file://.../resources/picture/ksharan.jpg";
Image image = new Image(imagePath, 200, 100, true, true);

int width = (int)image.getWidth();
int height = (int)image.getHeight();
```

769

```
// Create a copy of the image
WritableImage newImage =
    new WritableImage(image.getPixelReader(), width, height);
```

The third constructor lets you copy a rectangular region from a surface. The (x, y) value is coordinates of the upper-left corner of the rectangular region. The (width, height) value is the dimension of the rectangular region to be read using the reader and the desired dimension of the new image. An ArrayIndexOutOfBoundsException is thrown if the reader reads from a surface that does not have the necessary number of rows and columns to fill the new image.

The WritableImage is a read-write image. Its getPixelWriter() method returns a PixelWriter to write pixels to the image. It inherits the getPixelReader() method that returns a PixelReader to read data from the image.

The following snippet of code creates an Image and an empty WritableImage. It reads one pixel at a time from the Image, makes the pixel darker, and writes the same pixel to the new WritableImage. At the end, we have created a darker copy of the original image:

```
Image image = new Image("file://.../resources/picture/ksharan.jpg";);
PixelReader pixelReader = image.getPixelReader();
int width = (int)image.getWidth();
int height = (int)image.getHeight();

// Create a new, empty WritableImage
WritableImage darkerImage = new WritableImage(width, height);
PixelWriter darkerWriter = darkerImage.getPixelWriter();

// Read one pixel at a time from the source and
// write it to the destinations - one darker and one brighter
for(int y = 0; y < height; y++) {
        for(int x = 0; x < width; x++) {
                // Read the pixel from the source image
                Color color = pixelReader.getColor(x, y);

                // Write a darker pixel to the new image at the same
                    // location
                darkerWriter.setColor(x, y, color.darker());
        }
}
```

The program in Listing 21-6 creates an Image. It creates three instances of the WritableImage and copies the pixels from the original image to them. The copied pixels are modified before they are written to the destination. For one destination, pixels are darkened, for one brightened, and for one, made semitransparent. All four images are displayed in ImageViews as shown in Figure 21-4.

Listing 21-6. Writing Pixels to an Image

```
// CopyingImage.java
// ...find in the book's download area.
```

Figure 21-4. Original image and modified images

■ **Tip** It is easy to crop an image in JavaFX. Use one of the getPixels() methods of the PixelReader to read the needed area of the image in a buffer and write the buffer to a new image. This gives you a new image that is the cropped version of the original image.

Creating an Image from Scratch

In the previous section, we created new images by copying pixels from another image. We had altered the color and opacity of the original pixels before writing them to the new image. That was easy because we were working on one pixel at a time, and we received a pixel as a Color object. It is also possible to create pixels from scratch and then use them to create a new image. Anyone would admit that creating a new, meaningful image by defining its each pixel in code is not an easy task. However, JavaFX has made the process of doing so easy.

In this section, we will create a new image with a pattern of rectangles placed in a grid-like fashion. Each rectangle will be divided into two parts using the diagonal connecting the upper-left and lower-right corners. The upper triangle is painted in green and the lower in red. A new image will be created and filled with the rectangles.

Creating an image from scratch involves three steps:

- Create an instance of the WritableImage.

- Create buffer (a byte array, an int array, etc.) and populate it with pixel data depending on the pixel format you want to use for the pixel data.

- Write the pixels in the buffer to the image.

Let us write the code that creates the pixels for our rectangular region. Let us declare constants for the width and height of the rectangle:

```
static final int RECT_WIDTH = 20;
static final int RECT_HEIGHT = 20;
```

We need to define a buffer (a byte array) big enough to hold data for all pixels. Each pixel in BYTE_RGB format takes 2 bytes:

```
byte[] pixels = new byte[RECT_WIDTH * RECT_HEIGHT * 3];
```

If the region is rectangular, we need to know the height to width ratio to divide the region into upper and lower rectangles:

```
double ratio = 1.0 * RECT_HEIGHT/RECT_WIDTH;
```

The following snippet of code populates the buffer:

```
// Generate pixel data
for (int y = 0; y < RECT_HEIGHT; y++) {
        for (int x = 0; x < RECT_WIDTH; x++) {
            int i = y * RECT_WIDTH * 3 + x * 3;
            if (x <= y/ratio) {
                // Lower-half
                pixels[i] = -1;  // red -1 means 255 (-1 & 0xff = 255)
                pixels[i+1] = 0; // green = 0
                pixels[i+2] = 0; // blue = 0
            } else {
                // Upper-half
                pixels[i] = 0;     // red = 0
                pixels[i+1] = -1; // Green 255
                pixels[i+2] = 0;   // blue = 0
            }
        }
}
```

Pixels are stored in the buffer in the row-first order. The variable i inside the loop computes the position in the buffer where the 3-byte data starts for a pixel. For example, the data for the pixel at (0, 0) starts at index 0; the data for the pixel at (0, 1) starts at index 3; etc. The 3 bytes for a pixel store red, green, and blue values in order of increasing index. Encoded values for the color components are stored in the buffer, so that the expression "byteValue & 0xff" will produce the actual color component value between 0 and 255. If you want a red pixel, you need to set –1 for the red component as "-1 & 0xff" produces 255. For a red color, the green and blue components will be set to zero. A byte array initializes all elements to zero. However, we have explicitly set them to zero in our code. For the lower-half triangle, we set the color to green. The condition "x =<= y/ratio" is used to determine the position of a pixel whether it falls in the upper-half triangle or the lower-half triangle. If the y/ratio is not an integer, the division of the rectangle into two triangles may be a little off at the lower-right corner.

Once we get the pixel data, we need to write them to a WritableImage. The following snippet of code writes the pixels for the rectangle, once at the upper-left corner of the image:

```
WritableImage newImage = new WritableImage(350, 100);
PixelWriter pixelWriter = newImage.getPixelWriter();
byte[] pixels = generate pixel data...

// Our data is in BYTE_RGB format
PixelFormat<ByteBuffer> pixelFormat = PixelFormat.getByteRgbInstance();
Int xPos 0;
```

```
int yPos =0;
int offset = 0;
int scanlineStride = RECT_WIDTH * 3;
pixelWriter.setPixels(xPos, yPos,
                  RECT_WIDTH, RECT_HEIGHT,
                  pixelFormat,
                  pixels, offset,
                  scanlineStride);
```

The program in Listing 21-7 creates an image from scratch. It creates a pattern by writing row pixels for the rectangular region to fill the image. Figure 21-5 shows the image.

Listing 21-7. Creating an Image from Scratch

```
// CreatingImage.java
// ...find in the book's download area.
```

Figure 21-5. *An image created from scratch*

Saving a New Image to a File System

Saving an Image to the file system is easy:

- Convert the Image to a BufferedImage using the fromFXImage() method of the SwingFXUtils class.

- Pass the BufferedImage to the write() method of the ImageIO class.

Notice that we have to use two classes—BufferedImage and ImageIO—that are part of the standard Java library, not the JavaFX library. The following snippet of code shows the outline of the steps involved in saving an image to a file in the PNG format:

```
import java.awt.image.BufferedImage;
import java.io.File;
import java.io.IOException;
import javafx.embed.swing.SwingFXUtils;
import javafx.scene.image.Image;
import javax.imageio.ImageIO;
...
```

```
Image image = create an image...
BufferedImage bImage = SwingFXUtils.fromFXImage(image, null);

// Save the image to the file
File fileToSave = ...
String imageFormat = "png";
try {
        ImageIO.write(bImage, imageFormat, fileToSave);
}
catch (IOException e) {
        throw new RuntimeException(e);
}
```

The program in Listing 21-8 has code for a utility class `ImageUtil`. Its static `saveToFile(Image image)` method can be used to save an `Image` to a local file system. The method asks for a file name. The user can select a PNG or a JPEG format for the image.

Listing 21-8. A Utility Class to Save an Image to a File

```
// ImageUtil.java
// ...find in the book's download area.
```

The program in Listing 21-9 shows how to save an image to a file. Click the Save Image button to save the picture to a file. It opens a file chooser dialog to let you select a file name. If you cancel the file chooser dialog, the saving process is aborted.

Listing 21-9. Saving an Image to a File

```
// SaveImage.java
// ...find in the book's download area.
```

Taking the Snapshot of a Node and a Scene

JavaFX allows you to take a snapshot of a Node and a Scene as they will appear in the next frame. You get the snapshot in a `WritableImage`, which means you can perform all pixel-level operations after you take the snapshot. The Node and Scene classes contain a `snapshot()` method to accomplish this.

Taking the Snapshot of a Node

The Node class contains an overloaded `snapshot()` method:

- `WritableImage snapshot(SnapshotParameters params, WritableImage image)`
- `void snapshot(Callback<SnapshotResult,Void> callback, SnapshotParameters params, WritableImage image)`

The first version of the snapshot() method is synchronous, whereas the second one is asynchronous. The method lets you specify an instance of the SnapshotParameters class that contains the rendering attributes for the snapshot. If this is null, default values will be used. You can set the following attributes for the snapshot:

- A fill color

- A transform

- A viewport

- A camera

- A depth buffer

By default, the fill color is white; no transform and viewport are used; a ParallelCamera is used; and the depth buffer is set to false. Note that these attributes are used on the node only while taking its snapshot.

You can specify a WritableImage in the snapshot() method that will hold the snapshot of the node. If this is null, a new WritableImage is created. If the specified WritableImage is smaller than the node, the node will be clipped to fit the image size.

The first version of the snapshot() method returns the snapshot in a WritableImage. The image is either the one that is passed as the parameter or a new one created by the method.

The second, asynchronous version of the snapshot() method accepts a Callback object whose call() method is called. A SnapshotResult object is passed to the call() method, which can be used to obtain the snapshot image, the source node, and the snapshot parameters using the following methods:

- WritableImage getImage()

- SnapshotParameters getSnapshotParameters()

- Object getSource()

■ **Tip** The snapshot() method takes the snapshot of the node using the boundsInParent property of the node. That is, the snapshot contains all effects and transformations applied to the node. If the node is being animated, the snapshot will include the animated state of the node at the time it is taken.

The program in Listing 21-10 shows how to take a snapshot of a TextField node. It displays a Label, a TextField, and two Buttons in a GridPane. Buttons are used to take the snapshot of the TextField synchronously and asynchronously. Click one of the Buttons to take a snapshot. A file save dialog appears for you to enter the file name for the saved snapshot. The syncSnapshot() and asyncSnapshot() methods contain the logic to take the snapshot. For the snapshot, the fill is set to red, and a Scale and a Rotate transforms are applied. Figure 21-6 shows the snapshot.

Listing 21-10. Taking a Snapshot of a Node

```
// NodeSnapshot.java
// ...find in the book's download area.
```

Figure 21-6. *The snapshot of a node*

Taking the Snapshot of a Scene

The Scene class contains an overloaded snapshot() method:

- WritableImage snapshot(WritableImage image)

- void snapshot(Callback<SnapshotResult,Void> callback,
  WritableImage image)

Compare the snapshot() methods of the Scene class with that of the Node class. The only difference is that the snapshot() method in the Scene class does not contain the SnapshotParameters argument. This means that you cannot customize the scene snapshot. Except this, the method works the same way as it works for the Node class, as discussed in the previous section.

The first version of the snapshot() method is synchronous, whereas the second one is asynchronous. You can specify a WritableImage to the method that will hold the snapshot of the node. If this is null, a new WritableImage is created. If the specified WritableImage is smaller than the scene, the scene will be clipped to fit the image size.

The program in Listing 21-11 shows how to take a snapshot of a scene. The main logic in the program is essentially the same as that of the program in Listing 21-10, except that, this time, it takes a snapshot of a scene. Figure 21-7 shows the snapshot.

Listing 21-11. Taking a Snapshot of a Scene

```
// SceneSnapshot.java
// ...find in the book's download area.
```

Name:	Prema	Synchronous Snapshot
		Asynchronous Snapshot

Figure 21-7. *The snapshot of a scene*

Summary

JavaFX provides the Image API that lets you load and display images and read/write raw image pixels. All classes in the API are in the javafx.scene.image package. The API lets you perform the following operations on images: load an image in memory, display an image as a node in a scene graph, read pixels from an image, write pixels to an image, and convert a node in a scene graph to an image and save it to the local file system.

An instance of the Image class is an in-memory representation of an image. You can also construct an image in a JavaFX application by supplying pixels to a WritableImage instance. The Image class supports BMP, PNG, JPEG, and GIF image formats. It loads an image from a source, which can be specified as a string URL or an InputStream. It can also scale the original image while loading.

An instance of the ImageView class is used to display an image loaded in an Image object. The ImageView class inherits from the Node class, which makes an ImageView suitable to be added to a scene graph.

Images are constructed from pixels. JavaFX supports reading pixels from an image, writing pixels to an image, and creating a snapshot of the scene. It supports creating an image from scratch. If an image is writable, you can also modify the image in memory and save it to the file system. The Image API provides access to each pixel in the image. It supports reading and writing one pixel or a chunk of pixels at a time.

Data for pixels in an image may be stored in different formats. A PixelFormat defines how the data for a pixel for a given format is stored. A WritablePixelFormat represents a destination format to write pixels with full pixel color information.

The PixelReader and PixelWriter interfaces define methods to read data from an Image and write data to a WritableImage. Besides an Image, you can read pixels from and write pixels to any surface that contains pixels.

JavaFX allows you to take a snapshot of a Node and a Scene as they will appear in the next frame. You get the snapshot in a WritableImage, which means you can perform all pixel-level operations after you take the snapshot. The Node and Scene classes contain a snapshot() method to accomplish this.

The next chapter will discuss how to draw on a canvas using the Canvas API.

CHAPTER 22

■ ■ ■

Drawing on a Canvas

In this chapter, you will learn:

- What the Canvas API is
- How to create a canvas
- How to draw on a canvas such as basic shapes, text, paths, and images
- How to clear the canvas area
- How to save and restore the drawing states in a GraphicsContext

The examples of this chapter lie in the com.jdojo.canvas package. In order for them to work, you must add a corresponding line to the module-info.java file:

```
...
opens com.jdojo.canvas to javafx.graphics, javafx.base;
...
```

What Is the Canvas API?

Through the javafx.scene.canvas package, JavaFX provides the Canvas API that offers a drawing surface to draw shapes, images, and text using drawing commands. The API also gives pixel-level access to the drawing surface where you can write any pixels on the surface. The API consists of only two classes:

- Canvas
- GraphicsContext

A canvas is a bitmap image, which is used as a drawing surface. An instance of the Canvas class represents a canvas. It inherits from the Node class. Therefore, a canvas is a node. It can be added to a scene graph, and effects and transformations can be applied to it.

A canvas has a graphics context associated with it that is used to issue drawing commands to the canvas. An instance of the GraphicsContext class represents a graphics context.

© Kishori Sharan and Peter Späth 2022
K. Sharan and P. Späth, *Learn JavaFX 17*, https://doi.org/10.1007/978-1-4842-7848-2_22

Creating a Canvas

The Canvas class has two constructors. The no-args constructor creates an empty canvas. Later, you can set the size of the canvas using its width and height properties. The other constructor takes the width and height of the canvas as parameters:

```
// Create a Canvas of zero width and height
Canvas canvas = new Canvas();

// Set the canvas size
canvas.setWidth(400);
canvas.setHeight(200);

// Create a 400X200 canvas
Canvas canvas = new Canvas(400, 200);
```

Drawing on the Canvas

Once you create a canvas, you need to get its graphics context using the getGraphicsContext2D() method, as in the following snippet of code:

```
// Get the graphics context of the canvas
GraphicsContext gc = canvas.getGraphicsContext2D();
```

All drawing commands are provided in the GraphicsContext class as methods. Drawings that fall outside the bounds of the canvas are clipped. The canvas uses a buffer. The drawing commands push necessary parameters to the buffer. It is important to note that you should use the graphics context from any one thread before adding the Canvas to the scene graph. Once the Canvas is added to the scene graph, the graphics context should be used only on the JavaFX Application Thread. The GraphicsContext class contains methods to draw the following types of objects:

- Basic shapes
- Text
- Paths
- Images
- Pixels

Drawing Basic Shapes

The GraphicsContext class provides two types of methods to draw the basic shapes. The method fillXxx() draws a shape Xxx and fills it with the current fill paint. The method strokeXxx() draws a shape Xxx with the current stroke. Use the following methods for drawing shapes:

- fillArc()
- fillOval()
- fillPolygon()

- `fillRect()`
- `fillRoundRect()`
- `strokeArc()`
- `strokeLine()`
- `strokeOval()`
- `strokePolygon()`
- `strokePolyline()`
- `strokeRect()`
- `strokeRoundRect()`

The following snippet of code draws a rectangle. The stroke color is red, and the stroke width is 2px. The upper-left corner of the rectangle is at (0, 0). The rectangle is 100px wide and 50px high:

```
Canvas canvas = new Canvas(200, 100);
GraphicsContext gc = canvas.getGraphicsContext2D();
gc.setLineWidth(2.0);
gc.setStroke(Color.RED);
gc.strokeRect(0, 0, 100, 50);
```

Drawing Text

You can draw text using the `fillText()` and `strokeText()` methods of the `GraphicsContext` using the following snippets of code:

- `void strokeText(String text, double x, double y)`
- `void strokeText(String text, double x, double y, double maxWidth)`
- `void fillText(String text, double x, double y)`
- `void fillText(String text, double x, double y, double maxWidth)`

Both methods are overloaded. One version lets you specify the text and its position. The other version lets you specify the maximum width of the text as well. If the actual text width exceeds the specified maximum width, the text is resized to fit the specified maximum width. The following snippet of code draws two strings. Figure 22-1 shows the two strings on the canvas.

```
Canvas canvas = new Canvas(200, 50);
GraphicsContext gc = canvas.getGraphicsContext2D();
gc.setLineWidth(1.0);
gc.setStroke(Color.BLACK);
gc.strokeText("Drawing Text", 10, 10);
gc.strokeText("Drawing Text", 100, 10, 40);
```

Drawing Text   Drawing Text

Figure 22-1. Drawing text on a canvas

Drawing Paths

You can use path commands and SVG path strings to create a shape of your choice. A path consists of multiple subpaths. The following methods are used to draw paths:

- beginPath()
- lineTo(double x1, double y1)
- moveTo(double x0, double y0)
- quadraticCurveTo(double xc, double yc, double x1, double y1)
- appendSVGPath(String svgpath)
- arc(double centerX, double centerY, double radiusX, double radiusY, double startAngle, double length)
- arcTo(double x1, double y1, double x2, double y2, double radius)
- bezierCurveTo(double xc1, double yc1, double xc2, double yc2, double x1, double y1)
- closePath()
- stroke()
- fill()

The beginPath() and closePath() methods start and close a path, respectively. Methods such as arcTo() and lineTo() are the path commands to draw a specific type of subpath. Do not forget to call the stroke() or fill() method at the end, which will draw an outline or fill the path. The following snippet of code draws a triangle, as shown in Figure 22-2:

```
Canvas canvas = new Canvas(200, 50);
GraphicsContext gc = canvas.getGraphicsContext2D();
gc.setLineWidth(2.0);
gc.setStroke(Color.BLACK);

gc.beginPath();
gc.moveTo(25, 0);
gc.appendSVGPath("L50, 25L0, 25");
gc.closePath();
gc.stroke();
```

Figure 22-2. *Drawing a triangle*

Drawing Images

You can draw an image on the canvas using the drawImage() method. The method has three versions:

- void drawImage(Image img, double x, double y)

- void drawImage(Image img, double x, double y, double w, double h)

- void drawImage(Image img, double sx, double sy, double sw, double sh, double dx, double dy, double dw, double dh)

You can draw the whole or part of the image. The drawn image can be stretched or shortened on the canvas. The following snippet of code draws the whole image in its original size on the canvas at (10, 10):

```
Image image = new Image("your_image_URL");
Canvas canvas = new Canvas(400, 400);
GraphicsContext gc = canvas.getGraphicsContext2D();
gc.drawImage(image, 10, 10);
```

The following statement will draw the whole image on the canvas by resizing it to fit in a 100px wide by 150px high area. Whether the image is stretched or shortened depends on its original size:

```
// Draw the whole image in 100X150 area at (10, 10)
gc.drawImage(image, 10, 10, 100, 150);
```

The following statement will draw part of an image on the canvas. Here, it is assumed that the source image is bigger than 100px by 150px. The image part being drawn is 100px wide and 150px high, and its upper-left corner is at (0, 0) in the source image. The part of the image is drawn on the canvas at (10, 10), and it is stretched to fit 200px wide and 200px high area on the canvas:

```
// Draw part of the image in 200X200 area at (10, 10)
gc.drawImage(image, 0, 0, 100, 150, 10, 10, 200, 200);
```

Writing Pixels

You can also directly modify pixels on the canvas. The getPixelWriter() method of the GraphicsContext object returns a PixelWriter that can be used to write pixels to the associated canvas:

```
Canvas canvas = new Canvas(200, 100);
GraphicsContext gc = canvas.getGraphicsContext2D();
PixelWriter pw = gc.getPixelWriter();
```

Once you get a PixelWriter, you can write pixels to the canvas. Chapter 21 presented more details on how to write pixels using a PixelWriter.

Clearing the Canvas Area

The canvas is a transparent area. Pixels will have colors and opacity depending on what is drawn at those pixels. Sometimes, you may want to clear the whole or part of the canvas so the pixels are transparent again. The clearRect() method of the GraphicsContext lets you clear a specified area on the canvas:

```
// Clear the top-left 100X100 rectangular area from the canvas
gc.clearRect(0, 0, 100, 100);
```

Saving and Restoring the Drawing States

The current settings for the GraphicsContext are used for all subsequent drawing. For example, if you set the line width to 5px, all subsequent strokes will be 5px in width. Sometimes, you may want to modify the state of the graphics context temporarily and, after some time, restore the state that existed before the modification.

The save() and restore() methods of the GraphicsContext object let you save the current state and restore it afterward, respectively. Before you use these methods, let's discuss its need. Suppose you want to issue the following commands to the GraphicsContext object in order:

- Draw a rectangle without any effects

- Draw a string with a reflection effect

- Draw a rectangle without any effects

The following is the first (and incorrect) attempt of achieving this:

```
Canvas canvas = new Canvas(200, 120);
GraphicsContext gc = canvas.getGraphicsContext2D();
gc.strokeRect(10, 10, 50, 20);
gc.setEffect(new Reflection());
gc.strokeText("Chatar", 70, 20);
gc.strokeRect(120, 10, 50, 20);
```

Figure 22-3 shows the drawing of the canvas. Notice that the reflection effect was also applied to the second rectangle, which was not wanted.

Figure 22-3. *Drawing shapes and text*

You can fix the problem by setting the Effect to null after you draw the text. You had modified several properties for the GraphicsContext and then had to restore them all manually. Sometimes, a GraphicsContext may be passed to your code, but you do not want to modify its existing state.

The save() method stores the current state of the GraphicsContext on a stack. The restore() method restores the state of the GraphicsContext to the last saved state. Figure 22-4 shows the results of this. You can fix the problem using the following methods:

```
Canvas canvas = new Canvas(200, 120);
GraphicsContext gc = canvas.getGraphicsContext2D();

gc.strokeRect(10, 10, 50, 20);

// Save the current state
gc.save();

// Modify the current state to add an effect and darw the text
gc.setEffect(new Reflection());
gc.strokeText("Chatar", 70, 20);
```

```
// Restore the state what it was when the last save() was called and draw the
// second rectangle
gc.restore();
gc.strokeRect(120, 10, 50, 20);
```

Figure 22-4. *Drawing shapes and text using save() and restore() methods*

A Canvas Drawing Example

The program in Listing 22-1 shows how to draw basic shapes, text, images, and row pixels to a canvas. Figure 22-5 shows the resulting canvas with all drawings.

Listing 22-1. Drawing on a Canvas

```java
// CanvasTest.java
package com.jdojo.canvas;

import com.jdojo.util.ResourceUtil;
import java.nio.ByteBuffer;
import javafx.application.Application;
import javafx.scene.Scene;
import javafx.scene.canvas.Canvas;
import javafx.scene.canvas.GraphicsContext;
import javafx.scene.image.Image;
import javafx.scene.image.PixelFormat;
import javafx.scene.image.PixelWriter;
import javafx.scene.layout.Pane;
import javafx.scene.paint.Color;
import javafx.stage.Stage;

public class CanvasTest extends Application {
        private static final int RECT_WIDTH = 20;
        private static final int RECT_HEIGHT = 20;

        public static void main(String[] args) {
                Application.launch(args);
        }

        @Override
        public void start(Stage stage) {
                Canvas canvas = new Canvas(400, 100);
                GraphicsContext gc = canvas.getGraphicsContext2D();

                // Set line width and fill color
                gc.setLineWidth(2.0);
```

```
            gc.setFill(Color.RED);

            // Draw a rounded rectangle
            gc.strokeRoundRect(10, 10, 50, 50, 10, 10);

            // Fill an oval
            gc.fillOval(70, 10, 50, 20);

            // Draw text
            gc.strokeText("Hello Canvas", 10, 85);

            // Draw an Image
            String imagePath =
                    ResourceUtil.getResourceURLStr("picture/ksharan.jpg");
            Image image = new Image(imagePath);
            gc.drawImage(image, 130, 10, 60, 80);

            // Write custom pixels to create a pattern
            writePixels(gc);

            Pane root = new Pane();
            root.getChildren().add(canvas);
            Scene scene = new Scene(root);
            stage.setScene(scene);
            stage.setTitle("Drawing on a Canvas");
            stage.show();
    }

    private void writePixels(GraphicsContext gc) {
            byte[] pixels = this.getPixelsData();
            PixelWriter pixelWriter = gc.getPixelWriter();

            // Our data is in BYTE_RGB format
            PixelFormat<ByteBuffer> pixelFormat =
                    PixelFormat.getByteRgbInstance();

            int spacing = 5;
            int imageWidth = 200;
            int imageHeight = 100;

            // Roughly compute the number of rows and columns
            int rows = imageHeight/(RECT_HEIGHT + spacing);
            int columns = imageWidth/(RECT_WIDTH + spacing);

            // Write the pixels to the canvas
            for (int y = 0; y < rows; y++) {
                for (int x = 0; x < columns; x++) {
                    int xPos = 200 + x * (RECT_WIDTH + spacing);
                    int yPos = y * (RECT_HEIGHT + spacing);
                    pixelWriter.setPixels(xPos, yPos,
```

```
                   RECT_WIDTH, RECT_HEIGHT,
                   pixelFormat,
                   pixels, 0,
                   RECT_WIDTH * 3);
        }
     }
}

private byte[] getPixelsData() {
     // Each pixel in the w X h region will take 3 bytes
     byte[] pixels = new byte[RECT_WIDTH * RECT_HEIGHT * 3];

     // Height to width ration
     double ratio = 1.0 * RECT_HEIGHT/RECT_WIDTH;

     // Generate pixel data
     for (int y = 0; y < RECT_HEIGHT; y++) {
         for (int x = 0; x < RECT_WIDTH; x++) {
             int i = y * RECT_WIDTH * 3 + x * 3;
             if (x <= y/ratio) {
                 pixels[i] = -1;   // red -1 means
                                   // 255 (-1 & 0xff = 255)
                 pixels[i+1] = 0; // green = 0
                 pixels[i+2] = 0; // blue = 0
             } else {
                 pixels[i] = 0;     // red = 0
                 pixels[i+1] = -1; // Green 255
                 pixels[i+2] = 0;   // blue = 0
             }
         }
     }
     return pixels;
}
}
```

Figure 22-5. *A canvas with shapes, text, images, and raw pixels drawn on it*

Summary

Through the `javafx.scene.canvas` package, JavaFX provides the Canvas API that offers a drawing surface to draw shapes, images, and text using drawing commands. The API also gives pixel-level access to the drawing surface where you can write any pixels on the surface. The API consists of only two classes: `Canvas` and `GraphicsContext`. A canvas is a bitmap image, which is used as a drawing surface. An instance of the `Canvas` class represents a canvas. It inherits from the `Node` class. Therefore, a canvas is a node. It can be added to a scene graph, and effects and transformations can be applied to it. A canvas has a graphics context associated with it that is used to issue drawing commands to the canvas. An instance of the `GraphicsContext` class represents a graphics context.

The `Canvas` class contains a `getGraphicsContext2D()` method that returns an instance of the `GraphicsContext` class. After obtaining the `GraphicsContext` of a canvas, you issue drawing commands to the `GraphicsContext` that performs the drawing.

Drawings falling outside the bounds of the canvas are clipped. The canvas uses a buffer. The drawing commands push necessary parameters to the buffer. The `GraphicsContext` of a canvas can be used from any one thread before the canvas is added to the scene graph. Once the canvas is added to the scene graph, the graphics context should be used only on the JavaFX Application Thread. The `GraphicsContext` class contains methods to draw the following types of objects: basic shapes, text, paths, images, and pixels.

The next chapter will discuss how to use the drag-and-drop gesture to transfer data between nodes in the same JavaFX application, between two different JavaFX applications, and between a JavaFX application and a native application.

CHAPTER 23

■ ■ ■

Understanding Drag and Drop

In this chapter, you will learn:

- What a press-drag-release gesture is
- How to use a dragboard to facilitate data transfers
- How to initiate and detect a drag-and-drop gesture
- How to transfer data from the source to the target using a drag-and-drop gesture
- How to transfer images using a drag-and-drop gesture
- How to transfer custom data between the source and the target using a drag-and-drop gesture

The examples of this chapter lie in the com.jdojo.dnd package. In order for them to work, you must add a corresponding line to the module-info.java file:

```
...
opens com.jdojo.dnd to javafx.graphics, javafx.base;
...
```

What Is a Press-Drag-Release Gesture?

A press-drag-release gesture is a user action of pressing a mouse button, dragging the mouse with the pressed button, and releasing the button. The gesture can be initiated on a scene or a node. Several nodes and scenes may participate in a single press-drag-release gesture. The gesture is capable of generating different types of events and delivering those events to different nodes. The type of generated events and nodes receiving the events depends on the purpose of the gesture. A node can be dragged for different purposes:

- You may want to change the shape of a node by dragging its boundaries or move it by dragging it to a new location. In this case, the gesture involves only one node: the node on which the gesture was initiated.
- You may want to drag a node and drop it onto another node to connect them in some fashion, for example, connecting two nodes with a symbol in a flow chart. In this case, the drag gesture involves multiple nodes. When the source node is dropped onto the target node, an action takes place.

© Kishori Sharan and Peter Späth 2022
K. Sharan and P. Späth, *Learn JavaFX 17*, https://doi.org/10.1007/978-1-4842-7848-2_23

- You can drag a node and drop it onto another node to transfer data from the source node to the target node. In this case, the drag gesture involves multiple nodes. A data transfer occurs when the source node is dropped.

JavaFX supports three types of drag gestures:

- A simple press-drag-release gesture

- A full press-drag-release gesture

- A drag-and-drop gesture

This chapter will focus mainly on the third type of gesture: the drag-and-drop gesture. It is essential to understand the first two types of gestures to gain full insight into the drag-and-drop gesture. I will discuss the first two types of gestures briefly with a simple example of each type.

A Simple Press-Drag-Release Gesture

The *simple press-drag-release* gesture is the default drag gesture. It is used when the drag gesture involves only one node—the node on which the gesture was initiated. During the drag gesture, all MouseDragEvent types—mouse-drag entered, mouse-drag over, mouse-drag exited, mouse, and mouse-drag released—are delivered only to the gesture source node. In this case, when the mouse button is pressed, the topmost node is picked, and all subsequent mouse events are delivered to that node until the mouse button is released. When the mouse is dragged onto another node, the node on which the gesture was started is still under the cursor, and, therefore, no other nodes receive the events until the mouse button is released.

The program in Listing 23-1 demonstrates a case of the simple press-drag-release gesture. It adds two TextFields to a scene: one is called the source node and the other the target node. Event handlers are added to both nodes. The target node adds MouseDragEvent handlers to detect any mouse-dragged event on it. Run the program, press the mouse button on the source node, drag it onto the target node, and, finally, release the mouse button. The output that follows shows that the source node receives all mouse-dragged events. The target node does not receive any mouse-dragged events. This is the case of a simple press-drag-release gesture where the node initiating the drag gesture receives all mouse-dragged events.

Listing 23-1. Demonstrating a Simple Press-Drag-Release Gesture

```
// SimplePressDragRelease.java
package com.jdojo.dnd;

import javafx.application.Application;
import javafx.scene.Scene;
import javafx.scene.control.Label;
import javafx.scene.control.TextField;
import javafx.scene.layout.GridPane;
import javafx.stage.Stage;

public class SimplePressDragRelease extends Application {
        TextField sourceFld = new TextField("Source Node");
        TextField targetFld = new TextField("Target node");

        public static void main(String[] args) {
                Application.launch(args);
        }
```

```java
@Override
public void start(Stage stage) {
        // Build the UI
        GridPane root = getUI();

        // Add event handlers
        this.addEventHandlers();

        Scene scene = new Scene(root);
        stage.setScene(scene);
        stage.setTitle("A simple press-drag-release gesture");
        stage.show();
}

private GridPane getUI() {
        GridPane pane = new GridPane();
        pane.setHgap(5);
        pane.setVgap(20);
        pane.addRow(0, new Label("Source Node:"), sourceFld);
        pane.addRow(1, new Label("Target Node:"), targetFld);
        return pane;
}

private void addEventHandlers() {
        // Add mouse event handlers for the source
        sourceFld.setOnMousePressed(e ->
                print("Source: pressed"));
        sourceFld.setOnMouseDragged(e ->
                print("Source: dragged"));
        sourceFld.setOnDragDetected(e ->
                print("Source: dragged detected"));
        sourceFld.setOnMouseReleased(e ->
                print("Source: released"));

        // Add mouse event handlers for the target
        targetFld.setOnMouseDragEntered(e ->
                print("Target: drag entered"));
        targetFld.setOnMouseDragOver(e ->
                print("Target: drag over"));
        targetFld.setOnMouseDragReleased(e ->
                print("Target: drag released"));
        targetFld.setOnMouseDragExited(e ->
                print("Target: drag exited"));
}

private void print(String msg) {
        System.out.println(msg);
}
}
```

```
Source: Mouse pressed
Source: Mouse dragged
Source: Mouse dragged detected
Source: Mouse dragged
Source: Mouse dragged
...
Source: Mouse released
```

Note that the drag-detected event is generated once after the mouse is dragged. The `MouseEvent` object has a `dragDetect` flag, which can be set in the mouse-pressed and mouse-dragged events. If it is set to true, the subsequent event that is generated is the drag-detected event. The default is to generate it after the mouse-dragged event. If you want to generate it after the mouse-pressed event, not the mouse-dragged event, you need to modify the event handlers:

```
sourceFld.setOnMousePressed(e -> {
        print("Source: Mouse pressed");

        // Generate drag detect event after the current mouse pressed event
        e.setDragDetect(true);
});

sourceFld.setOnMouseDragged(e -> {
        print("Source: Mouse dragged");

        // Suppress the drag detected default event generation after mouse
          // dragged
        e.setDragDetect(false);
});
```

A Full Press-Drag-Release Gesture

When the source node of a drag gesture receives the drag-detected event, you can start a *full press-drag-release* gesture by calling the `startFullDrag()` method on the source node. The `startFullDrag()` method exists in both Node and Scene classes, allowing you to start a full press-drag-release gesture for a node and a scene. I will simply use only the term node during this discussion.

■ **Tip** The `startFullDrag()` method can only be called from the drag-detected event handler. Calling this method from any other place throws an `IllegalStateException`.

You need to do one more setup to see the full press-drag-release gesture in action. The source node of the drag gesture will still receive all mouse-dragged events as it is under the cursor when a drag is happening. You need to set the `mouseTransparent` property of the gesture source to false so the node below it will be picked and mouse-dragged events will be delivered to that node. Set this property to true in the mouse-pressed event and set it back to false in the mouse-released event.

The program in Listing 23-2 demonstrates a full press-drag-release gesture. The program is similar to the one shown in Listing 23-1, except for the following:

- In the mouse-pressed event handler for the source node, the `mouseTransparent` property for the source node is set to false. It is set back to true in the mouse-released event handler.

- In the drag-detected event handler, the `startFullDrag()` method is called on the source node.

Run the program, press the mouse button on the source node, drag it onto the target node, and, finally, release the mouse button. The output that follows shows that the target node receives mouse-dragged events as the mouse is dragged inside its bounds. This is the case of a full press-drag-release gesture where the node over which the mouse-dragged takes place receives the mouse-dragged events.

Listing 23-2. Demonstrating a Full Press-Drag-Release Gesture

```
// FullPressDragRelease.java
// ...find in the book's download area.
```

```
Source: Mouse pressed
Source: Mouse dragged
Source: Mouse dragged
Source: Mouse dragged detected
Source: Mouse dragged
Source: Mouse dragged
Target: drag entered
Target: drag over
Source: Mouse dragged
Target: drag over
Target: drag released
Source: Mouse released
Target: drag exited
```

A Drag-and-Drop Gesture

The third type of drag gesture is called a *drag-and-drop* gesture, which is a user action combining the mouse movement with a pressed mouse button. It is used to transfer data from the *gesture source* to a *gesture target*. A drag-and-drop gesture allows transferring data from

- One node to another node

- A node to a scene

- One scene to another scene

- A scene to a node

The source and target can be in the same Java or JavaFX application or two different Java or JavaFX applications. A JavaFX application and a native application may also participate in the gesture, for example:

- You can drag text from a Microsoft Word application to a JavaFX application to populate a TextArea and vice versa.

- You can drag an image file from Windows Explorer and drop it onto an ImageView in a JavaFX application. The ImageView can display the image.

- You can drag a text file from Windows Explorer and drop it onto a TextArea in a JavaFX application. The TextArea will read the file and display its content.

Several steps are involved in performing a drag-and-drop gesture:

- A mouse button is pressed on a node.

- The mouse is dragged with the button pressed.

- The node receives a drag-detected event.

- A drag-and-drop gesture is started on the node by calling the startDragAndDrop() method, making the node the gesture source. The data from the source node is placed in a dragboard.

- Once the system switches to a drag-and-drop gesture, it stops delivering MouseEvents and starts delivering DragEvents.

- The gesture source is dragged onto the potential gesture target. The potential gesture target checks whether it accepts the data placed in the dragboard. If it accepts the data, it may become the actual gesture target. The node indicates whether it accepts the data in one of its DragEvent handlers.

- The user releases the pressed button on the gesture target, sending it a drag-dropped event.

- The gesture target uses the data from the dragboard.

- A drag-done event is sent to the gesture source indicating that the drag-and-drop gesture is complete.

I will discuss all of these steps in detail in the sections that follow. The classes supporting the drag-and-drop gesture are included in the javafx.scene.input package.

Understanding the Data Transfer Modes

In a drag-and-drop gesture, the data can be transferred in three modes:

- Copy

- Move

- Link

The *copy* mode indicates that the data will be copied from the gesture source to the gesture target. You may drag a TextField and drop it onto another TextField. The latter gets a copy of the text contained in the former.

The *move* mode indicates that the data will be moved from the gesture source to the gesture target. You may drag a TextField and drop it onto another TextField. The text in the former is then moved to the latter.

The *link* mode indicates that the gesture target will create a link (or reference) to the data being transferred. The actual meaning of "link" depends on the application. You may drag and drop a URL to a WebView in the link mode. The WebView then loads the URL content.

The three data transfer modes are represented by the following three constants in the TransferMode enum:

- TransferMode.COPY

- TransferMode.MOVE

- TransferMode.LINK

Sometimes, you may need a combination of the three transfer modes. The TransferMode enum contains three convenience static fields that are arrays of its enum constants:

- TransferMode[] ANY

- TransferMode[] COPY_OR_MOVE

- TransferMode[] NONE

The ANY field is an array of COPY, MOVE, and LINK enum constants. The COPY_OR_MOVE field is an array of the COPY and MOVE enum constants. The NONE constant is an empty array.

Every drag-and-drop gesture includes the use of the TransferMode enum constants. The gesture source specifies the transfer modes that it supports for the data transfer. The gesture target specifies the modes in which it accepts the data transfer.

Understanding the *Dragboard*

In a drag-and-drop data transfer, the gesture source and the gesture target do not know each other. In fact, they may belong to two different applications: two JavaFX applications, or one JavaFX and one native. How does the data transfer take place between the gesture source and target if they do not know each other? In the real world, an intermediary is needed to facilitate a transaction between two unknown parties. In a drag-and-drop gesture, an intermediary is also used to facilitate the data transfer.

A dragboard acts as an intermediary between the gesture source and gesture target. A dragboard is the storage device that holds the data being transferred. The gesture source places the data into a dragboard; the dragboard is made available to the gesture target, so it can inspect the type of content that is available for transfer. When the gesture target is ready to transfer the data, it gets the data from the dragboard. Figure 23-1 shows the roles played by a dragboard.

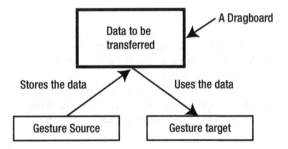

Figure 23-1. *Data transfer mechanism in a drag-and-drop gesture*

An instance of the Dragboard class represents a dragboard. The class is inherited from the Clipboard class. An instance of the Clipboard class represents an operating system clipboard. Typically, an operating system uses a clipboard to store data during cut, copy, and paste operations. You can get the reference of the general clipboard of the operating system using the static getSystemClipboard() method of the Clipboard class:

```
Clipboard systemClipboard = Clipboard.getSystemClipboard();
```

You can place data in the system clipboard that will be accessible to all applications in the system. You can read the data placed in the system clipboard, which can be placed there by any application. A clipboard can store different types of data, for example, rich text format (RTF) text, plain text, HTML, URL, images, or files. The class contains several methods to check if data in a specific format are available in the clipboard. These methods return true if the data in the specific format are available. For example, the hasString() method returns true if the clipboard contains a plain string; the hasRtf() method returns true for text in rich text format. The class contains methods to retrieve data in the specific format. For example, the getString() method returns data in plain text format; the getHtml() returns HTML text; the getImage() returns an image; and so forth. The clear() method clears the clipboard.

■ **Tip** You cannot create an instance of the Clipboard class directly. The clipboard is meant to store one *conceptual* item. The term conceptual means that the data in the clipboard may be stored in different formats representing the same item. For example, you may store RTF text and its plain text version. In this case, the clipboard has two copies of the same item in different formats.

The clipboard is not limited to store only a fixed number of data types. Any serializable data can be stored on the clipboard. Data stored on the clipboard has an associated data format. An instance of the DataFormat class represents a data format. The DataFormat class contains six static fields to represent the commonly used data formats:

- FILES
- HTML
- IMAGE
- PLAIN_TEXT
- RTF
- URL

The FILES represents a list of java.io.File objects. The HTML represents an HTML-formatted string. The IMAGE represents a platform-specific image type. The PLAIN_TEXT represents a plain text string. The RTF represents an RTF-formatted string. The URL represents a URL encoded as a string.

You may want to store data in the clipboard in a format other than those listed earlier. You can create a DataFormat object to represent any arbitrary format. You need to specify a list of mime types for your data format. The following statement creates a DataFormat with jdojo/person and jdojo/personlist as the mime types:

```
DataFormat myFormat = new DataFormat("jdojo/person", "jdojo/person");
```

The Clipboard class provides the following methods to work with the data and its format:

- boolean setContent(Map<DataFormat,Object> content)

- Object getContent(DataFormat dataFormat)

The content of the clipboard is a map with the DataFormat as keys and data as values. The getContent() method returns null if data in the specific data format are not available in the clipboard. The following snippet of code stores HTML and plain text version of data and, later, retrieves the data in both formats:

```
// Store text in HTML and plain-text formats in the system clipboard
Clipboard clipboard = Clipboard.getSystemClipboard();

Map<DataFormat,Object> data = new HashMap<>();
data.put(DataFormat.HTML, "<b>Yahoo!</b>");
data.put(DataFormat.PLAIN_TEXT, "Yahoo!");
clipboard.setContent(data);
...

// Try reading HTML text and plain text from the clipboard
If (clipboard.hasHtml()) {
        String htmlText = (String)clipboard.getContent(DataFormat.HTML);
        System.out.println(htmlText);
}

If (clipboard.hasString()) {
        String plainText = (String)clipboard.getContent(DataFormat.PLAIN_TEXT);
        System.out.println(plainText);
}
```

Preparing data to store in the clipboard requires writing a little bloated code. An instance of the ClipboardContent class represents the content of the clipboard, and it makes working with the clipboard data a little easier. The class inherits from the HashMap<DataFormat,Object> class. It provides convenience methods in the form putXxx() and getXxx() for commonly used data types. The following snippet of code rewrites the preceding logic to store data into the clipboard. The logic to retrieve the data remains the same:

```
Clipboard clipboard = Clipboard.getSystemClipboard();
ClipboardContent content = new ClipboardContent();
content.putHtml("<b>Yahoo!</b>");
content.putString("Yahoo!");
clipboard.setContent(content);
```

The Dragboard class inherits all the public methods available in the Clipboard class. It adds the following methods:

- Set<TransferMode> getTransferModes()

- void setDragView(Image image)

- void setDragView(Image image, double offsetX, double offsetY)

- void setDragViewOffsetX(double offsetX)

- void setDragViewOffsetY(double offsetY)

- Image getDragView()

- Double getDragViewOffsetX()

- double getDragViewOffsetY()

The getTransferModes() method returns the set of transfer modes supported by the gesture target. The setDragView() method sets an image as the drag view. The image is shown when the gesture source is dragged. The offsets are the x and y positions of the cursor over the image. Other methods involve getting the drag-view image and the cursor offsets.

■ **Tip** A dragboard is a special system clipboard used for the drag-and-drop gesture. You cannot create a dragboard explicitly. Whenever it is necessary to work with the dragboard, its reference is made available as the returned value from methods or the property of the event object. For example, the DragEvent class contains a getDragboard() method that returns the reference of the Dragboard containing the data being transferred.

The Example Application

In the following sections, I will discuss the steps in a drag-and-drop gesture in detail, and you will build an example application. The application will have two TextFields displayed in a scene. One text field is called the source node and the other the target node. The user can drag and drop the source node over to the target node. Upon completion of the gesture, the text from the source node is transferred (copied or moved) to the target node. I will refer to those nodes in the discussion. They are declared as follows:

```
TextField sourceFld = new TextField("Source node");
TextField targetFld = new TextField("Target node");
```

Initiating the Drag-and-Drop Gesture

The first step in a drag-and-drop gesture is to convert a simple press-drag-release gesture into a drag-and-drop gesture. This is accomplished in the mouse-drag detected event handler for the gesture source. Calling the startDragAndDrop() method on the gesture source initiates a drag-and-drop gesture. The method is available in the Node and Scene classes, so a node and a scene can be the gesture source of a drag-and-drop gesture. The method signature is

```
Dragboard startDragAndDrop(TransferMode... transferModes)
```

The method accepts the list of supported transfer modes by the gesture source and returns a dragboard. The gesture source needs to populate the dragboard with the data it intends to transfer. The following snippet of code initiates a drag-and-drop gesture, copies the source TextField text to the dragboard, and consumes the event. The drag-and-drop gesture is initiated only when the TextField contains text:

```
sourceFld.setOnDragDetected((MouseEvent e) -> {
        // User can drag only when there is text in the source field
        String sourceText = sourceFld.getText();
```

```java
    if (sourceText == null || sourceText.trim().equals("")) {
            e.consume();
            return;
    }

    // Initiate a drag-and-drop gesture
    Dragboard dragboard =
            sourceFld.startDragAndDrop(TransferMode.COPY_OR_MOVE);

    // Add the source text to the Dragboard
    ClipboardContent content = new ClipboardContent();
    content.putString(sourceText);
    dragboard.setContent(content);

    e.consume();
});
```

Detecting a Drag Gesture

Once the drag-and-drop gesture has been initiated, you can drag the gesture source over to any other node. The gesture source has already put the data in the dragboard declaring the transfer modes that it supports. It is now time for the potential gesture targets to declare whether they accept the data transfer offered by the gesture source. Note that there could be multiple potential gesture targets. One of them will become the actual gesture target when the gesture source is dropped on it.

The potential gesture target receives several types of drag events:

- It receives a drag-entered event when the gesture source enters its bounds.

- It receives a drag-over event when the gesture source is dragged around within its bounds.

- It receives a drag-exited event when the gesture source exits its bounds.

- It receives a drag-dropped event when the gesture source is dropped over it by releasing the mouse button.

In a drag-over event handler, the potential gesture target needs to declare that it intends to participate in the drag-and-drop gesture by calling the acceptTransferModes(TransferMode... modes) method of the DragEvent. Typically, the potential target checks the content of the dragboard before declaring whether it accepts the transfer modes. The following snippet of code accomplishes this. The target TextField checks the dragboard for plain text. It contains plain text, so the target declares that it accepts COPY and MOVE transfer modes:

```java
targetFld.setOnDragOver((DragEvent e) -> {
        // If drag board has a string, let the event know that the
          // target accepts copy and move transfer modes
        Dragboard dragboard = e.getDragboard();

        if(dragboard.hasString()) {
                e.acceptTransferModes(TransferMode.COPY_OR_MOVE);
        }

        e.consume();
});
```

Dropping the Source onto the Target

If the potential gesture target accepts the transfer mode supported by the gesture source, the gesture source can be dropped on the target. The dropping is accomplished by releasing the mouse button while the gesture source is still over the target. When the gesture source is dropped onto a target, the target becomes the actual gesture target. The actual gesture target receives the drag-dropped event. You need to add a drag-drop event handler for the gesture target in which it performs two tasks:

- It accesses the data in the dragboard.

- It calls the setDropCompleted(boolean isTransferDone) method of the DragEvent object.

Passing true to the method indicates that the data transfer was successful. Passing false indicates that the data transfer was unsuccessful. The dragboard cannot be accessed after calling this method.

The following snippet of code performs the data transfer and sets the appropriate completion flag:

```
targetFld.setOnDragDropped((DragEvent e) -> {
        // Transfer the data to the target
        Dragboard dragboard = e.getDragboard();
        if(dragboard.hasString()) {
                String text = dragboard.getString();
                targetFld.setText(text);

                // Data transfer is successful
                e.setDropCompleted(true);
        } else {
                // Data transfer is not successful
                e.setDropCompleted(false);
        }

        e.consume();
});
```

Completing the Drag-and-Drop Gesture

After the gesture source has been dropped, it receives a drag-done event. The DragEvent object contains a getTransferMode() method. When it is called from the drag-done event handler, it returns the transfer mode used for the data transfer. Depending on the transfer mode, you can clear or keep the content of the gesture source. For example, if the transfer mode is MOVE, it is better to clear the source content to give the user a real feel of the data move.

You may wonder what determines the data transfer mode. In this example, both the gesture source and the target support COPY and MOVE. When the target accessed the data from the dragboard in the drag-dropped event, it did not set any transfer mode. The system determines the data transfer mode depending on the state of certain keys and the source and target. For example, when you drag a TextField and drop it onto another TextField, the default data transfer mode is MOVE. When the same drag and drop is performed with the Ctrl key pressed, the COPY mode is used.

If the getTransferMode() method returns null or TransferMode.ONE, it indicates that no data transfer happened. The following snippet of code handles the drag-done event for the source TextField. The source text is cleared if the data transfer mode was MOVE:

```
sourceFld.setOnDragDone((DragEvent e) -> {
        // Check how the data transfer happened. If it was moved, clear the
            // text in the source.
        TransferMode modeUsed = e.getTransferMode();

        if (modeUsed == TransferMode.MOVE) {
                sourceFld.setText("");
        }

        e.consume();
});
```

This completes handling of a drag-and-drop gesture. If you need more information about the parties participating in the drag-and-drop gesture, please refer to the API documentation for the DragEvent class. For example, use the getGestureSource() and getGestureTarget() methods to get the reference of the gesture source and target, respectively.

Providing Visual Clues

There are several ways to provide visual clues during a drag-and-drop gesture:

- The system provides an icon under the cursor during the drag gesture. The icon changes depending on the transfer mode determined by the system and whether the drag target is a potential target for the drag-and-drop gesture.

- You can write code for the drag-entered and drag-exited events for the potential targets by changing its visual appearance. For example, in the drag-entered event handler, you can change the background color of the potential target to green if it allows the data transfer and to red if it does not. In the drag-exited event handler, you can change the background color back to normal.

- You can set a drag view in the dragboard in the drag-detected event handler for the gesture. The drag view is an image. For example, you can take a snapshot of the node or part of the node being dragged and set it as the drag view.

A Complete Drag-and-Drop Example

The program in Listing 23-3 has the complete source code for this example. It displays a window as shown in Figure 23-2. You can drag the gesture source TextField and drop it onto the target TextField. The text from the source will be copied or moved to the target. The transfer mode depends on the system. For example, on Windows, pressing the Ctrl key while dropping will copy the text, and dropping without pressing the Ctrl key will move the text. Notice that the drag icon is changed during the drag action. The icon gives you a clue as to what kind of data transfer is going to happen when you drop the source. For example, when you drag the source on a target that does not accept the data transfer offered by the source, a "not-allowed" icon, a circle with a diagonal solid line, is displayed.

Listing 23-3. Performing a Drag-and-Drop Gesture

```
// DragAndDropTest.java
// ...find in the book's download area.
```

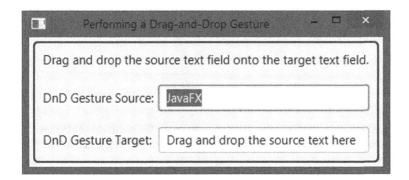

Figure 23-2. *A scene letting transfer text from a* `TextField` *to another using a drag-and-drop gesture*

Transferring an Image

The drag-and-drop gesture allows you to transfer an image. The image can be placed on the dragboard. You can also place a URL or a file on the dragboard that refers to the image location. Let's develop a simple application to demonstrate an image data transfer. To transfer an image, the user can drag and drop the following to a scene:

- An image
- An image file
- A URL pointing to an image

The program in Listing 23-4 opens a window with a text message, an empty `ImageView`, and a button. The `ImageView` will display the dragged and dropped image. Use the button to clear the image.

The entire scene is a potential target for a drag-and-drop gesture. A drag-over event handler is set for the scene. It checks whether the dragboard contains an image, a list of files, or a URL. If it finds one of these data types in the dragboard, it reports that it will accept ANY data transfer mode. In the drag-dropped event handler for the scene, the program attempts to read the image data, list of files, and the URL in order. If it is a list of files, you look at the mime type of each file to see if the name starts with `image/`. You use the first file with an image mime type and ignore the rest. If it is a URL, you simply try creating an `Image` object from it. You can play with the application in different ways:

- Run the program and open the HTML file `drag_and_drop.html` in a browser. The file is included in the `src/resources/html` directory. The HTML file contains two links: one pointing to a local image file and the other to a remote image file. Drag and drop the links onto the scene. The scene will show the images referred to by the links. Drag and drop the image from the web page. The scene will display the image. (Dragging and dropping of the image worked fine in Mozilla and Google Chrome browsers, but not in Windows Explorer.)

- Open a file explorer, for example, Windows Explorer on Windows. Select an image file and drag and drop the file onto the scene. The scene will display the image from the file. You can drop multiple files, but the scene will display only an image from one of those files.

You can enhance the application by allowing the user to drag multiple files onto the scene and showing them all in a TilePane. You can also add more error checks and feedbacks to the user about the drag-and-drop gesture.

Listing 23-4. Transferring an Image Using a Drag-and-Drop Gesture

```
// ImageDragAndDrop.java
// ...find in the book's download area.
```

Transferring Custom Data Types

You can transfer data in any format using the drag-and-drop gesture provided the data is Serializable. In this section, I will demonstrate how to transfer custom data. You will transfer an ArrayList<Item>. The Item class is shown in Listing 23-5; it is Serializable. The class is very simple. It contains one private field with its getter and setter methods.

Listing 23-5. Using a Custom Data Type in Data Transfer

```java
// Item.java
package com.jdojo.dnd;

import java.io.Serializable;

public class Item implements Serializable {
        private String name = "Unknown";

        public Item(String name) {
                this.name = name;
        }

        public String getName() {
                return name;
        }

        public void setName(String name) {
                this.name = name;
        }

        @Override
        public String toString() {
                return name;
        }
}
```

The program in Listing 23-6 shows how to use a custom data format in a drag-and-drop gesture. It displays a window as shown in Figure 23-3. The window contains two ListViews. Initially, only one of the ListViews is populated with a list of items. Both ListViews support multiple selection. You can select items in one ListView and drag and drop them into another ListView. The selected items will be copied or moved depending on the system-determined transfer mode. For example, on Windows, items will be moved by default. If you press the Ctrl key while dropping, the items will be copied instead.

Listing 23-6. Transferring Custom Data Using a Drag-and-Drop Gesture

```
// CustomDataTransfer.java
// ...find in the book's download area.
```

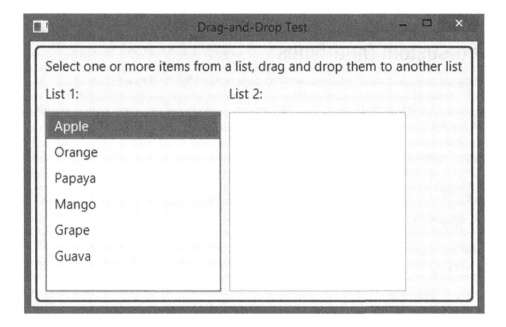

Figure 23-3. *Transferring a list of selected items between two ListViews*

Most of the program is similar to what you have seen before. The difference is in how you store and retrieve the ArrayList<Item> in the dragboard.

You define a new data format for this data transfer because the data do not fit into any of the categories available as the constants in the DataFormat class. You have to define the data as constants, as in the following code:

```
// Our custom Data Format
static final DataFormat ITEM_LIST = new DataFormat("jdojo/itemlist");
```

Now you have given a unique mime type jdojo/itemlist for the data format.

In the drag-detected event, you need to store the list of selected items onto the dragboard. The following snippet of code in the dragDetected() method stores the job. Notice that you have used the new data format while storing the data on the dragboard:

```
ArrayList<Item> selectedItems = this.getSelectedItems(listView);
ClipboardContent content = new ClipboardContent();
content.put(ITEM_LIST, selectedItems);
dragboard.setContent(content);
```

In the drag-over event, if the ListView is not being dragged over itself and the dragboard contains data in the ITEM_LIST data format, the ListView declares that it accepts a COPY or MOVE transfer. The following snippet of code in the dragOver() method does the job:

```
Dragboard dragboard = e.getDragboard();
if (e.getGestureSource() != listView && dragboard.hasContent(ITEM_LIST)) {
        e.acceptTransferModes(TransferMode.COPY_OR_MOVE);
}
```

Finally, you need to read the data from the dragboard when the source is dropped on the target. You need to use the getContent() method of the dragboard specifying the ITEM_LIST as the data format. The returned result needs to be cast to the ArrayList<Item>. The following snippet of code in the dragDropped() method does the job:

```
Dragboard dragboard = e.getDragboard();
if(dragboard.hasContent(ITEM_LIST)) {
        ArrayList<Item> list =
                (ArrayList<Item>)dragboard.getContent(ITEM_LIST);
        listView.getItems().addAll(list);

        // Data transfer is successful
        dragCompleted = true;
}
```

Finally, in the drag-done event handler, which is implemented in the dragDone() method, you remove the selected items from the source ListView if MOVE was used as the transfer mode. Notice that you have used an ArrayList<Item>, as both the ArrayList and Item classes are serializable.

Summary

A press-drag-release gesture is a user action of pressing a mouse button, dragging the mouse with the pressed button, and releasing the button. The gesture can be initiated on a scene or a node. Several nodes and scenes may participate in a single press-drag-release gesture. The gesture is capable of generating different types of events and delivering those events to different nodes. The type of generated events and the nodes receiving the events depend on the purpose of the gesture.

JavaFX supports three types of drag gestures: a simple press-drag-release gesture, a full press-drag-release gesture, and a drag-and-drop gesture.

The simple press-drag-release gesture is the default drag gesture. It is used when the drag gesture involves only one node—the node on which the gesture was initiated. During the drag gesture, all MouseDragEvent types—mouse-drag entered, mouse-drag over, mouse-drag exited, mouse, and mouse-drag released—are delivered only to the gesture source node.

When the source node of a drag gesture receives the drag-detected event, you can start a full press-drag-release gesture by calling the startFullDrag() method on the source node. The startFullDrag() method exists in both Node and Scene classes, allowing you to start a full press-drag-release gesture for a node and a scene.

The third type of drag gesture is called a drag-and-drop gesture, which is a user action combining the mouse movement with a pressed mouse button. It is used to transfer data from the gesture source to a gesture target. In a drag-and-drop gesture, the data can be transferred in three modes: copy, move, and link. The copy mode indicates that the data will be copied from the gesture source to the gesture target. The move mode indicates that the data will be moved from the gesture source to the gesture target. The link mode indicates that the gesture target will create a link (or reference) to the data being transferred. The actual meaning of "link" depends on the application.

In a drag-and-drop data transfer, the gesture source and the gesture target do not know each other—they may even belong to two different applications. A dragboard acts as an intermediary between the gesture source and the gesture target. A dragboard is the storage device to hold the data being transferred. The gesture source places the data onto a dragboard; the dragboard is made available to the gesture target, so it can inspect the type of content that is available for the transfer. When the gesture target is ready to transfer the data, it gets the data from the dragboard.

Using a drag-and-drop gesture, the data transfer takes place in three steps: initiating the drag-and-drop gesture by the source, detecting the drag gesture by the target, and dropping the source onto the target. Different types of events are generated for the source and target nodes during this gesture. You can also provide visual clues by showing icons during the drag-and-drop gesture. The drag-and-drop gesture supports transferring of any type of data, provided the data are serializable.

The next chapter discusses how to handle concurrent operations in JavaFX.

CHAPTER 24

■ ■ ■

Understanding Concurrency in JavaFX

In this chapter, you will learn:

- Why you need a concurrency framework in JavaFX

- How the Worker<V> interface represents a concurrent task

- How to run a one-time task

- How to run a reusable task

- How to run a scheduled task

The examples of this chapter lie in the com.jdojo.concurrent package. In order for them to work, you must add a corresponding line to the module-info.java file:

```
...
opens com.jdojo.concurrent to javafx.graphics, javafx.base;
...
```

The Need for a Concurrency Framework

Java (including JavaFX) GUI (graphical user interface) applications are inherently multithreaded. Multiple threads perform different tasks to keep the UI in sync with the user actions. JavaFX, like Swing and AWT, uses a single thread, called the JavaFX Application Thread, to process all UI events. The nodes representing the UI in a scene graph are not thread-safe. Designing nodes that are not thread-safe has advantages and disadvantages. They are faster, as no synchronization is involved. The disadvantage is that they need to be accessed from a single thread to avoid being in an illegal state. JavaFX puts a restriction that a live scene graph must be accessed from one and only one thread, the JavaFX Application Thread. This restriction indirectly imposes another restriction that a UI event should not process a long-running task, as it will make the application unresponsive. The user will get the impression that the application is hung.

The program in Listing 24-1 displays a window as shown in Figure 24-1. It contains three controls:

- A Label to display the progress of a task

- A *Start* button to start the task

- An *Exit* button to exit the application

this figure will be printed in b/w

Figure 24-1. *An example of an unresponsive UI*

Listing 24-1. Performing a Long-Running Task in an Event Handler

```java
// UnresponsiveUI.java
package com.jdojo.concurrent;

import javafx.application.Application;
import javafx.scene.Scene;
import javafx.scene.control.Button;
import javafx.scene.control.Label;
import javafx.scene.layout.HBox;
import javafx.scene.layout.VBox;
import javafx.stage.Stage;

public class UnresponsiveUI extends Application {
        Label statusLbl = new Label("Not Started...");
        Button startBtn = new Button("Start");
        Button exitBtn = new Button("Exit");

        public static void main(String[] args) {
                Application.launch(args);
        }

        @Override
        public void start(Stage stage) {
                // Add event handlers to the buttons
                startBtn.setOnAction(e -> runTask());
                exitBtn.setOnAction(e -> stage.close());

                HBox buttonBox = new HBox(5, startBtn, exitBtn);
                VBox root = new VBox(10, statusLbl, buttonBox);
                Scene scene = new Scene(root);
                stage.setScene(scene);
                stage.setTitle("An Unresponsive UI");
                stage.show();
        }

        public void runTask() {
                for(int i = 1; i <= 10; i++) {
```

```
                try {
                    String status = "Processing " + i + " of " + 10;
                    statusLbl.setText(status);
                    System.out.println(status);
                    Thread.sleep(1000);
                }
                catch (InterruptedException e) {
                    e.printStackTrace();
                }
            }
        }
    }
```

The program is very simple. When you click the *Start* button, a task lasting for ten seconds is started. The logic for the task is in the runTask() method, which simply runs a loop ten times. Inside the loop, the task lets the current thread, which is the JavaFX Application Thread, sleep for one second. The program has two problems.

Click the *Start* button and immediately try to click the *Exit* button. Clicking the *Exit* button has no effect until the task finishes. Once you click the *Start* button, you cannot do anything else on the window, except to wait for ten seconds for the task to finish. That is, the application becomes unresponsive for ten seconds. This is the reason you named the class UnresponsiveUI.

Inside the loop in the runTask() method, the program prints the status of the task on the standard output and displays the same in the Label in the window. You see the status updated on the standard output, but not in the Label.

It is repeated to emphasize that all UI event handlers in JavaFX run on a single thread, which is the JavaFX Application Thread. When the *Start* button is clicked, the runTask() method is executed in the JavaFX Application Thread. When the *Exit* button is clicked while the task is running, an ActionEvent event for the *Exit* button is generated and queued on the JavaFX Application Thread. The ActionEvent handler for the *Exit* button is run on the same thread after the thread is done running the runTask() method as part of the ActionEvent handler for the *Start* button.

A pulse event is generated when the scene graph is updated. The pulse event handler is also run on the JavaFX Application Thread. Inside the loop, the text property of the Label was updated ten times, which generated the pulse events. However, the scene graph was not refreshed to show the latest text for the Label, as the JavaFX Application Thread was busy running the task and it did not run the pulse event handlers.

Both problems arise because there is only one thread to process all UI event handlers, and you ran a long-running task in the ActionEvent handler for the *Start* button.

What is the solution? You have only one option. You cannot change the single-threaded model for handling the UI events. You must not run long-running tasks in the event handlers. Sometimes, it is a business need to process a big job as part of a user action. The solution is to run the long-running tasks in one or more background threads, instead of in the JavaFX Application Thread.

The program in Listing 24-2 is your first, incorrect attempt to provide a solution. The ActionEvent handler for the Start button calls the startTask() method, which creates a new thread and runs the runTask() method in the new thread.

Listing 24-2. A Program Accessing a Live Scene Graph from a Non-JavaFX Application Thread

```
// BadUI.java
package com.jdojo.concurrent;

import javafx.application.Application;
import javafx.scene.Scene;
import javafx.scene.control.Button;
```

```java
import javafx.scene.control.Label;
import javafx.scene.layout.HBox;
import javafx.scene.layout.VBox;
import javafx.stage.Stage;

public class BadUI extends Application {
        Label statusLbl = new Label("Not Started...");
        Button startBtn = new Button("Start");
        Button exitBtn = new Button("Exit");

        public static void main(String[] args) {
                Application.launch(args);
        }

        @Override
        public void start(Stage stage) {
                // Add event handlers to the buttons
                startBtn.setOnAction(e -> startTask());
                exitBtn.setOnAction(e -> stage.close());

                HBox buttonBox = new HBox(5, startBtn, exitBtn);
                VBox root = new VBox(10, statusLbl, buttonBox);
                Scene scene = new Scene(root);
                stage.setScene(scene);
                stage.setTitle("A Bad UI");
                stage.show();
        }

        public void startTask() {
                // Create a Runnable
                Runnable task = () -> runTask();

                // Run the task in a background thread
                Thread backgroundThread = new Thread(task);

                // Terminate the running thread if the application exits
                backgroundThread.setDaemon(true);

                // Start the thread
                backgroundThread.start();
        }

        public void runTask() {
            for(int i = 1; i <= 10; i++) {
              try {
                String status = "Processing " + i + " of " + 10;
                statusLbl.setText(status);
                System.out.println(status);
                Thread.sleep(1000);
              }
              catch (InterruptedException e) {
```

```
                e.printStackTrace();
            }
        }
    }
}
```

Run the program and click the *Start* button. A runtime exception is thrown. The partial stack trace of the exception is as follows:

```
Exception in thread "Thread-4" java.lang.IllegalStateException:
Not on FX application thread; currentThread = Thread-4
  at com.sun.javafx.tk.Toolkit.checkFxUserThread(Toolkit.java:209)
  at com.sun.javafx.tk.quantum.QuantumToolkit.checkFxUserThread(
      QuantumToolkit.java:393)...
  at com.jdojo.concurrent.BadUI.runTask(BadUI.java:47)...
```

The following statement in the `runTask()` method generated the exception:

```
statusLbl.setText(status);
```

The JavaFX runtime checks that a live scene must be accessed from the JavaFX Application Thread. The `runTask()` method is run on a new thread, named Thread-4 as shown in the stack trace, which is not the JavaFX Application Thread. The foregoing statement sets the `text` property for the `Label`, which is part of a live scene graph, from the thread other than the JavaFX Application Thread, which is not permissible.

How do you access a live scene graph from a thread other than the JavaFX Application Thread? The simple answer is that you cannot. The complex answer is that when a thread wants to access a live scene graph, it needs to run the part of the code that accesses the scene graph in the JavaFX Application Thread. The `Platform` class in the `javafx.application` package provides two static methods to work with the JavaFX Application Thread:

- `public static boolean isFxApplicationThread()`

- `public static void runLater(Runnable runnable)`

The `isFxApplicationThread()` method returns true if the thread calling this method is the JavaFX Application Thread. Otherwise, it returns false.

The `runLater()` method schedules the specified `Runnable` to be run on the JavaFX Application Thread at some unspecified time in future.

■ **Tip** If you have experience working with Swing, the `Platform.runLater()` in JavaFX is the counterpart of the `SwingUtilities.invokeLater()` in Swing.

Let us fix the problem in the `BadUI` application. The program in Listing 24-3 is the correct implementation of the logic to access the live scene graph. Figure 24-2 shows a snapshot of the window displayed by the program.

Listing 24-3. A Responsive UI That Runs Long-Running Tasks in a Background Thread

```java
// ResponsiveUI.java
package com.jdojo.concurrent;

import javafx.application.Application;
import javafx.application.Platform;
import javafx.scene.Scene;
import javafx.scene.control.Button;
import javafx.scene.control.Label;
import javafx.scene.layout.HBox;
import javafx.scene.layout.VBox;
import javafx.stage.Stage;

public class ResponsiveUI extends Application {
        Label statusLbl = new Label("Not Started...");
        Button startBtn = new Button("Start");
        Button exitBtn = new Button("Exit");

        public static void main(String[] args) {
                Application.launch(args);
        }

        @Override
        public void start(Stage stage) {
                // Add event handlers to the buttons
                startBtn.setOnAction(e -> startTask());
                exitBtn.setOnAction(e -> stage.close());

                HBox buttonBox = new HBox(5, startBtn, exitBtn);
                VBox root = new VBox(10, statusLbl, buttonBox);
                Scene scene = new Scene(root);
                stage.setScene(scene);
                stage.setTitle("A Responsive UI");
                stage.show();
        }

        public void startTask() {
                // Create a Runnable
                Runnable task = () -> runTask();

                // Run the task in a background thread
                Thread backgroundThread = new Thread(task);

                // Terminate the running thread if the application exits
                backgroundThread.setDaemon(true);

                // Start the thread
                backgroundThread.start();
        }
```

```java
    public void runTask() {
      for(int i = 1; i <= 10; i++) {
        try {
          String status = "Processing " + i + " of " + 10;

          // Update the Label on the JavaFx Application Thread
          Platform.runLater(() -> statusLbl.setText(status));
          System.out.println(status);
          Thread.sleep(1000);
        }
        catch (InterruptedException e) {
          e.printStackTrace();
        }
      }
    }
}
```

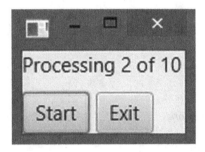

Figure 24-2. *A UI that runs a task in a background thread and updates the live scene graph correctly*

The program replaces the statement

```java
statusLbl.setText(status);
```

in the BadUI class with the statement

```java
// Update the Label on the JavaFx Application Thread
Platform.runLater(() -> statusLbl.setText(status));
```

Now, setting the text property for the Label takes place on the JavaFX Application Thread. The ActionEvent handler of the *Start* button runs the task in a background thread, thus freeing up the JavaFX Application Thread to handle user actions. The status of the task is updated in the Label regularly. You can click the *Exit* button while the task is being processed.

Did you overcome the restrictions imposed by the event-dispatching threading model of the JavaFX? The answer is yes and no. You used a trivial example to demonstrate the problem. You have solved the trivial problem. However, in the real world, performing a long-running task in a GUI application is not so trivial. For example, your task-running logic and the UI are tightly coupled as you are referencing the Label inside the runTask() method, which is not desirable in the real world. Your task does not return a result, nor does it have a reliable mechanism to handle errors that may occur. Your task cannot be reliably cancelled, restarted, or scheduled to be run at a future time.

The JavaFX concurrency framework has answers to all these questions. The framework provides a reliable way of running a task in one or multiple background threads and publishing the status and the result of the task in a GUI application. The framework is the topic of discussion in this chapter. I have taken several pages just to make the case for a concurrency framework in JavaFX. If you understand the background of the problem as presented in this section, understanding the framework will be easy.

Understanding the Concurrency Framework API

Java contains a comprehensive concurrency framework to the Java programming language through the libraries in the java.util.concurrent package. The JavaFX concurrency framework is very small. It is built on top of the Java language concurrency framework keeping in mind that it will be used in a GUI environment. Figure 24-3 shows a class diagram of the classes in the JavaFX concurrency framework.

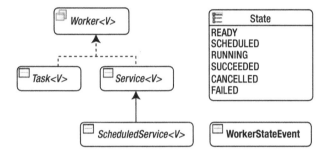

Figure 24-3. *A class diagram for classes in the JavaFX concurrency framework*

The framework consists of one interface, four classes, and one enum.

An instance of the Worker interface represents a task that needs to be performed in one or more background threads. The state of the task is observable from the JavaFX Application Thread.

The Task, Service, and ScheduledService classes implement the Worker interface. They represent different types of tasks. They are abstract classes. An instance of the Task class represents a one-shot task. A Task cannot be reused. An instance of the Service class represents a reusable task. The ScheduledService class inherits from the Service class. A ScheduledService is a task that can be scheduled to run repeatedly after a specified interval.

The constants in the Worker.State enum represent different states of a Worker.

An instance of the WorkerStateEvent class represents an event that occurs as the state of a Worker changes. You can add event handlers to all three types of tasks to listen to the change in their states.

Understanding the Worker<V> Interface

The Worker<V> interface provides the specification for any task performed by the JavaFX concurrency framework. A Worker is a task that is performed in one or more background threads. The generic parameter V is the data type of the result of the Worker. Use Void as the generic parameter if the Worker does not produce a result. The state of the task is observable. The state of the task is published on the JavaFX Application Thread, making it possible for the task to communicate with the scene graph, as is commonly required in a GUI application.

State Transitions for a Worker

During the life cycle, a Worker transitions through different states. The constants in the Worker.State enum represent the valid states of a Worker:

- Worker.State.READY
- Worker.State.SCHEDULED
- Worker.State.RUNNING
- Worker.State.SUCCEEDED
- Worker.State.CANCELLED
- Worker.State.FAILED

Figure 24-4 shows the possible state transitions of a Worker with the Worker.State enum constants representing the states.

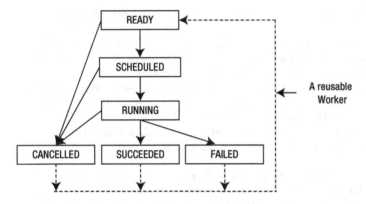

Figure 24-4. *Possible state transition paths for a Worker*

When a Worker is created, it is in the READY state. It transitions to the SCHEDULED state, before it starts executing. When it starts running, it is in the RUNNING state. Upon successful completion, a Worker transitions from the RUNNING state to the SUCCEEDED state. If the Worker throws an exception during its execution, it transitions to the FAILED state. A Worker may be cancelled using the cancel() method. It may transition to the CANCELLED state from the READY, SCHEDULED, and RUNNING states. These are the normal state transitions for a one-shot Worker.

A reusable Worker may transition from the CANCELLED, SUCCEEDED, and FAILED states to the READY state as shown in the figure by dashed lines.

Properties of a Worker

The Worker interface contains nine read-only properties that represent the internal state of the task:

- title
- message
- running
- state

- progress
- workDone
- totalWork
- value
- exception

When you create a Worker, you will have a chance to specify these properties. The properties can also be updated as the task progresses.

The title property represents the title for the task. Suppose a task generates prime numbers. You may give the task a title "Prime Number Generator."

The message property represents a detailed message during the task processing. Suppose a task generates several prime numbers; you may want to give feedback to the user at a regular interval or at appropriate times with a message such as "Generating X of Y prime numbers."

The running property tells whether the Worker is running. It is true when the Worker is in the SCHEDULED or RUNNING states. Otherwise, it is false.

The state property specifies the state of the Worker. Its value is one of the constants of the Worker. State enum.

The totalWork, workDone, and progress properties represent the progress of the task. The totalWork is the total amount of work to be done. The workDone is the amount of work that has been done. The progress is the ratio of workDone and totalWork. They are set to –1.0 if their values are not known.

The value property represents the result of the task. Its value is non-null only when the Worker finishes successfully reaching the SUCCEEDED state. Sometimes, a task may not produce a result. In those cases, the generic parameter V would be Void, and the value property will always be null.

A task may fail by throwing an exception. The exception property represents the exception that is thrown during the processing of the task. It is non-null only when the state of the Worker is FAILED. It is of the type Throwable.

Typically, when a task is in progress, you want to display the task details in a scene graph. The concurrency framework makes sure that the properties of a Worker are updated on the JavaFX Application Thread. Therefore, it is fine to bind the properties of the UI elements in a scene graph to these properties. You can also add Invalidation and ChangeListener to these properties and access a live scene graph from inside those listeners.

In subsequent sections, you will discuss specific implementations of the Worker interface. Let us create a reusable GUI to use in all examples. The GUI is based on a Worker to display the current values of its properties.

Utility Classes for Examples

Let us create the reusable GUI and non-GUI parts of the programs to use in examples in the subsequent sections. The WorkerStateUI class in Listing 24-4 builds a GridPane to display all properties of a Worker. It is used with a Worker<ObservableList<Long>>. It displays the properties of a Worker by UI elements to them. You can bind properties of a Worker to the UI elements by passing a Worker to the constructor or calling the bindToWorker() method.

Listing 24-4. A Utility Class to Build UI Displaying the Properties of a Worker

```
// WorkerStateUI.java
package com.jdojo.concurrent;
```

```java
import javafx.beans.binding.When;
import javafx.collections.ObservableList;
import javafx.concurrent.Worker;
import javafx.scene.control.Label;
import javafx.scene.control.ProgressBar;
import javafx.scene.control.TextArea;
import javafx.scene.layout.GridPane;
import javafx.scene.layout.HBox;

public class WorkerStateUI extends GridPane {
        private final Label title = new Label("");
        private final Label message = new Label("");
        private final Label running = new Label("");
        private final Label state = new Label("");
        private final Label totalWork = new Label("");
        private final Label workDone = new Label("");
        private final Label progress = new Label("");
        private final TextArea value = new TextArea("");
        private final TextArea exception = new TextArea("");
        private final ProgressBar progressBar = new ProgressBar();

        public WorkerStateUI() {
                addUI();
        }

        public WorkerStateUI(Worker<ObservableList<Long>> worker) {
                addUI();
                bindToWorker(worker);
        }

        private void addUI() {
                value.setPrefColumnCount(20);
                value.setPrefRowCount(3);
                exception.setPrefColumnCount(20);
                exception.setPrefRowCount(3);
                this.setHgap(5);
                this.setVgap(5);
                addRow(0, new Label("Title:"), title);
                addRow(1, new Label("Message:"), message);
                addRow(2, new Label("Running:"), running);
                addRow(3, new Label("State:"), state);
                addRow(4, new Label("Total Work:"), totalWork);
                addRow(5, new Label("Work Done:"), workDone);
                addRow(6, new Label("Progress:"),
                        new HBox(2, progressBar, progress));
                addRow(7, new Label("Value:"), value);
                addRow(8, new Label("Exception:"), exception);
        }
```

```java
    public void bindToWorker(final Worker<ObservableList<Long>> worker) {
        // Bind Labels to the properties of the worker
        title.textProperty().bind(worker.titleProperty());
        message.textProperty().bind(worker.messageProperty());
        running.textProperty().bind(
                worker.runningProperty().asString());
        state.textProperty().bind(
                worker.stateProperty().asString());
        totalWork.textProperty().bind(
                new When(worker.totalWorkProperty().isEqualTo(-1))
            .then("Unknown")
            .otherwise(worker.totalWorkProperty().asString()));
        workDone.textProperty().bind(
                new When(worker.workDoneProperty().isEqualTo(-1))
            .then("Unknown")
            .otherwise(worker.workDoneProperty().asString()));
        progress.textProperty().bind(
                new When(worker.progressProperty().isEqualTo(-1))
            .then("Unknown")
            .otherwise(worker.progressProperty().multiply(100.0)
                    .asString("%.2f%%")));
        progressBar.progressProperty().bind(
                worker.progressProperty());
        value.textProperty().bind(
                worker.valueProperty().asString());

        // Display the exception message when an exception occurs
            // in the worker
        worker.exceptionProperty().addListener(
                (prop, oldValue, newValue) -> {
                if (newValue != null) {
                    exception.setText(newValue.getMessage());
                } else {
                    exception.setText("");
                }
        });
    }
}
```

The PrimeUtil class in Listing 24-5 is a utility class to check whether a number is a prime number.

Listing 24-5. A Utility Class to Work with Prime Numbers

```java
// PrimeUtil.java
package com.jdojo.concurrent;

public class PrimeUtil {
    public static boolean isPrime(long num) {
        if (num <= 1 || num % 2 == 0) {
            return false;
        }
```

```
        int upperDivisor = (int)Math.ceil(Math.sqrt(num));
        for (int divisor = 3; divisor <= upperDivisor; divisor += 2) {
                if (num % divisor == 0) {
                        return false;
                }
        }
        return true;
    }
}
```

Using the Task<V> Class

An instance of the Task<V> class represents a one-time task. Once the task is completed, cancelled, or failed, it cannot be restarted. The Task<V> class implements the Worker<V> interface. Therefore, all properties and methods specified by the Worker<V> interface are available in the Task<V> class.

The Task<V> class inherits from the FutureTask<V> class, which is part of the Java concurrency framework. The FutureTask<V> implements the Future<V>, RunnableFuture<V>, and Runnable interfaces. Therefore, a Task<V> also implements all these interfaces.

Creating a Task

How do you create a Task<V>? Creating a Task<V> is easy. You need to subclass the Task<V> class and provide an implementation for the abstract method call(). The call() method contains the logic to perform the task. The following snippet of code shows the skeleton of a Task implementation:

```
// A Task that produces an ObservableList<Long>
public class PrimeFinderTask extends Task<ObservableList<Long>> {
        @Override
        protected ObservableList<Long>> call() {
                // Implement the task logic here...
        }
}
```

Updating Task Properties

Typically, you would want to update the properties of the task as it progresses. The properties must be updated and read on the JavaFX Application Thread, so they can be observed safely in a GUI environment. The Task<V> class provides special methods to update some of its properties:

- `protected void updateMessage(String message)`

- `protected void updateProgress(double workDone, double totalWork)`

- `protected void updateProgress(long workDone, long totalWork)`

- `protected void updateTitle(String title)`

- `protected void updateValue(V value)`

You provide the values for the workDone and the totalWork properties to the updateProgress() method. The progress property will be set to workDone/totalWork. The method throws a runtime exception if the workDone is greater than the totalWork or both are less than –1.0.

Sometimes, you may want to publish partial results of a task in its value property. The updateValue() method is used for this purpose. The final result of a task is the return value of its call() method.

All updateXxx() methods are executed on the JavaFX Application Thread. Their names indicate the property they update. They are safe to be called from the call() method of the Task. If you want to update the properties of the Task from the call() method directly, you need to wrap the code inside a Platform. runLater() call.

Listening to Task Transition Events

The Task class contains the following properties to let you set event handlers for its state transitions:

- onCancelled

- onFailed

- onRunning

- onScheduled

- onSucceeded

The following snippet of code adds an onSucceeded event handler, which would be called when the task transitions to the SUCCEEDED state:

```
Task<ObservableList<Long>> task = create a task...
task.setOnSucceeded(e -> {
        System.out.println("The task finished. Let us party!")
});
```

Cancelling a Task

Use one of the following two cancel() methods to cancel a task:

- public final boolean cancel()

- public boolean cancel(boolean mayInterruptIfRunning)

The first version removes the task from the execution queue or stops its execution. The second version lets you specify whether the thread running the task be interrupted. Make sure to handle the InterruptedException inside the call() method. Once you detect this exception, you need to finish the call() method quickly. Otherwise, the call to cancel(true) may not cancel the task reliably. The cancel() method may be called from any thread.

The following methods of the Task are called when it reaches a specific state:

- protected void scheduled()

- protected void running()

- protected void succeeded()

- protected void cancelled()

- protected void failed()

Their implementations in the Task class are empty. They are meant to be overridden by the subclasses.

Running a Task

A Task is Runnable as well as a FutureTask. To run it, you can use a background thread or an ExecutorService:

```
// Schedule the task on a background thread
Thread backgroundThread = new Thread(task);
backgroundThread.setDaemon(true);
backgroundThread.start();

// Use the executor service to schedule the task
ExecutorService executor = Executors.newSingleThreadExecutor();
executor.submit(task);
```

A Prime Finder Task Example

It is time to see a Task in action. The program in Listing 24-6 is an implementation of the Task<ObservableList<Long>>. It checks for prime numbers between the specified lowerLimit and upperLimit. It returns all the numbers in the range. Notice that the task thread sleeps for a short time before checking a number for a prime number. This is done to give the user an impression of a long-running task. It is not needed in a real-world application. The call() method handles an InterruptedException and finishes the task if the task was interrupted as part of a cancellation request.

The call to the method updateValue() needs little explanation:

```
updateValue(FXCollections.<Long>unmodifiableObservableList(results));
```

Every time a prime number is found, the results list is updated. The foregoing statement wraps the results list in an unmodifiable observable list and publishes it for the client. This gives the client access to the partial results of the task. This is a quick and dirty way of publishing the partial results. If the call() method returns a primitive value, it is fine to call the updateValue() method repeatedly.

■ **Tip**　In this case, you are creating a new unmodifiable list every time you find a new prime number, which is not acceptable in a production environment for performance reasons. The efficient way of publishing the partial results would be to declare a read-only property for the Task; update the read-only property regularly on the JavaFX Application Thread; let the client bind to the read-only property to see the partial results.

Listing 24-6. Finding Prime Numbers Using a Task<Long>

```
// PrimeFinderTask.java
// ...find in the book's download area.
```

The program in Listing 24-7 contains the complete code to build a GUI using your `PrimeFinderTask` class. Figure 24-5 shows the window when the task is running. You will need to click the *Start* button to start the task. Clicking the *Cancel* button cancels the task. Once the task finishes, it is cancelled or it fails; you cannot restart it, and both the `Start` and `Cancel` buttons are disabled. Notice that when the task finds a new prime number, it is displayed on the window immediately.

Listing 24-7. Executing a Task in a GUI Environment

```
// OneShotTask.java
// ...find in the book's download area.
```

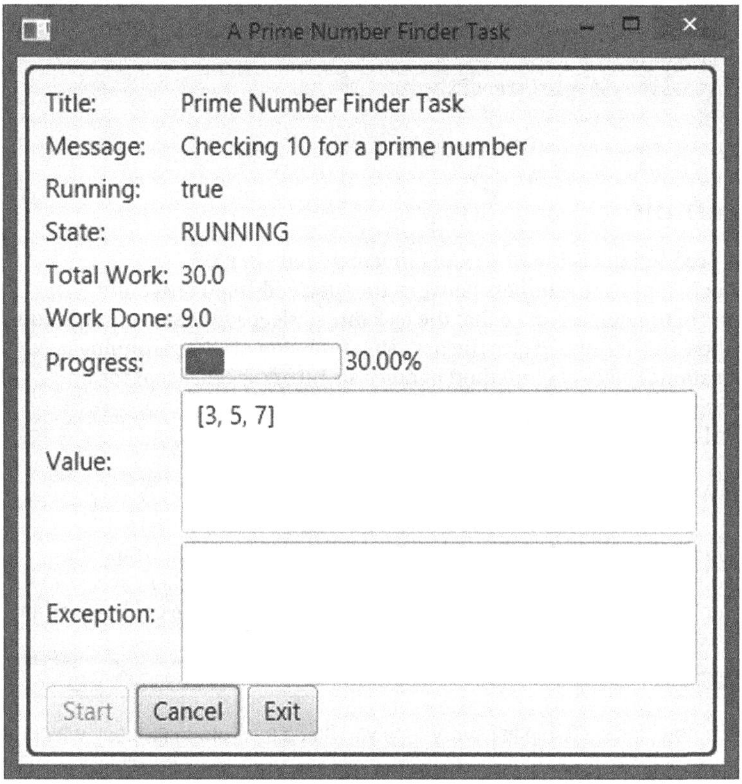

Figure 24-5. *A window using the prime number finder Task*

Using the Service<V> Class

The `Service<V>` class is an implementation of the `Worker<V>` interface. It encapsulates a `Task<V>`. It makes the `Task<V>` reusable by letting it be started, cancelled, reset, and restarted.

Creating the Service

Remember that a Service<V> encapsulates a Task<V>. Therefore, you need a Task<V> to have a Service<V>. The Service<V> class contains an abstract protected createTask() method that returns a Task<V>. To create a service, you need to subclass the Service<V> class and provide an implementation for the createTask() method.

The following snippet of code creates a Service that encapsulates a PrimeFinderTask, which you have created earlier:

```
// Create a service
Service<ObservableList<Long>> service = new Service<ObservableList<Long>>() {
        @Override
        protected Task<ObservableList<Long>> createTask() {
                // Create and return a Task
                return new PrimeFinderTask();
        }
};
```

The createTask() method of the service is called whenever the service is started or restarted.

Updating Service Properties

The Service class contains all properties (title, message, state, value, etc.) that represent the internal state of a Worker. It adds an executor property, which is a java.util.concurrent.Executor. The property is used to run the Service. If it is not specified, a daemon thread is created to run the Service.

Unlike the Task class, the Service class does not contain updateXxx() methods for updating its properties. Its properties are bound to the corresponding properties of the underlying Task<V>. When the Task updates its properties, the changes are reflected automatically to the Service and to the client.

Listening to Service Transition Events

The Service class contains all properties for setting the state transition listeners as contained by the Task class. It adds an onReady property. The property specifies a state transition event handler, which is called when the Service transitions to the READY state. Note that the Task class does not contain an onReady property as a Task is in the READY state when it is created, and it never transitions to the READY state again. However, a Service can be in the READY state multiple times. A Service transitions to the READY state when it is created, reset, and restarted. The Service class also contains a protected ready() method, which is intended to be overridden by subclasses. The ready() method is called when the Service transitions to the READY state.

Cancelling the Service

Use the cancel() methods to cancel a Service: the method sets the state of the Service to CANCELLED.

Starting the Service

Calling the start() method of the Service class starts a Service. The method calls the createTask() method to get a Task instance and runs the Task. The Service must be in the READY state when its start() method is called:

```
Service<ObservableList<Long>> service = create a service
...
// Start the service
service.start();
```

Resetting the Service

Calling the reset() method of the Service class resets the Service. Resetting puts all the Service properties back to their initial states. The state is set to READY. Resetting a Service is allowed only when the Service is in one of the finish states: SUCCEEDED, FAILED, CANCELLED, or READY. Calling the reset() method throws a runtime exception if the Service is in the SCHEDULED or RUNNING state.

Restarting the Service

Calling the restart() method of the Service class restarts a Service. It cancels the task if it exists, resets the service, and starts it. It calls the three methods on the Service object in sequence:

- cancel()
- reset()
- start()

The Prime Finder Service Example

The program in Listing 24-8 shows how to use a Service. The Service object is created and stored as an instance variable. The Service object manages a PrimeFinderTask object, which is a Task to find prime numbers between two numbers. Four buttons are added: *Start/Restart, Cancel, Reset,* and *Exit.* The *Start* button is labeled Restart after the Service is started for the first time. The buttons do what their labels indicate. Buttons are disabled when you cannot invoke them. Figure 24-6 shows a screenshot of the window after the *Start* button is clicked.

Listing 24-8. Using a Service to Find Prime Numbers

```
// PrimeFinderService.java
// ...find in the book's download area.
```

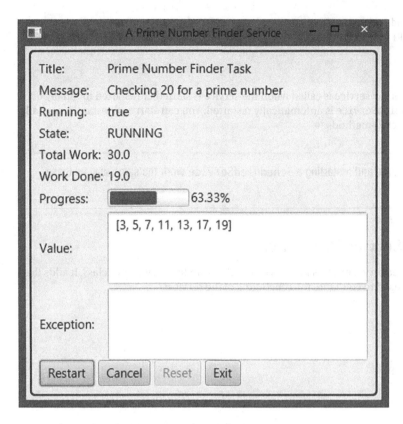

Figure 24-6. *A window using a Service to find prime numbers*

Using the ScheduledService<V> Class

The ScheduledService<V> is a Service<V>, which automatically restarts. It can restart when it finishes successfully or when it fails. Restarting on a failure is configurable. The ScheduledService<V> class inherits from the Service<V> class. The ScheduledService is suitable for tasks that use polling. For example, you may use it to refresh the score of a game or the weather report from the Internet after every ten minutes.

Creating the ScheduledService

The process of creating a ScheduledService is the same as that of creating a Service. You need to subclass the ScheduledService<V> class and provide an implementation for the createTask() method.

The following snippet of code creates a ScheduledService that encapsulates a PrimeFinderTask, which you have created earlier:

```
// Create a scheduled service
ScheduledService<ObservableList<Long>> service =
    new ScheduledService <ObservableList<Long>>() {
        @Override
        protected Task<ObservableList<Long>> createTask() {
```

```
            // Create and return a Task
            return new PrimeFinderTask();
    }
};
```

The createTask() method of the service is called when the service is started or restarted manually or automatically. Note that a ScheduledService is automatically restarted. You can start and restart it manually by calling the start() and restart() methods.

■ **Tip** Starting, cancelling, resetting, and restarting a ScheduledService work the same way as these operations on a Service.

Updating ScheduledService Properties

The ScheduledService<ScheduledService> class inherits properties from the Service<V> class. It adds the following properties that can be used to configure the scheduling of the service:

- lastValue
- delay
- period
- restartOnFailure
- maximumFailureCount
- backoffStrategy
- cumulativePeriod
- currentFailureCount
- maximumCumulativePeriod

A ScheduledService<V> is designed to run several times. The current value computed by the service is not very meaningful. Your class adds a new property lastValue, which is of the type V, and it is the last value computed by the service.

The delay is a Duration, which specifies a delay between when the service is started and when it begins running. The service stays in the SCHEDULED state for the specified delay. The delay is honored only when the service is started manually calling the start() or restart() method. When the service is restarted automatically, honoring the delay property depends on the current state of the service. For example, if the service is running behind its periodic schedule, it will rerun immediately, ignoring the delay property. The default delay is zero.

The period is a Duration, which specifies the minimum amount of time between the last run and the next run. The default period is zero.

The restartOnFailure specifies whether the service restarts automatically when it fails. By default, it is set to true.

The currentFailureCount is the number of times the scheduled service has failed. It is reset to zero when the scheduled service is restarted manually.

The `maximumFailureCount` specifies the maximum number of times the service can fail before it is transitioned into the `FAILED` state, and it is not automatically restarted again. Note that you can restart a scheduled service any time manually. By default, it is set to `Integer.MAX_VALUE`.

The `backoffStrategy` is a `Callback<ScheduledService<?>,Duration>` that computes the `Duration` to add to the period on each failure. Typically, if a service fails, you want to slow down before retrying it. Suppose a service runs every 10 minutes. If it fails for the first time, you may want to restart it after 15 minutes. If it fails for the second time, you want to increase the rerun time to 25 minutes, and so on. The `ScheduledService` class provides three built-in backoff strategies as constants:

- `EXPONENTIAL_BACKOFF_STRATEGY`

- `LINEAR_BACKOFF_STRATEGY`

- `LOGARITHMIC_BACKOFF_STRATEGY`

The rerun gaps are computed based on the nonzero period and the current failure count. The time between consecutive failed runs increases exponentially in the exponential `backoffStrategy`, linearly in the linear `backoffStrategy`, and logarithmically in the logarithmic `backoffStrategy`. The `LOGARITHMIC_BACKOFF_STRATEGY` is the default. When the `period` is zero, the following formulas are used. The computed duration is in milliseconds:

- Exponential: `Math.exp(currentFailureCount)`

- Linear: `currentFailureCount`

- Logarithmic: `Math.log1p(currentFailureCount)`

The following formulas are used for the non-null period:

- Exponential: `period + (period * Math.exp(currentFailureCount)`

- Linear: `period + (period * currentFailureCount)`

- Logarithmic: `period + (period * Math.log1p(currentFailureCount))`

The `cumulativePeriod` is a `Duration`, which is the time between the current failed run and the next run. Its value is computed using the `backoffStrategy` property. It is reset upon a successful run of the scheduled service. Its value can be capped using the `maximumCumulativePeriod` property.

Listening to ScheduledService Transition Events

The `ScheduledService` goes through the same transition states as the `Service`. It goes through the `READY`, `SCHEDULED`, and `RUNNING` states automatically after a successful run. Depending on how the scheduled service is configured, it may go through the same state transitions automatically after a failed run.

You can listen to the state transitions and override the transition-related methods (`ready()`, `running()`, `failed()`, etc.) as you can for a `Service`. When you override the transition-related methods in a `ScheduledService` subclass, make sure to call the super method to keep your `ScheduledService` working properly.

The Prime Finder ScheduledService Example

Let us use the `PrimeFinderTask` with a `ScheduledService`. Once started, the `ScheduledService` will keep rerunning forever. If it fails five times, it will quit by transitioning itself to the `FAILED` state. You can cancel and restart the service manually any time.

The program in Listing 24-9 shows how to use a ScheduledService. The program is very similar to the one shown in Listing 24-8, except at two places. The service is created by subclassing the ScheduledService class:

```
// Create the scheduled service
ScheduledService<ObservableList<Long>> service = new ScheduledService<ObservableList<
Long>>() {
        @Override
        protected Task<ObservableList<Long>> createTask() {
                return new PrimeFinderTask();
        }
};
```

The ScheduledService is configured in the beginning of the start() method, setting the delay, period, and maximumFailureCount properties:

```
// Configure the scheduled service
service.setDelay(Duration.seconds(5));
service.setPeriod(Duration.seconds(30));
service.setMaximumFailureCount(5);
```

Figures 24-7, 24-8, and 24-9 show the state of the ScheduledService when it is not started, when it is observing the delay period in the SCHEDULED state, and when it is running. Use the *Cancel* and Reset buttons to cancel and reset the service. Once the service is cancelled, you can restart it manually by clicking the Restart button.

Listing 24-9. Using a ScheduledService to Run a Task

```
// PrimeFinderScheduledService.java
// ...find in the book's download area.
```

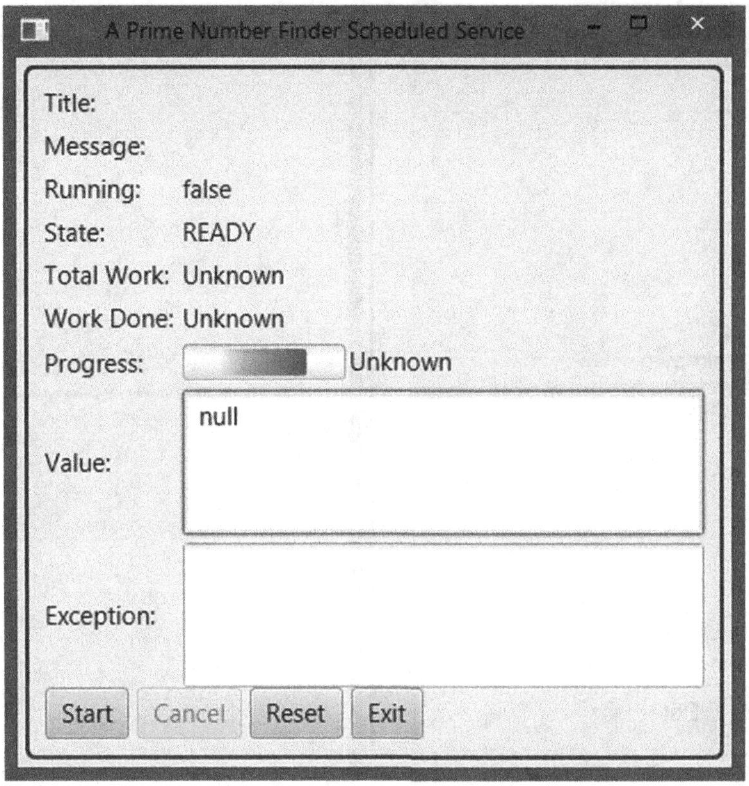

Figure 24-7. *The ScheduledService is not started*

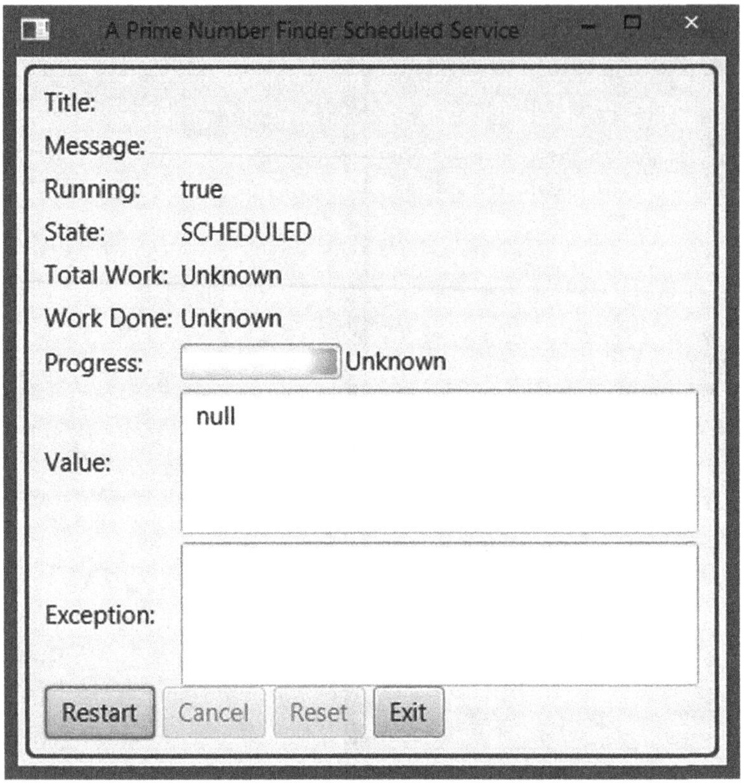

Figure 24-8. The ScheduledService is started for the first time, and it is observing the delay period

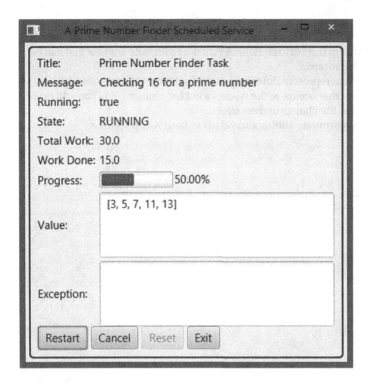

Figure 24-9. *The ScheduledService is started and running*

Summary

Java (including JavaFX) GUI applications are inherently multithreaded. Multiple threads perform different tasks to keep the UI in sync with the user actions. JavaFX, like Swing and AWT, uses a single thread, called the JavaFX Application Thread, to process all UI events. The nodes representing the UI in a scene graph are not thread-safe. Designing nodes that are not thread-safe has advantages and disadvantages. They are faster, as no synchronization is involved. The disadvantage is that they need to be accessed from a single thread to avoid being in an illegal state. JavaFX puts a restriction that a live scene graph must be accessed from one and only one thread, the JavaFX Application Thread. This restriction indirectly imposes another restriction that a UI event should not process a long-running task, as it will make the application unresponsive. The user will get the impression that the application is hung. The JavaFX concurrency framework is built on top of the Java language concurrency framework keeping in mind that it will be used in a GUI environment. The framework consists of one interface, four classes, and one enum. It provides a way to design a multithreaded JavaFX application that can perform long-running tasks in worker threads, keeping the UI responsive.

An instance of the Worker interface represents a task that needs to be performed in one or more background threads. The state of the task is observable from the JavaFX Application Thread. The Task, Service, and ScheduledService classes implement the Worker interface. They represent different types of tasks. They are abstract classes.

An instance of the Task class represents a one-shot task. A Task cannot be reused.

An instance of the Service class represents a reusable task.

The ScheduledService class inherits from the Service class. A ScheduledService is a task that can be scheduled to run repeatedly after a specified interval.

The constants in the Worker.State enum represent different states of a Worker. An instance of the WorkerStateEvent class represents an event that occurs as the state of a Worker changes. You can add event handlers to all three types of tasks to listen to the change in their states.

The next chapter will discuss how to incorporate audios and videos in JavaFX applications.

CHAPTER 25

Playing Audios and Videos

In this chapter, you will learn:

- What the Media API is

- How to play short audio clips

- How to play back media (audios and videos) and how to track different aspects of the playback such as playback rate, volume, playback time, repeating the playback, and media errors

The examples of this chapter lie in the com.jdojo.media package. In order for them to work, you must add a corresponding line to the module-info.java file:

```
...
opens com.jdojo.media to javafx.graphics, javafx.base;
...
```

Understanding the Media API

JavaFX supports playing audio and video through the JavaFX Media API. HTTP live streaming of static media files and live feeds are also supported. A number of media formats are supported, including AAC, AIFF, WAV, and MP3. FLV containing VP6 video and MP3 audio and MPEG-4 multimedia container with H.264/ AVC video formats are also supported. The support for a specific media format is platform dependent. Some media playback features and formats do not require any additional installations; some require third-party software to be installed. Please refer to the web page at https://openjfx.io/javadoc/17/javafx.media/ javafx/scene/media/package-summary.html#SupportedMediaTypes for details on the system requirements and supported media formats in JavaFX.

The Media API consists of several classes. Figure 25-1 shows a class diagram that includes only the core classes in the Media API. All classes in the API are included in the javafx.scene.media package.

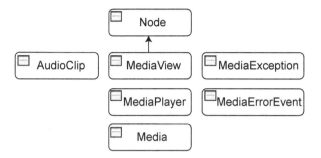

Figure 25-1. *A class diagram for core classes in the Media API*

AudioClip is used to play a short audio clip with minimal latency. Typically, this is useful for sound effects, which are usually short audio clips. Use the Media, MediaPlayer, and MediaView classes for playing audios and videos of longer length.

The Media and MediaPlayer classes are used to play audios as well as videos. An instance of the Media class represents a media resource, which could be an audio or a video. It provides the information about the media, for example, the duration of the media. An instance of the MediaPlayer class provides controls for playing a media.

An instance of the MediaView class provides the view of a media being played by a MediaPlayer. A MediaView is used for viewing a video.

Several things can go wrong when you attempt to play a media, for example, the media format may not be supported or the media content may be corrupt. An instance of the MediaException class represents a specific type of media error that may occur during media playback. When a media-related error occurs, a MediaErrorEvent is generated. You can handle the error by adding an appropriate event handler to the media objects.

I will cover the details of using these classes and other supporting classes in the Media API in this chapter.

Playing Short Audio Clips

An instance of the AudioClip class is used to play a short audio clip with minimal latency. Typically, this is useful for playing short audio clips, for example, a beep sound when the user makes an error or producing short sound effects in gaming applications.

The AudioClip class provides only one constructor that takes a URL in string form, which is the URL of the audio source. The audio clip is immediately loaded into memory in raw, uncompressed form. This is the reason why you should not use this class for long-playing audio clips. The source URL could use the HTTP, file, and JAR protocols. This means that you can play an audio clip from the Internet, the local file system, and a JAR file.

The following snippet of code creates an AudioClip using the HTTP protocol:

```
String clipUrl = "http://www.jdojo.com/myaudio.wav";
AudioClip audioClip = new AudioClip(clipUrl);
```

When an AudioClip object is created, the audio data are loaded into the memory, and they are ready to be played immediately. Use the play() method to play the audio and the stop() method to stop the playback:

```
// Play the audio
audioClip.play();
...
// Stop the playback
audioClip.stop();
```

The program in Listing 25-1 shows how to play an audio clip using the AudioClip class. It declares an instance variable to store the AudioClip reference. The AudioClip is created in the init() method to make sure the clip is ready to be played when the window is shown in the start() method. You could have also created the AudioClip in the constructor. The start() method adds Start and Stop buttons. Their action event handlers start and stop the playback, respectively.

Listing 25-1. Playing Back an Audio Clip Using an AudioClip Instance

```java
// AudioClipPlayer.java
package com.jdojo.media;

import com.jdojo.util.ResourceUtil;
import java.net.URL;
import javafx.application.Application;
import javafx.scene.Scene;
import javafx.scene.control.Button;
import javafx.scene.layout.HBox;
import javafx.scene.media.AudioClip;
import javafx.stage.Stage;

public class AudioClipPlayer extends Application {
        private AudioClip audioClip;

        public static void main(String[] args) {
            Application.launch(args);
        }

        @Override
        public void init() {
                URL mediaUrl =
                    ResourceUtil.getResourceURL("media/chimes.wav");

            // Create an AudioClip, which loads the audio data
                // synchronously
            audioClip = new AudioClip(mediaUrl.toExternalForm());
        }

        @Override
        public void start(Stage stage) {
            Button playBtn = new Button("Play");
            Button stopBtn = new Button("Stop");

            // Set event handlers for buttons
            playBtn.setOnAction(e -> audioClip.play());
            stopBtn.setOnAction(e -> audioClip.stop());
```

```
            HBox root = new HBox(5, playBtn, stopBtn);
            root.setStyle("-fx-padding: 10;");
            Scene scene = new Scene(root);
            stage.setScene(scene);
            stage.setTitle("Playing Short Audio Clips");
            stage.show();
        }
}
```

The AudioClip class supports setting some audio properties when the clip is played:

- cycleCount

- volume

- rate

- balance

- pan

- priority

All of the preceding properties, except the cycleCount, can be set on the AudioClip class. Subsequent calls to the play() method will use them as defaults. The play() method may also override the defaults for a specific playback. The cycleCount property must be specified on the AudioClip, and all subsequent playbacks will use the same value.

The cycleCount specifies the number of times the clip is played when the play() method is called. It defaults to one, which plays the clip only once. You can use one of the following three INDEFINITE constants as the cycleCount to play the AudioClip loop until stopped:

- AudioClip.INDEFINITE

- MediaPlayer.INDEFINITE

- Animation.INDEFINITE

The following snippet of code shows how to play an audio clip five times and indefinitely:

```
// Play five times
audioClip.setCycleCount(5);
...
// Loop forever
audioClip.setCycleCount(AudioClip.INDEFINITE);
```

The volume specifies the relative volume of the playback. The valid range is 0.0 to 1.0. A value of 0.0 represents muted, whereas 1.0 represents full volume.

The rate specifies the relative speed at which the audio is played. The valid range is 0.125 to 8.0. A value of 0.125 means the clip is played eight times slower, and the value of 8.0 means the clip will play eight times faster. The rate affects the playtime and the pitch. The default rate is 1.0, which plays the clip at the normal rate.

The balance specifies the relative volume for the left and right channels. The valid range is –1.0 to 1.0. A value of –1.0 sets the playback in the left channel at normal volume and mutes the right channel. A value of 1.0 sets the playback in the right channel at normal volume and mutes the left channel. The default value is 0.0, which sets the playback in both channels at normal volume.

The pan specifies the distribution of the clip between the left and right channels. The valid range is –1.0 to 1.0. A value of –1.0 shifts the clip entirely to the left channel. A value of 1.0 shifts the clip entirely to the right channel. The default value is 0.0, which plays the clip normally. Setting the value for pan for a mono clip has the same effect of setting the balance. You should change the default for this property only for audio clips using stereo sound.

The priority specifies the priority of the clip relative to other clips. It is used only when the number of playing clips exceeds the system limits. The playing clips with the lower priority will be stopped. It can be set to any integer. The default priority is set to zero.

The play() method is overloaded. It has three versions:

- Void play()

- void play(double volume)

- void play(double volume, double balance, double rate, double pan, int priority)

The no-args version of the method uses all of the properties set on the AudioClip. The other two versions can override the specified properties for a specific playback. Suppose the volume for the AudioClip is set to 1.0. Calling play() will play the clip at volume 1.0, and calling play(0.20) will play the clip at volume 0.20, leaving the volume property for the AudioClip unchanged at 1.0. That is, the play() method with parameters allows you to override the AudioClip properties on a per-playback basis.

The AudioClip class contains an isPlaying() method to check if the clip is still playing. It returns true if the clip is playing. Otherwise, it returns false.

Playing Media

JavaFX provides a unified API to work with audio and videos. You use the same classes to work with both. The Media API internally treats them as two different types of media that is transparent to the API users. From here onward, I will use the term media to mean both audio and video, unless specified otherwise.

The Media API contains three core classes to play back media:

- Media

- MediaPlayer

- MediaView

Creating a Media Object

An instance of the Media class represents a media resource, which could be an audio or a video. It provides the information related to the media, for example, the duration, metadata, data, and so forth. If the media is a video, it provides the width and height of the video. A Media object is immutable. It is created by supplying a string URL of the media resource, as in the following code:

```
// Create a Media
String mediaUrl = "http://www.jdojo.com/mymusic.wav";
Media media = new Media(mediaUrl);
```

The Media class contains the following properties, all (except onError) of which are read-only:

- duration

- width

- height

- error

- onError

The duration specifies the duration of the media in seconds. It is a Duration object. If the duration is unknown, it is Duration.UNKNOWN.

The width and height give the width and height of the source media in pixels, respectively. If the media does not have width and height, they are set as zero.

The error and onError properties are related. The error property represents the MediaException that occurs during the loading of the media. The onError is a Runnable object that you can set to get notified when an error occurs. The run() method of the Runnable is called when an error occurs:

```
// When an error occurs in loading the media, print it on the console
media.setOnError(() -> System.out.println(player.getError().getMessage()));
```

Creating a *MediaPlayer* Object

A MediaPlayer provides the controls, for example, play, pause, stop, seek, play speed, volume adjustment, for playing the media. The MediaPlayer provides only one constructor that takes a Media object as an argument:

```
// Create a MediaPlayer
MediaPlayer player = new MediaPlayer(media);
```

You can get the reference of the media from the MediaPlayer using the getMedia() method of the MediaPlayer class.

Like the Media class, the MediaPlayer class also contains error and onError properties to report errors. When an error occurs on the MediaPlayer, the same error is also reported on the Media object.

The MediaPlayer class contains many properties and methods. I will discuss them in subsequent sections.

Creating a *MediaView* Node

A MediaView is a node. It provides the view of a media being played by a MediaPlayer. Note that an audio clip does not have visuals. If you try creating a MediaView for an audio content, it would be empty. To watch a video, you create a MediaView and add it to a scene graph.

The MediaView class provides two constructors, one no-args constructor and one that takes a MediaPlayer as an argument:

- public MediaView()

- public MediaView(MediaPlayer mediaPlayer)

The no-args constructor creates a MediaView that is attached to any MediaPlayer. You will need to set a MediaPlayer using the setter for the mediaPlayer property:

```
// Create a MediaView with no MediaPlayer
MediaView mediaView = new MediaView();
mediaView.setMediaPlayer(player);
```

The other constructor lets you specify a MediaPlayer for the MediaView:

```
// Create a MediaView
MediaView mediaView = new MediaView(player);
```

Combining *Media, MediaPlayer,* and *MediaView*

The content of a media can be used simultaneously by multiple Media objects. However, one Media object can be associated with only one media content in its lifetime.

A Media object can be associated with multiple MediaPlayer objects. However, a MediaPlayer is associated with only one Media in its lifetime.

A MediaView may optionally be associated with a MediaPlayer. Of course, a MediaView that is not associated with a MediaPlayer does not have any visuals. The MediaPlayer for a MediaView can be changed. Changing the MediaPlayer for a MediaView is similar to changing the channel on a television. The view for the MediaView is provided by its current MediaPlayer. You can associate the same MediaPlayer with multiple MediaViews. Different MediaViews may display different parts of the same media during the playback. This relationship between the three types of objects involved in a media playback is shown in Figure 25-2.

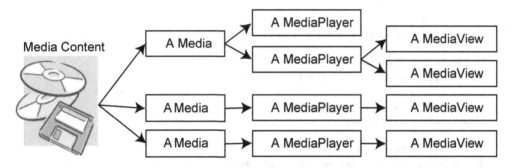

Figure 25-2. *Roles of different media-related objects in a media playback and the relation among them*

A Media Player Example

You now have enough background to understand the mechanism used to play an audio and a video. The program in Listing 25-2 plays a video clip using the ResourceUtil to find the file location. The program uses a video file resources/media/gopro.mp4. This file maybe is not included in the source code because it is approximately 50MB. You can substitute your own media file in this program if it is in a format supported by JavaFX.

Listing 25-2. Using the Media, MediaPlayer, and MediaView Classes to Play a Media

```
// QuickMediaPlayer.java
package com.jdojo.media;

import com.jdojo.util.ResourceUtil;
import java.net.URL;
import javafx.application.Application;
import javafx.scene.Scene;
```

```java
import javafx.scene.control.Button;
import javafx.scene.layout.BorderPane;
import javafx.scene.layout.HBox;
import javafx.scene.media.Media;
import javafx.scene.media.MediaPlayer;
import javafx.scene.media.MediaView;
import javafx.stage.Stage;
import static javafx.scene.media.MediaPlayer.Status.PLAYING;

public class QuickMediaPlayer extends Application {
        public static void main(String[] args) {
            Application.launch(args);
        }

        @Override
        public void start(Stage stage) {
            // Locate the media content
                URL mediaUrl = ResourceUtil.getResourceURL("media/gopro.mp4");
            String mediaStringUrl = mediaUrl.toExternalForm();

            // Create a Media
            Media media = new Media(mediaStringUrl);

            // Create a Media Player
            MediaPlayer player = new MediaPlayer(media);

            // Automatically begin the playback
            player.setAutoPlay(true);

            // Create a 400X300 MediaView
            MediaView mediaView = new MediaView(player);
            mediaView.setFitWidth(400);
            mediaView.setFitHeight(300);

            // Create Play and Stop player control buttons and add action
            // event handlers to them
            Button playBtn = new Button("Play");
            playBtn.setOnAction(e -> {
                    if (player.getStatus() == PLAYING) {
                            player.stop();
                            player.play();
                    } else {
                            player.play();
                    }
            });

            Button stopBtn = new Button("Stop");
            stopBtn.setOnAction(e -> player.stop());

            // Add an error handler
            player.setOnError(() ->
                    System.out.println(player.getError().getMessage()));
```

```
        HBox controlBox = new HBox(5, playBtn, stopBtn);
        BorderPane root = new BorderPane();

        // Add the MediaView and player controls to the scene graph
        root.setCenter(mediaView);
        root.setBottom(controlBox);

        Scene scene = new Scene(root);
        stage.setScene(scene);
        stage.setTitle("Playing Media");
        stage.show();
    }
}
```

The first two statements in the start() method prepare a string URL for the media file:

```
// Locate the media content
URL mediaUrl = ResourceUtil.getResourceURL("media/gopro.mp4");
String mediaStringUrl = mediaUrl.toExternalForm();
```

If you want to play a media from the Internet, you can replace the three statements with a statement similar to the following:

```
String mediaStringUrl = "http://www.jdojo.com/video.flv";
```

The program creates a Media, a MediaPlayer, and a MediaView. It sets the autoPlay property for the MediaPlayer to true, which will start playing the media as soon as possible:

```
// Automatically begin the playback
player.setAutoPlay(true);
```

The size of the MediaView is set 400px wide by 300px tall. If the media is a video, the video will be scaled to fit in this size. You will see an empty area for the audios. You can enhance the MediaView later, so it will take as much space as the media needs.

The Play and Stop buttons are created. Event handlers are added to them. They can be used to begin and stop the playback, respectively. When the media is already playing, clicking the Play button stops the playback and plays the media again.

A number of things can go wrong when playing a media. The program sets the onError property for the MediaPlayer, which is a Runnable. Its run() method is called when an error occurs. The run() method prints the error message on the console:

```
// Add an error handler
player.setOnError(() -> System.out.println(player.getError().getMessage()));
```

When you run the program, the video should play automatically. You can stop and replay it using the buttons at the bottom of the screen. If there is an error, you will see an error message on the console.

■ **Tip** The QuickMediaPlayer class can play audios as well as videos. All you need to do is change the URL of the source to point to the media you want to play.

Handling Playback Errors

An instance of the MediaException class, which inherits from the RuntimeException class, represents a media error that may occur in a Media, MediaPlayer, and MediaView. Media playback may fail for a number of reasons. The API users should be able to identify specific errors. The MediaException class defines a static enum MediaException.Type whose constants identify the type of error. The MediaException class contains a getType() method that returns one of the constants of the MediaException.Type enum.

- MEDIA_CORRUPTED

- MEDIA_INACCESSIBLE

- MEDIA_UNAVAILABLE

- MEDIA_UNSPECIFIED

- MEDIA_UNSUPPORTED

- OPERATION_UNSUPPORTED

- PLAYBACK_HALTED

- PLAYBACK_ERROR

- UNKNOWN

The MEDIA_CORRUPTED error type indicates that the media is corrupted or invalid. The MEDIA_INACCESSIBLE error type indicates that the media is inaccessible. However, the media may exist. The MEDIA_UNAVAILABLE error type indicates that the media does not exist or it is unavailable. The MEDIA_UNSPECIFIED error type indicates that the media has not been specified. The MEDIA_UNSUPPORTED error type indicates that the media is not supported by the platform. The OPERATION_UNSUPPORTED error type indicates that the operation performed on the media is not supported by the platform. The PLAYBACK_HALTED error type indicates an unrecoverable error that has halted the playback. The PLAYBACK_ERROR error type indicates a playback error that does not fall into any other described categories. The UNKNOWN error type indicates that an unknown error has occurred.

The Media and MediaPlayer classes contain an error property that is a MediaException. All three classes—Media, MediaPlayer, and MediaView—contain an onError property, which is an event handler that is invoked when an error occurs. The types of the onError properties in these classes are not consistent. It is a Runnable for the Media and MediaPlayer classes and the MediaErrorEvent for the MediaView class. The following snippet of code shows how to handle errors on a Media, MediaPlayer, and MediaView. They print the error details on the console:

```
player.setOnError(() -> {
        System.out.println(player.getError().getMessage());
});

media.setOnError(() -> {
        System.out.println(player.getError().getMessage());
});

mediaView.setOnError((MediaErrorEvent e) ->  {
        MediaException error = e.getMediaError();
        MediaException.Type errorType = error.getType();
        String errorMsg = error.getMessage();
        System.out.println("Error Type:" + errorType +
                ", error mesage:" + errorMsg);
});
```

Media error handlers are invoked on the JavaFX Application Thread. Therefore, it is safe to update the scene graph from the handlers.

It is recommended that you enclose the creation of the Media, MediaPlayer, and MediaView objects in a try-catch block and handle the exception appropriately. The onError handlers for these objects are involved after the objects are created. If an error occurs during the creation of these objects, those handlers will not be available. For example, if the media type you are trying to use is not supported, creating the Media object results in an error:

```
try {
        Media media = new Media(mediaStringUrl);
        ...
}
catch (MediaException e) {
        // Handle errors here
}
```

State Transitions of the *MediaPlayer*

A MediaPlayer always has a status. The current status of a MediaPlayer is indicated by the read-only status property. The status changes when an action is performed on the MediaPlayer. It cannot be set directly. The status of a MediaPlayer is defined by one of the eight constants in the MediaPlayer.Status enum:

- UNKNOWN
- READY
- PLAYING
- PAUSED
- STALLED
- STOPPED
- HALTED
- DISPOSED

The MediaPlayer transitions from one status to another when one of the following methods is called:

- play()
- pause()
- stop()
- dispose()

Figure 25-3 shows the status transition for a MediaPlayer. Figure 25-3 excludes the HALTED and DISPOSED statuses as these two statuses are terminal statuses.

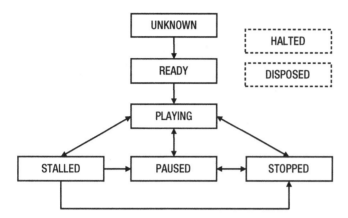

Figure 25-3. *Statuses of a MediaPlayer and the transition among them*

When a MediaPlayer is created, its status is UNKNOWN. Once the media is prerolled and it is ready to be played, the MediaPlayer transitions from UNKNOWN to READY. Once the MediaPlayer exits the UNKNOWN status, it cannot reenter it in its lifetime.

The MediaPlayer transitions to the PLAYING status when the play() method is called. This status indicates that the media is playing. Note if the autoPlay property is set to true, the MediaPlayer may enter the PLAYING status without calling the play() method explicitly after it is created.

When the MediaPlayer is playing, it may enter the STALLED status if it does not have enough data in its buffer to play. This status indicates that the MediaPlayer is buffering data. When enough data are buffered, it goes back to the PLAYING status. When a MediaPlayer is stalled, calling the pause() and stop() methods, it transitions to the PAUSED and STOPPED status, respectively. In that case, the buffering continues; however, the MediaPlayer does not transition to the PLAYING status once enough data are buffered. Rather, it stays in the PAUSED or STOPPED status.

Calling the pause() method transitions the MediaPlayer to the PAUSED status. Calling the stop() method transitions the MediaPlayer to the STOPPED status.

In cases of an unrecoverable error, the MediaPlayer transitions to the HALTED terminal status. This status indicates that the MediaPlayer cannot be used again. You must create a new MediaPlayer if you want to play the media again.

The dispose() method frees all of the resources associated with the MediaPlayer. However, the Media object used by the MediaPlayer can still be used. Calling the dispose() method transitions the MediaPlayer to the terminal status DISPOSED.

It is common to display the status of the MediaPlayer in an application. Add a ChangeListener to the status property to listen for any status changes.

Typically, you will be interested in receiving a notification when the status of the MediaPlayer changes. There are two ways to get the notifications:

- By adding a ChangeListener to the status property
- By setting status change handlers

The first method is suitable if you are interested in listening for any type of status change. The following snippet of code shows this method:

```
MediaPlayer player = new MediaPlayer(media);

// Add a ChangeListener to the player
player.statusProperty().addListener((prop, oldStatus, newStatus) -> {
        System.out.println("Status changed from " + oldStatus +
                " to " + newStatus);
});
```

The second method is suitable if you are interested in handling a specific type of status change. The MediaPlayer class contains the following properties that can be set to Runnable objects:

- onReady
- onPlaying
- onRepeat
- onStalled
- onPaused
- onStopped
- onHalted

The run() method of the Runnable object is called when the MediaPlayer enters into the specific status. For example, the run() method of the onPlaying handler is called when the player enters the PLAYING status. The following snippet of code shows how to set handlers for a specific type of status change:

```
// Add a handler for PLAYING status
player.setOnPlaying(() -> {
        System.out.println("Playing...");
});

// Add a handler for STOPPED status
player.setOnStopped(() -> {
        System.out.println("Stopped...");
});
```

Repeating Media Playback

A media can be played repeatedly for a specified number of times or even indefinitely. The cycleCount property specifies the number of times a playback will be repeated. By default, it is set to one. Set it to MediaPlayer.INDEFINITE to repeat the playback indefinitely until the player is paused or stopped. The read-only currentCount property is set to the number of completed playback cycles. It is set to zero when the media is playing the first cycle. At the end of the first cycle, it is set to one; it is incremented to two at the end of the second cycle; and so on. The following code would set a playback cycle of four times:

```
// The playback should repeat 4 times
player.setCycleCount(4);
```

You can receive a notification when the end of media for a cycle in playback is reached. Set a Runnable for the onEndOfMedia property of the MediaPlayer class to get the notification. Note that if a playback continues for four cycles, the end of the media notification will be sent four times:

```
player.setOnEndOfMedia(() -> {
        System.out.println("End of media...");
});
```

You can add an onRepeat event handler that is called when the end of media for a playback cycle is reached and the playback is going to repeat. It is called after the onEndOfMedia event handler:

```
player.setOnRepeat(() -> {
        System.out.println("Repeating...");
});
```

Tracking Media Time

Displaying the media duration and the elapsed time for a playback is an important feedback for the audience. A good understanding of these duration types is important in developing a good media playback dashboard. Different types of duration can be associated with a media:

- The current duration of a media playing media
- The duration of the media playback
- The duration of the media play for one cycle
- The start offset time
- The end offset time

By default, a media plays for its original duration. For example, if the duration of the media is 30 minutes, the media will play for 30 minutes in one cycle. The MediaPlayer lets you specify the length of the playback, which can be anywhere in the duration of the media. For example, for each playback cycle, you can specify that only the middle 10 minutes (11th to 12th) of the media should be played. The length of the media playback is specified by the following two properties of the MediaPlayer class:

- startTime
- stopTime

Both properties are of the Duration type. The startTime and stopTime are the time offsets where the media should start and stop playing for each cycle, respectively. By default, the startTime is set to Duration.ZERO, and the stopTime is set to the duration of the media. The following snippet of code sets these properties, so the media will be played from the 10th minute to the 21st minute:

```
player.setStartTime(Duration.minutes(10));
player.setStartTime(Duration.minutes(21));
```

The following constraints are applicable to the startTime and stopTime values:

```
0 ≤ startTime < stopTime
startTime < stopTime ≤ Media.duration
```

The read-only currentTime property is the current time offset in the media playback. The read-only cycleDuration property is the difference between the stopTime and startTime. It is the length of playback for each cycle. The read-only totalDuration property specifies the total duration of the playback if the playback is allowed to continue until finished. Its value is the cycleDuration multiplied by the cycleCount. If the cycleCount is INDEFINITE, the totalDuration will be INDEFINITE. If the media duration is UNKNOWN, the totalDuration will be UNKNOWN.

When you play a media from the network, the MediaPlayer may get stalled because it does not have enough data to continue the playback. The read-only bufferProgressTime property gives you the duration for which the media can be played without stalling.

Controlling the Playback Rate

The rate property of the MediaPlayer specifies the rate of the playback. The valid range is 0.0 to 8.0. For example, a rate of 2.0 plays the media two times faster than the normal rate. The default value is 1.0, which plays the media at the normal rate. The read-only currentRate property is the current rate of the playback. The following code would set the rate at three times the normal rate:

```
// Play the media at 3x
player.setRate(3.0);
```

Controlling the Playback Volume

Three properties in the MediaPlayer class control the volume of the audio in the media:

- volume

- mute

- balance

The volume specifies the volume of the audio. The range is 0.0 to 1.0. A value of 0.0 makes the audio inaudible, whereas a value of 1.0 plays it at full volume. The default value is 1.0.

The mute specifies whether the audio is produced by the MediaPlayer. By default, its value is false and the audio is produced. Setting it to true does not produce audio. Note that setting the mute property does not affect the volume property. Suppose the volume is set to 1.0, and the muted is set to true. There is no audio being produced. When the mute is set to false, the audio will use the volume property that is 1.0, and it will play at full volume. The following code would set the volume at half:

```
// Play the audio at half the full volumne
player.setVolumne(0.5);
...
// Mute the audio
player.setMute(true)
```

The balance specifies the relative volume for the left and right channels. The valid range is –1.0 to 1.0. A value of –1.0 sets the playback in the left channel at normal volume and mutes the right channel. A value of 1.0 sets the playback in the right channel at normal volume and mutes the left channel. The default value is 0.0, which sets the playback in both channels at normal volume.

Positioning the *MediaPlayer*

You can position a MediaPlayer at a specific playback time using the seek(Duration position) method:

```
// Position the media at the fifth minutes play time
player.seek(Duration.minutes(5.0));
```

Calling the seek() method has no effect if

- The MediaPlayer is in the STOPPED status.

- The media duration is Duration.INDEFINITE.

- You pass null or Duration.UNKNOWN to the seek() method.

- In all other cases, the position is clamped between the startTime and stopTime of the MediaPlayer.

Marking Positions in the Media

You can associate markers with specific points on the media timeline. Markers are simply text that are useful in a number of ways. You can use them to insert advertisements. For example, you can insert a URL as the marker text. When the marker is reached, you can pause playing the media and play another media. Note that playing another media involves creating new Media and MediaPlayer objects. You can reuse a MediaView. When you are playing the advertisement video, associate the MediaView with the new MediaPlayer. When the advertisement playback is finished, associate the MediaView back to the main MediaPlayer.

The Media class contains a getMarkers() method that returns an ObservableMap<String, Duration>. You need to add the (key, value) pairs in the map to add markers. The following snippet of code adds three markers to a media:

```
Media media = ...
ObservableMap<String, Duration> markers = media.getMarkers();
markers.put("START", Duration.ZERO);
markers.put("INTERVAL", media.getDuration().divide(2.0));
markers.put("END", media.getDuration());
```

The MediaPlayer fires a MediaMarkerEvent when a marker is reached. You can register a handler for this event in the onMarker property of the MediaPlayer. The following snippet of code shows how to handle the MediaMarkerEvent. The getMarker() method of the event returns a Pair<String, Duration> whose key and value are the marker text and marker duration, respectively:

```
// Add a marker event handler
player.setOnMarker((MediaMarkerEvent e) -> {
        Pair<String, Duration> marker = e.getMarker();
        String markerText = marker.getKey();
        Duration markerTime = marker.getValue();
        System.out.println("Reached the marker " + markerText +
                " at " + markerTime);
});
```

Showing Media Metadata

Some metadata may be embedded into a media that describe the media. Typically, the metadata contains the title, artist name, album name, genre, year, and so forth. The following snippet of code displays the metadata for the media when the MediaPlayer enters the READY status. Do not try reading the metadata just after creating the Media object, as the metadata may not be available:

```
Media media = ...
MediaPlayer player = new MediaPlayer(media);

// Display the metadata data on the console
player.setOnReady(() -> {
        ObservableMap<String, Object> metadata = media.getMetadata();
        for(String key : metadata.keySet()) {
            System.out.println(key + " = " + metadata.get(key));
        }
});
```

You cannot be sure whether there are metadata in a media or the type of metadata a media may contain. In your application, you can just look for the title, artist, album, and year. Alternatively, you could read all of the metadata and display them in a two-column table. Sometimes, the metadata may contain an embedded image of the artist. You would need to check the class name of the value in the map to use the image.

Customizing the *MediaView*

If the media has a view (e.g., a video), you can customize the size, area, and quality of the video using the following properties:

- fitHeight
- fitWidth
- preserveRatio
- smooth
- viewport
- x
- y

The fitWidth and fitHeight properties specify the resized width and height of the video, respectively. By default, they are zero, which means that the original width and height of the media will be used.

The preserveRatio property specifies whether to preserve the aspect ratio of the media while resizing. By default, it is false.

The smooth property specifies the quality of the filtering algorithm to be used in resizing the video. The default value is platform dependent. If it is set to true, a better-quality filtering algorithm is used. Note that a better-quality filtering takes more processing time. For smaller-sized videos, you may set it to false. For bigger-sized videos, it is recommended to set the property to true.

A viewport is a rectangular region to view part of a graphic. The viewport, x, and y properties together let you specify the rectangular area in the video that will be shown in the MediaView. The viewport is a Rectangle2D that is specified in the coordinate system of the original media frame. The x and y properties are the coordinates of the upper-left corner of the viewport. Recall that you can have multiple MediaViews associated with a MediaPlayer. Using multiple MediaViews with viewports, you can give the audience the impression of splitting the video. Using one MediaView with a viewport, you can let the audience view only part of the viewable area of the video.

A MediaView is a node. Therefore, to give a better visual experience to the audience, you can also apply effects and transformations to the MediaView.

Developing a Media Player Application

It requires a careful design to develop a good-looking, customizable media player application. I have covered most of the features offered by the Media API in JavaFX. Combining your knowledge of developing a user interface and the Media API, you can design and develop your own media player application. Keep the following points in mind while developing the application:

- The application should have the ability to specify a media source.

- The application should provide a UI to control the media playback.

- When the media source changes, you will need to create a new Media object and a MediaPlayer. You can reuse the MediaView by setting the new MediaPlayer using its setMediaPlayer() method.

Summary

JavaFX supports playing audio and video through the JavaFX Media API. HTTP live streaming of static media files and live feeds are also supported. A number of media formats are supported, such as AAC, AIFF, WAV, and MP3. FLV containing VP6 video and MP3 audio and MPEG-4 multimedia container with H.264/AVC video formats are supported. The support for a specific media format is platform dependent. Some media playback features and formats do not require any additional installations; but some require third-party software to be installed. The Media API consists of several classes. All classes in the API are included in the javafx.scene.media package.

An AudioClip is used to play a short audio clip with minimal latency. Typically, this is useful for sound effects, which are usually short audio clips. Use the Media, MediaPlayer, and MediaView classes for playing audios and videos of longer length.

The Media and MediaPlayer classes are used to play audios as well as videos. An instance of the Media class represents a media resource, which could be an audio or a video. It provides the information about the media, for example, the duration of the media. An instance of the MediaPlayer class provides controls for playing a media. A MediaPlayer always indicates the status of the playback. The current status of a MediaPlayer is indicated by the read-only status property. The status changes when an action is performed on the MediaPlayer. The status can be unknown, ready, playing, paused, stalled, stopped, halted, or disposed.

An instance of the MediaView class provides the view of a media being played by a MediaPlayer. A MediaView is used for viewing a video.

Several things can go wrong when you attempt to play a media, for example, the media format may not be supported or the media content may be corrupt. An instance of the MediaException class represents a specific type of media error that may occur during media playback. When a media-related error occurs, a MediaErrorEvent is generated. You can handle the error by adding an appropriate event handler to the media objects.

The next chapter will discuss FXML, which is an XML-based language to build user interfaces for a JavaFX application.

CHAPTER 26

■ ■ ■

Understanding FXML

In this chapter, you will learn:

- What FXML is
- How to edit an FXML document
- The structure of an FXML document
- How to create objects in an FXML document
- How to specify the location of resources in FXML documents
- How to use resource bundles in FXML documents
- How to refer to other FXML documents from an FXML document
- How to refer to constants in FXML documents
- How to refer to other elements and how to copy elements in FXML documents
- How to bind properties in FXML documents
- How to create custom controls using FXML

The examples of this chapter lie in the `com.jdojo.fxml` package. In order for them to work, you must add a corresponding line to the `module-info.java` file:

```
...
opens com.jdojo.fxml to javafx.graphics, javafx.base;
...
```

What Is FXML?

FXML is an XML-based language designed to build the user interface for JavaFX applications. You can use FXML to build an entire scene or part of a scene. FXML allows application developers to separate the logic for building the UI from the business logic. If the UI part of the application changes, you do not need to recompile the JavaFX code. Instead, you can change the FXML using a text editor and rerun the application. You still use JavaFX to write business logic using the Java language. An FXML document is an XML document. A basic knowledge of XML is required to understand this chapter.

A JavaFX scene graph is a hierarchical structure of Java objects. XML format is well suited for storing information representing some kind of hierarchy. Therefore, using FXML to store the scene graph is very

© Kishori Sharan and Peter Späth 2022
K. Sharan and P. Späth, *Learn JavaFX 17*, https://doi.org/10.1007/978-1-4842-7848-2_26

intuitive. It is common to use FXML to build a scene graph in a JavaFX application. However, the use of FXML is not limited to building only scene graphs. It can build a hierarchical object graph of Java objects. In fact, it can be used to create just one object, such as an object of a Person class.

Let's get a quick preview of what an FXML document looks like. First, create a simple UI, which consists of a VBox with a Label and a Button. Listing 26-1 contains the JavaFX code to build the UI, which is familiar to you. Listing 26-2 contains the FXML version for building the same UI.

Listing 26-1. A Code Snippet to Build an Object Graph in JavaFX

```
import javafx.scene.layout.VBox;
import javafx.scene.control.Label;
import javafx.scene.control.Button;

VBox root = new VBox();
root.getChildren().addAll(new Label("FXML is cool"), new Button("Say Hello"));
```

Listing 26-2. A Code Snippet to Build an Object Graph in FXML

```
<?xml version="1.0" encoding="UTF-8"?>

<?import javafx.scene.layout.VBox?>
<?import javafx.scene.control.Label?>
<?import javafx.scene.control.Button?>

<VBox>
        <children>
                <Label text="FXML is cool"/>
                <Button text="Say Hello"/>
        </children>
</VBox>
```

The first line in FXML is the standard XML declaration that is used by XML parsers. It is optional in FXML. If it is omitted, the version and encoding are assumed to be 1 and UTF-8, respectively. The next three lines are import statements that correspond to the import statements in Java code. Elements representing UI, such as VBox, Label, and Button, have the same name as the JavaFX classes. The <children> tag specifies the children of the VBox. The text properties for the Label and Button are specified using the text attributes of the respective elements.

Editing FXML Documents

An FXML document is simply a text file. Typically, the file name has a .fxml extension (e.g., hello.fxml). For example, you can use Notepad to create an FXML document in Windows. If you have used XML, you know that it is not easy to edit a large XML document in a text editor. The Gluon company provides a visual editor called *Scene Builder* for editing FXML documents. Scene Builder is open source. You can download its latest version from https://gluonhq.com/products/scene-builder/. Scene Builder can also be integrated into some IDEs, so you can edit FXML documents using Scene Builder from inside an IDE. Scene Builder is not discussed in this book.

FXML Basics

This section covers the basics of FXML. You will develop a simple JavaFX application, which consists of the following:

- A VBox
- A Label
- A Button

The spacing property for the VBox is set to 10px. The text properties for the Label and Button are set to "FXML is cool!" and "Say Hello". When the Button is clicked, the text in the Label changes to "Hello from FXML!". Figure 26-1 shows two instances of the window displayed by the application.

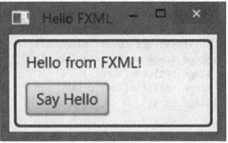

Figure 26-1. *Two instances of a window whose scene graphs are created using FXML*

The program in Listing 26-3 is the JavaFX implementation of the example application. The program should be easy if you have made it up to this chapter in the book.

Listing 26-3. The JavaFX Version of the FXML Example Application

```java
// HelloJavaFX.java
package com.jdojo.fxml;

import javafx.application.Application;
import javafx.event.ActionEvent;
import javafx.scene.Scene;
import javafx.scene.control.Button;
import javafx.scene.control.Label;
import javafx.scene.layout.VBox;
import javafx.stage.Stage;

public class HelloJavaFX extends Application {
        private final Label msgLbl = new Label("FXML is cool!");
        private final Button sayHelloBtn = new Button("Say Hello");

        public static void main(String[] args) {
                Application.launch(args);
        }
```

```java
        @Override
        public void start(Stage stage) {
                // Set the preferred width of the label
                msgLbl.setPrefWidth(150);

                // Set the ActionEvent handler for the button
                sayHelloBtn.setOnAction(this::sayHello);

                VBox root = new VBox(10);
                root.getChildren().addAll(msgLbl, sayHelloBtn);
                root.setStyle("""
                                -fx-padding: 10;
                        -fx-border-style: solid inside;
                        -fx-border-width: 2;
                        -fx-border-insets: 5;
                        -fx-border-radius: 5;
                        -fx-border-color: blue;""");
                Scene scene = new Scene(root);
                stage.setScene(scene);
                stage.setTitle("Hello FXML");
                stage.show();
        }

        public void sayHello(ActionEvent e) {
                msgLbl.setText("Hello from FXML!");
        }
}
```

Creating the FXML File

Let's create an FXML file sayhello.fxml. Store the file in the resources/fxml directory where the resources directory gets correctly addressed by the ResourceUtil class.

Adding UI Elements

The root element of the FXML document is the top-level object in the object graph. Your top-level object is a VBox. Therefore, the root element of your FXML would be

```
<VBox>
</VBox>
```

How do you know that to represent a VBox in the object graph, you need to use a <VBox> tag in FXML? It is both difficult and easy. It is difficult because there is no documentation for FXML tags. It is easy because FXML has a few rules explaining what constitutes a tag name. For example, if a tag name is the simple or full-qualified name of a class, the tag will create an object of that class. The preceding element will create an object of the VBox class. The preceding FXML can be rewritten using the fully qualified class name:

```
<javafx.scene.layout.VBox>
</javafx.scene.layout.VBox>
```

In JavaFX, layout panes have children. In FXML, layout panes have children as their child elements. You can add a Label and a Button to the VBox as follows:

```
<VBox>
        <Label></Label>
        <Button></Button>
</VBox>
```

This defines the basic structure of the object graph for this example application. It will create a VBox with a Label and a Button. The rest of the discussion will focus on adding details, for example, adding text for controls and setting styles for the VBox.

The preceding FXML shows that the Label and Button are children of the VBox. In the GUI sense, that is true. However, technically, they belong to the children property of the VBox object, not directly to the VBox. To be more technical (and a little verbose), you can rewrite the preceding FXML as shown in the following:

```
<VBox>
        <children>
                <Label></Label>
                <Button></Button>
        <children>
</VBox>
```

How do you know that you can ignore the <children> tag in the preceding FXML and still get the same results? The JavaFX library contains an annotation DefaultProperty in the javafx.beans package. It can be used to annotate classes. It contains a value element of the String type. The element specifies the property of the class, which should be treated as the default property in FXML. If a child element in FXML does not represent a property of its parent element, it belongs to the default property of the parent. The VBox class inherits from the Pane class, whose declaration is as follows:

```
@DefaultProperty(value="children")
public class Pane extends Region {...}
```

The annotation on the Pane class makes the children property the default property in FXML. The VBox inherits this annotation from the Pane class. This is the reason that the <children> tag can be omitted in the preceding FXML. If you see the DefaultProperty annotation on a class, it means you can omit the tag for the default property in FXML.

Importing Java Types in FXML

To use the simple names of Java classes in FXML, you must import the classes as you do in Java programs. There is one exception. In Java programs, you do not need to import classes from the java.lang package. However, in FXML, you need to import classes from all packages, including the java.lang package. An import processing instruction is used to import a class or all classes from a package. The following processing instructions import the VBox, Label, and Button classes:

```
<?import javafx.scene.layout.VBox?>
<?import javafx.scene.control.Label?>
<?import javafx.scene.control.Button?>
```

The following import processing instructions import all classes from the `javafx.scene.control` and `java.lang` packages:

```
<?import javafx.scene.control.*?>
<?import java.lang.*?>
```

Importing static members is not supported in FXML. Note that the import statement does not use a trailing semicolon.

Setting Properties in FXML

You can set properties for Java objects in FXML. A property for an object can be set in FXML if the property declaration follows the JavaBean conventions. There are two ways to set properties:

- Using attributes of an FXML element
- Using property elements

The attribute name or the property element name is the same as the name of the property being set. The following FXML creates a `Label` and sets its `text` property using an attribute:

```
<Label text="FXML is cool!"/>
```

The following FXML achieves the same using a property element:

```
<Label>
        <text>FXML is cool!</text>
</Label>
```

The following FXML creates a `Rectangle` and sets its `x`, `y`, `width`, `height`, and `fill` properties using attributes:

```
<Rectangle x="10" y="10" width="100" height="40" fill="red"/>
```

FXML specifies values for attributes as `String`s. Appropriate conversion is automatically applied to convert the `String` values to the required types. In the preceding case, the value "red" for the `fill` property will be automatically converted to a `Color` object, the value "100" for the `width` property will be converted to a double value, and so on.

Using property elements to set object properties is more flexible. Attributes can be used when the automatic type conversion from `String` is possible. Suppose you want to set an object of a `Person` class to a property of an object. It can be done using a property element. The following FXML sets the `person` property of an object of the class `MyCls`:

```
<MyCls>
        <person>
                <Person>
                        <!-- Configure the Person object here -->
                </Person>
        </person>
</MyCls>
```

A read-only property is a property that has a getter, but no setter. Two special types of read-only properties can be set in FXML using a property element:

- A read-only List property

- A read-only Map property

Use a property element for setting a read-only List property. All children of the property element will be added to the List returned by the getter of the property. The following FXML sets the read-only children property of a VBox:

```
<VBox>
        <children>
                <Label/>
                <Button/>
        <children>
</VBox>
```

You can use attributes of the property element to add entries to a read-only Map property. The names and values of the attributes become the keys and the values in the Map. The following snippet of code declares a class Item, which has a read-only map property:

```
public class Item {
        private Map<String, Integer> map = new HashMap<>();
        public Map getMap() {
                return map;
        }
}
```

The following FXML creates an Item object and sets its map property with two entries ("n1", 100) and ("n2", 200). Notice that the names of the attributes n1 and n2 become the keys in the Map:

```
<Item>
        <map n1="100" n2="200"/>
</Item>
```

There is one special type of property for Java objects known as the static property. The static property is not declared on the class of the object. Rather, it is set using a static method of another class. Suppose you want to set the margin for a Button that will be placed in a VBox. The JavaFX code is shown as follows:

```
Button btn = new Button("OK");
Insets insets = new Insets(20.0);;
VBox.setMargin(btn, insets);
VBox vbox = new VBox(btn);
```

You can achieve the same in FXML by setting a VBox.margin property for the Button:

```
<?import javafx.scene.layout.VBox?>
<?import javafx.scene.control.Button?>
<?import javafx.geometry.Insets?>
```

```
<VBox>
    <Button text="OK">
        <VBox.margin>
            <Insets top="20.0" right="20.0" bottom="20.0" left="20.0"/>
        </VBox.margin>
    </Button>
</VBox>
```

You cannot create an Insets object from a String, and, therefore, you cannot use an attribute to set the margin property. You need to use a property element to set it. When you use a GridPane in FXML, you can set the rowIndex and columnIndex static as shown in the following:

```
<?import javafx.scene.layout.GridPane?>
<?import javafx.scene.control.Button?>

<GridPane>
        <Button text="OK">
                <GridPane.rowIndex>0</GridPane.rowIndex>
                <GridPane.columnIndex>0</GridPane.columnIndex>
        </Button>
</GridPane>
```

Because the rowIndex and columnIndex properties can also be represented as Strings, you can use attributes to set them:

```
<GridPane>
        <Button text="OK" GridPane.rowIndex="0" GridPane.columnIndex="0"/>
</GridPane>
```

Specifying FXML Namespace

FXML does not have an XML schema. It uses a namespace that needs to be specified using the namespace prefix "fx". For the most part, the FXML parser will figure out the tag names such as tag names that are classes, properties of the classes, and so on. FXML uses special elements and attribute names, which must be qualified with the "fx" namespace prefix. The following FXML declares the "fx" namespace prefix:

```
<VBox xmlns:fx="http://javafx.com/fxml">...</VBox>
```

Optionally, you can append the version of the FXML in the namespace URI. The FXML parser will verify that it can parse the specified XML code. At the time of this writing, the only supported version is 1.0:

```
<VBox xmlns:fx="http://javafx.com/fxml/1.0">...</VBox>
```

The FXML version can include dots, underscores, and dashes. Only the numbers before the first occurrence of the underscores and dashes are compared. All of the following three declarations specify the FXML version as 1.0:

```
<VBox xmlns:fx="http://javafx.com/fxml/1">...</VBox>
<VBox xmlns:fx="http://javafx.com/fxml/1.0-ea">...</VBox>
<VBox xmlns:fx="http://javafx.com/fxml/1.0-rc1-2014_03_02">...</VBox>
```

■ **Tip** The <fx:script> tag is an example for such a namespaced tag. It is for adding scripting logic to the FXML file. However, try to avoid it. First, scripting support in FXML seems to be not very stable. Second, adding processing logic to the FXML front-end definition is not considered to be a good programming style. Better use controllers, which we describe shorty.

Assigning an Identifier to an Object

An object created in FXML can be referred to somewhere else in the same document. It is common to get the reference of UI objects created in FXML inside the JavaFX code. You can achieve this by first identifying the objects in FXML with an fx:id attribute. The value of the fx:id attribute is the identifier for the object. If the object type has an id property, the value will be also set for the property. Note that each Node in JavaFX has an id property that can be used to refer to them in CSS. The following is an example of specifying the fx:id attribute for a Label:

```
<Label fx:id="msgLbl" text="FXML is cool!"/>
```

Now, you can refer to the Label using the msgLbl. The fx:id attribute has several uses. It is, for example, used to inject the reference of UI elements into the instance variables of a JavaFX class at the time FXML is loaded. I will discuss this in separate sections.

Adding Event Handlers

You can set event handlers for nodes in FXML. Setting an event handler is similar to setting any other properties. JavaFX classes define onXxx properties to set an event handler for an Xxx event. For example, the Button class contains an onAction property to set an ActionEvent handler. In FXML, you can specify two types of event handlers:

- Script event handlers
- Controller event handlers

In this book, we only talk about controller event handlers, because it is generally better to keep programming logic away from the GUI. I will discuss how to specify controller event handlers in the section "Using a Controller in FXML."

Loading FXML Documents

An FXML document defines the view (the GUI) part of a JavaFX application. You need to load the FXML document to get the object graph it represents. Loading an FXML is performed by an instance of the FXMLLoader class, which is in the javafx.fxml package.

The FXMLLoader class provides several constructors that let you specify the location, charset, resource bundle, and other elements to be used for loading the document. You need to specify at least the location of the FXML document, which is a URL. The class contains load() methods to perform the actual loading of the document. The following snippet of code loads an FXML document from a local file system in Windows:

```
String fxmlDocUrl = "file:///C:/resources/fxml/test.fxml";
URL fxmlUrl = new URL(fxmlDocUrl);
FXMLLoader loader = new FXMLLoader();
loader.setLocation(fxmlUrl);
VBox root = loader.<VBox>load();
```

The load() method has a generic return type. In the preceding snippet of code, you have made your intention clear in the call to the load() method (loader.<VBox>load()) that you are expecting a VBox instance from the FXML document. If you prefer, you may omit the generic parameter:

```
// Will work
VBox root = loader.load();
```

FXMLLoader supports loading a FXML document using an InputStream. The following snippet of code loads the same FXML document using an InputStream:

```
FXMLLoader loader = new FXMLLoader();
String fxmlDocPath = "C:\\resources\\fxml\\test.fxml";
FileInputStream fxmlStream = new FileInputStream(fxmlDocPath);
VBox root = loader.<VBox>load(fxmlStream);
```

Internally, the FXMLLoader reads the document using streams, which may throw an IOException. All versions of the load() method in the FXMLLoader class throw IOException. You have omitted the exception handling code in the preceding sample code. In your application, you will need to handle the exception.

The FXMLLoader class contains several versions of the load() method. Some of them are instance methods and some static methods. You need to create an FXMLLoader instance and use the instance load() method, if you want to retrieve more information from the loader, such as the controller reference, resource bundle, the location, charset, and root object. If you just want to load an FXML document without regard for any other details, you need to use the static load() methods. The following snippet of code uses a static load() method to load an FXML document:

```
String fxmlDocUrl = "file:///C:/resources/fxml/test.fxml";
URL fxmlUrl = new URL(fxmlDocUrl);
VBox root = FXMLLoader.<VBox>load(fxmlUrl);
```

What do you do next after loading an FXML document? At this point, the role of FXML is over, and your JavaFX code should take over. I will discuss the loader later in the text.

The program in Listing 26-4 has the JavaFX code for this example. It loads the FXML document stored in the *sayHello.fxml* file. The program loads the document using the ResourceUtil utility class. The loader returns a VBox, which is set as the root for the scene. The rest of the code is the same as you have been using except for one difference in the declaration of the start() method. The method declares that it may throw an IOException, which you had to add because you have called the load() method of the FXMLLoader inside the method. When you run the program, it displays a window as shown in Figure 26-1.

Listing 26-4. Using FXML to Build the GUI

```java
// SayHelloFXML.java
package com.jdojo.fxml;

import javafx.application.Application;
import javafx.fxml.FXMLLoader;
import java.io.IOException;
import java.net.URL;
import com.jdojo.util.ResourceUtil;
import javafx.scene.Scene;
import javafx.scene.layout.VBox;
import javafx.stage.Stage;

public class SayHelloFXML extends Application {
        public static void main(String[] args) {
                Application.launch(args);
        }

        @Override
        public void start(Stage stage) throws IOException {
            // Construct a URL for the FXML document
                URL fxmlUrl =
                    ResourceUtil.getResourceURL("fxml/sayhello.fxml");

                // Load the FXML document
                VBox root = FXMLLoader.<VBox>load(fxmlUrl);
                Scene scene = new Scene(root);
                stage.setScene(scene);
                stage.setTitle("Hello FXML");
                stage.show();
        }
}
```

If you click the button, nothing happens yet. We talk about connecting the UI to the Java code in the next section.

Using a Controller in FXML

A controller is simply a class name whose object is created by FXML and used to initialize the UI elements. FXML lets you specify a controller on the root element using the fx:controller attribute. Note that only one controller is allowed per FXML document, and if specified, it must be specified on the root element.

The following FXML specifies a controller for the VBox element:

```xml
<VBox fx:controller="com.jdojo.fxml.SayHelloController"
     xmlns:fx="http://javafx.com/fxml">
</VBox>
```

A controller needs to conform to some rules, and it can be used for different reasons:

- The controller is instantiated by the FXML loader.

- The controller must have a public no-args constructor. If it does not exist, the FXML loader will not be able to instantiate it, which will throw an exception at the load time.

- The controller can have accessible methods, which can be specified as event handlers in FXML. Please refer to the following discussion for the meaning of "accessible."

- The FXML loader will automatically look for accessible instance variables of the controller. If the name of an accessible instance variable matches the fx:id attribute of an element, the object reference from FXML is automatically copied into the controller instance variable. This feature makes the references of UI elements in FXML available to the controller. The controller can use them later, such as binding them to the model.

- The controller can have an accessible initialize() method, which should take no arguments and have a return type of void. The FXML loader will call the initialize() method after the loading of the FXML document is complete.

Listing 26-5 shows the code for a controller class that you will use for this example.

Listing 26-5. A Controller Class

```java
// SayHelloController.java
package com.jdojo.fxml;

import java.net.URL;
import java.util.ResourceBundle;
import javafx.fxml.FXML;
import javafx.scene.control.Label;

public class SayHelloController {
        // The reference of msgLbl will be injected by the FXML loader
        @FXML
        private Label msgLbl;

        // location and resources will be automatically injected by the
            // FXML loader
        @FXML
        private URL location;

        @FXML
        private ResourceBundle resources;

        // Add a public no-args constructor explicitly just to
        // emphasize that it is needed for a controller
        public SayHelloController() {
        }
```

```
@FXML
private void initialize() {
        System.out.println("Initializing SayHelloController...");
        System.out.println("Location = " + location);
        System.out.println("Resources = " + resources);
}

@FXML
private void sayHello() {
        msgLbl.setText("Hello from FXML!");
}
}
```

The controller class uses an @FXML annotation on some members. The @FXML annotation can be used on fields and methods. It cannot be used on classes and constructors. By using an @FXML annotation on a member, you are declaring that the FXML loader can access the member even if it is private. A public member used by the FXML loader does not need to be annotated with @FXML. However, annotating a public member with @FXML is not an error. It is better to annotate all members, public and private, used by the FXML loader with @FXML annotation. This tells the reader of your code how the members are being used.

The following FXML sets the sayHello() method of the controller class as the event handler for the Button:

```
<VBox fx:controller="com.jdojo.fxml.SayHelloController"
    xmlns:fx="http://javafx.com/fxml">
        <Button fx:id="sayHelloBtn" text="Say Hello" onAction="#sayHello"/>
...
</VBox>
```

There two special instance variables that can be declared in the controller, and they are automatically injected by the FXML loader:

- @FXML private URL location;

- @FXML private ResourceBundle resources;

The location is the location of the FXML document. The resources is the reference of the ResourceBundle used, if any, in the FXML.

When the event handler attribute value starts with a hash symbol (#), it indicates to the FXML loader that sayHello is the method in the controller. The event handler method in the controller should conform to some rules:

- The method may take no arguments or a single argument. If it takes an argument, the argument type must be a type assignment compatible with the event it is supposed to handle.

- It is not an error to have both versions of the method: one that takes no arguments and with a single argument. In such a case, the method with a single argument is used.

- Conventionally, the method return type should be void, because there is no taker of the returned value.

- The method must be accessible to the FXML loader: make it public or annotate it with @FXML.

When the FXML loader is done loading the FXML document, it calls the `initialize()` method of the controller. The method should not take any argument. It should be accessible to the FXML loader. In the controller, you used the @FXML annotation to make it accessible to the FXML loader.

The FXMLLoader class lets you set a controller for the root element in the code using the `setController()` method. Use the `getController()` method to get the reference of the controller from the loader. Developers make a common mistake in getting the reference of the controller. The mistake is made because of the way the `load()` method is designed. There are seven overloaded versions of the `load()` method: two of them are instance methods and five are static methods. To use the `getController()` method, you must create an object of the FXMLLoader class and make sure that you use one of the instance methods of the class to load the document. The following is an example of the common mistake:

```
URL fxmlUrl = new URL("file:///C:/resources/fxml/test.fxml");

// Create an FXMLLoader object - a good start
FXMLLoader loader = new FXMLLoader();

// Load the document -- mistake
VBox root = loader.<VBox>load(fxmlUrl);

// loader.getController() will return null
Test controller = loader.getController();
// controller is null here
```

The preceding code creates an object of the FXMLLoader class. However, the `load(URL url)` method that is called in the loader variable is the static `load()` method, not the instance `load()` method. Therefore, the loader instance never got a controller, and when you ask it for a controller, it returns `null`. To clear the confusion, the following are the instance and static versions of the `load()` method of which only the first two versions are instance methods:

- `<T> T load()`
- `<T> T load(InputStream inputStream)`
- `static <T> T load(URL location)`
- `static <T> T load(URL location, ResourceBundle resources)`
- `static <T> T load(URL location, ResourceBundle resources, BuilderFactory builderFactory)`
- `static <T> T load(URL location, ResourceBundle resources, BuilderFactory builderFactory, Callback<Class<?>,Object> controllerFactory)`
- `static <T> T load(URL location, ResourceBundle resources, BuilderFactory builderFactory, Callback<Class<?>,Object> controllerFactory, Charset charset)`

The following snippet of code is the correct way of using the `load()` method, so you can get the reference of the controller in JavaFX code:

```
URL fxmlUrl = new URL("file:///C:/resources/fxml/test.fxml");

// Create an FXMLLoader object - a good start
FXMLLoader loader = new FXMLLoader();
loader.setLocation(fxmlUrl);
```

```
// Calling the no-args instance load() method - Correct
VBox root = loader.<VBox>load();

// loader.getController() will return the controller
Test controller = loader.getController();
```

You now have the controller for this example application. Let's modify the FXML to match the controller. Listing 26-6 shows the modified FXML. It is saved in the sayhellowithcontroller.fxml file under the *resources/fxml* directory.

Listing 26-6. The Contents of the sayhellowithcontroller.fxml File

```
<?xml version="1.0" encoding="UTF-8"?>
<?language javascript?>

<?import javafx.scene.Scene?>
<?import javafx.scene.layout.VBox?>
<?import javafx.scene.control.Label?>
<?import javafx.scene.control.Button?>

<VBox fx:controller="com.jdojo.fxml.SayHelloController" spacing="10" xmlns:fx="http://
javafx.com/fxml">
        <Label fx:id="msgLbl" text="FXML is cool!" prefWidth="150"/>
        <Button fx:id="sayHelloBtn" text="Say Hello" onAction="#sayHello"/>
        <style>
                -fx-padding: 10;
                -fx-border-style: solid inside;
                -fx-border-width: 2;
                -fx-border-insets: 5;
                -fx-border-radius: 5;
                -fx-border-color: blue;
        </style>
</VBox>
```

The program in Listing 26-7 is the JavaFX application for this example. The code is very similar to the one shown in Listing 26-4. The main difference is the FXML document that uses a controller. When the document is loaded, the initialize() method of the controller is called by the loader. The method prints a message, including the location of the resource bundle reference used. When you click the button, the sayHello() method of the controller is called that sets the text in the Label. Note that the Label reference is automatically injected into the controller by the FXML loader.

Listing 26-7. A JavaFX Application Class Using FXML and a Controller

```
// SayHelloFXMLMain.java
package com.jdojo.fxml;

import java.io.IOException;
import java.net.URL;
import com.jdojo.util.ResourceUtil;
import javafx.application.Application;
import javafx.fxml.FXMLLoader;
import javafx.scene.Scene;
```

```java
import javafx.scene.layout.VBox;
import javafx.stage.Stage;

public class SayHelloFXMLMain extends Application {
        public static void main(String[] args) {
                Application.launch(args);
        }

        @Override
        public void start(Stage stage) throws IOException {
                // Construct a URL for the FXML document
                    URL fxmlUrl = ResourceUtil.getResourceURL(
                        "fxml/sayhellowithcontroller.fxml");
                VBox root = FXMLLoader.<VBox>load(fxmlUrl);
                Scene scene = new Scene(root);
                stage.setScene(scene);
                stage.setTitle("Hello FXML");
                stage.show();
        }
}
```

Creating Objects in FXML

The main purpose of using FXML is creating an object graph. Objects of all classes are not created the same way. For example, some classes provide constructors to create their objects, some static valueOf() method, and some factory methods. FXML should be able to create objects of all classes, or at least it should give you some control over deciding how to create those objects. In the following sections, I will discuss different ways of creating objects in FXML.

Using the no-args Constructor

Using the no-args constructor to create objects in FXML is easy. If an element name is a class name, which has a no-args constructor, the element will create an object of that class. The following element creates a VBox object as the VBox class has a no-args constructor:

```
<VBox>
        ...
</VBox>
```

Using the static valueOf() Method

Sometimes, immutable classes provide a valueOf() method to construct an object. If the valueOf() method is declared static, it can accept a single String argument and returns an object. You can use the fx:value attribute to create an object using the method. Suppose you have an Xxx class, which contains a static valueOf(String s) method. The following is the Java code:

```
Xxx x = Xxx.valueOf("a value");
```

You can do the same in FXML as

```
<Xxx fx:value="a value"/>
```

Note that you have stated that the valueOf() method should be able to accept a String argument, which qualifies both of the following methods in this category:

- public static Xxx valueOf(String arg)
- public static Xxx valueOf(Object arg)

The following elements create Long and String objects with 100 and "Hello" as their values:

```
<Long fx:value="100"/>
<String fx:value="Hello"/>
```

Note that the String class contains a no-args constructor that creates an empty string. If you need a String object with an empty string as the content, you can still use the no-args constructor:

```
<!-- Will create a String object with "" as the content -->
<String/>
```

Do not forget to import classes, Long and String, when you use the preceding elements as FXML does not automatically import classes from the java.lang package.

It is worth noting that the object type the fx:value attribute creates is the type of the returned object from the valueOf() object, not of the class type of the element. Consider the following method declaration for a class Yyy:

```
public static Zzz valueOf(String arg);
```

What type of object will the following element create?

```
<Yyy fx:value="hello"/>
```

If your answer is Yyy, it is wrong. It is commonly thought that the element name is Yyy, so it creates a Yyy type object. The preceding element is the same as invoking Yyy.valueOf("Hello"), which returns an object of the Zzz type. Therefore, the preceding element creates an object of the Zzz type, not the Yyy type. Although it is possible to have this use case, this is a confusing way to design your class. Typically, a valueOf() method in the class Xxx returns an object of the Xxx type.

Using a Factory Method

Sometimes, a class provides factory methods to create its object. If a class contains a static, no-args method that returns an object, you can use the method with the fx:factory attribute. The following element creates a LocalDate in FXML using the now() factory method of the LocalDate class:

```
<?import java.time.LocalDate?>
<LocalDate fx:factory="now"/>
```

Sometimes, you need to create JavaFX collections in FXML. The FXCollections class contains several factory methods to create collections. The following snippet of FXML creates an ObservableList<String> that adds four fruit names to the list:

```
<?import java.lang.String?>
<?import javafx.collections.FXCollections?>
<FXCollections fx:factory="observableArrayList">
        <String fx:value="Apple"/>
        <String fx:value="Banana"/>
        <String fx:value="Grape"/>
        <String fx:value="Orange"/>
</FXCollections>
```

The FXML in Listing 26-8 is an example of using the fx:factory attribute to create an ObservableList. The list is used to set the items property of a ComboBox. The value "Orange" from the list is set as the default value. The VBox will show a Label and a ComboBox with the list of four fruit names.

Listing 26-8. Creating a ComboBox, Populating It, and Selecting an Item

```
<?import javafx.scene.layout.VBox?>
<?import javafx.scene.control.Label?>
<?import javafx.scene.control.Button?>
<?import javafx.scene.control.ComboBox?>
<?import java.lang.String?>
<?import javafx.collections.FXCollections?>

<VBox xmlns:fx="http://javafx.com/fxml">
        <Label text="List of Fruits"/>
        <ComboBox>
            <items>
                <FXCollections fx:factory="observableArrayList">
                        <String fx:value="Apple"/>
                        <String fx:value="Banana"/>
                        <String fx:value="Grape"/>
                        <String fx:value="Orange"/>
                </FXCollections>
            </items>
            <value>
                <String fx:value="Orange"/>
            </value>
        </ComboBox>
</VBox>
```

Using Builders

If the FXMLLoader cannot create an object of a class, it looks for a builder that can create the object. A builder is an implementation of the Builder interface. The interface is in the javafx.util package, and it contains one method build():

```
public interface Builder<T> {
    public T build();
}
```

A Builder knows how to build an object of a specific type. A Builder is used with a BuilderFactory, which is another interface in the same package:

```
public interface BuilderFactory {
    public Builder<?> getBuilder(Class<?> type);
}
```

The FXMLLoader allows you to use a BuilderFactory. When it cannot create the object of a class using all other methods, it calls the getBuilder() method of the BuilderFactory by passing the type of the object as the method argument. If the BuilderFactory returns a non-null Builder, the loader sets all the properties of the object being created in the Builder. Finally, it calls the build() method of the Builder to get the object. The FXMLLoader class uses an instance of the JavaFXBuilderFactory as a default BuilderFactory.

FXMLLoader supports two types of Builders:

- If the Builder implements the Map interface, the put() method is used to pass the object properties to the Builder. The put() method is passed the name and value of the property.

- If the Builder does not implement the Map interface, the Builder should contain the getter and setter methods, based on the JavaBeans convention, for all properties specified in the FXML.

Consider the declaration of the Item class in Listing 26-9. By default, FXML will not be able to create an Item object as it does not have a no-args constructor. The class has two properties, id and name.

Listing 26-9. An Item Class That Does Not Have a no-args Constructor

```java
// Item.java
package com.jdojo.fxml;

public class Item {
        private Long id;
        private String name;

        public Item(Long id, String name) {
                this.id = id;
                this.name = name;
        }

        public Long getId() {
                return id;
        }

        public void setId(Long id) {
                this.id = id;
        }

        public String getName() {
                return name;
        }
```

```java
        public void setName(String name) {
                this.name = name;
        }

        @Override
        public String toString() {
                return "id=" + id + ", name=" + name;
        }
}
```

Listing 26-10 contains the content of an FXML file items.fxml. It creates an ArrayList with three objects of the Item class. If you load this file using FXMLLoader, you would receive an error that the loader cannot instantiate the Item class.

Listing 26-10. FXML to Create a List of Item Objects

```xml
<!-- items.fxml -->
<?import com.jdojo.fxml.Item?>
<?import java.util.ArrayList?>
<ArrayList>
        <Item name="Kishori" id="100"/>
        <Item name="Ellen" id="200"/>
        <Item name="Kannan" id="300"/>
</ArrayList>
```

Let's create a Builder to build an object of the Item class. The ItemBuilder class in Listing 26-11 is the Builder for the Item class. It declares id and name instance variables. As the FXMLLoader comes across these properties, the loader will call the corresponding setters. The setters store the values in the instance variable. When the loader needs the object, it calls the build() method, which builds and returns an Item object.

Listing 26-11. A Builder for the Item Class That Uses Property Setters to Build an Object

```java
// ItemBuilder.java
package com.jdojo.fxml;

import javafx.util.Builder;

public class ItemBuilder implements Builder<Item> {
        private Long id;
        private String name;

        public Long getId() {
                return id;
        }

        public String getName() {
                return name;
        }

        public void setId(Long id) {
                this.id = id;
        }
```

```java
        public void setName(String name) {
                this.name = name;
        }

        @Override
        public Item build() {
                return new Item(id, name);
        }
}
```

Now, you need to create a BuilderFactory for the Item type. The ItemBuilderFactory class shown in Listing 26-12 implements the BuilderFactory interface. When the getBuilder() is passed the Item type, it returns an ItemBuilder object. Otherwise, it returns the default JavaFX builder.

Listing 26-12. A BuilderFactory to Get a Builder for the Item Type

```java
// ItemBuilderFactory.java
package com.jdojo.fxml;

import javafx.util.Builder;
import javafx.util.BuilderFactory;
import javafx.fxml.JavaFXBuilderFactory;

public class ItemBuilderFactory implements BuilderFactory {
        private final JavaFXBuilderFactory fxFactory =
                new JavaFXBuilderFactory();

        @Override
        public Builder<?> getBuilder(Class<?> type) {
                // You supply a Builder only for Item type
                if (type == Item.class) {
                        return new ItemBuilder();
                }

                // Let the default Builder do the magic
                return fxFactory.getBuilder(type);
        }
}
```

Listings 26-13 and 26-14 have code for the Builder and BuilderFactory implementation for the Item type. This time, the Builder implements the Map interface by extending the AbstractMap class. It overrides the put() method to read the passed in properties and their values. The entrySet() method needs to be overridden as it is defined as abstract in the AbstractMap class. You do not have any useful implementation for it. You just throw a runtime exception. The build() method creates and returns an object of the Item type. The BuilderFactory implementation is similar to the one in Listing 26-12, except that it returns an ItemBuilderMap as the Builder for the Item type.

Listing 26-13. A Builder for the Item Class That Implements the Map Interface

```java
// ItemBuilderMap.java
package com.jdojo.fxml;

import java.util.AbstractMap;
import java.util.Map;
import java.util.Set;
import javafx.util.Builder;

public class ItemBuilderMap extends AbstractMap<String, Object> implements Builder<Item> {
        private String name;
        private Long id;

        @Override
        public Object put(String key, Object value) {
                if ("name".equals(key)) {
                    this.name = (String)value;
                } else if ("id".equals(key)) {
                    this.id = Long.valueOf((String)value);
                } else {
                    throw new IllegalArgumentException(
                            "Unknown Item property: " + key);
                }

                return null;
        }

        @Override
        public Set<Map.Entry<String, Object>> entrySet() {
                throw new UnsupportedOperationException();
        }

        @Override
        public Item build() {
                return new Item(id, name);
        }
}
```

Listing 26-14. Another BuilderFactory to Get a Builder for the Item Type

```java
// ItemBuilderFactoryMap.java
package com.jdojo.fxml;

import javafx.fxml.JavaFXBuilderFactory;
import javafx.util.Builder;
import javafx.util.BuilderFactory;

public class ItemBuilderFactoryMap implements BuilderFactory {
        private final JavaFXBuilderFactory fxFactory =
                new JavaFXBuilderFactory();
```

```
        @Override
        public Builder<?> getBuilder(Class<?> type) {
                if (type == Item.class) {
                        return new ItemBuilderMap();
                }
                return fxFactory.getBuilder(type);
        }
}
```

Let's test both Builders for the Item class. The program in Listing 26-15 uses both Builders for the Item class. It loads the list of Items from the items.fxml file, assuming that the file is located in the resources/fxml directory.

Listing 26-15. Using Builders to Instantiate Item Objects in FXML

```java
// BuilderTest.java
package com.jdojo.fxml;

import java.io.IOException;
import java.net.URL;
import com.jdojo.util.ResourceUtil;
import java.util.ArrayList;
import javafx.fxml.FXMLLoader;
import javafx.util.BuilderFactory;

public class BuilderTest {
        public static void main(String[] args) throws IOException {
            // Use the Builder with property getter and setter
            loadItems(new ItemBuilderFactory());

            // Use the Builder with Map
            loadItems(new ItemBuilderFactoryMap());
        }

        public static void
          loadItems(BuilderFactory builderFactory) throws IOException {
                URL fxmlUrl = ResourceUtil.getResourceURL("fxml/items.fxml");

            FXMLLoader loader = new FXMLLoader();
            loader.setLocation(fxmlUrl);
            loader.setBuilderFactory(builderFactory);
            ArrayList items = loader.<ArrayList>load();
            System.out.println("List:" + items);
        }
}
```

```
List:[id=100, name=Kishori, id=200, name=Ellen, id=300, name=Kannan]
List:[id=100, name=Kishori, id=200, name=Ellen, id=300, name=Kannan]
```

■ **Tip** The BuilderFactory you supply to the FXMLLoader replaces the default BuilderFactory. You need to make sure that your BuilderFactory returns a specific Builder for your custom type and returns the default Builder for the rest. Currently, FXMLLoader does not allow using more than one BuilderFactory.

Creating Reusable Objects in FXML

Sometimes, you need to create objects that are not directly part of the object graph. However, they may be used somewhere else in the FXML document. For example, you may want to create an Insets or a Color once and reuse them in several places. Using a ToggleGroup is a typical use case. A ToggleGroup is created once and used with several RadioButton objects.

You can create an object in FXML without making it part of the object group using the <fx:define> block. You can refer to the objects created in the <fx:define> block by their fx:id in the attribute value of other elements. The attribute value must be prefixed with a dollar symbol ($):

```
<?import javafx.scene.layout.VBox?>
<?import javafx.scene.control.Label?>
<?import javafx.scene.control.Button?>
<?import javafx.geometry.Insets?>
<?import javafx.scene.control.ToggleGroup?>
<?import javafx.scene.control.RadioButton?>

<VBox fx:controller="com.jdojo.fxml.Test" xmlns:fx="http://javafx.com/fxml">
    <fx:define>
        <Insets fx:id="margin" top="5.0" right="5.0"
                bottom="5.0" left="5.0"/>
        <ToggleGroup fx:id="genderGroup"/>
    </fx:define>
    <Label text="Gender" VBox.margin="$margin"/>
    <RadioButton text="Male" toggleGroup="$genderGroup"/>
    <RadioButton text="Female" toggleGroup="$genderGroup"/>
    <RadioButton text="Unknown" toggleGroup="$genderGroup" selected="true"/>
    <Button text="Close" VBox.margin="$margin"/>
</VBox>
```

The preceding FXML creates two objects, an Insets and a ToggleGroup, in an <fx:define> block. They are given an fx:id of "margin" and "genderGroup". They are referred to in controls, which are part of the object graph, by "$margin" and "$genderGroup".

■ **Tip** If the value of an attribute starts with a $ symbol, it is considered a reference to an object. If you want to use a leading $ symbol as part of the value, escape it with a backslash ("\$hello").

Specifying Locations in Attributes

An attribute value starting with an @ symbol refers to a location. If the @ symbol is followed by a forward slash (@/), the location is considered relative to the CLASSPATH. If the @ symbol is not followed by a forward slash, the location is considered relative to the location of the FXML file being processed.

In the following FXML, the image URL will be resolved relative to the location of the FXML file that contains the element:

```
<ImageView>
        <Image url="@resources/picture/ksharan.jpg"/>
</ImageView>
```

In the following FXML, the image URL will be resolved relative to the CLASSPATH:

```
<ImageView>
        <Image url="@/resources/picture/ksharan.jpg"/>
</ImageView>
```

If you want to use a leading @ symbol as part of the attribute value, escape it with a backward slash ("\@not-a-location").

Using Resource Bundles

Using a ResourceBundle in FXML is much easier than using it in Java code. Specifying the keys from a ResourceBundle in attribute values uses the corresponding values for the default Locale. If an attribute value starts with a % symbol, it is considered as the key name from the resource bundle. At runtime, the attribute value will come from the specified ResourceBundle in the FXMLLoader. If you want to use a leading % symbol in an attribute value, escape it with a backward slash (e.g., "\%hello").

Consider the FXML content in Listing 26-16. It uses "%greetingText" as the value for the text property of the Label. The attribute value starts with a % symbol. The FXMLLoader will look up the value of the "greetingText" in the ResourceBundle and use it for the text property. It is all done for you without writing even a single line of code!

Listing 26-16. The Contents of the greetings.fxml File

```
<?import javafx.scene.control.Label?>
<Label text="%greetingText"/>
```

Listings 26-17 and 26-18 have contents for ResourceBundle files: one for default Locale named greetings.properties and one for Indian Locale named greetings_hi.properties. The suffix _hi in the file name means the Indian language Hindi.

Listing 26-17. The Contents of the greetings.properties File

```
# The default greeting
greetingText = Hello
```

Listing 26-18. The Contents of the greetings_hi.properties File

```
# The Indian greeting
greetingText = Namaste
```

The program in Listing 26-19 uses a ResourceBundle with the FXMLLoader. The ResourceBundle is loaded from the resources/resourcebundles directory in CLASSPATH. The FXML file is loaded from the resources/fxml/greetings.fxml in the folder referred to in class ResourceUtil. The program loads the Label from the FXML file twice: once for the default Locale US and once by changing the default Locale to India Hindi. Both Labels are displayed in the VBox as shown in Figure 26-2.

Listing 26-19. Using a Resource Bundle with the FXMLLoader

```
// ResourceBundleTest.java
package com.jdojo.fxml;

import java.io.IOException;
import java.net.URL;
import com.jdojo.util.ResourceUtil;
import java.util.Locale;
import java.util.ResourceBundle;
import javafx.application.Application;
import javafx.fxml.FXMLLoader;
import javafx.scene.Scene;
import javafx.scene.control.Label;
import javafx.scene.layout.VBox;
import javafx.stage.Stage;

public class ResourceBundleTest extends Application {
        public static void main(String[] args) {
                Application.launch(args);
        }

        @Override
        public void start(Stage stage) throws IOException {
                URL fxmlUrl =
                    ResourceUtil.getResourceURL("fxml/greetings.fxml");

            // Create a ResourceBundle to use in FXMLLoader
            String resourcePath = "resources/resourcebundles/greetings";
            ResourceBundle resourceBundle =
                    ResourceBundle.getBundle(resourcePath);

            // Load the Label for default Locale
            Label defaultGreetingLbl =
                    FXMLLoader.<Label>load(fxmlUrl, resourceBundle);

            // Change the default Locale and load the Label again
            Locale.setDefault(new Locale("hi", "in"));
```

```
        // We need to recreate the ResourceBundler to pick up the
           // new default Locale
        resourceBundle = ResourceBundle.getBundle(resourcePath);

        Label indianGreetingLbl =
                FXMLLoader.<Label>load(fxmlUrl, resourceBundle);

        // Add both Labels to a Vbox
        VBox root =
                new VBox(5, defaultGreetingLbl, indianGreetingLbl);
        Scene scene = new Scene(root);
        stage.setScene(scene);
        stage.setTitle("Using a ResourceBundle in FXML");
        stage.show();
    }
}
```

Figure 26-2. *Labels using a resource bundle to populate their text properties*

Including FXML Files

An FXML document can include another FXML document using the <fx:include> element. The object graph generated by the nested document is included at the position where the nested document occurs in the containing document. The <fx:include> element takes a source attribute whose value is the path of the nested document:

```
<fx:include source="nested_document_path"/>
```

If the nested document path starts with a leading forward slash, the path is resolved relative to the CLASSPATH. Otherwise, it is resolved relative to the containing document path.

The <fx:include> element can have the fx:id attribute and all attributes that are available for the included object. The attributes specified in the containing document override the corresponding attributes in the included document. For example, if you include an FXML document, which creates a Button, you can specify the text property in the included document as well as the containing document. When the containing document is loaded, the text property from the containing document will be used.

An FXML document may optionally specify a controller using the fx:controller attribute for the root element. The rule is that you can have a maximum of one controller per FXML document. When you nest documents, each document can have its own controller. FXMLLoader lets you inject the nested controller reference into the controller of the main document. You need to follow a naming convention to inject the nested controller. The controller for the main document should have an accessible instance variable with the name as

```
Instance variable name = "fx:id of the fx:include element" + "Controller"
```

If the fx:id for the <fx:include> element is "xxx," the instance variable name should be xxxController.

Consider the two FXML documents shown in Listings 26-20 and 26-21. The closebutton.fxml file creates a Button, sets its text property to Close, and attaches an action event handler. The event handler uses the JavaScript language. It closes the containing window.

The maindoc.fxml includes the closebutton.fxml, assuming that both files are in the same directory. It specifies text and fx:id attributes for the <fx:include> element. Note that the included FXML specifies "Close" as the test property, and the maindoc.fxml overrides it and sets it to "Close."

Listing 26-20. An FXML Document That Creates a Close Button to Close the Containing Window

```
<!-- closebutton.fxml -->
<?language javascript?>
<?import javafx.scene.control.Button?>
<Button fx:controller="com.jdojo.fxml.CloseBtnController"
        text="Close"
        fx:id="closeBtn"
        onAction="#closeWindow"
        xmlns:fx="http://javafx.com/fxml">
</Button>
```

Listing 26-21. An FXML Document Using an <fx:include> Element

```
<!-- maindoc.fxml -->
<?import javafx.scene.layout.VBox?>
<?import javafx.scene.control.Label?>

<VBox fx:controller="com.jdojo.fxml.MainDocController" xmlns:fx="http://javafx.com/fxml">
        <Label text="Testing fx:include"/>

        <!-- Override the text property of the included Button -->
        <fx:include source="closebutton.fxml" fx:id="includedCloseBtn"
                text="Hide"/>
</VBox>
```

Both FXML documents specify a controller listed in Listings 26-22 and 26-23. Note that the controller for the main document declares two instance variables: one will refer to the included Button, and the other will refer to the controller of the included document. Note that the reference of the Button will also be included in the controller of the nested document.

Listing 26-22. The ControllerClass for the FXML Defining the Close Button

```
// CloseBtnController.java
package com.jdojo.fxml;

import javafx.fxml.FXML;
import javafx.scene.control.Button;

public class CloseBtnController {
        @FXML
        private Button closeBtn;
```

```
        @FXML
        public void initialize() {
                System.out.println("CloseBtnController.initialize()");
        }
}
```

Listing 26-23. The Controller Class for the Main Document

```
// MainDocController.java
package com.jdojo.fxml;

import javafx.fxml.FXML;
import javafx.scene.control.Button;

public class MainDocController {
        @FXML
        private Button includedCloseBtn;

        @FXML
        private CloseBtnController includedCloseBtnController;

        @FXML
        public void initialize() {
                System.out.println("MainDocController.initialize()");
                // You can use the nested controller here
        }
}
```

The program in Listing 26-24 loads the maindoc.fxml and adds the loaded VBox to the scene. It displays a window with the *Hide* button from the closebutton.fxml file. Clicking the Hide button will close the window.

Listing 26-24. Loading and Using a Nested FXML Document

```
// FxIncludeTest.java
package com.jdojo.fxml;

import java.io.IOException;
import java.net.MalformedURLException;
import java.net.URL;
 import com.jdojo.util.ResourceUtil;
import javafx.application.Application;
import javafx.fxml.FXMLLoader;
import javafx.scene.Scene;
import javafx.scene.layout.VBox;
import javafx.stage.Stage;
```

```
public class FxIncludeTest  extends Application {
        public static void main(String[] args) {
                Application.launch(args);
        }

        @Override
        public void
           start(Stage stage) throws MalformedURLException, IOException {
                   URL fxmlUrl = ResourceUtil.getResourceURL(
                       "fxml/maindoc.fxml");

                FXMLLoader loader = new FXMLLoader();
                loader.setLocation(fxmlUrl);
                VBox root = loader.<VBox>load();
                Scene scene = new Scene(root);
                stage.setScene(scene);
                stage.setTitle("Nesting Documents in FXML");
                stage.show();
        }
}
```

Using Constants

Classes, interfaces, and enums may define constants, which are static, final variables. You can refer to those constants using the fx:constant attribute. The attribute value is the name of the constant. The name of the element is the name of the type that contains the constant. For example, for Long.MAX_VALUE, you can use the following element:

```
<Long fx:constant="MAX_VALUE"/>
```

Note that all enum constants belong to this category, and they can be accessed using the fx:constant attribute. The following element accesses the Pos.CENTER enum constant:

```
<Pos fx:constant="CENTER"/>
```

The following FXML content accesses constants from the Integer and Long classes and the Pos enum. It sets the alignment property of a VBox to Pos.CENTER:

```
<?import javafx.scene.layout.VBox?>
<?import javafx.scene.control.TextField?>
<?import java.lang.Integer?>
<?import java.lang.Long?>
<?import javafx.scene.text.FontWeight?>
<?import javafx.geometry.Pos?>

<VBox xmlns:fx="http://javafx.com/fxml">
        <fx:define>
                <Integer fx:constant="MAX_VALUE" fx:id="minInt"/>
        </fx:define>
```

```
            <alignment><Pos fx:constant="CENTER"/></alignment>
            <TextField text="$minInt"/>
            <TextField>
                    <text><Long fx:constant="MIN_VALUE"/></text>
            </TextField>
</VBox>
```

Referencing Another Element

You can reference another element in the document using the `<fx:reference>` element. The `fx:id` attribute specifies the `fx:id` of the referred element:

```
<fx:reference source="fx:id of the source element"/>
```

The following FXML content uses an `<fx:reference>` element to refer to an Image:

```
<?import javafx.scene.layout.VBox?>
<?import javafx.scene.image.Image?>
<?import javafx.scene.image.ImageView?>
<VBox xmlns:fx="http://javafx.com/fxml">
        <fx:define>
            <Image url="resources/picture/ksharan.jpg" fx:id="myImg"/>
        </fx:define>
        <ImageView>
            <image>
                <fx:reference source="myImg"/>
            </image>
        </ImageView>
</VBox>
```

Note that you can also rewrite the preceding FXML content using the variable dereferencing method as follows:

```
<VBox xmlns:fx="http://javafx.com/fxml">
        <fx:define>
            <Image url="resources/picture/ksharan.jpg" fx:id="myImg"/>
        </fx:define>
        <ImageView image="$myImg"/>
</VBox>
```

Copying Elements

Sometimes, you want to copy an element. Copying in this context is creating a new object by copying the attributes of the source object. You can do so using the <fx:copy> element:

```
<fx:copy source="fx:id of the source object" />
```

To copy an object, the class must provide a copy constructor. A copy constructor takes an object of the same class. Suppose you have an Item class that contains a copy constructor:

```java
public class Item {
        private Long id;
        private String name;

        public Item() {
        }

        // The copy constructor
        public Item(Item source) {
                this.id = source.id + 100;
                this.name = source.name + " (Copied)";
        }
        ...
}
```

The following FXML document creates an Item object inside the <fx:define> block. It copies the Item object several times and adds them to the items list for a ComboBox. Note that the source Item itself is added to the items list using a <fx:reference> element:

```xml
<?import javafx.scene.layout.VBox?>
<?import javafx.scene.control.ComboBox?>
<?import javafx.collections.FXCollections?>
<?import com.jdojo.fxml.Item?>

<VBox xmlns:fx="http://javafx.com/fxml">
        <fx:define>
                <Item name="Kishori" id="100" fx:id="myItem"/>
        </fx:define>
        <ComboBox value="$myItem">
            <items>
                <FXCollections fx:factory="observableArrayList">
                    <fx:reference source="myItem"/>
                    <fx:copy source="myItem" />
                    <fx:copy source="myItem" />
                    <fx:copy source="myItem" />
                    <fx:copy source="myItem" />
                </FXCollections>
            </items>
        </ComboBox>

</VBox>
```

Binding Properties in FXML

FXML supports simple property bindings. You need to use an attribute for the property to bind it to the property of another element or a document variable. The attribute value starts with a $ symbol, which is followed with a pair of curly braces. The following FXML content creates a VBox with two TextFields. The text property of the mirrorText field is bound to the text property of the mainText field:

```
<?import javafx.scene.layout.VBox?>
<?import javafx.scene.control.TextField?>

<VBox xmlns:fx="http://javafx.com/fxml">
        <TextField fx:id="mainText" text="Hello"/>
        <TextField fx:id="mirrorText" text="${mainText.text}" disable="true"/>
</VBox>
```

Creating Custom Controls

You can create custom controls using FXML. Let's create a login form with two Labels, a TextField, a PasswordField, and two Buttons. Listing 26-25 contains the FXML content for the form. Note that the root element is an <fx:root>. The <fx:root> element creates a reference to the previously created element. The value for the <fx:root> element is set in the FXMLLoader using the setRoot() method. The type attribute specifies the type of the root that will be injected.

Listing 26-25. The FXML Contents for a Custom Login Form

```
<!-- login.fxml -->
<?import javafx.scene.layout.GridPane?>
<?import javafx.scene.control.Label?>
<?import javafx.scene.control.Button?>
<?import javafx.scene.control.TextField?>
<?import javafx.scene.control.PasswordField?>

<fx:root type="javafx.scene.layout.GridPane"
            xmlns:fx="http://javafx.com/fxml">
        <Label text="User Id:" GridPane.rowIndex="0"
            GridPane.columnIndex="0"/>
        <TextField fx:id="userId" GridPane.rowIndex="0"
            GridPane.columnIndex="1"/>
        <Label text="Password:" GridPane.rowIndex="1"
            GridPane.columnIndex="0"/>
        <PasswordField fx:id="pwd" GridPane.rowIndex="1"
            GridPane.columnIndex="1"/>
        <Button fx:id="okBtn" text="OK" onAction="#okClicked"
            GridPane.rowIndex="0" GridPane.columnIndex="2"/>
        <Button fx:id="cancelBtn" text="Cancel" onAction="#cancelClicked"
            GridPane.rowIndex="1" GridPane.columnIndex="2"/>
</fx:root>
```

The class in Listing 26-26 represents the JavaFX part of the custom control. You will create an object of the LoginControl class and use it as any other standard control. This class is also used as a controller for the login.fxml. In the constructor, the class loads the FXML content. Before loading the content, it sets itself as the root and the controller in the FXMLLoader. Instance variables allow for the userId and pwd control injection in the class. When the Buttons are clicked, you simply print a message on the console. This control needs more work, if you want to use it in a real-world application. You will need to provide a way for the users to hook event notification when the *OK* and *Cancel* buttons are clicked.

Listing 26-26. A Class Implementing the Custom Control

```java
// LoginControl.java
package com.jdojo.fxml;

import java.io.IOException;
import java.net.URL;
import com.jdojo.util.ResourceUtil;
import javafx.fxml.FXML;
import javafx.fxml.FXMLLoader;
import javafx.scene.control.PasswordField;
import javafx.scene.control.TextField;
import javafx.scene.layout.GridPane;

public class LoginControl extends GridPane {
        @FXML
        private TextField userId;

        @FXML
        private PasswordField pwd;

        public LoginControl() {
                // Load the FXML
                    URL fxmlUrl =
                        ResourceUtil.getResourceURL("fxml/login.fxml");
                FXMLLoader loader = new FXMLLoader();
                loader.setLocation(fxmlUrl);
                loader.setRoot(this);
                loader.setController(this);
                try {
                        loader.load();
                }
                catch (IOException exception) {
                    throw new RuntimeException(exception);
                }
        }

        @FXML
        private void initialize() {
                // Do some work
        }
```

```
@FXML
private void okClicked() {
        System.out.println("Ok clicked");
}

@FXML
private void cancelClicked() {
    System.out.println("Cancel clicked");
}

public String getUserId() {
        return userId.getText();
}

public String getPassword() {
        return pwd.getText();
}
}
```

The program in Listing 26-27 shows how to use the custom control. Using the custom control is as easy as creating a Java object. The custom control extends the GridPane; therefore, it can be used as a GridPane. Using the control in FXML is no different than using other controls. The control provides a no-args constructor, which will allow creating it in FXML by using an element with the class name <LoginControl>.

Listing 26-27. Using the Custom Control

```
// LoginTest.java
package com.jdojo.fxml;

import javafx.application.Application;
import javafx.scene.Scene;
import javafx.scene.layout.GridPane;
import javafx.stage.Stage;

public class LoginTest extends Application {
        public static void main(String[] args) {
                Application.launch(args);
        }

        @Override
        public void start(Stage stage) {
                // Create the Login custom control
                GridPane root = new LoginControl();
                Scene scene = new Scene(root);
                stage.setScene(scene);
                stage.setTitle("Using FXMl Custom Control");
                stage.show();
        }
}
```

Summary

FXML is an XML-based language to build a user interface for a JavaFX application. You can use FXML to build an entire scene or part of a scene. FXML allows application developers to separate the logic for building the UI from the business logic. If the UI part of the application changes, you do not need to recompile the JavaFX code: change the FXML using a text editor and rerun the application. You still use JavaFX to write business logic using the Java language. An FXML document is an XML document.

It is common to use FXML to build a scene graph in a JavaFX application. However, the use of FXML is not limited to building only scene graphs. It can build a hierarchical object graph of Java objects. In fact, it can be used to create just one object, such as an object of a Person class.

An FXML document is simply a text file. Typically, the file name has a .fxml extension (e.g., hello. fxml). You can use any text editor to edit an FXML document. The Gluon company provides an open source visual editor called *Scene Builder* for editing FXML documents. Scene Builder can also be integrated into some IDEs.

FXML lets you create an object using the no-args constructor, the valueOf() method, a factory method, and a builder.

Sometimes, you need to create objects that are not directly part of the object graph. However, they may be used somewhere else in the FXML document. You can create an object in FXML without making it part of the object group using the <fx:define> block. You can refer to the objects created in the <fx:define> block by their fx:id in the attribute value of other elements. The attribute value must be prefixed with a dollar symbol ($).

FXML lets you refer to resources by specifying their locations. An attribute value starting with an @ symbol refers to a location. If the @ symbol is followed with a forward slash (@/), the location is considered relative to the CLASSPATH. If the @ symbol is not followed by a forward slash, the location is considered relative to the location of the FXML file being processed.

Using a ResourceBundle in FXML is much easier than using it in Java code. Specifying the keys from a ResourceBundle in attribute values uses the corresponding values for the default Locale. If an attribute value starts with a % symbol, it is considered as the key name from the resource bundle. At runtime, the attribute value will come from the specified ResourceBundle in the FXMLLoader. If you want to use a leading % symbol in an attribute value, escape it with a backward slash (e.g., "\%hello").

An FXML document can include another FXML document using the <fx:include> element. The object graph generated by the nested document is included at the position where the nested document occurs in the containing document.

Classes, interfaces, and enums may define constants, which are static, final variables. You can refer to those constants using the fx:constant attribute. The attribute value is the name of the constant. The name of the element is the name of the type that contains the constant. For example, for Long.MAX_VALUE, you can use the element <Long fx:constant="MAX_VALUE"/>.

You can reference another element in the document using the <fx:reference> element. The fx:id attribute specifies the fx:id of the referred element. You can copy an element using the <fx:copy> element. It will create a new object by copying the attributes of the source object.

FXML supports simple property bindings. You need to use an attribute for the property to bind it to the property of another element or a document variable. The attribute value starts with a $ symbol, which is followed with a pair of curly braces. You can create custom controls using FXML.

The next chapter will discuss the Print API in JavaFX that lets you configure printers and print nodes in JavaFX applications.

CHAPTER 27

Understanding the Print API

In this chapter, you will learn:

- What the Print API is
- How to obtain the list of available printers
- How to get the default printer
- How to print nodes
- How to show the page setup and print dialog to users
- How to customize the setting for the printer jobs
- How to set up the page layout for printing
- How to print web pages displayed in a WebView

The examples of this chapter lie in the com.jdojo.print package. In order for them to work, you must add a corresponding line to the module-info.java file:

```
...
opens com.jdojo.print to javafx.graphics, javafx.base;
...
```

What Is the Print API?

JavaFX includes support for printing nodes through the Print API in the javafx.print package. The API consists of the following classes and a number of enums (not listed):

- Printer
- PrinterAttributes
- PrintResolution
- PrinterJob
- JobSettings
- Paper
- PaperSource
- PageLayout
- PageRange

© Kishori Sharan and Peter Späth 2022
K. Sharan and P. Späth, *Learn JavaFX 17*, https://doi.org/10.1007/978-1-4842-7848-2_27

Instances of the above-listed classes represent different parts of the printing process. For example, a Printer represents a printer that can be used for printing jobs; a PrinterJob represents a print job that can be sent to a Printer for printing; and a Paper represents the paper sizes available on printers.

The Print API provides support for printing nodes that may or may not be attached to a scene graph. It is a common requirement to print the content of a web page, not the WebView node that contains the web page. The javafx.scene.web.WebEngine class contains a print(PrinterJob job) method that prints the contents of the web page, not the WebView node.

If a node is modified during the printing process, the printed node may not appear correct. Note that the printing of a node may span multiple pulse events resulting in concurrent change in the content being printed. To ensure correct printing, please make sure that the node being printed is not modified during the print process.

Nodes can be printed on any thread including the JavaFX Application Thread. It is recommended that large, time-consuming print jobs be submitted on a background thread to keep the UI responsive.

Classes in the Print API are final as they represent existing printing device properties. Most of them do not provide any public constructor as you cannot make up a printing device. Rather, you obtain their references using factory methods in various classes.

■ **Note**   The Print API provides the basic printing support only to print nodes and web pages. You will not be able to use it to print reports in JavaFX applications.

Listing Available Printers

The Printer.getAllPrinters() static method returns an observable list of installed printers on the machine. Note that the list of printers returned by the method may change over time as new printers are installed or old printers are removed. Use the getName() method of the Printer to get the name of the printer. The following snippet of code lists all installed printers on the machine running the code. You may get a different output:

```
import javafx.collections.ObservableSet;
import javafx.print.Printer;
...
ObservableSet<Printer> allPrinters = Printer.getAllPrinters();
for(Printer p : allPrinters) {
        System.out.println(p.getName());
}
```

```
ImageRight Printer
Microsoft XPS Document Writer
PDF995
Sybase DataWindow PS
\\pro-print1\IS-CANON1
\\pro-print1\IS-HP4000
\\pro-print1\IS-HP4015
\\pro-print1\IS-HP4050
\\pro-print1\IS-HP4650
\\pro-print1\IS-HP4650(Color)
```

Getting the Default Printer

The `Printer.getDefaultPrinter()` method returns the default `Printer`. The method may return `null` if no printer is installed. The default printer may be changed on a machine. Therefore, the method may return different printers from call to call, and the printer returned may not be valid after some time. The following snippet of code shows how to get the default printer:

```
Printer defaultprinter = Printer.getDefaultPrinter();
if (defaultprinter != null) {
        String name = defaultprinter.getName();
        System.out.println("Default printer name: " + name);
} else {
        System.out.println("No printers installed.");
}
```

Printing Nodes

Printing a node is easy: create a `PrinterJob` and call its `printPage()` method passing the node to be printed. Printing a node using the default printer with all default settings takes only three lines of code:

```
PrinterJob printerJob = PrinterJob.createPrinterJob();
printerJob.printPage(node); // node is the node to be printed
printerJob.endJob();
```

In a real-world application, you want to handle the errors. You can rewrite the code to handle errors as follows:

```
// Create a printer job for the default printer
PrinterJob printerJob = PrinterJob.createPrinterJob();
if (printerJob!= null) {
        // Print the node
        boolean printed = printerJob.printPage(node);
        if (printed) {
                // End the printer job
                printerJob.endJob();
        } else {
                System.out.println("Printing failed.");
        }
} else {
        System.out.println("Could not create a printer job.");
}
```

You can use the `createPrinterJob()` static method of the `PrinterJob` class to create a printer job:

- `public static PrinterJob createPrinterJob()`
- `public static PrinterJob createPrinterJob(Printer printer)`

The method with no-args creates a printer job for the default printer. You can use the other version of the method to create a printer job for the specified printer.

You can change the printer for a `PrinterJob` by calling its `setPrinter()` method. If the current printer job settings are not supported by the new printer, the settings are reset automatically for the new printer:

```
// Set a new printer for the printer job
printerJob.setPrinter(myNewPrinter);
```

Setting a `null` printer for the job will use the default printer.

Use one of the following `printPage()` methods to print a node:

- `boolean printPage(Node node)`
- `boolean printPage(PageLayout pageLayout, Node node)`

The first version of the method takes only the node to be printed as the parameter. It uses the default page layout for the job for printing.

The second version lets you specify a page layout for printing the node. The specified `PageLayout` will override the `PageLayout` for the job, and it will be used only for printing the specified node. For subsequent printing, the default `PageLayout` for the job will be used. You can create a `PageLayout` using the `Printer` class. I will discuss an example of this kind later.

The `printPage()` method returns true if the printing was successful. Otherwise, it returns false. When you are done printing, call the `endJob()` method. The method returns true if the job can be successfully spooled to the printer queue. Otherwise, it returns false, which may indicate that the job could not be spooled or it was already completed. After successful completion of the job, the job can no longer be reused.

■ **Tip** You can call the `printPage()` method on a `PrinterJob` as many times as you want. Calling the `endJob()` method tells the job that no more printing will be performed. The method transitions the job status to `DONE`, and the job should no longer be reused.

You can cancel a print job using the `cancelJob()` method of the `PrinterJob`. The printing may not be cancelled immediately, for example, when a page is in the middle of printing. The cancellation occurs as soon as possible. The method does not have any effect if

- The job has already been requested to be cancelled.
- The job is already completed.
- The job has an error.

A `PrinterJob` has a read-only status, which is defined by one of the constants of the `PrinterJob.JobStatus` enum:

- `NOT_STARTED`
- `PRINTING`
- `CANCELED`
- `DONE`
- `ERROR`

The NOT_STARTED status indicates a new job. In this status, the job can be configured, and printing can be initiated. The PRINTING status indicates that the job has requested to print at least one page, and it has not terminated printing. In this status, the job cannot be configured.

The other three statuses, CANCELED, DONE, and ERROR, indicate the termination state of the job. Once the job is in one of these statuses, it should not be reused. There is no need to call the endJob() method when the status goes to CANCELED or ERROR. The DONE status is entered when the printing was successful and the endJob() method was called. The PrinterJob class contains a read-only jobStatus property that indicates the current status of the print job.

The program in Listing 27-1 shows how to print nodes. It displays a TextArea where you can enter text. Two Buttons are provided: one prints the TextArea node and the other the entire scene. When printing is initiated, the print job status is displayed in a Label. The code in the print() method is the same as previously discussed. The method includes the logic to display the job status in the Label. The program displays the window shown in Figure 27-1. Run the program; enter text in the TextArea; and click one of the two buttons to print.

Listing 27-1. Printing Nodes

```java
// PrintingNodes.java
package com.jdojo.print;

import javafx.application.Application;
import javafx.print.PrinterJob;
import javafx.scene.Node;
import javafx.scene.Scene;
import javafx.scene.control.Button;
import javafx.scene.control.Label;
import javafx.scene.control.TextArea;
import javafx.scene.layout.HBox;
import javafx.scene.layout.VBox;
import javafx.stage.Stage;

public class PrintingNodes  extends Application {
        private Label jobStatus = new Label();

        public static void main(String[] args) {
                Application.launch(args);
        }

        @Override
        public void start(Stage stage) {
                VBox root = new VBox(5);

                Label textLbl = new Label("Text:");
                TextArea text = new TextArea();
                text.setPrefRowCount(10);
                text.setPrefColumnCount(20);
                text.setWrapText(true);

                // Button to print the TextArea node
                Button printTextBtn = new Button("Print Text");
                printTextBtn.setOnAction(e -> print(text));
```

```
                // Button to print the entire scene
                Button printSceneBtn = new Button("Print Scene");
                printSceneBtn.setOnAction(e -> print(root));

                HBox jobStatusBox = new HBox(5,
                        new Label("Print Job Status:"), jobStatus);
                HBox buttonBox = new HBox(5,
                        printTextBtn, printSceneBtn);

                root.getChildren().addAll(
                        textLbl, text, jobStatusBox, buttonBox);
                Scene scene = new Scene(root);
                stage.setScene(scene);
                stage.setTitle("Printing Nodes");
                stage.show();
        }

        private void print(Node node) {
                jobStatus.textProperty().unbind();
                jobStatus.setText("Creating a printer job...");

                // Create a printer job for the default printer
                PrinterJob job = PrinterJob.createPrinterJob();
                if (job != null) {
                    // Show the printer job status
                    jobStatus.textProperty().bind(
                            job.jobStatusProperty().asString());

                    // Print the node
                    boolean printed = job.printPage(node);
                    if (printed) {
                        // End the printer job
                        job.endJob();
                    } else {
                        jobStatus.textProperty().unbind();
                        jobStatus.setText("Printing failed.");
                    }
                } else {
                    jobStatus.setText(
                            "Could not create a printer job.");
                }
        }
    }
}
```

Figure 27-1. *A window letting the user print text in a TextArea and the scene*

Showing the Page Setup and Print Dialogs

The Print API allows users to interact with the printing process. Users can change the printer settings interactively before the printing is initiated. The API lets you show Page Setup and Print Setup dialogs for setting the page properties and printer settings for the job.

You can let the user configure the page layout by showing a Page Setup dialog. Use the showPageSetupDialog(Window owner) method of the PrinterJob to show a Page Setup dialog. The user can set the page size, source, orientation, and margin. The dialog may allow the user to access other printing properties such as the list of printers. Once the user confirms the settings on the dialog, the PrinterJob has the new settings. The method returns true if the user confirms the settings on the dialog. It returns false if the user cancels the dialog. It also returns false if the dialog cannot be displayed, such as when the job is not in the NOT_STARTED state.

The owner parameter to the method is the window that will be the owner of the dialog box. It can be null. If specified, the inputs to the window will be blocked, while the dialog is displayed:

```
PrinterJob job = PrinterJob.createPrinterJob();

// Show the page setup dialog
boolean proceed = job.showPageSetupDialog(null);
if (proceed) {
        // Start printing here or you can print later
}
```

You can use the showPrintDialog(Window owner) method to show a Print dialog where the user can modify the printer and settings for the PrinterJob. The return value and parameter of this method have meanings similar to that of the showPageSetupDialog() method:

```
PrinterJob job = PrinterJob.createPrinterJob();

// Show the print setup dialog
boolean proceed = job.showPrintDialog(null);
if (proceed) {
        // Start printing here or you can print later
}
```

The program in Listing 27-2 shows a similar window as shown by the program in Listing 27-1. This time, clicking the print buttons displays a Page Setup and Print Setup dialogs (as shown in Figure 27-2). Once the user confirms the settings on the dialogs, the text in the TextArea is printed. Notice that even though you create a PrinterJob for the default printer before showing the dialogs, you can change the printer using the dialogs, and the text will print using the changed printer.

Listing 27-2. Showing the Page Setup and Print Dialogs to the User

```
// PrintDialogs.java
// ...find in the book's download area
```

Figure 27-2. *A window letting users use print dialogs to customize the printer settings*

Customizing PrinterJob Settings

The Print API contains two classes that are related to printer and printer job settings:

- PrinterAttributes
- JobSettings

A printer has attributes, which indicate the printing capabilities of the printer. Examples of printer attributes are default paper size, supported paper sizes, maximum number of copies, and default collation. A PrinterAttributes object encapsulates the attributes of a printer. The Print API does not let you change the printer attributes as you cannot change the capabilities of a printer. You can only use its capabilities. You cannot create a PrinterAttributes object directly. You need to get it from a Printer object using the getPrinterAttributes() method. The following snippet of code prints some attributes of the default printer in the machine. You may get a different output:

```
import javafx.print.Collation;
import javafx.print.PageOrientation;
import javafx.print.PrintSides;
import javafx.print.Printer;
import javafx.print.PrinterAttributes;
...
Printer printer = Printer.getDefaultPrinter();
PrinterAttributes attribs = printer.getPrinterAttributes();

// Read some printer attributes
int maxCopies = attribs.getMaxCopies();
PrintSides printSides = attribs.getDefaultPrintSides();
Set<PageOrientation> orientations = attribs.getSupportedPageOrientations();
Set<Collation> collations = attribs.getSupportedCollations();

// Print the printer attributes
System.out.println("Max. Copies: " + maxCopies);
System.out.println("Print Sides: " + printSides);
System.out.println("Supported Orientation: " + orientations);
System.out.println("Supported Collations: " + collations);
```

```
Max. Copies: 999
Print Sides: ONE_SIDED
Supported Orientation: [PORTRAIT, LANDSCAPE, REVERSE_LANDSCAPE]
Supported Collations: [UNCOLLATED, COLLATED]
```

■ **Tip** A PrinterAttributes is an immutable object. It contains the default and supported attributes of a printer. You obtain PrinterAttributes from a Printer object.

A JobSettings contains the printer attributes to be used for a print job for a specific printer. You can obtain the JobSettings of a print job using the getJobSettings() method of the PrinterJob object. A JobSettings is a mutable object. It contains a property for each printer attribute that can be set for a print job. By default, its properties are initialized to the default properties of the printer. You can change the

895

property that will be used for the current print job. If you change the property of a JobSettings that is not supported by the printer, the property reverts to the default value for the printer. The following snippet of code sets the printSides property to DUPLEX. In this case, the printer supports only ONE_SIDED printing. Therefore, the printSides property is set to ONE_SIDED, which is the default, and only supported printSides value by the printer. You may get a different output:

```
// Create a printer job for the default printer
PrinterJob job = PrinterJob.createPrinterJob();

// Get the JobSettings for the print job
JobSettings jobSettings = job.getJobSettings();
System.out.println(jobSettings.getPrintSides());

// Set the printSides to DUPLEX
jobSettings.setPrintSides(PrintSides.DUPLEX);
System.out.println(jobSettings.getPrintSides());
```

```
ONE_SIDED
ONE_SIDED
```

For a print job, you can specify the page ranges using the pageRanges property of the JobSettings. The pageRanges property is an array of PageRange. A PageRange has startPage and endPage properties that define the range. The following snippet of code sets the page ranges for a job to 1-5 and 20-25:

```
PrinterJob job = PrinterJob.createPrinterJob();
JobSettings jobSettings = job.getJobSettings();
jobSettings.setPageRanges(new PageRange(1, 5), new PageRange(20, 25));
```

Most of the printer attributes are represented by enum constants. For example, the collation attribute is represented by Collation.COLLATED and Collation.UNCOLLATED constants. Some attributes, such as the number of copies to be printed, are specified as an int. Please refer to the list of properties in the JobSettings class that you can set for a print job.

Setting Page Layout

An instance of the PageLayout class represents the page setup for a print job. By default, it is set to the printer default value. You have already seen setting up the page layout using the Page Setup dialog. A PageLayout encapsulates three things:

- The paper size
- The page orientation
- The page margins

A PageLayout is used to configure the printable area of the page, which must lie within the printable area of the hardware. If a page is rendered outside the printable area of the hardware, the content is clipped.

You cannot create a PageLayout object directly. You need to use one of the createPageLayout() methods of the Printer to get a PageLayout:

- PageLayout createPageLayout(Paper paper, PageOrientation orient, double lMargin, double rMargin, double tMargin, double bMargin)

- PageLayout createPageLayout(Paper paper, PageOrientation orient, Printer.MarginType mType)

The margins can be specified as numbers or as one of the following constants of the Printer. MarginType enum:

- DEFAULT

- EQUAL

- EQUAL_OPPOSITES

- HARDWARE_MINIMUM

The DEFAULT margin type requests default 0.75 inch on all sides.

The EQUAL margin type uses the largest of the four hardware margins on all four sides, so the margins are equal on all four sides.

The EQUAL_OPPOSITES margin type uses the larger of left and right hardware margins for the left and right sides, and the larger of the top and bottom hardware margins for the top and bottom sides.

The HARDWARE_MINIMUM requests that the minimum hardware allowed margins should be set on all sides.

The following snippet of code creates a PageLayout for A4 size paper, LANDSCAPE page orientation, and equal margins on all sides. The PageLayout is set to a print job:

```
import javafx.print.JobSettings;
import javafx.print.PageLayout;
import javafx.print.PageOrientation;
import javafx.print.Paper;
import javafx.print.Printer;
import javafx.print.PrinterJob;
...
PrinterJob job = PrinterJob.createPrinterJob();
Printer printer = job.getPrinter();
PageLayout pageLayout = printer.createPageLayout(Paper.A4,
                                                 PageOrientation.LANDSCAPE,
                                                 Printer.MarginType.EQUAL);
JobSettings jobSettings = job.getJobSettings();
jobSettings.setPageLayout(pageLayout);
```

Sometimes, you want to know the size of the printable area on the page. You can get it using the getPrintableWidth() and getPrintableHeight() methods of the PageLayout. This is useful if you want to resize a node before printing, so it fits the printable area. The following snippet of code prints an Ellipse that fits the printable area:

```
PrinterJob job = PrinterJob.createPrinterJob();
JobSettings jobSettings = job.getJobSettings();
PageLayout pageLayout = jobSettings.getPageLayout();
double pgW = pageLayout.getPrintableWidth();
double pgH = pageLayout.getPrintableHeight();
```

```
// Make the Ellipse fit the printable are of the page
Ellipse node = new Ellipse(pgW/2, pgH/2, pgW /2, pgH/2);
node.setFill(null);
node.setStroke(Color.BLACK);
node.setStrokeWidth(1);

boolean printed = job.printPage(node);
if (printed) {
        // End the printer job
        job.endJob();
}
```

Printing a Web Page

There is a special way to print the contents of a web page. Use the print(PrinterJob job) method of the WebEngine class to print the web page loaded by the engine. The method does not modify the specified job. The job can be used for more printing after the print() method call:

```
WebView webView = new WebView();
WebEngine webEngine = webView.getEngine();
...
PrinterJob job = PrinterJob.createPrinterJob();
webEngine.print(job);
```

The program in Listing 27-3 shows how to print web pages. There is nothing new in the program that you have not already covered. The program displays a window with a URL field, a *Go* button, a *Print* button, and a WebView. The Print button is enabled when a web page is successfully loaded. You can enter a web page URL and click the *Go* button to navigate to the page. Click the *Print* button to print the web page.

Listing 27-3. Printing a Web Page

```
// PrintingWebPage.java
// ...find in the book's download area.
```

Summary

JavaFX includes support for printing nodes through the Print API in the javafx.print package. The API consists of a few classes and a number of enums. The Print API provides support for printing nodes that may or may not be attached to a scene graph. It is a common requirement to print the content of a web page, not the WebView node that contains the web page. The javafx.scene.web.WebEngine class contains a print(PrinterJob job) method that prints the contents of the web page, not the WebView node.

If a node is modified during the printing process, the printed node may not appear correct. Note that the printing of a node may span multiple pulse events resulting in concurrent change in the content being printed. To ensure correct printing, make sure that the node being printed is not modified during the print process.

Nodes can be printed on any thread including the JavaFX Application Thread. It is recommended that large, time-consuming print jobs be submitted on a background thread to keep the UI responsive.

Classes in the Print API are final as they represent existing printing device properties. Most of them do not provide any public constructor as you cannot make up a printing device. Rather, you obtain their references using factory methods in various classes.

An instance of the `Printer` class represents a printer. The `Printer.getAllPrinters()` static method returns an observable list of installed printers on the machine. Note that the list of printers returned by the method may change over time as new printers are installed or old printers are removed. Use the `getName()` method of the `Printer` to get the name of the printer.

The `Printer.getDefaultPrinter()` method returns the default `Printer`. The method may return `null` if no printer is installed. The default printer may be changed on a machine. Therefore, the method may return different printers from call to call, and the printer returned may not be valid after some time.

You can create a printer job by calling the `PrinterJob.createPrinterJob()` method. It returns an object of the `PrinterJob` class. Once you get a `PrinterJob` object, call its `printPage()` method to print a node. The node to be printed is passed as an argument to the method.

The Print API allows users to interact with the printing process. Users can change the printer settings interactively before the printing is initiated. The API lets you show Page Setup and Print Setup dialogs for setting the page properties and printer settings for the job. You can let the user configure the page layout by showing a Page Setup dialog. Use the `showPageSetupDialog(Window owner)` method of the `PrinterJob` to show a Page Setup dialog. The user can set the page size, source, orientation, and margins. The dialog may allow the user to access other printing properties such as the list of printers.

The Print API lets you customize the printer job settings. The API contains two classes that are related to printer and printer job settings: `PrinterAttributes` and `JobSettings` classes. A printer has attributes, which indicate the printing capabilities of the printer such as default paper size, supported paper sizes, maximum number of copies, and default collation. A `PrinterAttributes` object encapsulates the attributes of a printer. The Print API does not let you change the printer attributes as you cannot change the capabilities of a printer. You cannot create a `PrinterAttributes` object directly. You need to get it from a `Printer` object using the `getPrinterAttributes()` method.

An instance of the `PageLayout` class represents the page setup for a print job. By default, it is set to the printer default value. A `PageLayout` is used to configure the printable area of the page, which must lie within the printable area of the hardware. If a page is rendered outside the printable area of the hardware, the content is clipped. You cannot create a `PageLayout` object directly. You need to use one of the `createPageLayout()` methods of the `Printer` to get a `PageLayout`.

There is a special way to print the contents of a web page. Use the `print(PrinterJob job)` method of the `WebEngine` class to print the web page loaded by the engine. The method does not modify the specified job. The job can be used for more printing after the `print()` method call.

Additional Controls and Resources

In the appendix, we introduce additional controls, which did not make their way to the main text. Also, we talk about online resources for further reading.

Additional Controls

Some controls were omitted in the main text, because we didn't want the book to become too lengthy. They are not unimportant, though, so we present a short introduction to them here in the appendix.

The TreeView Control

A TreeView is a control that displays hierarchical data in a tree-like structure, as shown in Figure A-1. You can think of a TreeView as displaying a tree upside down—the root of the tree being at the top. Each item in a TreeView is an instance of the TreeItem class. TreeItems form parent-child relationships. In Figure A-1, Departments, IS, and Doug Dyer are instances of a TreeItem.

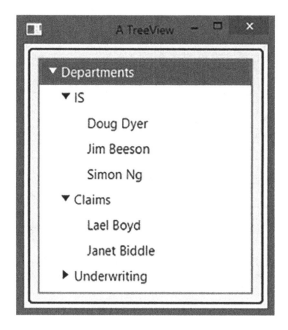

Figure A-1. *A window with a* TreeView *control*

A TreeItem is also referred to as a *node*. The TreeItem class does not inherit from the Node class. Therefore, a TreeItem is not a JavaFX Node, and it cannot be added to a scene graph.

A TreeItem is categorized as a *branch* or *leaf node*. If a TreeItem contains other instances of TreeItem, which are called its children, it is called a branch node. Otherwise, it is called a leaf node. In Figure A-1, Departments, IS, and Claims are examples of branch nodes, whereas Doug Dyer and Lael Boyd are examples of leaf nodes. Notice that leaf nodes are those that occur at the tips of the tree hierarchy. A leaf node has a parent but no children. A branch node has a parent as well as children, except a special branch node, which is called the *root node*. The root node has no parent, but children only, and it is the first node in the TreeView. Departments is the root node in Figure A-1.

A branch node can be in an *expanded* or *collapsed* state. In Figure A-1, the Departments, IS, and Claims nodes are in the expanded state, whereas the Underwriting node is in the collapsed state. A triangle, which is called a *disclosure node*, is used to show the expanded and collapsed state of a branch node.

A TreeItem serves as the data model in a TreeView. Each TreeItem uses an instance of the TreeCell class to render its value. A TreeCell in a TreeView can be customized using a cell factory. By default, a TreeCell is not editable.

TreeView is a virtualized control. It creates only as many instances of TreeCell as needed to display the items for its current height. Cells are recycled as you scroll through items. Virtualization makes it possible to use TreeView for viewing very large number of items without using a large amount of memory. Note, however, that loading TreeItems always takes memory. Virtualization helps only in viewing the items by recycling the cells used in viewing them.

The first item in a TreeView that does not have a parent is known as the root node. By default, the root node is visible. Calling the setShowRoot(false) method of the TreeView hides the root node. Hiding the root node makes traversing the TreeView a little easier because the user has one less level of indentation to traverse. Hiding the root node shows its child nodes at the first level.

A TreeItem fires events as it is modified, for example, by adding or removing children or expanding or collapsing. An instance of the TreeModificationEvent class, which is a static inner class of the TreeItem class, represents all kinds of modification events.

Adding and removing TreeItems is as easy as adding or removing them in the children list of their parents. The root node does not have a parent. To delete the root node, you need to set the root property of the TreeView to null.

A TreeView uses a TreeCell to render a TreeItem. A TreeCell is an IndexedCell. You can visualize items in a TreeView from top to bottom arranged in rows. Each row has exactly one item. Each item is given a row index. The first item, which is the root item, has an index of zero. The row indices are given only to the visible items. TreeView contains a read-only expandedItemCount property that is the number of visible items. Use the getExpandedItemCount() method to get the number of visible items. If a node above an item is expanded or collapsed, the index of the item changes to reflect new visible items. The index of a TreeCell in a TreeView and the row index of an item are the same. Use the getIndex() method of the TreeCell or the getRow(TreeItem<T> item) method of the TreeView to get the row index of an item. A TreeCell is a Labeled control. By default, it uses the following rules to render its TreeItem: If the value in the TreeItem is an instance of the Node class, the value is displayed using the graphic property of the cell. Otherwise, the toString() method of the value is called, and the returned string is displayed using the text property of the cell.

A cell in a TreeView can be editable. An editable cell may switch between editing and nonediting mode. In editing mode, cell data can be modified by the user. For a cell to enter editing mode, the TreeView must be editable. TreeView has an editable property, which can be set to true using the setEditable(true) method. By default, TreeView is not editable. Creating a TreeView does not let you edit its cells. Cell-editing capability is provided through specialized implementations of the TreeCell class. The JavaFX library provides some of these implementations. Set the cell factory for a TreeView, which is a Callback object, to use one of the following implementations of the TreeCell to make cells in a TreeView editable: CheckBoxTreeCell, ChoiceBoxTreeCell, ComboBoxTreeCell, or TextFieldTreeCell.

TreeView lets you load all items at once or items on demand. TreeView automatically provides vertical and horizontal scrollbars when needed. TreeView uses a selection model to select one or multiple TreeItems. The selectionModel property represents the selection model. TreeView supports styling using CSS.

There are a number of examples available in the book's download area. Watch out for classes TreeView*, TreeItem*, PathTreeItem*, and FileSystemBrowser in package com.jdojo.control.

The TreeTableView Control

The TreeTableView control combines the features of the TableView and TreeView controls. It displays a TreeView inside a TableView. A TreeView is used to view hierarchical data; a TableView is used to view tabular data. A TreeTableView is used to view hierarchical data in a tabular form, as shown in Figure A-2.

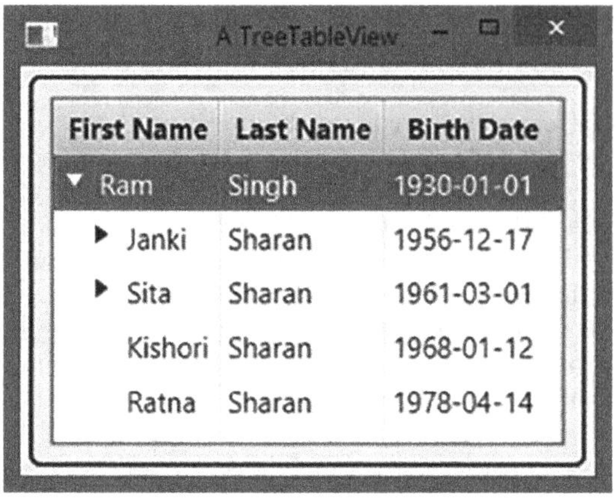

Figure A-2. *A TreeTableView showing a family hierarchy with details*

An instance of the TreeTableColumn class represents a column in a TreeTableView. The getColumns() method of the TreeTableView class returns an ObservableList of TreeTableColumns, which are the columns added to the TreeTableView. You need to add columns to this columns list.

TreeItems act as models in a TreeView. Each node in the TreeView derives its data from the corresponding TreeItem. Recall that you can visualize each node (or TreeItem) in a TreeView as a row with only one column. An ObservableList provides the model in a TableView. Each item in the observable list provides data for a row in the TableView. A TableView can have multiple columns. TreeTableView also uses models for its data. Because it is a combination of TreeView and TableView, it has to decide which type of model it uses. It uses the model based on TreeView. That is, each row in a TreeTableView is defined by a TreeItem in a TreeView. TreeTableView supports multiple columns. Data for columns in a row are derived from the TreeItem for that row.

An instance of the TreeTableView represents a TreeTableView control. The class takes a generic type argument, which is the type of the item contained in the TreeItems. Recall that TreeItems provide the model for a TreeTableView. The generic type of the controls and its TreeItems are the same.

The TreeTableView class provides two constructors. The default constructor creates a TreeTableView with no data. The control displays a placeholder, similar to the one shown by TableView. Like a TableView, TreeTableView contains a placeholder property, which is Node, and if you need to, you can supply your own placeholder. You can add columns and data to a TreeTableView. TreeTableView supports sorting the same way TableView supports sorting.

Showing and hiding columns in a TreeTableView work the same way they do for TableView. By default, all columns in a TreeTableView are visible. The TreeTableColumn class has a visible property to set the visibility of a column. If you turn off the visibility of a parent column, a column with nested columns, all its nested columns will be invisible.

TreeTableView lets you customize rendering of its cells, using different selection models for its cells and rows. It also allows editing data in its cells and adding and deleting rows. You can also style TreeTableView using CSS.

There are a number of examples available in the book's download area. Watch out for classes TreeTable* in package com.jdojo.control.

The WebView Control

JavaFX provides a web component that can be used as an embedded web browser in a JavaFX application. It is based on WebKit, which is an open source web browser engine. It supports

- Viewing HTML5 content with CSS and JavaScript

- Access to the DOM of the HTML content

- Browsing history maintenance

- Executing JavaScript code from JavaFX and vice versa

The component handles most of the work of web browsing, for example, rendering the HTML content, maintaining a history of the visited web pages, navigating to a URL when links are clicked, and displaying pop-up contents, among others. You would need to write code to handle other web-related features, for example, displaying an alert, prompt, or confirmation dialog using JavaScript. I will discuss all of the features of this component in this chapter.

The web browser component comprises a simple API consisting of a few classes in the `javafx.scene.web` package:

- `WebView`

- `WebEngine`

- `WebHistory`

- `WebHistory.Entry`

- `WebEvent`

- `PopupFeatures`

- `PromptData`

The `WebView` class inherits from the `Parent` class. It is a node, not a control. It is added to a scene graph for viewing web pages using local or remote URLs. A `WebView` displays one web page at a time, and it can be styled using a CSS.

A `WebView` uses a `WebEngine` for the core processing of its content. A `WebEngine` manages one web page at a time. The `WebView` handles user input events such as mouse and keyboard events and other tasks, for example, loading the web page content, applying a CSS, and creating a DOM, that are performed by the `WebEngine`. When using a `WebView` component, you will be working with its `WebEngine` most of the time.

A `WebEngine` maintains the browsing history of all visited web pages for a session in an instance of the `WebHistory` class. An instance of the inner class `WebHistory.Entry` represents an entry in the browsing history. An instance of the `WebEvent` class represents an event generated by a `WebEngine` while it processes a web page. Examples of such events are a resized event that occurs when JavaScript running on a web page resizes or moves the window and an alert event that occurs when JavaScript running on the web page calls the `window.alert()` function, among others.

When JavaScript running on a web page opens a pop-up window, an instance of the `PopupFeatures` class encapsulates the details of the pop-up window. The `WebEngine` lets you register a pop-up handler to handle the displaying of the pop-up window.

An instance of the `PromptData` class encapsulates the details of a prompt window (a message and an initial value) displayed by JavaScript code using the `window.prompt()` function. The `WebEngine` lets you register a prompt handler to handle the prompt. In the prompt handler, you can display a JavaFX dialog window to prompt the user for input. Figure A-3 shows the architecture of the web browser component.

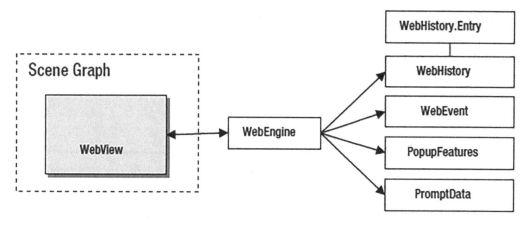

Figure A-3. *Architecture of the web browser component*

There are a number of examples available in the book's download area. Watch out for classes in package com.jdojo.web.

Further Reading

The first address you would go to get further information is the Gluon company's online documentation at

```
https://openjfx.io/
https://openjfx.io/openjfx-docs/
```

And of course visit the Wikipedia article at

```
https://en.wikipedia.org/wiki/JavaFX
```

To see some more technical and release-related information, you can point your browser at

```
https://github.com/openjdk/jfx
https://gluonhq.com/products/javafx/openjfx-11-release-notes/
https://gluonhq.com/products/javafx/openjfx-12-release-notes/
https://gluonhq.com/products/javafx/openjfx-13-release-notes/
https://gluonhq.com/products/javafx/openjfx-14-release-notes/
https://gluonhq.com/products/javafx/openjfx-15-release-notes/
https://gluonhq.com/products/javafx/openjfx-16-release-notes/
https://gluonhq.com/products/javafx/openjfx-17-release-notes/
```

■ **Caution** If you enter "javafx" in a search engine, you would often find outdated information about JavaFX. Make sure you get actual documentation of JavaFX releases at least showing version 11.

Index

G

Printed in the United States
by Baker & Taylor Publisher Services

Printed in the United States
by Baker & Taylor Publisher Services